WEBSTER'S **WORD POWER** ✓

English
Thesaurus

GEDDES & GROSSET

Published 2015 by Geddes & Grosset,
an imprint of The Gresham Publishing Company, Academy Park, Building 4000,
Gower Street, Glasgow G51 1PR
www.geddesandgrosset.com
info@geddesandgrosset.co.uk
Find us on ﬁ facebook/pages/geddesandgrosset

First published 2001, reprinted 2001, 2002, 2003, 2004 (four times), 2005,
2007 (three times), 2008, 2009 (three times), 2010 (twice), 2011 (three times),
this revised and updated edition 2014, reprinted 2014, 2015

ISBN 978-1-84205-763-6

Printed and bound in Spain, Novoprint S.A.

This book is not published by the original publishers of
Webster's Dictionary or by their successors.

ENGLISH THESAURUS

This book is an accessible and comprehensive 'word-finder'. It provides over 150,000 synonyms (words that have similar meanings), arranged in A–Z style.

Thesauruses are invaluable if you want to make your writing varied and interesting.

This thesaurus provides an alphabetical listing of 10,000 words with their related synonyms. Here's how to use the book: imagine you want to say that a joke is 'funny' but that you have used the word once before in your paragraph. Look up 'funny' in the thesaurus and it will tell you that you could also use the words 'amusing', 'comical', 'humorous', 'hilarious', 'entertaining', or a number of other words instead.

Many words have more than one sense or meaning. 'Funny', for example, does not only apply to things that make you laugh. It can also be applied to things or people that are rather odd, and under this meaning the thesaurus lists 'odd', 'peculiar', 'weird', 'bizarre', and so on.

> **funny** *adj* **1** amusing, comic, comical, diverting, droll, entertaining, facetious, hilarious, humorous, jocose, jocular, witty. **2** farcical, laughable, ludicrous. **3** bizarre, curious, odd, peculiar, strange. • *n* **1** jest, joke. **2** cartoon, comic.

In this book, you will find that those words that have more than one meaning have more than one list of synonyms and that these are numbered **1**, **2**, and so on. Thus, 'funny' meaning 'amusing' is under **1**, 'funny' meaning 'deserving mockery' is under **2**, and 'funny' meaning 'odd' is under **3**. Some words have quite a few different synonym lists depending on the number of meanings attached to them.

Antonyms

Antonyms are the opposite of synonyms. They refer to words that have the opposite meaning. There are antonyms for some of the headwords in this book. You'll find them below the main entry, labelled with a part of speech.

> **abbreviate** *vb* abridge, compress, condense, contract, cut, curtail, epitomize, reduce, retrench, shorten.
> *vb antonyms* amplify, extend.

Other features:

Strict alphabetical order is followed. All compound words and hyphenated words are alphabetized as if they are one word.

Variant spellings appear in bold type next to the headword.

Parts of speech are indicated in italic, after the bold headword, by the abbreviations shown on the following page. Other parts of speech after the main headword are indicated by a full point (.) and •.

Different senses within parts of speech are numbered. Parts of speech are separated by full points (.) and •.

Words of **different origins** but with the same spelling are given separate, numbered entries.

Registers are indicated by the following labels: *fml, inf, sl, derog, off*.

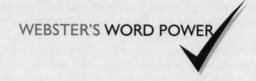

WEBSTER'S **WORD POWER**

Abbreviations

abbr	abbreviation
adj	adjective
adv	adverb
approx	approximately
aux	auxiliary
conj	conjunction
derog	derogatory, derogatorily
dial	dialect
e.g.	exempli gratis, for example
etc	etcetera, and so on
f	feminine
fml	formal
gram	grammar
hum	humorous
i.e.	id est, that is
inf	informal
lit	literary
m	masculine
math	mathematics
med	medicine
mus	music
myth	mythology
n	noun
naut	nautical
neut	neuter
npl	noun plural
obs	obsolete
off	offensive
p	participle
pl	plural
poet	poetical
poss	possessive
prep	preposition
pron	pronoun
reflex	reflexive
sing	singular
sl	slang
usu	usually
vb	verb
zool	zoology

A

aback *adv* back, backward, regressively.

abandon *vb* 1 abdicate, abjure, desert, drop, evacuate, forsake, forswear, leave, quit, relinquish, yield. 2 cede, forgo, give up, let go, renounce, resign, surrender, vacate, waive. • *n* careless freedom, dash, impetuosity, impulse, wildness.
vb antonyms continue, persist, support.
n antonym restraint.

abandoned *adj* 1 depraved, derelict, deserted, discarded, dropped, forsaken, left, outcast, rejected, relinquished. 2 corrupt, demoralized, depraved, dissolute, graceless, impenitent, irreclaimable, lost, obdurate, profligate, reprobate, shameless, sinful, unprincipled, vicious, wicked.
adj antonyms cherished, restrained.

abandonment *n* desertion, dereliction, giving up, leaving, relinquishment, renunciation, surrender.

abase *vb* 1 depress, drop, lower, reduce, sink. 2 debase, degrade, disgrace, humble, humiliate.
vb antonyms elevate, honour.

abasement *n* abjection, debasement, degradation, disgrace, humbleness, humiliation, shame.

abash *vb* affront, bewilder, confound, confuse, dash, discompose, disconcert, embarrass, humiliate, humble, shame, snub.

abashment *n* confusion, embarrassment, humiliation, mortification, shame.

abate *vb* 1 diminish, decrease, lessen, lower, moderate, reduce, relax, remove, slacken. 2 allow, bate, deduct, mitigate, rebate, remit. 3 allay, alleviate, appease, assuage, blunt, calm, compose, dull, mitigate, moderate, mollify, pacify, qualify, quiet, quell, soften, soothe, tranquillize.
vb antonyms increase, strengthen.

abatement *n* 1 alleviation, assuagement, decrement, decrease, extenuation, mitigation, moderation, remission. 2 cessation, decline, diminution, ebb, fading, lowering, sinking, settlement. 3 allowance, deduction, rebate, reduction.

abbey *n* convent, monastery, priory.

abbreviate *vb* abridge, compress, condense, contract, cut, curtail, epitomize, reduce, retrench, shorten.
vb antonyms amplify, extend.

abbreviation *n* abridgment, compression, condensation, contraction, curtailment, cutting, reduction, shortening.
n antonyms expansion, extension.

abdicate *vb* abandon, cede, forgo, forsake, give up, quit, relinquish, renounce, resign, retire, surrender.

abdication *n* abandonment, abdicating, relinquishment, renunciation, resignation, surrender.

abdomen *n* belly, gut, paunch, stomach, (*inf*) tummy.

abduct *vb* carry off, kidnap, spirit away, take away.

abduction *n* carrying off, kidnapping, removal, seizure, withdrawal.

aberrant *adj* 1 deviating, devious, divergent, diverging, erratic, rambling, wandering. 2 abnormal, anomalous, disconnected, eccentric, erratic, exceptional, inconsequent, peculiar, irregular, preternatural, singular, strange, unnatural, unusual.
adj antonyms normal, straight.

aberration *n* 1 departure, deviation, divergence, rambling, wandering. 2 abnormality, anomaly, eccentricity, irregularity, peculiarity, singularity, unconformity. 3 delusion, disorder, hallucination, illusion, instability.
n antonym conformity.

abet *vb* 1 aid, assist, back, help, support, sustain, uphold. 2 advocate, condone, countenance, encourage, favour, incite, sanction.
vb antonym discourage.

abettor *n* 1 ally, assistant. 2 adviser, advocate, promoter. 3 accessory, accomplice, associate, confederate.

abeyance *n* 1 anticipation, calculation, expectancy, waiting. 2 dormancy, inactivity, intermission, quiescence, remission, reservation, suppression, suspension.
n antonyms activity, continuation.

abhor *vb* abominate, detest, dislike intensely, execrate, hate, loathe, nauseate, view with horror.
vb antonyms adore, love.
abhorrence *n* abomination, antipathy, aversion, detestation, disgust, hatred, horror, loathing.
abhorrent *adj* **1** abominating, detesting, hating, loathing. **2** hateful, horrifying, horrible, loathsome, nauseating, odious, offensive, repellent, repugnant, repulsive, revolting, shocking.
adj antonym attractive.
abide *vb* **1** lodge, rest, sojourn, stay, wait. **2** dwell, inhabit, live, reside. **3** bear, continue, persevere, persist, remain. **4** endure, last, suffer, tolerate. **5** (*with* **by**) act up to, conform to, discharge, fulfil, keep, persist in.
vb antonyms dispute, quit.
abiding *adj* changeless, constant, continuing, durable, enduring, immutable, lasting, permanent, stable, unchangeable.
ability *n* **1** ableness, adroitness, aptitude, aptness, cleverness, dexterity, efficacy, efficiency, facility, might, ingenuity, knack, power, readiness, skill, strength, talent, vigour. **2** competency, qualification. **3** calibre, capability, capacity, expertness, faculty, gift, parts.
n antonyms inability, incompetence.
abject *adj* base, beggarly, contemptible, cringing, degraded, despicable, dirty, grovelling, ignoble, low, mean, menial, miserable, paltry, pitiful, poor, servile, sneaking, slavish, vile, worthless, wretched.
adj antonym exalted.
abjectness *n* abasement, abjection, baseness, contemptibleness, meanness, pitifulness, servility, vileness.
abjuration *n* **1** abandonment, abnegation, discarding, disowning, rejection, relinquishment, renunciation, repudiation. **2** disavowal, disclaimer, disclaiming, recall, recantation, repeal, retraction, reversal, revocation.
abjure *vb* **1** abandon, discard, disclaim, disown, forgo, forswear, give up, reject, relinquish, renounce, repudiate. **2** disavow, disclaim, recall, recant, renounce, repeal, retract, revoke, withdraw.
able *adj* **1** accomplished, adroit, apt, clever, expert, ingenious, practical, proficient, qualified, quick, skilful, talented, versed.

2 competent, effective, efficient, fitted, quick. **3** capable, gifted, mighty, powerful, talented. **4** athletic, brawny, muscular, robust, stalwart, strong, vigorous.
adj antonyms incapable, incompetent.
ablution *n* baptism, bathing, cleansing, lavation, purification, washing.
abnegation *n* abandonment, denial, renunciation, surrender.
n antonyms acceptance, support.
abnormal *adj* aberrant, anomalous, divergent, eccentric, exceptional, peculiar, odd, singular, strange, uncomfortable, unnatural, unusual, weird.
adj antonyms normal, straight.
abnormality *n* abnormity, anomaly, deformity, idiosyncrasy, irregularity, monstrosity, peculiarity, oddity, singularity, unconformity.
aboard *adv* inside, within, on.
abode *n* domicile, dwelling, habitation, home, house, lodging, quarters, residence, residency, seat.
abolish *vb* **1** abrogate, annul, cancel, eliminate, invalidate, nullify, quash, repeal, rescind, revoke. **2** annihilate, destroy, end, eradicate, extirpate, extinguish, obliterate, overthrow, suppress, terminate.
vb antonyms continue, retain.
abolition *n* **1** abrogation, annulling, annulment, cancellation, cancelling, nullification, repeal, rescinding, rescission, revocation. **2** annihilation, destruction, eradication, extinction, extinguishment, extirpation, obliteration, overthrow, subversion, suppression.
n antonyms continuance, retention.
abominable *adj* **1** accursed, contemptible, cursed, damnable, detestable, execrable, hellish, horrid, nefarious, odious. **2** abhorrent, detestable, disgusting, foul, hateful, loathsome, nauseous, obnoxious, shocking, revolting, repugnant, repulsive. **3** shabby, vile, wretched.
adj antonyms delightful, desirable.
abominate *vb* abhor, detest, execrate, hate, loathe, recoil from, revolt at, shrink from, shudder at.
abomination *n* **1** abhorrence, antipathy, aversion, detestation, disgust, execration, hatred, loathing. **2** contamination, corruption, corruptness, defilement, foulness, impurity, loathsomeness, odiousness, pollution, taint, uncleanness. **3** annoyance,

curse, evil, infliction, nuisance, plague, torment.

n antonyms adoration, delight.

aboriginal *adj* first, indigenous, native, original.

aborigine *n* aboriginal, local, original inhabitant, native.

abortion *n* 1 miscarriage, premature labour. 2 termination. 3 disappointment, failure.

n antonyms continuation, success.

abortive *adj* 1 immature, incomplete, rudimental, rudimentary, stunted, untimely. 2 futile, fruitless, idle, ineffectual, inoperative, nugatory, profitless, unavailing, unsuccessful, useless, vain.

adj antonym successful.

abound *vb* 1 flow, flourish, increase, swarm, swell. 2 exuberate, luxuriate, overflow, proliferate, swarm, teem.

vb antonym be in short supply.

about *prep* 1 around, encircling, surrounding, round. 2 near. 3 concerning, referring to, regarding, relating to, relative to, respecting, touching, with regard to, with respect to. 4 all over, over, through. • *adv* 1 around, before. 2 approximately, near, nearly.

above *adj* above-mentioned, aforementioned, aforesaid, foregoing, preceding, previous, prior. • *adv* 1 aloft, overhead. 2 before, previously. 3 of a higher rank. • *prep* 1 higher than, on top of. 2 exceeding, greater than, more than, over. 3 beyond, superior to.

adj, adv antonym below.

prep antonyms below, under.

above-board *adj* candid, frank, honest, open, straightforward, truthful, upright. • *adv* candidly, fairly, openly, sincerely.

adj antonyms shady, underhand.

abrade *vb* erase, erode, rub off, scrape out, wear away

abrasion *n* 1 attrition, disintegration, friction, wearing down. 2 scrape, scratch.

abreast *adv* aligned, alongside.

adv antonyms out of touch, unaware.

abridge *vb* 1 abbreviate, condense, compress, shorten, summarize. 2 contract, diminish, lessen, reduce.

vb antonyms amplify, pad.

abridgment *n* 1 compression, condensation, contraction, curtailment, diminution, epitomizing, reduction, shortening. 2 abstract, brief, compendium, digest,

epitome, outline, précis, summary, syllabus, synopsis. 3 deprivation, limitation, restriction.

n antonyms expansion, padding.

abroad *adv* 1 overseas. 2 expansively, unrestrainedly, ubiquitously, widely. 3 forth, out of doors. 4 extensively, publicly.

abrogate *vb* abolish, annul, cancel, invalidate, nullify, overrule, quash, repeal, rescind, revoke, set aside, vacate, void.

abrogation *n* abolition, annulling, annulment, cancellation, cancelling, repeal rescinding, rescission, revocation, voidance, voiding.

abrupt *adj* 1 broken, craggy, jagged, rough, rugged. 2 precipitous, steep. 3 hasty, illtimed, precipitate, sudden, unanticipated, unexpected. 4 blunt, brusque, curt, discourteous. 5 cramped, harsh, jerky, stiff.

adj antonyms ceremonious, expansive, leisurely.

abscess *n* boil, fester, pustule, sore, ulcer.

abscond *vb* bolt, decamp, elope, escape, flee, fly, retreat, run off, sneak away, steal away, withdraw.

absence *n* 1 nonappearance, nonattendance. 2 abstraction, distraction, inattention, musing, preoccupation, reverie. 3 default, defect, deficiency, lack, privation.

n antonyms existence, presence.

absent *adj* 1 abroad, away, elsewhere, gone, not present. 2 abstracted, dreaming, inattentive, lost, musing, napping, preoccupied.

adj antonyms aware, present.

absolute *adj* 1 complete, ideal, independent, perfect, supreme, unconditional, unconditioned, unlimited, unqualified, unrestricted. 2 arbitrary, authoritative, autocratic, despotic, dictatorial, imperious, irresponsible, tyrannical, tyrannous. 3 actual, categorical, certain, decided, determinate, genuine, positive, real, unequivocal, unquestionable, veritable.

adj antonyms conditional, partial.

absolutely *adv* 1 completely, definitely, unconditionally. 2 actually, downright, indeed, indubitably, infallibly, positively, really, truly, unquestionably.

absoluteness *n* 1 actuality, completeness, ideality, perfection, positiveness, reality, supremeness. 2 absolutism, arbitrariness, despotism, tyranny.

absolution *n* acquittal, clearance,

deliverance, discharge, forgiveness, liberation, pardon, release, remission, shrift, shriving.
n antonym condemnation.

absolutism *n* absoluteness, arbitrariness, autocracy, despotism, tyranny.

absolve *vb* acquit, clear, deliver, discharge, exculpate, excuse, exonerate, forgive, free, liberate, loose, pardon, release, set free.
vb antonym charge.

absorb *vb* **1** appropriate, assimilate, drink in, imbibe, soak up. **2** consume, destroy, devour, engorge, engulf, exhaust, swallow up, take up. **3** arrest, engage, engross, fix, immerse, occupy, rivet.
vb antonyms dissipate, exude.

absorbent *adj* absorbing, imbibing, penetrable, porous, receptive.

absorption *adj* **1** appropriation, assimilation, imbibing, osmosis, soaking up. **2** consumption, destroying, devouring, engorgement, engulfing, exhaustion, swallowing up. **3** concentration, engagement, engrossment, immersion, occupation, preoccupation.

abstain *vb* avoid, cease, deny oneself, desist, forbear, refrain, refuse, stop, withhold.
vb antonym indulge.

abstemious *adj* abstinent, frugal, moderate, self-denying, sober, temperate.
adj antonyms gluttonous, intemperate, luxurious.

abstinence *n* abstemiousness, avoidance, forbearance, moderation, self-restraint, soberness, sobriety, teetotalism, temperance.
n antonym self-indulgence.

abstinent *adj* **1** abstaining, fasting. **2** abstemious, restraining, self-denying, self-restraining, sober, temperate.

abstract *vb* **1** detach, disengage, disjoin, dissociate, disunite, isolate, separate. **2** appropriate, purloin, seize, steal, take. **3** abbreviate, abridge, epitomize. • *adj* **1** isolated, separate, simple, unrelated. **2** abstracted, occult, recondite, refined, subtle, vague. **3** nonobjective, nonrepresentational. • *n* abridgment, condensation, digest, excerpt, extract, précis, selection, summary, synopsis.
vb antonyms expand, insert.
adj antonym concrete.

abstracted *adj* **1** absent, absent-minded, dreaming, inattentive, lost, musing, preoccupied. **2** abstruse, refined, subtle.

abstraction *n* **1** absence, absent-mindedness, inattention, muse, musing, preoccupation, reverie. **2** disconnection, disjunction, isolation, separation. **3** abduction, appropriation, pilfering, purloining, seizure, stealing, taking.

abstruse *adj* abstract, attenuated, dark, difficult, enigmatic, hidden, indefinite, mysterious, mystic, mystical, obscure, occult, profound, recondite, remote, subtle, transcendental, vague.
adj antonyms concrete, obvious.

absurd *adj* egregious, fantastic, foolish, incongruous, ill-advised, ill-judged, irrational, ludicrous, nonsensical, nugatory, preposterous, ridiculous, self-annulling, senseless, silly, stupid, unreasonable.
adj antonyms logical, rational, sensible.

absurdity *n* drivel, extravagance, fatuity, folly, foolery, foolishness, idiocy, nonsense.

abundance *n* affluence, amplitude, ampleness, copiousness, exuberance, fertility, flow, flood, largeness, luxuriance, opulence, overflow, plenitude, profusion, richness, store, wealth.
n antonyms dearth, scarcity.

abundant *adj* abounding, ample, bountiful, copious, exuberant, flowing, full, good, large, lavish, rich, liberal, much, overflowing, plentiful, plenteous, replete, teeming, thick.
adj antonyms scarce, sparse.

abuse *vb* **1** betray, cajole, deceive, desecrate, dishonour, misapply, misemploy, misuse, pervert, pollute, profane, prostitute, violate, wrong. **2** harm, hurt, ill-use, ill-treat, injure, maltreat, mishandle. **3** asperse, berate, blacken, calumniate, defame, disparage, lampoon, lash, malign, revile, reproach, satirize, slander, traduce, upbraid, vilify. • *n* **1** cruelty, ill-treatment, maltreatment, sadism. **2** desecration, dishonour, ill-use, misuse. **3** aspersion, defamation, disparagement, insult, invective, opprobrium, railing, rating, reviling, ribaldry, rudeness, scurrility, upbraiding, vilification, vituperation.
vb antonyms cherish, compliment, praise.
n antonyms attention, care.

abusive *adj* **1** condemnatory, insolent, insulting, offensive, opprobrious, reproachful, reviling, ribald, rude, scurrilous, vilificatory, vituperative. **2** barbaric, barbarous, brutal, cruel, harmful, injurious, inhuman, nasty, sadistic, savage, vicious.

adj antonym complimentary.

abut *vb* adjoin, border, impinge, meet, project.

abutment *n* **1** bank, bulwark, buttress, embankment, fortification. **2** abutting, abuttal, adjacency, contiguity, juxtaposition.

abuttal *n* adjacency, boundary, contiguity, juxtaposition, nearness, next, terminus.

abyss *n* abysm, chasm, gorge, gulf, pit.

academic *adj* collegiate, lettered, scholastic. • *n* academician, classicist, doctor, fellow, pundit, savant, scholar, student, teacher.

academy *n* college, high school, institute, school.

accede *vb* accept, acquiesce, agree, assent to, comply with, concur, consent, yield.

vb antonyms demur, object.

accelerate *vb* dispatch, expedite, forward, hasten, hurry, precipitate, press on, quicken, speed, urge on.

vb antonyms delay, slow down.

acceleration *n* expedition, hastening, hurrying, quickening, pickup, precipitation, speeding up, stepping up.

accent *vb* accentuate, emphasize, stress. • *n* **1** cadence, inflection, intonation, tone. **2** beat, emphasis, ictus.

accentuate *vb* **1** accent, emphasize, mark, point up, punctuate, stress. **2** highlight, overemphasize, overstress, underline, underscore.

accept *vb* **1** acquire, derive, get, gain, obtain, receive, take. **2** accede to, acknowledge, acquiesce in, admit, agree to, approve, assent to, avow, embrace. **3** estimate, construe, interpret, regard, value.

vb antonyms demur, reject.

acceptable *adj* agreeable, gratifying, pleasant, pleasing, pleasurable, welcome.

adj antonyms unsatisfactory, unwelcome.

acceptance *n* **1** accepting, acknowledgment, receipt, reception, taking. **2** approbation, approval, gratification, satisfaction.

acceptation *n* **1** construction, import, interpretation, meaning, sense, significance, signification, understanding. **2** adoption, approval, currency, vogue.

access *vb* broach, enter, open, open up. • *n* **1** approach, avenue, entrance, entry, passage, way. **2** admission, admittance, audience, interview. **3** addition, accession,

aggrandizement, enlargement, gain, increase, increment.

n antonyms egress, outlet.

accession *n* **1** addition, augmentation, enlargement, extension, increase. **2** succession.

accessory *adj* abetting, additional, additive, adjunct, aiding, ancillary, assisting, contributory, helping, subsidiary, subordinate, supplemental. • *n* **1** abettor, accomplice, assistant, associate, confederate, helper. **2** accompaniment, attendant, concomitant, detail, subsidiary.

accident *n* **1** calamity, casualty, condition, contingency, disaster, fortuity, incident, misadventure, miscarriage, mischance, misfortune, mishap. **2** affection, alteration, chance, contingency, mode, modification, property, quality, state.

accidental *adj* **1** casual, chance, contingent, fortuitous, undesigned, unintended. **2** adventitious, dispensable, immaterial, incidental, nonessential.

adj antonyms intentional, premeditated.

acclamation *n* acclaim, applause, cheer, cry, plaudit, outcry, salutation, shouting.

acclimatization *n* adaptation, adjustment, conditioning, familiarization, habituation, inurement, naturalization.

acclimatize *vb* accustom, adapt, adjust, condition, familiarize, habituate, inure, naturalize, season.

acclivity *n* ascent, height, hill, rising ground, steep, upward slope.

accommodate *vb* **1** contain, furnish, hold, oblige, serve, supply. **2** adapt, fit, suit. **3** adjust, compose, harmonize, reconcile, settle.

accommodation *n* **1** advantage, convenience, privilege. **2** adaptation, agreement, conformity, fitness, suitableness. **3** adjustment, harmonization, harmony, pacification, reconciliation, settlement.

accompaniment *n* adjunct, appendage, attachment, attendant, concomitant.

accompany *vb* attend, chaperon, convoy, escort, follow, go with.

accomplice *n* abettor, accessory, ally, assistant, associate, confederate, partner.

accomplish *vb* **1** achieve, bring about, carry, carry through, complete, compass, consummate, do, effect, execute, perform, perfect. **2** conclude, end, finish, terminate.

accomplished *adj* **1** achieved, completed,

done, effected, executed, finished, fulfilled, realized. **2** able, adroit, apt, consummate, educated, experienced, expert, finished, instructed, practised, proficient, qualified, ripe, skilful, versed. **3** elegant, fashionable, fine, polished, polite, refined. *adj antonym* inexpert.

accomplishment *n* **1** achievement, acquirement, attainment, qualification. **2** completion, fulfilment.

accord *vb* **1** admit, allow, concede, deign, give, grant, vouchsafe, yield. **2** agree, assent, concur, correspond, harmonize, quadrate, tally. • *n* accordance, agreement, concord, concurrence, conformity, consensus, harmony, unanimity, unison. *vb antonym* disagree. *n antonym* discord.

accordant *adj* agreeable, agreeing, congruous, consonant, harmonious, suitable, symphonious.

accordingly *adv* **1** agreeably, conformably, consistently, suitably. **2** consequently, hence, so, thence, therefore, thus, whence, wherefore.

accost *vb* address, confront, greet, hail, salute, speak to, stop.

account *vb* **1** assess, appraise, estimate, evaluate, judge, rate. **2** (*with* **for**) assign, attribute, explain, expound, justify, rationalize, vindicate. • *n* **1** inventory, record, register, score. **2** bill, book, charge. **3** calculation, computation, count, reckoning, score, tale, tally. **4** chronicle, detail, description, narration, narrative, portrayal, recital, rehearsal, relation, report, statement, tidings, word. **5** elucidation, explanation, exposition. **6** consideration, ground, motive, reason, regard, sake. **7** consequence, consideration, dignity, distinction, importance, note, repute, reputation, worth.

accountable *adj* amenable, answerable, duty-bound, liable, responsible.

accoutre *vb* arm, dress, equip, fit out, furnish.

accredit *vb* authorize, depute, empower, entrust.

accrue *vb* arise, come, follow, flow, inure, issue, proceed, result.

accumulate *vb* agglomerate, aggregate, amass, bring together, collect, gather, grow, hoard, increase, pile, store. *vb antonyms* diffuse, disseminate.

accumulation *n* agglomeration, aggregation, collection, heap, hoard, mass, pile, store.

accuracy *n* carefulness, correctness, exactness, fidelity, precision, strictness.

accurate *adj* close, correct, exact, faithful, nice, precise, regular, strict, true, truthful. *adj antonyms* inaccurate, wrong.

accusation *n* arraignment, charge, incrimination, impeachment, indictment.

accuse *vb* arraign, charge, censure, impeach, indict, tax.

accustom *vb* discipline, drill, familiarize, habituate, harden, inure, train, use.

ace *n* (*cards, dice*) **1** one spot, single pip, single point. **2** atom, bit, grain, iota, jot, particle, single, unit, whit. **3** expert, master, virtuoso. • *adj* best, expert, fine, outstanding, superb.

acerbity *n* **1** acidity, acridity, acridness, astringency, bitterness, roughness, sourness, tartness. **2** acrimony, bitterness, harshness, severity, venom.

achieve *vb* **1** accomplish, attain, complete, do, effect, execute, finish, fulfil, perform, realize. **2** acquire, gain, get, obtain, win. *vb antonyms* fail, miss.

achievement *n* **1** accomplishment, acquirement, attainment, completion, consummation, performance, realization. **2** deed, exploit, feat, work.

acid *adj* pungent, sharp, sour, stinging, tart, vinegary.

acknowledge *vb* **1** recognize. **2** accept, admit, accept, allow, concede, grant. **3** avow, confess, own, profess.

acme *n* apex, climax, height, peak, pinnacle, summit, top, vertex, zenith. *n antonym* nadir.

acquaint *vb* **1** familiarize. **2** announce, apprise, communicate, enlighten, disclose, inform, make aware, make known, notify, tell.

acquaintance *n* **1** companionship, familiarity, fellowship, intimacy, knowledge. **2** associate, companion, comrade, friend.

acquiesce *vb* **1** bow, comply, consent, give way, rest, submit, yield. **2** agree, assent, concur, consent. *vb antonyms* disagree, object.

acquire *vb* **1** achieve, attain, earn, gain, get, have, obtain, procure, realize, secure, win. **2** learn thoroughly, master. *vb antonyms* forfeit, forgo, relinquish.

acquirement *n* **1** acquiring, gaining, gathering, mastery. **2** acquisition, accomplishment, attainment.

acquit *vb* absolve, clear, discharge, exculpate, excuse, exonerate, forgive, liberate, pardon, pay, quit, release, set free, settle. *vb antonym* convict.

acquittal *n* absolution, acquittance, clearance, deliverance, discharge, exoneration, liberation, release.

acquittance *n* **1** discharge. **2** quittance, receipt.

acrid *adj* biting, bitter, caustic, pungent, sharp.

acrimonious *adj* acrid, angry, bitter, caustic, harsh, malignant, petulant, sarcastic, severe, testy, virulent. *adj antonyms* kindly, peaceable.

acrimony *n* **1** bitterness, churlishness, harshness, rancour, severity, spite, venom. **2** causticity, causticness, corrosiveness, sharpness.

act *vb* **1** do, execute, function, make, operate, work. **2** enact, feign, perform, play. • *n* **1** achievement, deed, exploit, feat, performance, proceeding, turn. **2** bill, decree, enactment, law, ordinance, statute. **3** actuality, existence, fact, reality.

acting *adj* interim, provisional, substitute, temporary. • *n* **1** enacting, impersonation, performance, portrayal, theatre. **2** counterfeiting, dissimulation, imitation, pretence.

action *n* **1** achievement, activity, agency, deed, exertion, exploit, feat. **2** battle, combat, conflict, contest, encounter, engagement, operation. **3** lawsuit, prosecution.

active *adj* **1** effective, efficient, influential, living, operative. **2** assiduous, bustling, busy, diligent, industrious, restless. **3** agile, alert, brisk, energetic, lively, nimble, prompt, quick, smart, spirited, sprightly, supple. **4** animated, ebullient, fervent, vigorous. *adj antonyms* dormant, inactive, inert, passive.

actual *adj* **1** certain, decided, genuine, objective, real, substantial, tangible, true, veritable. **2** perceptible, present, sensible, tangible. **3** absolute, categorical, positive. *adj antonyms* apparent, imaginary, theoretical.

actuate *vb* impel, incite, induce, instigate, move, persuade, prompt.

acumen *n* acuteness, astuteness, discernment, ingenuity, keenness, penetration, sagacity, sharpness, shrewdness.

acute *adj* **1** pointed, sharp. **2** astute, bright, discerning, ingenious, intelligent, keen, quick, penetrating, piercing, sagacious, sage, sharp, shrewd, smart, subtle. **3** distressing, fierce, intense, piercing, pungent, poignant, severe, violent. **4** high, high-toned, sharp, shrill. **5** (*med*) sudden, temporary, violent.

adage *n* aphorism, dictum, maxim, proverb, saw, saying.

adapt *vb* accommodate, adjust, conform, coordinate, fit, qualify, proportion, suit, temper.

add *vb* **1** adjoin, affix, annex, append, attach, join, tag. **2** sum, sum up, total. *vb antonym* subtract.

addict *vb* accustom, apply, dedicate, devote, habituate. • *n* **1** devotee, enthusiast, fan. **2** head, junkie, user.

addicted *adj* attached, devoted, given up to, inclined, prone, wedded.

addition *n* **1** augmentation, accession, enlargement, extension, increase, supplement. **2** adjunct, appendage, appendix, extra.

address *vb* accost, apply to, court, direct. • *n* **1** appeal, application, entreaty, invocation, memorial, petition, request, solicitation, suit. **2** discourse, oration, lecture, sermon, speech. **3** ability, adroitness, art, dexterity, expertness, skill. **4** courtesy, deportment, demeanour, tact.

adduce *vb* **1** advance, allege, assign, offer, present. **2** cite, mention, name.

adept *adj* accomplished, experienced, practised, proficient, skilled. • *n* expert, master, virtuoso. *adj antonyms* bungling, incompetent, inept. *n antonyms* bungler, incompetent.

adequate *adj* able, adapted, capable, competent, equal, fit, requisite, satisfactory, sufficient, suitable. *adj antonyms* inadequate, insufficient.

adhere *vb* **1** cling, cleave, cohere, hold, stick. **2** appertain, belong, pertain.

adherent *adj* adhering, clinging, sticking. • *n* acolyte, dependant, disciple, follower, partisan, supporter, vassal.

adhesion *n* adherence, attachment, clinging, coherence, sticking.

adhesive *adj* **1** clinging, sticking. **2** glutinous, gummy, sticky, tenacious, viscous. • *n* binder, cement, glue, paste.

adieu *n* farewell, goodbye, parting, valediction.

adipose *adj* fat, fatty, greasy, oily, oleaginous, sebaceous.

adjacent *adj* adjoining, bordering, conterminous, contiguous, near, near to, neighbouring, touching.

adjoin *vb* abut, add, annex, append, border, combine, neighbour, unite, verge.

adjourn *vb* 1 defer, delay, postpone, procrastinate. 2 close, dissolve, end, interrupt, prorogue, suspend.
vb antonym convene.

adjudge *vb* 1 allot, assign, award. 2 decide, decree, determine, settle.

adjunct *n* addition, advantage, appendage, appurtenance, attachment, attribute, auxiliary, dependency, help.

adjure *vb* beg, beseech, entreat, pray, supplicate.

adjust *vb* 1 adapt, arrange, dispose, rectify. 2 regulate, set right, settle, suit. 3 compose, harmonize, pacify, reconcile, settle. 4 accommodate, adapt, fit, suit.
vb antonyms derange, disarrange, upset.

administer *vb* 1 contribute, deal out, dispense, supply. 2 conduct, control, direct, govern, manage, oversee, superintend. 3 conduce, contribute.

admirable *adj* 1 astonishing, striking, surprising, wonderful. 2 excellent, fine, rare, superb.
adj antonym despicable.

admiration *n* affection, approbation, approval, astonishment, delight, esteem, pleasure, regard.
n antonym contempt.

admirer *n* 1 beau, gallant, suitor, sweetheart. 2 fan, follower, supporter.

admissible *adj* allowable, lawful, permissible, possible.
adj antonyms illegitimate, inadmissible.

admission *n* 1 access, admittance, entrance, introduction. 2 acceptance, acknowledgement, allowance, assent, avowal, concession.
n antonyms denial, exclusion.

admit *vb* 1 give access to, let in, receive. 2 agree to, accept, acknowledge, concede, confess. 3 allow, bear, permit, suffer, tolerate.
vb antonyms exclude, gainsay.

admonish *vb* 1 censure, rebuke, reprove. 2 advise caution, counsel, enjoin, fore-

warn, warn. 3 acquaint, apprise, inform, instruct, notify, remind.

admonition *n* 1 censure, rebuke, remonstrance. 2 advice, caution, chiding, counsel, instruction, monition.

adolescence *n* minority, teens, youth.
n antonym senescence.

adolescent *adj* juvenile, young, youthful. • *n* minor, teenager, youth.

adopt *vb* 1 appropriate, assume. 2 accept, approve, avow, espouse, maintain, support. 3 affiliate, father, foster.
vb antonyms disown, repudiate.

adore *vb* 1 worship. 2 esteem, honour, idolize, love, revere, venerate.
vb antonyms abhor, hate.

adorn *vb* beautify, decorate, embellish, enrich, garnish, gild, grace, ornament.

adroit *adj* apt, dextrous, expert, handy, ingenious, ready, skilful.
adj antonyms clumsy, inept, maladroit.

adulation *n* blandishment, cajolery, fawning, flattery, flummery, praise, sycophancy.

adult *adj* grown-up, mature, ripe, ripened. • *n* grown-up person.
adj antonym immature.

adulterate *vb* alloy, contaminate, corrupt, debase, deteriorate, vitiate.

advance *adj* 1 beforehand, forward, leading. • *vb* propel, push, send forward. 2 aggrandize, dignify, elevate, exalt, promote. 3 benefit, forward, further, improve, promote. 4 adduce, allege, assign, offer, propose, propound. 5 augment, increase. 6 proceed, progress. 7 grow, improve, prosper, thrive. • *n* 1 march, progress. 2 advancement, enhancement, growth, promotion, rise. 3 offer, overture, proffering, proposal, proposition, tender. 4 appreciation, rise.
vb antonyms impede, retard, retreat.
n antonym recession.

advancement *n* advance, benefit, gain, growth, improvement, profit.

advantage *n* 1 ascendancy, precedence, preeminence, superiority, upper-hand. 2 benefit, blessing, emolument, gain, profit, return. 3 account, behalf, interest. 4 accommodation, convenience, prerogative, privilege.
n antonyms disadvantage, hindrance.

advantageous *adj* beneficial, favourable, profitable.

advent *n* accession, approach, arrival, coming, visitation.

adventitious *adj* accidental, extraneous, extrinsic, foreign, fortuitous, nonessential.

adventure *vb* dare, hazard, imperil, peril, risk, venture. • *n* **1** chance, contingency, experiment, fortuity, hazard, risk, venture. **2** crisis, contingency, event, incident, occurrence, transaction.

adventurous *adj* **1** bold, chivalrous, courageous, daring, doughty. **2** foolhardy, headlong, precipitate, rash, reckless. **3** dangerous, hazardous, perilous.

adj antonyms cautious, chary, prudent.

adversary *n* antagonist, enemy, foe, opponent.

n antonyms ally, supporter.

adverse *adj* **1** conflicting, contrary, opposing. **2** antagonistic, harmful, hostile, hurtful, inimical, unfavourable, unpropitious. **3** calamitous, disastrous, unfortunate, unlucky, untoward.

adj antonyms advantageous, propitious.

adversity *n* affliction, calamity, disaster, distress, misery, misfortune, sorrow, suffering, woe.

n antonym prosperity.

advertise *vb* advise, announce, declare, inform, placard, proclaim, publish.

advertisement *n* announcement, information, notice, proclamation.

advice *n* **1** admonition, caution, counsel, exhortation, persuasion, suggestion, recommendation. **2** information, intelligence, notice, notification. **3** care, counsel, deliberation, forethought.

advisable *adj* advantageous, desirable, expedient, prudent.

adj antonyms inadvisable, injudicious.

advise *vb* **1** admonish, counsel, commend, recommend, suggest, urge. **2** acquaint, apprise, inform, notify. **3** confer, consult, deliberate.

adviser *n* counsellor, director, guide, instructor.

advocate *vb* countenance, defend, favour, justify, maintain, support, uphold, vindicate. • *n* **1** apologist, counsellor, defender, maintainer, patron, pleader, supporter. **2** attorney, barrister, counsel, lawyer, solicitor.

vb antonyms deprecate, disparage, impugn.

n antonyms critic, opponent.

aegis *n* defence, protection, safeguard, shelter.

aesthetic *adj* appropriate, beautiful, tasteful.

affable *adj* **1** accessible, approachable, communicative, conversable, cordial, easy, familiar, frank, free, sociable, social. **2** complaisant, courteous, civil, obliging, polite, urbane.

adj antonyms cool, reserved, reticent, unfriendly.

affair *n* **1** business, circumstance, concern, matter, office, question. **2** event, incident, occurrence, performance, proceeding, transaction. **3** battle, combat, conflict, encounter, engagement, skirmish.

affairs *npl* **1** administration, relations. **2** business, estate, finances, property.

affect *vb* **1** act upon, alter, change, influence, modify, transform. **2** concern, interest, regard, relate. **3** improve, melt, move, overcome, subdue, touch. **4** aim at, aspire to, crave, yearn for. **5** adopt, assume, feign.

affectation *n* affectedness, airs, artificiality, foppery, pretension, simulation.

affected *adj* **1** artificial, assumed, feigned, insincere, theatrical. **2** assuming, conceited, foppish, vain.

affection *n* **1** bent, bias, feeling, inclination, passion, proclivity, propensity. **2** accident, attribute, character, mark, modification, mode, note, property. **3** attachment, endearment, fondness, goodwill, kindness, partiality, love.

n antonyms antipathy, dislike.

affectionate *adj* attached, devoted, fond, kind, loving, sympathetic, tender.

adj antonyms cold, undemonstrative.

affiliate *vb* ally, annex, associate, connect, incorporate, join, unite. • *n* ally, associate, confederate.

affinity *n* **1** connection, propinquity, relationship. **2** analogy, attraction, correspondence, likeness, relation, resemblance, similarity, sympathy.

affirm *vb* **1** allege, assert, asseverate, aver, declare, state. **2** approve, confirm, establish, ratify.

affix *vb* annex, attach, connect, fasten, join, subjoin, tack.

afflict *vb* agonize, distress, grieve, pain, persecute, plague, torment, trouble, try, wound.

vb antonyms comfort, solace.

affliction *n* **1** adversity, calamity, disaster, misfortune, stroke, visitation. **2** bitterness, depression, distress, grief, misery, plague, scourge, sorrow, trial, tribulation, wretchedness, woe.

n antonyms comfort, consolation, solace.

affluent *adj* **1** abounding, abundant, bounteous, plenteous. **2** moneyed, opulent, rich, wealthy.

adj antonyms impecunious, impoverished, poor.

afford *vb* **1** furnish, produce, supply, yield. **2** bestow, communicate, confer, give, grant, impart, offer. **3** bear, endure, support.

affray *n* brawl, conflict, disturbance, feud, fight, quarrel, scuffle, struggle.

affright *vb* affray, alarm, appal, confound, dismay, shock, startle. • *n* alarm, consternation, fear, fright, panic, terror.

affront *vb* **1** abuse, insult, outrage. **2** annoy, chafe, displease, fret, irritate, offend, pique, provoke, vex. • *n* abuse, contumely, insult, outrage, vexation, wrong.

vb antonyms appease, compliment.

n antonym compliment.

afraid *adj* aghast, alarmed, anxious, apprehensive, frightened, scared, timid.

adj antonyms confident, unafraid.

after *prep* **1** later than, subsequent to. **2** behind, following. **3** about, according to. **4** because of, in imitation of. • *adj* **1** behind, consecutive, ensuing, following, later, succeeding, successive, subsequent. **2** aft, back, hind, rear, rearmost, tail.• *adv* afterwards, later, next, since, subsequently, then, thereafter.

prep antonym before.

again *adv* **1** afresh, anew, another time, once more. **2** besides, further, in addition, moreover.

against *prep* **1** adverse to, contrary to, in opposition to, resisting. **2** abutting, close up to, facing, fronting, off, opposite to, over. **3** in anticipation of, for, in expectation of. **4** in compensation for, to counterbalance, to match.

prep antonyms for, pro.

age *vb* decline, grow old, mature. • *n* **1** aeon, date, epoch, period, time. **2** decline, old age, senility. **3** antiquity, oldness.

n antonyms salad days, youth.

agency *n* **1** action, force, intervention, means, mediation, operation, procurement. **2** charge, direction, management, superintendence, supervision.

agent *n* **1** actor, doer, executor, operator,

performer. **2** active element, cause, force. **3** attorney, broker, commissioner, deputy, factor, intermediary, manager, middleman.

agglomeration *n* accumulation, aggregation, conglomeration, heap, lump, pile.

agglutinate *vb* cement, fasten, glue, unite.

aggrandize *vb* advance, dignify, elevate, enrich, exalt, promote.

aggravate *vb* **1** heighten, increase, worsen. **2** colour, exaggerate, magnify, overstate. **3** enrage, irritate, provoke, tease.

vb antonyms alleviate, appease, mollify.

aggravation *n* exaggeration, heightening, irritation.

aggregate *vb* accumulate, amass, collect, heap, pile. • *adj* collected, total. • *n* amount, gross, total, whole.

adj antonyms individual, particular.

aggressive *adj* **1** assailing, assailant, assaulting, attacking, invading, offensive. **2** pushing, self-assertive.

adj antonyms peaceable, submissive.

aggressor *n* assailant, assaulter, attacker, invader.

aggrieve *vb* **1** afflict, grieve, pain. **2** abuse, ill-treat, impose, injure, oppress, wrong.

aghast *adj* **1** appalled, dismayed, frightened, horrified, horror-struck, panic-stricken, terrified. **2** amazed, astonished, startled, thunderstruck.

agile *adj* active, alert, brisk, lively, nimble, prompt, smart, ready.

adj antonyms clumsy, stiff, torpid.

agitate *vb* **1** disturb, jar, rock, shake, trouble. **2** disquiet, excite, ferment, rouse, trouble. **3** confuse, discontent, flurry, fluster, flutter. **4** canvass, debate, discuss, dispute, investigate.

vb antonyms calm, tranquilize.

agitation *n* **1** concussion, shake, shaking. **2** commotion, convulsion, disturbance, ferment, jarring, storm, tumult, turmoil. **3** discomposure, distraction, emotion, excitement, flutter, perturbation, ruffle, tremor, trepidation. **4** controversy, debate, discussion.

agnostic *n* doubter, empiricist, sceptic.

agonize *vb* distress, excruciate, rack, torment, torture.

agony *n* anguish, distress, pangs.

agree *vb* **1** accord, concur, harmonize, unite. **2** accede, acquiesce, assent, comply, concur, subscribe. **3** bargain, contract, covenant, engage, promise, undertake.

4 compound, compromise. **5** chime, cohere, conform, correspond, match, suit, tally.
vb antonyms conflict, disagree.

agreeable *adj* charming, pleasant, pleasing.
adj antonyms disagreeable, distasteful, incompatible, nasty.

agreement *n* **1** accordance, compliance, concord, harmony, union. **2** bargain, compact, contract, pact, treaty.

agriculture *n* cultivation, culture, farming, geoponics, husbandry, tillage.

aid *vb* **1** assist, help, serve, support. **2** relieve, succour. **3** advance, facilitate, further, promote. • *n* **1** assistance, cooperation, help, patronage. **2** alms, subsidy, succour, relief.
vb antonyms impede, obstruct.
n antonyms impediment, obstruction.

ailment *n* disease, illness, sickness.

aim *vb* **1** direct, level, point, train. **2** design, intend, mean, purpose, seek. • *n* **1** bearing, course, direction, tendency. **2** design, object, view, reason.

air *vb* expose, display, ventilate. • *n* **1** atmosphere, breeze. **2** appearance, aspect, manner. **3** melody, tune.

aisle *n* passage, walk.

akin *adj* **1** allied, kin, related. **2** analogous, cognate, congenial, connected.
adj antonym alien.

alacrity *n* **1** agility, alertness, activity, eagerness, promptitude. **2** cheerfulness, gaiety, hilarity, liveliness, vivacity.

alarm *vb* daunt, frighten, scare, startle, terrify. • *n* **1** alarm-bell, tocsin, warning. **2** apprehension, fear, fright, terror.
vb antonyms calm, reassure, soothe.
n antonym composure.

alert *adj* **1** awake, circumspect, vigilant, watchful, wary. **2** active, brisk, lively, nimble, quick, prompt, ready, sprightly. • *vb* alarm, arouse, caution, forewarn, signal, warn. • *n* alarm, signal, warning.
adj antonyms listless, slow.

alertness *n* **1** circumspection, vigilance, watchfulness, wariness. **2** activity, briskness, nimbleness, promptness, readiness, spryness.

alien *adj* **1** foreign, not native. **2** differing, estranged, inappropriate, remote, unallied, separated. • *n* foreigner, stranger.
adj antonym akin.
n antonym native.

alienate *vb* (*legal*) **1** assign, demise, transfer. **2** disaffect, estrange, wean, withdraw.

alienation *n* (*legal*) **1** assignment, conveyance, transfer. **2** breach, disaffection, division, estrangement, rupture. **3** (*med*) aberration, delusion, derangement, hallucination, insanity, madness.

alike *adj* akin, analogous, duplicate, identical, resembling, similar. • *adv* equally.

aliment *n* diet, fare, meat, nutriment, provision, rations, sustenance.

alive *adj* **1** animate, breathing, live. **2** aware, responsive, sensitive, susceptible. **3** brisk, cheerful, lively, sprightly.
adj antonyms dead, lifeless.

allay *vb* **1** appease, calm, check, compose. **2** alleviate, assuage, lessen, moderate, solace, temper.
vb antonyms exacerbate, intensify.

allege *vb* **1** affirm, assert, declare, maintain, say. **2** adduce, advance, assign, cite, plead, produce, quote.

allegiance *n* duty, homage, fealty, fidelity, loyalty, obligation.
n antonyms disloyalty, enmity.

allegory *n* apologue, fable, myth, parable, story, tale.

alleviate *vb* assuage, lighten, mitigate, mollify, moderate, quell, quiet, quieten, soften, soothe.
vb antonym aggravate.

alliance *n* **1** affinity, intermarriage, relation. **2** coalition, combination, confederacy, league, treaty, union. **3** affiliation, connection, relationship, similarity.
n antonyms divorce, enmity, estrangement, hostility.

allot *vb* **1** divide, dispense, distribute. **2** assign, fix, prescribe, specify.

allow *vb* **1** acknowledge, admit, concede, confess, grant, own. **2** authorize, grant, let, permit. **3** bear, endure, suffer, tolerate. **4** grant, yield, relinquish, spare. **5** approve, justify, sanction. **6** abate, bate, deduct, remit.
vb antonyms deny, forbid.

allude *vb* glance, hint, mention, imply, insinuate, intimate, refer, suggest, touch.

allure *vb* attract, beguile, cajole, coax, entice, lure, persuade, seduce, tempt. • *n* appeal, attraction, lure, temptation.
vb antonym repel.

allusion *n* hint, implication, intimation, insinuation, mention, reference, suggestion.

ally *vb* combine, connect, join, league, marry, unite. • *n* aider, assistant, associate, coadjutor, colleague, friend, partner.
n antonyms antagonist, enemy.
vb antonym estrange.

almighty *adj* all-powerful, omnipotent.
adj antonyms impotent, insignificant, weak.

alms *npl* benefaction, bounty, charity, dole, gift, gratuity.

alone *adj* companionless, deserted, forsaken, isolated, lonely, only, single, sole, solitary.

along *adv* **1** lengthways, lengthwise. **2** forward, onward. **3** beside, together, simultaneously.

aloud *adv* audibly, loudly, sonorously, vociferously.

alter *vb* change, conform, modify, shift, turn, transform, transmit, vary.
vb antonym fix.

altercation *n* bickering, contention, controversy, dispute, dissension, strife, wrangling.

alternating *adj* intermittent, interrupted.

alternative *adj* another, different, second, substitute. • *n* choice, option, preference.

although *conj* albeit, even if, for all that, notwithstanding, though.

altitude *n* elevation, height, loftiness.
n antonym depth.

altogether *adv* completely, entirely, totally, utterly.

always *adv* continually, eternally, ever, evermore, perpetually, unceasingly.
adv antonym never.

amalgamate *vb* blend, combine, commingle, compound, incorporate, mix.
vb antonym separate.

amass *vb* accumulate, aggregate, collect, gather, heap, scrape together.

amateur *n* dilettante, nonprofessional.
n antonym professional.

amaze *vb* astonish, astound, bewilder, confound, confuse, dumbfound, perplex, stagger, stupefy.

amazement *n* astonishment, bewilderment, confusion, marvel, surprise, wonder.

ambassador *n* deputy, envoy, legate, minister, plenipotentiary.

ambiguous *adj* dubious, doubtful, enigmatic, equivocal, uncertain, indefinite, indistinct, obscure, vague.
adj antonyms clear.

ambition *n* aspiration, emulation, longing, yearning.
n antonyms apathy, diffidence.

ambitious *adj* aspiring, avid, eager, intent.
adj antonym unassuming.

ameliorate *vb* amend, benefit, better, elevate, improve, mend.

amenability *n* **1** amenableness, responsiveness. **2** accountability, liability, responsibility.

amenable *adj* **1** acquiescent, agreeable, persuadable, responsive, susceptible. **2** accountable, liable, responsible.

amend *vb* better, correct, improve, mend, redress, reform.
vb antonyms impair, worsen.

amends *npl* atonement, compensation, expiation, indemnification, recompense, reparation, restitution.

amenity *n* **1** agreeableness, mildness, pleasantness, softness. **2** affability, civility, courtesy, geniality, graciousness, urbanity.

amiable *adj* attractive, benign, charming, genial, good-natured, harmonious, kind, lovable, lovely, pleasant, pleasing, sweet, winning, winsome.
adj antonyms hostile, unfriendly.

amicable *adj* amiable, cordial, friendly, harmonious, kind, kindly, peaceable.

amiss *adj* erroneous, inaccurate, incorrect, faulty, improper, wrong. • *adv* erroneously, inaccurately, incorrectly, wrongly.
adj antonyms right, well.

amnesty *n* absolution, condonation, dispensation, forgiveness, oblivion.

amorous *adj* **1** ardent, enamoured, fond, longing, loving, passionate, tender. **2** erotic, impassioned.
adj antonyms cold, indifferent.

amorphous *adj* **1** formless, irregular, shapeless, unshapen. **2** noncrystalline, structureless. **3** chaotic, characterless, clumsy, disorganized, misshapen, unorganized, vague.

amount *n* aggregate, sum, total.

ample *adj* **1** broad, capacious, extended, extensive, great, large, roomy, spacious. **2** abounding, abundant, copious, generous, liberal, plentiful. **3** diffusive, unrestricted.
adj antonyms insufficient, meager.

amputate *vb* clip, curtail, prune, lop, remove, separate, sever.

amuse *vb* **1** charm, cheer, divert, enliven,

entertain, gladden, relax, solace. **2** beguile, cheat, deceive, delude, mislead.

vb antonym bore.

amusement *n* diversion, entertainment, frolic, fun, merriment, pleasure.

n antonyms bore, boredom.

analeptic *adj* comforting, invigorating, restorative.

analogy *n* correspondence, likeness, parallelism, parity, resemblance, similarity.

analysis *n* decomposition, dissection, resolution, separation.

anarchy *n* chaos, confusion, disorder, misrule, lawlessness, riot.

anathema *n* ban, curse, denunciation, excommunication, execration, malediction, proscription.

anatomy *n* **1** dissection. **2** form, skeleton, structure.

ancestor *n* father, forebear, forefather, progenitor.

ancestry *n* **1** family, house, line, lineage. **2** descent, genealogy, parentage, pedigree, stock.

anchor *vb* **1** fasten, fix, secure. **2** cast anchor, take firm hold. • *n* **1** (*naut*) ground tackle. **2** defence, hold, security, stay.

ancient *adj* **1** old, primitive, pristine. **2** antiquated, antique, archaic, obsolete.

adj antonym modern.

ancillary *adj* accessory, auxiliary, contributory, helpful, instrumental.

angelic *adj* **1** adorable, celestial, cherubic, heavenly, saintly, seraphic. **2** entrancing, enrapturing, rapturous, ravishing.

adj antonyms devilish, fiendish.

anger *vb* chafe, displease, enrage, gall, infuriate, irritate, madden. • *n* choler, exasperation, fury, gall, indignation, ire, passion, rage, resentment, spleen, wrath.

vb antonyms appease, calm, please.

n antonym forbearance.

angle *vb* fish. • *n* **1** divergence, flare, opening. **2** bend, corner, crotch, cusp, point. **3** fish-hook, hook.

angry *adj* chafed, choleric, exasperated, furious, galled, incensed, irritated, nettled, piqued, provoked, resentful.

adj antonyms calm, content.

anguish *n* agony, distress, grief, pang, rack, torment, torture.

n antonyms happiness, solace.

anile *adj* aged, decrepit, doting, imbecile, senile.

animadversion *n* **1** comment, notice, observation, remark. **2** blame, censure, condemnation, reproof, stricture.

animate *vb* **1** inform, quicken, vitalize, vivify. **2** fortify, invigorate, revive. **3** activate, enliven, excite, heat, impel, kindle, rouse, stimulate, stir, waken. **4** elate, embolden, encourage, exhilarate, gladden, hearten. • *adj* alive, breathing, live, living, organic, quick.

vb antonyms dull, inhibit.

adj antonyms dull, spiritless.

animosity *n* bitterness, enmity, grudge, hatred, hostility, rancour, rankling, spleen, virulence.

n antonym goodwill.

annals *npl* archives, chronicles, records, registers, rolls.

annex *vb* **1** affix, append, attach, subjoin, tag, tack. **2** connect, join, unite.

annihilate *vb* abolish, annul, destroy, dissolve, exterminate, extinguish, kill, obliterate, raze, ruin.

annotation *n* comment, explanation, illustration, note, observation, remark.

announce *vb* advertise, communicate, declare, disclose, proclaim, promulgate, publish, report, reveal, trumpet.

vb antonym suppress.

announcement *n* advertisement, annunciation, bulletin, declaration, manifesto, notice, notification, proclamation.

annoy *vb* badger, chafe, disquiet, disturb, fret, hector, irk, irritate, molest, pain, pester, plague, trouble, vex, worry, wound.

vb antonyms gratify, please.

annul *vb* abolish, abrogate, cancel, countermand, nullify, overrule, quash, repeal, recall, reverse, revoke.

anoint *vb* consecrate, oil, sanctify, smear.

anonymous *adj* nameless, unacknowledged, unsigned.

answer *vb* fulfil, rejoin, reply, respond, satisfy. • *n* **1** rejoinder, reply, response, retort. **2** confutation, rebuttal, refutation.

answerable *adj* accountable, amenable, correspondent, liable, responsible, suited.

antagonism *n* contradiction, discordance, disharmony, dissonant, incompatibility, opposition.

n antonyms rapport, sympathy.

antecedent *adj* anterior, foregoing, forerunning, precedent, preceding, previous. • *n* forerunner, precursor.

anterior *adj* **1** antecedent, foregoing, preceding, previous, prior. **2** fore, front.

anticipate *vb* **1** antedate, forestall, foretaste, prevent. **2** count upon, expect, forecast, foresee.

anticipation *n* **1** apprehension, contemplation, expectation, hope, prospect, trust. **2** expectancy, forecast, foresight, foretaste, preconception, presentiment.

antidote *n* **1** corrective, counteractive, counter-poison. **2** cure, remedy, restorative, specific.

antipathy *n* abhorrence, aversion, disgust, detestation, hate, hatred, horror, loathing, repugnance.
n antonyms rapport, sympathy.

antique *adj* ancient, archaic, bygone, old, old-fashioned.

anxiety *n* apprehension, care, concern, disquiet, fear, foreboding, misgiving, perplexity, trouble, uneasiness, vexation, worry.
n antonym composure.

anxious *adj* apprehensive, restless, solicitous, uneasy, unquiet, worried.
adj antonym composed.

apart *adv* **1** aloof, aside, separately. **2** asunder.

apathetic *adj* cold, dull, impassive, inert, listless, obtuse, passionless, sluggish, torpid, unfeeling.

ape *vb* **1** counterfeit, imitate, mimic. **2** affect. • *n* **1** simian, troglodyte. **2** imitator, mimic. **3** image, imitation, likeness, type.

aperture *n* chasm, cleft, eye, gap, opening, hole, orifice, passage.

aphorism *n* adage, apothegm, byword, maxim, proverb, saw, saying.

apish *adj* **1** imitative, mimicking. **2** affected, foppish, trifling.

aplomb *n* composure, confidence, equanimity, self-confidence.

apocryphal *adj* doubtful, fabulous, false, legendary, spurious, uncanonical.

apologetic *adj* **1** exculpatory, excusatory. **2** defensive, vindictive.
adj antonym defiant.

apology *n* **1** defence, justification, vindication. **2** acknowledgement, excuse, explanation, plea, reparation.
n antonym defiance.

apostate *adj* backsliding, disloyal, faithless, false, perfidious, recreant, traitorous, untrue. • *n* backslider, deserter, pervert, renegade, turncoat.

adj antonym faithful.
n antonyms adherent, convert, loyalist.

apostle *n* **1** angel, herald, messenger, missionary, preacher. **2** advocate, follower, supporter.

apothegm *n* aphorism, byword, dictum, maxim, proverb, saw, saying.

appal *vb* affright, alarm, daunt, dismay, frighten, horrify, scare, shock.
vb antonyms encourage, reassure.

apparel *n* attire, array, clothes, clothing, dress, garments, habit, raiment, robes, suit, trappings, vestments.

apparent *adj* **1** discernible, perceptible, visible. **2** conspicuous, evident, legible, manifest, obvious, open, patent, plain, unmistakable. **3** external, ostensible, seeming, superficial.
adj antonyms obscure, real.

apparition *n* **1** appearance, appearing, epiphany, manifestation. **2** being, form. **3** ghost, phantom, spectre, spirit, vision.

appeal *vb* address, entreat, implore, invoke, refer, request, solicit. • *n* application, entreaty, invocation, solicitation, suit.

appear *vb* **1** emerge, loom. **2** break, open. **3** arise, occur, offer. **4** look, seem, show.
vb antonym disappear.

appearance *n* **1** advent, arrival, apparition, coming. **2** form, shape. **3** colour, face, fashion, feature, guise, pretence, pretext. **4** air, aspect, complexion, demeanour, manner, mien.
n antonyms disappearance, reality.

appease *vb* abate, allay, assuage, calm, ease, lessen, mitigate, pacify, placate, quell, soothe, temper, tranquillize.
vb antonym aggravate.

appellation *n* address, cognomen, denomination, epithet, style, title.

append *vb* **1** attach, fasten, hang. **2** add, annex, subjoin, tack, tag.

appendix *n* **1** addition, adjunct, appurtenance, codicil. **2** excursus, supplement.

appetite *n* **1** craving, desire, longing, lust, passion. **2** gusto, relish, stomach, zest. **3** hunger.
n antonym distaste.

applaud *vb* acclaim, cheer, clap, compliment, encourage, extol, magnify.
vb antonyms censure, disparage.

applause *n* acclamation, approval, cheers, commendation, plaudit.

applicable *adj* adapted, appropriate, apt,

befitting, fitting, germane, pertinent, proper, relevant.

adj antonym inapplicable.

application *n* **1** emollient, lotion, ointment, poultice, wash. **2** appliance, exercise, practice, use. **3** appeal, petition, request, solicitation, suit. **4** assiduity, constancy, diligence, effort, industry.

apply *vb* **1** bestow, lay upon. **2** appropriate, convert, employ, exercise, use. **3** addict, address, dedicate, devote, direct, engage.

appoint *vb* **1** determine, establish, fix, prescribe. **2** bid, command, decree, direct, order, require. **3** allot, assign, delegate, depute, detail, destine, settle. **4** constitute, create, name, nominate. **5** equip, furnish, supply.

vb antonyms dismiss, reject.

apportion *vb* allocate, allot, allow, assign, deal, dispense, divide, share.

apposite *adj* apt, fit, germane, pertinent, relevant, suitable, pertinent.

appraise *vb* appreciate, estimate, prize, rate, value.

appreciate *vb* appreciate, esteem, estimate, rate, realize, value.

apprehend *vb* **1** arrest, catch, detain, seize, take. **2** conceive, imagine, regard, view. **3** appreciate, perceive, realize, see, take in. **4** fear, forebode. **5** conceive, fancy, hold, imagine, presume, understand.

apprehension *n* **1** arrest, capture, seizure. **2** intellect, intelligence, mind, reason. **3** discernment, intellect, knowledge, perception, sense. **4** belief, fancy, idea, notion, sentiment, view. **5** alarm, care, dread, distrust, fear, misgiving, suspicion.

apprise *vb* acquaint, inform, notify, tell.

approach *vb* **1** advance, approximate, come close. **2** broach. **3** resemble. • *n* **1** advance, advent. **2** approximation, convergence, nearing, tendency. **3** entrance, path, way.

approbation *n* **1** approval, commendation, liking, praise. **2** assent, concurrence, consent, endorsement, ratification, sanction.

appropriate *vb* **1** adopt, arrogate, assume, set apart. **2** allot, apportion, assign, devote. **3** apply, convert, employ, use. • *adj* adapted, apt, befitting, fit, opportune, seemly, suitable.

adj antonym inappropriate.

approve *vb* **1** appreciate, commend, like, praise, recommend, value. **2** confirm, countenance, justify, ratify, sustain, uphold.

vb antonym disapprove.

approximate *vb* approach, be tantamount to, border on, resemble, verge on. • *adj* **1** approaching, proximate. **2** almost exact, inexact, rough.

adj antonym exact.

apt *adj* **1** applicable, apposite, appropriate, befitting, fit, felicitous, germane. **2** disposed, inclined, liable, prone, subject. **3** able, adroit, clever, dextrous, expert, handy, happy, prompt, ready, skilful.

adj antonym inapt.

aptitude *n* **1** applicability, appropriateness, felicity, fitness, pertinence, suitability. **2** inclination, tendency, turn. **3** ability, address, adroitness, quickness, readiness, tact.

n antonym inaptitude.

arbitrary *adj* **1** absolute, autocratic, despotic, domineering, imperious, overbearing, unlimited. **2** capricious, discretionary, fanciful, voluntary, whimsical.

adj antonyms circumspect, rational, reasoned.

arcade *n* colonnade, loggia.

arch[1] *adj* **1** cunning, knowing, frolicsome, merry, mirthful, playful, roguish, shrewd, sly. **2** consummate, chief, leading, pre-eminent, prime, primary, principal.

arch[2] *vb* **1** span, vault. **2** bend, curve. • *n* archway, span, vault.

archaic *adj* ancient, antiquated, antique, bygone, obsolete, old.

archives *npl* documents, records, registers, rolls.

ardent *adj* **1** burning, fiery, hot. **2** eager, earnest, fervent, impassioned, keen, passionate, warm, zealous.

adj antonym dispassionate.

ardour *n* **1** glow, heat, warmth. **2** eagerness, enthusiasm, fervour, heat, passion, soul, spirit, warmth, zeal.

arduous *adj* **1** high, lofty, steep, uphill. **2** difficult, fatiguing, hard, laborious, onerous, tiresome, toilsome, wearisome.

adj antonym easy.

area *n* circle, circuit, district, domain, field, range, realm, region, tract.

argue *vb* **1** plead, reason upon. **2** debate, dispute. **3** denote, evince, imply, indicate, mean, prove. **4** contest, debate, discuss, sift.

arid *adj* **1** barren, dry, parched, sterile, unfertile. **2** dry, dull, jejune, pointless, uninteresting.

adj antonyms fertile, lively.

aright *adv* correctly, justly, rightly, truly.

arise *vb* 1 ascend, mount, soar, tower. 2 appear, emerge, rise, spring. 3 begin, originate. 4 rebel, revolt, rise. 5 accrue, come, emanate, ensue, flow, issue, originate, proceed, result.

aristocracy *n* gentry, nobility, noblesse, peerage.

arm[1] *n* 1 bough, branch, limb, protection. 2 cove, creek, estuary, firth, fjord, frith, inlet.

arm[2] *vb* 1 array, equip, furnish. 2 clothe, cover, fortify, guard, protect, strengthen.

arms *npl* 1 accoutrements, armour, array, harness, mail, panoply, weapons. 2 crest, escutcheon.

army *n* 1 battalions, force, host, legions, troops. 2 host, multitude, throng, vast assemblage.

around *prep* about, encircling, encompassing, round, surrounding. • *adv* about, approximately, generally, near, nearly, practically, round, thereabouts.

arouse *vb* animate, awaken, excite, incite, kindle, provoke, rouse, stimulate, warm, whet.

vb antonyms calm, lull, quieten.

arraign *vb* accuse, censure, charge, denounce, impeach, indict, prosecute, tax.

arrange *vb* 1 array, class, classify, dispose, distribute, group, range, rank. 2 adjust, determine, fix upon, settle. 3 concoct, construct, devise, plan, prepare, project.

arrant *adj* bad, consummate, downright, gross, notorious, rank, utter.

array *vb* 1 arrange, dispose, place, range, rank. 2 accoutre, adorn, attire, decorate, dress, enrobe, embellish, equip, garnish, habit, invest. • *n* 1 arrangement, collection, disposition, marshalling, order. 2 apparel, attire, clothes, dress, garments. 3 army, battalions, soldiery, troops.

arrest *vb* 1 check, delay, detain, hinder, hold, interrupt, obstruct, restrain, stay, stop, withhold. 2 apprehend, capture, catch, seize, take. 3 catch, engage, engross, fix, occupy, secure, rivet. • *n* 1 check, checking, detention, hindrance, interruption, obstruction, restraining, stay, staying, stopping. 2 apprehension, capture, detention, seizure.

arrive *vb* attain, come, get to, reach.

vb antonyms depart.

arrogance *n* assumption, assurance, disdain,

effrontery, haughtiness, loftiness, lordliness, presumption, pride, scornfulness, superciliousness.

n antonym humility.

arrogate *vb* assume, claim unduly, demand, usurp.

arrow *n* bolt, dart, reed, shaft.

art *n* 1 business, craft, employment, trade. 2 address, adroitness, aptitude, dexterity, ingenuity, knack, readiness, sagacity, skill. 3 artfulness, artifice, astuteness, craft, deceit, duplicity, finesse, subtlety.

artful *adj* crafty, cunning, disingenuous, insincere, sly, tricky, wily.

adj antonyms artless, ingenuous, naïve.

article *n* 1 branch, clause, division, head, item, member, paragraph, part, point, portion. 2 essay, paper, piece. 3 commodity, substance, thing.

artifice *n* art, chicanery, contrivance, cunning, deception, deceit, duplicity, effort, finesse, fraud, imposture, invention, stratagem, subterfuge, trick, trickery.

artificial *adj* 1 counterfeit, sham, spurious. 2 assumed, affected, constrained, fictitious, forced, laboured, strained.

adj antonyms genuine, natural.

artless *adj* 1 ignorant, rude, unskilful, untaught. 2 natural, plain, simple. 3 candid, fair, frank, guileless, honest, plain, simple, sincere, truthful, unsuspicious.

adj antonym artful.

ascend *vb* arise, aspire, climb, mount, soar, tower.

vb antonym descend.

ascendancy, ascendency *n* authority, control, domination, mastery, power, predominance, sovereignty, superiority, sway.

ascertain *vb* 1 certify, define, determine, establish, fix, settle, verify. 2 discover, find out, get at.

ashamed *adj* abashed, confused.

adj antonyms defiant, shameless.

ask *vb* 1 interrogate, inquire, question. 2 adjure, beg, conjure, crave, desire, dun, entreat, implore, invite, inquire, petition, request, solicit, supplicate, seek, sue.

aspect *n* 1 air, bearing, countenance, expression, feature, look, mien, visage. 2 appearance, attitude, condition, light, phase, position, posture, situation, state, view. 3 angle, direction, outlook, prospect.

asperity *n* 1 ruggedness, roughness, unevenness. 2 acrimony, causticity, corrosiveness, sharpness, sourness, tartness. **3** acerbity, bitterness, churlishness, harshness, sternness, sullenness, severity, virulence.

aspersion *n* abuse, backbiting, calumny, censure, defamation, detraction, slander, vituperation, reflection, reproach.

n antonyms commendation, compliment.

aspiration *n* aim, ambition, craving, hankering, hope, longing.

aspire *vb* **1** desire, hope, long, yearn. **2** ascend, mount, rise, soar, tower.

assail *vb* **1** assault, attack, invade, oppugn. **2** impugn, malign, maltreat. **3** ply, storm.

assassinate *vb* dispatch, kill, murder, slay.

assault *vb* assail, attack, charge, invade. • *n* **1** aggression, attack, charge, incursion, invasion, onset, onslaught. **2** storm.

assemble *vb* **1** call, collect, congregate, convene, convoke, gather, levy, muster. **2** converge, forgather.

vb antonym disperse.

assembly *n* **1** company, collection, concourse, congregation, gathering, meeting, rout, throng. **2** caucus, congress, conclave, convention, convocation, diet, legislature, meeting, parliament, synod.

assent *vb* accede, acquiesce, agree, concur, subscribe, yield. • *n* accord, acquiescence, allowance, approval, approbation, consent.

vb antonym disagree.

assert *vb* **1** affirm, allege, aver, asseverate, declare, express, maintain, predicate, pronounce, protest. **2** claim, defend, emphasize, maintain, press, uphold, vindicate.

vb antonym deny.

assertion *n* **1** affirmation, allegation, asseveration, averment, declaration, position, predication, remark, statement, word. **2** defence, emphasis, maintenance, pressing, support, vindication.

n antonym denial.

assess *vb* **1** appraise, compute, estimate, rate, value. **2** assign, determine, fix, impose, levy.

asseverate *vb* affirm, aver, avow, declare, maintain, protest.

assiduous *adj* active, busy, careful, constant, diligent, devoted, indefatigable, industrious, sedulous, unremitting, untiring.

assign *vb* **1** allot, appoint, apportion, appropriate. **2** fix, designate, determine, specify. **3** adduce, advance, allege, give, grant, offer, present, show.

assist *vb* **1** abet, aid, befriend, further, help, patronize, promote, second, speed, support, sustain. **2** aid, relieve, succour. **3** alternate with, relieve, spell.

vb antonym thwart.

associate *vb* **1** affiliate, combine, conjoin, couple, join, link, relate, yoke. **2** consort, fraternize, mingle, sort. • *n* **1** chum, companion, comrade, familiar, follower, mate. **2** ally, confederate, friend, partner, fellow.

association *n* combination, company, confederation, connection, partnership, society.

assort *vb* **1** arrange, class, classify, distribute, group, rank, sort. **2** agree, be adapted, consort, suit.

assuage *vb* allay, alleviate, appease, calm, ease, lessen, mitigate, moderate, mollify, pacify, quell, relieve, soothe, tranquillize.

vb antonym exacerbate.

assume *vb* **1** take, undertake. **2** affect, counterfeit, feign, pretend, sham. **3** arrogate, usurp. **4** beg, hypothesize, imply, postulate, posit, presuppose, suppose, simulate.

assurance *n* **1** assuredness, certainty, conviction, persuasion, pledge, security, surety, warrant. **2** engagement, pledge, promise. **3** averment, assertion, protestation. **4** audacity, confidence, courage, firmness, intrepidity. **5** arrogance, brass, boldness, effrontery, face, front, impudence.

n antonym uncertainty.

assure *vb* **1** encourage, embolden, hearten. **2** certify, insure, secure against loss, vouch for.

astonish *vb* amaze, astound, confound, daze, dumbfound, overwhelm, startle, stun, stupefy, surprise.

astute *adj* acute, cunning, deep, discerning, ingenious, intelligent, penetrating, perspicacious, quick, sagacious, sharp, shrewd.

adj antonym stupid.

asylum *n* refuge, retreat, sanctuary, shelter.

athletic *adj* brawny, lusty, muscular, powerful, robust, sinewy, stalwart, stout, strapping, strong, sturdy.

adj antonym puny.

athletics *npl* aerobics, eurythmics, exercise, exercising, gymnastics, sports, track and field, workout.

atom *n* bit, molecule, monad, particle, scintilla.

atone *vb* answer, compensate, expiate, satisfy.

atonement *n* amends, expiation, propitiation, reparation, satisfaction.

atrocity *n* depravity, enormity, flagrancy, ferocity, savagery, villainy.

attach *vb* **1** affix, annex, connect, fasten, join, hitch, tie. **2** charm, captivate, enamour, endear, engage, win. **3** (*legal*) distress, distrain, seize, take.
vb antonyms detach, unfasten.

attack *vb* **1** assail, assault, charge, encounter, invade, set upon, storm, tackle. **2** censure, criticise, impugn. • *n* aggression, assault, charge, offence, onset, onslaught, raid, thrust.

attain *vb* **1** accomplish, achieve, acquire, get, obtain, secure. **2** arrive at, come to, reach.

attempt *vb* **1** assail, assault, attack. **2** aim, endeavour, seek, strive, try. • *n* **1** effort, endeavour, enterprise, experiment, undertaking, venture. **2** assault, attack, onset.

attend *vb* **1** accompany, escort, follow. **2** guard, protect, watch. **3** minister to, serve, wait on. **4** give heed, hear, harken, listen. **5** be attendant, serve, tend, wait.

attention *n* **1** care, circumspection, heed, mindfulness, observation, regard, watch, watchfulness. **2** application, reflection, study. **3** civility, courtesy, deference, politeness, regard, respect. **4** addresses, courtship, devotion, suit, wooing.
n antonyms disregard, inattention.

attentive *adj* alive, awake, careful, civil, considerate, courteous, heedful, mindful, observant, watchful.
adj antonyms heedless, inattentive, inconsiderate.

attenuate *vb* contract, dilute, diminish, elongate, lengthen, lessen, rarefy, reduce, slim, thin, weaken.

attest *vb* **1** authenticate, certify, corroborate, confirm, ratify, seal, vouch. **2** adjure, call to witness, invoke. **3** confess, display, exhibit, manifest, prove, show, witness.

attic *n* garret, loft, upper storey.

Attic *adj* **1** delicate, subtle, penetrating, pointed, pungent. **2** chaste, classic, correct, elegant, polished, pure.

attire *vb* accoutre, apparel, array, clothe, dress, enrobe, equip, rig, robe. • *n* clothes, clothing, costume, dress, garb, gear, habiliment, outfit, toilet, trapping, vestment, vesture, wardrobe.

attitude *n* **1** pose, position, posture. **2** aspect, conjuncture, condition, phase, prediction, situation, standing, state.

attract *vb* **1** draw, pull. **2** allure, captivate, charm, decoy, enamour, endear, entice, engage, fascinate, invite, win.

attraction *n* **1** affinity, drawing, pull. **2** allurement, charm, enticement, fascination, magnetism, lure, seduction, witchery.

attribute *vb* ascribe, assign, impute, refer. • *n* characteristic, mark, note, peculiarity, predicate, property, quality.

attrition *n* abrasion, friction, rubbing.

attune *vb* **1** accord, harmonize, modulate, tune. **2** accommodate, adapt, adjust, attempt.

audacity *n* **1** boldness, courage, daring, fearlessness, intrepidity. **2** assurance, brass, effrontery, face, front, impudence, insolence, presumption, sauciness.
n antonyms caution, reserve, timidity.

audience *n* **1** assemblage, congregation. **2** hearing, interview, reception.

augment *vb* add to, enhance, enlarge, increase, magnify, multiply, swell.
vb antonym decrease.

augmentation *n* accession, addition, enlargement, extension, increase.

augury *n* **1** prediction, prognostication, prophecy, soothsaying. **2** auspice, forerunner, harbinger, herald, omen, precursor, portent, sign.

august *adj* awe-inspiring, awful, dignified, grand, imposing, kingly, majestic, noble, princely, regal, solemn, stately, venerable.

auspicious *adj* **1** fortunate, happy, lucky, prosperous, successful. **2** bright, favourable, golden, opportune, promising, prosperous.
adj antonyms inauspicious, ominous.

austere *adj* ascetic, difficult, formal, hard, harsh, morose, relentless, rigid, rigorous, severe, stern, stiff, strict, uncompromising, unrelenting.
adj antonyms elaborate, extravagant, genial.

authentic *adj* **1** genuine, pure, real, true, unadulterated, uncorrupted, veritable. **2** accurate, authoritative, reliable, true, trustworthy.
adj antonyms counterfeit, inauthentic, spurious.

authority *n* **1** dominion, empire, government, jurisdiction, power, sovereignty. **2** ascendency, control, influence, rule, supremacy, sway. **3** authorization, liberty, order, permit, precept, sanction, warranty. **4** testimony, witness. **5** connoisseur, expert, master.

authorize *vb* **1** empower, enable, entitle. **2** allow, approve, confirm, countenance, permit, ratify, sanction.

auxiliary *adj* aiding, ancillary, assisting, helpful, subsidiary. • *n* ally, assistant, confederate, help.

avail *vb* assist, benefit, help, profit, use, service.

available *adj* accessible, advantageous, applicable, beneficial, profitable, serviceable, useful.

   adj antonym unavailable.

avarice *n* acquisitiveness, covetousness, greediness, penuriousness, rapacity.

n antonym generosity.

avaricious *adj* grasping, miserly, niggardly, parsimonious.

avenge *vb* punish, retaliate, revenge, vindicate.

avenue *n* **1** access, entrance, entry, passage. **2** alley, path, road, street, walk. **3** channel, pass, route, way.

aver *vb* allege, assert, asseverate, avouch, declare, pronounce, protest, say.

averse *adj* adverse, backward, disinclined, indisposed, opposed, unwilling.

adj antonyms sympathetic, willing.

aversion *n* abhorrence, antipathy, disgust, dislike, hate, hatred, loathing, reluctance, repugnance.

n antonyms liking, sympathy.

avid *adj* eager, greedy, voracious.

adj antonym indifferent.

avocation *n* **1** business, calling, employ-

ment, occupation, trade, vocation. **2** distraction, hindrance, interruption.

avoid *vb* **1** dodge, elude, escape, eschew, shun. **2** forebear, refrain from.

avouch *vb* allege, assert, declare, maintain, say.

avow *vb* admit, acknowledge, confess, own.

awaken *vb* **1** arouse, excite, incite, kindle, provoke, spur, stimulate. **2** wake, waken. **3** begin, be excited.

award *vb* adjudge, allot, assign, bestow, decree, grant. • *n* adjudication, allotment, assignment, decision, decree, determination, gift, judgement.

aware *adj* acquainted, apprised, conscious, conversant, informed, knowing, mindful, sensible.

adj antonyms insensitive, unaware.

away *adv* absent, not present. • *adj* **1** at a distance. **2** elsewhere. **3** out of the way.

awe *vb* cow, daunt, intimidate, overawe. • *n* **1** abashment, fear, reverence. **2** dread, fear, fearfulness, terror.

n antonym contempt.

awful *adj* **1** august, awesome, dread, grand, inspired. **2** abashed, alarming, appalled, dire, frightful, portentous, tremendous.

awkward *adj* **1** bungling, clumsy, inept, maladroit, unskilful. **2** lumbering, unfit, ungainly, unmanageable. **3** boorish. **4** inconvenient, unsuitable.

adj antonyms amenable, convenient, elegant, graceful, straightforward.

axiom *n* adage, aphorism, apothegm, maxim, postulation, truism.

axis *n* axle, shaft, spindle.

azure *adj* blue, cerulean, sky-coloured.

B

babble *vb* blather, chatter, gibber, jabber, prate, prattle. • *n* chat, gossip, palaver, prate, tattle.

babel *n* clamour, confusion, din, discord, disorder, hubbub, jargon, pother.

baby *vb* coddle, cosset, indulge, mollycoddle, pamper, spoil. • *adj* 1 babyish, childish, infantile, puerile. 2 diminutive, doll-like, miniature, pocket, pocket-sized, small-scale. • *n* 1 babe, brat, child, infant, suckling, nursling. 2 chicken, coward, milksop, namby-pamby, sad sack, weakling. 3 miniature. 4 innocent.

back *vb* 1 abet, aid, countenance, favour, second, support, sustain. 2 go back, move back, retreat, withdraw. • *adj* hindmost. •*adv* 1 in return, in consideration. 2 ago, gone, since. 3 aside, away, behind, by. 4 abaft, astern, backwards, hindwards, rearwards. •*n* end, hind part, posterior, rear.
vb antonym discourage.

backbite *vb* abuse, asperse, blacken, defame, libel, malign, revile, scandalize, slander, traduce, vilify.

backbone *n* 1 chine, spine. 2 constancy, courage, decision, firmness, nerve, pluck, resolution, steadfastness.
n antonyms spinelessness, weakness.

backward *adj* 1 disinclined, hesitating, indisposed, loath, reluctant, unwilling, wavering. 2 dull, slow, sluggish, stolid, stupid. •*adv* aback, behind, rearward.
adj antonyms forward, precocious.

bad *adj* 1 baleful, baneful, detrimental, evil, harmful, hurtful, injurious, noxious, pernicious, unwholesome, vicious. 2 abandoned, corrupt, depraved, immoral, sinful, unfair, unprincipled, wicked. 3 unfortunate, unhappy, unlucky, miserable. 4 disappointing, discouraging, distressing, sad, unwelcoming. 5 abominable, mean, shabby, scurvy, vile, wretched. 6 defective, inferior, imperfect, incompetent, poor, unsuitable. 7 hard, heavy, serious, severe.

badge *n* brand, emblem, mark, sign, symbol, token.

badger *vb* annoy, bait, bother, hector, harry, pester, persecute, tease, torment, trouble, vex, worry.

baffle *vb* 1 balk, block, check, circumvent, defeat, foil, frustrate, mar, thwart, undermine, upset. 2 bewilder, confound, disconcert, perplex.
vb antonyms enlighten, help.

bait *vb* harry, tease, worry. •*n* allurement, decoy, enticement, lure, temptation.
vb antonym disincentive

balance *vb* 1 equilibrate, pose, (*naut*) trim. 2 compare, weigh. 3 compensate, counteract, estimate. 4 adjust, clear, equalize, square. •*n* 1 equilibrium, liberation. 2 excess, remainder, residue, surplus.
vb antonyms overbalance, unbalance.
n antonyms imbalance, instability.

bald *adj* 1 bare, naked, uncovered, treeless. 2 dull, inelegant, meagre, prosaic, tame, unadorned, vapid.
adj antonyms adorned, hirsute.

baleful *adj* baneful, deadly, calamitous, hurtful, injurious, mischievous, noxious, pernicious, ruinous.
adj antonyms auspicious, favorable.

balk *vb* baffle, defeat, disappoint, disconcert, foil, frustrate, thwart.

ball *n* 1 drop, globe, orb, pellet, marble, sphere. 2 bullet, missile, projectile, shot. 3 assembly, dance.

balmy *adj* aromatic, fragrant, healing, odorous, perfumed.

ban *vb* 1 anathematize, curse, execrate. 2 interdict, outlaw. •*n* 1 edict, proclamation. 2 anathema, curse, denunciation, execration. 3 interdiction, outlawry, penalty, prohibition
vb antonym permit.
n antonyms dispensation, permission.

band[1] *vb* 1 belt, bind, cinch, encircle, gird, girdle. 2 ally, associate, combine, connect, join, league. 3 bar, marble, streak, stripe, striate, vein. •*n* 1 crew, gang, horde, society, troop. 2 ensemble, group, orchestra.

band[2] *n* 1 ligament, ligature, tie. 2 bond, chain, cord, fetter, manacle, shackle, trammel. 3 bandage, belt, binding, cincture, girth, tourniquet.
n antonyms disband, disperse.

bandit *n* brigand, freebooter, footpad, gangster, highwayman, outlaw, robber.

baneful *adj* **1** poisonous, venomous. **2** deadly, destructive, hurtful, mischievous, noxious, pernicious.

bang *vb* **1** beat, knock, maul, pommel, pound, strike, thrash, thump. **2** slam. **3** clatter, rattle, resound, ring. •*n* **1** clang, clangour, whang. **2** blow, knock, lick, thump, thwack, whack.

banish *vb* **1** exile, expatriate, ostracize. **2** dismiss, exclude, expel.
vb antonyms recall, welcome.

bank¹ *vb* **1** incline, slope, tilt. **2** embank. •*n* **1** dike, embankment, escarpment, heap, knoll, mound. **2** border, bound, brim, brink, margin, rim, strand. **3** course, row, tier.
n antonym spend.

bank² *vb* deposit, keep, save. •*n* depository, fund, reserve, savings, stockpile.

banner *n* colours, ensign, flag, standard, pennon, standard, streamer.

banter *vb* chaff, deride, jeer, joke, mock, quiz, rally, ridicule. •*n* badinage, chaff, derision, jesting, joking, mockery, quizzing, raillery, ridicule.

bar *vb* exclude, hinder, obstruct, prevent, prohibit, restrain, stop. •*n* **1** grating, pole, rail, rod. **2** barricade, hindrance, impediment, obstacle, obstruction, stop. **3** bank, sand bar, shallow, shoal, spit. **4** (*legal*) barristers, counsel, court, judgement, tribunal.

barbarian *adj* brutal, cruel, ferocious, fierce, fell, inhuman, ruthless, savage, truculent, unfeeling. •*n* brute, ruffian, savage.

barbaric *adj* **1** barbarous, rude, savage, uncivilized, untamed. **2** capricious, coarse, gaudy, riotous, showy, outlandish, uncouth, untamed, wild.

bare *vb* **1** denude, depilate, divest, strip, unsheathe. **2** disclose, manifest, open, reveal, show. •*adj* **1** denuded, exposed, naked, nude, stripped, unclothed, uncovered, undressed, unsheltered. **2** alone, mere, sheer, simple. **3** bald, meagre, plain, unadorned, uncovered, unfurnished. **4** empty, destitute, indigent, poor.

bargain *vb* **1** agree, contract, covenant, stipulate. **2** convey, sell, transfer. •*n* **1** agreement, compact, contract, covenant, convention, indenture, transaction, stipulation, treaty. **2** proceeds, purchase, result.

barren *adj* **1** childless, infecund, sterile. **2** (*bot*) acarpous, sterile. **3** bare, infertile, poor, sterile, unproductive. **4** ineffectual, unfruitful, uninstructive.
adj antonyms fertile, productive, useful.

barricade *vb* block up, fortify, protect, obstruct. •*n* barrier, obstruction, palisade, stockade.

barrier *n* bar, barricade, hindrance, impediment, obstacle, obstruction, stop.

barter *vb* bargain, exchange, sell, trade, traffic.

base¹ *adj* **1** cheap, inferior, worthless. **2** counterfeit, debased, false, spurious. **3** baseborn, humble, lowly, mean, nameless, plebeian, unknown, untitled, vulgar. **4** abject, beggarly, contemptible, degraded, despicable, low, menial, pitiful, servile, sordid, sorry, worthless.

base² *vb* establish, found, ground. •*n* **1** foundation, fundament, substructure, underpinning. **2** pedestal, plinth, stand. **3** centre, headquarters, HQ, seat. **4** starting point. **5** basis, cause, grounds, reason, standpoint. **6** bottom, foot, foundation, ground.

bashful *adj* coy, diffident, shy, timid.
adj antonym confident.

basis *n* **1** agreement, arrangement, system, way. **2** base, bottom, ground, groundwork, foundation, theory, premise, principle, starting point.

base *n* bottom, foundation, fundament, ground, groundwork.

bastard *adj* adulterated, baseborn, counterfeit, false, illegitimate, sham. •*n* love child.

batch *vb* assemble, bunch, bundle, collect, gather, group. •*n* amount, collection, crowd, lot, quantity.

bathe *vb* **1** immerse, lave, wash. **2** cover, enfold, enwrap, drench, flood, infold, suffuse. •*n* bath, shower, swim.

batter¹ *vb* **1** beat, pelt, smite. **2** break, bruise, demolish, destroy, shatter, shiver, smash. **3** abrade, deface, disfigure, indent, mar. **4** incline, recede, retreat, slope. •*n* batsman, striker.

batter² *n* dough, goo, goop, gunk, paste, pulp.

battle *vb* contend, contest, engage, fight, strive, struggle. •*n* action, affair, brush, combat, conflict, contest, engagement, fight, fray.

bauble *n* gewgaw, gimcrack, knick-knack, plaything, toy, trifle, trinket.

bawdy *adj* obscene, filthy, impure, indecent, lascivious, lewd, smutty, unchaste.
adj antonyms chaste, clean.

bawl *vb* clamour, cry, hoot, howl, roar, shout, squall, vociferate, yell.

bay[1] *vb* bark, howl, wail, yell, yelp.

bay[2] *n* alcove, compartment, niche, nook, opening, recess.

bay[3] *n* bight, cove, gulf, inlet.

bays *npl* applause, chaplet, fame, garland, glory, honour, plaudits, praise, renown.

beach *vb* ground, maroon, strand. •*n* coast, margin, rim, sands, seashore, seaside, shore, shoreline, strand, waterfront.

beacon *vb* **1** brighten, flame, shine, signal. **2** enlighten, illuminate, illumine, guide, light, signal. •*n* **1** lighthouse, pharos, watchtower. **2** sign, signal.

beadle *n* apparitor, church officer, crier, servitor, summoner.

beak *n* **1** bill, mandible, (*sl*) nose. **2** (*naut*) bow, prow, stem.

beam *vb* beacon, gleam, glisten, glitter, shine. •*n* **1** balk, girder, joist, scantling, stud. **2** gleam, pencil, ray, streak.

bear *vb* **1** support, sustain, uphold. **2** carry, convey, deport, transport, waft. **3** abide, brook, endure, stand, suffer, tolerate, undergo. **4** carry on, keep up, maintain. **5** cherish, entertain, harbour. **6** produce. **7** cast, drop, sustain. **8** endure, submit, suffer. **9** act, operate, work.

bearable *adj* endurable, sufferable, supportable, tolerable.

bearing *n* **1** air, behaviour, demeanour, deportment, conduct, carriage, conduct, mien, port. **2** connection, dependency, relation. **3** endurance, patience, suffering. **4** aim, course, direction. **5** bringing forth, producing. **6** bed, receptacle, socket.

beastly *adj* abominable, brutish, ignoble, low, sensual, vile.

beat *vb* **1** bang, baste, buffet, cane, hammer, hit, knock, maul, pound, pummel, punch, strike, thrash, thump, thwack, whack, whip. **2** bray, bruise, pound, pulverize. **3** batter, pelt. **4** conquer, defeat, overcome, rout, subdue, surpass, vanquish. **5** pulsate, throb. **6** dash, strike. •*adj* **1** baffled, bamboozled, confounded, mystified, nonplussed, perplexed, puzzled, stumped. **2** done, dog-tired, exhausted, tired out, worn out. **3** beaten, defeated, licked. •*n* **1** blow, striking, stroke. **2** beating, pulsation, throb. **3** accent, metre, rhythm. **4** circuit, course, round.

beatific *adj* ecstatic, enchanting, enraptured, ravishing, rapt.

beatitude *n* blessing, ecstasy, felicity, happiness.

beau *n* **1** coxcomb, dandy, exquisite, fop, popinjay. **2** admirer, lover, suitor, sweetheart.

beautiful *adj* charming, comely, fair, fine, exquisite, handsome, lovely, pretty.
adj antonyms plain, ugly.

beautify *vb* adorn, array, bedeck, deck, decorate, embellish, emblazon, garnish, gild, grace, ornament, set.

beauty *n* **1** elegance, grace, symmetry. **2** attractiveness, comeliness, fairness, loveliness, seemliness. **3** belle.

become *vb* **1** change to, get, go, wax. **2** adorn, befit, set off, suit.

becoming *adj* **1** appropriate, apt, congruous, decent, decorous, due, fit, proper, right, seemly, suitable. **2** comely, graceful, neat, pretty.
adj antonym unbecoming.

bed *vb* **1** embed, establish, imbed, implant, infix, inset, plant. **2** harbour, house, lodge. •*n* **1** berth, bunk, cot, couch. **2** channel, depression, hollow. **3** base, foundation, receptacle, support, underlay. **4** accumulation, layer, seam, stratum, vein.

befall *vb* **1** betide, overtake. **2** chance, happen, occur, supervene.

befitting *adj* appropriate, apt, becoming, decorous, fit, proper, right, suitable, seemly.

befool *vb* bamboozle, beguile, cheat, circumvent, delude, deceive, dupe, fool, hoax, hoodwink, infatuate, stupefy, trick.

befriend *vb* aid, benefit, countenance, encourage, favour, help, patronize.
vb antonym neglect.

beg *vb* adjure, ask, beseech, conjure, crave, entreat, implore, importune, petition, pray, request, solicit, supplicate.

beggarly *adj* **1** destitute, needy, poor. **2** abject, base, despicable, grovelling, low, mean, miserable, miserly, paltry, pitiful, scant, servile, shabby, sorry, stingy, vile, wretched.

begin *vb* **1** arise, commence, enter, open. **2** inaugurate, institute, originate, start.
vb antonyms end, finish.

beginning *n* **1** arising, commencement, dawn, emergence, inauguration, inception, initiation, opening, outset, start, rise. **2** origin, source.
n antonyms end, finish.

beguile *vb* **1** cheat, deceive, delude. **2** amuse, cheer, divert, entertain, solace.

behaviour *n* air, bearing, carriage, comportment, conduct, demeanour, deportment, manner, manners, mien.

behest *n* bidding, charge, command, commandment, direction, hest, injunction, mandate, order, precept.

behind *prep* abaft, after, following. •*adv* abaft, aft, astern, rearward. •*adj* **1** arrested, backward, checked, detained, retarded. **2** after, behind. •*n* **1** rear, stern, tail. **2** back, back side, reverse. **3** bottom, buttocks, posterior, rump.

behold *vb* consider, contemplate, eye, observe, regard, see, survey, view.

behoove *vb* **1** become, befit, suit. **2** be binding, be obligatory.

being *n* **1** actuality, existence, reality, subsistence. **2** core, essence, heart, root.

beleaguer *vb* **1** besiege, blockade, invest. **2** beset, block, encumber, encompass, encounter, obstruct, surround.

belief *n* **1** assurance, confidence, conviction, persuasion, trust. **2** acceptance, assent, credence, credit, currency. **3** creed, doctrine, dogma, faith, opinion, tenet.
n antonym disbelief.

bellow *vb* bawl, clamour, cry, howl, vociferate, yell.

belt *n* **1** band, cincture, girdle, girth, zone. **2** region, stretch, strip.

bemoan *vb* bewail, deplore, lament, mourn.
vb antonym gloat.

bemused *adj* bewildered, confused, fuddled, muddled, muzzy, stupefied, tipsy.

bend *vb* **1** bow, crook, curve, deflect, draw. **2** direct, incline, turn. **3** bend, dispose, influence, mould, persuade, subdue. **4** (*naut*) fasten, make fast. **5** crook, deflect, deviate, diverge, swerve. **6** bow, lower, stoop. **7** condescend, deign. •*n* angle, arc, crook, curvature, curve, elbow, turn.

beneath *prep* **1** below, under, underneath. **2** unbecoming, unbefitting, unworthy. •*adv* below, underneath.

benediction *n* beatitude, benefit, benison, blessing, boon, grace, favour.
n antonyms anathema, curse, execration.

benefaction *n* alms, boon, charity, contribution, donation, favour, gift, grant, gratuity, offering, present.

beneficent *adj* benevolent, bounteous, bountiful, charitable, generous, kind, liberal.

beneficial *adj* advantageous, favourable, helpful, profitable, salutary, serviceable, useful, wholesome.
adj antonym harmful.

benefit *vb* **1** befriend, help, serve. **2** advantage, avail, profit. • *n* **1** favour, good turn, kindness, service. **2** account, advantage, behalf, gain, good, interest, profit, utility.
vb antonyms harm, hinder, undermine.
n antonym harm.

benevolence *n* beneficence, benignity, generosity, goodwill, humanity, kindliness, kindness.
n antonym meanness.

benevolent *adj* altruistic, benign, charitable, generous, humane, kind, kind-hearted, liberal, obliging, philanthropic, tender, unselfish.
adj antonym mean.

benign *adj* amiable, amicable, beneficent, benevolent, complaisant, friendly, gentle, good, gracious, humane, kind, kindly, obliging.

bent *adj* **1** angled, angular, bowed, crooked, curved, deflected, flexed, hooked, twisted. **2** disposed, inclined, prone, minded. **3** (*with* on) determined, fixed on, resolved, set on. • *n* bias, inclination, leaning, partiality, penchant, predilection, prepossession, proclivity, propensity
adj antonym straight.

bequeath *vb* **1** devise, give, grant, leave, will. **2** impart, transmit.

berate *vb* chide, rate, reprimand, reprove, scold.
vb antonym praise.

bereave *vb* afflict, deprive of, despoil, dispossess, divest, rob, spoil, strip.

beseech *vb* **1** beg, conjure, entreat, implore, importune, petition, supplicate. **2** ask, beg, crave, solicit.

beset *vb* **1** besiege, encompass, enclose, environ, encircle, hem in, surround. **2** decorate, embarrass, embellish, entangle, garnish, ornament, perplex, set.

beside *prep* **1** at the side of, by the side of, close to, near. **2** aside from, not according to, out of the course of, out of the way of. **3** not in possession of, out of. **4** *also* **besides** barring, distinct from, excluding, except, excepting, in addition to, other than, over and above, save. • *adv also* **besides** additionally, also, further, furthermore, in addition, more, moreover, over and above, too, yet.

besiege *vb* beset, blockade, encircle, encompass, environ, invest, surround.

besot *vb* **1** drench, intoxicate, soak, steep. **2** befool, delude, infatuate, stultify, stupefy.

bespatter *vb* bedaub, befoul, besmirch, smear, spatter.

bespeak *vb* accost, address, declare, evince, forestall, imply, indicate, prearrange, predict, proclaim, solicit.

best *vb* **1** better, exceed, excel, predominate, rival, surpass. **2** beat, defeat, outdo, worst. •*adj* chief, first, foremost, highest, leading, utmost. •*adv* **1** advantageously, excellently. **2** extremely, greatly. •*n* choice, cream, flower, pick.
adj antonym worst.
adv antonym worst.
n antonym worst.

bestial *adj* **1** beast-like, beastly, brutal, degraded, depraved, irrational, low, vile. **2** sensual.
adj antonyms civilized, humane.

bestow *vb* **1** deposit, dispose, put, place, store, stow. **2** accord, give, grant, impart.
vb antonym deprive.

bet *vb* gamble, hazard, lay, pledge, stake, wage, wager. •*n* gamble, hazard, stake, wager.

bethink *vb* cogitate, consider, ponder, recall, recollect, reflect, remember.

betide *vb* befall, happen, occur, overtake.

betimes *adv* beforehand, early, forward, soon.

betoken *vb* argue, betray, denote, evince, imply, indicate, prove, represent, show, signify, typify.

betray *vb* **1** be false to, break, violate. **2** blab, discover, divulge, expose, reveal, show, tell. **3** argue, betoken, display, evince, expose, exhibit, imply, indicate, manifest, reveal. **4** beguile, delude, ensnare, lure, mislead. **5** corrupt, ruin, seduce, undo.
vb antonyms defend, fulfil, protect.

betroth *vb* affiance, engage to marry, pledge in marriage, plight.

better *vb* advance, amend, correct, exceed, improve, promote, rectify, reform. •*adj* bigger, fitter, greater, larger, less ill, preferable. •*n* **1** advantage, superiority, upper hand, victory. **2** improvement, greater good.
vb antonyms deteriorate, worsen.
adj antonym worse.

between *prep* amidst, among, betwixt.

bewail *vb* bemoan, deplore, express, lament, mourn over, rue, sorrow.

beware *vb* avoid, heed, look out, mind.
vb antonyms brave, dare.

bewilder *vb* confound, confuse, daze, distract, embarrass, entangle, muddle, mystify, nonplus, perplex, pose, puzzle, stagger.

bewitch *vb* captivate, charm, enchant, enrapture, entrance, fascinate, spellbind, transport.

beyond *prep* above, before, farther, over, past, remote, yonder.

bias *vb* bend, dispose, incline, influence, predispose, prejudice. •*n* bent, inclination, leaning, partiality, penchant, predilection, prepossession, proclivity, propensity, slant, tendency, turn.
n antonyms fairness, impartiality.

bicker *vb* argue, dispute, jangle, quarrel, spar, spat, squabble, wrangle.
vb antonym agree.

bid *vb* **1** charge, command, direct, enjoin, order, require, summon. **2** ask, call, invite, pray, request, solicit. **3** offer, propose, proffer, tender. •*n* bidding, offer, proposal.

big *adj* **1** bumper, bulking, bulky, great, huge, large, massive, monstrous. **2** important, imposing. **3** distended, inflated, full, swollen, tumid. **4** fecund, fruitful, productive, teeming.
adj antonyms little, small.

bigoted *adj* dogmatic, hidebound, intolerant, obstinate, narrow-minded, opinionated, prejudiced.
adj antonyms broad-minded, enlightened, liberal.

bill[1] *vb* **1** charge, dun, invoice. **2** programme, schedule. **3** advertise, boost, plug, promote, publicize. • *n* **1** account, charges, reckoning, score. **2** advertisement, banner, hoarding, placard, poster. **3** playbill, programme, schedule. **4** bill of exchange, certificate, money. **5** account, reckoning, statement.

bill[2] *n* **1** beak, mandible, (*sl*) nose. **2** billhook, brush-cutter, hedge-bill, hedging knife. **3** caress, fondle, kiss, toy.

billet *vb* allot, apportion, assign, distribute, quarter, station. •*n* accommodation, lodgings, quarters.

billow *vb* **1** surge, wave. **2** heave, roll. **3** bag, balloon, bulge, dilate, swell. •*n* roller, surge, swell, wave.

bin *n* box, bunker, crib, frame, receptacle.

bind *vb* **1** confine, enchain, fetter, restrain, restrict. **2** bandage, tie up, wrap. **3** fasten, lash, pinion, secure, tie, truss. **4** engage, hold, oblige, obligate, pledge. **5** contract, harden, shrink, stiffen.

birth *n* **1** ancestry, blood, descent, extraction, lineage, race. **2** being, creation, creature, offspring, production, progeny.

bit *n* **1** crumb, fragment, morsel, mouthful, piece, scrap. **2** atom, grain, jot, mite, particle. **3** instant, minute, moment, second.

bite *vb* **1** champ, chew, crunch, gnaw. **2** burn, make smart, sting. **3** catch, clutch, grapple, grasp, grip. **4** bamboozle, cheat, cozen, deceive, defraud, dupe, gull, mislead, outwit, overreach, trick. • *n* **1** grasp, hold. **2** punch, relish, spice, pungency, tang, zest. **3** lick, morsel, sip, taste. **4** crick, nip, pain, pang, prick, sting.

bitter *adj* **1** acrid. **2** dire, fell, merciless, relentless, ruthless. **3** harsh, severe, stern. **4** afflictive, calamitous, distressing, galling, grievous, painful, poignant, sore, sorrowful.

adj antonyms contented, genial, sweet.

black *adj* **1** dark, ebony, inky, jet, sable, swarthy. **2** dingy, dusky, lowering, murky, pitchy. **3** calamitous, dark, depressing, disastrous, dismal, doleful, forbidding, gloomy, melancholy, mournful, sombre, sullen.

blacken *vb* **1** darken. **2** deface, defile, soil, stain, sully. **3** asperse, besmirch, calumniate, defame, malign, revile, slander, traduce, vilify.

vb antonyms enhance, praise.

blamable *adj* blameable, blameworthy, censurable, culpable, delinquent. faulty, remiss, reprehensible.

blame *vb* accuse, censure, condemn, disapprove, reflect upon, reprehend, reproach, reprove, upbraid. • *n* **1** animadversion, censure, condemnation, disapproval, dispraise, disapprobation, reprehension, reproach, reproof. **2** defect, demerit, fault, guilt, misdeed, shortcoming, sin, wrong.

n antonym exonerate.

blameless *adj* faultless, guiltless, inculpable, innocent, irreproachable, unblemished, undefiled, unimpeachable, unspotted, unsullied, spotless, stainless.

adj antonym guilty.

blanch *vb* bleach, fade, etiolate, whiten.

vb antonyms blush, color, redden.

bland *adj* **1** balmy, demulcent, gentle, mild, soothing, soft. **2** affable, amiable, complaisant, kindly, mild, suave.

adv antonyms piquant, sharp.

blandishment *n* cajolery, coaxing, compliment, fascination, fawning, flattery, wheedling

blank *adj* **1** bare, empty, vacuous, void. **2** amazed, astonished, confounded, confused, dumbfounded, nonplussed. **3** absolute, complete, entire, mere, perfect, pure, simple, unabated, unadulterated, unmitigated, unmixed, utter, perfect.

blare *vb* blazon, blow, peal, proclaim, trumpet. • *n* blast, clang, clangour, peal.

blasphemy *n* **1** impiousness, sacrilege, heresy, irreverence. **2** cursing, profanity, swearing.

blast *vb* **1** annihilate, blight, destroy, kill, ruin, shrivel, wither. **2** burst, explode, kill. • *n* **1** blow, gust, squall. **2** blare, clang, peal. **3** burst, discharge, explosion.

blaze *vb* **1** blazon, proclaim, publish. **2** burn, flame, glow. • *n* flame, flare, flash, glow, light.

bleach *vb* blanch, etiolate, render white, whiten.

bleak *adj* **1** bare, exposed, unprotected, unsheltered, storm-beaten, windswept. **2** biting, chill, cold, piercing, raw. **3** cheerless, comfortless, desolate, dreary, uncongenial, *adj antonyms* cheerful, congenial.

blemish *vb* **1** blur, injure, mar, spot, stain, sully, taint, tarnish. **2** asperse, calumniate, defame, malign, revile, slander, traduce, vilify. • *n* **1** blot, blur, defect, disfigurement, fault, flaw, imperfection, soil, speck, spot, stain, tarnish. **2** disgrace, dishonour, reproach, stain, taint.

blend *vb* amalgamate, coalesce, combine, commingle, fuse, mingle, mix, unite. • *n* amalgamation, combination, compound, fusion, mix, mixture, union.

vb antonym separate.

bless *vb* **1** beatify, delight, gladden. **2** adore, celebrate, exalt, extol, glorify, magnify, praise.

vb antonyms condemn, curse.

blessedness *n* beatitude, bliss, blissfulness, felicity, happiness, joy.

blight *vb* **1** blast, destroy, kill, ruin, shrivel, wither. **2** annihilate, annul, crush, disappoint, frustrate. • *n* blast, mildew, pestilence.

vb antonym bless.

n antonyms blessing, boon.

blind *vb* **1** blear, darken, deprive of sight. **2** blindfold, hoodwink. •*adj* **1** eyeless, sightless, stone-blind, unseeing. **2** benighted, ignorant, injudicious, purblind, undiscerning, unenlightened. **3** concealed, confused, dark, dim, hidden, intricate, involved, labyrinthine, obscure, private, remote. **4** careless, headlong, heedless, inconsiderate, indiscriminate, thoughtless. **5** blank, closed, shut. •*n* **1** cover, curtain, screen, shade, shutter. **2** blinker. **3** concealment, disguise, feint, pretence, pretext, ruse, stratagem, subterfuge.
adj antonyms aware, clear, sighted.

blink *vb* **1** nictate, nictitate, wink. **2** flicker, flutter, gleam, glitter, intermit, twinkle. **3** avoid, disregard, evade, gloss over, ignore, overlook, pass over. •*n* **1** glance, glimpse, sight, view, wink. **2** gleam, glimmer, sheen, shimmer, twinkle.

bliss *n* beatification, beatitude, blessedness, blissfulness, ecstasy, felicity, happiness, heaven, joy, rapture, transport.
n antonyms damnation, misery.

blithe *adj* airy, animated, blithesome, buoyant, cheerful, debonair, elated, happy, jocund, joyful, joyous, lively, mirthful, sprightly, vivacious.
adj antonym morose.

bloat *vb* dilate, distend, inflate, swell.

block *vb* **1** arrest, bar, blockade, check, choke, close, hinder, impede, jam, obstruct, stop. **2** form, mould, shape. **3** brace, stiffen. •*n* **1** lump, mass. **2** blockhead, dunce, fool, simpleton. **3** pulley, tackle. **4** execution, scaffold. **5** jam, obstruction, pack, stoppage.

blood *n* **1** children, descendants, offspring, posterity, progeny. **2** family, house, kin, kindred, line, relations. **3** consanguinity, descent, kinship, lineage, relationship. **4** courage, disposition, feelings, mettle, passion, spirit, temper.

bloom *vb* **1** blossom, blow, flower. **2** thrive, prosper. •*n* **1** blossom, blossoming, blow, efflorescence, florescence, flowering. **2** delicacy, delicateness, flush, freshness, heyday, prime, vigour. **3** flush, glow, rose.
vb antonym wither.

blossom *vb* bloom, blow, flower. •*n* bloom, blow, efflorescence, flower.
vb antonym wither.

blot *vb* **1** cancel, efface, erase, expunge, obliterate, rub out. **2** blur, deface, disfigure, obscure, spot, stain, sully. **3** disgrace, dishonour, tarnish. •*n* **1** blemish, blur, erasure, spot, obliteration, stain. **2** disgrace, dishonour, stigma.

blow[1] *n* **1** bang, beat, buffet, dab, impact, knock, pat, punch, rap, slam, stroke, thump, wallop, buffet, impact. **2** affliction, calamity, disaster, misfortune, setback.

blow[2] *vb* **1** breathe, gasp, pant, puff. **2** flow, move, scud, stream, waft. •*n* blast, gale, gust, squall, storm, wind.

blue *adj* **1** azure, cerulean, cobalt, indigo, sapphire, ultramarine. **2** ghastly, livid, pallid. **3** dejected, depressed, dispirited, downcast, gloomy, glum, mopey, melancholic, melancholy, sad.

bluff[1] *adj* **1** abrupt, blunt, blustering, coarse, frank, good-natured, open, outspoken. **2** abrupt, precipitous, sheer, steep. •*n* cliff, headland, height.
n antonyms diplomatic, refined.

bluff[2] *vb* deceive, defraud, lie, mislead. •*n* deceit, deception, feint, fraud, lie.

blunder *vb* err, flounder, stumble. •*n* error, fault, howler, mistake, solecism.

blunt *adj* **1** dull, edgeless, obtuse, pointless, unsharpened. **2** insensible, stolid, thickwitted. **3** abrupt, bluff, downright, plainspoken, outspoken, unceremonious, uncourtly. •*vb* deaden, dull, numb, weaken.
adj antonyms sharp, tactful.
vb antonyms intensify, sharpen.

blur *vb* **1** darken, dim, obscure. **2** blemish, blot, spot, stain, sully, tarnish. •*n* **1** blemish, blot, soil, spot, stain, tarnish. **2** disgrace, smear.

blush *vb* colour, flush, glow, redden. •*n* bloom, flush, glow, colour, reddening, suffusion.
vb antonym blanch.

bluster *vb* boast, brag, bully, domineer, roar, swagger, swell, vaunt. •*n* **1** boisterousness, noise, tumult, turbulence. **2** braggadocio, bravado, boasting, gasconade, swaggering.

board *n* **1** deal, panel, plank. **2** diet, entertainment, fare, food, meals, provision, victuals. **3** cabinet, conclave, committee, council. **4** directorate. **5** panel.

boast *vb* bluster, brag, crack, flourish, crow, vaunt. •*n* blustering, boasting, bombast, brag, braggadocio, bravado, bombast, swaggering, vaunt.
vb antonym deprecate.

bode *vb* augur, betoken, forebode,

foreshadow, foretell, portend, predict, prefigure, presage, prophesy.

bodily *adj* carnal, corporeal, fleshly, physical. •*adv* altogether, completely, entirely, wholly.

body *n* 1 carcass, corpse, remains. 2 stem, torso, trunk. 3 aggregate, bulk, corpus, mass. 4 being, individual, mortal creature, person. 5 assemblage, association, band, company, corporation, corps, coterie, force, party, society, troop. 6 consistency, substance, thickness.

boggle *vb* demur, falter, hang fire, hesitate, shrink, vacillate, waver.

boil[1] *vb* agitate, bubble, foam, froth, rage, seethe, simmer. •*n* ebullience, ebullition.

boil[2] (*med*) gathering, pimple, pustule, swelling, tumour.

boisterous *adj* 1 loud, roaring, stormy. 2 clamouring, loud, noisy, obstreperous, tumultuous, turbulent.
adj antonyms calm, quiet, restrained.

bold *adj* 1 adventurous, audacious, courageous. 2 brave, daring, dauntless, doughty, fearless, gallant, hardy, heroic, intrepid, mettlesome, manful, manly, spirited, stouthearted, undaunted, valiant, valorous. 3 assured, confident, self-reliant. 4 assuming, forward, impertinent, impudent, insolent, push, rude, saucy. 5 conspicuous, projecting, prominent, striking. 6 abrupt, precipitous, prominent, steep.
adj antonyms diffident, restrained.

bolster *vb* aid, assist, defend, help, maintain, prop, stay, support. •*n* 1 cushion, pillow. 2 prop, support.

bolt *vb* abscond, flee, fly. •*n* 1 arrow, dart, missile, shaft. 2 thunderbolt.

bombast *n* bluster, brag, braggadocio, fustian, gasconade, mouthing, pomposity, rant.

bond *vb* bind, connect, fuse, glue, join. •*adj* captive, enslaved, enthralled, subjugated. •*n* 1 band, cord, fastening, ligament, ligature, link, nexus. 2 bondage, captivity, chains, constraint, fetters, prison, shackle. 3 attachment, attraction, connection, coupling, link, tie, union. 4 compact, obligation, pledge, promise.

bondage *n* captivity, confinement, enslavement, enthralment, peonage, serfdom, servitude, slavery, thraldom, vassalage.
n antonyms freedom, independence.

bonny *adj* 1 beautiful, handsome, fair, fine,

pretty. 2 airy, blithe, buoyant, buxom, cheerful, jolly, joyous, merry. playful, sporty, sprightly, winsome.

bonus *n* gift, honorarium, premium, reward, subsidy.

booby *n* blockhead, dunce, fool, idiot, simpleton.

book *vb* 1 bespeak, engage, reserve. 2 programme, schedule. 3 list, log, record, register. •*n* booklet, brochure, compendium, handbook, manual, monograph, pamphlet, textbook, tract, treatise, volume, work.
vb antonym cancel.

bookish *adj* erudite, learned, literary, scholarly, studious.

boon *adj* 1 convivial, jolly, jovial, hearty. 2 close, intimate. •*n* 1 benefaction, favour, grant, gift, present. 2 advantage, benefit, blessing, good, privilege.
n antonyms blight, disadvantage.

boor *n* bumpkin, clodhopper, clown, lout, lubber, peasant, rustic, swain.
n antonyms aesthete, charmer.

boorish *adj* awkward, bearish, clownish, course, gruff, ill-bred, loutish, lubberly, rude, rustic, uncivilized, uncouth, uneducated.
adj antonyms cultured, polite, refined.

bootless *adj* abortive, fruitless, futile, profitless, vain, worthless, useless.
adj antonyms profitable, useful.

booty *n* loot, pillage, plunder, spoil.

border *vb* 1 bound, edge, fringe, line, march, rim, skirt, verge. 2 abut, adjoin, butt, conjoin, connect, neighbour. •*n* 1 brim, brink, edge, fringe, hem, margin, rim, skirt, verge. 2 boundary, confine, frontier, limit, march, outskirts.

bore[1] *vb* annoy, fatigue, plague, tire, trouble, vex, weary, worry. •*n* bother, nuisance, pest, worry.

bore[2] *vb* drill, perforate, pierce, sink, tunnel. •*n* calibre, hole, shaft, tunnel.
vb antonyms charm, interest.
n antonym pleasure.

borrow *vb* 1 take and return, use temporarily. 2 adopt, appropriate, imitate. 3 dissemble, feign, simulate.

boss[1] *vb* 1 emboss, stud. 2 •*n* knob, protuberance, stud.

boss[2] *vb* command, direct, employ, run. •*n* employer, foreman, master, overseer, superintendent.

botch *vb* blunder, bungle, cobble, mar,

mend, mess, patch, spoil. •*n* **1** blotch, pustule, sore. **2** failure, miscarriage.
vb antonyms accomplish, succeed.
n antonyms success.

bother *vb* annoy, disturb, harass, molest, perplex, pester, plague, tease, trouble, vex, worry. •*n* annoyance, perplexity, plague, trouble, vexation.

bottom *vb* build, establish, found. •*adj* base, basic, ground, lowermost, lowest, nethermost, undermost. •*n* **1** base, basis, foot, foundation, groundwork. **2** dale, meadow, valley. **3** buttocks, fundament, seat. **4** dregs, grounds, lees, sediment.

bounce *vb* bound, jump, leap, rebound, recoil, spring. •*n* **1** knock, thump. **2** bound, jump, leap, spring, vault.

bound¹ *adj* **1** assured, certain, decided, determined, resolute, resolved. **2** confined, hampered, restricted, restrained. **3** committed, contracted, engaged, pledged, promised. **4** beholden, duty-bound, obligated, obliged.

bound² *vb* border, delimit, circumscribe, confine, demarcate, limit, restrict, terminate. •*n* boundary, confine, edge, limit, march, margin, periphery, term, verge.

bound³ *vb* jump, leap, spring. •*n* bounce, jump, leap, spring, vault.

boundary *n* border, bourn, circuit, circumference, confine, limit, march, periphery, term, verge.

boundless *adj* endless, immeasurable, infinite, limitless, unbounded, unconfined, undefined, unlimited, vast.
adj antonym limited.

bountiful *adj* beneficent, bounteous, generous, liberal, munificent, princely.

bounty *n* beneficence, benevolence, charity, donation, generosity, gift, kindness, premium, present, reward.

bourn *n* **1** border, boundary, confine, limit. **2** brook, burn, rill, rivulet, stream, torrent.

bow¹ *n* (*naut*) beak, prow, stem.

bow² *vb* **1** arc, bend, buckle, crook, curve, droop, flex, yield. **2** crush, depress, subdue. **3** curtsy, genuflect, kowtow, submit. •*n* **1** arc, bend, bilge, bulge, convex, curve, flexion. **2** bob, curtsy, genuflection, greeting, homage, obeisance. **3** coming out, debut, introduction. **4** curtain call, encore.

bowels *npl* **1** entrails, guts, insides, viscera. **2** compassion, mercy, pity, sympathy, tenderness.

box¹ *vb* fight, hit, mill, spar. •*n* blow, buffet, fight, hit, spar.

box² *vb* barrel, crate, pack, parcel. •*n* case, chest, container, crate, portmanteau, trunk.

boy *n* lad, stripling, youth.

brace *vb* **1** make tight, tighten. **2** buttress, fortify, reinforce, shore, strengthen, support, truss. •*n* **1** couple, pair. **2** clamp, girder, prop, shore, stay, support, tie, truss.

brag *vb* bluster, boast, flourish, gasconade, vaunt.
vb antonym deprecate.

branch *vb* diverge, fork, bifurcate, ramify, spread. •*n* **1** bough, offset, limb, shoot, sprig, twig. **2** arm, fork, ramification, spur. **3** article, department, member, part, portion, section, subdivision.

brand *vb* denounce, stigmatize, mark. •*n* **1** firebrand, torch. **2** bolt, lightning flash. **3** cachet, mark, stamp, tally. **4** blot, reproach, stain, stigma.

brave *vb* dare, defy. •*adj* bold, courageous, fearless, heroic, intrepid, stalwart.
vb antonyms capitulate, crumple.
adj antonyms cowardly, timid.

bravery *n* courage, daring, fearlessness, gallantry, valour.

brawl *vb* bicker, dispute, jangle, quarrel, squabble. •*n* broil, dispute, feud, fracas, fray, jangle, quarrel, row, scuffle, squabble, uproar, wrangle.

brawny *adj* athletic, lusty, muscular, powerful, robust, sinewy, stalwart, strapping, strong, sturdy.

bray *vb* clamour, hoot, roar, trumpet, vociferate. •*n* blare, crash, roar, shout.

breach *n* **1** break, chasm, crack, disruption, fissure, flaw, fracture, opening, rent, rift, rupture. **2** alienation, difference, disaffection, disagreement, split.

bread *n* aliment, diet, fare, food, nourishment, nutriment, provisions, regimen, victuals.

break *vb* **1** crack, disrupt, fracture, part, rend, rive, sever. **2** batter, burst, crush, shatter, smash, splinter. **3** cashier, degrade, discard, discharge, dismiss. **4** disobey, infringe, transgress, violate. **5** intermit, interrupt, stop. **6** disclose, open, unfold. •*n* **1** aperture, breach, chasm, fissure, gap, rent, rip, rupture. **2** break-up, crash, debacle.

breast *vb* face, oppose, resist, stem, withstand. •*n* **1** bosom, chest, thorax. **2** affections, conscience, heart. **3** mammary gland, mammary organ, pap, udder.

breath *n* **1** exhaling, inhaling, pant, sigh, respiration, whiff. **2** animation, existence, life. **3** pause, respite, rest. **4** breathing space, instant, moment.

breathe *vb* **1** live, exist. **2** emit, exhale, give out. **3** diffuse, express, indicate, manifest, show.

breed *vb* **1** bear, beget, engender, hatch, produce. **2** bring up, foster, nourish, nurture, raise, rear. **3** discipline, educate, instruct, nurture, rear, school, teach, train. **4** generate, originate. •*n* extraction, family, lineage, pedigree, progeny, race, strain.

brevity *n* briefness, compression, conciseness, curtness, pithiness, shortness, terseness, transiency.
n antonyms longevity, permanence, verbosity.

brew *vb* concoct, contrive, devise, excite, foment, instigate, plot. •*n* beverage, concoction, drink, liquor, mixture, potation.

bribe *vb* buy, corrupt, influence, pay off, suborn. •*n* allurement, corruption, enticement, graft, pay-off, subornation.

bridle *vb* check, curb, control, govern, restrain. •*n* check, control, curb.

brief *vb* **1** direct, give directions, instruct. **2** capsulate, summarize, delineate, describe, draft, outline, sketch. **3** (*law*) retain. •*adj* **1** concise, curt, inconsiderable, laconic, pithy, short, succinct, terse. **2** fleeting, momentary, short, temporary, transient. •*n* **1** abstract, breviary, briefing, epitome, compendium, summary, syllabus. **2** (*law*) precept, writ.
adj antonyms long, long-lived, verbose.

brigand *n* bandit, footpad, freebooter, gangster, highwayman, marauder, outlaw, robber, thug.

bright *adj* **1** blazing, brilliant, dazzling, gleaming, glowing, light, luminous, radiant, shining, sparkling, sunny. **2** clear, cloudless, lambent, lucid, transparent. **3** famous, glorious, illustrious. **4** acute, discerning, ingenious, intelligent, keen. **5** auspicious, cheering, encouraging, exhilarating, favourable, inspiring, promising, propitious. **6** cheerful, genial, happy, lively, merry, pleasant, smiling, vivacious.
adj antonyms depressing, dull, stupid.

brilliant *adj* **1** beaming, bright, effulgent,

gleaming, glistening, glittering, lustrous, radiant, resplendent, shining, sparkling splendid. **2** admirable, celebrated, distinguished, famous, glorious, illustrious, renowned. **3** dazzling, decided, prominent, signal, striking, unusual.
adj antonyms dull, restrained, stupid, undistinguished.

brim *n* **1** border, brink, edge, rim, margin, skirt, verge. **2** bank, border, coast, shore.

bring *vb* **1** bear, convey, fetch. **2** accompany, attend, conduct, convey, convoy, guide, lead. **3** gain, get, obtain, procure, produce.

brisk *adj* active, alert, agile, lively, nimble, perky, quick, smart, spirited, spry.
adj antonym sluggish.

brittle *adj* brash, breakable, crisp, crumbling, fragile, frangible, frail, shivery.
adj antonyms durable, resilient, sturdy.

broach *vb* **1** open, pierce, set. **2** approach, break, hint, suggest. **3** proclaim, publish, utter.

broad *adj* **1** ample, expansive, extensive, large, spacious, sweeping, vast, wide. **2** enlarged, hospitable, liberal, tolerant. **3** diffused, open, spread. **4** coarse, gross, indecent, indelicate, unrefined, vulgar.
adj antonym narrow.

broaden *vb* augment, enlarge, expand, extend, increase, spread, stretch, widen.

broken *adj* **1** fractured, rent, ruptured, separated, severed, shattered, shivered, torn. **2** exhausted, feeble, impaired, shaken, shattered, spent, wasted. **3** defective, halting, hesitating, imperfect, stammering, stumbling. **4** contrite, humble, lowly, penitent. **5** abrupt, craggy, precipitous, rough.

broker *n* agent, factor, go-between, middleman.

brood *vb* incubate, sit. •*n* **1** issue, offspring, progeny. **2** breed, kind, line, lineage, sort, strain.

brook *vb* abide, bear, endure, suffer, tolerate. •*n* burn, beck, creek, rill, rivulet, run, streamlet.

brotherhood *n* association, clan, clique, coterie, fraternity, junta, society.

brotherly *adj* affectionate, amicable, cordial, friendly, kind.
adj antonyms callous, unbrotherly.

browbeat *vb* bully, intimidate, overawe, overbear.
vb antonym coax.

bruise *vb* **1** contuse, crunch, squeeze. **2** batter, break, maul, pound, pulverize. **3** batter, deface, indent. •*n* blemish, contusion, swelling.

brush¹ *n* brushwood, bush, scrub, scrubwood, shrubs, thicket, wilderness.

brush² *vb* **1** buff, clean, polish, swab, sweep, wipe. **2** curry, groom, rub down. **3** caress, flick, glance, graze, scrape, skim, touch. •*n* **1** besom, broom. **2** action, affair, collision, contest, conflict, encounter, engagement, fight, skirmish.

brutal *adj* **1** barbaric, barbarous, brutish, cruel, ferocious, inhuman, ruthless, savage. **2** bearish, brusque, churlish, gruff, impolite, harsh, rude, rough, truculent, uncivil.
adj antonyms humane, kindly.

brute *n* **1** barbarian, beast, monster, ogre, savage. **2** animal, beast, creature. •*adj* **1** carnal, mindless, physical. **2** bestial, coarse, gross.
n antonym gentleman
adj antonym refined.

bubble *vb* boil, effervesce, foam. •*n* bead, **1** blob, fluid, globule. **2** bagatelle, trifle. **3** cheat, delusion, hoax.

buccaneer *n* corsair, freebooter, pirate.

buck *vb* jump, leap. •*n* **1** beau, blade, blood, dandy, fop, gallant, spark. **2** male.

bud *vb* burgeon, germinate, push, shoot, sprout, vegetate. •*n* burgeon, gem, germ, shoot, sprout.
vb antonyms waste away, wither.

budget *vb* allocate, cost, estimate. •*n* **1** account, estimate, financial statement. **2** assets, finances, funds, means, resources. **3** bag, bundle, pack, packet, parcel, roll. **4** assortment, batch, collection, lot, set, store.

buffet¹ *vb* **1** beat, box, cuff, slap, smite, strike. **2** resist, struggle against. •*n* blow, box, cuff, slap, strike.

buffet² *n* **1** cupboard, sideboard. **2** refreshment counter.

buffoon *n* antic, clown, droll, fool, harlequin, jester, mountebank.

build *vb* construct, erect, establish, fabricate, fashion, model, raise, rear. •*n* **1** body, figure, form, frame, physique. **2** construction, shape, structure.
vb antonyms destroy, knock down, lessen, weaken.

building *n* **1** construction, erection,

fabrication. **2** edifice, fabric, house, pile, substructure, structure,
n antonym destruction.

bulk *n* **1** dimension, magnitude, mass, size, volume. **2** amplitude, bulkiness, massiveness. **3** body, majority, mass.

bully *vb* browbeat, bulldoze, domineer, haze, hector, intimidate, overbear. •*n* blusterer, browbeater, bulldozer, hector, swaggerer, roisterer, tyrant.
vb antonyms coax, persuade.

bulwark *n* **1** barrier, fortification, parapet, rampart, wall. **2** palladium, safeguard, security.

bump *vb* collide, knock, strike, thump. •*n* **1** blow, jar, jolt, knock, shock, thump. **2** lump, protuberance, swelling.

bunch *vb* assemble, collect, crowd, group, herd, pack. •*n* **1** bulge, bump, bundle, hump, knob, lump, protuberance. **2** cluster, hand, fascicle. **3** assortment, batch, collection, group, lot, parcel, set. **4** knot, tuft.
vb antonyms scatter, spread out.

bundle *vb* bale, pack, package, parcel, truss, wrap. •*n* bale, batch, bunch, collection, heap, pack, package, packet, parcel, pile, roll, truss.

bungle *vb* blow, bodge, botch, bumble, flub, fluff, fumble.

bungler *n* botcher, duffer, fumbler, lout, lubber, mis-manager, muddler.

burden *vb* encumber, grieve, load, oppress, overlay, overload, saddle, surcharge, try. •*n* **1** capacity, cargo, freight, lading, load, tonnage, weight. **2** affliction, charge, clog, encumbrance, impediment, grievance, sorrow, trial, trouble. **3** drift, point, substance, tenor, surcharge.
vb antonyms disburden, lighten, relieve.

bureau *n* **1** chest of drawers, dresser. **2** counting room, office.

burial *n* burying, entombment, inhumation, interment, sepulture.

burlesque *vb* ape, imitate, lampoon, mock, ridicule, satirize. •*n* caricature, extravaganza, parody, send-up, take-off, travesty.

burn¹ *n* beck, brook, gill, rill, rivulet, runnel, runlet, stream. water

burn² *vb* **1** blaze, conflagrate, enflame, fire, flame, ignite, kindle, light, smoulder. **2** cremate, incinerate. **3** scald, scorch, singe. **4** boil, broil, cook, roast, seethe, simmer, stew, swelter, toast. **5** bronze, brown, sunburn, suntan, tan. **6** bake, desiccate, dry, parch, sear, shrivel, wither. **7** glow, tingle, warm. •*n* **1** scald, scorch, singe. **2** sunburn.

burning *adj* **1** aflame, fiery, hot, scorching. **2** ardent, earnest, fervent, fervid, impassioned, intense.

burnish *vb* brighten, buff, polish, shine. •*n* glaze, gloss, patina, polish, shine.
vb antonym tarnish.

burst *vb* break open, be rent, explode, shatter, split open. •*adj* broken, kaput, punctured, ruptured, shattered, split. •*n* **1** break, breakage, breach, fracture, rupture. **2** blast, blowout, blowup, discharge, detonation, explosion. **3** spurt. **4** blaze, flare, flash. **5** cloudburst, downpour. **6** bang, crack, crash, report, sound. **7** fusillade, salvo, spray, volley, outburst, outbreak flare-up, blaze, eruption.

bury *vb* **1** entomb, inter. **2** conceal, hide, secrete, shroud.
vb antonyms disinter, uncover.

business *n* **1** calling, employment, job, line, occupation, profession, pursuit, vocation. **2** commerce, dealing, trade, traffic. **3** affair, concern, engagement, matter, transaction, undertaking. **4** duty, function, office, task, work.

bustle *vb* fuss, hurry, scurry. •*n* ado, commotion, flurry, fuss, hurry, hustle, pother, stir, tumult.

busy *vb* devote, employ, engage, occupy, spend, work. •*adj* **1** employed, engaged, occupied. **2** active, assiduous, diligent, engrossed, industrious, sedulous, working. **3** agile, brisk, nimble, spry, stirring. **4** meddling, officious.
adj antonyms idle, quiet.

but *conj* except, excepting, further, moreover, still, unless, yet. •*adv* all the same, even, notwithstanding, still, yet.

butchery *n* massacre, murder, slaughter.

butt[1] *vb* **1** bunt, push, shove, shunt, strike. **2** encroach, impose, interfere, intrude, invade, obtrude. •*n* buck, bunt, push, shove, shunt, thrust.

butt[2] *n* barrel, cask.

butt[3] *n* **1** aim, goal, mark, object, point, target. **2** dupe, gull, victim.

butt[4] *vb* abut, adjoin, conjoin, connect, neighbour. •*n* **1** end, piece, remainder, stub, stump. **2** buttocks, posterior, rump.

buttonhole *vb* bore, catch, detain in conversation, importune.

buttress *vb* brace, prop, shore, stay, support. •*n* brace, bulwark, prop, stay, support.
vb antonyms weaken.

buxom *adj* comely, fresh, healthy, hearty, plump, rosy, ruddy, vigorous.
adj antonyms petite, slim, small.

byword *n* adage, aphorism, apothegm, dictum, maxim, proverb, saying, saw.

C

cabal *vb* conspire, intrigue, machinate, plot. • *n* **1** clique, combination, confederacy, coterie, faction, gang, junta, league, party, set. **2** conspiracy, intrigue, machination, plot.

cabbalistic, cabalistic *adj* dark, fanciful, mysterious, mystic, occult, secret.

cabaret *n* **1** floor show, nightclub, show. **2** (*archaic*) tavern, inn, public house, wine shop.

cabin *n* berth, bunk, cot, cottage, crib, dwelling, hovel, hut, shack, shanty, shed.

cabinet *n* **1** apartment, boudoir, chamber, closet. **2** case, davenport, desk, escritoire. **3** council, ministry.

cackle *vb* **1** giggle, laugh, snicker, titter. **2** babble, chatter, gabble, palaver, prate, prattle, titter. • *n* babble, chatter, giggle, prate, prattle, snigger, titter.

cacophonous *adj* discordant, grating, harsh, inharmonious, jarring, raucous.

cadaverous *adj* bloodless, deathlike, ghastly, pale, pallid, wan.

cage *vb* confine, immure, imprison, incarcerate. • *n* coop, pen, pound.

cajole *vb* **1** blandish, coax, flatter, jolly, wheedle. **2** beguile, deceive, delude, entrap, inveigle, tempt.

calamity *n* adversity, affliction, blow, casualty, cataclysm, catastrophe, disaster, distress, downfall, evil, hardship, mischance, misery, misfortune, mishap, reverse, ruin, stroke, trial, visitation.
n antonyms blessing, godsend.

calculate *vb* **1** cast, compute, count, estimate, figure, rate, reckon, weigh. **2** tell.

calculating *adj* **1** crafty, designing, scheming, selfish. **2** careful, cautious, circumspect, far-sighted, politic, sagacious, wary.
adj antonyms artless, naïve, open.

calefaction *n* **1** heating, warming. **2** hotness, incandescence, warmth.

calendar *n* **1** almanac, ephemeris, register. **2** catalogue, list, schedule.

calibre *n* **1** bore, capacity, diameter, gauge. **2** ability, capacity, endowment, faculty, gifts, parts, scope, talent.

call *vb* **1** christen, denominate, designate, dub, entitle, name, phrase, style, term.
2 bid, invite, summons. **3** assemble, convene, convoke, muster. **4** cry, exclaim. **5** arouse, awaken, proclaim, rouse, shout, waken. **6** appoint, elect, ordain. • *n* **1** cry, outcry, voice. **2** appeal, invitation, summons. **3** claim, demand, summons. **4** appointment, election, invitation.

calling *n* business, craft, employment, occupation, profession, pursuit, trade.

callous *adj* **1** hard, hardened, indurated. **2** apathetic, dull, indifferent, insensible, inured, obdurate, obtuse, sluggish, torpid, unfeeling.
adj antonyms kind, sensitive, sympathetic.

callow *adj* **1** naked, unfeathered, unfledged. **2** green, immature, inexperienced, sappy, silly, soft, unfledged, unsophisticated.

calm *vb* **1** allay, becalm, compose, hush, lull, smooth, still, tranquillize. **2** alleviate, appease, assuage, moderate, mollify, pacify, quiet, soften, soothe, tranquillize. • *adj* **1** halcyon, mild, peaceful, placid, quiet, reposeful, serene, smooth, still, tranquil, unruffled. **2** collected, cool, composed, controlled, impassive, imperturbable, sedate, self-possessed, undisturbed, unperturbed, unruffled, untroubled. • *n* **1** lull. **2** equanimity, peace, placidity, quiet, repose, serenity, stillness, tranquillity.
vb antonyms excite, irritate, worry.
adj antonyms excitable, rough, stormy, wild, worried.
n antonyms restlessness, storminess.

calorific *adj* heat, heat-producing.

calumniate *vb* abuse, asperse, backbite, blacken, blemish, defame, discredit, disparage, lampoon, libel, malign, revile, slander, traduce, vilify.

calumny *n* abuses, aspersion, backbiting, defamation, detraction, evil-speaking, insult, libel, lying, obloquy, slander, vilification, vituperation.

camber *vb* arch, bend, curve. • *n* arch, arching, convexity.

camp[1] *vb* bivouac, encamp, lodge, pitch, tent. • *n* **1** bivouac, cantonment, encampment, laager. **2** cabal, circle, clique, coterie, faction, group, junta, party, ring, set.

40

camp² *adj* affected, artificial, effeminate, exaggerated, mannered, theatrical.

canal *n* channel, duct, pipe, tube.

cancel *vb* 1 blot, efface, erase, expunge, obliterate. 2 abrogate, annul, countermand, nullify, quash, repeal, rescind, revoke.

candelabrum *n* candlestick, chandelier, lustre.

candid *adj* 1 fair, impartial, just, unbiased, unprejudiced. 2 artless, frank, free, guileless, honest, honourable, ingenuous, naive, open, plain, sincere, straightforward.
adj antonyms cagey, devious, evasive.

candidate *n* applicant, aspirant, claimant, competitor, probationer.

candour *n* 1 fairness, impartiality, justice. 2 artlessness, frankness, guilelessness, honesty, ingenuousness, openness, simplicity, sincerity, straightforwardness, truthfulness.

canker *vb* 1 corrode, erode, rot, rust, waste. 2 blight, consume, corrupt, embitter, envenom, infect, poison, sour. •*n* 1 gangrene, rot. 2 bale, bane, blight, corruption, infection, irritation.

canon *n* catalogue, criterion, formula, formulary, law, regulation, rule, standard, statute.

canorous *adj* musical, tuneful.

cant¹ *vb* whine. •*adj* 1 current, partisan, popular, rote, routine, set. 2 argotic, slangy. •*n* 1 hypocrisy. 2 argot, jargon, lingo, slang.

cant² *vb* bevel, incline, list, slant, tilt, turn. •*n* bevel, inclination, leaning, list, pitch, slant, tilt, turn.

cantankerous *adj* contumacious, crabbed, cross-grained, dogged, headstrong, heady, intractable, obdurate, obstinate, perverse, refractory, stiff, stubborn, wilful, unyielding.
adj antonyms good-natured, pleasant.

canting *adj* affected, pious, sanctimonious, whining.

canvas *n* burlap, scrim, tarpaulin.

canvass *vb* 1 discuss, dispute. 2 analyse, consider, examine, investigate, review, scrutinize, sift, study. 3 campaign, electioneer, solicit votes. •*n* 1 debate, discussion, dispute. 2 examination, scrutiny, sifting.

canyon *n* gorge, gulch, ravine.

cap *vb* 1 cover, surmount. 2 complete, crown, finish. 3 exceed, overtop, surpass,

transcend. 4 match, parallel, pattern. •*n* 1 beret, head-cover, head-dress. 2 acme, chief, crown, head, peak, perfection, pitch, summit, top.

capability *n* ability, brains, calibre, capableness, capacity, competency, efficiency, faculty, force, power, scope, skill.

capable *adj* 1 adapted, fitted, qualified, suited. 2 able, accomplished, clever, competent, efficient, gifted, ingenious, intelligent, sagacious, skilful.
adj antonyms incapable, incompetent, useless.

capacious *adj* ample, broad, comprehensive, expanded, extensive, large, roomy, spacious, wide.

capacitate *vb* enable, qualify.

capacity *n* 1 amplitude, dimensions, magnitude, volume. 2 aptitude, aptness, brains, calibre, discernment, faculty, forte, genius, gift, parts, power, talent, turn, wit. 3 ability, capability, calibre, cleverness, competency, efficiency, skill. 4 character, charge, function, office, position, post, province, service, sphere.

caper *vb* bound, caracole, frisk, gambol, hop, leap, prank, romp, skip, spring. •*n* bound, dance, gambol, frisk, hop, jump, leap, prance, romp, skip.

capillary *adj* delicate, fine, minute, slender.

capital *adj* 1 cardinal, chief, essential, important, leading, main, major, pre-eminent, principal, prominent. 2 fatal. 3 excellent, first-class, first-rate, good, prime, splendid. •*n* 1 chief city, metropolis, seat. 2 money, estate, investments, shares, stock.
adj antonyms minor, sad, unfortunate.

caprice *n* crotchet, fancy, fickleness, freak, humour, inconstancy, maggot, phantasy, quirk, vagary, whim, whimsy.

capricious *adj* changeable, crotchety, fanciful, fantastical, fickle, fitful, freakish, odd, puckish, queer, uncertain, variable, wayward, whimsical.
adj antonyms sensible, steady.

capsize *vb* overturn, upset.

capsule *n* 1 case, covering, envelope, sheath, shell, wrapper. 2 pericarp, pod, seed-vessel.

captain *vb* command, direct, head, lead, manage, officer, preside. •*n* chief, chieftain, commander, leader, master, officer, soldier, warrior.

captious *adj* **1** censorious, critical, fault-finding, hypercritical. **2** acrimonious, cantankerous, contentious, crabbed, cross, snappish, snarling, splenetic, testy, touchy, waspish. **3** ensnaring, insidious.

captivate *vb* allure, attract, bewitch, catch, capture, charm, enamour, enchant, enthral, fascinate, gain, hypnotize, infatuate, win.
vb antonyms appal, repel.

captivity *n* **1** confinement, durance, duress, imprisonment. **2** bondage, enthralment, servitude, slavery, subjection, thraldom, vassalage.
n antonym freedom.

capture *vb* apprehend, arrest, catch, seize. •*n* **1** apprehension, arrest, catch, catching, imprisonment, seizure. **2** bag, prize.

carcass *n* body, cadaver, corpse, corse, remains.

cardinal *adj* capital, central, chief, essential, first, important, leading, main, pre-eminent, primary, principal, vital.

care *n* **1** anxiety, concern, perplexity, trouble, solicitude, worry. **2** attention, carefulness, caution, circumspection, heed, regard, vigilance, wariness, watchfulness. **3** charge, custody, guardianship, keep, oversight, superintendence, ward. **4** burden, charge, concern, responsibility.
n antonyms carelessness, inattention, thoughtlessness.

careful *adj* **1** anxious, solicitous, concerned, troubled, uneasy. **2** attentive, heedful, mindful, regardful, thoughtful. **3** cautious, canny, circumspect, discreet, leery, vigilant, watchful.
adj antonyms careless, inattentive, thoughtless.

careless *adj* **1** carefree, nonchalant, unapprehensive, undisturbed, unperplexed, unsolicitous, untroubled. **2** disregardful, heedless, inattentive, incautious, inconsiderate, neglectful, negligent, regardless, remiss, thoughtless, unobservant, unconcerned, unconsidered, unmindful, unthinking.
adj antonyms accurate, careful, meticulous, thoughtful.

carelessness *n* heedlessness, inadvertence, inattention, inconsiderateness, neglect, negligence, remissness, slackness, thoughtlessness, unconcern.

caress *vb* coddle, cuddle, cosset, embrace, fondle, hug, kiss, pet. •*n* cuddle, embrace, fondling, hug, kiss.

caressing *n* blandishment, dalliance, endearment, fondling.

cargo *n* freight, lading. load.

caricature *vb* burlesque, parody, send-up, take-off, travesty. •*n* burlesque, farce, ludicrous, parody, representation, take-off, travesty.

carious *adj* decayed, mortified, putrid, rotten, ulcerated.

cark *vb* annoy, fret, grieve, harass, perplex, worry.

carnage *n* bloodshed, butchery, havoc, massacre, murder, slaughter.

carnal *adj* **1** animal, concupiscent, fleshly, lascivious, lecherous, lewd, libidinous, lubricous, lustful, salacious, sensual, voluptuous. **2** bodily, earthy, mundane. natural, secular, temporal, unregenerate, unspiritual.
adj antonyms chaste, pure, spiritual.

carol *vb* chant, hum, sing, warble. •*n* canticle, chorus, ditty, hymn, lay, song, warble.

carousal *n* **1** banquet, entertainment, feast, festival, merry-making, regale. **2** bacchanal, carouse, debauch, jamboree, jollification, orgy, revel, revelling, revelry, saturnalia, spree, wassail.

carp *vb* cavil, censure, criticize, fault.
vb antonym praise.

carping *adj* captious, cavilling, censorious, hypercritical. •*n* cavil, censure, fault-finding, hypercriticism.
n antonyms compliments, praise.

carriage *n* **1** conveyance, vehicle. **2** air, bearing, behaviour, conduct, demeanour, deportment, front, mien, port.

carry *vb* **1** bear, convey, transfer, transmit, transport. **2** impel, push forward, urge. **3** accomplish, compass, effect, gain, secure. **4** bear up, support, sustain. **5** infer, involve, imply, import, signify.

cart *n* conveyance, tumbril, van, vehicle, wagon.

carte-blanche *n* authority, power.

carve *vb* **1** chisel, cut, divide, engrave, grave, hack, hew, indent, incise, sculpt, sculpture. **2** fashion, form, mould, shape.

cascade *vb* cataract, descend, drop, engulf, fall, inundate, overflow, plunge, tumble. •*n* cataract, fall, falls, force, linn, waterfall.

case¹ *vb* **1** cover, encase, enclose, envelop, protect, wrap. **2** box, pack. •*n* **1** capsule, covering, sheathe. 2 box, cabinet, container, holder, receptacle.

case² *n* 1 condition, plight, predicament, situation, state. 2 example, instance, occurrence. 3 circumstance, condition, contingency, event. 4 action, argument, cause, lawsuit, process, suit, trial.

case-hardened *adj* 1 hardened, indurated, steeled. 2 brazen, brazen-faced, obdurate, reprobate.

cash *n* banknotes, bullion, coin, currency, money, payment, specie.

cashier *vb* break, discard, discharge, dismiss.

cast *vb* 1 fling, hurl, pitch, send, shy, sling, throw, toss. 2 drive, force, impel, thrust. 3 lay aside, put off, shed. 4 calculate, compute, reckon. 5 communicate, diffuse, impart, shed, throw. •*n* 1 fling, throw, toss. 2 shade, tinge, tint, touch. 3 air, character, look, manner, mien, style, tone, turn. 4 form, mould.

castaway *adj* abandoned, cast-off, discarded, rejected. •*n* derelict, outcast, reprobate, vagabond.

caste *n* class, grade, lineage, order, race, rank, species, status.

castigate *vb* 1 beat, chastise, flog, lambaste, lash, thrash, whip. 2 chaste, correct, discipline, punish. 3 criticize, flagellate, upbraid.

castle *n* citadel, fortress, stronghold.

castrate *vb* 1 caponize, emasculate, geld. 2 mortify, subdue, suppress, weaken.

casual *adj* 1 accidental, contingent, fortuitous, incidental, irregular, occasional, random, uncertain, unforeseen, unintentional, unpremeditated. 2 informal, relaxed.
adj antonyms deliberate, painstaking, planned.

casualty *n* 1 chance, contingency, fortuity, mishap. 2 accident, catastrophe, disaster, mischance, misfortune.

cat *n* felid, feline, grimalkin, kitten, puss, pussycat, tabby, tomcat.

cataclysm *n* 1 deluge, flood, inundation. 2 disaster, upheaval.

catacomb *n* crypt, tomb, vault.

catalogue *vb* alphabetize, categorize, chronicle, class, classify, codify, file, index, list, record, tabulate. •*n* enumeration, index, inventory, invoice, list, record, register, roll, schedule.

cataract *n* cascade, fall, waterfall.

catastrophe *n* 1 conclusion, consummation, denouement, end, finale, issue, termination, upshot. 2 adversity, blow, calamity, cataclysm, debacle, disaster, ill, misfortune, mischance, mishap, trial, trouble.

catch *vb* 1 clutch, grasp, gripe, nab, seize, snatch. 2 apprehend, arrest, capture. 3 overtake. 4 enmesh, ensnare, entangle, entrap, lime, net. 5 bewitch, captivate, charm, enchant, fascinate, win. 6 surprise, take unawares. •*n* 1 arrest, capture, seizure. 2 bag, find, haul, plum, prize. 3 drawback, fault, hitch, obstacle, rub, snag. 4 captive, conquest.
vb antonyms drop, free, miss.

catching *adj* 1 communicable, contagious, infectious, pestiferous, pestilential. 2 attractive, captivating, charming, enchanting, fascinating, taking, winning, winsome.
adj antonyms boring, ugly, unattractive.

catechize *adj* examine, interrogate, question, quiz.

catechumen *n* convert, disciple, learner, neophyte, novice, proselyte, pupil, tyro.

categorical *adj* absolute, direct, downright, emphatic, explicit, express, positive, unconditional, unqualified, unreserved, utter.

category *n* class, division, head, heading, list, order, rank, sort.

catenation *n* conjunction, connection, union.

cater *vb* feed, provide, purvey.

cathartic *adj* abstergent, aperient, cleansing, evacuant, laxative, purgative. •*n* aperient, laxative, physic, purgative, purge.

catholic *adj* 1 general, universal, worldwide. 2 charitable, liberal, tolerant, unbigoted, unexclusive.

cause *vb* 1 breed, create, originate, produce. 2 effect, effectuate, occasion, produce. •*n* 1 agent, creator, mainspring, origin, original, producer, source, spring. 2 account, agency, consideration, ground, incentive, incitement, inducement, motive, reason. 3 aim, end, object, purpose. 4 action, case, suit, trial.
n antonyms effect, result.

caustic *adj* 1 acrid, cathartic, consuming, corroding, corrosive, eating, erosive, mordant, virulent. 2 biting, bitter, burning, cutting, sarcastic, satirical, scalding, scathing, severe, sharp, stinging.
adj antonyms mild, soothing.

caution *vb* admonish, forewarn, warn. •*n* **1** care, carefulness, circumspection, discretion, forethought, heed, heedfulness, providence, prudence, wariness, vigilance, watchfulness. **2** admonition, advice, counsel, injunction, warning.

cautious *adj* careful, chary, circumspect, discreet, heedful, prudent, wary, vigilant, wary, watchful.

adj antonyms heedless, imprudent, incautious.

cavalier *adj* **1** arrogant, curt, disdainful, haughty, insolent, scornful, supercilious. **2** debonair, gallant, gay. •*n* chevalier, equestrian, horseman, horse-soldier, knight.

cave *n* cavern, cavity, den, grot, grotto.

cavil *vb* carp, censure, hypercriticize, object.

cavilling *adj* captious, carping, censorious, critical, hypercritical.

cavity *n* hollow, pocket, vacuole, void.

cease *vb* **1** desist, intermit, pause, refrain, stay, stop. **2** fail. **3** discontinue, end, quit, terminate.

vb antonyms begin, start.

ceaseless *adj* **1** continual, continuous, incessant, unceasing, uninterrupted, unremitting. **2** endless, eternal, everlasting, perpetual.

cede *vb* **1** abandon, abdicate, relinquish, resign, surrender, transfer, yield. **2** convey, grant.

celebrate *vb* **1** applaud, bless, commend, emblazon, extol, glorify, laud, magnify, praise, trumpet. **2** commemorate, honour, keep, observe. **3** solemnize.

celebrated *adj* distinguished, eminent, famed, famous, glorious, illustrious, notable, renowned.

adj antonyms obscure, unknown.

celebrity *n* **1** credit, distinction, eminence, fame, glory, honour, renown, reputation, repute. **2** lion, notable, star.

n antonyms nobody, obscurity.

celestial *adj* **1** empyreal, empyrean. **2** angelic, divine, god-like, heavenly, seraphic, supernal, supernatural.

adj antonyms earthly, mundane.

celibate *adj* single, unmarried. •*n* bachelor, single, virgin.

cellular *adj* alveolate, honeycombed.

cement *vb* **1** attach, bind, join, combine, connect, solder, unite, weld. **2** cohere, stick. •*n* glue, paste, mortar, solder.

cemetery *n* burial-ground, burying-ground, churchyard, god's acre, graveyard, necropolis.

censor *vb* **1** blue-pencil, bowdlerize, cut, edit, expurgate. **2** classify, kill, quash, squash, suppress. •*n* caviller, censurer, faultfinder.

censorious *adj* captious, carping, caviling, condemnatory, faultfinding, hypercritical, severe.

censure *vb* abuse, blame, chide, condemn, rebuke, reprehend, reprimand, reproach, reprobate, reprove, scold, upbraid. •*n* animadversion, blame, condemnation, criticism, disapprobation, disapproval, rebuke, remonstrance, reprehension, reproach, reproof, stricture.

n antonyms approval, compliments, praise.

vb antonyms approve, compliment, praise.

ceremonious *adj* **1** civil, courtly, lofty, stately. **2** formal, studied. **3** exact, formal, punctilious, precise, starched, stiff.

adj antonyms informal, relaxed, unceremonious.

ceremony *n* **1** ceremonial, etiquette, form, formality, observance, solemnity, rite. **2** parade, pomp, show, stateliness.

certain *adj* **1** absolute, incontestable, incontrovertible, indisputable, indubitable, positive, undeniable, undisputed, unquestionable, unquestioned. **2** assured, confident, sure, undoubting. **3** infallible, never-failing, unfailing. **4** actual, existing, real. **5** constant, determinate, fixed, settled, stated.

adj antonyms doubtful, hesitant, uncertain, unsure.

certainty *n* **1** indubitability, indubitableness, inevitableness, inevitability, surety, unquestionability, unquestionableness. **2** assurance, assuredness, certitude, confidence, conviction, surety.

n antonyms doubt, hesitation, uncertainty.

certify *vb* **1** attest, notify, testify, vouch. **2** ascertain, determine, verify, show.

cerulean *adj* azure, blue, sky-blue.

cessation *n* ceasing, discontinuance, intermission, pause, remission, respite, rest, stop, stoppage, suspension.

n antonym commencement.

cession *n* abandonment, capitulation, ceding, concession, conveyance, grant, relinquishment, renunciation, surrender, yielding.

chafe *vb* **1** rub. **2** anger, annoy, chagrin, enrage, exasperate, fret, gall, incense, irritate, nettle, offend, provoke, ruffle, tease, vex. **3** fret, fume, rage.

chaff *vb* banter, deride, jeer, mock, rally, ridicule, scoff. •*n* **1** glumes, hulls, husks. **2** refuse, rubbish, trash, waste.

chaffer *n* bargain, haggle, higgle, negotiate.

chagrin *vb* annoy, chafe, displease, irritate, mortify, provoke, vex. •*n* annoyance, displeasure, disquiet, dissatisfaction, fretfulness, humiliation, ill-humour, irritation, mortification, spleen, vexation.
n antonyms delight, pleasure.

chain *vb* **1** bind, confine, fetter, manacle, restrain, shackle, trammel. **2** enslave. •*n* bond, fetter, manacle, shackle, union.
vb antonyms free, release.

chalice *n* bowl, cup, goblet.

challenge *vb* **1** brave, call out, dare, defy, dispute. **2** demand, require. •*n* **1** defiance, interrogation, question. **2** exception, objection.

chamber *n* **1** apartment, hall, room. **2** cavity, hollow.

champion *vb* advocate, defend, uphold. •*n* **1** defender, promoter, protector, vindicator. **2** belt-holder, hero, victor, warrior, winner.

chance *vb* befall, betide, happen, occur. •*adj* accidental, adventitious, casual, fortuitous, incidental, unexpected, unforeseen. •*n* **1** accident, cast, fortuity, fortune, hap, luck. **2** contingency, possibility. **3** occasion, opening, opportunity. **4** contingency, fortuity, gamble, peradventure, uncertainty. **5** hazard, jeopardy, peril, risk.
n antonyms certainty, law, necessity.
adj antonyms certain, deliberate, intentional.

change *vb* **1** alter, fluctuate, modify, vary. **2** displace, remove, replace, shift, substitute. **3** barter, commute, exchange. •*n* **1** alteration, mutation, revolution, transition, transmutation, turning, variance, variation. **2** innovation, novelty, variety, vicissitude.

changeable *adj* **1** alterable, inconstant, modifiable, mutable, uncertain, unsettled, unstable, unsteady, variable, variant. **2** capricious, fickle, fitful, flighty, giddy, mercurial, vacillating, volatile, wavering.
adj antonyms constant, reliable, unchangeable.

changeless *adj* abiding, consistent, constant, fixed, immutable, permanent, regular, reliable, resolute, settled, stationary, unalterable, unchanging.

channel *vb* chamfer, cut, flute, groove. •*n* **1** canal, conduit, duct, passage. **2** aqueduct, canal, chute, drain, flume, furrow. **3** chamfer, groove, fluting, furrow, gutter.

chant *vb* **1** carol, sing, warble. **2** intone, recite. **3** canticle, song.

chaos *n* anarchy, confusion, disorder.
n antonym order.

char *vb* burn, scorch.

character *n* **1** emblem, figure, hieroglyph, ideograph, letter, mark, sign, symbol. **2** bent, constitution, cast, disposition, nature, quality. **3** individual, original, person, personage. **4** reputation, repute. **5** nature, traits. **6** eccentric, trait.

characteristic *adj* distinctive, peculiar, singular, special, specific, typical. •*n* attribute, feature, idiosyncrasy, lineament, mark, peculiarity, quality, trait.
adj antonyms uncharacteristic, untypical.

charge *vb* **1** burden, encumber, freight, lade, load. **2** entrust. **3** ascribe, impute, lay. **4** accuse, arraign, blame, criminate, impeach, inculpate, indict, involve. **5** bid, command, exhort, enjoin, order, require, tax. **6** assault, attack bear down. •*n* **1** burden, cargo, freight, lading, load. **2** care, custody, keeping, management, ward. **3** commission, duty, employment, office, trust. **4** responsibility, trust. **5** command, direction, injunction, mandate, order, precept. **6** exhortation, instruction. **7** cost, debit, expense, expenditure, outlay. **8** price, sum. **9** assault, attack, encounter, onset, onslaught.

charger *n* **1** dish, platter. **2** mount, steed, war-horse.

charily *adv* carefully, cautiously, distrustfully, prudently, sparingly, suspiciously, warily.

charitable *adj* **1** beneficial, beneficent, benignant, bountiful, generous, kind, liberal, open-handed. **2** candid, considerate, lenient, mild.
adj antonyms uncharitable, unforgiving.

charity *n* **1** benevolence, benignity, fellow-feeling, good-nature, goodwill, kind-heartedness, kindness, tenderheartedness. **2** beneficence, bounty, generosity, humanity, philanthropy, liberality.

charlatan *n* cheat, empiric, impostor, mountebank, pretender, quack.

charm *vb* allure, attract, becharm, bewitch,

captivate, catch, delight, enamour, enchain, enchant, enrapture, enravish, fascinate, transport, win. •*n* **1** enchantment, incantation, magic, necromancy, sorcery, spell, witchery. **2** amulet, talisman. **3** allurement, attraction, attractiveness, fascination.

charming *adj* bewitching, captivating, delightful, enchanting, enrapturing, fascinating, lovely.

adj antonyms ugly, unattractive.

charter *vb* **1** incorporate. **2** hire, let. •*n* **1** franchise, immunity, liberty, prerogation, privilege, right. **2** bond, deed, indenture, instrument, prerogative.

chary *adj* **1** careful, cautious, circumspect, shy, wary. **2** abstemious, careful, choice, economical, frugal, provident, saving, sparing, temperate, thrifty, unwasteful.

chase *vb* **1** follow, hunt, pursue, track. **2** emboss. •*n* course, field-sport, hunt, hunting.

chasm *n* cavity, cleft, fissure, gap, hollow, hiatus, opening.

chaste *adj* **1** clean, continent, innocent, modest, pure, pure-minded, undefiled, virtuous. **2** chastened, pure, simple, unaffected, uncorrupt.

adj antonyms indecorous, lewd.

chasten *vb* **1** correct, humble. **2** purify, refine, render, subdue.

chastening *n* chastisement, correction, discipline, humbling.

chastise *vb* **1** castigate, correct, flog, lash, punish, whip. **2** chasten, correct, discipline, humble, punish, subdue.

chastity *n* **1** abstinence, celibacy, continence, innocence, modesty, pure-mindedness, purity, virtue. **2** cleanness, decency. **3** chasteness, refinement, restrainedness, simplicity, sobriety, unaffectedness.

chat *vb* babble, chatter, confabulate, gossip, prate, prattle. •*n* chit-chat, confabulation, conversation, gossip, prattle.

chatter *vb* babble, chat, confabulate, gossip, prate, prattle. •*n* babble, chat, gabble, jabber, patter, prattle.

cheap *adj* **1** inexpensive, low-priced. **2** common, indifferent, inferior, mean, meretricious, paltry, poor.

adj antonyms costly, excellent, noble, superior.

cheapen *vb* belittle, depreciate.

cheat *vb* **1** cozen, deceive, dissemble, juggle, shuffle. **2** bamboozle, befool, beguile, cajole, circumvent, deceive, defraud, chouse, delude, dupe, ensnare, entrap, fool, gammon, gull, hoax, hoodwink, inveigle, jockey, mislead, outwit, overreach, trick. •*n* **1** artifice, beguilement, blind, catch, chouse, deceit, deception, fraud, imposition, imposture, juggle, pitfall, snare, stratagem, swindle, trap, trick, wile. **2** counterfeit, deception, delusion, illusion, mockery, paste, sham, tinsel. **3** beguiler, charlatan, cheater, cozener, impostor, jockey, knave, mountebank, trickster, rogue, render, sharper, seizer, shuffler, swindler, taker, tearer.

check *vb* **1** block, bridle, control, counteract, curb, hinder, obstruct, repress, restrain. **2** chide, rebuke, reprimand, reprove. •*n* bar, barrier, block, brake, bridle, clog, control, curb, damper, hindrance, impediment, interference, obstacle, obstruction, rebuff, repression, restraint, stop, stopper.

cheep *vb* chirp, creak, peep, pipe, squeak.

cheer *vb* **1** animate, encourage, enliven, exhilarate, gladden, incite, inspirit. **2** comfort, console, solace. **3** applaud, clap. •*n* **1** cheerfulness, gaiety, gladness, glee, hilarity, jollity, joy, merriment, mirth. **2** entertainment, food, provision, repast, viands, victuals. **3** acclamation, hurrah, huzza.

vb antonyms boo, dishearten, jeer.

cheerful *adj* **1** animated, airy, blithe, buoyant, cheery, gay, glad, gleeful, happy, joyful, jocund, jolly, joyous, light-hearted, lightsome, lively, merry, mirthful, sprightly, sunny. **2** animating, cheering, cheery, encouraging, enlivening, glad, gladdening, gladsome, grateful, inspiriting, jocund, pleasant.

adj antonym sad.

cheerless *adj* dark, dejected, desolate, despondent, disconsolate, discouraged, dismal, doleful, dreary, forlorn, gloomy, joyless, low-spirited, lugubrious, melancholy, mournful, rueful, sad, sombre, spiritless, woe-begone.

cherish *vb* **1** comfort, foster, nourish, nurse, nurture, support, sustain. **2** treasure. **3** encourage, entertain, indulge, harbour.

chest *n* **1** box, case, coffer. **2** breast, thorax, trunk.

chew *vb* **1** crunch, masticate, munch. **2** bite, champ, gnaw. **3** meditate, ruminate.

chicanery *n* chicane, deception, duplicity, intrigue, intriguing, sophistication, sophistry, stratagems, tergiversation, trickery, wiles, wire-pulling.

chide *vb* **1** admonish, blame, censure, rebuke, reprimand, reprove, scold, upbraid. **2** chafe, clamour, fret, fume, scold.
vb antonym praise.

chief *adj* **1** first, foremost, leading, master, supereminent, supreme, top. **2** capital, cardinal, especial, essential, grand, great, main, master, paramount, prime, principal, supreme, vital. •*n* **1** chieftain, commander. **2** head, leader.
adj antonyms junior, minor, unimportant.

chiffonier *n* cabinet, sideboard.

child *n* **1** babe, baby, bairn, bantling, brat, chit, infant, nursling, suckling, wean. **2** issue, offspring, progeny.

childbirth *n* child-bearing, delivery, labour, parturition, travail.

childish *adj* **1** infantile, juvenile, puerile, tender, young. **2** foolish, frivolous, silly, trifling, weak.
adj antonyms adult, sensible.

childlike *adj* **1** docile, dutiful, gentle, meek, obedient, submissive. **2** confiding, guileless, ingenuous, innocent, simple, trustful.

chill *vb* dampen, depress, deject, discourage, dishearten. •*adj* bleak, chilly, cold, frigid, gelid. •*n* **1** chilliness, cold, coldness, frigidity. **2** ague, rigour, shiver. **3** damp, depression.
adj antonyms friendly, warm.

chime *vb* accord, harmonize. •*n* accord, consonance.

chimera *n* crochet, delusion, dream, fantasy, hallucination, illusion, phantom.

chimerical *adj* delusive, fanciful, fantastic, illusory, imaginary, quixotic, shadowy, unfounded, visionary, wild.

chink[1] *vb* cleave, crack, fissure, crevasse, incise, split, slit. •*n* aperture, cleft, crack, cranny, crevice, fissure, gap, opening, slit.

chink[2] *vb, n* jingle, clink, ring, ting, tink, tinkle.

chip *vb* flake, fragment, hew, pare, scrape. •*n* flake, fragment, paring, scrap.

chirp *vb* cheep, chirrup, peep, twitter.

chirrup *vb* animate, cheer, encourage, inspirit.

chisel *vb* carve, cut, gouge, sculpt, sculpture.

chivalrous *adj* **1** adventurous, bold, brave, chivalric, gallant, knightly, valiant, warlike. **2** gallant, generous, high-minded, magnanimous.
adj antonyms cowardly, ungallant.

chivalry *n* **1** knighthood, knight-errantry. **2** courtesy, gallantry, politeness. **3** courage, valour.

choice *adj* **1** excellent, exquisite, precious, rare, select, superior, uncommon, unusual, valuable. **2** careful, chary, frugal, sparing. •*n* **1** alternative, election, option, selection. **2** favourite, pick, preference.
adj antonym inferior.

choke *vb* **1** gag, smother, stifle, strangle, suffocate, throttle. **2** overcome, overpower, smother, suppress. **3** bar, block, close, obstruct, stop.

choleric *adj* angry, fiery, hasty, hot, fiery, irascible, irritable, passionate, petulant, testy, touchy, waspish.

choose *vb* adopt, co-opt, cull, designate, elect, pick, predestine, prefer, select.

chop *vb* **1** cut, hack, hew. **2** mince. **3** shift, veer. •*n* **1** slice. **2** brand, quality. **3** chap, jaw.

chouse *vb* bamboozle, beguile, cheat, circumvent, cozen, deceive, defraud, delude, dupe, gull, hoodwink, overreach, swindle, trick, victimize. •*n* **1** cully, dupe, gull, simpleton, tool. **2** artifice, cheat, circumvention, deceit, deception, delusion, double-dealing, fraud, imposition, imposture, ruse, stratagem, trick, wile.

christen *vb* **1** baptize. **2** call, dub, denominate, designate, entitle, name, style, term, title.

chronic *adj* confirmed, continuing, deepseated, inveterate, rooted.
adj antonym temporary.

chronicle *vb* narrate, record, register. •*n* **1** diary, journal, register. **2** account, annals, history, narration, recital, record.

chuckle *vb* crow, exult, giggle, laugh, snigger, titter. •*n* giggle, laughter, snigger, titter.

chum *n* buddy, companion, comrade, crony, friend, mate, pal.

churl *n* **1** boor, bumpkin, clodhopper, clown, countryman, lout, peasant, ploughman, rustic. **2** curmudgeon, hunks, miser, niggard, scrimp, skinflint.

churlish *adj* **1** brusque, brutish, cynical, harsh, impolite, rough, rude, snappish, snarling, surly, uncivil, waspish. **2** crabbed, ill-tempered, morose, sullen. **3** close,

close-fisted, illiberal, mean, miserly, niggardly, penurious, stingy.

churn *vb* agitate, jostle.

cicatrice *n* cicatrix, mark, scar, seam.

cincture *n* band, belt, cestos, cestus, girdle.

cipher *n* **1** naught, nothing, zero. **2** character, device, monogram, symbol. **3** nobody, nonentity.

circle *vb* **1** compass, encircle, encompass, gird, girdle, ring. **2** gyrate, revolve, rotate, round, turn. •*n* **1** circlet, corona, gyre, hoop, ring, rondure. **2** circumference, cordon, periphery. **3** ball, globe, orb, sphere. **4** compass, enclosure. **5** class, clique, company, coterie, fraternity, set, society. **6** bounds, circuit, compass, field, province, range, region, sphere.

circuit *n* **1** cycle, revolution, turn. **2** bounds, district, field, province, range, region, space, sphere, tract. **3** boundary, compass. **4** course, detour, perambulation, round, tour.

circuitous *adj* ambiguous, devious, indirect, roundabout, tortuous, turning, winding.
adj antonyms direct, straight.

circulate *vb* diffuse, disseminate, promulgate, propagate, publish, spread.

circumference *n* bound, boundary, circuit, girth, outline, perimeter, periphery.

circumlocution *n* circuitousness, obliqueness, periphrase, periphrasis, verbosity, wordiness.

circumscribe *vb* **1** bound, define, encircle, enclose, encompass, limit, surround. **2** confine, restrict.

circumspect *adj* attentive, careful, cautious, considerate, discreet, heedful, judicious, observant, prudent, vigilant, wary, watchful.

circumstance *n* **1** accident, incident. **2** condition, detail, event, fact, happening, occurrence, position, situation.

circumstantial *adj* **1** detailed, particular. **2** indirect, inferential, presumptive.

circumvent *vb* **1** check, checkmate, outgeneral, thwart. **2** bamboozle, beguile, cheat, chouse, cozen, deceive, defraud, delude, dupe, gull, hoodwink, inveigle, mislead, outwit, overreach, trick.

circumvention *n* cheat, cheating, chicanery, deceit, deception, duplicity, fraud, guile, imposition, imposture, indirection, trickery, wiles.

cistern *n* basin, pond, reservoir, tank.

citation *n* **1** excerpt, extract, quotation.

2 enumeration, mention, quotation, quoting.

cite *vb* **1** adduce, enumerate, extract, mention, name, quote. **2** call, summon.

citizen *n* burgess, burgher, denizen, dweller, freeman, inhabitant, resident, subject, townsman.

civil *adj* **1** civic, municipal, political. **2** domestic. **3** accommodating, affable, civilized, complaisant, courteous, courtly, debonair, easy, gracious, obliging, polished, polite, refined, suave, urbane, wellbred, well-mannered.
adj antonym uncivil.

civility *n* affability, amiability, complaisance, courteousness, courtesy, good-breeding, politeness, suavity, urbanity.

civilize *vb* cultivate, educate, enlighten, humanize, improve, polish, refine.

claim *vb* ask, assert, challenge, demand, exact, require. •*n* **1** call, demand, lien, requisition. **2** pretension, privilege, right, title.

clammy *adj* **1** adhesive, dauby, glutinous, gummy, ropy, smeary, sticky, viscid, viscous. **2** close, damp, dank, moist, sticky, sweaty.

clamour *vb* shout, vociferate. •*n* blare, din, exclamation, hullabaloo, noise, outcry, uproar, vociferation.

clan *n* **1** family, phratry, race, sect, tribe. **2** band, brotherhood, clique, coterie, fraternity, gang, set, society, sodality.

clandestine *adj* concealed, covert, fraudulent, furtive, hidden, private, secret, sly, stealthy, surreptitious, underhand.
adj antonym open.

clap *vb* **1** pat, slap, strike. **2** force, slam. **3** applaud, cheer. •*n* **1** blow, knock, slap. **2** bang, burst, explosion, peal, slam.

clarify *vb* cleanse, clear, depurate, purify, strain.
vb antonym obscure.

clash *vb* **1** collide, crash, strike. **2** clang, clank, clatter, crash, rattle. **3** contend, disagree, interfere. •*n* **1** collision. **2** clang, clangour, clank, clashing, clatter, crash, rattle. **3** contradiction, disagreement, interference, jar, jarring, opposition.

clasp *vb* **1** clutch, entwine, grasp, grapple, grip, seize. **2** embrace, enfold, fold, hug. •*n* **1** buckle, catch, hasp, hook. **2** embrace, hug.

class *vb* arrange, classify, dispose, distribute, range, rank. •*n* **1** form, grade, order, rank, status. **2** group, seminar. **3** breed, kind, sort. **4** category, collection, denomination, division, group, head.

classical *adj* **1** first-rate, master, masterly, model, standard. **2** Greek, Latin, Roman. **3** Attic, chaste, elegant, polished, pure, refined.

classify *vb* arrange, assort, categorize, class, dispose, distribute, group, pigeonhole, rank, systematize, tabulate.

clatter *vb* **1** clash, rattle. **2** babble, clack, gabble, jabber, prate, prattle. •*n* clattering, clutter, rattling.

clause *n* article, condition, provision, stipulation.

claw *vb* lacerate, scratch, tear. •*n* talon, ungula.

clean *vb* cleanse, clear, purge, purify, rinse, scour, scrub, wash, wipe. •*adj* **1** immaculate, spotless, unsmirched, unsoiled, unspotted, unstained, unsullied, white. **2** clarified, pure, purified, unadulterated, unmixed. **3** adroit, delicate, dextrous, graceful, light, neat, shapely. **4** complete, entire, flawless, faultless, perfect, unabated, unblemished, unimpaired, whole. **5** chaste, innocent, moral, pure, undefiled. •*adv* altogether, completely, entirely, perfectly, quite, thoroughly, wholly.

adj antonyms dirty, indecent, polluted, unsterile.

vb antonyms defile, dirty.

cleanse *vb* clean, clear, elutriate, purge, purify, rinse, scour, scrub, wash, wipe.

vb antonyms defile, dirty.

clear *vb* **1** clarify, cleanse, purify, refine. **2** emancipate, disenthral, free, liberate, loose. **3** absolve, acquit, discharge, exonerate, justify, vindicate. **4** disembarrass, disengage, disentangle, extricate, loosen, rid. **5** clean up, scour, sweep. **6** balance. **7** emancipate, free, liberate. •*adj* **1** bright, crystalline, light, limpid, luminous, pellucid, transparent. **2** pure, unadulterated, unmixed. **3** free, open, unencumbered, unobstructed. **4** cloudless, fair, serene, sunny, unclouded, undimmed, unobscured. **5** distinct, intelligible, lucid, luminous, perspicuous. **6** apparent, conspicuous, distinct, evident, indisputable, manifest, obvious, palpable, unambiguous, undeniable, unequivocal, unmistakable, unquestionable, visible. **7** clean, guiltless, immaculate, innocent, irreproachable, sinless, spotless, unblemished, undefiled,

unspotted, unsullied. **8** unhampered, unimpeded, unobstructed. **9** euphonious, liquid, mellifluous, musical, silvery, sonorous.

adj antonyms cloudy, fuzzy, guilty, vague.

vb antonyms block, condemn, defile, dirty.

cleave[1] *vb* crack, divide, open, part, rend, rive, sever, split, sunder.

cleave[2] *vb* adhere, cling, cohere, hold, stick.

cleft *adj* bifurcated, cloven, forked. •*n* breach, break, chasm, chink, cranny, crevice, fissure, fracture, gap, interstice, opening, rent, rift.

clemency *n* **1** mildness, softness. **2** compassion, fellow-feeling, forgivingness, gentleness, kindness, lenience, leniency, lenity, mercifulness, mercy, mildness, tenderness.

n antonyms harshness, ruthlessness.

clement *adj* compassionate, forgiving, gentle, humane, indulgent, kind, kind-hearted, lenient, merciful, mild, tender, tenderhearted.

clench *vb* **1** close tightly, grip. **2** fasten, fix, rivet, secure.

clergy *n* clergymen, the cloth, ministers.

clever *adj* **1** able, apt, gifted, talented. **2** adroit, capable, dextrous, discerning, expert, handy, ingenious, knowing, quick, ready, skilful, smart, talented.

adj antonyms foolish, naïve, senseless.

click *vb* beat, clack, clink, tick. •*n* **1** beat, clack, clink, tick. **2** catch, detent, pawl, ratchet.

cliff *n* crag, palisade, precipice, scar, steep.

climate *n* **1** clime, temperature, weather. **2** country, region.

climax *vb* consummate, crown, culminate, peak. •*n* acme, consummation, crown, culmination, head, peak, summit, top, zenith.

n antonyms bathos, low point, nadir.

clinch *vb* **1** clasp, clench, clutch, grapple, grasp, grip. **2** fasten, secure. **3** confirm, establish, fix. •*n* **1** catch, clutch, grasp, grip. **2** clincher, clamp, cramp, holdfast.

cling *vb* **1** adhere, clear, stick. **2** clasp, embrace, entwine.

clink *vb, n* **1** chink, jingle, ring, tinkle. **2** chime, rhyme.

clip *vb* **1** cut, shear, snip. **2** curtail, cut, dock, pare, prune, trim. •*n* **1** cutting, shearing. **2** blow, knock, lick, rap, thump, thwack, thump.

clique *n* association, brotherhood, cabal, camarilla, clan, club, coterie, gang, junta, party, ring, set, sodality.

cloak *vb* conceal, cover, dissemble, hide, mask, veil. •*n* 1 mantle, surcoat. 2 blind, cover, mask, pretext, veil.

clock *vb* 1 mark time, measure, stopwatch. 2 clock up, record, register. •*n* chronometer, horologue, timekeeper, timepiece, timer, watch.

clog *vb* 1 fetter, hamper, shackle, trammel. 2 choke, obstruct. 3 burden, cumber, embarrass, encumber, hamper, hinder, impede, load, restrain, trammel. •*n* 1 deadweight, drag-weight, fetter, shackle, trammel. 2 check, drawback, encumbrance, hindrance, impediment, obstacle, obstruction.
vb antonym unblock.

cloister *n* 1 abbey, convent, monastery, nunnery, priory. 2 arcade, colonnade, piazza.

close¹ *adj* 1 closed, confined, snug, tight. 2 hidden, private, secret. 3 incommunicative, reserved, reticent, secretive, taciturn. 4 concealed, retired, secluded, withdrawn. 5 confined, motionless, stagnant. 6 airless, oppressive, stale, stifling, stuffy, sultry. 7 compact, compressed, dense, form, solid, thick. 8 adjacent, adjoining, approaching, immediately, near, nearly, neighbouring. 9 attached, dear, confidential, devoted, intimate. 10 assiduous, earnest, fixed, intense, intent, unremitting. 11 accurate, exact, faithful, nice, precise, strict. 12 churlish, close-fisted, curmudgeonly, mean, illiberal, miserly, niggardly, parsimonious, penurious, stingy, ungenerous. •*n* courtyard, enclosure, grounds, precinct, yard.
adj antonyms careless, cool, far, unfriendly.

close² *vb* 1 occlude, seal, shut. 2 choke, clog, estop, obstruct, stop. 3 cease, complete, concede, end, finish, terminate. 4 coalesce, unite. 5 cease, conclude, finish, terminate. 6 clinch, grapple. 7 agree. •*n* cessation, conclusion, end, finish, termination.

closet *n* 1 cabinet, retiring-room. 2 cupboard, press, store-room, wardrobe.

clot *vb* coagulate, concrete. •*n* coagulation, concretion, lump.

clothe *vb* 1 array, attire, deck, dress, rig. 2 cover, endow, envelop, enwrap, invest with, swathe.
vb antonyms unclothe, undress.

clothes *n* apparel, array, attire, clothing, costume, dress, garb, garments, gear, habiliments, habits, raiment, rig, vestments, vesture.

cloud *vb* 1 becloud, obnubilate, overcast, overspread. 2 befog, darken, dim, obscure, shade, shadow. •*n* 1 cirrus, cumulus, fog, haze, mist, nebulosity, scud, stratus, vapour. 2 army, crowd, horde, host, multitude, swarm, throng. 3 darkness, eclipse, gloom, obscuration, obscurity.
vb antonym clear.

cloudy *adj* 1 clouded, filmy, foggy, hazy, lowering, lurid, murky, overcast. 2 confused, dark, dim, obscure. 3 depressing, dismal, gloomy, sullen. 4 clouded, mottled. 5 blurred, dimmed, lustreless, muddy.
adj antonyms clear, sunny.

clown *n* 1 churl, clod-breaker, clodhopper, hind, husbandman, lubber. 2 boor, bumpkin, churl, fellow, lout. 3 blockhead, dolt, clodpoll, dunce, dunderhead, numbskull, simpleton, thickhead. 4 buffoon, droll, farceur, fool, harlequin, jack-a-dandy, jester, mime, pantaloon, punch, scaramouch.

clownish *adj* 1 awkward, boorish, clumsy, coarse, loutish, ungainly, rough, rustic. 2 churlish, ill-bred, ill-mannered, impolite, rude, uncivil.

cloy *vb* glut, pall, sate, satiate, surfeit.

club *vb* 1 combine, unite. 2 beat, bludgeon, cudgel. •*n* 1 bat, bludgeon, cosh, cudgel, hickory, shillelagh, stick, truncheon. 2 association, company, coterie, fraternity, set, society, sodality.

clump *vb* 1 assemble, batch, bunch, cluster, group, lump. 2 lumber, stamp, stomp, stump, trudge. •*n* assemblage, bunch, cluster, collection, group, patch, tuft.

clumsy *adj* 1 botched, cumbrous, heavy, ill-made, ill-shaped, lumbering, ponderous, unwieldy. 2 awkward, blundering, bungling, elephantine, heavy-handed, inapt, mal adroit, unhandy, unskilled.
adj antonym graceful.

cluster *vb* assemble, batch, bunch, clump, collect, gather, group, lump, throng. •*n* agglomeration, assemblage, batch, bunch, clump, collection, gathering, group, throng.

clutch¹ *vb* catch, clasp, clench, clinch, grab, grapple, grasp, grip, hold, seize, snatch, squeeze. •*n* clasp, clench, clinch, grasp, grip, hold, seizure, squeeze.

clutch² *n* aerie, brood, hatching, nest.

clutches *npl* **1** claws, paws, talons. **2** hands, power.

clutter *vb* **1** confuse, disarrange, disarray, disorder, jumble, litter, mess, muss. **2** clatter. •*n* **1** bustle, clatter, clattering, racket. **2** confusion, disarray, disorder, jumble, litter, mess, muss.

coadjutor *n* abettor, accomplice, aider, ally, assistant, associate, auxiliary, collaborator, colleague, cooperator, fellow-helper, helper, helpmate, partner.

coagulate *vb* clot, congeal, concrete, curdle, thicken.

coalesce *vb* **1** amalgamate, blend, cohere, combine, commix, incorporate, mix, unite. **2** concur, fraternize.

coalition *n* alliance, association, combination, compact, confederacy, confederation, conjunction, conspiracy, co-partnership, federation, league, union.

coarse *adj* **1** crude, impure, rough, unpurified. **2** broad, gross, indecent, indelicate, ribald, vulgar. **3** bearish, bluff, boorish, brutish, churlish, clownish, gruff, impolite, loutish, rude, unpolished. **4** crass, inelegant.
adj antonyms fine, polite, refined, sophisticated.

coast *vb* flow, glide, roll, skim, sail, slide, sweep. •*n* **1** littoral, seaboard, sea-coast, seaside, shore, strand. **2** border.

coat *vb* cover, spread. •*n* **1** cut-away, frock, jacket. **2** coating, cover, covering. **3** layer.

coax *vb* allure, beguile, cajole, cog, entice, flatter, persuade, soothe, wheedle.
vb antonym force.

cobble *vb* **1** botch, bungle. **2** mend, patch, repair, tinker.
vb antonym force.

cobweb *adj* flimsy, gauzy, slight, thin, worthless. •*n* entanglement, meshes, snare, toils.

cochleate *adj* cochlear, cochleary, cochleous, cochleated, spiral.

cockle *vb* corrugate, pucker, wrinkle.

coddle *vb* caress, fondle, humour, indulge, nurse, pamper, pet.

codger *n* churl, curmudgeon, hunks, lickpenny, miser, niggard, screw, scrimp, skinflint.

codify *vb* condense, digest, summarize, systematize, tabulate.

coerce *vb* **1** check, curb, repress, restrain, subdue. **2** compel, constrain, drive, force, urge.
vb antonyms coax, persuade.

coercion *n* **1** check, curb, repression, restraint. **2** compulsion, constraint, force.
n antonym persuasion.

coeval *adj* coetaneous, coexistent, contemporaneous, contemporary, synchronous.

coexistent *adj* coetaneous, coeval, simultaneous, synchronous.

coffer *n* **1** box, casket, chest, trunk. **2** money-chest, safe, strongbox. **3** caisson.

cogent *adj* compelling, conclusive, convincing, effective, forcible, influential, irresistible, persuasive, potent, powerful, resistless, strong, trenchant, urgent.

cogitate *vb* consider, deliberate, meditate, ponder, reflect, ruminate, muse, think, weigh.

cognate *adj* affiliated, affined, akin, allied, alike, analogous, connected, kindred, related, similar.

cognizance *n* cognition, knowing, knowledge, notice, observation.
n antonym unawareness.

cohere *vb* agree, coincide, conform, fit, square, suit.

coherence *n* **1** coalition, cohesion, connection, dependence, union. **2** agreement, congruity, consistency, correspondence, harmony, intelligibility, intelligible, meaning, rationality, unity.

coherent *adj* **1** adherent, connected, united. **2** congruous, consistent, intelligible, logical.

cohort *n* band, battalion, line, squadron. •*n* **1** convolution, curlicue, helix, knot, roll, spiral, tendril, twirl, volute, whorl. **2** bustle, care, clamour, confusion, entanglements, perplexities, tumult, turmoil, uproar.

coil *vb* curl, twine, twirl, twist, wind.

coin *vb* **1** counterfeit, create, devise, fabricate, forge, form, invent, mint, originate, mould, stamp. •*n* **1** corner, quoin. **2** key, plug, prop, wedge. **3** cash, money, specie.

coincide *vb* **1** cohere, correspond, square, tally. **2** acquiesce, agree, harmonize, concur.

coincidence *n* **1** corresponding, squaring, tallying. **2** agreeing, concurrent, concurring.

cold *adj* **1** arctic, biting, bleak, boreal, chill, chilly, cutting, frosty, gelid, glacial, icy, nipping, polar, raw, wintry. **2** frost-bitten,

shivering. **3** apathetic, cold-blooded, dead, freezing, frigid, indifferent, lukewarm, passionless, phlegmatic, sluggish, stoical, stony, torpid, unconcerned, unfeeling, unresponsive, unsympathetic. **4** dead, dull, spiritless, unaffecting, uninspiring, uninteresting. •*n* chill, chilliness, coldness. *adj antonyms* friendly, warm.
n antonyms friendliness, warmth.

collapse *vb* break down, fail, fall. •*n* depression, exhaustion, failure, faint, prostration, sinking, subsidence.

collar *vb* apprehend, arrest, capture, grab, nab, seize. •*n* **1** collarette, gorget, neckband, ruff, torque. **2** band, belt, fillet, guard, ring, yoke.

collate *vb* adduce, collect, compare, compose.

collateral *adj* **1** contingent, indirect, secondary, subordinate. **2** concurrent, parallel. **3** confirmatory, corroborative. **4** accessory, accompanying, additional, ancillary, auxiliary, concomitant, contributory, simultaneous, supernumerary. **5** consanguineous, related. •*n* **1** guarantee, guaranty, security, surety, warranty. **2** accessory, extra, nonessential, unessential. **3** consanguinean, relative.

collation *n* luncheon, repast, meal.

colleague *n* aider, ally, assistant, associate, auxiliary, coadjutor, collaborator, companion, confederate, confrere, cooperator, helper, partner.

collect *vb* **1** assemble, compile, gather, muster. **2** accumulate, aggregate, amass, garner.

collected *adj* calm, composed, cool, placid, self-possessed, serene, unperturbed.
adj antonyms disorganized, dithery, worried.

collection *n* **1** aggregation, assemblage, cluster, crowd, drove, gathering, group, pack. **2** accumulation, congeries, conglomeration, heap, hoard, lot, mass, pile, store. **3** alms, contribution, offering, offertory.

collision *n* **1** clash, concussion, crash, encounter, impact, impingement, shock. **2** conflict, crashing, interference, opposition.

collocate *vb* arrange, dispose, place, set.

colloquy *n* conference, conversation, dialogue, discourse, talk.

collude *vb* concert, connive, conspire.

collusion *n* connivance, conspiracy, coven, craft, deceit.

collusive *adj* conniving, conspiratorial, dishonest, deceitful, deceptive, fraudulent.

colossal *adj* Cyclopean, enormous, gigantic, Herculean, huge, immense, monstrous, prodigious, vast.

colour *vb* **1** discolour, dye, paint, stain, tinge, tint. **2** disguise, varnish. **3** disguise, distort, garble, misrepresent, pervert. **4** blush, flush, redden, show. •*n* **1** hue, shade, tinge, tint, tone. **2** paint, pigment, stain. **3** redness, rosiness, ruddiness. **4** complexion. **5** appearance, disguise, excuse, guise, plea, pretence, pretext, semblance.

colourless *adj* **1** achromatic, uncoloured, untinged. **2** blanched, hueless, livid, pale, pallid. **3** blank, characterless, dull, expressionless, inexpressive, monotonous.

colours *n* banner, ensign, flag, standard.

column *n* **1** pillar, pilaster. **2** file, line, row.

coma *n* **1** drowsiness, lethargy, somnolence, stupor, torpor. **2** bunch, clump, cluster, tuft.

comatose *adj* drowsy, lethargic, sleepy, somnolent, stupefied.

comb *vb* **1** card, curry, dress, groom, rake, unknot, untangle. **2** rake, ransack, rummage, scour, search. •*n* **1** card, hatchel, ripple. **2** harrow, rake.

combat *vb* **1** contend, contest, fight, struggle, war. **2** battle, oppose, resist, struggle, withstand. •*n* action, affair, battle, brush, conflict, contest, encounter, fight, skirmish.

combative *adj* belligerent, contentious, militant, pugnacious, quarrelsome.

combination *n* **1** association, conjunction, connection, union. **2** alliance, cartel, coalition, confederacy, consolidation, league, merger, syndicate. **3** cabal, clique, conspiracy, faction, junta, ring. **4** amalgamation, compound, mixture.

combine *vb* **1** cooperate, merge, pool, unite. **2** amalgamate, blend, incorporate, mix.
vb antonym separate.

combustible *adj* consumable, inflammable.

come *vb* **1** advance, approach. **2** arise, ensue, flow, follow, issue, originate, proceed, result. **3** befall, betide, happen, occur.
vb antonyms depart, go, leave.

comely *adj* **1** becoming, decent, decorous, fitting, seemly, suitable. **2** beautiful, fair, graceful, handsome, personable, pretty, symmetrical.

comfort *vb* alleviate, animate, cheer, console,

encourage, enliven, gladden, inspirit, invigorate, refresh, revive, solace, soothe, strengthen. •*n* **1** aid, assistance, countenance, help, support, succour. **2** consolation, solace, encouragement, relief. **3** ease, enjoyment, peace, satisfaction.
n antonyms distress, torment.

comfortable *adj* **1** acceptable, agreeable, delightful, enjoyable, grateful, gratifying, happy, pleasant, pleasurable, welcome. **2** commodious, convenient, easeful, snug. **3** painless.
adj antonyms poor, uncomfortable.

comfortless *adj* **1** bleak, cheerless, desolate, drear, dreary, forlorn, miserable, wretched. **2** broken-hearted, desolate, disconsolate, forlorn, heart-broken, inconsolable, miserable, woe-begone, wretched.

comical *adj* amusing, burlesque, comic, diverting, droll, farcical, funny, humorous, laughable, ludicrous, sportive, whimsical.
adj antonyms sad, unamusing.

coming *adj* **1** approaching, arising, arriving, ensuing, eventual, expected, forthcoming, future, imminent, issuing, looming, nearing, prospective, ultimate. **2** emergent, emerging, successful. **3** due, owed, owing. •*n* **1** advent, approach, arrival. **2** imminence, imminency, nearness. **3** apparition, appearance, disclosure, emergence, manifestation, materialization, occurrence, presentation, revelation, rising.

command *vb* **1** bid, charge, direct, enjoin, order, require. **2** control, dominate, govern, lead, rule, sway. **3** claim, challenge, compel, demand, exact. •*n* **1** behest, bidding, charge, commandment, direction, hest, injunction, mandate, order, requirement, requisition. **2** ascendency, authority, dominion, control, government, power, rule, sway, supremacy.

commander *n* captain, chief, chieftain, commandment, head, leader.

commemorate *vb* celebrate, keep, observe, solemnize.

commence *vb* begin, inaugurate, initiate, institute, open, originate, start.
vb antonyms cease, finish.

commend *vb* **1** assign, bespeak, confide, recommend, remit. **2** commit, entrust, yield. **3** applaud, approve, eulogize, extol, laud, praise.
vb antonym criticize.

commendation *n* **1** approbation, approval,

good opinion, recommendation. **2** praise, encomium, eulogy, panegyric.
n antonyms blame, criticism.

commensurate *adj* **1** commeasurable, commensurable. **2** co-extensive, conterminous, equal. **3** adequate, appropriate, corresponding, due, proportionate, proportioned, sufficient.
adj antonym inappropriate.

comment *vb* annotate, criticize, explain, interpret, note, remark. •*n* **1** annotation, elucidation, explanation, exposition, illustration, commentary, note, gloss. **2** observation, remark.

commentator *n* annotator, commentator, critic, expositor, expounder, interpreter.

commerce *n* **1** business, exchange, dealing, trade, traffic. **2** communication, communion, intercourse.

commercial *adj* mercantile, trading.

commination *n* denunciation, menace, threat, threatening.

commingle *vb* amalgamate, blend, combine, commix, intermingle, intermix, join, mingle, mix, unite.

comminute *vb* bray, bruise, grind, levigate, powder, pulverize, triturate.

commiserate *vb* compassionate, condole, pity, sympathize.

commiseration *n* **1** compassion, pitying. **2** condolence, pity, sympathy.

commission *vb* **1** authorize, empower. **2** delegate, depute. •*n* **1** doing, perpetration. **2** care, charge, duty, employment, errand, office, task, trust. **3** allowance, compensation, fee, rake-off.

commissioner *n* agent, delegate, deputy.

commit *vb* **1** confide, consign, delegate, entrust, remand. **2** consign, deposit, lay, place, put, relegate, resign. **3** do, enact, perform, perpetrate. **4** imprison. **5** engage, implicate, pledge.

commodious *adj* advantageous, ample, comfortable, convenient, fit, proper, roomy, spacious, suitable, useful.
adj antonym cramped.

commodity *n* goods, merchandise, produce, wares.

common *adj* **1** collective, public. **2** general, useful. **3** common-place, customary, everyday, familiar, frequent, habitual, usual. **4** banal, hackneyed, stale, threadbare, trite. **5** indifferent, inferior, low, ordinary, plebeian, popular, undistinguished, vulgar.

adj antonyms noteworthy, uncommon.

commonplace *adj* common, hackneyed, ordinary, stale, threadbare, trite. •*n* **1** banality, cliché, platitude. **2** jotting, memoir, memorandum, note, reminder.

adj antonyms exceptional, rare.

common-sense *adj* practical, sagacious, sensible, sober.

adj antonym foolish.

commotion *n* **1** agitation, disturbance, ferment, perturbation, welter. **2** ado, bustle, disorder, disturbance, hurly-burly, pother, tumult, turbulence, turmoil.

communicate *vb* **1** bestow, confer, convey, give, impart, transmit. **2** acquaint, announce, declare, disclose, divulge, publish, reveal, unfold. **3** commune, converse, correspond.

communication *n* **1** conveyance, disclosure, giving, imparting, transmittal. **2** commence, conference, conversation, converse, correspondence, intercourse. **3** announcement, dispatch, information, message, news.

communicative *adj* affable, chatty, conversable, free, open, sociable, unreserved.

adj antonym reticent.

communion *n* **1** converse, fellowship, intercourse, participation. **2** Eucharist, holy communion, Lord's Supper, sacrament.

community *n* **1** commonwealth, people, public, society. **2** association, brotherhood, college, society. **3** likeness, participancy, sameness, similarity.

compact[1] *n* agreement, arrangement, bargain, concordant, contract, covenant, convention, pact, stipulation, treaty.

adj antonyms diffuse, rambling, rangy.

compact[2] *vb* **1** compress, condense, pack, press. **2** bind, consolidate, unite. •*adj* **1** close, compressed, condensed, dense, firm, solid. **2** brief, compendious, concise, laconic, pithy, pointed, sententious, short, succinct, terse.

companion *n* **1** accomplice, ally, associate, comrade, compeer, confederate, consort, crony, friend, fellow, mate. **2** partaker, participant, participator, partner, sharer.

companionable *adj* affable, conversable, familiar, friendly, genial, neighbourly, sociable.

companionship *n* association, fellowship, friendship, intercourse, society.

company *n* **1** assemblage, assembly, band, bevy, body, circle, collection, communication, concourse, congregation, coterie, crew, crowd, flock, gang, gathering, group, herd, rout, set, syndicate, troop. **2** party. **3** companionship, fellowship, guests, society, visitor, visitors. **4** association, copartnership, corporation, firm, house, partnership.

compare *vb* **1** assimilate, balance, collate, parallel. **2** liken, resemble.

comparison *n* **1** collation, compare, estimate. **2** simile, similitude.

compartment *n* bay, cell, division, pigeonhole, section.

compass *vb* **1** embrace, encompass, enclose, encircle, environ, surround. **2** beleaguer, beset, besiege, block, blockade, invest. **3** accomplish, achieve, attain, carry, consummate, effect, obtain, perform, procure, realize. **4** contrive, devise, intend, meditate, plot, purpose. •*n* **1** bound, boundary, extent, gamut, limit, range, reach, register, scope, stretch. **2** circuit, round.

compassion *n* clemency, commiseration, condolence, fellow-feeling, heart, humanity, kind-heartedness, kindness, kindliness, mercy, pity, rue, ruth, sorrow, sympathy, tenderheartedness, tenderness.

n antonym indifference.

compassionate *adj* benignant, clement, commiserative, gracious, kind, merciful, pitying, ruthful, sympathetic, tender.

adj antonym indifferent.

compatible *adj* accordant, agreeable to, congruous, consistent, consonant, reconcilable, suitable.

adj antonyms antagonistic, antipathetic, incompatible.

compeer *n* associate, comrade, companion, equal, fellow, mate, peer.

compel *vb* **1** constrain, force, coerce, drive, necessitate, oblige. **2** bend, bow, subdue, subject.

compend *n* abbreviation, abridgement, abstract, breviary, brief, compendium, conspectus, digest, epitome, précis, summary, syllabus, synopsis.

compendious *adj* abbreviated, abridged, brief, comprehensive, concise, short, succinct, summary.

compensate *vb* **1** counterbalance, counterpoise, countervail. **2** guerdon, recompense, reimburse, remunerate, reward. **3** indemnify, reimburse, repay, requite. **4** atone.

compensation *n* 1 pay, payment, recompense, remuneration, reward, salary. 2 amends, atonement, indemnification, indemnity, reparation, requital, satisfaction. 3 balance, counterpoise, equalization, offset.

compete *vb* contend, contest, cope, emulate, rival, strive, struggle, vie.

competence *n* 1 ability, capability, capacity, fitness, qualification, suitableness. 2 adequacy, adequateness, enough, sufficiency. *n antonym* incompetence.

competent *adj* 1 able, capable, clever, equal, endowed, qualified. 2 adapted, adequate, convenient, fit, sufficient, suitable. *adj antonym* incompetent.

competition *n* contest, emulation, rivalry, rivals.

competitor *n* adversary, antagonist, contestant, emulator, opponent.

compile *vb* 1 compose, prepare, write. 2 arrange, collect, select.

complacency *n* 1 content, contentment, gratification, pleasure, satisfaction. 2 affability, civility, complaisance, courtesy, politeness.

complacent *adj* 1 contented, gratified, pleased, satisfied. 2 affable, civil, complaisant, courteous, easy, gracious, grateful, obliging, polite, urbane.

complain *vb* bemoan, bewail, deplore, grieve, groan, grouch, grumble, lament, moan, murmur, repine, whine.

complainant *n* accuser, plaintiff.

complaining *adj* fault-finding, murmuring, querulous.

complaint *n* 1 grievance, gripe, grumble, lament, lamentation, plaint, murmur, wail. 2 ail, ailment, annoyance, disease, disorder, illness, indisposition, malady, sickness. 3 accusation, charge, information.

complete *vb* accomplish, achieve, conclude, consummate, do, effect, effectuate, end, execute, finish, fulfil, perfect, perform, realize, terminate. •*adj* 1 clean, consummate, faultless, full, perfect, perform, thorough. 2 all, entire, integral, total, unbroken, undiminished, undivided, unimpaired, whole. 3 accomplished, achieved, completed, concluded, consummated, ended, finished. *adj antonyms* imperfect, incomplete.

completion *n* accomplishing, accomplishment, achieving, conclusion, consummation, effecting, effectuation, ending, execution, finishing, perfecting, performance, termination.

complex *adj* 1 composite, compound, compounded, manifold, mingled, mixed. 2 complicate, complicated, entangled, intricate, involved, knotty, mazy, tangled. •*n* 1 complexus, complication, involute, skein, tangle. 2 entirety, integration, network, totality, whole. 3 compulsion, fixation, obsession, preoccupation, prepossession. 4 prejudice. *adj antonym* simple.

complexion *n* colour, hue, tint.

complexity *n* complication, entanglement, intricacy, involution.

compliance *n* 1 concession, obedience, submission. 2 acquiescence, agreement, assent, concurrence, consent. 3 compliancy, yieldingness.

complicate *vb* confuse, entangle, interweave, involve.

complication *n* 1 complexity, confusion, entanglement, intricacy. 2 combination, complexus, mixture.

compliment *vb* commend, congratulate, eulogize, extol, flatter, laud, praise. •*n* admiration, commendation, courtesy, encomium, eulogy, favour, flattery, honour, laudation, praise, tribute. *n antonyms* criticism, insult. *vb antonyms* condemn, insult.

complimentary *adj* commendatory, congratulatory, encomiastic, eulogistic, flattering, laudatory, panegyrical. *adj antonyms* critical, insulting, unflattering.

comply *vb* 1 adhere to, complete, discharge, fulfil, meet, observe, perform, satisfy. 2 accede, accord, acquiesce, agree to, assent, consent to, yield. *vb antonyms* disobey, resist.

component *adj* composing, constituent, constituting. •*n* constituent, element, ingredient, part.

comport *vb* accord, agree, coincide, correspond, fit, harmonize, square, suit, tally.

compose *vb* 1 build, compact, compound, constitute, form, make, synthesize. 2 contrive, create, frame, imagine, indite, invent, write. 3 adjust, arrange, regulate, settle. 4 appease, assuage, calm, pacify, quell, quiet, soothe, still, tranquillize.

composed *adj* calm, collected, cool,

imperturbable, placid, quiet, sedate, self-possessed, tranquil, undisturbed, unmoved, unruffled.

adj antonym agitated.

composite *adj* 1 amalgamated, combined, complex, compounded, mixed. 2 integrated, unitary. •*n* admixture, amalgam, blend, combination, composition, compound, mixture, unification.

composition *n* 1 constitution, construction, formation, framing, making. 2 compound, mixture. 3 arrangement, combination, conjunction, make-up, synthesize, union. 4 invention, opus, piece, production, writing. 5 agreement, arrangement, compromise.

compost *n* fertilizer, fertilizing, manure, mixture.

composure *n* calmness, coolness, equanimity, placidity, sedateness, quiet, self-possession, serenity, tranquillity.

n antonym discomposure.

compotation *n* 1 conviviality, frolicking, jollification, revelling, revelry, rousing, wassailling. 2 bacchanal, carousal, carouse, debauch, orgy, revel, saturnalia, wassail.

compound[1] *vb* 1 amalgamate, blend, combine, intermingle, intermix, mingle, mix, unite. 2 adjust, arrange, compose, compromise, settle. •*adj* complex, composite. •*n* 1 combination, composition, mixture. 2 farrago, hodgepodge, jumble, medley, mess, olio.

compound[2] *n* enclosure, garden, yard.

comprehend *vb* 1 comprise, contain, embrace, embody, enclose, include, involve. 2 apprehend, conceive, discern, grasp, know, imagine, master, perceive, see, understand.

vb antonym misunderstand.

comprehension *n* 1 comprising, embracing, inclusion. 2 compass, domain, embrace, field, limits, province, range, reach, scope, sphere, sweep. 3 connotation, depth, force, intention. 4 conception, grasp, intelligence, understanding. 5 intellect, intelligence, mind, reason, understanding.

n antonym incomprehension.

comprehensive *adj* all-embracing, ample, broad, capacious, compendious, extensive, full, inclusive, large, sweeping, wide.

adj antonyms incomplete, selective.

compress *vb* abbreviate, condense, constrict, contract, crowd, press, shorten, squeeze, summarize.

vb antonyms diffuse, expand, separate.

compression *n* 1 condensation, confining, pinching, pressing, squeezing. 2 brevity, pithiness, succinctness, terseness.

comprise *vb* comprehend, contain, embody, embrace, enclose, include, involve.

compromise *vb* 1 adjust, arbitrate, arrange, compose, compound, settle. 2 jeopardize, prejudice. 3 commit, engage, implicate, pledge. 4 agree, compound. •*n* adjustment, agreement, composition, settlement.

vb antonyms differ, quarrel.

n antonyms disagreement, intransigence.

compulsion *n* coercion, constraint, force, forcing, pressure, urgency.

n antonyms freedom, liberty.

compulsory *adj* 1 coercive, compelling, constraining. 2 binding, enforced, imperative, necessary, obligatory, unavoidable.

adj antonyms optional, voluntary.

compunction *n* contrition, misgiving, penitence, qualm, regret, reluctance, remorse, repentance, sorrow.

computable *adj* calculable, numerable, reckonable.

computation *n* account, calculation, estimate, reckoning, score, tally.

compute *vb* calculate, count, enumerate, estimate, figure, measure, number, rate, reckon, sum.

comrade *n* accomplice, ally, associate, chum, companion, compatriot, compeer, crony, fellow, mate, pal.

concatenate *vb* connect, join, link, unite.

concatenation *n* 1 connection. 2 chain, congeries, linking, series, sequence, succession.

concave *adj* depressed, excavated, hollow, hollowed, scooped.

conceal *vb* 1 bury, cover, screen, secrete. 2 disguise, dissemble, mask.

vb antonym reveal.

concede *vb* 1 grant, surrender, yield. 2 acknowledge, admit, allow, confess, grant.

vb antonyms deny, dispute.

conceit *n* 1 belief, conception, fancy, idea, image, imagination, notion, thought. 2 caprice, illusion, vagary, whim. 3 estimate, estimation, impression, judgement, opinion. 4 conceitedness, egoism, self-complacency, priggishness, priggery, self-conceit, self-esteem, self-sufficiency, vanity. 5 crotchet, point, quip, quirk.

n antonyms diffidence, modesty.

conceited *adj* egotistical, opinionated, opinionative, overweening, self-conceited, vain.
adj antonyms diffident, modest.

conceivable *adj* **1** imaginable, picturable. **2** cogitable, comprehensible, intelligible, rational, thinkable.

conceive *vb* **1** create, contrive, devise, form, plan, purpose. **2** fancy, imagine. **3** comprehend, fathom, think, understand. **4** assume, imagine, suppose. **5** bear, become pregnant.

concern *vb* **1** affect, belong to, interest, pertain to, regard, relate to, touch. **2** disquiet, disturb, trouble. •*n* **1** affair, business, matter, transaction. **2** concernment, consequence, importance, interest, moment, weight. **3** anxiety, care, carefulness, solicitude, worry. **4** business, company, establishment, firm, house.
n antonym unconcern.

concert *vb* combine, concoct, contrive, design, devise, invent, plan, plot, project. •*n* agreement, concord, concordance, cooperation, harmony, union, unison.

concession *n* **1** acquiescence, assent, cessation, compliance, surrender, yielding. **2** acknowledgement, allowance, boon, confession, grant, privilege.

conciliate *vb* **1** appease, pacify, placate, propitiate, reconcile. **2** engage, gain, secure, win, win over.

concise *adj* brief, compact, compendious, comprehensive, compressed, condensed, crisp, laconic, pithy, pointed, pregnant, sententious, short, succinct, summary, terse.
adj antonyms diffuse, expansive.

conclave *n* assembly, cabinet, council.

conclude *vb* **1** close, end, finish, terminate. **2** deduce, gather, infer, judge. **3** decide, determine, judge. **4** arrange, complete, settle. **5** bar, hinder, restrain, stop. **6** decide, determine, resolve.

conclusion *n* **1** deduction, inference. **2** decision, determination, judgement. **3** close, completion, end, event, finale, issue, termination, upshot. **4** arrangement, closing, effecting, establishing, settlement.

conclusive *adj* **1** clinching, convincing, decisive, irrefutable, unanswerable. **2** final, ultimate.
adj antonym inconclusive.

concoct *vb* brew, contrive, design, devise, frame, hatch, invent, mature, plan, plot, prepare, project.

concomitant *adj* accessory, accompanying, attendant, attending, coincident, concurrent, conjoined. •*n* accessory, accompaniment, attendant.

concord *n* **1** agreement, amity, friendship, harmony, peace, unanimity, union, unison, unity. **2** accord, adaptation, concordance, consonance, harmony.
n antonym discord.

concordant *adj* accordant, agreeable, agreeing, harmonious.

concordat *n* agreement, bargain, compact, convention, covenant, stipulation, treaty.

concourse *n* **1** confluence, conflux, congress. **2** assemblage, assembly, collection, crowd, gathering, meeting, multitude, throng.

concrete *vb* cake, congeal, coagulate, harden, solidify, thicken. •*adj* **1** compact, consolidated, firm, solid, solidified. **2** agglomerated, complex, conglomerated, compound, concreted. **3** completely, entire, individualized, total. •*n* **1** compound, concretion, mixture. **2** cement.
adj antonym abstract.

concur *vb* **1** accede, acquiesce, agree, approve, assent, coincide, consent, harmonize. **2** combine, conspire, cooperate, help.
vb antonym disagree.

concurrent *adj* **1** agreeing, coincident, harmonizing, meeting, uniting. **2** associate, associated, attendant, concomitant, conjoined, united.

concussion *n* **1** agitation, shaking. **2** clash, crash, shock.

condemn *vb* **1** adjudge, convict, doom, sentence. **2** disapprove, proscribe, reprobate. **3** blame, censure, damn, deprecate, disapprove, reprehend, reprove, upbraid.
vb antonyms approve, praise.

condemnation *n* **1** conviction, doom, judgement, penalty, sentence. **2** banning, disapproval, proscription. **3** guilt, sin, wrong. **4** blame, censure, disapprobation, disapproval, reprobation, reproof.

condemnatory *adj* blaming, censuring, damnatory, deprecatory, disapproving, reproachful.

condense *vb* **1** compress, concentrate, consolidate, densify, thicken. **2** abbreviate, abridge, contract, curtail, diminish, epitomize, reduce, shorten, summarize. **3** liquefy.

vb antonyms dilute, expand.

condescend *vb* **1** deign, vouchsafe. **2** descend, stoop, submit.

condescension *n* affability, civility, courtesy, deference, favour, graciousness, obeisance.

condign *adj* adequate, deserved, just, merited, suitable.

condiment *n* appetizer, relish, sauce, seasoning.

condition *vb* **1** postulate, specify, stipulate. **2** groom, prepare, qualify, ready, train. **3** acclimatize, accustom, adapt, adjust, familiarize, habituate, naturalize. **4** attune, commission, fix, overhaul, prepare, recondition, repair, service, tune. •*n* **1** case, circumstances, plight, predicament, situation, state. **2** class, estate, grade, rank, station. **3** arrangement, consideration, provision, proviso, stipulation. **4** attendant, necessity, postulate, precondition, prerequisite.

condole *vb* commiserate, compassionate, console, sympathize.

condonation *n* forgiveness, overlooking, pardon.

condone *vb* excuse, forgive, pardon.

conduce *vb* **1** contribute, lead, tend. **2** advance, aid.

conducive *adj* conducting, contributing, instrumental, promotive, subservient, subsidiary.

conduct *vb* **1** convoy, direct, escort, lead. **2** administer, command, govern, lead, preside, superintend. **3** manage, operate, regulate. **4** direct, lead. •*n* **1** administration, direction, guidance, leadership, management. **2** convoy, escort, guard. **3** actions, bearing, behaviour, career, carriage, demeanour, deportment, manners.

conductor *n* **1** guide, lead. **2** director, leader, manager. **3** propagator, transmitter.

conduit *n* canal, channel, duct, passage, pipe, tube.

confederacy *n* alliance, coalition, compact, confederation, covenant, federation, league, union.

confer *vb* **1** advise, consult, converse, deliberate, discourse, parley, talk. **2** bestow, give, grant, vouchsafe.

confess *vb* **1** acknowledge, admit, avow, own. **2** admit, concede, grant, recognize. **3** attest, exhibit, manifest, prove, show. **4** shrive.

vb antonyms conceal, deny.

confession *n* acknowledgement, admission, avowal.

n antonyms concealment, denial.

confide *vb* commit, consign, entrust, trust.

confidence *n* **1** belief, certitude, dependence, faith, reliance, trust. **2** aplomb, assurance, boldness, cocksureness, courage, firmness, intrepidity, self-reliance. **3** secrecy.

n antonyms diffidence, distrust.

confident *adj* **1** assured, certain, cocksure, positive, sure. **2** bold, presumptuous. sanguine, undaunted.

adj antonyms diffident, sceptical.

confidential *adj* **1** intimate, private, secret. **2** faithful, trustworthy.

adj antonyms common, public.

configuration *n* conformation, contour, figure, form, gestalt, outline, shape.

confine *vb* **1** restrain, shut in, shut up. **2** immure, imprison, incarcerate, impound, jail, mew. **3** bound, circumscribe, limit, restrict. •*n* border, boundary, frontier, limit.

vb antonym free.

confinement *n* **1** restraint. **2** captivity, duress, durance, immurement, imprisonment, incarceration. **3** childbirth, delivery, lying-in, parturition.

confines *npl* borders, boundaries, edges, frontiers, limits, marches, precincts.

confirm *vb* **1** assure, establish, fix, settle. **2** strengthen. **3** authenticate, avouch, corroborate, countersign, endorse, substantiate, verify. **4** bind, ratify, sanction.

vb antonym deny.

confirmation *n* **1** establishment, settlement. **2** corroboration, proof, substantiation, verification.

n antonym denial.

confiscate *vb* appropriate, forfeit, seize.

conflict *vb* clash, combat, contend, contest, disagree, fight, interfere, strive, struggle. •*n* **1** battle, collision, combat, contention, contest, encounter, fight, struggle. **2** antagonism, clashing, disagreement, discord, disharmony, inconsistency, interference, opposition.

n antonyms agreement, concord.

vb antonym agree.

confluence *n* **1** conflux, junction, meeting, union. **2** army, assemblage, assembly, concourse, crowd, collection, horde, host, multitude, swarm.

confluent *adj* blending, concurring, flowing, joining, meeting, merging, uniting.

conform *vb* **1** accommodate, adapt, adjust. **2** agree, comport, correspond, harmonize, square, tally.

vb antonym differ.

conformation *n* **1** accordance, agreement, compliance, conformity. **2** configuration, figure, form, manner, shape, structure.

confound *vb* **1** confuse. **2** baffle, bewilder, embarrass, flurry, mystify, nonplus, perplex, pose. **3** amaze, astonish, astound, bewilder, dumfound, paralyse, petrify, startle, stun, stupefy, surprise. **4** annihilate, demolish, destroy, overthrow, overwhelm, ruin. **5** abash, confuse, discompose, disconcert, mortify, shame.

confront *vb* **1** face. **2** challenge, contrapose, encounter, oppose, threaten.

vb antonym evade.

confuse *vb* **1** blend, confound, intermingle, mingle, mix. **2** derange, disarrange, disorder, jumble, mess, muddle. **3** darken, obscure, perplex. **4** befuddle, bewilder, embarrass, flabbergast, flurry, fluster, mystify, nonplus, pose. **5** abash, confound, discompose, disconcert, mortify, shame.

vb antonyms clarify, enlighten, explain, reassure.

confusion *n* **1** anarchy, chaos, clutter, confusedness, derangement, disarrangement, disarray, disorder, jumble, muddle. **2** agitation, commotion, ferment, stir, tumult, turmoil. **3** astonishment, bewilderment, distraction, embarrassment, fluster, fuddle, perplexity. **4** abashment, discomfiture, mortification, shame. **5** annihilation, defeat, demolition, destruction, overthrow, ruin.

n antonyms clarity, composure, order.

confute *vb* disprove, oppugn, overthrow, refute, silence.

congeal *vb* benumb, condense, curdle, freeze, stiffen, thicken.

congenial *adj* **1** kindred, similar, sympathetic. **2** adapted, agreeable, natural, suitable, suited. **3** agreeable, favourable, genial.

congenital *adj* connate, connatural, inborn.

congratulate *vb* compliment, felicitate, gratulate, greet, hail, salute.

vb antonym commiserate.

congregate *vb* **1** assemble, collect, convene, convoke, gather, muster. **2** gather, meet, swarm, throng.

vb antonyms dismiss, disperse.

congregation *n* assemblage, assembly, collection, gathering, meeting.

congress *n* assembly, conclave, conference, convention, convocation, council, diet, meeting.

congruity *n* agreement, conformity, consistency, fitness, suitableness.

n antonym incongruity.

congruous *adj* **1** accordant, agreeing, compatible, consistent, consonant, suitable. **2** appropriate, befitting, fit, meet, proper, seemly.

conjecture *vb* **1** assume, guess, hypothesize, imagine, suppose. surmise, suspect. **2** dare say, fancy, presume. •*n* assumption, guess, hypothesis, supposition, surmise, theory.

conjoin *vb* associate, combine, connect, join, unite.

conjugal *adj* bridal, connubial, hymeneal, matrimonial, nuptial.

conjuncture *n* **1** combination, concurrence, connection. **2** crisis, emergency, exigency, juncture.

conjure *vb* **1** adjure, beg, beseech, crave, entreat, implore, invoke, pray, supplicate. **2** bewitch, charm, enchant, fascinate. **3** juggle.

connect *vb* **1** associate, conjoin, combine, couple, hyphenate, interlink, join, link, unite. **2** cohere, interlock.

vb antonym disconnect.

connected *adj* **1** associated, coupled, joined, united. **2** akin, allied, related. **3** communicating.

connection *n* **1** alliance, association, dependence, junction, union. **2** commerce, communication, intercourse. **3** affinity, relationship. **4** kindred, kinsman, relation, relative.

n antonym disconnection.

connive *vb* collude, conspire, plot, scheme.

connoisseur *n* critic, expert, virtuoso.

connotation *n* comprehension, depth, force, intent, intention, meaning.

connubial *adj* bridal, conjugal, hymeneal, matrimonial, nuptial.

conquer *vb* **1** beat, checkmate, crush, defeat, discomfit, humble, master, overcome, overpower, overthrow, prevail, quell, reduce, rout, subdue, subjugate, vanquish. **2** overcome, surmount.

vb antonyms surrender, yield.

conqueror *n* **1** humbler, subduer, subjugator, vanquisher. **2** superior, victor, winner.

conquest *n* **1** defeat, discomfiture, mastery, overthrow, reduction, subjection, subjugation. **2** triumph, victor. **3** winning.

consanguinity *n* affinity, kinship, blood-relationship, kin, kindred, relationship.

conscientious *adj* careful, exact, fair, faithful, high-principled, honest, honourable, incorruptible, just, scrupulous, straightforward, uncorrupt, upright.
adj antonyms careless, irresponsible.

conscious *adj* 1 intelligent, knowing, percipient, sentient. 2 intellectual, rational, reasoning, reflecting, self-conscious, thinking. 3 apprised, awake, aware, cognizant, percipient, sensible. 4 self-admitted, self-accusing.
adj antonym unconscious.

consecrate *vb* 1 dedicate, devote, ordain. 2 hallow, sanctify, venerate.

consecutive *adj* following, succeeding.
adj antonym discontinuous.

consent *vb* 1 agree, allow, assent, concur, permit, yield. 2 accede, acquiesce, comply. •*n* 1 approval, assent, concurrence, permission. 2 accord, agreement, consensus, concord, cooperation, harmony, unison. 3 acquiescence, compliance.
vb antonyms oppose, refuse.
n antonyms opposition, refusal.

consequence *n* 1 effect, end, event, issue, result. 2 conclusion, deduction, inference. 3 concatenation, connection, consecution. 4 concern, distinction, importance, influence, interest, moment, standing, weight.
n antonym cause.

consequential *adj* 1 consequent, following, resulting, sequential. 2 arrogant, conceited, inflated, pompous, pretentious, self-important, self-sufficient, vainglorious.
adj antonyms inconsequential, unimportant.

conservation *n* guardianship, maintenance, preservation, protection.

conservative *adj* 1 conservatory, moderate, moderationist. 2 preservative. 3 reactionary, unprogressive. •*n* 1 die-hard, reactionary, redneck, rightist, right-winger. 2 moderate. 3 preservative.
adj antonyms left-wing, radical.
n antonyms left-winger, radical.

conserve *vb* keep, maintain, preserve, protect, save, sustain, uphold. •*n* confit, confection, jam, preserve, sweetmeat.
vb antonyms squander, use, waste.

consider *vb* 1 attend, brood, contemplate, examine, heed, mark, mind, ponder, reflect, revolve, study, weigh. 2 care for,

consult, envisage, regard, respect. 3 cogitate, deliberate, mediate, muse, ponder, reflect, ruminate, think. 4 account, believe, deem, hold, judge, opine.
vb antonym ignore.

considerate *adj* 1 circumspect, deliberate, discrete, judicious, provident, prudent, serious, sober, staid, thoughtful. 2 charitable, forbearing, patient.
adj antonyms selfish, thoughtless.

consideration *n* 1 attention, cogitation, contemplation, deliberation, notice, heed, meditation, pondering, reflection, regard. 2 consequence, importance, important, moment, significant, weight. 3 account, cause, ground, motive, reason, sake, score.
n antonyms disdain, disregard.

consign *vb* 1 deliver, hand over, remand, resign, transfer, transmit. 2 commit, entrust. 3 ship.

consignor *n* sender, shipper, transmitter.

consistency *n* 1 compactness, consistence, density, thickness. 2 agreement, compatibility, congruity, consonance, correspondence, harmony.

consistent *adj* accordant, agreeing, comfortable, compatible, congruous, consonant, correspondent, harmonious, logical.
adj antonyms erratic, inconsistent.

consolation *n* alleviation, comfort, condolence, encouragement, relief, solace.
n antonym discouragement.

console *vb* assuage, calm, cheer, comfort, encourage, solace, relieve, soothe.
vb antonyms agitate, upset.

consolidate *vb* 1 cement, compact, compress, condense, conduce, harden, solidify, thicken. 2 combine, conjoin, fuse, unite.

consolidation *n* 1 solidification. 2 combination, union.

consonance *n* 1 accord, concord, conformity, harmony. 2 accord, accordance, agreement, congruence, congruity, consistency, unison.

consonant *adj* 1 accordant, according, harmonious. 2 compatible, congruous, consistent. •*n* articulation, letter-sound.

consort *vb* associate, fraternize. •*n* associate, companion, fellow, husband, spouse, partner.

conspectus *n* abstract, brief, breviary, compend, compendium, digest, epitome, outline, precis, summary, syllabus, synopsis.

conspicuous *adj* 1 apparent, clear, discernible,

glaring, manifest, noticeable, perceptible, plain, striking, visible. **2** celebrated, distinguished, eminent, famed, famous, illustrious, marked, noted, outstanding. pre-eminent, prominent, remarkable, signal.
adj antonym inconspicuous.

conspiracy *n* cabal, collusion, confederation, intrigue, league, machination, plot, scheme.

conspire *vb* **1** concur, conduce, cooperate. **2** combine, compass, contrive, devise, project. **3** confederate, contrive, hatch, plot, scheme.

constancy *n* **1** immutability, permanence, stability, unchangeableness. **2** regularity, unchangeableness. **3** decision, determination, firmness, inflexibility, resolution, steadfastness, steadiness. **4** devotion, faithfulness, fidelity, loyalty, trustiness, truth.
n antonyms inconstancy, irregularity.

constant *adj* **1** abiding, enduring, fixed, immutable, invariable, invariant, permanent, perpetual, stable, unalterable, unchanging, unvaried. **2** certain, regular, stated, uniform. **3** determined, firm, resolute, stanch, steadfast, steady, unanswering, undeviating, unmoved, unshaken, unwavering. **4** assiduous, diligent, persevering, sedulous, tenacious, unremitting. **5** continual, continuous, incessant, perpetual, sustained, unbroken, uninterrupted. **6** devoted, faithful, loyal, true, trusty.
adj antonyms fickle, fitful, irregular, occasional, variable.

consternation *n* alarm, amazement, awe, bewilderment, dread, fear, fright, horror, panic, terror.
n antonym composure.

constituent *adj* **1** component, composing, constituting, forming. **2** appointing, electoral. •*n* **1** component, element, ingredient, principal. **2** elector, voter.

constitute *vb* **1** compose, form, make. **2** appoint, delegate, depute, empower. **3** enact, establish, fix, set up.

constitution *n* **1** establishment, formation, make-up, organization, structure. **2** character, characteristic, disposition, form, habit, humour, peculiarity, physique, quality, spirit, temper, temperament.

constitutional *adj* **1** congenital, connate, inborn, inbred, inherent, innate, natural, organic. **2** lawful, legal, legitimate. •*n* airing, exercise, promenade, stretch, walk.

constrain *vb* **1** coerce, compel, drive, force. **2** chain, confine, curb, enthral, hold, restrain. **3** draw, impel, urge.

constriction *n* compression, constraint, contraction.

construct *vb* **1** build, fabricate, erect, raise, set up. **2** arrange, establish, form, found, frame, institute, invent, make, organize, originate.
vb antonyms demolish, destroy.

construction *n* **1** building, erection, fabrication. **2** configuration, conformation, figure, form, formation, made, shape, structure. **3** explanation, interpretation, rendering, version.
n antonym destruction.

construe *vb* analyse, explain, expound, interpret, parse, render, translate.

consult *vb* **1** advise, ask, confer, counsel, deliberate, interrogate, question. **2** consider, regard.

consume *vb* absorb, decay, destroy, devour, dissipate, exhaust, expend, lavish, lessen, spend, squander, vanish, waste.

consummate[1] *vb* accomplish, achieve, compass, complete, conclude, crown, effect, effectuate, end, execute, finish, perfect, perform.
vb antonym imperfect.

consummate[2] *adj* complete, done, effected, finished, fulfilled, perfect, supreme.

consumption *n* **1** decay, decline, decrease, destruction, diminution, expenditure, use, waste. **2** atrophy, emaciation.

contact *vb* **1** hit, impinge, touch. **2** approach, be heard, communicate with, reach. •*n* approximation, contiguity, junction, juxtaposition, taction, tangency, touch.

contagion *n* **1** infection. **2** contamination, corruption, infection, taint.

contagious *adj* **1** catching, epidemic, infectious. **2** deadly, pestiferous, pestilential, poisonous.

contain *vb* **1** accommodate, comprehend, comprise, embody, embrace, enclose, include. **2** check, restrain.
vb antonym exclude.

contaminate *vb* corrupt, defile, deprave, infect, poison, pollute, soil, stain, sully, taint, tarnish, vitiate.
vb antonym purify.

contamination *n* **1** contaminating, defilement, defiling, polluting, pollution. **2** abomination, defilement, impurity, foulness, infection, pollution, stain, taint, uncleanness.

contemn *vb* despise, disdain, disregard, neglect, scorn, scout, slight, spurn.

contemplate *vb* **1** behold, gaze upon, observe, survey. **2** consider, dwell on, meditate on, muse on, ponder, reflect upon, study, survey, think about. **3** design, intend, mean, plan, purpose.

contemplation *n* **1** cogitation, deliberation, meditation, pondering, reflection, speculation, study, thought. **2** prospect, prospective, view. **3** expectation.

contemporaneous *adj* coetaneous, coeval, coexistent, coexisting, coincident, concomitant, contemporary, simultaneous, synchronous.

contemporary *adj* **1** coetaneous, coeval, coexistent, coexisting, coincident, concomitant, concurrent, contemporaneous, current, present, simultaneous, synchronous. **2** advanced, modern, modernistic, progressive, up-to-date. •*n* coeval, coexistent, compeer, fellow.

adj antonyms preceding, succeeding.

contempt *n* contumely, derision, despite, disdain, disregard, misprision, mockery, scorn, slight.

n antonyms admiration, regard.

contemptible *adj* abject, base, despicable, haughty, insolent, insulting, low, mean, paltry, pitiful, scurvy, sorry, supercilious, vile, worthless.

adj antonyms admirable, honorable.

contemptuous *adj* arrogant, contumelious, disdainful, haughty, insolent, insulting, scornful, sneering, supercilious.

adj antonyms humble, polite, respectful.

contend *vb* **1** battle, combat, compete, contest, fight, strive, struggle, vie. **2** argue, debate, dispute, litigate. **3** affirm, assert, contest, maintain.

content[1] *n* **1** essence, gist, meaning, meat, stuff, substance. **2** capacity, measure, space, volume.

content[2] *vb* appease, delight, gladden, gratify, humour, indulge, please, satisfy, suffice. •*adj* agreeable, contented, happy, pleased, satisfied. •*n* contentment, ease, peace, satisfaction.

vb antonym displease.

n antonym discontent.

adj antonym dissatisfied.

contention *n* **1** discord, dissension, feud, squabble, strife, quarrel, rapture, wrangle, wrangling. **2** altercation, bickering, contest, controversy, debate, dispute, litigation, logomachy.

contentious *adj* **1** belligerent, cross, litigious, peevish, perverse, petulant, pugnacious, quarrelsome, wrangling. **2** captious, caviling, disputatious.

conterminous *adj* **1** adjacent, adjoining, contiguous. **2** co-extensive, coincident, commensurate.

contest *vb* **1** argue, contend, controvert, debate, dispute, litigate, question. **2** strive, struggle. **3** compete, cope, fight, vie. •*n* **1** altercation, contention, controversy, difference, dispute, debate, quarrel. **2** affray, battle, bout, combat, conflict, encounter, fight, match, scrimmage, struggle, tussle. **3** competition, contention, rivalry.

context *n* **1** circumstances, conditions, times, situation. **2** background, frame of reference, framework.

contexture *n* composition, constitution, framework, structure, texture.

contiguous *adj* abutting, adjacent, adjoining, beside, bordering, conterminous, meeting, near, neighbouring, touching.

continent[1] *n* mainland, mass, tract.

continent[2] *adj* abstemious, abstinent, chaste, restrained, self-commanding, self-controlled, moderate, sober, temperate.

contingency *n* **1** chance, fortuity, uncertainty. **2** accident, casualty, event, incident, occurrence.

contingent *adj* **1** accidental, adventitious, casual, fortuitous, incidental. **2** conditional, dependent, uncertain. •*n* proportion, quota, share.

continual *adj* **1** constant, constant, perpetual, unceasing, uninterrupted, unremitting. **2** endless, eternal, everlasting, interminable, perennial, permanent, perpetual, unending. **3** constant, oft-repeated.

adj antonyms intermittent, occasional, temporary.

continuance *n* **1** abiding, continuation, duration, endurance, lasting, persistence, stay. **2** continuation, extension, perpetuation, prolongation, protraction. **3** concatenation, connection, sequence, succession. **4** constancy, endurance, perseverance, persistence.

continue *vb* **1** endure, last, remain. **2** abide, linger, remain, stay, tarry. **3** endure, persevere, persist, stick. **4** extend, prolong, perpetuate, protract.

vb antonyms discontinue, stop.

continuous *adj* connected, continued, extended, prolonged, unbroken, uninterrupted.

adj antonyms discontinuous, intermittent, sporadic.

contour *n* outline, profile.

contraband *adj* banned, forbidden, illegal, illicit, interdicted, prohibited, smuggled, unlawful.

contract *vb* **1** abbreviate, abridge, condense, confine, curtail, diminish, epitomize, lessen, narrow, reduce, shorten. **2** absorb, catch, incur, get, make, take. **3** constrict, shrink, shrivel, wrinkle. **4** agree, bargain, covenant, engage, pledge, stipulate. •*n* agreement, arrangement, bargain, bond, compact, concordat, covenant, convention, engagement, pact, stipulation, treaty.

vb antonyms enlarge, expand, lengthen.

contradict *vb* **1** assail, challenge, controvert, deny, dispute, gainsay, impugn, traverse. **2** abrogate, annul, belie, counter, disallow, negative, contravene, counteract, oppose, thwart.

vb antonyms agree, confirm, corroborate.

contradiction *n* **1** denial, negation, rejection. **2** antinomy, clashing, incongruity, opposition.

contradictory *adj* antagonistic, contrary, incompatible, inconsistent, negating, opposed, opposite, repugnant.

adj antonym consistent.

contrariety *n* antagonism, clashing, contradiction, contrast, opposition, repugnance.

contrary *adj* **1** adverse, counter, discordant, opposed, opposing, opposite. **2** antagonistic, conflicting, contradictory, repugnant, retroactive. **3** forward, headstrong, obstinate, refractory, stubborn, unruly, wayward, perverse. •*n* antithesis, converse, obverse, opposite, reverse.

adj antonyms like, obliging, similar.

contrast *vb* compare, differentiate, distinguish, oppose. •*n* **1** contrariety, difference, opposition. **2** comparison, distinction.

n antonym similarity.

contravene *vb* abrogate, annul, contradict, counteract, countervail, cross, go against, hinder, interfere, nullify, oppose, set aside, thwart.

contravention *n* abrogation, contradiction,

interference, opposition, transgression, traversal, violation.

contretemps *n* accident, mischance, mishap.

contribute *vb* **1** bestow, donate, give, grant, subscribe. **2** afford, aid, furnish, supply. **3** concur, conduce, conspire, cooperate, minister, serve, tend.

vb antonyms subtract, withhold.

contribution *n* **1** bestowal, bestowment, grant. **2** donation, gift, offering, subscription.

contrite *adj* humble, penitent, repentant, sorrowful.

contrition *n* compunction, humiliation, penitence, regret, remorse, repentance, self-condemnation, self-reproach, sorrow.

contrivance *n* **1** design, inventive, inventiveness. **2** contraption, device, gadget, invention, machine. **3** artifice, device, fabrication, machination, plan, plot, scheme, shift, stratagem.

contrive *vb* **1** arrange, brew, concoct, design, devise, effect, form, frame, hatch, invent, plan, project. **2** consider, plan, plot, scheme. **3** manage, make out.

control *vb* **1** command, direct, dominate, govern, manage, oversee, sway, regulate, rule, superintend. **2** bridle, check, counteract, curb, check, hinder, repress, restrain. •*n* ascendency, command, direction, disposition, dominion, government, guidance, mastery, oversight, regiment, regulation, rule, superintendence, supremacy, sway.

controversy *n* **1** altercation, argument, contention, debate, discussion, disputation, dispute, logomachy, polemics, quarrel, strife. **2** lawsuit.

n antonyms accord, agreement.

contumacious *adj* disobedient, cross-grained, disrespectful, haughty, headstrong, intractable, obdurate, obstinate, pertinacious, perverse, rebellious, refractory, stiff-necked, stubborn.

contumacy *n* **1** doggedness, haughtiness, headiness, obduracy, obstinacy, pertinacity, perverseness, stubbornness. **2** contempt, disobedience, disrespect, insolence, insubordination, rebelliousness.

contumelious *adj* abusive, arrogant, calumnious, contemptuous, disdainful, insolent, insulting, opprobrious, overbearing, rude, scornful, supercilious.

contumely *n* abuse, affront, arrogance,

contempt, contemptuousness, disdain, indignity, insolence, insult, obloquy, opprobrium, reproach, rudeness, scorn, superciliousness.

contuse *vb* bruise, crush, injure, knock, squeeze, wound.

contusion *n* bruise, crush, injury, knock, squeeze, wound.

convalescence *n* recovery, recuperation.

convene *vb* 1 assemble, congregate, gather, meet, muster. 2 assemble, call, collect, convoke, muster, summon.

convenience *n* 1 fitness, propriety, suitableness. 2 accessibility, accommodation, comfort, commodiousness, ease, handiness, satisfaction, serviceability, serviceableness.

convenient *adj* 1 adapted, appropriate, fit, fitted, proper, suitable, suited. 2 advantageous, beneficial, comfortable, commodious, favourable, handy, helpful, serviceable, timely, useful.

adj antonyms awkward, inconvenient.

convent *n* abbey, cloister, monastery, priory.

convention *n* 1 assembly, congress, convocation, meeting. 2 agreement, bargain, compact, contract, pact, stipulation, treaty. 3 custom, formality, usage.

conventional *adj* 1 agreed on, bargained for, stipulated. 2 accustomed, approved, common, customary, everyday, habitual, ordinary, orthodox, regular, standard, traditional, usual, wonted.

adj antonyms exotic, unconventional, unusual.

conversable *adj* affable, communicative, free, open, sociable, social, unreversed.

conversation *n* chat, colloquy, communion, confabulation, conference, converse, dialogue, discourse, intercourse, interlocution, parley, talk.

converse[1] *vb* 1 commune. 2 chat, confabulate, discourse, gossip, parley, talk. •*n* 1 commerce, communication, intercourse. 2 colloquy, conversation, talk.

converse[2] *adj* 1 adverse, contradictory, contrary, counter, opposed, opposing, opposite. 2 *n* antithesis, contrary, opposite, reverse.

conversion *n* 1 change, reduction, resolution, transformation, transmutation. 2 interchange, reversal, transposition.

convert *vb* 1 alter, change, transform, transmute. 2 interchange, reverse, transpose.

3 apply, appropriate, convince. •*n* disciple, neophyte, proselyte.

convey *vb* 1 bear, bring, carry, fetch, transmit, transport, waft. 2 abalienate, alienate, cede, consign, deliver, demise, devise, devolve, grant, sell, transfer.

conveyance *n* 1 alienation, cession, transfer, transference, transmission. 2 carriage, carrying, conveying, transfer, transmission.

convict *vb* condemn, confute, convince, imprison, sentence. •*n* criminal, culprit, felon, malefactor, prisoner.

convivial *adj* festal, festive, gay, jolly, jovial, merry, mirthful, social.

adj antonym taciturn.

convocation *n* 1 assembling, convening, convoking, gathering, summoning. 2 assembly, congress, convention, council, diet, meeting, synod.

convoke *vb* assemble, convene, muster, summon.

convoy *vb* accompany, attend, escort, guard, protect. •*n* attendance, attendant, escort, guard, protection.

convulse *vb* agitate, derange, disorder, disturb, shake, shatter.

convulsion *n* 1 cramp, fit, spasm. 2 agitation, commotion, disturbance, shaking, tumult.

cook *vb* 1 bake, boil, broil, fry, grill, microwave, roast, spit-roast, steam, stir-fry. 2 falsify, garble.

cool *vb* 1 chill, ice, refrigerate. 2 abate, allay, calm, damp, moderate, quiet, temper. •*adj* 1 calm, collected, composed, dispassionate, placid, sedate, self-possessed, quiet, staid, unexcited, unimpassioned, undisturbed, unruffled. 2 cold-blooded, indifferent, lukewarm, unconcerned. 3 apathetic, chilling, freezing, frigid, repellent. 4 bold, impertinent, impudent, self-possessed, shameless. •*n* 1 chill, chilliness, coolness. 2 calmness, composure, coolheadedness, countenance, equanimity, poise, self-possession, self-restraint.

adj antonyms excited, friendly, hot, warm.

vb antonyms excite, heat, warm.

coop *vb* cage, confine, encage, immure, imprison. •*n* barrel, box, cage, pen.

cooperate *vb* abet, aid, assist, co-act, collaborate, combine, concur, conduce, conspire, contribute, help, unite.

cooperation *n* aid, assistance, co-action, concert, concurrence, collaboration, synergy.

coordinate *vb* accord, agree, arrange, equalize, harmonize, integrate, methodize, organize, regulate, synchronize, systematize. •*adj* **1** coequal, equal, equivalent, tantamount. **2** coincident, synchronous. •*n* **1** complement, counterpart, like, pendant. **2** companion, fellow, match, mate.

copartnership *n* **1** association, fraternity, partnership. **2** company, concern, establishment, firm, house.

cope *vb* combat, compete, contend, encounter, engage, strive, struggle, vie.

copious *adj* abundant, ample, exuberant, full, overflowing, plenteous, plentiful, profuse, rich.

adj antonyms meagre, scarce.

copiousness *n* abundance, exuberance, fullness, plenty, profusion, richness.

copse *n* coppice, grove, thicket.

copulation *n* coition, congress, coupling.

copy *vb* **1** duplicate, reproduce, trace, transcribe. **2** follow, imitate, pattern. •*n* counterscript, duplicate, facsimile, off-1 print, replica, reproduction, transcript. **2** archetype, model, original, pattern. **3** manuscript, typescript.

n antonym original.

cord *n* braid, gimp, line, string.

cordate *adj* cordiform, heart-shaped.

cordial *adj* **1** affectionate, ardent, earnest, heartfelt, hearty, sincere, warm, warmhearted. **2** grateful, invigorating, restorative, pleasant, refreshing. •*n* **1** balm, balsam, elixir, tisane, tonic. **2** liqueur.

adj antonyms aloof, cool, hostile.

core *n* centre, essence, heart, kernel.

n antonyms exterior, perimeter, surface.

corner *vb* confound, confuse, nonplus, perplex, pose, puzzle. •*n* **1** angle, bend, crutch, cusp, elbow, joint, knee. **2** niche, nook, recess, retreat.

corollary *n* conclusion, consequence, deduction, induction, inference.

coronal *n* bays, chaplet, crown, garland, laurel, wreath.

corporal *adj* **1** bodily. **2** corporeal, material, physical.

corporeal *adj* **1** bodily, fleshly, substantial. **2** corporal, material, nonspiritual, physical.

corps *n* band, body, company, contingent, division, platoon, regiment, squad, squadron, troop.

corpse *n* **1** body, carcass, remains. **2** ashes, dust.

corpulent *adj* big, burly, fat, fleshy, large, lusty, obese, plump, portly, pursy, rotund, stout.

adj antonym thin.

corpuscle *n* atom, bit, grain, iota, jot, mite, molecule, monad, particle, scintilla, scrap, whit.

correct *vb* **1** adjust, amend, cure, improve, mend, reclaim, rectify, redress, reform, regulate, remedy. **2** chasten, discipline, punish. •*adj* accurate, equitable, exact, faultless, just, precise, proper, regular, right, true, upright.

adj antonyms inaccurate, incorrect, wrong.

correction *n* **1** amendment, improvement, redress. **2** chastening, discipline, punishment.

corrective *adj* alternative, counteractive, emendatory, improving, modifying, rectifying, reformative, reformatory.

correctness *n* accuracy, exactness, faultlessness, nicety, precision, propriety, rectitude, regularity, rightness, truth.

correlate *n* complement, correlative, counterpart.

correspond *vb* **1** accord, agree, answer, comport, conform, fit, harmonize, match, square, suit, tally. **2** answer, belong, correlate. **3** communicate.

correspondence *n* **1** accord, agreement, coincidence, concurrence, conformity, congruity, fitness, harmony, match. **2** correlation, counterposition. **3** communication, letters, writing.

corroborate *vb* confirm, establish, ratify, substantiate, support, sustain, strengthen.

corrode *vb* **1** canker, erode, gnaw. **2** consume, deteriorate, rust, waste. **3** blight, embitter, envenom, poison.

corrosive *adj* **1** acrid, biting, consuming, cathartic, caustic, corroding, eroding, erosive, violent. **2** consuming, corroding, gnawing, mordant, wasting, wearing. **3** blighting, cankerous, carking, embittering, envenoming, poisoning.

corrugate *vb* cockle, crease, furrow, groove, pucker, rumple, wrinkle.

corrupt *vb* **1** putrefy, putrid, render. **2** contaminate, defile, infect, pollute, spoil, taint, vitiate. **3** degrade, demoralize, deprave, pervert. **4** adulterate, debase, falsify, sophisticate. **5** bribe, entice. •*adj* **1** contaminated, corrupted, impure, infected, putrid, rotten, spoiled, tainted,

unsound. **2** abandoned, debauched, depraved, dissolute, profligate, reprobate, vicious, wicked. **3** bribable, buyable.
adj antonyms honest, trustworthy, upright.
vb antonym purify.
corruption *n* **1** putrefaction, putrescence, rottenness. **2** adulteration, contamination, debasement, defilement, infection, perversion, pollution, vitiation. **3** demoralization, depravation, depravity, immorality, laxity, sinfulness, wickedness. **4** bribery, dishonesty.
n antonyms honesty, purification.
corsair *n* buccaneer, picaroon, pirate, rover, sea-robber, sea-rover.
corset *n* bodice, girdle, stays.
cosmonaut *n* astronaut, spaceman.
cosmos *n* **1** creation, macrocosm, universe, world. **2** harmony, order, structure.
cost *vb* absorb, consume, require. •*n* **1** amount, charge, expenditure, expense, outlay, price. **2** costliness, preciousness, richness, splendour, sumptuousness. **3** damage, detriment, loss, pain, sacrifice, suffering.
costly *adj* **1** dear, expensive, high-priced. **2** gorgeous, luxurious, precious, rich, splendid, sumptuous, valuable.
adj antonyms cheap, inexpensive.
costume *n* apparel, attire, dress, robes, uniform.
cosy, cozy *adj* **1** comfortable, easy, snug. **2** chatty, conversable, social, talkative.
coterie *n* association, brotherhood, circle, club, set, society, sodality.
cottage *n* cabin, chalet, cot, hut, lodge, shack, shanty.
couch *vb* **1** lie, recline. **2** crouch, squat. **3** bend down, stoop. **4** conceal, cover up, hide. **5** lay, level. •*n* bed, davenport, divan, lounge, seat, settee, settle, sofa.
council *n* **1** advisers, cabinet, ministry. **2** assembly, congress, conclave, convention, convocation, diet, husting, meeting, parliament, synod.
counsel *vb* admonish, advise, caution, recommend, warn. •*n* **1** admonition, advice, caution, instruction, opinion, recommendation, suggestion. **2** deliberation, forethought. **3** advocate, barrister, counsellor, lawyer.
count *vb* **1** enumerate, number, score. **2** calculate, cast, compute, estimate, reckon. **3** account, consider, deem, esteem, hold,

judge, regard, think. **4** tell. •*n* reckoning, tally.
countenance *vb* abet, aid, approve, assist, befriend, encourage, favour, patronize, sanction, support. •*n* **1** aspect, look, men. **2** aid, approbation, approval, assistance, encouragement, favour, patronage, sanction, support.
counter[1] *n* **1** abacus, calculator, computer, meter, reckoner, tabulator. **2** bar, buffet, shopboard, table. **3** (*naut*) end, poop, stern, tail. **4** chip, token.
counter[2] *vb* contradict, contravene, counteract, oppose, retaliate. •*adj* adverse, against, contrary, opposed, opposite. •*adv* contrariwise, contrary. •*n* **1** antithesis, contrary, converse, opposite, reverse. **2** counterblast, counterblow, retaliation.
counteract *vb* **1** check, contrapose, contravene, cross, counter, counterpose, defeat, foil, frustrate, hinder, oppose, resist, thwart, traverse. **2** annul, countervail, counterbalance, destroy, neutralize, offset.
vb antonyms assist, support.
counteractive *adj* antidote, corrective, counteragent, medicine, remedy, restorative.
counterbalance *vb* **1** balance, counterpoise. **2** compensate, countervail.
counterfeit *vb* **1** forge, imitate. **2** fake, feign, pretend, sham, simulate. **3** copy, imitate. •*adj* **1** fake, forged, fraudulent, spurious. **2** false, feigned, hypocritical, mock, sham, simulated, spurious. **3** copied, imitated, resembling. •*n* copy, fake, forgery, sham.
vb antonym genuine.
countermand *vb* abrogate, annul, cancel, recall, repeal, rescind, revoke.
counterpane *n* coverlet, duvet, quilt.
counterpart *n* **1** copy, duplicate. **2** complement, correlate, correlative, reverse, supplement. **3** fellow, mate, match, tally, twin.
counterpoise *vb* balance, counteract, countervail, counterbalance, equilibrate, offset. •*n* balance, counterweight.
countersign *n* password, watchword.
countervail *vb* balance, compensate, counterbalance.
country *n* **1** land, region. **2** countryside. **3** fatherland, home, kingdom, state, territory. **4** nation, people, population. •*adj* **1** rural, rustic. **2** countrified, rough, rude, uncultivated, unpolished, unrefined.
adj antonyms urban.
countryman *n* **1** compatriot, fellow-citizen.

2 boor, clown, farmer, hind, husbandman, peasant, rustic, swain.

couple *vb* **1** pair, unite. **2** copulate, embrace. **3** buckle, clasp, conjoin, connect, join, link, pair, yoke. •*n* **1** brace, pair, twain, two. **2** bond, coupling, lea, link, tie.

courage *n* audaciousness, audacity, boldness, bravery, daring, derring-do, dauntlessness, fearlessness, firmness, fortitude, gallantry, hardihood, heroism, intrepidity, manhood, mettle, nerve, pluck, prowess, resolution, spirit, spunk, valorousness, valour.

n antonym cowardice.

courageous *adj* audacious, brave, bold, chivalrous, daring, dauntless, fearless, gallant, hardy, heroic, intrepid, lion-hearted, mettlesome, plucky, resolute, reliant, staunch, stout, undismayed, valiant, valorous.

adj antonym cowardly.

course *vb* chase, follow, hunt, pursue, race, run. •*n* **1** career, circuit, race, run. **2** road, route, track, way. **3** bearing, direction, path, tremor, track. **4** ambit, beat, orbit, round. **5** process, progress, sequence. **6** order, regularity, succession, turn. **7** behaviour, conduct, deportment. **8** arrangement, series, system.

court *vb* **1** fawn, flatter, flirt, ingratiate. **2** address, woo. **3** seek. **4** invite, solicit. •*n* **1** area, courtyard, patio, quadrangle. **2** addresses, civilities, homage, respects, solicitations. **3** retinue, palace, tribunal.

courteous *adj* affable, attentive, ceremonious, civil, complaisant, courtly, debonair, elegant, gracious, obliging, polished, polite, refined, respected, urbane, well-bred, well-mannered.

adj antonyms discourteous, rude.

courtesy *n* affability, civility, complaisance, courteousness, elegance, good-breeding, graciousness, polish, politeness, refine, urbanity.

n antonyms discourtesy, rudeness.

courtly *adj* affable, ceremonious, civil, elegant, flattering, lordly, obliging, polished, polite, refined, urbane.

courtyard *n* area, court, patio, quadrangle, yard.

cove¹ *n* anchorage, bay, bight, creek, firth, fjord, inlet.

cove² *n* bloke, chap, character, customer, fellow, type.

covenant *vb* agree, bargain, contract, stipu-

late. •*n* **1** bond, deed. **2** arrangement, bargain, compact, concordat, contract, convention, pact, stipulation, treaty.

cover *vb* **1** overlay, overspread. **2** cloak, conceal, curtain, disguise, hide, mask, screen, secrete, shroud, veil. **3** defend, guard, protect, shelter, shield. **4** case, clothe, envelop, invest, jacket, sheathe. **5** comprehend, comprise, contain, embody, embrace, include. •*n* **1** capsule, case, covering, integument, tegument, top. **2** cloak, disguise, screen, veil. **3** guard, defence, protection, safeguard, shelter, shield. **4** shrubbery, thicket, underbrush, undergrowth, underwood, woods.

covert *adj* clandestine, concealed, disguised, hidden, insidious, private, secret, sly, stealthy, underhand. •*n* **1** coppice, shade, shrubbery, thicket, underwood. **2** asylum. **3** defence, harbour, hiding-place, refuge, retreat, sanctuary, shelter.

adj antonym open.

covet *vb* **1** aim after, desire, long for, yearn for. **2** hanker after, lust after.

covetous *adj* acquisitive, avaricious, closefisted, grasping, greedy, miserly, niggardly, parsimonious, penurious, rapacious.

cow¹ *n* bovine, heifer.

cow² *vb* abash, break, daunt, discourage, dishearten, frighten, intimidate, overawe, subdue.

coward *adj* cowardly, timid. •*n* caitiff, craven, dastard, milksop, poltroon, recreant, skulker, sneak, wheyface.

adj antonym hero.

cowardly *adj* base, chicken-hearted, coward, craven, dastardly, faint-hearted, fearful, lily-livered, mean, pusillanimous, timid, timorous, white-livered, yellow.

adj antonym courageous.

cower *vb* bend, cringe, crouch, fawn, shrink, squat, stoop.

coxcomb *n* beau, dandy, dude, exquisite, fop, jackanapes, popinjay, prig.

coy *adj* backward, bashful, demure, diffident, distant, modest, reserved, retiring, self-effacing, shrinking, shy, timid.

adj antonyms forward, impudent, sober.

coyness *n* affectation, archness, backwardness, bashfulness, coquettishness, demureness, diffidence, evasiveness, modesty, primness, reserve, shrinking, shyness, timidity.

cozy *see* **cosy.**

crabbed *adj* **1** acrid, rough, sore, tart.
2 acrimonious, cantankerous, captious,
caustic, censorious, churlish, cross, growl-
ing, harsh, ill-tempered, morose, peevish,
petulant, snappish, snarling, splenetic,
surly, testy, touchy, waspish. **3** difficult,
intractable, perplexing, tough, trying, unmanageable.

crabbedness *n* **1** acridity, acridness, roughness, sourness, tartness. **2** acerbity, acrimonious, asperity, churlishness, harshness, ill-tempered, moodiness, moroseness, sullenness. **3** difficulty, intractability,
perplexity.

crack *vb* **1** break. **2** chop, cleave, split. **3** snap.
4 craze, madden. **5** boast, brag, bluster,
crow, gasconade, vapour, vaunt. •*adj* capital, excellent, first-class, first-rate, tip-top.
•*n* **1** breach, break, chink, cleft, cranny,
crevice, fissure, fracture, opening, rent,
rift, split. **2** burst, clap, explosion, pop, report. **3** snap.

cracked *adj* **1** broken, crackled, split.
2 crack-brained, crazed, crazy, demented,
deranged, flighty, insane.

crackle *vb* crepitate, decrepitate, snap.

craft *n* **1** ability, aptitude, cleverness, dexterity, expertness, power, readiness, skill,
tact, talent. **2** artifice, artfulness, cunning,
craftiness, deceitfulness, deception, guile,
shrewdness, subtlety. **3** art, avocation,
business, calling, employment, handicraft,
trade, vocation. **4** vessel.
n antonyms naïvety, openness.

crafty *adj* arch, artful, astute, cunning,
crooked, deceitful, designing, fraudulent,
guileful, insidious, intriguing, scheming,
shrewd, sly, subtle, tricky, wily.
adj antonyms naïve, open.

crag *n* **1** rock. **2** neck, throat.

craggy *adj* broken, cragged, jagged, rough,
rugged, scraggy, uneven.
adj antonyms pleasant, smooth.

cram *vb* **1** fill, glut, gorge, satiate, stuff.
2 compress, crowd, overcrowd, press,
squeeze. **3** coach, grind.

cramp *vb* **1** convulse. **2** check, clog, confine, hamper, hinder, impede, obstruct,
restrain, restrict. •*n* **1** convulsion, crick,
spasm. **2** check, restraint, restriction, obstruction.

crank *vb* bend, crankle, crinkle, turn, twist,
wind. •*n* bend, quirk, turn, twist, winding.

cranny *n* breach, break, chink, cleft, crack,
crevice, fissure, gap, hole, interstice, nook,
opening, rift.

crapulous *adj* crapulent, drunk, drunken,
inebriated, intoxicated, tipsy.

crash *vb* break, shatter, shiver, smash,
splinter. •*adj* emergency, fast, intensive,
rushed, speeded-up. •*n* clang, clash, collision concussion, jar.

crass *adj* coarse, gross, raw, thick, unabated,
unrefined.

cravat *n* neckcloth, neckerchief, necktie.

crave *vb* **1** ask, beg, beseech, entreat, implore, petition, solicit, supplicate. **2** desire,
hanker after, long for, need, want, yearn
for.
vb antonyms dislike, spurn.

craven *n* coward, dastard, milk-sop, poltroon, recreant. •*adj* cowardly, chicken-
hearted, lily-livered, pusillanimous, yellow.

craving *n* hankering, hungering, longing,
yearning.
n antonyms dislike, distaste.

craw *n* crop, gullet, stomach, throat.

craze *vb* **1** bewilder, confuse, dement, derange, madden. **2** disorder, impair, weak-
en. •*n* fashion, mania, mode, novelty.

crazy *adj* **1** broken, crank, rickety, shaky,
shattered, tottering. **2** crack-brained, delirious, demented, deranged, distracted,
idiotic, insane, lunatic, mad, silly.
adj antonyms sane, sensible.

create *vb* **1** originate, procreate. **2** cause, design, fashion, form, invent, occasion, pro-
duce. **3** appoint, constitute, make.
vb antonym destroy.

creation *n* **1** formation, invention, origination, production. **2** cosmos, universe. **3** appointment, constitution, establishment,
nomination.

creator *n* **1** author, designer, inventor, fash-
ioner, maker, originator. **2** god.

creature *n* **1** animal, beast, being, body,
brute, man, person. **2** dependant,
hanger-on, minion, parasite, retainer, vassal. **3** miscreant, wretch.

credence *n* acceptance, belief, confidence,
credit, faith, reliance, trust.
n antonym distrust.

credentials *npl* certificate, diploma, missive,
passport, recommendation, testament,
testimonial, title, voucher, warrant.

credibility *n* believability, plausibility, ten-
ability, trustworthiness.

credit *vb* **1** accept, believe, trust. **2** loan,

trust. •*n* **1** belief, confidence, credence, faith, reliance, trust. **2** esteem, regard, reputableness, reputation. **3** influence, power. **4** honour, merit. **5** loan, trust.
n antonym discredit.
vb antonym disbelieve.

creditable *adj* estimable, honourable, meritorious, praiseworthy, reputable, respectable.
adj antonyms blameworthy, shameful.

credulity *n* credulousness, gullibility, silliness, simplicity, stupidity.

credulous *adj* dupable, green, gullible, naive, over-trusting, trustful, uncritical, unsuspecting, unsuspicious.
adj antonym skeptical.

creed *n* belief, confession, doctrine, dogma, opinion, profession, tenet.

creek *n* **1** bay, bight, cove, fjord, inlet. **2** rivulet, streamlet.

creep *vb* **1** crawl. **2** steal upon. **3** cringe, fawn, grovel, insinuate. •*n* **1** crawl, scrabble, scramble. **2** fawner, groveller, sycophant, toady.

crest *n* **1** comb, plume, topknot, tuft. **2** apex, crown, head, ridge, summit, top. **3** arms, badge, bearings.

crestfallen *adj* dejected, depressed, despondent, discouraged, disheartened, dispirited, downcast, down-hearted, low-spirited, melancholy, sad.

crevice *n* chink, cleft, crack, cranny, fissure, fracture, gap, hole, interstice, opening, rent, rift.

crew *n* **1** company, complement, hands. **2** company, corps, gang, horde, mob, party, posse, set, squad, team, throng.

crib *vb* **1** cage, confine, encage, enclose, imprison. **2** pilfer, purloin. •*n* **1** manger, rack. **2** bin, bunker. **3** plagiarism, plunder, theft.

crick *vb* jar, rick, wrench, wrick. •*n* convulsion, cramp, jarring, spasm, rick, wrench, wrick.

crime *n* **1** felony, misdeed, misdemeanour, offence, violation. **2** delinquency, fault, guilt, iniquity, sin, transgression, unrighteousness, wickedness, wrong.

criminal *adj* culpable, felonious, flagitious, guilty, illegal, immoral, iniquitous, nefarious, unlawful, vicious, wicked, wrong. •*n* convict, culprit, delinquent, felon, malefactor, offender, sinner, transgressor.
adj antonyms honest, upright.

crimp *vb* crisp, curl.

cringe *vb* bend, bow, cower, crouch, fawn, grovel, kneel, sneak, stoop, truckle.

cripple *vb* cramp, destroy, disable, enfeeble, impair, lame, maim, mutilate, paralyse, ruin, weaken.

crisis *n* **1** acme, climax, height. **2** conjuncture, emergency, exigency, juncture, pass, pinch, push, rub, strait, urgency.

crisp *adj* brittle, curled, friable, frizzled.
adj antonyms flabby, limp, vague.

criterion *n* canon, gauge, measure, principle, proof, rule, standard, test, touchstone.

critic *n* arbiter, caviller, censor, connoisseur, judge, nit-picker, reviewer.

critical *adj* **1** accurate, exact, nice. **2** captious, carping, censorious, exacting. **3** crucial, decisive, determining, important, turning. **4** dangerous, dubious, exigent, hazardous, imminent, momentous, precarious, ticklish.
adj antonyms uncritical, unimportant.

criticism *n* analysis, animadversion, appreciation, comment, critique, evaluation, judgement, review, strictures.

criticize *vb* appraise, evaluate, examine, judge.
vb antonym praise.

croak *vb* **1** complain, groan, grumble, moan, mumble, repine. **2** die.

crone *n* hag, witch.

crony *n* ally, associate, chum, friend, mate, mucker, pal.

crook *vb* bend, bow, curve, incurvate, turn, wind. •*n* **1** bend, curvature, flexion, turn. **2** artifice, machination, trick. **3** criminal, thief, villain

crooked *adj* **1** angular, bent, bowed, curved, winding, zigzag. **2** askew, aslant, awry, deformed, disfigured, distorted, twisted, wry. **3** crafty, deceitful, devious, dishonest, dishonourable, fraudulent, insidious, intriguing, knavish, tricky, underhanded, unfair, unscrupulous.

crop *vb* **1** gather, mow, pick, pluck, reap. **2** browse, nibble. **3** clip, curtail, lop, reduce, shorten. •*n* harvest, produce, yield.

cross *vb* **1** intersect, pass over, traverse. **2** hinder, interfere, obstruct, thwart. **3** interbred, intermix. •*adj* **1** transverse. **2** cantankerous, captious, crabbed, churlish, crusty, cynical, fractious, fretful, grouchy, ill-natured, ill-tempered, irascible, irritable, morose, peevish, pettish, petulant, snappish, snarling, sour, spleeny, splenetic, sulky, sullen, surly, testy, touchy, waspish. •*n* **1** crucifix, gibbet, rood. **2** affliction, misfortune, trial, trouble, vexation. **3** cross-breeding, hybrid, intermixture.

adj antonyms calm, placid, pleasant.

cross-grained *adj* cantankerous, headstrong, obdurate, peevish, perverse, refractory, stubborn, untractable, wayward.

crossing *n* intersection, overpass, traversing, under-pass.

crossways, crosswise *adv* across, over, transversely.

crotchet *n* caprice, fad, fancy, freak, quirk, vagary, whim, whimsy.

crouch *vb* **1** cower, cringe, fawn, truckle. **2** crouch, kneel, stoop, squat. **3** bow, curtsy, genuflect.

croup *n* buttocks, crupper, rump.

crow *vb* bluster, boast, brag, chuckle, exult, flourish, gasconade, swagger, triumph, vapour, vaunt.

crowd *vb* **1** compress, cram, jam, pack, press. **2** collect, congregate, flock, herd, huddle, swarm. •*n* **1** assembly, company, concourse, flock, herd, horde, host, jam, multitude, press, throng. **2** mob, pack, populace, rabble, rout.

crown *vb* **1** adorn, dignify, honour. **2** recompense, requite, reward. **3** cap, complete, consummate, finish, perfect. •*n* **1** bays, chaplet, coronal, coronet, garland, diadem, laurel, wreath. **2** monarchy, royalty, sovereignty. **3** diadem. **4** dignity, honour, recompense, reward. **5** apex, crest, summit, top.

crowning *adj* completing, consummating, dignifying, finishing, perfecting.

crucial *adj* **1** intersecting, transverse. **2** critical, decisive, searching, severe, testing, trying.

crude *adj* **1** raw, uncooked, undressed, unworked. **2** harsh, immature, rough, unripe. **3** crass, coarse, unrefined. **4** awkward, immature, indigestible, rude, uncouth, unpolished, unpremeditated.

adj antonyms finished, polite, refined, tasteful.

cruel *adj* **1** barbarous, blood-thirsty, dire, fell, ferocious, inexorable, hard-hearted, inhuman, merciless, pitiless, relentless, ruthless, sanguinary, savage, truculent, uncompassionate, unfeeling, unmerciful, unrelenting. **2** bitter, cold, hard, severe, sharp, unfeeling.

adj antonyms compassionate, kind, merciful.

crumble *vb* bruise, crush, decay, disintegrate, perish, pound, pulverize, triturate.

crumple *vb* rumple, wrinkle.

crush *vb* **1** bruise, compress, contuse, squash, squeeze. **2** bray, comminute, crumble, disintegrate, mash. **3** demolish, raze, shatter. **4** conquer, overcome, overpower, overwhelm, quell, subdue.

crust *n* coat, coating, incrustation, outside, shell, surface.

crusty *adj* **1** churlish, crabbed, cross, cynical, fretful, forward, morose, peevish, pettish, petulant, snappish, snarling, surly, testy, touchy, waspish. **2** friable, hard, short.

cry *vb* **1** call, clamour, exclaim. **2** blubber, snivel, sob, wail, weep, whimper. **3** bawl, bellow, hoot, roar, shout, vociferate, scream, screech, squawk, squall, squeal, yell. **4** announce, blazon, proclaim, publish. •*n* **1** acclamation, clamour, ejaculation, exclamation, outcry. **2** crying, lament, lamentation, plaint, weeping. **3** bawl, bellow, howl, roar, scream, screech, shriek, yell. **4** announcement, proclamation, publication.

crypt *n* catacomb, tomb, vault.

cuddle *vb* **1** cosset, nestle, snuggle, squat. **2** caress, embrace, fondle, hug, pet. •*n* caress, embrace, hug.

cudgel *vb* bang, baste, batter, beat, cane, drub, thrash, thump. •*n* bastinado, baton, bludgeon, club, shillelagh, stick, truncheon.

cue *vb* intimate, prompt, remind, sign, signal. •*n* catchword, hint, intimation, nod, prompting, sign, signal, suggestion.

cuff *vb* beat, box, buffet, knock, pummel, punch, slap, smack, strike, thump. •*n* blow, box, punch, slap, smack, strike, thump.

cul-de-sac *n* alley, dead end, impasse, pocket.

cull *vb* **1** choose, elect, pick, select. **2** collect, gather, glean, pluck.

culmination *n* acme, apex, climax, completion, consummation, crown, summit, top, zenith.

culpability *n* blame, criminality, culpableness, guilt, remissness, sinfulness.

culpable *adj* blameable, blameworthy, censurable, faulty, guilty, reprehensible, sinful, transgressive, wrong.

adj antonyms blameless, innocent.

culprit *n* delinquent, criminal, evil-doer, felon, malefactor, offender.

cultivate *vb* 1 farm, fertilize, till, work. 2 civilize, develop, discipline, elevate, improve, meliorate, refine, train. 3 investigate, prosecute, pursue, search, study. 4 cherish, foster, nourish, patronize, promote.
vb antonym neglect.

culture *n* 1 agriculture, cultivation, farming, husbandry, tillage. 2 cultivation, elevation, improvement, refinement.

cumber *vb* 1 burden, clog, encumber, hamper, impede, obstruct, oppress, overload. 2 annoy, distract, embarrass, harass, perplex, plague, torment, trouble, worry.

cumbersome *adj* burdensome, clumsy, cumbrous, embarrassing, heavy, inconvenient, oppressive, troublesome, unmanageable, unwieldy, vexatious.
adj antonyms convenient, manageable.

cuneiform *adj* cuneate, wedge-shaped.

cunning *adj* 1 artful, astute, crafty, crooked, deceitful, designing, diplomatic, foxy, guileful, intriguing, machiavellian, sharp, shrewd, sly, subtle, tricky, wily. 2 curious, ingenious. •*n* 1 art, artfulness, artifice, astuteness, craft, shrewdness, subtlety. 2 craftiness, chicane, chicanery, deceit, deception, intrigue, slyness.
adj antonyms gullible, naïve.
n antonyms openness, simplicity.

cup *n* 1 beaker, bowl, chalice, goblet, mug. 2 cupful, draught, potion.

cupboard *n* buffet, cabinet, closet.

cupidity *n* 1 avidity, greed, hankering, longing, lust. 2 acquisitiveness, avarice, covetousness, greediness, stinginess.

curative *adj* healing, medicinal, remedial, restorative.

curator *n* custodian, guardian, keeper, superintendent.

curb *vb* bridle, check, control, hinder, moderate, repress, restrain. •*n* bridle, check, control, hindrance, rein, restraint.
vb antonyms encourage, foster, goad.

cure *vb* 1 alleviate, correct, heal, mend, remedy, restore. 2 kipper, pickle, preserve. •*n* 1 antidote, corrective, help, remedy, reparative, restorative, specific. 2 alleviation, healing, restorative.

curiosity *n* 1 interest, inquiringness, inquisitiveness. 2 celebrity, curio, marvel, novelty, oddity, phenomenon, rarity, sight, spectacle, wonder.

curious *adj* 1 interested, inquiring, inquisitive, meddling, peering, prying, scrutinizing. 2 extraordinary, marvellous, novel, queer, rare, singular, strange, unique, unusual. 3 cunning, elegant, fine, finished, neat, skilful, well-wrought.
adj antonyms incurious, indifferent, normal, ordinary, uninterested.

curl *vb* 1 coil, twist, wind, writhe. 2 bend, buckle, ripple, wave. •*n* 1 curlicue, lovelock, ringlet. 2 flexure, sinuosity, undulation, wave, waving, winding.

curmudgeon *n* churl, lick-penny, miser, niggard, screw, scrimp, skinflint.

currency *n* 1 publicity. 2 acceptance, circulation, transmission. 3 bills, coins, money, notes.

current *adj* 1 common, general, popular, rife. 2 circulating, passing. 3 existing, instant, present, prevalent, widespread. •*n* course, progression, river, stream, tide, undertow. •*adv* commonly, generally, popularly, publicly.
adj antonyms antiquated, old-fashioned.

curry *vb* 1 comb, dress. 2 beat, cudgel, drub, thrash.

curse *vb* 1 anathematize, damn, denounce, execrate, imprecate, invoke, maledict. 2 blast, blight, destroy, doom. 3 afflict, annoy, harass, injure, plague, scourge, torment, vex. 4 blaspheme, swear. •*n* 1 anathema, ban, denunciation, execration, fulmination, imprecation, malediction, malison. 2 affliction, annoyance, plague, scourge, torment, trouble, vexation. 3 ban, condemnation, penalty, sentence.
vb antonym bless.
n antonyms advantage, blessing.

cursed *adj* 1 accursed, banned, blighted, curse-laden, unholy. 2 abominable, detestable, execrable, hateful, villainous. 3 annoying, confounded, plaguing, scourging, tormenting, troublesome, vexatious.

cursory *adj* brief, careless, desultory, hasty, passing, rapid, slight, summary, superficial, transient, transitory.
adj antonyms painstaking, thorough.

curt *adj* 1 brief, concise, laconic, short, terse. 2 crusty, rude, snappish, tart.
adj antonym voluble.

curtail *vb* 1 abridge, dock, lop, retrench, shorten. 2 abbreviate, contract, decrease, diminish, lessen.
vb antonyms extend, lengthen, prolong.

curtain *vb* cloak, cover, drape, mantle, screen, shade, shield, veil. •*n* arras, drape, drop, portière, screen, shade.

curvature *n* arcuation, bend, bending, camber, crook, curve, flexure, incurvation.

curve *vb* bend, crook, inflect, turn, twist, wind. •*n* arcuation, bend, bending, camber, crook, flexure, incurvation.

curvet *vb* **1** bound, leap, vault. **2** caper, frisk.

cushion *vb* **1** absorb, damp, dampen, deaden, dull, muffle, mute, soften, subdue, suppress. **2** cradle, pillow, support. •*n* bolster, hassock, pad, pillow, woolsack.

cusp *n* angle, horn, point.

custodian *n* curator, guardian, keeper, sacristan, superintendent, warden.

custody *n* **1** care, charge, guardianship, keeping, safe-keeping, protection, watch, ward. **2** confinement, durance, duress, imprisonment, prison.

custom *n* **1** consuetude, convention, fashion, habit, manner, mode, practice, rule, usage, use, way. **2** form, formality, observation. **3** patronage. **4** duty, impost, tax, toll, tribute.

customary *adj* accustomed, common, conventional, familiar, fashionable, general, habitual, gnomic, prescriptive, regular, usual, wonted.

adj antonyms occasional, rare, unusual.

cut *vb* **1** chop, cleave, divide, gash, incise, lance, sever, slice, slit, wound. **2** carve, chisel, sculpture. **3** hurt, move, pierce, touch. **4** ignore, slight. **5** abbreviate, abridge, curtail, shorten. •*n* **1** gash, groove, incision, nick, slash, slice, slit. **2** channel, passage. **3** piece, slice. **4** fling, sarcasm, taunt. **5** fashion, form, mode, shape, style.

cutthroat *adj* **1** barbarous, cruel, ferocious, murderous. **2** competitive, exacting, exorbitant, extortionate, rivalling, ruthless, usurious.•*n* assassin, murderer, ruffian.

cutting *adj* **1** keen, sharp. **2** acid, biting, bitter, caustic, piercing, sarcastic, sardonic, satirical, severe, trenchant, wounding.

cycle *n* age, circle, era, period, revolution, round.

cynical *adj* **1** captious, carping, censorious, churlish, crabbed, cross, crusty, fretful, ill-natured, ill-tempered, morose, peevish, pettish, petulant, sarcastic, satirical, snappish, snarling, surly, testy, touchy, waspish. **2** contemptuous, derisive, misanthropic, pessimistic, scornful.

cyst *n* pouch, sac.

D

dab *vb* **1** box, rap, slap, strike, tap touch. **2** coat, daub, smear. • *adj* **1** adept, expert, proficient. **2** pat. • *n* lump, mass, pat.

dabble *vb* **1** dip, moisten, soak, spatter, splash, sprinkle, wet. **2** meddle, tamper, trifle.

daft *adj* **1** absurd, delirious, foolish, giddy, idiotic, insane, silly, simple, stupid, witless. **2** frolicsome, merry, mirthful, playful, sportive.
adj antonyms bright, sane.

dagger *n* bayonet, dirk, poniard, stiletto.

dainty *adj* **1** delicate, delicious, luscious, nice, palatable, savoury, tender, toothsome. **2** beautiful, charming, choice, delicate, elegant, exquisite, fine, neat. **3** fastidious, finical, finicky, over-nice, particular, scrupulous, squeamish. • *n* delicacy, titbit, treat.
adj antonyms clumsy, gross.

dale *n* bottom, dell, dingle, glen, vale, valley.

dalliance *n* caressing, endearments, flirtation, fondling.

dally *vb* **1** dawdle, fritter, idle, trifle, waste time. **2** flirt, fondle, toy.
vb antonyms hasten, hurry.

damage *vb* harm, hurt, impair, injure, mar. • *n* detriment, harm, hurt, injury, loss, mischief.
vb antonyms fix, repair.
n antonym repair.

damages *npl* compensation, fine, forfeiture, indemnity, reparation, satisfaction.

dame *n* **1** babe, baby, broad, doll, girl. **2** lady, madam, matron, mistress.

damn *vb* condemn, doom, kill, ruin. • *n* bean, curse, fig, hoot, rap, sou, straw, whit.
vb antonym bless.

damnable *adj* abominable, accursed, atrocious, cursed, detestable, hateful, execrable, odious, outrageous.
adj antonyms admirable, praiseworthy.

damp *vb* **1** dampen, moisten. **2** allay, abate, check, discourage, moderate, repress, restrain. **3** chill, cool, deaden, deject, depress, dispirit. • *adj* dank, humid, moist, wet. • *n* **1** dampness, dank, fog, mist, moisture, vapour. **2** chill, dejection, depression.

vb antonym dry.
adj antonyms arid, dry.
n antonym dryness.

damper *n* **1** check, hindrance, impediment, obstacle. **2** damp, depression, discouragement, wet blanket.

dandle *vb* **1** amuse, caress, fondle, pet, toss. **2** dance.

danger *n* jeopardy, insecurity, hazard, peril, risk, venture.
n antonyms safety, security.

dangerous *adj* critical, hazardous, insecure, perilous, risky, ticklish, unsafe.
adj antonyms harmless, safe, secure.

dangle *vb* **1** drape, hang, pend, sway, swing. **2** fawn.

dank *adj* damp, humid, moist, wet.
adj antonym dry.

dapper *adj* **1** active, agile, alert, brisk, lively, nimble, quick, ready, smart, spry. **2** neat, nice, pretty, spruce, trim.
adj antonyms dishevelled, dowdy, scruffy, shabby, sloppy.

dapple *vb* diversify, spot, variegate. • *adj* dappled, spotted, variegated.

dare *vb* challenge, defy, endanger, hazard, provoke, risk. • *n* challenge, defiance, gage.

daring *adj* adventurous, bold, brave, chivalrous, courageous, dauntless, doughty, fearless, gallant, heroic, intrepid, valiant, valorous. • *n* adventurousness, boldness, bravery, courage, dauntlessness, doughtiness, fearlessness, intrepidity, undauntedness, valour.
adj antonyms afraid, timid.
n antonyms cowardice, timidity.

dark *adj* **1** black, cloudy, darksome, dusky, inky, lightless, lurid, moonless, murky, opaque, overcast, pitchy, rayless, shady, shadowy, starless, sunless, swart, tenebrous, umbrageous, unenlightened, unilluminated. **2** abstruse, cabbalistic, enigmatical, incomprehensible, mysterious, mystic, mystical, obscure, occult, opaque, recondite, transcendental, unintelligible. **3** cheerless, discouraging, dismal, disheartening, funereal, gloomy. **4** benighted, darkened, ignorant, rude, unlettered, untaught. **5** atrocious, damnable, infamous, flagitious, foul, horrible, infernal, nefarious, vile, wicked. • *n* **1** darkness, dusk, murkiness, obscurity. **2** concealment, privacy, secrecy. **3** blindness, ignorance.

adj antonyms bright, happy, light, lucid.

n antonyms brightness, light.

darken *vb* **1** cloud, dim, eclipse, obscure, shade, shadow. **2** chill, damp, depress, gloom, sadden. **3** benight, stultify, stupefy. **4** obscure, perplex. **5** defile, dim, dull, stain, sully.

darkness *n* **1** blackness, dimness, gloom, obscurity. **2** blindness, ignorance. **3** cheerlessness, despondency, gloom, joylessness. **4** privacy, secrecy.

darling *adj* beloved, cherished, dear, loved, precious, treasured. • *n* dear, favourite, idol, love, sweetheart.

dart *vb* **1** dash, rush, scoot, spring. **2** hurl, launch, propel, sling, throw. **3** emit, shoot.

dash *vb* **1** break, destroy, disappoint, frustrate, ruin, shatter, spoil, thwart. **2** abash, confound, disappoint, surprise. **3** bolt, dart, fly, run, speed, rush. • *n* **1** blow, stroke. **2** advance, onset, rush. **3** infusion, smack, spice, sprinkling, tincture, tinge, touch. **4** flourish, show.

dashing *adj* **1** headlong, impetuous, precipitate, rushing. **2** brilliant, gay, showy, spirited.

adj antonym drab.

dastardly *adj* base, cowardly, coward, cowering, craven, pusillanimous, recreant. • *n* coward, craven, milksop, poltroon, recreant.

adj antonyms heroic, noble.

data *npl* conditions, facts, information, premises.

date *n* **1** age, cycle, day, generation, time. **2** epoch, era, period. **3** appointment, arrangement, assignation, engagement, interview, rendezvous, tryst. **4** catch, steady, sweetheart.

daub *vb* bedaub, begrime, besmear, blur, cover, deface, defile, grime, plaster, smear, smudge, soil, sully. • *n* smear, smirch, smudge.

daunt *vb* alarm, appal, check, cow, deter, discourage, frighten, intimate, scare, subdue, tame, terrify, thwart.

vb antonyms encourage, hearten.

dauntless *adj* bold, brave, chivalrous, courageous, daring, doughty, gallant, heroic,

indomitable, intrepid, unconquerable, undaunted, undismayed, valiant, valorous.

adj antonyms discouraged, disheartened.

dawdle *vb* dally, delay, fiddle, idle, lag, loiter, potter, trifle.

dawn *vb* appear, begin, break, gleam, glimmer, open, rise. • *n* daybreak, dawning, cockcrow, sunrise, sun-up.

n antonyms dusk, sundown, sunset.

day *n* **1** daylight, sunlight, sunshine. **2** age, epoch, generation, lifetime, time.

daze *vb* **1** blind, dazzle. **2** bewilder, confound, confuse, perplex, stun, stupefy. • *n* **1** bewilderment, confusion, discomposure, perturbation, pother. **2** coma, stupor, swoon, trance.

dazzle *vb* **1** blind, daze. **2** astonish, confound, overpower, surprise. • *n* brightness, brilliance, splendour.

dead *adj* **1** breathless, deceased, defunct, departed, gone, inanimate, lifeless. **2** apathetic, callous, cold, dull, frigid, indifferent, inert, lukewarm, numb, obtuse, spiritless, torpid, unfeeling. **3** flat, insipid, stagnant, tasteless, vapid. **4** barren, inactive, sterile, unemployed, unprofitable, useless. • *adv* **1** absolutely, completely, downright, fundamentally, quite. **2** direct, directly, due, exactly, just, right, squarely, straight. • *n* **1** depth, midst. **2** hush, peace, quietude, silence, stillness.

deaden *vb* **1** abate, damp, dampen, dull, impair, muffle, mute, restrain, retard, smother, weaken. **2** benumb, blunt, hebetate, obtund, paralyse.

vb antonym enliven.

deadly *adj* **1** deleterious, destructive, fatal, lethal, malignant, mortal, murderous, noxious, pernicious, poisonous, venomous. **2** implacable, mortal, rancorous, sanguinary.

adj antonyms harmless, healthy.

deal *vb* **1** allot, apportion, assign, bestow, dispense, distribute, divide, give, reward, share. **2** bargain, trade, traffic, treat with. • *n* **1** amount, degree, distribution, extent, lot, portion, quantity, share. **2** bargain, transaction.

dear *adj* **1** costly, expensive, high-priced. **2** beloved, cherished, darling, esteemed, precious, treasured. • *n* beloved, darling, deary, honey, love, precious, sweet, sweetie, sweetheart.

adj antonyms cheap, hateful.

dearth n 1 deficiency, insufficiency, scarcity. 2 famine, lack, need, shortage, want.
n antonyms abundance, excess.

death n cessation, decease, demise, departure, destruction, dissolution, dying, end, exit, mortality, passing.
n antonyms birth, life.

deathless adj 1 eternal, everlasting, immortal, imperishable, undying. 2 boring, dull, turgid.

debacle n 1 breakdown, cataclysm, collapse. 2 rout, stampede.

debar vb blackball, deny, exclude, hinder, prevent, prohibit, restrain, shut out, stop, withhold.

debase vb 1 adulterate, alloy, depress, deteriorate, impair, injure, lower, pervert, reduce, vitiate. 2 abase, degrade, disgrace, dishonour, humble, humiliate, mortify, shame. 3 befoul, contaminate, corrupt, defile, foul, pollute, soil, taint.
vb antonyms elevate, upgrade.

debate vb 1 argue, canvass, contest, discuss, dispute. 2 contend, deliberate, wrangle. • n 1 controversy, discussion, disputation. 2 altercation, contention, contest, dispute, logomachy.
vb antonym agree.
n antonym agreement.

debauch vb 1 corrupt, deprave, pollute, vitiate. 2 deflower, ravish, seduce, violate. • n carousal, orgy, revel, saturnalia.

debauchery n 1 dissipation, dissoluteness, excesses, intemperance. 2 debauch, excess, intemperance, lewdness, licentiousness, lust. 3 bacchanal, carousal, indulgence, orgies, potation, revelry, revels, saturnalia, spree.

debilitate vb enervate, enfeeble, exhaust, prostrate, relax, weaken.

debility n enervation, exhaustion, faintness, feebleness, frailty, imbecility, infirmity, languor, prostration, weakness.

debonair adj affable, civil, complaisant, courteous, easy, gracious, kind, obliging, polite, refined, urbane, well-bred.

debris n detritus, fragments, remains, rubbish, rubble, ruins, wreck, wreckage.

debt n 1 arrears, debit, due, liability, obligation. 2 fault, misdoing, offence, shortcoming, sin, transgression, trespass.
n antonyms asset, credit.

decadence n caducity, decay, declension, decline, degeneracy, degeneration, deterioration, fall, retrogression.

decamp vb abscond, bolt, escape, flee, fly.

decapitate vb behead, decollate, guillotine.

decay vb 1 decline, deteriorate, disintegrate, fail, perish, wane, waste, wither. 2 decompose, putrefy, rot. • n caducity, decadence, declension, decline, decomposition, decrepitude, degeneracy, degeneration, deterioration, dilapidation, disintegration, fading, failing, perishing, putrefaction, ruin, wasting, withering.
vb antonyms flourish, grow, ripen.

deceased adj dead, defunct, departed, gone, late, lost.

deceit n artifice, cheating, chicanery, cozenage, craftiness, deceitfulness, deception, double-dealing, duplicity, finesse, fraud, guile, hypocrisy, imposition, imposture, pretence, sham, treachery, tricky, underhandedness, wile.
n antonyms honesty, openness.

deceitful adj 1 counterfeit, deceptive, delusive, fallacious, hollow, illusive, illusory, insidious, misleading. 2 circumventive, cunning, designing, dissembling, dodgy, double-dealing, evasive, false, fraudulent, guileful, hypocritical, insincere, tricky, underhanded, wily.
adj antonyms honest, open, trustworthy.

deceive vb befool, beguile, betray, cheat, chouse, circumvent, cozen, defraud, delude, disappoint, double-cross, dupe, ensnare, entrap, fool, gull, hoax, hoodwink, humbug, mislead, outwit, overreach, trick.
vb antonym enlighten.

deceiver n charlatan, cheat, humbug, hypocrite, knave, impostor, pretender, rogue, sharper, trickster.

decent adj 1 appropriate, becoming, befitting, comely, seemly, decorous, fit, proper, seemly. 2 chaste, delicate, modest, pure. 3 moderate, passable, respectable, tolerable.
adj antonyms disobliging, indecent, poor.

deception n 1 artifice, cheating, chicanery, cozenage, craftiness, deceitfulness, deception, double-dealing, duplicity, finesse, fraud, guile, hoax, hypocrisy, imposition, imposture, pretence, sham, treachery, trick, underhandedness, wile. 2 cheat, chouse, ruse, stratagem, wile.
n antonyms artlessness, openness.

deceptive adj deceitful, deceiving, delusive, disingenuous, fallacious, false, illusive, illusory, misleading.
adj antonyms artless, genuine, open.

decide *vb* **1** close, conclude, determine, end, settle, terminate. **2** resolve. **3** adjudge, adjudicate, award.

decided *adj* **1** determined, firm, resolute, unhesitating, unwavering. **2** absolute, categorical, positive, unequivocal. **3** certain, clear, indisputable, undeniable, unmistakable, unquestionable.

deciduous *adj* caducous, nonperennial, temporary.

decipher *vb* **1** explain, expound, interpret, reveal, solve, unfold, unravel. **2** read.
vb antonym encode.

decision *n* **1** conclusion, determination, judgement, settlement. **2** adjudication, award, decree, pronouncement, sentence. **3** firmness, resolution.

decisive *adj* conclusive, determinative, final.
adj antonyms indecisive, insignificant.

deck *vb* **1** adorn, array, beautify, decorate, embellish, grace, ornament. **2** apparel, attire, bedeck, clothe, dress, robe.

declaim *vb* harangue, mouth, rant, speak, spout.

declamation *n* declaiming, haranguing, mouthing, ranting, spouting.

declamatory *adj* bombastic, discursive, fustian, grandiloquent, high-flown, high-sounding, incoherent, inflated, pompous, pretentious, rhetorical, swelling, turgid.

declaration *n* **1** affirmation, assertion, asseveration, averment, avowal, protestation, statement. **2** announcement, proclamation, publication.

declaratory *adj* **1** affirmative, annunciatory, assertive, declarative, definite, enunciative, enunciatory, expressive. **2** explanatory, expository.

declare *vb* advertise, affirm, announce, assert, asseverate, aver, blazon, bruit, proclaim, promulgate, pronounce, publish, state, utter.

declension *n* **1** decadence, decay, decline, degeneracy, deterioration, diminution. **2** inflection, variation. **3** declination, nonacceptance, refusal.

declination *n* **1** bending, descent, inclination. **2** decadence, decay, decline, degeneracy, degeneration, degradation, deterioration, diminution. **3** aberration, departure, deviation, digression, divagation, divergence. **4** declinature, nonacceptance, refusal.

decline *vb* **1** incline, lean, slope. **2** decay, droop, fail, flag, languish, pine, sink. **3** degenerate, depreciate, deteriorate. **4** decrease, diminish, dwindle, fade, ebb, lapse, lessen, wane. **5** avoid, refuse, reject. **6** inflect, vary. • *n* **1** decadence, decay, declension, declination, degeneracy, deterioration, diminution, wane. **2** atrophy, consumption, marasmus, phthisis. **3** declivity, hill, incline, slope.

declivity *n* declination, descent, incline, slope.

decompose *vb* **1** analyse, disintegrate, dissolve, distil, resolve, separate. **2** corrupt, decay, putrefy, rot.
v antonyms combine, unite.

decomposition *n* **1** analysis, break-up, disintegration, resolution. **2** caries, corruption, crumbling, decay, disintegration, dissolution, putrescence, rotting.

decorate *vb* adorn, beautify, bedeck, deck, embellish, enrich, garnish, grace, ornament.

decoration *n* **1** adorning, beautifying, bedecking, decking, enriching, garnishing, ornamentation, ornamenting. **2** adornment, enrichment, embellishment, ornament.

decorous *adj* appropriate, becoming, befitting, comely, decent, fit, suitable, proper, sedate, seemly, staid.

decorum *n* appropriate behaviour, courtliness, decency, deportment, dignity, gravity, politeness, propriety, sedateness, seemliness.

decoy *vb* allure, deceive, ensnare, entice, entrap, inveigle, lure, seduce, tempt. • *n* allurement, lure, enticement.

decrease *vb* **1** abate, contract, decline, diminish, dwindle, ebb, lessen, subside, wane. **2** curtail, diminish, lessen, lower, reduce, retrench. • *n* abatement, contraction, declension, decline, decrement, diminishing, diminution, ebb, ebbing, lessening, reduction, subsidence, waning.
vb antonym increase.
n antonym increase.

decree *vb* adjudge, appoint, command, decide, determine, enact, enjoin, order, ordain. • *n* act, command, edict, enactment, fiat, law, mandate, order, ordinance, precept, regulation, statute.

decrement *n* decrease, diminution, lessening, loss, waste.

decrepit *adj* **1** feeble, effete, shattered,

wasted, weak. **2** aged, crippled, superannuated.

adj antonyms fit, well-cared-for, youthful.

decry *vb* abuse, belittle, blame, condemn, denounce, depreciate, detract, discredit, disparage, run down, traduce, underrate, undervalue.

vb antonyms praise, value.

dedicate *vb* **1** consecrate, devote, hallow, sanctify. **2** address, inscribe.

deduce *vb* conclude, derive, draw, gather, infer.

deducible *adj* derivable, inferable.

deduct *vb* **1** remove, subtract, withdraw. **2** abate, detract.

vb antonym add.

deduction *n* **1** removal, subtraction, withdrawal. **2** abatement, allowance, defalcation, discount, rebate, reduction, reprise. **3** conclusion, consequence, corollary, inference.

deed *n* **1** achievement, act, action, derringdo, exploit, feat, performance. **2** fact, truth, reality. **3** charter, contract, document, indenture, instrument, transfer.

deem *vb* **1** account, believe, conceive, consider, count, estimate, hold, imagine, judge, regard, suppose, think. **2** fancy, opine.

deep *adj* **1** abysmal, extensive, great, profound. **2** abstruse, difficult, hard, intricate, knotty, mysterious, recondite, unfathomable. **3** astute, cunning, designing, discerning, intelligent, insidious, penetrating, sagacious, shrewd. **4** absorbed, engrossed. **5** bass, grave, low. **6** entire, great, heartfelt, thorough. • *n* **1** main, ocean, water, sea. **2** abyss, depth, profundity. **3** enigma, mystery, riddle. **4** silence, stillness.

adj antonyms open, shallow.

deeply *adv* **1** profoundly. **2** completely, entirely, extensively, greatly, thoroughly. **3** affectingly, distressingly, feelingly, mournfully, sadly.

deface *vb* blotch, deform, disfigure, injure, mar, mutilate, obliterate, soil, spoil, sully, tarnish.

vb antonym repair.

de facto *adj* actual, real. • *adv* actually, in effect, in fact, really, truly.

defalcate *vb* abate, curtail, retrench, lop.

defalcation *n* **1** abatement, deduction, diminution, discount, reduction. **2** default, deficiency, deficit, shortage, shortcoming. **3** embezzlement, fraud.

defamation *n* abuse, aspersion, back-biting, calumny, detraction, disparagement, libel, obloquy, opprobrium, scandal, slander.

n antonym praise.

defamatory *adj* abusive, calumnious, libellous, slanderous.

defame *vb* abuse, asperse, blacken, belie, besmirch, blemish, calumniate, detract, disgrace, dishonour, libel, malign, revile, slander, smirch, traduce, vilify.

default *vb* defalcate, dishonour, fail, repudiate, welsh. • *n* **1** defalcation, failure, lapse, neglect, offence, omission, oversight, shortcoming. **2** defect, deficiency, deficit, delinquency, destitution, fault, lack, want.

defaulter *n* delinquent, embezzler, offender, peculator.

defeat *vb* **1** beat, checkmate, conquer, discomfit, overcome, overpower, overthrow, repulse, rout, ruin, vanquish. **2** baffle, balk, block, disappoint, disconcert, foil, frustrate, thwart. • *n* **1** discomfiture, downfall, overthrow, repulse, rout, vanquishment. **2** bafflement, checkmate, frustration.

defect *vb* abandon, desert, rebel, revolt. • *n* **1** default, deficiency, destitution, lack, shortcoming, spot, taint, want. **2** blemish, blotch, error, flaw, imperfection, mistake. **3** failing, fault, foible.

defection *n* **1** abandonment, desertion, rebellion, revolt. **2** apostasy, backsliding, dereliction.

defective *adj* **1** deficient, inadequate, incomplete, insufficient, scant, short. **2** faulty, imperfect, marred.

adj antonyms normal, operative.

defence *n* **1** defending, guarding, holding, maintaining, maintenance, protection. **2** buckler, bulwark, fortification, guard, protection, rampart, resistance, shield. **3** apology, excuse, justification, plea, vindication.

defenceless *adj* exposed, helpless, unarmed, unprotected, unguarded, unshielded, weak.

defend *vb* **1** cover, fortify, guard, preserve, protect, safeguard, screen, secure, shelter, shield. **2** assert, espouse, justify, maintain, plead, uphold, vindicate.

defender *n* **1** asserter, maintainer, pleader, upholder. **2** champion, protector, vindicator.

defer[1] *vb* adjourn, delay, pigeonhole, procrastinate, postpone, prorogue, protract, shelve, table.

defer² *vb* **1** abide by, acknowledge, bow to, give way, submit, yield. **2** admire, esteem, honour, regard, respect.

deference *n* **1** esteem, homage, honour, obeisance, regard, respect, reverence, veneration. **2** complaisance, consideration. **3** obedience, submission.

deferential *adj* respectful, reverential.

defiance *n* **1** challenge, daring. **2** contempt, despite, disobedience, disregard, opposition, spite.

defiant *adj* **1** contumacious, recalcitrant, resistant. **2** bold, courageous, resistant.

adj antonyms acquiescent, submissive.

deficiency *n* **1** dearth, default, deficit, insufficiency, lack, meagreness, scantiness, scarcity, shortage, shortness, want. **2** defect, error, failing, falling, fault, foible, frailty, imperfection, infirmity, weakness.

deficient *adj* defective, faulty, imperfect, inadequate, incomplete, insufficient, lacking, scant, scanty, scarce, short, unsatisfactory, wanting.

adj antonyms excessive, superfluous.

deficit *n* deficiency, lack, scarcity, shortage, shortness.

defile¹ *vb* **1** dirty, foul, soil, stain, tarnish. **2** contaminate, debase, poison, pollute, sully, taint, vitiate. **3** corrupt, debauch, deflower, ravish, seduce, violate.

vb antonym cleanse.

defile² *vb* file, march, parade, promenade. • *n* col, gorge, pass, passage, ravine, strait.

define *vb* bound, circumscribe, designate, delimit, demarcate, determine, explain, limit, specify.

definite *adj* **1** defined, determinate, determined, fixed, restricted. **2** assured, certain, clear, exact, explicit, positive, precise, specific, unequivocal.

adj antonyms indefinite, vague.

definitive *adj* **1** categorical, determinate, explicit, express, positive, unconditional. **2** conclusive, decisive, final.

deflect *vb* bend, deviate, diverge, swerve, turn, twist, waver, wind.

deflower *vb* corrupt, debauch, defile, seduce.

deform *vb* deface, disfigure, distort, injure, mar, misshape, ruin, spoil.

deformity *n* abnormality, crookedness, defect, disfigurement, distortion, inelegance, irregularity, malformation, misproportion, misshapenness, monstrosity, ugliness.

defraud *vb* beguile, cheat, chouse, circumvent, cozen, deceive, delude, diddle, dupe, embezzle, gull, overreach, outwit, pilfer, rob, swindle, trick.

defray *vb* bear, discharge, liquidate, meet, pay, settle.

deft *adj* adroit, apt, clever, dab, dextrous, expert, handy, ready, skilful.

adj antonym clumsy.

defunct *adj* **1** dead, deceased, departed, extinct, gone. **2** abrogated, annulled, cancelled, inoperative.

adj antonyms alive, live, operative.

defy *vb* **1** challenge, dare. **2** brave, contemn, despise, disregard, face, flout, provoke, scorn, slight, spurn.

vb antonyms flinch, quail, yield.

degeneracy *n* **1** abasement, caducity, corruption, debasement, decadence, decay, declension, decline, decrease, degenerateness, degeneration, degradation, depravation, deterioration. **2** inferiority, meanness, poorness.

degenerate *vb* decay, decline, decrease, deteriorate, retrograde, sink. • *adj* base, corrupt, decayed, degenerated, deteriorated, fallen, inferior, low, mean, perverted.

vb antonym improve.

adj antonyms upright, virtuous.

degeneration *n* debasement, decline, degeneracy, deterioration.

degradation *n* **1** deposition, disgrace, dishonour, humiliation, ignominy. **2** abasement, caducity, corruption, debasement, decadence, decline, degeneracy, degeneration, deterioration, perversion, vitiation.

degrade *vb* **1** abase, alloy, break, cashier, corrupt, debase, demote, discredit, disgrace, dishonour, disparage, downgrade, humiliate, humble, lower, pervert, vitiate. **2** deteriorate, impair, lower, sink.

vb antonyms enhance, improve.

degree *n* **1** stage, step. **2** class, grade, order, quality, rank, standing, station. **3** extent, measure. **4** division, interval, space.

deify *vb* **1** apotheosize, idolize, glorify, revere. **2** elevate, ennoble, exalt.

deign *vb* accord, condescend, grant, vouchsafe.

deject *vb* depress, discourage, dishearten, dispirit, sadden.

dejected *adj* blue, chapfallen, crestfallen, depressed, despondent, disheartened, dispirited, doleful, downcast, down-hearted, gloomy, low-spirited, miserable, sad, wretched.

adj antonyms bright, happy, high-spirited.

delay *vb* **1** defer, postpone, procrastinate. **2** arrest, detain, check, hinder, impede, retard, stay, stop. **3** prolong, protract. **4** dawdle, linger, loiter, tarry. • *n* **1** deferment, postponement, procrastination. **2** check, detention, hindrance, impediment, retardation, stoppage. **3** prolonging, protraction. **4** dallying, dawdling, lingering, tarrying, stay, stop.

delectable *adj* agreeable, charming, delightful, enjoyable, gratifying, pleasant, pleasing.

adj antonyms horrid, unpleasant.

delectation *n* delight, ecstasy, gladness, joy, rapture, ravishment, transport.

delegate *vb* **1** appoint, authorize, mission, depute, deputize, transfer. **2** commit, entrust. • *n* ambassador, commissioner, delegate, deputy, envoy, representative.

delete *vb* cancel, efface, erase, expunge, obliterate, remove.

vb antonym add in.

deleterious *adj* **1** deadly, destructive, lethal, noxious, poisonous. **2** harmful, hurtful, injurious, pernicious, unwholesome.

adj antonyms enhancing, helpful.

deliberate *vb* cogitate, consider, consult, meditate, muse, ponder, reflect, ruminate, think, weigh. • *adj* **1** careful, cautious, circumspect, considerate, heedful, purposeful, methodical, thoughtful, wary. **2** well-advised, well-considered. **3** aforethought, intentional, premeditated, purposed, studied.

adj antonyms chance, unintentional.

deliberation *n* **1** caution, circumspection, cogitation, consideration, coolness, meditation, prudence, reflection, thought, thoughtfulness, wariness. **2** purpose.

delicacy *n* **1** agreeableness, daintiness, deliciousness, pleasantness, relish, savouriness. **2** bonne bouche, dainty, tidbit. **3** elegance, fitness, lightness, niceness, nicety, smoothness, softness, tenderness. **4** fragility, frailty, slenderness, slightness, tenderness, weakness. **5** carefulness, discrimination, fastidiousness, finesse, nicety, scrupulousness, sensitivity, subtlety, tact. **6** purity, refinement, sensibility.

delicate *adj* **1** agreeable, delicious, pleasant, pleasing, palatable, savoury. **2** elegant,

exquisite, fine, nice. **3** careful, dainty, discriminating, fastidious, scrupulous. **4** fragile, frail, slender, slight, tender, delicate. **5** pure, refined.

adj antonyms harsh, imprecise, strong.

delicious *adj* **1** dainty, delicate, luscious, nice, palatable, savoury. **2** agreeable, charming, choice, delightful, exquisite, grateful, pleasant.

adj antonym unpleasant.

delight *vb* charm, enchant, enrapture, gratify, please, ravish, rejoice, satisfy, transport. • *n* charm, delectation, ecstasy, enjoyment, gladness, gratification, happiness, joy, pleasure, rapture, ravishment, satisfaction, transport.

vb antonyms dismay, displease.

n antonyms dismay, displeasure.

delightful *adj* agreeable, captivating, charming, delectable, enchanting, enjoyable, enrapturing, rapturous, ravishing, transporting.

adj antonym horrible.

delineate *vb* **1** design, draw, figure, paint, sketch, trace. **2** depict, describe, picture, portray.

delineation *n* **1** design, draught, drawing, figure, outline, sketch. **2** account, description, picture, portrayal.

delinquency *n* crime, fault, misdeed, misdemeanour, offence, wrong-doing.

delinquent *adj* negligent, offending. • *n* criminal, culprit, defaulter, malefactor, miscreant, misdoer, offender, transgressor, wrong-doer.

delirious *adj* crazy, demented, deranged, frantic, frenzied, light-headed, mad, insane, raving, wandering.

adj antonym sane.

delirium *n* aberration, derangement, frenzy, hallucination, incoherence, insanity, lunacy, madness, raving, wandering.

deliver *vb* **1** emancipate, free, liberate, release. **2** extricate, redeem, rescue, save. **3** commit, give, impart, transfer. **4** cede, grant, relinquish, resign, yield. **5** declare, emit, promulgate, pronounce, speak, utter. **6** deal, discharge.

deliverance *n* emancipation, escape, liberation, redemption, release.

delivery *n* **1** conveyance, surrender. **2** commitment, giving, rendering, transference, transferral, transmission. **3** elocution, enunciation, pronunciation, speech, utterance. **4** childbirth, confinement, labour, parturition, travail.

dell *n* dale, dingle, glen, valley, ravine.

delude *vb* beguile, cheat, chouse, circumvent, cozen, deceive, dupe, gull, misguide, mislead, overreach, trick.

deluge *vb* drown, inundate, overflow, overwhelm, submerge. • *n* cataclysm, downpour, flood, inundation, overflow, rush.

delusion *n* **1** artifice, cheat, clap-trap, deceit, dodge, fetch, fraud, imposition, imposture, ruse, snare, trick, wile. **2** deception, error, fallacy, fancy, hallucination, illusion, mistake, mockery, phantasm.

delusive *adj* deceitful, deceiving, deceptive, fallacious, illusional, illusionary, illusive.

demand *vb* **1** challenge, exact, require. **2** claim, necessitate, require. **3** ask, inquire. • *n* **1** claim, draft, exaction, requirement, requisition. **2** call, want. **3** inquiry, interrogation, question.

vb antonyms cede, supply.

n antonym supply.

demarcation *n* bound, boundary, confine, distinction, division, enclosure, limit, separation.

demeanour *n* air, bearing, behaviour, carriage, deportment, manner, mien.

demented *adj* crack-brained, crazed, crazy, daft, deranged, dotty, foolish, idiotic, infatuated, insane, lunatic.

adj antonym sane.

dementia *n* idiocy, insanity, lunacy.

demerit *n* delinquency, fault, ill-desert.

demise *vb* **1** alienate, consign, convey, devolve, grant, transfer. **2** bequeath, devise, leave, will. • *n* **1** alienation, conveyance, transfer, transference, transmission. **2** death, decease.

demolish *vb* annihilate, destroy, dismantle, level, over-throw, overturn, pulverize, raze, ruin.

vb antonym build up.

demon *n* devil, fiend, kelpie, goblin, troll.

demoniac, demoniacal *adj* **1** demonic, demonical, devilish, diabolic, diabolical, fiendish, hellish, infernal, Mephistophelean, Mephistophelian, satanic. **2** delirious, distracted, frantic, frenzied, feverish, hysterical, mad, overwrought, rabid.

demonstrate *vb* establish, exhibit, illustrate, indicate, manifest, prove, show.

demonstration *n* display, exhibition, manifestation, show.

demonstrative *adj* **1** affectionate, communicative, effusive, emotional, expansive, expressive, extroverted, open, outgoing, passionate, sentimental, suggestive, talkative, unreserved. **2** absolute, apodictic, certain, conclusive, probative. **3** exemplificative, illustrative.

demoralize *vb* **1** corrupt, debase, debauch, deprave, vitiate. **2** depress, discourage, dishearten, weaken.

demulcent *adj* emollient, lenitive, mild, mollifying, sedative, soothing.

demur *vb* **1** halt, hesitate, pause, stop, waver. **2** doubt, object, scruple. • *n* demurral, hesitance, hesitancy, hesitation, objection, pause, qualm, scruple.

demure *adj* **1** prudish. **2** coy, decorous, grave, modest, priggish, prudish, sedate, sober, staid.

adj antonym forward.

den *n* **1** cavern, cave. **2** haunt, lair, resort, retreat.

denial *n* **1** contradiction, controverting, negation. **2** abjuration, disavowal, disclaimer, disowning. **3** disallowance, refusal, rejection.

denizen *n* citizen, dweller, inhabitant, resident.

denominate *vb* call, christen, designate, dub, entitle, name, phrase, style, term.

denomination *n* **1** appellation, designation, name, style, term, title. **2** class, kind, sort. **3** body, persuasion, school, sect.

denote *vb* betoken, connote, designate, imply, indicate, mark, mean, note, show, signify, typify.

dénouement *n* **1** catastrophe, unravelling. **2** consummation, issue, finale, upshot, conclusion, termination.

denounce *vb* **1** menace, threaten. **2** arraign, attack, brand, censure, condemn, proscribe, stigmatize, upbraid. **3** accuse, inform, denunciate.

vb antonym praise.

dense *adj* **1** close, compact, compressed, condensed, thick. **2** dull, slow, stupid.

adj antonyms clever, sparse.

dent *vb* depress, dint, indent, pit. • *n* depression, dint, indentation, nick, notch.

dentate *adj* notched, serrate, toothed.

denude *vb* bare, divest, strip.

denunciation *n* **1** menace, threat. **2** arraignment, censure, fulmination, invective. **3** exposure.

deny *vb* **1** contradict, gainsay, oppose, refute, traverse. **2** abjure, abnegate, disavow, disclaim, disown, renounce. **3** disallow, refuse, reject, withhold.
vb antonyms admit, allow.

depart *vb* **1** absent, disappear, vanish. **2** abandon, decamp, go, leave, migrate, quit, remove, withdraw. **3** decease, die. **4** deviate, diverge, vary.
vb antonyms arrive, keep to.

department *n* **1** district, division, part, portion, province. **2** bureau, function, office, province, sphere, station. **3** branch, division, subdivision.

departure *n* **1** exit, leaving, parting, removal, recession, removal, retirement, withdrawal. **2** abandonment, forsaking. **3** death, decease, demise, deviation, exit.
n antonym arrival.

depend *vb* hang, hinge, turn.

dependant *n* **1** client, hanger-on, henchman, minion, retainer, subordinate, vassal. **2** attendant, circumstance, concomitant, consequence, corollary.

dependence *n* **1** concatenation, connection, interdependence. **2** confidence, reliance, trust. **3** buttress, prop, staff, stay, support, supporter. **4** contingency, need, subjection, subordination.

dependency *n* **1** adjunct, appurtenance. **2** colony, province.

dependent *adj* **1** hanging, pendant. **2** conditioned, contingent, relying, subject, subordinate.
adj antonym independent.

depict *vb* **1** delineate, limn, outline, paint, pencil, portray, sketch. **2** describe, render, represent.

deplete *vb* drain, empty, evacuate, exhaust, reduce.

deplorable *adj* calamitous, distressful, distressing, grievous, lamentable, melancholy, miserable, mournful, pitiable, regrettable, sad, wretched.

deplore *vb* bemoan, bewail, grieve for, lament, mourn, regret.
vb antonym praise.

deploy *vb* display, expand, extend, open, unfold.

deportment *n* air, bearing, behaviour, breeding, carriage, comportment, conduct, demeanour, manner, mien, port.

depose *vb* **1** break, cashier, degrade, dethrone, dismiss, displace, oust, reduce. **2** avouch, declare, depone, testify.

deposit *vb* **1** drop, dump, precipitate. **2** lay, put. **3** bank, hoard, lodge, put, save, store. **4** commit, entrust. • *n* **1** dregs, lees, precipitate, precipitation, sediment, settlement, settlings, silt. **2** money, pawn, pledge, security, stake.

depositary *n* fiduciary, guardian, trustee.

deposition *n* **1** affidavit, evidence, testimony. **2** deposit, precipitation, settlement. **3** dethroning, displacement, removal.

depository *n* deposit, depot, storehouse, warehouse.

depot *n* depository, magazine, storehouse, warehouse.

depravation *n* **1** abasement, corruption, deterioration, impairing, injury, vitiation. **2** debasement, degeneracy, degeneration, depravity, impairment.

depraved *adj* abandoned, corrupt, corrupted, debased, debauched, degenerate, dissolute, evil, graceless, hardened, immoral, lascivious, lewd, licentious, lost, perverted, profligate, reprobate, shameless, sinful, vicious, wicked.

depravity *n* **1** corruption, degeneracy, depravedness. **2** baseness, contamination, corruption, corruptness, criminality, demoralization, immorality, iniquity, license, perversion, vice, viciousness, wickedness.

depreciate *vb* **1** underestimate, undervalue, underrate. **2** belittle, censure, decry, degrade, disparage, malign, traduce.
vb antonyms appreciate, overrate, praise.

depreciation *n* belittling, censure, derogation, detraction, disparagement, maligning, traducing.

depredation *n* despoiling, devastation, pilfering, pillage, plunder, rapine, robbery, spoliation, theft.

depress *vb* **1** bow, detrude, drop, lower, reduce, sink. **2** abase, abash, degrade, debase, disgrace, humble, humiliate. **3** chill, damp, dampen, deject, discourage, dishearten, dispirit, sadden. **4** deaden, lower.
vb antonym cheer.

depression *n* **1** cavity, concavity, dent, dimple, dint, excavation, hollow, hollowness, indentation, pit. **2** blues, cheerlessness, dejection, dejectedness, despondency, disconsolateness, disheartenment, dispiritedness, dole, dolefulness, downheartedness, dumps, gloom, gloominess, hypochondria, melancholy, sadness, vapours. **3** inactivity, lowness, stagnation.

4 abasement, debasement, degradation, humiliation.

deprivation *n* bereavement, dispossession, loss, privation, spoliation, stripping.

deprive *vb* bereave, denude, despoil, dispossess, divest, rob, strip.
vb antonyms bestow.

depth *n* **1** abyss, deepness, drop, profundity. **2** extent, measure. **3** middle, midst, stillness. **4** astuteness, discernment, penetration, perspicacity, profoundness, profundity, sagacity, shrewdness.

deputation *n* **1** commission, delegation. **2** commissioners, deputies, delegates, delegation, embassies, envoys, legation.

depute *vb* accredit, appoint, authorize, charge, commission, delegate, empower, entrust.

deputy *adj* acting, assistant, vice, subordinate. • *n* agent, commissioner, delegate, envoy, factor, legate, lieutenant, proxy, representative, substitute, viceregent.

derange *vb* **1** confound, confuse, disarrange, disconcert, disorder, displace, madden, perturb, unsettle. **2** discompose, disconcert, disturb, perturb, ruffle, upset. **3** craze, madden, unbalance, unhinge.

derangement *n* **1** confusion, disarrangement, disorder, irregularity. **2** discomposure, disturbance, perturbation. **3** aberration, alienation, delirium, dementia, hallucination, insanity, lunacy, madness, mania.

derelict *adj* **1** abandoned, forsaken, left, relinquished. **2** delinquent, faithless, guilty, neglectful, negligent, unfaithful. • *n* castaway, castoff, outcast, tramp, vagrant, wreck, wretch.

dereliction *n* **1** abandonment, desertion, renunciation. **2** delinquency, failure, faithlessness, fault, neglect, negligence.
n antonyms devotion, faithfulness, fulfillment.

deride *vb* chaff, flout, gibe, insult, jeer, lampoon, mock, ridicule, satirize, scoff, scorn, sneer, taunt.

derision *n* contempt, disrespect, insult, laughter, mockery, ridicule, scorn.
n antonym praise.

derisive *adj* contemptuous, contumelious, mocking, ridiculing, scoffing, scornful.

derivation *n* **1** descent, extraction, genealogy. **2** etymology. **3** deducing, deriving, drawing, getting, obtaining. **4** beginning, foundation, origination, source.

derive *vb* **1** draw, get, obtain, receive. **2** deduce, follow, infer, trace.

derogate *vb* compromise, depreciate, detract, diminish, disparage, lessen.

derogatory *adj* belittling, depreciative, deprecatory, detracting, dishonouring, disparaging, injurious.

descant *vb* amplify, animadvert, dilate, discourse, discuss, enlarge, expatiate. • *n* **1** melody, soprano, treble. **2** animadversion, commentary, remarks. **3** discourse, discussion.

descend *vb* **1** drop, fall, pitch, plunge, sink, swoop. **2** alight, dismount. **3** go, pass, proceed, devolve. **4** derive, issue, originate.

descendants *npl* offspring, issue, posterity, progeny.

descent *n* **1** downrush, drop, fall. **2** descending. **3** decline, declivity, dip, pitch, slope. **4** ancestry, derivation, extraction, genealogy, lineage, parentage, pedigree. **5** assault, attack, foray, incursion, invasion, raid.

describe *vb* **1** define, delineate, draw, illustrate, limn, sketch, specify, trace. **2** detail. **3** depict, explain, narrate, portray, recount, relate, represent. **4** characterize.

description *n* **1** delineation, tracing. **2** account, depiction, explanation, narration, narrative, portrayal, recital, relation, report, representation. **3** class, kind, sort, species.

descry *vb* **1** behold, discover, discern, distinguish, espy, observe, perceive, see. **2** detect, recognize.

desecrate *vb* abuse, pervert, defile, pollute, profane, violate.

desert[1] *n* **1** due, excellence, merit, worth. **2** punishment, reward.

desert[2] *vb* abandon, abscond, forsake, leave, quit, relinquish, renounce, resign, quit, vacate.

desert[3] *adj* barren, desolate, forsaken, lonely, solitary, uncultivated, uninhabited, unproductive, untilled, waste, wild.

deserted *adj* abandoned, forsaken, relinquished.

deserter *n* **1** abandoner, forsaker, quitter, runaway. **2** apostate, backslider, fugitive, recreant, renegade, revolter, traitor, turncoat.

desertion *n* abandonment, dereliction, recreancy, relinquishment.

deserve *vb* earn, gain, merit, procure, win.

desiderate *vb* desire, lack, miss, need, want.

design *vb* **1** brew, concoct, contrive, devise, intend, invent, mean, plan, project, scheme. **2** intend, mean, purpose. **3** delineate, describe, draw, outline, sketch, trace. • *n* **1** aim, device, drift, intent, intention, mark, meaning, object, plan, proposal, project, purport, purpose, scheme, scope. **2** delineation, draught, drawing, outline, plan, sketch. **3** adaptation, artifice, contrivance, invention, inventiveness.

designate *vb* **1** denote, distinguish, indicate, particularize, select, show, specify, stipulate. **2** characterize, define, describe. **3** call, christen, denominate, dub, entitle, name, style. **4** allot, appoint, christen.

designation *n* **1** indication, particularization, selection, specification. **2** class, description, kind. **3** appellation, denomination, name, style, title.

designing *adj* artful, astute, crafty, crooked, cunning, deceitful, insidious, intriguing, Machiavellian, scheming, sly, subtle, treacherous, trickish, tricky, unscrupulous, wily.

desirable *adj* agreeable, beneficial, covetable, eligible, enviable, good, pleasing, preferable.
adj antonyms undesirable.

desire *vb* **1** covet, crave, desiderate, fancy, hanker after, long for, lust after, want, wish, yearn for. **2** ask, entreat, request, solicit. • *n* **1** eroticism, lasciviousness, libidinousness, libido, lust, lustfulness, passion. **2** eagerness, fancy, hope, inclination, mind, partiality, penchant, pleasure, volition, want, wish.

desirous *adj* avid, eager, desiring, longing, solicitous, wishful.

desist *vb* cease, discontinue, forbear, pause, stay, stop.
vb antonyms continue, resume.

desolate *vb* depopulate, despoil, destroy, devastate, pillage, plunder, ravage, ruin, sack. • *adj* **1** bare, barren, bleak, desert, forsaken, lonely, solitary, unfrequented, uninhabited, waste, wild. **2** companionable, lonely, lonesome, solitary. **3** desolated, destroyed, devastated, ravaged, ruined. **4** cheerless, comfortless, companionless, disconsolate, dreary, forlorn, forsaken, miserable, wretched.
adj antonym cheerful.

desolation *n* **1** destruction, devastation, havoc, ravage, ruin. **2** barrenness, bleakness,

desolateness, dreariness, loneliness, solitariness, solitude, wildness. **3** gloom, gloominess, misery, sadness, unhappiness, wretchedness.

despair *vb* despond, give up, lose hope. • *n* dejection, desperation, despondency, disheartenment, hopelessness.
vb antonym hope.
n antonyms cheerfulness, resilience.

despatch *see* **dispatch**.

desperado *n* daredevil, gangster, marauder, ruffian, thug, tough.

desperate *adj* **1** despairing, despondent, desponding, hopeless. **2** forlorn, irretrievable. **3** extreme. **4** audacious, daring, foolhardy, frantic, furious, headstrong, precipitate, rash, reckless, violent, wild, wretched. **5** extreme, great, monstrous, prodigious, supreme.

desperation *n* **1** despair, hopelessness. **2** fury, rage.

despicable *adj* abject, base, contemptible, degrading, low, mean, paltry, pitiful, shameful, sordid, vile, worthless.
adj antonyms laudable, noble.

despise *vb* contemn, disdain, disregard, neglect, scorn, slight, spurn, undervalue.
vb antonyms appreciate, prize.

despite *n* **1** malevolence, malice, malignity, spite. **2** contempt, contumacy, defiance. • *prep* notwithstanding.

despoil *vb* **1** bereave, denude, deprive, dispossess, divest, strip. **2** devastate, fleece, pillage, plunder, ravage, rifle, rob.
vb antonyms adorn, enrich.

despond *vb* despair, give up, lose hope, mourn, sorrow.

despondency *n* blues, dejection, depression, discouragement, gloom, hopelessness, melancholy, sadness.

despondent *adj* dejected, depressed, discouraged, disheartened, dispirited, lowspirited, melancholy.
adj antonyms cheerful, hopeful.

despot *n* **1** autocrat, dictator. **2** oppressor, tyrant.
n antonyms democrat, egalitarian, liberal.

despotic *adj* **1** absolute, arrogant, autocratic, dictatorial, imperious. **2** arbitrary, oppressive, tyrannical, tyrannous.
adj antonyms democratic, egalitarian, liberal, tolerant.

despotism *n* **1** absolutism, autocracy, dictatorship. **2** oppression, tyranny.

destination *n* **1** appointment, decree, destiny, doom, fate, foreordainment, foreordination, fortune, lot, ordination, star. **2** aim, design, drift, end, intention, object, purpose, scope. **3** bourne, goal, harbour, haven, journey's end, resting-place, terminus.

destine *vb* **1** allot, appoint, assign, consecrate, devote, ordain. **2** design, intend, predetermine. **3** decree, doom, foreordain, predestine.

destitute *adj* distressed, indigent, moneyless, necessitous, needy, penniless, penurious, pinched, poor, reduced, wanting.
adj antonyms prosperous, wealthy.

destitution *n* indigence, need, penury, poverty, privation, want.

destroy *vb* **1** demolish, overthrow, overturn, subvert, raze, ruin. **2** annihilate, dissolve, efface, quench. **3** desolate, devastate, devour, ravage, waste. **4** eradicate, extinguish, extirpate, kill, uproot, slay.
vb antonym create.

destruction *n* **1** demolition, havoc, overthrow, ruin, subversion. **2** desolation, devastation, holocaust, ravage. **3** annihilation, eradication, extinction, extirpation. **4** death, massacre, murder, slaughter.
n antonym creation.

destructive *adj* **1** baleful, baneful, deadly, deleterious, detrimental, fatal, hurtful, injurious, lethal, mischievous, noxious, pernicious, ruinous. **2** annihilatory, eradicative, exterminative, extirpative.
adj antonyms creative, positive, productive.

desultory *adj* capricious, cursory, discursive, erratic, fitful, inconstant, inexact, irregular, loose, rambling, roving, slight, spasmodic, unconnected, unmethodical, unsettled, unsystematic, vague, wandering.

detach *vb* **1** disengage, disconnect, disjoin, dissever, disunite, divide, part, separate, sever, unfix. **2** appoint, detail, send.
vb antonym attach.

detail *vb* **1** delineate, depict, describe, enumerate, narrate, particularize, portray, recount, rehearse, relate, specify. **2** appoint, detach, send. • *n* **1** account, narration, narrative, recital, relation. **2** appointment, detachment. **3** item, part.

details *npl* facts, minutiae, particulars, parts.

detain *vb* **1** arrest, check, delay, hinder, hold, keep, restrain, retain, stay, stop. **2** confine.
vb antonym release.

detect *vb* ascertain, catch, descry, disclose, discover, expose, reveal, unmask.

detention *n* confinement, delay, hindrance, restraint, withholding.

deter *vb* debar, discourage, frighten, hinder, prevent, restrain, stop, withhold.

deteriorate *vb* **1** corrupt, debase, degrade, deprave, disgrace, impair, spoil, vitiate. **2** decline, degenerate, depreciate, worsen.

deterioration *n* **1** corruption, debasement, degradation, depravation, vitiation, perversion. **2** caducity, decadence, decay, decline, degeneracy, degeneration, impairment.
n antonym improvement.

determinate *adj* **1** absolute, certain, definite, determined, established, explicit, express, fixed, limited, positive, settled. **2** conclusive, decided, decisive, definitive.

determination *n* **1** ascertainment, decision, deciding, determining, fixing, settlement, settling. **2** conclusion, judgment, purpose, resolution, resolve, result. **3** direction, leaning, tendency. **4** firmness, constancy, effort, endeavour, exertion, grit, persistence, stamina, resoluteness. **5** definition, limitation, qualification.
n antonym irresolution.

determine *vb* **1** adjust, conclude, decide, end, establish, fix, resolve, settle. **2** ascertain, certify, check, verify. **3** impel, incline, induce, influence, lead, turn. **4** decide, resolve. **5** condition, define, limit. **6** compel, necessitate.

detest *vb* abhor, abominate, despise, execrate, hate, loathe, nauseate, recoil from.
vb antonym adore.

detestable *adj* **1** abhorred, abominable, accursed, cursed, damnable, execrable, hateful, odious. **2** disgusting, loathsome, nauseating, offensive, repulsive, sickening, vile.

dethrone *vb* depose, uncrown.

detract *vb* **1** abuse, asperse, belittle, calumniate, debase, decry, defame, depreciate, derogate, disparage, slander, traduce, vilify. **2** deprecate, deteriorate, diminish, lessen.

detraction *n* abuse, aspersion, calumny, censure, defamation, depreciation, derogation, disparagement, slander.

detriment *n* cost, damage, disadvantage, evil, harm, hurt, injury, loss, mischief, prejudice.
n antonym advantage.

detrimental *adj* baleful, deleterious, destructive, harmful, hurtful, injurious, mischievous, pernicious, prejudicial.
adj antonym advantageous.

devastate *vb* desolate, despoil, destroy, lay waste, harry, pillage, plunder, ravage, sack, spoil, strip, waste.

devastation *n* **1** despoiling, destroying, harrying, pillaging, plundering, ravaging, sacking, spoiling, stripping, wasting. **2** desolation, destruction, havoc, pillage, rapine, ravage, ruin, waste.

develop *vb* **1** disentangle, disclose, evolve, exhibit, explicate, uncover, unfold, unravel. **2** cultivate, grow, mature, open, progress.

development *n* **1** disclosure, disentanglement, exhibition, unfolding, unravelling. **2** growth, increase, maturation, maturing. **3** evolution, growth, progression. **4** elaboration, expansion, explication.

deviate *vb* **1** alter, deflect, digress, diverge, sheer off, slew, tack, turn aside, wheel, wheel about. **2** err, go astray, stray, swerve, wander. **3** differ, vary.

deviation *n* **1** aberration, departure, depression, divarication, divergence, turning. **2** alteration, change, difference, variance, variation.

device *n* **1** contraption, contrivance, gadget, invention. **2** design, expedient, plan, project, resort, resource, scheme, shift. **3** artifice, evasion, fraud, manoeuvre, ruse, stratagem, trick, wile. **4** blazon, emblazonment, emblem, sign, symbol, type.

devil *n* **1** demon, fiend, goblin. **2** Apollyon, Belial, Beezelbub, Deuce, Evil One, Lucifer, Mephistopheles, Old Harry, Old Nick, Old Serpent, Prince of Darkness, Satan.

devilish *adj* **1** demon, demonic, demonical, demoniac, demoniacal, diabolic, diabolical, fiendish, hellish, infernal, Mephistophelean, Mephistophelian, satanic. **2** atrocious, barbarous, cruel, malevolent, malicious, malign, malignant, wicked.

devilry *n* **1** devilment, diablerie, mischief. **2** devilishness, fiendishness, wickedness.

devious *adj* **1** deviating, erratic, roundabout, wandering. **2** circuitous, confusing, crooked, labyrinthine, mazy, obscure. **3** crooked, disingenuous, misleading, treacherous.
adj antonyms artless, candid, straightforward.

devise *vb* **1** brew, compass, concert, concoct, contrive, dream up, excogitate, imagine, invent, plan, project, scheme. **2** bequeath, demise, leave, will.

devoid *adj* bare, destitute, empty, vacant, void.

devolve *vb* alienate, consign, convey, deliver over, demise, fall, hand over, make over, pass, transfer.

devote *vb* **1** appropriate, consecrate, dedicate, destine. **2** set apart. **3** addict, apply, give up, resign. **4** consign, doom, give over.

devoted *adj* **1** affectionate, attached, loving. **2** ardent, assiduous, earnest, zealous.
adj antonyms inconstant, indifferent, negligent.

devotee *n* bigot, enthusiast, fan, fanatic, zealot.

devotion *n* **1** consecration, dedication, duty. **2** devotedness, devoutness, fidelity, godliness, holiness, piety, religion, religiousness, saintliness, sanctity. **3** adoration, prayer, worship. **4** affection, attachment, love. **5** ardour, devotedness, eagerness, earnestness, fervour, passion, spirit, zeal.
n antonyms inconstancy, negligence.

devotional *adj* devout, godly, pious, religious, saintly.

devour *vb* **1** gorge, gulp down, swallow eagerly, wolf. **2** annihilate, consume, destroy, expend, spend, swallow up, waste.

devout *adj* **1** devotional, godly, holy, pious, religious, saint-like, saintly. **2** earnest, grave, serious, sincere, solemn.
adj antonyms insincere, uncommitted.

dexterity *n* ability, address, adroitness, aptitude, aptness, art, cleverness, expertness, facility, knack, quickness, readiness, skilfulness, skill, tact.
n antonyms clumsiness, ineptitude.

dexterous, dextrous *adj* able, adept, adroit, apt, deft, clever, expert, facile, handy, nimble-fingered, quick, ready, skilful.
adj antonyms clumsy, inept.

diabolic, diabolical *adj* atrocious, barbarous, cruel, devilish, fiendish, hellish, impious, infernal, malevolent, malign, malignant, satanic, wicked.

diagram *n* chart, delineation, figure, graph, map, outline, plan, sketch.

dialect *n* **1** idiom, localism, provincialism. **2** jargon, lingo, patois, patter. **3** language, parlance, phraseology, speech, tongue.

dialectal *adj* idiomatic, local, provincial.

dialectic, dialectical *adj* analytical, critical, logical, rational, rationalistic.

dialogue *n* **1** colloquy, communication, conference, conversation, converse, intercourse, interlocution. **2** playbook, script, speech, text, words.

diaphanous *adj* clear, filmy, gossamer, pellucid, sheer, translucent, transparent.

diarrhoea *n* (*med*) flux, looseness, purging, relaxation.

diary *n* chronicle, daybook, journal, register.

diatribe *n* **1** disputation, disquisition, dissertation. **2** abuse, harangue, invective, reviling, tirade.
n antonyms praise.

dictate *vb* bid, direct, command, decree, enjoin, ordain, order, prescribe, require. • *n* **1** bidding, command, decree, injunction, order. **2** maxim, precept, rule.

dictation *n* direction, order, prescription.

dictator *n* autocrat, despot, tyrant.

dictatorial *adj* **1** absolute, unlimited, unrestricted. **2** authoritative, despotic, dictatory, domineering, imperious, overbearing, peremptory, tyrannical.

dictatorship *n* absolutism, authoritarianism, autocracy, despotism, iron rule, totalitarianism, tyranny.

diction *n* expression, language, phraseology, style, vocabulary, wording.

dictionary *n* **1** glossary, lexicon, thesaurus, vocabulary, wordbook. **2** encyclopedia.

dictum *n* **1** affirmation, assertion, saying. **2** (*law*) award, arbitrament, decision, opinion.

didactic, didactical *adj* educational, instructive, pedagogic, preceptive.

die *vb* **1** decease, demise, depart, expire, pass on. **2** decay, decline, fade, fade out, perish, wither. **3** cease, disappear, vanish. **4** faint, fall, sink.

diet[1] *vb* **1** eat, feed, nourish. **2** abstain, fast, regulate, slim. • *n* aliment, fare, food, nourishment, nutriment, provision, rations, regimen, subsistence, viands, victuals.

diet[2] *n* assembly, congress, convention, convocation, council, parliament.

differ *vb* **1** deviate, diverge, vary. **2** disagree, dissent. **3** bicker, contend, dispute, quarrel, wrangle.

difference *n* **1** contrariety, contrast, departure, deviation, disagreement, disparity, dissimilarity, dissimilitude, divergence, diversity, heterogeneity, inconformity, nuance, opposition, unlikeness, variation.
2 alienation, altercation, bickering, breach, contention, contest, controversy, debate, disaccord, disagreement, disharmony, dispute, dissension, embroilment, falling out, irreconcilability, jarring, misunderstanding, quarrel, rupture, schism, strife, variance, wrangle. **3** discrimination, distinction.
n antonyms agreement, conformity, uniformity.

different *adj* **1** distinct, nonidentical, separate, unlike. **2** contradistinct, contrary, contrasted, deviating, disagreeing, discrepant, dissimilar, divergent, diverse, incompatible, incongruous, unlike, variant, various. **3** divers, heterogeneous, manifold, many, sundry.
adj antonyms conventional, normal, same, similar, uniform.

difficult *adj* **1** arduous, exacting, hard, Herculean, stiff, tough, uphill. **2** abstruse, complex, intricate, knotty, obscure, perplexing. **3** austere, rigid, unaccommodating, uncompliant, unyielding. **4** dainty, fastidious, squeamish.
adj antonyms easy, straightforward.

difficulty *n* **1** arduousness, laboriousness. **2** bar, barrier, crux, deadlock, dilemma, embarrassment, emergency, exigency, fix, hindrance, impediment, knot, obstacle, obstruction, perplexity, pickle, pinch, predicament, stand, standstill, thwart, trial, trouble. **3** cavil, objection. **4** complication, controversy, difference, embarrassment, embroilment, imbroglio, misunderstanding.
n antonyms advantage, ease.

diffidence *n* **1** distrust, doubt, hesitance, hesitancy, hesitation, reluctance. **2** bashfulness, modesty, sheepishness, shyness, timidity.
n antonym confidence.

diffident *adj* **1** distrustful, doubtful, hesitant, hesitating, reluctant. **2** bashful, modest, over-modest, sheepish, shy, timid.

diffuse[1] *vb* circulate, disperse, disseminate, distribute, intermingle, propagate, scatter, spread, strew.

diffuse[2] *adj* **1** broadcast, dispersed, scattered, sparse, sporadic, widespread. **2** broad, extensive, liberal, profuse, wide. **3** copious, loose, prolix, rambling, verbose, wordy.

diffusion *n* circulation, dispersion, dissemination, distribution, extension, propagation, spread, strewing.

diffusive *adj* **1** expansive, permeating, wide-reaching. **2** spreading, dispersive, disseminative, distributive, distributory.

dig *vb* channel, delve, excavate, grub, hollow out, quarry, scoop, tunnel. • *n* poke, punch, thrust.

digest[1] *vb* **1** arrange, classify, codify, dispose, methodize, systemize, tabulate. **2** concoct. **3** assimilate, consider, contemplate, meditate, ponder, reflect upon, study. **4** master. **5** macerate, soak, steep.

digest[2] *n* **1** code, system. **2** abridgement, abstract, brief, breviary, compend, compendium, conspectus, epitome, summary, synopsis.

dignified *adj* august, courtly, decorous, grave, imposing, majestic, noble, stately. *adj antonym* undignified.

dignify *vb* **1** advance, aggrandize, elevate, ennoble, exalt, promote. **2** adorn, grace, honour. *vb antonyms* degrade, demean.

dignity *n* **1** elevation, eminence, exaltation, excellence, glory, greatness, honour, place, rank, respectability, standing, station. **2** decorum, grandeur, majesty, nobleness, stateliness. **3** preferment. **4** dignitary, magistrate. **5** elevation, height.

digress *vb* depart, deviate, diverge, expatiate, wander.

digression *n* **1** departure, deviation, divergence. **2** episode, excursus.

dilapidate *vb* demolish, destroy, disintegrate, ruin, waste.

dilapidated *adj* decayed, ruined, run down, wasted.

dilapidation *n* decay, demolition, destruction, disintegration, disrepair, dissolution, downfall, ruin, waste.

dilate *vb* **1** distend, enlarge, expand, extend, inflate, swell, tend, widen. **2** amplify, descant, dwell, enlarge, expatiate. *vb antonyms* abbreviate, constrict, curtail.

dilation *n* amplification, bloating, distension, enlargement, expanding, expansion, spreading, swelling.

dilatory *adj* backward, behind-hand, delaying, laggard, lagging, lingering, loitering, off-putting, procrastinating, slack, slow, sluggish, tardy.

dilemma *n* difficulty, fix, plight, predicament, problem, quandary, strait.

diligence *n* activity, application, assiduity, assiduousness, attention, care, constancy, earnestness, heedfulness, industry, laboriousness, perseverance, sedulousness.

diligent *adj* active, assiduous, attentive, busy, careful, constant, earnest, hardworking, indefatigable, industrious, laborious, notable, painstaking, persevering, persistent, sedulous, tireless. *adj antonyms* dilatory, lazy.

dilly-dally *vb* dally, dawdle. delay, lag, linger, loiter, saunter, trifle.

dilute *vb* attenuate, reduce, thin, weaken. • *adj* attenuated, diluted, thin, weak, wishy-washy.

dim *vb* blur, cloud, darken, dull, obscure, sully, tarnish. • *adj* **1** cloudy, dark, dusky, faint, ill-defined, indefinite, indistinct, mysterious, obscure, shadowy. **2** dull, obtuse. **3** clouded, confused, darkened, faint, obscured. **4** blurred, dulled, sullied, tarnished. *vb antonyms* brighten, illuminate. *adj antonyms* bright, distinct.

dimension *n* extension, extent, measure.

dimensions *npl* **1** amplitude, bigness, bulk, capacity, greatness, largeness, magnitude, mass, massiveness, size, volume. **2** measurements.

diminish *vb* **1** abate, belittle, contract, decrease, lessen, reduce. **2** curtail, cut, dwindle, melt, narrow, shrink, shrivel, subside, taper off, weaken. *vb antonyms* enhance, enlarge, increase.

diminution *n* abatement, abridgement, attenuation, contraction, curtailment, decrescendo, cut, decay, decrease, deduction, lessening, reduction, retrenchment, weakening.

diminutive *adj* contracted, dwarfish, little, minute, puny, pygmy, small, tiny. *adj antonyms* big, great, huge, large.

din *vb* beat, boom, clamour, drum, hammer, pound, repeat, ring, thunder. • *n* bruit, clamour, clash, clatter, crash, crashing, hubbub, hullabaloo, hurly-burly, noise, outcry, racket, row, shout, uproar.

dingle *n* dale, dell, glen, vale, valley.

dingy *adj* **1** brown, dun, dusky. **2** bedimmed, colourless, dimmed, dulled, faded, obscure, smirched, soiled, sullied. *adj antonyms* bright, clean.

dint *n* **1** blow, stroke. **2** dent, indentation, nick, notch. **3** force, power.

diocese *n* bishopric, charge, episcopate, jurisdiction, see.

dip *vb* **1** douse, duck, immerse, plunge, souse. **2** bail, ladle. **3** dive, pitch. **4** bend, incline, slope. • *n* **1** decline, declivity, descent, drop, fall. **2** concavity, depression, hole, hollow, pit, sink. **3** bathe, dipping, ducking, sousing, swim.

diplomat *n* diplomatist, envoy, legate, minister, negotiator.

dire *adj* alarming, awful, calamitous, cruel, destructive, disastrous, dismal, dreadful, fearful, gloomy, horrible, horrid, implacable, inexorable, portentous, shocking, terrible, terrific, tremendous, woeful.

direct *vb* **1** aim, cast, level, point, turn. **2** advise, conduct, control, dispose, guide, govern, manage, regulate, rule. **3** command, bid, enjoin, instruct, order. **4** lead, show. **5** address, superscribe. • *adj* **1** immediate, straight, undeviating. **2** absolute, categorical, express, plain, unambiguous. **3** downright, earnest, frank, ingenuous, open, outspoken, sincere, straightforward, unequivocal.

direction *n* **1** aim. **2** tendency. **3** bearing, course. **4** administration, conduct, control, government, management, oversight, superintendence. **5** guidance, lead. **6** command, order, prescription. **7** address, superscription.

directly *adv* **1** absolutely, expressly, openly, unambiguously. **2** forthwith, immediately, instantly, quickly, presently, promptly, soon, speedily.

adv antonym indirectly.

director *n* **1** boss, manager, superintendent. **2** adviser, counsellor, guide, instructor, mentor, monitor.

direful *adj* awful, calamitous, dire, dreadful, fearful, gloomy, horrible, shocking, terrible, terrific, tremendous.

dirge *n* coronach, elegy, lament, monody, requiem, threnody.

dirty *vb* befoul, defile, draggle, foul, pollute, soil, sully. • *adj* **1** begrimed, defiled, filthy, foul, mucky, nasty, soiled, unclean. **2** clouded, cloudy, dark, dull, muddy, sullied. **3** base, beggarly, contemptible, despicable, grovelling, low, mean, paltry, pitiful, scurvy, shabby, sneaking, squalid. **4** disagreeable, rainy, sloppy, uncomfortable.

vb antonyms clean, cleanse.

adj antonyms clean, spotless.

disability *n* disablement, disqualification, impotence, impotency, inability, incapacity, incompetence, incompetency, unfitness, weakness.

disable *vb* **1** cripple, enfeeble, hamstring, impair, paralyse, unman, weaken. **2** disenable, disqualify, incapacitate, unfit.

disabuse *vb* correct, undeceive.

disadvantage *n* **1** disadvantageousness, inconvenience, unfavourableness. **2** damage, detriment, disservice, drawback, harm, hindrance, hurt, injury, loss, prejudice.

n antonyms advantage, benefit.

vb antonyms aid, help.

disadvantageous *adj* **1** inconvenient, inexpedient, unfavourable. **2** deleterious, detrimental, harmful, hurtful, injurious, prejudicial.

disaffect *vb* alienate, disdain, dislike, disorder, estrange.

disaffected *adj* alienated, disloyal, dissatisfied, estranged.

disaffection *n* alienation, breach, disagreement, dislike, disloyalty, dissatisfaction, estrangement, repugnance, ill will, unfriendliness.

disagree *vb* **1** deviate, differ, diverge, vary. **2** dissent. **3** argue, bicker, clash, debate, dispute, quarrel, wrangle.

vb antonym agree.

disagreeable *adj* contrary, displeasing, distasteful, nasty, offensive, unpleasant, unpleasing, unsuitable.

disagreement *n* **1** deviation, difference, discrepancy, dissimilarity, dissimilitude, divergence, diversity, incongruity, unlikeness. **2** disaccord, dissent. **3** argument, bickering, clashing, conflict, contention, dispute, dissension, disunion, disunity, jarring, misunderstanding, quarrel, strife, variance, wrangle.

n antonym agreement.

disallow *vb* **1** forbid, prohibit. **2** disapprove, reject. **3** deny, disavow, disclaim, dismiss, disown, repudiate.

disappear *vb* **1** depart, fade, vanish. **2** cease, dissolve.

vb antonym appear.

disappoint *vb* baffle, balk, deceive, defeat, delude, disconcert, foil, frustrate, mortify, tantalize, thwart, vex.

vb antonyms delight, please, satisfy.

disappointment *n* baffling, balk, failure,

foiling, frustration, miscarriage, mortification, unfulfilment.

disapprobation n blame, censure, condemnation, disapproval, dislike, displeasure, reproof.

disapprove vb 1 blame, censure, condemn, deprecate, dislike. 2 disallow, reject.

disarrange vb agitate, confuse, derange, disallow, dishevel, dislike, dislocate, disorder, disorganize, disturb, jumble, reject, rumple, tumble, unsettle.

disarray n 1 confusion, disorder. 2 dishabille.

disaster n accident, adversity, blow, calamity, casualty, catastrophe, misadventure, mischance, misfortune, mishap, reverse, ruin, stroke.

n antonyms success, triumph.

disastrous adj adverse, calamitous, catastrophic, destructive, hapless, ill-fated, ill-starred, ruinous, unfortunate, unlucky, unpropitious, unprosperous, untoward.

disavow vb deny, disallow, disclaim, disown.

disband vb break up, disperse, scatter, separate.

vb antonyms assemble, band, combine.

disbelief n agnosticism, doubt, nonconviction, rejection, unbelief.

n antonym belief.

disburden vb alleviate, diminish, disburden, discharge, disencumber, ease, free, relieve, rid.

disbursement n expenditure, spending.

discard vb 1 abandon, cast off, lay aside, reject. 2 banish, break, cashier, discharge, dismiss, remove, repudiate.

vb antonyms adopt, embrace, espouse.

discern vb 1 differentiate, discriminate, distinguish, judge. 2 behold, descry, discover, espy, notice, observe, perceive, recognize, see.

discernible adj detectable, discoverable, perceptible.

discerning adj acute, astute, clear-sighted, discriminating, discriminative, eagle-eyed, ingenious, intelligent, judicious, knowing, perspicacious, piercing, sagacious, sharp, shrewd.

discernment n 1 acumen, acuteness, astuteness, brightness, cleverness, discrimination, ingenuity, insight, intelligence, judgement, penetration, perspicacity, sagacity, sharpness, shrewdness. 2 beholding, descrying, discerning, discovery, espial, notice, perception.

discharge vb 1 disburden, unburden, unload. 2 eject, emit, excrete, expel, void. 3 cash, liquidate, pay. 4 absolve, acquit, clear, exonerate, free, release, relieve. 5 cashier, discard, dismiss, sack. 6 destroy, remove. 7 execute, perform, fulfil, observe. 8 annul, cancel, invalidate, nullify, rescind. • n 1 disburdening, unloading. 2 acquittal, dismissal, displacement, ejection, emission, evacuation, excretion, expulsion, vent, voiding. 3 blast, burst, detonation, explosion, firing. 4 execution, fulfilment, observance. 5 annulment, clearance, liquidation, payment, satisfaction, settlement. 6 exemption, liberation, release. 7 flow, flux, execration.

vb antonyms employ, engage, hire.

disciple n 1 catechumen, learner, pupil, scholar, student. 2 adherent, follower, partisan, supporter.

discipline vb 1 breed, drill, educate, exercise, form, instruct, teach, train. 2 control, govern, regulate, school. 3 chasten, chastise, punish. • n 1 culture, drill, drilling, education, exercise, instruction, training. 2 control, government, regulation, subjection. 3 chastisement, correction, punishment.

n antonyms carelessness, negligence.

disclaim vb 1 abandon, disallow, disown, disavow. 2 reject, renounce, repudiate.

vb antonyms accept, acknowledge, claim.

disclose vb 1 discover, exhibit, expose, manifest, uncover. 2 bare, betray, blab, communicate, divulge, impart, publish, reveal, show, tell, unfold, unveil, utter.

vb antonyms conceal, hide.

disclosure n betrayal, discovery, exposé, exposure, revelation, uncovering. • vb discolour, stain, tarnish, tinge.

discomfit vb 1 beat, checkmate, conquer, defeat, overcome, overpower, overthrow, rout, subdue, vanquish, worst. 2 abash, baffle, balk, confound, disconcert, foil, frustrate, perplex, upset.

discomfiture n confusion, defeat, frustration, overthrow, rout, vexation.

discomfort n annoyance, disquiet, distress, inquietude, malaise, trouble, uneasiness, unpleasantness, vexation.

n antonyms comfort, ease.

discommode vb annoy, disquiet, disturb, harass, incommode, inconvenience, molest, trouble.

discompose vb **1** confuse, derange, disarrange, disorder, disturb, embroil, jumble, unsettle. **2** agitate, annoy, chafe, displease, disquiet, fret, harass, irritate, nettle, plague, provoke, ruffle, trouble, upset, vex, worry. **3** abash, bewilder, disconcert, embarrass, fluster, perplex.

disconcert vb **1** baffle, balk, contravene, defeat, disarrange, frustrate, interrupt, thwart, undo, upset. **2** abash, agitate, bewilder, confuse, demoralize, discompose, disturb, embarrass, faze, perplex, perturb, unbalance, worry.

disconnect vb detach, disengage, disjoin, dissociate, disunite, separate, sever, uncouple, unlink.

vb antonyms attach, connect, engage.

disconsolate adj broken-hearted, cheerless, comfortless, dejected, desolate, forlorn, gloomy, heartbroken, inconsolable, melancholy, miserable, sad, sorrowful, unhappy, woeful, wretched.

adj antonyms cheerful, cheery.

discontent n discontentment, displeasure, dissatisfaction, inquietude, restlessness, uneasiness.

n antonym content.

discontinuance n cessation, discontinuation, disjunction, disruption, intermission, interruption, separation, stop, stoppage, stopping, suspension.

discontinue vb cease, intermit, interrupt, quit, stop.

vb antonym continue.

discord n **1** contention, difference, disagreement, dissension, opposition, quarrelling, rupture, strife, variance, wrangling. **2** cacophony, discordance, dissonance, harshness, jangle, jarring.

n antonyms agreement, concord, harmony.

discordance n **1** conflict, disagreement, incongruity, inconsistency, opposition, repugnance. **2** discord, dissonance.

discordant adj **1** contradictory, contrary, disagreeing, incongruous, inconsistent, opposite, repugnant. **2** cacophonous, dissonant, harsh, inharmonious, jangling, jarring.

discount vb **1** allow for, deduct, lower, rebate, reduce, subtract. **2** disregard, ignore, overlook. • n abatement, drawback. **3** allowance, deduction, rebate, reduction.

discourage vb **1** abase, awe, damp, daunt, deject, depress, deject, dismay, dishearten, dispirit, frighten, intimidate. **2** deter, dissuade, hinder. **3** disfavour, discountenance.

vb antonyms encourage, favour, hearten, inspire.

discouragement n **1** disheartening. **2** dissuasion. **3** damper, deterrent, embarrassment, hindrance, impediment, obstacle, wet blanket.

discourse vb **1** expiate, hold forth, lucubrate, sermonize, speak. **2** advise, confer, converse, parley, talk. **3** emit, utter. • n **1** address, disquisition, dissertation, homily, lecture, preachment, sermon, speech, treatise. **2** colloquy, conversation, converse, talk.

discourteous adj abrupt, brusque, curt, disrespectful, ill-bred, ill-mannered, impolite, inurbane, rude, uncivil, uncourtly, ungentlemanly, unmannerly.

adj antonyms courteous, polite, respectful.

discourtesy n abruptness, brusqueness, ill-breeding, impoliteness, incivility, rudeness.

discover vb **1** communicate, disclose, exhibit, impart, manifest, show, reveal, tell. **2** ascertain, behold, discern, espy, see. **3** descry, detect, determine, discern. **4** contrive, invent, originate.

vb antonyms conceal, hide.

discredit vb **1** disbelieve, doubt, question. **2** depreciate, disgrace, dishonour, disparage, reproach. • n **1** disbelief, distrust. **2** disgrace, dishonour, disrepute, ignominy, notoriety, obloquy, odium, opprobrium, reproach, scandal.

vb antonyms believe, credit.

n antonym credit.

discreditable adj derogatory, disgraceful, disreputable, dishonourable, ignominious, infamous, inglorious, scandalous, unworthy.

discreet adj careful, cautious, circumspect, considerate, discerning, heedful, judicious, prudent, sagacious, wary, wise.

adj antonyms careless, indiscreet, tactless.

discrepancy n contrariety, difference, disagreement, discordance, dissonance, divergence, incongruity, inconsistency, variance, variation.

discrete adj **1** discontinuous, disjunct, distinct, separate. **2** disjunctive.

discretion n **1** care, carefulness, caution, circumspection, considerateness,

consideration, heedfulness, judgement, judicious, prudence, wariness. **2** discrimination, maturity, responsibility. **3** choice, option, pleasure, will.
n antonym indiscretion.

discrimination *n* **1** difference, distinction. **2** acumen, acuteness, discernment, insight, judgement, penetration, sagacity.

discriminatory *adj* characteristic, characterizing, discriminating, discriminative, distinctive, distinguishing.

discursive *adj* **1** argumentative, reasoning. **2** casual, cursory, desultory, digressive, erratic, excursive, loose, rambling, roving, wandering, wave.

discus *n* disk, quoit.

discuss *vb* agitate, argue, canvass, consider, debate, deliberate, examine, sift, ventilate.

disdain *vb* deride, despise, disregard, reject, scorn, slight, scout, spurn. • *n* arrogance, contempt, contumely, haughtiness, hauteur, scorn, sneer, superciliousness.
vb antonyms admire, respect.
n antonyms admiration, respect.

disdainful *adj* cavalier, contemptuous, contumelious, haughty, scornful, supercilious.
adj antonyms admiring, respectful.

disease *n* affection, affliction, ail, ailment, complaint, disorder, distemper, illness, indisposition, infirmity, malady, sickness.
n antonym health.

disembarrass *vb* clear, disburden, disencumber, disengage, disentangle, extricate, ease, free, release, rid.

disembodied *adj* bodiless, disincarnate, immaterial, incorporeal, spiritual, unbodied.

disembowel *vb* degut, embowel, eviscerate.

disengage *vb* **1** clear, deliver, discharge, disembarrass, disembroil, disencumber, disentangle, extricate, liberate, release. **2** detach, disjoin, dissociate, disunite, divide, separate. **3** wean, withdraw.

disentangle *vb* **1** loosen, separate, unfold, unravel, untwist. **2** clear, detach, disconnect, disembroil, disengage, extricate, liberate, loose, unloose.
vb antonym entangle.

disfavour *n* **1** disapproval, disesteem, dislike, disrespect. **2** discredit, disregard, disrepute, unacceptableness. **3** disservice, unkindness. •*vb* disapprove, dislike, object, oppose.

disfigure *vb* blemish, deface, deform, injure, mar, spoil.

disfigurement *n* **1** blemishing, defacement, deforming, disfiguration, injury, marring, spoiling. **2** blemish, defect, deformity, scar, spot, stain.

disgorge *vb* **1** belch, cast up, spew, throw up, vomit. **2** discharge, eject. **3** give up, relinquish, surrender, yield.

disgrace *vb* **1** degrade, humble, humiliate. **2** abase, debase, defame, discredit, disfavour, dishonour, disparage, reproach, stain, sully, taint, tarnish. • *n* abomination, disrepute, humiliation, ignominy, infamy, mortification, shame, scandal.
vb antonyms honour, respect.
n antonyms esteem, honour, respect.

disgraceful *adj* discreditable, dishonourable, disreputable, ignominious, infamous, opprobrious, scandalous, shameful.
adj antonyms honourable, respectable.

disguise *vb* cloak, conceal, cover, dissemble, hide, mask, muffle, screen, secrete, shroud, veil. • *n* **1** concealment, cover, mask, veil. **2** blind, cloak, masquerade, pretence, pretext, veneer.
vb antonyms expose, reveal, uncover.

disguised *adj* cloaked, masked, veiled.

disgust *vb* **1** nauseate, sicken. **2** abominate, detest, displease, offend, repel, repulse, revolt. • *n* **1** disrelish, distaste, loathing, nausea. **2** abhorrence, abomination, antipathy, aversion, detestation, dislike, repugnance, revulsion.
vb antonyms delight, gratify, tempt.
n antonyms admiration, liking.

dish *vb* **1** deal out, give, ladle, serve. **2** blight, dash, frustrate, mar, ruin, spoil. • *n* bowl, plate, saucer, vessel.

dishearten *vb* cast down, damp, dampen, daunt, deject, depress, deter, discourage, dispirit.

dished *adj* baffled, balked, disappointed, disconcerted, foiled, frustrated, upset.

dishevelled *adj* disarranged, disordered, messed, tousled, tumbled, unkempt, untidy, untrimmed.

dishonest *adj* cheating, corrupt, crafty, crooked, deceitful, deceiving, deceptive, designing, faithless, false, falsehearted, fraudulent, guileful, knavish, perfidious, slippery, treacherous, unfair, unscrupulous.
adj antonym fair, honest, scrupulous, trustworthy.

dishonesty *n* deceitfulness, faithlessness,

falsehood, fraud, fraudulence, fraudulency, improbity, knavery, perfidious, treachery, trickery.

dishonour *vb* abase, defame, degrade, discredit, disfavour, dishonour, disgrace, disparage, reproach, shame, taint. • *n* abasement, basement, contempt, degradation, discredit, disesteem, disfavour, disgrace, dishonour, disparagement, disrepute, ignominy, infamy, obloquy, odium, opprobrium, reproach, scandal, shame.
vb antonym honour.
n antonym honour.

dishonourable *adj* 1 discreditable, disgraceful, disreputable, ignominious, infamous, scandalous, shameful. 2 base, false, false-hearted, shameless.

disinclination *n* alienation, antipathy, aversion, dislike, indisposition, reluctance, repugnance, unwillingness.

disinfect *vb* cleanse, deodorize, fumigate, purify, sterilize.

disingenuous *adj* artful, deceitful, dishonest, hollow, insidious, insincere, uncandid, unfair, wily.
adj antonyms artless, frank, ingenuous, naïve.

disintegrate *vb* crumble, decompose, dissolve, disunite, pulverize, separate.
vb antonyms combine, merge, unite.

disinter *vb* dig up, disentomb, disinhume, exhume.

disinterested *adj* 1 candid, fair, high-minded, impartial, indifferent, unbiased, unselfish, unprejudiced. 2 generous, liberal, magnanimous.
adj antonyms biased, concerned, interested, prejudiced.

disjoin *vb* detach, disconnect, dissever, dissociate, disunite, divide, part, separate, sever, sunder.

disjointed *adj* desultory, disconnected, incoherent, loose.

disjunction *n* disassociation, disconnection, disunion, isolation, parting, separation, severance.

dislike *vb* abominate, detest, disapprove, disrelish, hate, loathe. • *n* antagonism, antipathy, aversion, disapproval, disfavour, disgust, disinclination, displeasure, disrelish, distaste, loathing, repugnance.
vb antonyms favour, like, prefer.
n antonyms attachment, liking, predilection.

dislocate *vb* 1 disarrange, displace, disturb. 2 disarticulate, disjoint, luxate, slip.

dislodge *vb* dismount, dispel, displace, eject, expel, oust, remove.

disloyal *adj* disaffected, faithless, false, perfidious, traitorous, treacherous, treasonable, undutiful, unfaithful, unpatriotic, untrue.
adj antonym loyal.

disloyalty *n* faithlessness, perfidy, treachery, treason, undutifulness, unfaithfulness.

dismal *adj* 1 cheerless, dark, dreary, dull, gloomy, lonesome. 2 blue, calamitous, doleful, dolorous, funereal, lugubrious, melancholy, mournful, sad, sombre, sorrowful.
adj antonyms bright, cheerful.

dismantle *vb* divest, strip, unrig.
vb antonym assemble.

dismay *vb* affright, alarm, appal, daunt, discourage, dishearten, frighten, horrify, intimidate, paralyse, scare, terrify. • *n* affright, alarm, consternation, fear, fright, horror, terror.
vb antonym encourage.
n antonyms boldness, encouragement.

dismember *vb* 1 disjoint, dislimb, dislocate, mutilate. 2 divide, separate, rend, sever.

dismiss *vb* banish, cashier, discard, discharge, disperse, reject, release, remove.
vb antonyms accept, appoint.

dismount *vb* 1 alight, descend, dismantle, unhorse. 2 dislodge, displace.

disobedient *adj* froward, noncompliant, noncomplying, obstinate, rebellious, refractory, uncomplying, undutiful, unruly, unsubmissive.
adj antonym obedient.

disobey *vb* infringe, transgress, violate.
vb antonym obey.

disobliging *adj* ill-natured, unaccommodating, unamiable, unfriendly, unkind.

disorder *vb* confound, confuse, derange, disarrange, discompose, disorganize, disturb, unsettle, upset. • *n* 1 confusion, derangement, disarrangement, disarray, disorganization, irregularity, jumble, litter, mess, topsy-turvy. 2 brawl, commotion, disturbance, fight, quarrel, riot, tumult. 3 riotousness, tumultuousness, turbulence. 4 ail, ailment, complaint, distemper, illness, indisposition, malady, sickness.
vb antonyms arrange, organize.
n antonym order.

disorderly *adj* **1** chaotic, confused, intemperate, irregular, unmethodical, unsystematic, untidy. **2** lawless, rebellious, riotous, tumultuous, turbulent, ungovernable, unmanageable, unruly.

disorganization *n* chaos, confusion, demoralization, derangement, disorder.
n antonyms order, tidiness.

disorganize *vb* confuse, demoralize, derange, disarrange, discompose, disorder, disturb, unsettle, upset.

disown *vb* **1** disavow, disclaim, reject, renounce, repudiate. **2** abnegate, deny, disallow.
vb antonym accept.

disparage *vb* **1** belittle, decry, depreciate, derogate from, detract from, doubt, question, run down, underestimate, underpraise, underrate, undervalue. **2** asperse, defame, inveigh against, reflect on, reproach, slur, speak ill of, traduce, vilify.
vb antonym praise.

disparagement *n* **1** belittlement, depreciation, derogation, detraction, underrating, undervaluing. **2** derogation, detraction, diminution, harm, impairment, injury, lessening, prejudice, worsening. **3** aspersion, calumny, defamation, reflection, reproach, traduction, vilification. **4** blackening, disgrace, dispraise, indignity, reproach.
n antonym praise.

disparity *n* **1** difference, disproportion, inequality. **2** dissimilarity, dissimilitude, unlikeness.

dispassionate *adj* **1** calm, collected, composed, cool, imperturbable, inexcitable, moderate, quiet, serene, sober, staid, temperate, undisturbed, unexcitable, unexcited, unimpassioned, unruffled. **2** candid, disinterested, fair, impartial, neutral, unbiased.
adj antonyms biased, emotional.

dispatch, despatch *vb* **1** assassinate, kill, murder, slaughter, slay. **2** accelerate, conclude, dismiss, expedite, finish, forward, hasten, hurry, quicken, speed. • *n* **1** dispatching, sending. **2** diligence, expedition, haste, rapidity, speed. **3** completion, conduct, doing, transaction. **4** communication, document, instruction, letter, message, missive, report.

dispel *vb* banish, disperse, dissipate, scatter.
vb antonym give rise to.

dispensation *n* **1** allotment, apportioning, apportionment, dispensing, distributing, distribution. **2** administration, stewardship. **3** economy, plan, scheme, system. **4** exemption, immunity, indulgence, licence, privilege.

dispense *vb* **1** allot, apportion, assign, distribute. **2** administer, apply, execute. **3** absolve, excuse, exempt, exonerate, release, relieve.

disperse *vb* **1** dispel, dissipate, dissolve, scatter, separate. **2** diffuse, disseminate, spread. **3** disappear, vanish.
vb antonym gather.

dispirit *vb* damp, dampen, depress, deject, discourage, dishearten.

dispirited *adj* chapfallen, dejected, depressed, discouraged, disheartened, down-cast, down-hearted.
adj antonym encouraged.

displace *vb* **1** dislocate, mislay, misplace, move. **2** dislodge, remove. **3** cashier, depose, discard, discharge, dismiss, oust, replace, unseat.

display *vb* **1** expand, extend, open, spread, unfold. **2** exhibit, show. **3** flaunt, parade. • *n* **1** exhibition, manifestation, show. **2** flourish, ostentation, pageant, parade, pomp.
vb antonym hide.

displease *vb* **1** disgruntle, disgust, disoblige, dissatisfy, offend. **2** affront, aggravate, anger, annoy, chafe, chagrin, fret, irritate, nettle, pique, provoke, vex.

displeasure *n* **1** disaffection, disapprobation, disapproval, dislike, dissatisfaction, distaste. **2** anger, annoyance, indignation, irritation, pique, resentment, vexation, wrath. **3** injury, offence.
n antonyms gratification, pleasure.

disport *vb* **1** caper, frisk, frolic, gambol, play, sport, wanton. **2** amuse, beguile, cheer, divert, entertain, relax, solace.

disposal *n* **1** arrangement, disposition. **2** conduct, control, direction, government, management, ordering, regulation. **3** bestowment, dispensation, distribution.
n antonym provision.

dispose *vb* **1** arrange, distribute, marshal, group, place, range, rank, set. **2** adjust, determine, regulate, settle. **3** bias, incline, induce, lead, move, predispose. **4** control, decide, regulate, rule, settle. **5** arrange, bargain, compound. **6** alienate, convey, demise, sell, transfer.

disposed *adj* apt, inclined, prone, ready, tending.

disposition *n* **1** arrangement, arranging, classification, disposing, grouping, location, placing. **2** adjustment, control, direction, disposure, disposal, management, ordering, regulation. **3** aptitude, bent, bias, inclination, nature, predisposition, proclivity, proneness, propensity, tendency. **4** character, constitution, humour, native, nature, temper, temperament, turn. **5** inclination, willingness. **6** bestowal, bestowment, dispensation, distribution.

dispossess *vb* **1** deprive, divest, expropriate, strip. **2** dislodge, eject, oust. **3** disseise, disseize, evict, oust.
vb antonyms give, provide.

dispraise *n* **1** blame, censure. **2** discredit, disgrace, dishonour, disparagement, opprobrium, reproach, shame.

disproportion *n* **1** disparity, inadequacy, inequality, insufficiency, unsuitableness. **2** incommensurateness.

disprove *vb* confute, rebel, rebut.
vb antonym prove.

disputable *adj* controvertible, debatable, doubtful, questionable.

dispute *vb* **1** altercate, argue, debate, litigate, question. **2** bicker, brawl, jangle, quarrel, spar, spat, squabble, tiff, wrangle. **3** agitate, argue, debate, ventilate. **4** challenge, contradict, controvert, deny, impugn. **5** contest, struggle for. • *n* **1** controversy, debate, discussion, disputation. **2** altercation, argument, bickering, brawl, disagreement, dissension, spat, squabble, tiff, wrangle.
vb antonym agree.
n antonym agreement.

disqualification *n* disability, incapitation.

disqualify *vb* **1** disable, incapacitate, unfit. **2** disenable, preclude, prohibit.
vb antonyms accept, allow.

disquiet *vb* agitate, annoy, bother, discompose, disturb, excite, fret, harass, incommode, molest, plague, pester, trouble, vex, worry. • *n* anxiety, discomposure, disquietude, disturbance, restlessness, solicitude, trouble, uneasiness, unrest, vexation, worry.

disquisition *n* dissertation, discourse, essay, paper, thesis, treatise.

disregard *vb* contemn, despise, disdain, disobey, disparage, ignore, neglect, overlook, slight. • *n* **1** contempt, ignoring, inattention, neglect, pretermit, oversight, slight. **2** disesteem, disfavour, indifference.
vb antonyms note, pay attention to.
n antonym attention.

disreputable *adj* **1** derogatory, discreditable, dishonourable, disgraceful, infamous, opprobrious, scandalous, shameful. **2** base, contemptible, low, mean, vicious, vile, vulgar.
adj antonyms decent, honourable.

disrepute *n* abasement, degradation, derogation, discredit, disgrace, dishonour, illrepute, odium.

disrespect *n* disesteem, disregard, irreverence, neglect, slight.

disrespectful *adj* discourteous, impertinent, impolite, rude, uncivil, uncourteous.
adj antonym respectful.

dissatisfaction *n* **1** discontent, disquiet, inquietude, uneasiness. **2** disapprobation, disapproval, dislike, displeasure.

dissect *vb* **1** analyze, examine, explore, investigate, scrutinize, sift. **2** cut apart.

dissemble *vb* **1** cloak, conceal, cover, disguise, hide. **2** counterfeit, dissimulate, feign, pretend.

dissembler *n* dissimulator, feigner, hypocrite, pretender, sham.

disseminate *vb* circulate, diffuse, disperse, proclaim, promulgate, propagate, publish, scatter, spread.

dissension *n* contention, difference, disagreement, discord, quarrel, strife, variance.

dissent *vb* decline, differ, disagree, refuse. • *n* difference, disagreement, nonconformity, opposition, recusancy, refusal.
vb antonyms agree, consent.
n antonym agreement.

dissentient *adj* disagreeing, dissenting, dissident, factious.

dissertation *n* discourse, disquisition, essay, thesis, treatise.

disservice *n* disadvantage, disfavour, harm, hurt, ill-turn, injury, mischief.

dissidence *n* disagreement, dissent, nonconformity, sectarianism.

dissimilar *adj* different, divergent, diverse, heterogeneous, unlike, various.
adj antonyms compatible, similar.

dissimilarity *n* dissimilitude, disparity, divergent, diversity, unlikeness, variation.

dissimulation *n* concealment, deceit,

dissembling, double-dealing, duplicity, feigning, hypocrisy, pretence.
n antonym openness.

dissipate *vb* 1 dispel, disperse, scatter. 2 consume, expend, lavish, spend, squander, waste. 3 disappear, vanish.
vb antonym accumulate.

dissipation *n* 1 dispersion, dissemination, scattering, vanishing. 2 squandering, waste. 3 crapulence, debauchery, dissoluteness, drunkenness, excess, profligacy.

dissociate *vb* disjoin, dissever, disunite, divide, separate, sever, sunder.

dissolute *adj* abandoned, corrupt, debauched, depraved, disorderly, dissipated, graceless, lax, lewd, licentious, loose, profligate, rakish, reprobate, shameless, vicious, wanton, wild.
adj antonym virtuous.

dissolution *n* 1 liquefaction, melting, solution. 2 decomposition, putrefaction. 3 death, disease. 4 destruction, overthrow, ruin. 5 termination.

dissolve *vb* 1 liquefy, melt. 2 disorganize, disunite, divide, loose, separate, sever. 3 destroy, ruin. 4 disappear, fade, scatter, vanish. 5 crumble, decompose, disintegrate, perish.

dissonance *n* 1 cacophony, discord, discordance, harshness, jarring. 2 disagreement, discrepancy, incongruity, inconsistency.

dissonant *adj* 1 discordant, grating, harsh, jangling, jarring, unharmonious. 2 contradictory, disagreeing, discrepant, incongruous, inconsistent.

distance *vb* excel, outdo, outstrip, surpass.
• *n* 1 farness, remoteness. 2 aloofness, coldness, frigidity, reserve, stiffness, offishness. 3 absence, separation, space.

distant *adj* 1 far, far-away, remote. 2 aloof, ceremonious, cold, cool, frigid, haughty, reserved, stiff, uncordial. 3 faint, indirect, obscure, slight.
adj antonyms close, friendly.

distaste *n* 1 disgust, disrelish. 2 antipathy, aversion, disinclination, dislike, displeasure, dissatisfaction, repugnance.

distasteful *adj* 1 disgusting, loathsome, nauseating, nauseous, unpalatable, unsavoury. 2 disagreeable, displeasing, offensive, repugnant, repulsive, unpleasant.
adj antonym pleasing.

distemper *n* ail, ailment, complaint, disease,

disorder, illness, indisposition, malady, sickness.

distempered *adj* 1 diseased, disordered. 2 immoderate, inordinate, intemperate, unregulated.

distend *vb* bloat, dilate, enlarge, expand, increase, inflate, puff, stretch, swell, widen.
vb antonym deflate.

distil *vb* 1 dribble, drip, drop. 2 extract, separate.

distinct *adj* 1 definite, different, discrete, disjunct, individual, separate, unconnected. 2 clear, defined, manifest, obvious, plain, unconfused, unmistakable, well-defined.
adj antonyms fuzzy, hazy, indistinct.

distinction *n* 1 discernment, discrimination, distinguishing. 2 difference. 3 account, celebrity, credit, eminence, fame, name, note, rank, renown, reputation, repute, respectability, superiority.

distinctive *adj* characteristic, differentiating, discriminating, distinguishing.
adj antonym common.

distinctness *n* 1 difference, separateness. 2 clearness, explicitness, lucidity, lucidness, perspicuity, precision.

distinguish *vb* 1 characterize, mark. 2 differentiate, discern, discriminate, perceive, recognize, see, single out, tell. 3 demarcate, divide, separate. 4 celebrate, honour, signalize.

distinguished *adj* 1 celebrated, eminent, famous, illustrious, noted. 2 conspicuous, extraordinary, laureate, marked, shining, superior, transcendent.
adj antonyms insignificant, ordinary.

distort *vb* 1 contort, deform, gnarl, screw, twist, warp, wrest. 2 falsify, misrepresent, pervert.

distortion *n* 1 contortion, deformation, deformity, twist, wryness. 2 falsification, misrepresentation, perversion, wresting.

distract *vb* 1 divert, draw away. 2 bewilder, confound, confuse, derange, discompose, disconcert, disturb, embarrass, harass, madden, mystify, perplex, puzzle.

distracted *adj* crazed, crazy, deranged, frantic, furious, insane, mad, raving, wild.
adj antonyms calm, untroubled.

distraction *n* 1 abstraction, bewilderment, confusion, mystification, embarrassment, perplexity. 2 agitation, commotion, discord, disorder, disturbance, division, perturbation, tumult, turmoil. **3** aberration, alienation, delirium, derangement, frenzy, hallucination, incoherence, insanity, lunacy, madness, mania, raving, wandering.

distress *vb* **1** afflict, annoy, grieve, harry, pain, perplex, rack, trouble. **2** distrain, seize, take. • *n* **1** affliction, calamity, disaster, misery, misfortune, adversity, hardship, perplexity, trial, tribulation. **2** agony, anguish, dolour, grief, sorrow, suffering. **3** gnawing, gripe, griping, pain, torment, torture. **4** destitution, indigence, poverty, privation, straits, want.

vb antonyms assist, comfort.

n antonyms comfort, ease, security.

distribute *vb* **1** allocate, allot, apportion, assign, deal, dispense, divide, dole out, give, mete, partition, prorate, share. **2** administer, arrange, assort, class, classify, dispose.

vb antonyms collect, gather in.

distribution *n* **1** allocation, allotment, apportionment, assignment, assortment, dispensation, dispensing. **2** arrangement, disposal, disposition, classification, division, dole, grouping, partition, sharing.

district *n* circuit, department, neighbourhood, province, quarter, region, section, territory, tract, ward.

distrust *vb* disbelieve, discredit, doubt, misbelieve, mistrust, question, suspect. • *n* doubt, misgiving, mistrust, question, suspicion.

vb antonym trust.

n antonym trust.

distrustful *adj* doubting, dubious, suspicious.

disturb *vb* **1** agitate, shake, stir. **2** confuse, derange, disarrange, disorder, unsettle, upset. **3** annoy, discompose, disconcert, disquiet, distract, fuss, incommode, molest, perturb, plague, trouble, ruffle, vex, worry. **4** impede, interrupt, hinder.

vb antonyms calm, quiet, reassure.

disturbance *n* **1** agitation, commotion, confusion, convulsion, derangement, disorder, perturbation, unsettlement. **2** annoyance, discomposure, distraction, excitement, fuss. **3** hindrance, interruption, molestation. **4** brawl, commotion, disorder, excitement, fracas, hubbub, riot, rising, tumult, turmoil, uproar.

n antonyms peace, quiet.

disunion *n* **1** disconnection, disjunction, division, separation, severance. **2** breach, feud, rupture, schism.

disunite *vb* **1** detach, disconnect, disjoin, dissever, dissociate, divide, part, rend, separate, segregate, sever, sunder. **2** alienate, estrange.

disuse *n* discontinuance, disusage, neglect, nonobservance.

n antonym use.

ditch *vb* **1** canalize, dig, excavate, furrow, gouge, trench. **2** abandon, discard, dump, jettison, scrap. • *n* channel, drain, fosse, moat, trench.

divan *n* bed, chesterfield, couch, settee, sofa.

divaricate *vb* diverge, fork, part.

dive *vb* explore, fathom, penetrate, plunge, sound. • *n* **1** drop, fall, header, plunge. **2** bar, den, dump, joint, saloon.

diverge *vb* **1** divide, radiate, separate. **2** divaricate, separate. **3** deviate, differ, disagree, vary.

vb antonyms agree, come together, join.

divers *adj* different, manifold, many, numerous, several, sundry, various.

diverse *adj* different, differing, disagreeing, dissimilar, divergent, heterogeneous, multifarious, multiform, separate, unlike, variant, various, varying.

adj antonym identical.

diversion *n* **1** deflection, diverting. **2** amusement, delight, distraction, enjoyment, entertainment, game, gratification, pastime, play, pleasure, recreation, sport. **3** detour, digression.

diversity *n* **1** difference, dissimilarity, dissimilitude, divergence, unlikeness, variation. **2** heterogeneity, manifoldness, multifariousness, multiformity, variety.

divert *vb* **1** deflect, distract, disturb. **2** amuse, beguile, delight, entertain, exhilarate, give pleasure, gratify, recreate, refresh, solace.

vb antonyms direct, irritate.

divest *vb* **1** denude, disrobe, strip, unclothe, undress. **2** deprive, dispossess, strip.

divide *vb* **1** bisect, cleave, cut, dismember, dissever, disunite, open, part, rend, segregate, separate, sever, shear, split, sunder. **2** allocate, allot, apportion, assign, dispense, distribute, dole, mete, portion, share. **3** compartmentalize, demarcate, partition. **4** alienate, disunite, estrange.

vb antonyms collect, gather, join.

divination *n* **1** augury, divining, foretelling, incantation, magic, sooth-saying, sorcery. **2** prediction, presage, prophecy.

divine *vb* **1** foretell, predict, presage, prognosticate, vaticinate, prophesy. **2** believe, conjecture, fancy, guess, suppose, surmise, suspect, think. • *adj* **1** deiform, godlike, superhuman, supernatural. **2** angelic, celestial, heavenly, holy, sacred, seraphic, spiritual. **3** exalted, exalting, rapturous, supreme, transcendent. • *n* churchman, clergyman, ecclesiastic, minister, parson, pastor, priest.

division *n* **1** compartmentalization, disconnection, disjunction, dismemberment, segmentation, separation, severance. **2** category, class, compartment, head, parcel, portion, section, segment. **3** demarcation, partition. **4** alienation, allotment, apportionment, distribution. **5** breach, difference, disagreement, discord, disunion, estrangement, feud, rupture, variance.
n antonyms agreement, multiplication, unification.

divorce *vb* disconnect, dissolve, disunite, part, put away, separate, sever, split up, sunder, unmarry. • *n* disjunction, dissolution, disunion, division, divorcement, parting, separation, severance.
vb antonyms marry, unify.

divulge *vb* communicate, declare, disclose, discover, exhibit, expose, impart, proclaim, promulgate, publish, reveal, tell, uncover.

dizzy *adj* **1** giddy, vertiginous. **2** careless, heedless, thoughtless.

do *vb* **1** accomplish, achieve, act, commit, effect, execute, perform. **2** complete, conclude, end, finish, settle, terminate. **3** conduct, transact. **4** observe, perform, practise. **5** translate, render. **6** cook, prepare. **7** cheat, chouse, cozen, hoax, swindle. **8** serve, suffice. • *n* **1** act, action, adventure, deed, doing, exploit, feat, thing. **2** banquet, event, feast, function, party.

docile *adj* amenable, obedient, pliant, teachable, tractable, yielding.
adj antonyms truculent, unco-operative.

dock[1] *vb* **1** clip, curtail, cut, deduct, truncate. **2** lessen, shorten.

dock[2] *vb* **1** anchor, moor. **2** join, meet. • *n* anchorage, basin, berth, dockage, dockyard, dry dock, harbour, haven, marina, pier, shipyard, wharf.

doctor *vb* **1** adulterate, alter, cook, falsify, manipulate, tamper with. **2** attend, minister to, cure, heal, remedy, treat. **3** fix, mend, overhaul, repair, service. • *n* **1** general practitioner, GP, healer, leech, medic, physician. **2** adept, savant.

doctrinaire *adj* impractical, theoretical. • *n* ideologist, theorist, thinker.

doctrine *n* article, belief, creed, dogma, opinion, precept, principle, teaching, tenet.

dodge *vb* equivocate, evade, prevaricate, quibble, shuffle. • *n* artifice, cavil, evasion, quibble, subterfuge, trick.

dogged *adj* **1** cantankerous, headstrong, inflexible, intractable, mulish, obstinate, pertinacious, perverse, resolute, stubborn, tenacious, unyielding, wilful. **2** churlish, morose, sour, sullen, surly.
adj antonym irresolute.

dogma *n* article, belief, creed, doctrine, opinion, precept, principle, tenet.

dogmatic *adj* **1** authoritative, categorical, formal, settled. **2** arrogant, confident, dictatorial, imperious, magisterial, opinionated, oracular, overbearing, peremptory, positive. **3** doctrinal.

dole *vb* allocate, allot, apportion, assign, deal, distribute, divide, share. • *n* **1** allocation, allotment, apportionment, distribution. **2** part, portion, share. **3** alms, donation, gift, gratuity, pittance. **4** affliction, distress, grief, sorrow, woe.

doleful *adj* **1** lugubrious, melancholy, piteous, rueful, sad, sombre, sorrowful, woebegone, woeful. **2** cheerless, dark, dismal, dolorous, dreary, gloomy.
adj antonym cheerful.

dolorous *adj* **1** cheerless, dark, dismal, gloomy. **2** doleful, lugubrious, mournful, piteous, rueful, sad, sorrowful, woeful.

dolt *n* blockhead, booby, dullard, dunce, fool, ignoramus, simpleton.

domain *n* **1** authority, dominion, jurisdiction, province, sway. **2** empire, realm, territory. **3** lands, estate. **4** branch, department, region.

domestic *n* charwoman, help, home help, maid, servant. • *adj* **1** domiciliary, family, home, household, private. **2** domesticated. **3** internal, intestine.

domesticate *vb* **1** tame. **2** adopt, assimilate, familiarize, naturalize.

domicile *vb* domiciliate, dwell, inhabit, live, remain, reside. • *n* abode, dwelling, habitation, harbour, home, house, residence.

dominant *adj* ascendant, ascending, chief, controlling, governing, influential, outstanding, paramount, predominant, preeminent, preponderant, presiding, prevailing, ruling.

dominate *vb* **1** control, rule, sway. **2** command, overlook, overtop, surmount.

domineer *vb* **1** rule, tyrannize. **2** bluster, bully, hector, menace, swagger, swell, threaten.

dominion *n* **1** ascendancy, authority, command, control, domain, domination, government, jurisdiction, mastery, rule, sovereign, sovereignty, supremacy, sway. **2** country, kingdom, realm, region, territory.

donation *n* alms, benefaction, boon, contribution, dole, donative, gift, grant, gratuity, largesse, offering, present, subscription.

done *adj* **1** accomplished, achieved, effected, executed, performed. **2** completed, concluded, ended, finished, terminated. **3** carried on, transacted. **4** rendered, translated. **5** cooked, prepared. **6** cheated, cozened, hoaxed, swindled. **7** (*with* **for**) damned, dished, *hors de combat*, ruined, shelved, spoiled, wound up.

donkey *n* **1** ass, mule. **2** dunce, fool, simpleton.

donor *n* **1** benefactor, bestower, giver. **2** donator.

double *vb* **1** fold, plait. **2** duplicate, geminate, increase, multiply, repeat. **3** return. • *adj* **1** binary, coupled, geminate, paired. **2** dual, twice, twofold. **3** deceitful, dishonest, double-dealing, false, hollow, insincere, knavish, perfidious, treacherous, two-faced. • *adv* doubly, twice, twofold. • *n* **1** doubling, fold, plait. **2** artifice, manoeuvre, ruse, shift, stratagem, trick, wile. **3** copy, counterpart, twin.

doublet *n* jacket, jerkin.

doubt *vb* **1** demur, fluctuate, hesitate, vacillate, waver. **2** distrust, mistrust, query, question, suspect. • *n* **1** dubiety, dubiousness, dubitation, hesitance, hesitancy, hesitation, incertitude, indecision, irresolution, question, suspense, uncertainty, vacillation. **2** distrust, misgiving, mistrust, scepticism, suspicion.
vb antonyms believe, trust.
n antonyms belief, certainty, confidence, trust.

doubtful *adj* **1** dubious, hesitating, sceptical, undecided, undetermined, wavering. **2** ambiguous, dubious, enigmatical, equivocal, hazardous, obscure, problematical, unsure. **3** indeterminate, questionable, undecided, unquestioned.
adj antonyms certain, definite.

doubtless *adv* **1** certainly, unquestionably. **2** clearly, indisputably, precisely.

doughty *adj* adventurous, bold, brave, chivalrous, courageous, daring, dauntless, fearless, gallant, heroic, intrepid, redoubtable, valiant, valorous.
adj antonyms cowardly, weak.

douse *see* **dowse**.

dowdy *adj* **1** awkward, dingy, ill-dressed, shabby, slatternly, slovenly. **2** old-fashioned, unfashionable.
adj antonyms dressy, smart, spruce.

dowel *n* peg, pin, pinion, tenon.

dower *n* **1** endowment, gift. **2** dowry. **3** portion, share.

downcast *adj* chapfallen, crestfallen, dejected, depressed, despondent, discouraged, disheartened, dispirited, downhearted, low-spirited, sad, unhappy.
adj antonyms cheerful, elated, happy.

downfall *n* descent, destruction, fall, ruin.

downhearted *adj* chapfallen, crestfallen, dejected, depressed, despondent, discouraged, disheartened, dispirited, downcast, low-spirited, sad, unhappy.
adj antonyms cheerful, enthusiastic, happy.

downright *adj* **1** absolute, categorical, clear, explicit, plain, positive, sheer, simple, undisguised, unequivocal, utter. **2** aboveboard, artless, blunt, direct, frank, honest, ingenuous, open, sincere, straightforward, unceremonious.

downy *adj* lanate, lanated, lanose.

dowse, **douse** *vb* dip, immerse, plunge, souse, submerge.

doze *vb* drowse, nap, sleep, slumber. • *n* drowse, forty-winks, nap.

dozy *adj* drowsy, heavy, sleepy, sluggish.

draft *vb* **1** detach, select. **2** commandeer, conscript, impress. **3** delineate, draw, outline, sketch. • *n* **1** conscription, drawing, selection. **2** delineation, outline, sketch. **3** bill, cheque, order.

drag *vb* **1** draw, haul, pull, tow, tug. **2** trail. **3** linger, loiter. • *n* **1** favour, influence, pull. **2** brake, check, curb, lag, resistance, retardation, scotch, skid, slackening, slack-off, slowing.

draggle vb befoul, bemire, besmirch, dangle, drabble, trail.

dragoon vb compel, drive, force, harass, harry, persecute. • n cavalier, equestrian, horse-soldier.

drain vb 1 milk, sluice, tap. 2 empty, evacuate, exhaust. 3 dry. • n 1 channel, culvert, ditch, sewer, sluice, trench, watercourse. 2 exhaustion, withdrawal.
vb antonym fill.

draught n 1 current, drawing, pulling, traction. 2 cup, dose, drench, drink, potion. 3 delineation, design, draft, outline, sketch.

draw vb 1 drag, haul, tow, tug, pull. 2 attract. 3 drain, suck, syphon. 4 extract, extort. 5 breathe in, inhale, inspire. 6 allure, engage, entice, induce, influence, lead, move, persuade. 7 extend, protract, stretch. 8 delineate, depict, sketch. 9 deduce, derive, infer. 10 compose, draft, formulate, frame, prepare, write.

drawback n 1 defect, deficiency, detriment, disadvantage, fault, flaw, imperfection, injury. 2 abatement, allowance, deduction, discount, rebate, reduction.
n antonym advantage.

drawing n 1 attracting, draining, inhaling, pulling, traction. 2 delineation, draught, outline, picture, plan, sketch.

dread vb apprehend, fear. • adj 1 dreadful, frightful, horrible, terrible. 2 awful, venerable. • n 1 affright, alarm, apprehension, fear, terror. 2 awe, veneration.
n antonyms confidence, security.

dreadful adj 1 alarming, appalling, awesome, dire, direful, fearful, formidable, frightful, horrible, horrid, terrible, terrific, tremendous. 2 awful, venerable.
adj antonym comforting.

dream vb fancy, imagine, think. • n conceit, day-dream, delusion, fancy, fantasy, hallucination, illusion, imagination, reverie, vagary, vision.

dreamer n enthusiast, visionary.
n antonyms pragmatist, realist.

dreamy adj absent, abstracted, fanciful, ideal, misty, shadowy, speculative, unreal, visionary.

dreary adj 1 cheerless, chilling, comfortless, dark, depressing, dismal, drear, gloomy, lonely, lonesome, sad, solitary, sorrowful. 2 boring, dull, monotonous, tedious, tiresome, uninteresting, wearisome.

adj antonyms bright, interesting.

dregs npl 1 feculence, grounds, lees, offscourings, residuum, scourings, sediment, waste. 2 draff, dross, refuse, scum, trash.

drench vb 1 dowse, drown, imbrue, saturate, soak, souse, steep, wet. 2 physic, purge.

dress vb 1 align, straighten. 2 adjust, arrange, dispose. 3 fit, prepare. 4 accoutre, apparel, array, attire, clothe, robe, rig. 5 adorn, bedeck, deck, decorate, drape, embellish, trim. • n 1 apparel, attire, clothes, clothing, costume, garb, guise, garments, habiliment, habit, raiment, suit, toilet, vesture. 2 frock, gown, rob.
vb antonyms disrobe, strip, undress.

dressing n 1 compost, fertilizer, manure. 2 forcemeat, stuffing.

dressy adj flashy, gaudy, showy.
adj antonyms dowdy, scruffy.

drift vb accumulate, drive, float, wander. • n 1 bearing, course, direction. 2 aim, design, intent, intention, mark, object, proposal, purpose, scope, tendency. 3 detritus, deposit, diluvium. 4 gallery, passage, tunnel. 5 current, rush, sweep. 6 heap, pile.

drill[1] vb 1 bore, perforate, pierce. 2 discipline, exercise, instruct, teach, train. • n 1 borer. 2 discipline, exercise, training.

drill[2] n channel, furrow, trench.

drink vb 1 imbibe, sip, swill. 2 carouse, indulge, revel, tipple, tope. 3 swallow, quaff. 4 absorb. • n 1 beverage, draught, liquid, potation, potion. 2 dram, nip, sip, snifter, refreshment.

drip vb 1 dribble, drop, leak, trickle. 2 distil, filter, percolate. 3 ooze, reek, seep, weep. • n 1 dribble, drippings, drop, leak, leakage, leaking, trickle. 2 bore, nuisance, wet blanket.

drive vb 1 hurl, impel, propel, send, shoot, thrust. 2 actuate, incite, press, urge. 3 coerce, compel, constrain, force, harass, oblige, overburden, press, rush. 4 go, guide, ride, travel. 5 aim, intend. • n 1 effort, energy, pressure. 2 airing, ride. 3 road.

drivel vb babble, blether, dote, drool, slaver, slobber. • n balderdash, drivelling, fatuity, nonsense, prating, rubbish, slaver, stuff, twaddle.

drizzle vb mizzle, rain, shower, sprinkle. • n haar, mist, mizzle, rain, sprinkling.

droll adj 1 comic, comical, farcical, funny, jocular, ludicrous, laughable, ridiculous. 2 amusing, diverting, facetious, odd, quaint, queer, waggish. • *n* buffoon, clown, comedian, fool, harlequin, jester, punch, Punchinello, scaramouch, wag, zany.

drollery *n* archness, buffoonery, fun, humour, jocularity, pleasantry, waggishness, whimsicality.

drone *vb* **1** dawdle, drawl, idle, loaf, lounge. **2** hum. • *n* idler, loafer, lounger, sluggard.

drool *vb* drivel, slaver.

droop *vb* **1** fade, wilt, wither. **2** decline, fail, faint, flag, languish, sink, weaken. **3** bend, hang.

vb antonyms rise, straighten.

drop *vb* **1** distil, drip, shed. **2** decline, depress, descend, dump, lower, sink. **3** abandon, desert, forsake, forswear, leave, omit, relinquish, quit. **4** cease, discontinue, intermit, remit. **5** fall, precipitate. • *n* **1** bead, droplet, globule. **2** earring, pendant.

vb antonyms mount, rise.

dross *n* **1** cinder, lees, recrement, scoria, scum, slag. **2** refuse, waste.

drought *n* aridity, drouth, dryness, thirstiness.

drove *n* **1** flock, herd. **2** collection, company, crowd.

drown *vb* **1** deluge, engulf, flood, immerse, inundate, overflow, sink, submerge, swamp. **2** overcome, overpower, overwhelm.

drowse *vb* doze, nap, sleep, slumber, snooze. • *n* doze, forty winks, nap, siesta, sleep, snooze.

drowsy *adj* **1** dozy, sleepy. **2** comatose, lethargic, stupid. **3** lulling, soporific.

adj antonyms alert, awake.

drub *vb* bang, beat, cane, cudgel, flog, hit, knock, pommel, pound, strike, thrash, thump, whack.

drubbing *n* beating, caning, cudgelling, flagellation, flogging, pommelling, pounding, thrashing, thumping, whacking.

drudge *vb* grub, grind, plod, slave, toil, work. • *n* grind, hack, hard worker, menial, plodder, scullion, servant, slave, toiler, worker.

vb antonyms idle, laze.

n antonyms shirker, lazybones

drug *vb* **1** dose, medicate. **2** disgust, surfeit. • *n* **1** medicine, physic, remedy. **2** poison.

drunk *adj* **1** drunken, inebriated, intoxicated, maudlin, soaked, tiddly, tipsy. **2** ablaze, aflame, delirious, fervent, suffused. • *n* **1** alcoholic, boozer, carouser, dipsomaniac, drinker, drunkard, inebriate, lush, reveller,

soak, sot, tippler, toper. **2** bacchanal, bender, binge.

adj antonym sober.

dry *vb* dehydrate, desiccate, drain, parch. • *adj* **1** desiccated, dried, juiceless, sapless, unmoistened. **2** arid, droughty, parched. **3** drouthy, thirsty. **4** barren, dull, insipid, jejune, plain, pointless, tame, tedious, tiresome, unembellished, uninteresting, vapid. **5** cutting, keen, sarcastic, severe, sharp, sly.

vb antonyms soak, wet.

adj antonyms interesting, sweet, wet.

dub *vb* call, christen, denominate, designate, entitle, name, style, term.

dubious *adj* **1** doubtful, fluctuating, hesitant, irresolute, skeptical, uncertain, undecided, unsettled, wavering. **2** ambiguous, doubtful, equivocal, improbable, questionable, uncertain.

adj antonyms certain, reliable, trustworthy.

duck *vb* **1** dip, dive, immerse, plunge, submerge, souse. **2** bend, bow, dodge, stoop.

duct *n* **1** canal, channel, conduit, pipe, tube. **2** blood-vessel.

ductile *adj* **1** compliant, docile, facile, tractable, yielding. **2** flexible, malleable, pliant. **3** extensible, tensile.

dudgeon *n* anger, indignation, ill will, ire, malice, resentment, umbrage, wrath.

due *adj* **1** owed, owing. **2** appropriate, becoming, befitting, bounden, fit, proper, suitable, right. • *adv* dead, direct, directly, exactly, just, right, squarely, straight. • *n* claim, debt, desert, right.

dulcet *adj* **1** delicious, honeyed, luscious, sweet. **2** harmonious, melodious. **3** agreeable, charming, delightful, pleasant, pleasing.

dull *vb* **1** blunt. **2** benumb, besot, deaden, hebetate, obtund, paralyse, stupefy. **3** dampen, deject, depress, discourage, dishearten, dispirit. **4** allay, alleviate, assuage, mitigate, moderate, quiet, soften. **5** deaden, dim, sully, tarnish. • *adj* **1** blockish, brutish, doltish, obtuse, stolid, stupid, unintelligent. **2** apathetic, callous, dead, insensible, passionless, phlegmatic, unfeeling, unimpassioned, unresponsive. **3** heavy, inactive, inanimate, inert, languish, lifeless, slow, sluggish, torpid. **4** blunt, dulled, hebetate, obtuse. **5** cheerless, dismal, dreary, gloomy, sad, sombre. **6** dim, lack-lustre, lustreless, matt, obscure, opaque, tarnished. **7** dry, flat, insipid, irksome, jejune, prosy, tedious, tiresome, uninteresting, wearisome.

vb antonyms brighten, sharpen, stimulate.

adj antonyms alert, bright, clear, exciting, sharp.

duly *adv* **1** befittingly, decorously, fitly, properly, rightly. **2** regularly.

dumb *adj* inarticulate, mute, silent, soundless, speechless, voiceless.

adj antonym intelligent.

dumbfound *vb* amaze, astonish, astound, bewilder, confound, confuse, nonplus, pose.

dumps *npl* blues, dejection, depression, despondency, gloom, gloominess, melancholy, sadness.

dun[1] *adj* greyish-brown, brown, drab.

dun[2] *vb* beset, importune, press, urge.

dunce *n* ass, block, blockhead, clodpole, dolt, donkey, dullard, dunderhead, fool, goose, halfwit, ignoramus, jackass, lackwit, loon, nincompoop, numskull, oaf, simpleton, thickhead, witling.

n antonyms brain, intellectual.

dupe *vb* beguile, cheat, chouse, circumvent, cozen, deceive, delude, gull, hoodwink, outwit, overreach, swindle, trick. • *n* gull, simpleton.

duplicate *vb* copy, double, repeat, replicate, reproduce. • *adj* doubled, twofold. • *n* copy, counterpart, facsimile, replica, transcript.

duplicity *n* artifice, chicanery, circumvention, deceit, deception, dishonesty, dissimulation, double-dealing, falseness, fraud, guile, hypocrisy, perfidy.

durable *adj* abiding, constant, continuing, enduring, firm, lasting, permanent, persistent, stable.

adj antonyms fragile, impermanent, perishable, weak.

duration *n* **1** continuance, continuation, permanency, perpetuation, prolongation. **2** period, time.

duress *n* **1** captivity, confinement, constraint, durance, hardship, imprisonment, restraint. **2** compulsion.

dusky *adj* **1** cloudy, darkish, dim, murky, obscure, overcast, shady, shadowy. **2** dark, swarthy, tawny.

adj antonyms bright, light, white.

dutiful *adj* **1** duteous, obedient, submissive. **2** deferential, respectful, reverential.

duty *n* **1** allegiance, devoirs, obligation, responsibility, reverence. **2** business, engagement, function, office, service. **3** custom, excise, impost, tariff, tax, toll.

dwarf *vb* **1** dominate, overshadow, overlook. **2** lower, stunt. • *n* **1** achondroplasic, little person, (*derog*, *off*) midget, person of short stature, person with dwarfism. **2** (*myth*) gnome, fairy.

adj antonym large.

dwell *vb* abide, inhabit, live, lodge, remain, reside, rest, sojourn, stay, stop, tarry, tenant.

dwelling *n* abode, cot, domicile, dugout, establishment, habitation, home, house, hutch, lodging, mansion, quarters, residence.

dwindle *vb* **1** decrease, diminish, lessen, shrink. **2** decay, decline, deteriorate, pine, sink, waste away.

vb antonym increase.

dye *vb* colour, stain, tinge. • *n* cast, colour, hue, shade, stain, tinge, tint.

dying *adj* **1** expiring. **2** mortal, perishable. • *n* death, decease, demise, departure, dissolution, exit.

adj antonyms coming, reviving.

dynasty *n* dominion, empire, government, rule, sovereignty.

dyspepsia *n* indigestion.

E

eager *adj* **1** agog, avid, anxious, desirous, fain, greedy, impatient, keen, longing, yearning. **2** animated, ardent, earnest, enthusiastic, fervent, fervid, forward, glowing, hot, impetuous, sanguine, vehement, zealous.
adj antonyms apathetic, unenthusiastic.

eagerness *n* ardour, avidity, earnestness, enthusiasm, fervour, greediness, heartiness, hunger, impatience, impetuosity, intentness, keenness, longing, thirst, vehemence, yearning, zeal.

eagle-eyed *adj* discerning, hawk-eyed, sharp-sighted.

ear¹ *n* attention, hearing, heed, regard.

ear² *n* head, spike.

early *adj* **1** opportune, seasonable, timely. **2** forward, premature. **3** dawning, matutinal. • *adv* anon, beforehand, betimes, ere, seasonably, shortly, soon.
adv antonym late.

earn *vb* **1** acquire, gain, get, obtain, procure, realize, reap, win. **2** deserve, merit.
vb antonyms lose, spend.

earnest *adj* **1** animated, ardent, eager, cordial, fervent, fervid, glowing, hearty, impassioned, importune, warm, zealous. **2** fixed, intent, steady. **3** sincere, true, truthful. **4** important, momentous, serious, weighty. • *n* **1** reality, seriousness, truth. **2** foretaste, pledge, promise. **3** handsel, payment.
adj antonyms apathetic, flippant, unenthusiastic.

earnings *npl* allowance, emoluments, gains, income, pay, proceeds, profits, remuneration, reward, salary, stipend.
n antonyms expenses, outgoings.

earth *n* **1** globe, orb, planet, world. **2** clay, clod, dirt, glebe, ground, humus, land, loam, sod, soil, turf. **3** mankind, world.

earthborn *adj* abject, base, earthly, grovelling, low, mean, unspiritual.

earthly *adj* **1** terrestrial. **2** base, carnal, earthborn, low, gross, grovelling, sensual, sordid, unspiritual, worldly. **3** bodily, material, mundane, natural, secular, temporal.
adj antonyms heavenly, spiritual.

earthy *adj* **1** clayey, earth-like, terrene.

2 earthly, terrestrial. **3** coarse, gross, material, unrefined.
adj antonyms cultured, refined.

ease *vb* **1** disburden, disencumber, pacify, quiet, relieve, still. **2** abate, allay, alleviate, appease, assuage, diminish, mitigate, soothe. **3** loosen, release. **4** facilitate, favour. • *n* **1** leisure, quiescence, repose, rest. **2** calmness, content, contentment, enjoyment, happiness, peace, quiet, quietness, quietude, relief, repose, satisfaction, serenity, tranquillity. **3** easiness, facility, readiness. **4** flexibility, freedom, liberty, lightness, naturalness, unconcern, unconstraint. **5** comfort, elbowroom.
n antonyms difficulty, discomfort.
vb antonyms hinder, retard, torment.

easy *adj* **1** light. **2** careless, comfortable, contented, effortless, painless, quiet, satisfied, tranquil, untroubled. **3** accommodating, complaisant, compliant, complying, facile, indolent, manageable, pliant, submissive, tractable, yielding. **4** graceful, informal, natural, unconstrained. **5** flowing, ready, smooth, unaffected. **6** gentle, lenient, mild, moderate. **7** affluent, loose, unconcerned, unembarrassed.
adj antonyms demanding, difficult, fast, impossible, intolerant.

eat *vb* **1** chew, consume, devour, engorge, ingest, ravage, swallow. **2** corrode, demolish, erode. **3** breakfast, dine, feed, lunch, sup.

eatable *adj* edible, esculent, harmless, wholesome.

ebb *vb* **1** abate, recede, retire, subside. **2** decay, decline, decrease, degenerate, deteriorate, sink, wane. • *n* **1** refluence, reflux, regress, regression, retrogression, return. **2** caducity, decay, decline, degeneration, deterioration, wane, waning. **3** abatement, decrease, decrement, diminution.
vb antonyms increase, rise.
n antonyms flow, increase, rising.

ebullience *n* ebullition, effervescence. **2** burst, bursting, overenthusiasm, overflow, rush, vigour.

ebullition *n* **1** boiling, bubbling. **2** effervescence, fermentation. **3** burst, fit, outbreak, outburst, paroxysm.

eccentric *adj* **1** decentred, parabolic. **2** aberrant, abnormal, anomalous, cranky, erratic, fantastic, irregular, odd, outlandish, peculiar, singular, strange, uncommon, unnatural, wayward, whimsical. • *n* crank, curiosity, original.

adj antonyms normal, sane.

eccentricity *n* **1** ellipticity, flattening, flatness, oblateness. **2** aberration, irregularity, oddity, oddness, peculiarity, singularity, strangeness, waywardness.

n antonyms normalcy, normality, ordinariness.

ecclesiastic¹, ecclesiastical *adj* churchish, churchly, clerical, ministerial, nonsecular, pastoral, priestly, religious, sacerdotal.

ecclesiastic² *n* chaplain, churchman, clergyman, cleric, clerk, divine, minister, parson, pastor, priest, reverend, shepherd.

echo *vb* **1** reply, resound, reverberate, ring. **2** re-echo, repeat. • *n* **1** answer, repetition, reverberation. **2** imitation.

éclat *n* acclamation, applause, brilliancy, effect, glory, lustre, pomp, renown, show, splendour.

eclipse *vb* **1** cloud, darken, dim, obscure, overshadow, veil. **2** annihilate, annul, blot out, extinguish. • *n* **1** clouding, concealment, darkening, dimming, disappearance, hiding, obscuration, occultation, shrouding, vanishing, veiling. **2** annihilation, blotting out, destruction, extinction, extinguishment, obliteration.

economize *vb* **1** husband, manage, save. **2** retrench.

vb antonym squander.

economy *n* **1** frugality, husbandry, parsimony, providence, retrenchment, saving, skimping, stinginess, thrift, thriftiness. **2** administration, arrangement, management, method, order, plan, regulation, system. **3** dispensation.

n antonym improvidence.

ecstasy *n* **1** frenzy, madness, paroxysm, trance. **2** delight, gladness, joy, rhapsody, rapture, ravishment, transport.

n antonym torment.

eddy *vb* **1** gurgle, surge, spin, swirl, whirl. • *n* countercurrent. **2** swirl, vortex, whirlpool.

edge *vb* **1** sharpen. **2** border, fringe, rim. • *n* **1** border, brim, brink, bound, crest, fringe, hem, lip, margin, rim, verge. **2** animation, intensity, interest, keenness, sharpness,

zest. **3** acrimony, bitterness, gall, sharpness, sting.

edging *n* border, frill, fringe, trimming.

edible *adj* eatable, esculent, harmless, wholesome.

edict *n* act, command, constitution, decision, decree, law, mandate, manifesto, notice, order, ordinance, proclamation, regulation, rescript, statute.

edifice *n* building, fabric, habitation, house, structure.

edify *vb* educate, elevate, enlightenment, improve, inform, instruct, nurture, teach, upbuild.

edition *n* impression, issue, number.

educate *vb* breed, cultivate, develop, discipline, drill, edify, exercise, indoctrinate, inform, instruct, mature, nurture, rear, school, teach, train.

educated *adj* cultured, lettered, literate.

education *n* breeding, cultivation, culture, development, discipline, drilling, indoctrination, instruction, nurture, pedagogics, schooling, teaching, training, tuition.

educe *vb* bring out, draw out, elicit, evolve, extract.

eerie *adj* awesome, fearful, frightening, strange, uncanny, weird.

adj antonyms natural, ordinary.

efface *vb* blot, blot out, cancel, delete, destroy, erase, expunge, obliterate, remove, sponge.

effect *vb* **1** cause, create, effectuate, produce. **2** accomplish, achieve, carry, compass, complete, conclude, consummate, contrive, do, execute, force, negotiate, perform, realize, work. • *n* **1** consequence, event, fruit, issue, outcome, result. **2** efficiency, fact, force, power, reality. **3** validity, weight. **4** drift, import, intent, meaning, purport, significance, tenor.

effective *adj* **1** able, active, adequate, competent, convincing, effectual, sufficient. **2** cogent, efficacious, energetic, forcible, potent, powerful.

adj antonyms ineffective, useless.

effects *npl* chattels, furniture, goods, movables, property.

effectual *adj* **1** operative, successful. **2** active, effective, efficacious, efficient.

effectuate *vb* accomplish, achieve, complete, do, effect, execute, fulfil, perform, secure.

effeminate *adj* **1** delicate, feminine, soft,

tender, timorous, unmanly, womanish, womanlike, womanly. **2** camp.

effervesce *vb* bubble, ferment, foam, froth.

effete *adj* **1** addle, barren, fruitless, sterile, unfruitful, unproductive, unprolific. **2** decayed, exhausted, spent, wasted.

efficacious *adj* active, adequate, competent, effective, effectual, efficient, energetic, operative, powerful.

efficacy *n* ability, competency, effectiveness, efficiency, energy, force, potency, power, strength, vigour, virtue.

efficient *adj* **1** active, capable, competent, effective, effectual, efficacious, operative, potent. **2** able, energetic, ready, skilful.
adj antonym inefficient.

effigy *n* figure, image, likeness, portrait, representation, statue.

effloresce *vb* bloom, flower.

efflorescence *n* blooming, blossoming, flowering.

effluence *n* discharge, efflux, effluvium, emanation, emission, flow, outflow, outpouring.

effort *n* application, attempt, endeavour, essay, exertion, pains, spurt, strain, strife, stretch, struggle, trial, trouble.

effrontery *n* assurance, audacity, boldness, brass, disrespect, hardihood, impudence, incivility, insolence, presumption, rudeness, sauciness, shamelessness.

effulgent *adj* burning, beaming, blazing, bright, brilliant, dazzling, flaming, glowing, lustrous, radiant, refulgent, resplendent, shining, splendid.

effusion *n* **1** discharge, efflux, emission, gush, outpouring. **2** shedding, spilling, waste. **3** address, speech, talk, utterance.

egg *vb* (*with* on) **1** encourage, incite, instigate, push, stimulate, urge. **2** harass, harry, provoke.

ego *n* id, self, me, subject, superego.

egotism *n* **1** self-admiration, self-assertion, self-commendation, self-conceit, self-esteem, self-importance, self-praise. **2** egoism, selfishness.

egotistic, egotistical *adj* bumptious, conceited, egoistical, opinionated, self-asserting, self-admiring, self-centred, self-conceited, self-important, self-loving, vain.

egregious *adj* appalling, flagrant, glaring, grievous, gross, heinous, horrifying, insufferable, monstrous, outrageous, outstandingly bad.

egress *n* departure, emergence, exit, outlet, way out.

eject *vb* **1** belch, discharge, disgorge, emit, evacuate, puke, spew, spit, spout, spurt, void, vomit. **2** bounce, cashier, discharge, dismiss, disposes, eliminate, evict, expel, fire, oust. **3** banish, reject, throw out.

elaborate *vb* develop, improve, mature, produce, refine, ripen. • *adj* complicated, decorated, detailed, dressy, laboured, laborious, ornate, perfected, studied.
adj antonyms plain, simple.
vb antonyms précis, simplify.

elapse *vb* go, lapse, pass.

elastic *adj* **1** rebounding, recoiling, resilient, springy. **2** buoyant, recuperative.
adj antonym rigid.

elated *adj* animated, cheered, elate, elevated, excited, exhilarated, exultant, flushed, puffed up, roused.
adj antonym downcast.

elbow *vb* crowd, force, hustle, jostle, nudge, push, shoulder. • *n* angle, bend, corner, flexure, joining, turn.

elder *adj* **1** older, senior. **2** ranking. **3** ancient, earlier, older. • *n* **1** ancestor, senior. **2** presbyter, prior, senator.
adj antonym younger.

elect *vb* appoint, choose, cull, designate, pick, prefer, select. • *adj* **1** choice, chosen, picked, selected. **2** appointed, elected. **3** predestinated, redeemed.

election *n* **1** appointment, choice, preference, selection. **2** alternative, freedom, freewill, liberty. **3** predestination.

elector *n* chooser, constituent, selector, voter.

electrify *vb* **1** charge, galvanize. **2** astonish, enchant, excite, rouse, startle, stir, thrill.
vb antonym bore.

elegance, elegancy *n* **1** beauty, grace, propriety, symmetry. **2** courtliness, daintiness, gentility, nicety, polish, politeness, refinement, taste.

elegant *adj* **1** beautiful, chaste, classical, dainty, graceful, fine, handsome, neat, symmetrical, tasteful, trim, well-made, well-proportioned. **2** accomplished, courtly, cultivated, fashionable, genteel, polished, polite, refined.
adj antonym inelegant.

elegiac *adj* dirgeful, mournful, plaintive, sorrowful.

elegy *n* dirge, epicedium, lament, ode, threnody.

element *n* **1** basis, component, constituent, factor, germ, ingredient, part, principle, rudiment, unit. **2** environment, milieu, sphere.

elementary *adj* **1** primordial, simple, uncombined, uncomplicated, uncompounded. **2** basic, component, fundamental, initial, primary, rudimental, rudimentary.
adj antonyms advanced, complex.

elevate *vb* **1** erect, hoist, lift, raise. **2** advance, aggrandize, exalt, promote. **3** dignify, ennoble, exalt, greaten, improve, refine. **4** animate, cheer, elate, excite, exhilarate, rouse.
vb antonyms lessen, lower.

elfin *adj* elflike, elvish, mischievous, weird.

elicit *vb* **1** draw out, educe, evoke, extort, fetch, obtain, pump, wrest, wring. **2** deduce, educe.

eligible *adj* **1** desirable, preferable. **2** qualified, suitable, worthy.
adj antonym ineligible.

eliminate *vb* **1** disengage, eradicate, exclude, expel, remove, separate. **2** ignore, omit, reject.
vb antonym accept.

ellipsis *n* gap, hiatus, lacuna, omission.

elliptical *adj* **1** oval. **2** defective, incomplete.

elocution *n* declamation, delivery, oratory, rhetoric, speech, utterance.

elongate *vb* draw, draw out, extend, lengthen, protract, stretch.

elope *vb* abscond, bolt, decamp, disappear, leave.

eloquence *n* fluency, oratory, rhetoric.

else *adv* besides, differently, otherwise.

elucidate *vb* clarify, demonstrate, explain, expound, illuminate, illustrate, interpret, unfold.

elucidation *n* annotation, clarification, comment, commentary, elucidating, explaining, explanation, exposition, gloss, scholium.

elude *vb* **1** avoid, escape, evade, shun, slip. **2** baffle, balk, disappoint, disconcert, escape, foil, frustrate, thwart.

elusive *adj* **1** deceptive, deceitful, delusive, evasive, fallacious, fraudulent, illusory. **2** equivocatory, equivocating, shuffling.

Elysian *adj* blissful, celestial, delightful, enchanting, heavenly, ravishing, seraphic.

emaciation *n* attenuation, lankness, leanness, meagreness, tabes, tabescence, thinness.

emanate *vb* arise, come, emerge, flow, issue, originate, proceed, spring.

emancipate *vb* deliver, discharge, disenthral, enfranchise, free, liberate, manumit, release, unchain, unfetter, unshackle.
vb antonym enslave.

emancipation *n* deliverance, enfranchisement, deliverance, freedom, liberation, manumission, release.

emasculate *vb* **1** castrate, geld. **2** debilitate, effeminize, enervate, unman, weaken.

embalm *vb* **1** cherish, consecrate, conserve, enshrine, preserve, store, treasure. **2** perfume, scent.

embargo *vb* ban, bar, blockade, debar, exclude, prohibit, proscribe, restrict, stop, withhold. • *n* ban, bar, blockade, exclusion, hindrance, impediment, prohibition, prohibitory, proscription, restraint, restriction, stoppage.
vb antonym allow.
n antonym pass, allowance.

embark *vb* engage, enlist.
vb antonym disembark.

embarrass *vb* **1** beset, entangle, perplex. **2** annoy, clog, bother, distress, hamper, harass, involve, plague, trouble, vex. **3** abash, confound, confuse, discomfit, disconcert, dumbfound, mortify, nonplus, pose, shame.

embellish *vb* adorn, beautify, bedeck, deck, decorate, emblazon, enhance, enrich, garnish, grace, ornament.
vb antonyms denude, simplify.

embellishment *n* adornment, decoration, enrichment, ornament, ornamentation.

embezzle *vb* appropriate, defalcate, filch, misappropriate, peculate, pilfer, purloin, steal.

embitter *vb* **1** aggravate, envenom, exacerbate. **2** anger, enrage, exasperate, madden.
vb antonym pacify.

emblem *n* badge, cognizance, device, mark, representation, sign, symbol, token, type.

embody *vb* **1** combine, compact, concentrate, incorporate. **2** comprehend, comprise, contain, embrace, include. **3** codify, methodize, systematize.

embolden *vb* animate, cheer, elate, encourage, gladden, hearten, inspirit, nerve, reassure.

embosom *vb* bury, cherish, clasp, conceal, enfold, envelop, enwrap, foster, hide, nurse, surround.

embrace *vb* **1** clasp. **2** accept, seize, welcome. **3** comprehend, comprise, contain, cover, embody, encircle, enclose, encompass, enfold, hold, include. • *n* clasp, fold, hug.

embroil *vb* **1** commingle, encumber, ensnarl, entangle, implicate, involve. **2** confuse, discompose, disorder, distract, disturb, perplex, trouble.

embryo *n* beginning, germ, nucleus, root, rudiment.

embryonic *adj* incipient, rudimentary, undeveloped.

emendation *n* amendment, correction, improvement, rectification.

emerge *vb* **1** rise. **2** emanate, escape, issue. **3** appear, arise, outcrop.
vb antonyms disappear, fade.

emergency *n* **1** crisis, difficulty, dilemma, exigency, extremity, necessity, pass, pinch, push, strait, urgency. **2** conjuncture, crisis, juncture, pass.

emigration *n* departure, exodus, migration, removal.

eminence *n* **1** elevation, hill, projection, prominence, protuberance. **2** celebrity, conspicuousness, distinction, exaltation, fame, loftiness, note, preferment, reputation, repute, renown.

eminent *adj* **1** elevated, high, lofty. **2** celebrated, conspicuous, distinguished, exalted, famous, illustrious, notable, prominent, remarkable, renowned.
adj antonyms unimportant, unknown.

emissary *n* messenger, scout, secret agent, spy.

emit *vb* breathe out, dart, discharge, eject, emanate, exhale, gust, hurl, jet, outpour, shed, shoot, spurt, squirt.
vb antonym absorb.

emollient *adj* relaxing, softening, soothing. • *n* softener.

emolument *n* **1** compensation, gain, hire, income, lucre, pay, pecuniary, profits, salary, stipend, wages. **2** advantage, benefit, profit, perquisites.

emotion *n* agitation, excitement, feeling, passion, perturbation, sentiment, sympathy, trepidation.

emphasis *n* **1** accent, stress. **2** force, importance, impressiveness, moment, significance, weight.

emphatic *adj* decided, distinct, earnest, energetic, expressive, forcible, impressive, intensive, positive, significant, strong, unequivocal.

adj antonyms quiet, understated, unemphatic.

empire *n* **1** domain, dominion, sovereignty, supremacy. **2** authority, command, control, government, rule, sway.

empirical, empiric *adj* **1** experimental, experiential. **2** hypothetical, provisional, tentative. **3** charlatanic, quackish.

employ *vb* **1** busy, devote, engage, engross, enlist, exercise, occupy, retain. **2** apply, commission, use. • *n* employment, service.

employee *n* agent, clerk, employee, hand, servant, workman.

employment *n* avocation, business, calling, craft, employ, engagement, occupation, profession, pursuit, trade, vocation, work.
n antonym unemployment.

emporium *n* market, mart, shop, store.

empower *vb* **1** authorize, commission, permit, qualify, sanction, warrant. **2** enable.

empty *vb* **1** deplete, drain, evacuate, exhaust. **2** discharge, disembogue. **3** flow, embogue. • *adj* **1** blank, hollow, unoccupied, vacant, vacuous, void. **2** deplete, destitute, devoid, hungry. **3** unfilled, unfurnished, unsupplied. **4** unsatisfactory, unsatisfying, unsubstantial, useless, vain. **5** clear, deserted, desolate, exhausted, free, unburdened, unloaded, waste. **6** foolish, frivolous, inane, senseless, silly, stupid, trivial, weak.
adj antonyms filled, full, replete.
vb antonym fill.

empyrean, empyreal *adj* aerial, airy, ethereal, heavenly, refined, sublimated, sublimed.

emulation *n* **1** competition, rivalry, strife, vying. **2** contention, envy, jealousy.

enable *vb* authorize, capacitate, commission, empower, fit, permit, prepare, qualify, sanction, warrant.
vb antonyms inhibit, prevent.

enact *vb* **1** authorize, command, decree, establish, legislate, ordain, order, sanction. **2** act, perform, personate, play, represent.
vb antonym repeal.

enactment *n* act, decree, law, edict, ordinance.

enamour *vb* bewitch, captivate, charm, enchant, endear, fascinate.

enchain *vb* bind, confine, enslave, fetter, hold, manacle, restrain, shackle.

enchant *vb* **1** beguile, bewitch, charm, delude, fascinate. **2** captivate, catch, enamour, win. **3** beatify, delight, enrapture, rapture, ravish, transport.

vb antonyms bore, disenchant.

enchanting *adj* bewitching, blissful, captivating, charming, delightful, enrapturing, fascinating, rapturous, ravishing.

enchantment *n* **1** charm, conjuration, incantation, magic, necromancy, sorcery, spell, witchery. **2** bliss, delight, fascination, rapture, ravishment, transport.

encase *vb* **1** encircle, enclose, incase, infix, set. **2** chase, emboss, engrave, inlay, ornament.

encage *vb* confine, coop up, impound, imprison, shut up.

encircle *vb* **1** belt, circumscribe, encompass, enclose, engird, enring, environ, gird, ring, span, surround, twine. **2** clasp, embrace, enfold, fold.

enclose, inclose *vb* **1** circumscribe, corral, coop, embosom, encircle, encompass, environ, fence in, hedge, include, pen, shut in, surround. **2** box, cover, encase, envelop, wrap.

encomium *n* applause, commendation, eulogy, laudation, panegyric, praise.

encompass *vb* **1** belt, compass, encircle, enclose, engird, environ, gird, surround. **2** beset, besiege, hem in, include, invest, surround.

encounter *vb* **1** confront, face, meet. **2** attack, combat, contend, engage, strive, struggle. • *n* **1** assault, attack, clash, collision, meeting, onset. **2** action, affair, battle, brush, combat, conflict, contest, dispute, engagement, skirmish.

encourage *vb* **1** animate, assure, cheer, comfort, console, embolden, enhearten, fortify, hearten, incite, inspirit, instigate, reassure, stimulate, strengthen. **2** abet, aid, advance, approve, countenance, favour, foster, further, help, patronize, promote, support.

vb antonyms depress, discourage, dissuade.

encroach *vb* infringe, invade, intrude, tench, trespass, usurp.

encumber *vb* **1** burden, clog, hamper, hinder, impede, load, obstruct, overload, oppress, retard. **2** complicate, embarrass, entangle, involve, perplex.

encumbrance *n* **1** burden, clog, deadweight, drag, embarrassment, hampering, hindrance, impediment, incubus, load. **2** claim, debt, liability, lien.

end *vb* **1** abolish, close, conclude, discontinue, dissolve, drop, finish, stop, terminate. **2** annihilate, destroy, kill. **3** cease, terminate. • *n* **1** extremity, tip. **2** cessation, close, denouement, ending, expiration, finale, finis, finish, last, period, stoppage, wind-up. **3** completion, conclusion, consummation. **4** annihilation, catastrophe, destruction, dissolution. **5** bound, limit, termination, terminus. **6** consequence, event, issue, result, settlement, sequel, upshot. **7** fragment, remnant, scrap, stub, tag, tail. **8** aim, design, goal, intent, intention, object, objective, purpose.

n antonyms beginning, opening, start.

vb antonyms begin, start.

endanger *vb* compromise, hazard, imperil, jeopardize, peril, risk.

vb antonyms protect, shelter, shield.

endear *vb* attach, bind, captivate, charm, win.

endearment *n* **1** attachment, fondness, love, tenderness. **2** caress, blandishment, fondling.

endeavour *vb* aim, attempt, essay, labour, seek, strive, struggle, study, try. • *n* aim, attempt, conatus, effort, essay, exertion, trial, struggle, trial.

endless *adj* **1** boundless, illimitable, immeasurable, indeterminable, infinite, interminable, limitless, unlimited. **2** dateless, eternal, everlasting, never-ending, perpetual, unending. **3** deathless, everenduring, ever-living, immortal, imperishable, undying.

endorse, indorse *vb* **1** approve, back, confirm, guarantee, ratify, sanction, superscribe, support, visé, vouch for, warrant. **2** superscribe.

vb antonyms denounce, disapprove.

endow *vb* bequeath, clothe, confer, dower, endue, enrich, gift, indue, invest, supply.

vb antonym divest.

endowment *n* **1** bequest, boon, bounty, gift, grant, largesse, present. **2** foundation, fund, property, revenue. **3** ability, aptitude, capability, capacity, faculty, genius, gift, parts, power, qualification, quality, talent.

endurance *n* **1** abiding, bearing, sufferance, suffering, tolerance, toleration. **2** backbone, bottom, forbearance, fortitude, guts, patience, resignation.

endure *vb* **1** bear, support, sustain. **2** experience, suffer, undergo, weather. **3** abide, brook, permit, pocket, swallow, tolerate, stomach, submit, withstand. **4** continue, last, persist, remain, wear.

vb antonyms cease, end.

enemy *n* **1** adversary, foe. **2** antagonist, foeman, opponent, rival.

n antonyms ally, friend.

energetic *adj* active, effective, efficacious, emphatic, enterprising, forceful, forcible, hearty, mettlesome, potent, powerful, strenuous, strong, vigorous.

energy *n* **1** activity, dash, drive, efficacy, efficiency, force, go, impetus, intensity, mettle, might, potency, power, strength, verve, vim. **2** animation, life, manliness, spirit, spiritedness, stamina, vigour, zeal.

n antonyms inertia, lethargy, weakness.

enervate *vb* break, debilitate, devitalize, emasculate, enfeeble, exhaust, paralyse, relax, soften, unhinge, unnerve, weaken.

vb antonyms activate, energize.

enfeeble *vb* debilitate, devitalize, enervate, exhaust, relax, unhinge, unnerve, weaken.

enfold, infold *vb* **1** enclose, envelop, fold, enwrap, wrap. **2** clasp, embrace.

enforce *vb* compel, constrain, exact, force, oblige, require, urge.

enfranchise *vb* emancipate, free, liberate, manumit, release.

engage *vb* **1** bind, commit, obligate, pledge, promise. **2** affiance, betroth, plight. **3** book, brief, employ, enlist, hire, retain. **4** arrest, allure, attach, draw, entertain, fix, gain, win. **5** busy, commission, contract, engross, occupy. **6** attack, encounter. **7** combat, contend, contest, fight, interlock, struggle. **8** embark, enlist. **9** agree, promise, stipulate, undertake, warrant.

vb antonyms discharge, disengage, dismiss.

engagement *n* **1** appointment, assurance, contract, obligation, pledge, promise, stipulation. **2** betrothment, betrothal, plighting. **3** avocation, business, calling, employment, enterprise, occupation. **4** action, battle, combat, encounter, fight.

engender *vb* **1** bear, beget, breed, create, generate, procreate, propagate. **2** cause, excite, incite, occasion, produce.

engine *n* **1** invention, machine. **2** agency, agent, device, implement, instrument, means, method, tool, weapon.

engorge *vb* **1** bolt, devour, eat, gobble, gorge, gulp, swallow. **2** glut, obstruct, stuff.

engrave *vb* **1** carve, chisel, cut, etch, grave, hatch, incise, sculpt. **2** grave, impress, imprint, infix.

engross *vb* **1** absorb, engage, occupy, take up. **2** buy up, forestall, monopolize.

engrossment *n* absorption, forestalling, monopoly.

engulf *vb* absorb, overwhelm, plunge, swallow up.

enhance *vb* advance, aggravate, augment, elevate, heighten, increase, intensify, raise, swell.

vb antonyms decrease, minimize.

enhearten *vb* animate, assure, cheer, comfort, console, embolden, encourage, hearten, incite, inspirit, reassure, stimulate.

enigma *n* conundrum, mystery, problem, puzzle, riddle.

enigmatic *adj* ambiguous, dark, doubtful, equivocal, hidden, incomprehensible, mysterious, mystic, obscure, occult, perplexing, puzzling, recondite, uncertain, unintelligible.

adj antonyms simple, straightforward.

enjoin *vb* **1** admonish, advise, urge. **2** bid, command, direct, order, prescribe, require. **3** prohibit, restrain.

enjoy *vb* like, possess, relish.

vb antonyms abhor, detest.

enjoyment *n* **1** delight, delectation, gratification, happiness, indulgence, pleasure, satisfaction. **2** possession.

n antonyms displeasure, dissatisfaction.

enkindle *vb* **1** inflame, ignite, kindle. **2** excite, incite, instigate, provoke, rouse, stimulate.

enlarge *vb* **1** amplify, augment, broaden, develop, dilate, distend, expand, extend, grow, increase, magnify, widen. **2** aggrandize, engreaten, ennoble, expand, exaggerate, greaten. **3** swell.

vb antonyms decrease, diminish, shrink.

enlighten *vb* **1** illume, illuminate, illumine. **2** counsel, educate, civilize, inform, instruct, teach.

vb antonyms confuse, puzzle.

enlist *vb* **1** enrol, levy, recruit, register. **2** enrol, list. **3** embark, engage.

enliven *vb* **1** animate, invigorate, quicken, reanimate, rouse, wake. **2** exhilarate, cheer, brighten, delight, elate, gladden, inspire, inspirit, rouse.

vb antonyms subdue.

enmity *n* animosity, aversion, bitterness,

hate, hatred, hostility, ill-will, malevolence, malignity, rancour.

n antonyms amity, friendship.

ennoble *vb* aggrandize, dignify, elevate, engreaten, enlarge, exalt, glorify, greaten, raise.

ennui *n* boredom, irksomeness, languor, lassitude, listlessness, tedium, tiresomeness, weariness.

enormity *n* atrociousness, atrocity, depravity, flagitiousness, heinousness, nefariousness, outrageousness, villainy, wickedness.

n antonyms triviality, unimportance.

enormous *adj* 1 abnormal. exceptional, inordinate, irregular. 2 colossal, Cyclopean, elephantine, Herculean, huge, immense, monstrous, vast, gigantic, prodigious, titanic, tremendous.

adj antonyms small, tiny.

enough *adj* abundant, adequate, ample, plenty, sufficient. • *adv* satisfactorily, sufficiently. • *n* abundance, plenty, sufficiency.

enquire *see* **inquire**.

enrage *vb* anger, chafe, exasperate, incense, inflame, infuriate, irritate, madden, provoke.

vb antonyms calm, placate, soothe.

enrapture *vb* beatify, bewitch, delight, enchant, enravish, entrance, surpassingly, transport.

enrich *vb* 1 endow. 2 adorn, deck, decorate, embellish, grace, ornament.

vb antonym impoverish.

enrobe *vb* clothe, dress, apparel, array, attire, invest, robe.

enrol *vb* 1 catalogue, engage, engross, enlist, list, register. 2 chronicle, record.

vb antonyms leave, reject.

ensconce *vb* conceal, cover, harbour, hide, protect, screen, secure, settle, shelter, shield, snugly.

enshrine *vb* 1 embalm, enclose, entomb. 2 cherish, treasure.

ensign *n* 1 banner, colours, eagle, flag, gonfalcon, pennon, standard, streamer. 2 sign, signal, symbol. 3 badge, hatchment.

enslave *vb* captivate, dominate, master, overmaster, overpower, subjugate.

vb antonyms emancipate, free.

ensnare *vb* 1 catch, entrap. 2 allure, inveigle, seduce. 3 bewilder, confound, embarrass, encumber, entangle, perplex.

ensue *vb* 1 follow, succeed. 2 arise, come, flow, issue, proceed, result, spring.

vb antonym precede.

entangle *vb* 1 catch, ensnare, entrap. 2 confuse, enmesh, intertwine, intertwist, interweave, knot, mat, ravel, tangle. 3 bewilder, embarrass, encumber, ensnare, involve, nonplus, perplex, puzzle.

vb antonym disentangle.

enterprise *n* 1 adventure, attempt, cause, effort, endeavour, essay, project, undertaking, scheme, venture. 2 activity, adventurousness, daring, dash, energy, initiative, readiness, push.

n antonyms apathy, inertia.

enterprising *adj* 1 adventurous, audacious, bold, daring, dashing, venturesome, venturous. 2 active, adventurous, alert, efficient, energetic, prompt, resourceful, smart, spirited, stirring, strenuous, zealous.

adj antonyms lethargic, unadventurous.

entertain *vb* 1 fete, receive, regale, treat. 2 cherish, foster, harbour, hold, lodge, shelter. 3 admit, consider. 4 amuse, cheer, divert, please, recreate.

vb antonyms bore, reject.

entertainment *n* 1 hospitality. 2 banquet, collation, feast, festival, reception, treat. 3 amusement, diversion, pastime, recreation, sport.

enthusiasm *n* 1 ecstasy, exaltation, fanaticism. 2 ardour, earnestness, devotion, eagerness, fervour, passion, warmth, zeal.

n antonym apathy.

enthusiast *n* 1 bigot, devotee, fan, fanatic, freak, zealot. 2 castle-builder, dreamer, visionary.

entice *vb* allure, attract, bait, cajole, coax, decoy, inveigle, lure, persuade, prevail on, seduce, tempt, wheedle, wile.

enticement *n* allurement, attraction, bait, blandishment, inducement, inveiglement, lure, persuasion, seduction.

entire *adj* 1 complete, integrated, perfect, unbroken, undiminished, undivided, unimpaired, whole. 2 complete, full, plenary, thorough. 3 mere, pure, sheer, unalloyed, unmingled, unmitigated, unmixed.

adj antonyms impaired, incomplete, partial.

entitle *vb* 1 call, characterize, christen, denominate, designate, dub, name, style. 2 empower, enable, fit for, qualify for.

entomb *vb* bury, inhume, inter.

entrails *npl* bowels, guts, intestines, inwards, offal, viscera.

entrance¹ *n* 1 access, approach, avenue,

incoming, ingress. 2 adit, avenue, aperture, door, doorway, entry, gate, hallway, inlet, lobby, mouth, passage, portal, stile, vestibule. 3 beginning, commencement, debut, initiation, introduction. 4 admission, entrée.

n antonyms departure, exit.

entrance[2] *vb* bewitch, captivate, charm, delight, enchant, enrapture, fascinate, ravish, transport.

vb antonyms bore, repel.

entrap *vb* 1 catch, ensnare. 2 allure, entice, inveigle, seduce. 3 embarrass, entangle, involve, nonplus, perplex, pose, stagger.

entreat *vb* adjure, beg, beseech, crave, enjoin, implore, importune, petition, pray, solicit, supplicate.

entreaty *n* adjuration, appeal, importunity, petition, prayer, request, solicitation, suit, supplication.

entrée *n* access, admission, admittance.

entrench, intrench *vb* 1 furrow. 2 circumvallate, fortify. 2 encroach, infringe, invade, trench, trespass.

entrenchment, intrenchment *n* 1 entrenching. 2 earthwork, fortification. 3 defence, protection, shelter. 4 encroachment, inroad, invasion.

entrust *vb* commit, confide, consign.

entwine *vb* 1 entwist, interlace, intertwine, interweave, inweave, twine, twist, weave. 2 embrace, encircle, encumber, interlace, surround.

enumerate *vb* calculate, cite, compute, count, detail, mention, number, numerate, reckon, recount, specify, tell.

enunciate *vb* articulate, declare, proclaim, promulgate, pronounce, propound, publish, say, speak, utter.

envelop *vb* 1 encase, enfold, enwrap, fold, pack, wrap. 2 cover, encircle, encompass, enshroud, hide, involve, surround.

envelope *n* capsule, case, covering, integument, shroud, skin, wrapper, veil, vesture, wrap.

envenom *vb* 1 poison, taint. 2 embitter, malign. 3 aggravate, enrage, exasperate, incense, inflame, irritate, madden, provoke.

environ *vb* 1 begird, belt, embrace, encircle, encompass, enclose, engird, envelop, gird, hedge, hem, surround. 2 beset, besiege, encompass, invest.

environs *npl* neighbourhood, vicinage, vicinity.

envoy *n* 1 ambassador, legate, minister, plenipotentiary. 2 courier, messenger.

envy *vb* 1 hate. 2 begrudge, grudge. 3 covet, emulate, desire. • *n* 1 enviousness, hate, hatred, ill-will, jealousy, malice, spite. 2 grudge, grudging.

enwrap *vb* absorb, cover, encase, engross, envelop, infold, involve, wrap, wrap up.

ephemeral *adj* brief, diurnal, evanescent, fleeting, flitting, fugacious, fugitive, momentary, occasional, short-lived, transient, transitory.

epic *adj* Homeric, heroic, narrative.

epicure *n* 1 gastronome, glutton, gourmand, gourmet. 2 epicurean, sensualist, Sybarite, voluptuary.

epidemic *adj* general, pandemic, prevailing, prevalent. • *n* outbreak, pandemia, pestilence, plague, spread, wave.

epidermis *n* cuticle, scarf-skin.

epigrammatic *adj* antithetic, concise, laconic, piquant, poignant, pointed, pungent, sharp, terse.

episcopal *adj* Episcopalian, pontifical, prelatic.

epistle *n* communication, letter, missive, note.

epithet *n* appellation, description, designation, name, predicate, title.

epitome *n* abbreviation, abridgement, abstract, breviary, brief, comment, compendium, condensation, conspectus, digest, summary, syllabus, synopsis.

epitomize *vb* abbreviate, abridge, abstract, condense, contract, curtail, cut, reduce, shorten, summarize.

vb antonyms elaborate, expand.

epoch *n* age, date, era, period, time.

equable *adj* calm, equal, even, even-tempered, regular, steady, uniform, serene, tranquil, unruffled.

equal *vb* equalize, even, match. • *adj* 1 alike, coordinate, equivalent, like, tantamount. 2 even, level, equable, regular, uniform. 3 equitable, even-handed, fair, impartial, just, unbiased. 4 co-extensive, commensurate, corresponding, parallel, proportionate. 5 adequate, competent, fit, sufficient. • *n* 1 compeer, fellow, match, peer. 2 rival.

adj antonyms different, inequitable, unequal.

equanimity *n* calmness, composure, coolness, peace, regularity, self-possession, serenity, steadiness.

n antonyms alarm, anxiety, discomposure.

equestrian *adj* equine, horse-like, horsy. • *n*

1 horseman, rider. **2** cavalier, cavalryman, chevalier, horse soldier, knight.

equilibrist *n* acrobat, balancer, funambulist, rope-walker.

equip *vb* **1** appoint, arm, furnish, provide, rig, supply. **2** accoutre, array, dress.

equipage *n* **1** accoutrements, apparatus, baggage, effects, equipment, furniture. **2** carriage, turnout, vehicle. **3** attendance, procession, retinue, suite, train.

equipment *n* accoutrement, apparatus, baggage, equipage, furniture, gear, outfit, rigging.

equipoise *n* balance, equilibrium.

equitable *adj* **1** even-handed, candid, honest, impartial, just, unbiased, unprejudiced, upright. **2** adequate, fair, proper, reasonable, right.
adj antonyms inequitable, unfair.

equity *n* **1** just, right. **2** fair play, fairness, impartiality, justice, rectitude, reasonableness, righteousness, uprightness.
n antonym inequity.

equivalent *adj* **1** commensurate, equal, equipollent, tantamount. **2** interchangeable, synonymous. • *n* complement, coordinate, counterpart, double, equal, fellow, like, match, parallel, pendant, quid pro quo.
adj antonyms dissimilar, unlike.

equivocal *adj* **1** ambiguous. **2** doubtful, dubious, enigmatic, indeterminate, problematical, puzzling, uncertain.
adj antonyms clear, unequivocal.

equivocate *vb* dodge, evade, fence, palter, prevaricate, shuffle, quibble.

equivocation *n* **1** evasion, paltering, prevarication, quibbling, shuffling. **2** double entendre, double meaning, quibble.

era *n* age, date, epoch, period, time.

eradicate *vb* **1** extirpate, root, uproot. **2** abolish, annihilate, destroy, obliterate.

erase *vb* blot, cancel, delete, efface, expunge, obliterate, scrape out.

erasure *n* cancellation, cancelling, effacing, expunging, obliteration.

erect *vb* **1** build, construct, raise, rear. **2** create, establish, form, found, institute, plant. • *adj* **1** standing, unrecumbent, uplifted, upright. **2** elevated, vertical, perpendicular, straight. **3** bold, firm, undaunted, undismayed, unshaken, unterrified.
adj antonyms limp, relaxed.

erelong *adv* early, quickly, shortly, soon, speedily.

ergo *adv* consequently, hence, therefore.

erode *vb* canker, consume, corrode, destroy, eat away, fret, rub.

erosive *adj* acrid, cathartic, caustic, corroding, corrosive, eating, virulent.

erotic *adj* amorous, amatory, arousing, seductive, stimulating, titillating.

err *vb* **1** deviate, ramble, rove, stray, wander. **2** blunder, misjudge, mistake. **3** fall, lapse, nod, offend, sin, stumble, trespass, trip.

errand *n* charge, commission, mandate, message, mission, purpose.

errant *adj* adventurous, rambling, roving, stray, wandering.

erratic *adj* **1** nomadic, rambling, roving, wandering. **2** moving, planetary. **3** abnormal, capricious, deviating, eccentric, irregular, odd, queer, strange.
adj antonyms consistent, reliable, stable, straight.

erratum *n* correction, corrigendum, error, misprint, mistake.

erroneous *adj* false, incorrect, inaccurate, inexact, mistaken untrue, wrong.
adj antonym correct.

error *n* **1** blunder, fallacy, inaccuracy, misapprehension, mistake, oversight. **2** delinquency, fault, iniquity, misdeed, misdoing, misstep, obliquity, offence, shortcoming, sin, transgression, trespass, wrongdoing.

erudition *n* knowledge, learning, lore, scholarship.

eruption *n* **1** explosion, outbreak, outburst. **2** sally. **3** rash.

escape *vb* **1** avoid, elude, evade, flee from, shun. **2** abscond, bolt, decamp, flee, fly. **3** slip. • *n* **1** flight. **2** release. **3** passage, passing. **4** leakage.

eschew *vb* abstain, avoid, elude, flee from, shun.

escort *vb* **1** convey, guard, protect. **2** accompany, attend, conduct. • *n* **1** attendant, bodyguard, cavalier, companion, convoy, gallant, guard, squire. **2** protection, safe conduct, safeguard. **3** attendance, company.

esculent *adj* eatable, edible, wholesome.

esoteric *adj* hidden, inmost, inner, mysterious, private, recondite, secret.

especial *adj* **1** absolute, chief, distinct, distinguished, marked, particular, peculiar, principal, singular, special, specific, uncommon, unusual. **2** detailed, minute, noteworthy.

espousal *n* **1** affiancing, betrothing, espousing, plighting. **2** adoption, defence, maintenance, support.

espouse *vb* **1** betroth, plight, promise. **2** marry, wed. **3** adopt, champion, defend, embrace, maintain, support.

espy *vb* descry, detect, discern, discover, observe, perceive, spy, watch.

esquire *n* armiger, attendant, escort, gentleman, squire.

essay[1] *vb* attempt, endeavour, try. • *n* aim, attempt, effort, endeavour, exertion, struggle, trial.

essay[2] *n* article, composition, disquisition, dissertation, paper, thesis.

essence *n* **1** nature, quintessence, substance. **2** extract, part. **3** odour, perfume, scent. **4** being, entity, existence, nature.

essential *adj* **1** fundamental, indispensable, important, inward, intrinsic, necessary, requisite, vital. **2** diffusible, pure, rectified, volatile.
adj antonym inessential.
n antonym inessential.

establish *vb* **1** fix, secure, set, settle. **2** decree, enact, ordain. **3** build, constitute, erect, form, found, institute, organize, originate, pitch, plant, raise. **4** ensconce, ground, install, place, plant, root, secure. **5** approve, confirm, ratify, sanction. **6** prove, substantiate, verify.

estate *n* **1** condition, state. **2** position, rank, standing. **3** division, order. **4** effects, fortune, possessions, property. **5** interest.

esteem *vb* **1** appreciate, estimate, rate, reckon, value. **2** admire, honour, like, prize, respect, revere, reverence, value, venerate, worship. **3** account, believe, consider, deem, fancy, hold, imagine, suppose, regard, think. • *n* **1** account, appreciation, consideration, estimate, estimation, judgement, opinion, reckoning, valuation. **2** credit, honour, regard, respect, reverence.

estimable *adj* **1** appreciable, calculable, computable. **2** admirable, credible, deserving, excellent, good, meritorious, precious, respectful, valuable, worthy.

estimate *vb* **1** appraise, appreciate, esteem, prise, rate, value. **2** assess, calculate, compute, count, gauge, judge, reckon. • *n* **1** estimation, judgement, valuation. **2** calculation, computation.

estimation *n* **1** appreciation, estimate, valuation. **2** esteem, estimate, judgement, opinion. **3** honour, reckoning, regard, respect, reverence.

estop *vb* bar, impede, preclude, stop.

estrange *vb* **1** withdraw, withhold. **2** alienate, divert. **3** disaffect, destroy.

estuary *n* creek, inlet, fiord, firth, frith, mouth.

etch *vb* corrode, engrave.

eternal *adj* **1** absolute, inevitable, necessary, self-active, self-existent, self-originated. **2** abiding, ceaseless, endless, ever-enduring, everlasting, incessant, interminable, never-ending, perennial, permanent, perpetual, sempiternal, unceasing, unending. **3** deathless, immortal, imperishable, incorruptible, indestructible, never-dying, undying. **4** immutable, unchangeable. **5** constant, continual, continuous, incessant, persistent, unbroken, uninterrupted.
adj antonyms changeable, ephemeral, temporary.

ethereal *adj* **1** aerial, airy, celestial, empyreal, heavenly, unworldly. **2** attenuated, light, subtle, tenuous, volatile. **3** delicate, fairy, flimsy, fragile, rare, refined, subtle.

eulogize *vb* applaud, commend, extol, laud, magnify, praise.

eulogy *n* **1** discourse, eulogium, panegyric, speech. **2** applause, encomium, commendation, laudation, praise.
n antonym condemnation.

euphonious *adj* clear, euphonic, harmonious, mellifluous, mellow, melodious, musical, silvery, smooth, sweet-toned.

evacuant *adj* abstergent, cathartic, cleansing, emetic, purgative. • *n* cathartic, purgative.

evacuate *vb* **1** empty. **2** discharge, clean out, clear out, eject, excrete, expel, purge, void. **3** abandon, desert, forsake, leave, quit, relinquish, withdraw.

evade *vb* **1** elude, escape. **2** avoid, decline, dodge, funk, shun. **3** baffle, elude, foil. **4** dodge, equivocate, fence, palter, prevaricate, quibble, shuffle.
vb antonym face.

evanescence *n* **1** disappearance, evanishing, evanishment, vanishing. **2** transience, transientness, transitoriness.

evanescent *adj* ephemeral, fleeting, flitting, fugitive, passing, short-lived, transient, transitory, vanishing.

evaporate *vb* **1** distil, volatilize. **2** dehydrate, dry, vaporize. **3** disperse, dissolve, fade, vanish.

evaporation *n* **1** distillation, volatilization. **2** dehydration, drying, vaporization. **3** disappearance, dispersal, dissolution.

evasion *n* artifice, avoidance, bluffing, deceit, dodge, equivocation, escape, excuse, funking, prevarication, quibble, shift, subterfuge, shuffling, sophistical, tergiversation.

evasive *adj* elusive, elusory, equivocating, prevaricating, shuffling, slippery, sophistical.
adj antonyms direct, frank.

even *vb* **1** balance, equalize, harmonize, symmetrize. **2** align, flatten, flush, level, smooth, square. • *adj* **1** flat, horizontal, level, plane, smooth. **2** calm, composed, equable, equal, peaceful, placid, regular, steady, uniform, unruffled. **3** direct, equitable, fair, impartial, just, straightforward. • *adv* **1** exactly, just, verily. **2** likewise. • *n* eve, evening, eventide, vesper.
adj antonyms unequal, uneven.

evening *n* dusk, eve, even, eventide, nightfall, sunset, twilight.

event *n* **1** circumstance, episode, fact, happening, incident, occurrence. **2** conclusion, consequence, end, issue, outcome, result, sequel, termination. **3** adventure, affair.

eventful *adj* critical, important, memorable, momentous, remarkable, signal, stirring.

eventual *adj* **1** final, last, ultimate. **2** conditional, contingent, possible. • *adv* always, aye, constantly, continually, eternally, ever evermore, forever, incessantly, perpetually, unceasingly.

everlasting *adj* **1** ceaseless, constant, continual, endless, eternal, ever-during, incessant, interminable, never-ceasing, never-ending, perpetual, unceasing, unending, unintermitting, uninterrupted. **2** deathless, ever-living, immortal, imperishable, never-dying, undying.
adj antonyms temporary, transient.

evermore *adv* always, constantly, continually, eternally, ever, forever, perpetually.

everyday *adj* accustomed, common, commonplace, customary, habitual, routine, usual, wonted.
adj antonyms exceptional, special.

evict *vb* dispossess, eject, thrust out.

evidence *vb* evince, make clear, manifest, prove, show, testify, vouch. • *n* affirmation, attestation, averment, confirmation, corroboration, deposition, grounds, indication, proof, testimony, token, trace, voucher, witness.

evident *adj* apparent, bald, clear, conspicuous, distinct, downright, incontestable, indisputable, manifest, obvious, open, overt, palpable, patent, plain, unmistakable.
adj antonym uncertain.

evil *adj* **1** bad, ill. **2** base, corrupt, malicious, malevolent, malign, nefarious, perverse, sinful, vicious, vile, wicked, wrong. **3** bad, deleterious, baleful, baneful, destructive, harmful, hurtful, injurious, mischievous, noxious, pernicious, profane. **4** adverse, calamitous, diabolic, disastrous, unfortunate, unhappy, unpropitious, woeful. • *n* **1** calamity, disaster, ill, misery, misfortune, pain, reverse, sorrow, suffering, woe. **2** badness, baseness, corruption, depravity, malignity, sin, viciousness, wickedness. **3** bale, bane, blast, canker, curse, harm, injury, mischief, wrong.

evince *vb* **1** establish, evidence, manifest, prove, show. **2** disclose, display, exhibit, indicate, reveal.

eviscerate *vb* disembowel, embowel, gut.

evoke *vb* arouse, elicit, excite, provoke, rouse.
vb antonyms quell, suppress.

evolve *vb* develop, educe, exhibit, expand, open, unfold, unroll.

exacerbate *vb* aggravate, embitter, enrage, exasperate, excite, inflame, infuriate, irritate, provoke, vex.

exact *vb* **1** elicit, extort, mulch, require, squeeze. **2** ask, claim, compel, demand, enforce, requisition, take. • *adj* **1** rigid, rigorous, scrupulous, severe, strict. **2** diametric, express, faultless, precise, true. **3** accurate, close, correct, definite, faithful, literal, undeviating. **4** accurate, critical, delicate, fine, nice, sensitive. **5** careful, methodical, punctilious, orderly, punctual, regular.
adj antonym inexact.

exacting *adj* critical, difficult, exactive, rigid, extortionary.

exaction *n* contribution, extortion, oppression, rapacity, tribute.

exactness *n* **1** accuracy, correctness, exactitude, faithfulness, faultlessness, fidelity, nicety, precision, rigour. **2** carefulness, method, precision, regularity, rigidness, scrupulosity, scrupulousness, strictness.

exaggerate *vb* enlarge, magnify, overcharge, overcolour, overstate, romance, strain, stretch.
vb antonyms belittle, understate.

exalt *vb* **1** elevate, erect, heighten, lift up, raise. **2** aggrandize, dignify, elevate, ennoble. **3** bless, extol, glorify, magnify, praise.
vb antonym debase.

exalted *adj* elated, elevated, high, high-flown, lofty, lordly, magnificent.

examination *n* **1** inspection, observation. **2** exploration, inquiry, inquisition, investigation, perusal, research, search, scrutiny, survey. **3** catechism, probation, review, test, trial.

examine *vb* **1** inspect, observe. **2** canvass, consider, explore, inquire, investigate, scrutinize, study, test. **3** catechize, interrogate.

example *n* **1** archetype, copy, model, pattern, piece, prototype, representative, sample, sampler, specimen, standard. **2** exemplification, illustration, instance, precedent, warning.

exanimate *adj* **1** dead, defunct, inanimate, lifeless. **2** inanimate, inert, sluggish, spiritless, torpid.

exasperate *vb* **1** affront, anger, chafe, enrage, incense, irritate, nettle, offend, provoke, vex. **2** aggravate, exacerbate, inflame, rouse.
vb antonyms calm, soothe.

exasperation *n* **1** annoyance, exacerbation, irritation, provocation. **2** anger, fury, ire, passion, rage, wrath. **3** aggravation, heightening, increase, worsening.

excavate *vb* burrow, cut, delve, dig, hollow, hollow out, scoop, trench.

exceed *vb* **1** cap, overstep, surpass, transcend. **2** excel, outdo, outstrip, outvie, pass.

excel *vb* **1** beat, eclipse, outdo, outrival, outstrip, outvie, surpass. **2** cap, exceed, transcend.

excellence *n* **1** distinction, eminence, preeminence, superiority, transcendence. **2** fineness, fitness, goodness, perfection, purity, quality, superiority. **3** advantage. **4** goodness, probity, uprightness, virtue, worth.
n antonym inferiority.

excellent *adj* **1** admirable, choice, crack, eminent, first-rate, prime, sterling, superior, tiptop, transcendent. **2** deserving, estimable, praiseworthy, virtuous, worthy.
adj antonym inferior.

except *vb* exclude, leave out, omit, reject. • *conj* unless. • *prep* bar, but, excepting, excluding, save.

exceptional *adj* aberrant, abnormal, anomalous, exceptive, irregular, peculiar, rare, special, strange, superior, uncommon, unnatural, unusual.
adj antonyms mediocre, unexceptional.

excerpt *vb* cite, cull, extract, quote, select, take. • *n* citation, extract, quotation, selection.

excess *adj* excessive, unnecessary, redundant, spare, superfluous, surplus. • *n* **1** disproportion, fulsomeness, glut, oversupply, plethora, redundance, redundancy, surfeit, superabundance, superfluity. **2** overplus, remainder, surplus. **3** debauchery, dissipation, dissoluteness, intemperance, immoderation, overindulgence, unrestraint. **4** extravagance, immoderation, overdoing.
n antonym dearth.

excessive *adj* **1** disproportionate, exuberant, superabundant, superfluous, undue. **2** extravagant, enormous, inordinate, outrageous, unreasonable. **3** extreme, immoderate, intemperate. **4** vehement, violent.

exchange *vb* **1** barter, change, commute, shuffle, substitute, swap, trade, truck. **2** bandy, interchange. • *n* **1** barter, change, commutation, dealing, shuffle, substitution, trade, traffic. **2** interchange, reciprocity. **3** bazaar, bourse, fair, market.

excise[1] *n* capitation, customs, dues, duty, tariff, tax, taxes, toll.

excise[2] *vb* cancel, cut, delete, edit, efface, eradicate, erase, expunge, extirpate, remove, strike out.

excision *n* destruction, eradication, extermination, extirpation.

excitable *adj* **1** impressible, nervous, sensitive, susceptible. **2** choleric, hasty, hotheaded, hot-tempered, irascible, irritable, passionate, quick-tempered.

excite *vb* **1** animate, arouse, awaken, brew, evoke, impel, incite, inflame, instigate, kindle, move, prompt, provoke, rouse, spur, stimulate. **2** create, elicit, evoke, raise. **3** agitate, discompose, disturb, irritate.
vb antonyms bore, quell.

excitement *n* **1** excitation, exciting. **2** incitement, motive, stimulus. **3** activity,

agitation, bustle, commotion, disturbance, ferment, flutter, perturbation, sensation, stir, tension. **4** choler, heat, irritation, passion, violence, warmth.
n antonyms apathy, calm.

exclaim *vb* call, cry, declare, ejaculate, shout, utter, vociferate.

exclude *vb* **1** ban, bar, blackball, debar, ostracize, preclude, reject. **2** hinder, prevent, prohibit, restrain, withhold. **3** except, omit. **4** eject, eliminate, expel, extrude.
vb antonyms admit, allow, include.

exclusive *adj* **1** debarring, excluding. **2** illiberal, narrow, narrow-minded, selfish, uncharitable. **3** aristocratic, choice, clannish, cliquish, fastidious, fashionable, select, snobbish. **4** only, sole, special.

excommunicate *vb* anathematize, ban, curse, denounce, dismiss, eject, exclude, expel, exscind, proscribe, unchurch.

excoriate *vb* abrade, flay, gall, scar, scarify, score, skin, strip.

excrement *n* dejections, dung, faeces, excreta, excretion, ordure, stool.

excrescence *n* fungus, growth, knob, lump, outgrowth, protuberance, tumour, wart.

excrete *vb* discharge, eject, eliminate, separate.

excruciate *vb* agonize, rack, torment, torture.

exculpate *vb* absolve, acquit, clear, discharge, exonerate, free, justify, release, set right, vindicate.

excursion *n* **1** drive, expedition, jaunt, journey, ramble, ride, sally, tour, trip, voyage, walk. **2** digression, episode.

excursive *adj* devious, diffuse, digressive, discursive, erratic, rambling, roaming, roving, wandering.

excusable *adj* allowable, defensible, forgivable, justifiable, pardonable, venial, warrantable.

excursus *n* discussion, disquisition, dissertation.

excuse *vb* **1** absolve, acquit, exculpate, exonerate, forgive, pardon, remit. **2** extenuate, justify. **3** exempt, free, release. **4** overlook. • *n* **1** absolution, apology, defence, extenuation, justification, plea. **2** colour, disguise, evasion, guise, pretence, pretext, makeshift, semblance, subterfuge.

execrable *adj* **1** abhorrent, abominable, accursed, cursed, damnable, detestable, hateful, odious. **2** disgusting, loathsome, nauseating, nauseous, obnoxious, offensive, repulsive, revolting, sickening, vile.

execrate *vb* **1** curse, damn, imprecate. **2** abhor, abominate, detest, hate, loathe.
vb antonyms commend, praise.

execute *vb* **1** accomplish, achieve, carry out, complete, consummate, do, effect, effectuate, finish, perform, perpetrate. **2** administer, enforce, seal, sign. **3** behead, electrocute, guillotine, hang.

execution *n* **1** accomplishment, achievement, completion, consummation, operation, performance. **2** warrant, writ. **3** beheading, electrocution, hanging.

executive *adj* administrative, commanding, controlling, directing, managing, ministerial, officiating, presiding, ruling. • *n* administrator, director, manager.

exegetic, exegetical *adj* explanatory, explicative, explicatory, expository, hermeneutic, interpretative.

exemplary *adj* **1** assiduous, close, exact, faithful, punctual, punctilious, rigid, rigorous, scrupulous. **2** commendable, correct, good, estimable, excellent, praiseworthy, virtuous. **3** admonitory, monitory, warning.

exemplify *vb* evidence, exhibit, illustrate, manifest, show.

exempt *vb* absolve, except, excuse, exonerate, free, release, relieve. • *adj* absolved, excepted, excused, exempted, free, immune, liberated, privileged, released.
adj antonym liable.

exemption *n* absolution, dispensation, exception, immunity, privilege, release.

exercise *vb* **1** apply, busy, employ, exert, praxis, use. **2** effect, exert, produce, wield. **3** break in, discipline, drill, habituate, school, train. **4** practise, prosecute, pursue. **5** task, test, try. **6** afflict, agitate, annoy, burden, pain, trouble. • *n* **1** appliance, application, custom, employment, operation, performance, play, plying, practice, usage, use, working. **2** action, activity, effort, exertion, labour, toil, work. **3** discipline, drill, drilling, schooling, training. **4** lesson, praxis, study, task, test, theme.

exert *vb* employ, endeavour, exercise, labour, strain, strive, struggle, toil, use, work.

exertion *n* **1** action, exercise, exerting, use. **2** attempt, effort, endeavour, labour, strain, stretch, struggle, toil, trial.
n antonyms idleness, rest.

exhalation *n* **1** emission, evaporation. **2** damp, effluvium, fog, fume, mist, reek, smoke, steam, vapour.

exhale *vb* **1** breathe, discharge, elect, emanate, emit, evaporate, reek. **2** blow, expire, puff.
vb antonym inhale.

exhaust *vb* **1** drain, draw, empty. **2** consume, destroy, dissipate, expend, impoverish, lavish, spend, squander, waste. **3** cripple, debilitate, deplete, disable, enfeeble, enervate, overtire, prostrate, weaken.
vb antonym refresh.

exhaustion *n* debilitation, enervation, fatigue, lassitude, weariness.

exhibit *vb* **1** demonstrate, disclose, display, evince, expose, express, indicate, manifest, offer, present, reveal, show. **2** offer, present, propose.
vb antonym hide.

exhibition *n* **1** demonstration, display, exposition, manifestation, representation, spectacle, show. **2** allowance, benefaction, grant, pension, scholarship.

exhilarate *vb* animate, cheer, elate, enliven, gladden, inspire, inspirit, rejoice, stimulate.
vb antonyms bore, discourage.

exhilaration *n* **1** animating, cheering, elating, enlivening, gladdening, rejoicing, stimulating. **2** animation, cheer, cheerfulness, gaiety, gladness, glee, good spirits, hilarity, joyousness.

exhort *vb* **1** advise, caution, encourage, incite, persuade, stimulate, urge, warm. **2** preach.

exhume *vb* disentomb, disinhume, disinter, unbury, unearth.

exigency, exigence *n* **1** demand, necessity, need, requirement, urgency, want. **2** conjuncture, crisis, difficulty, distress, emergency, extremity, juncture, nonplus, quandary, pass, pinch, pressure, strait.

exiguous *adj* attenuated, diminutive, fine, small, scanty, slender, tiny.

exile *vb* banish, expatriate, expel, ostracize, proscribe. • *n* **1** banishment, expatriation, expulsion, ostracism, proscription, separation. **2** outcast, refugee.

exist *vb* **1** be, breathe, live. **2** abide, continue, endure, last, remain.

existence *n* **1** being, subsisting, subsistence. **2** being, creature, entity, essence, thing. **3** animation, continuation, life, living, vitality, vivacity.

exit *vb* depart, egress, go, leave. • *n* **1** departure, withdrawal. **2** death, decrease, demise, end. **3** egress, outlet.
n antonym entrance.

exonerate *vb* **1** absolve, acquit, clear, exculpate, justify, vindicate. **2** absolve, discharge, except, exempt, free, release.
vb antonym incriminate.

exorbitant *adj* enormous, excessive, extravagant, inordinate, unreasonable.
adj antonyms fair, reasonable.

exorcise *vb* **1** cast out, drive away, expel. **2** deliver, purify. **3** address, conjure.

exordium *n* introduction, opening, preamble, preface, prelude, proem, prologue.

exotic *adj* **1** extraneous, foreign. **2** extravagant.
adj antonym ordinary.

expand *vb* **1** develop, open, spread, unfold, unfurl. **2** diffuse, enlarge, extend, increase, stretch. **3** dilate, distend, enlarge.
vb antonyms contract, précis.

expanse *n* area, expansion, extent, field, stretch.

expansion *n* **1** expansion, opening, spreading. **2** diastole, dilation, distension, swelling. **3** development, diffusion, enlargement, increase. **4** expanse, extent, stretch.

ex parte *adj* biased, one-sided, partisan.

expatiate *vb* amplify, decant, dilate, enlarge, range, rove.

expatriate *vb* banish, exile, expel, ostracize, proscribe. • *adj* banished, exiled, refugee. • *n* displaced person, emigrant, exile.

expect *vb* anticipate, await, calculate, contemplate, forecast, foresee, hope, reckon, rely.

expectancy *n* **1** expectance, expectation. **2** abeyance, prospect.

expectation *n* **1** anticipation, expectance, expectancy, hope, prospect. **2** assurance, confidence, presumption, reliance, trust.

expedient *adj* **1** advisable, appropriate, convenient, desirable, fit, proper, politic, suitable. **2** advantageous, profitable, useful. • *n* contrivance, device, means, method, resort, resource, scheme, shift, stopgap, substitute.
adj antonym inexpedient.

expedite *vb* accelerate, advance, dispatch, facilitate, forward, hasten, hurry, precipitate, press, quicken, urge.

expedition *n* **1** alacrity, alertness, celerity, dispatch, haste, promptness, quickness, speed.

2 enterprise, undertaking. **3** campaign, excursion, journey, march, quest, voyage.
n antonym delay.

expeditious *adj* **1** quick, speedy, swift, rapid. **2** active, alert, diligent, nimble, prompt, punctual, swift.

expel *vb* **1** dislodge, egest, eject, eliminate, excrete. **2** discharge, eject, evacuate, void. **3** bounce, discharge, exclude, exscind, fire, oust, relegate, remove. **4** banish, disown, excommunicate, exile, expatriate, ostracize, proscribe, unchurch.
vb antonym admit.

expend *vb* **1** disburse, spend. **2** consume, employ, exert, use. **3** dissipate, exhaust, scatter, waste.
vb antonym save.

expenditure *n* **1** disbursement, outlay, outlaying, spending. **2** charge, cost, expenditure, outlay.

expensive *adj* **1** costly, dear, high-priced. **2** extravagant, lavish, wasteful.
adj antonyms cheap, inexpensive.

experience *vb* **1** endure, suffer. **2** feel, know. **3** encounter, suffer, undergo. • *n* **1** endurance, practice, trial. **2** evidence, knowledge, proof, test, testimony.
n antonym inexperience.

experienced *adj* able, accomplished, expert, instructed, knowing, old, practised, qualified, skilful, trained, thoroughbred, versed, veteran, wise.
adj antonym inexperienced.

experiment *vb* examine, investigate, test, try. • *n* assay, examination, investigation, ordeal, practice, proof, test, testimony, touchstone, trial.

expert *adj* able, adroit, apt, clever, dextrous, proficient, prompt, quick, ready, skilful. • *n* adept, authority, connoisseur, crack, master, specialist.
n antonym novice.

expertise *n* adroitness, aptness, dexterity, facility, promptness, skilfulness, skill.

expiate *vb* atone, redeem, satisfy.

expiration *n* **1** death, decease, demise, departure, exit. **2** cessation, close, conclusion, end, termination.

expire *vb* **1** cease, close, conclude, end, stop, terminate. **2** emit, exhale. **3** decease, depart, die, perish.
vb antonyms begin, continue.

explain *vb* **1** demonstrate, elucidate, expound, illustrate, interpret, resolve, solve, unfold, unravel. **2** account for, justify, warrant.
vb antonyms obfuscate, obscure.

explanation *n* **1** clarification, description, elucidation, exegesis, explication, exposition, illustration, interpretation. **2** account, answer, deduction, justification, key, meaning, secret, solution, warrant.

explicit *adj* absolute, categorical, clear, definite, determinate, exact, express, plain, positive, precise, unambiguous, unequivocal, unreserved.
adj antonyms inexplicit, vague.

explode *vb* **1** burst, detonate, discharge, displode, shatter, shiver. **2** contemn, discard, repudiate, scorn, scout.

exploit *vb* befool, milk, use, utilize. • *n* achievement, act, deed, feat.

explore *vb* examine, fathom, inquire, inspect, investigate, prospect, scrutinize, seek.

explosion *n* blast, burst, bursting, clap, crack, detonation, discharge, fulmination, pop.

exponent *n* **1** example, illustration, index, indication, specimen, symbol, type. **2** commentator, demonstrator, elucidator, expounder, illustrator, interpreter.

expose *vb* **1** bare, display, uncover. **2** descry, detect, disclose, unearth. **3** denounce, mask. **4** subject. **5** endanger, jeopardize, risk, venture.
vb antonym cover.

exposé *n* **1** exhibit, exposition, manifesto. **2** denouncement, divulgement, exposure, revelation.

exposition *n* **1** disclosure, interpretation. **2** commentary, critique, elucidation, exegesis, explanation, explication, interpretation. **3** display, show.

expound *vb* **1** develop, present, rehearse, reproduce, unfold. **2** clear, elucidate, explain, interpret.

express *vb* **1** air, assert, asseverate, declare, emit, enunciate, manifest, utter, vent, signify, speak, state, voice. **2** betoken, denote, equal, exhibit, indicate, intimate, present, represent, show, symbolize. • *adj* **1** categorical, clear, definite, determinate, explicit, outspoken, plain, positive, unambiguous. **2** accurate, close, exact, faithful, precise, true. **3** particular, special. **4** fast, nonstop, quick, rapid, speedy, swift. • *n* dispatch, message.
adj antonym vague.

expression *n* **1** assertion, asseveration,

communication, declaration, emission, statement, utterance, voicing. **2** language, locution, phrase, remark, saying, term, word. **3** air, aspect, look, mien.

expressive *adj* **1** indicative, meaningful, significant. **2** demonstrative, eloquent, emphatic, energetic, forcible, lively, strong, vivid. **3** appropriate, sympathetic, well-modulated.

adj antonyms expressionless, poker-faced.

expulsion *n* **1** discharge, eviction, expelling, ousting. **2** elimination, evacuation, excretion. **3** ejection, excision, excommunication, extrusion, ostracism, separation.

expunge *vb* annihilate, annul, cancel, delete, destroy, efface, erase, obliterate, wipe out.

expurgate *vb* **1** clean, cleanse, purge, purify. **2** bowdlerize, emasculate.

exquisite *adj* **1** accurate, delicate, discriminating, exact, fastidious, nice, refined. **2** choice, elect, excellent, precious, rare, valuable. **3** complete, consummate, matchless, perfect. **4** acute, keen, intense, poignant. • *n* beau, coxcomb, dandy, fop, popinjay.

adj antonyms flawed, imperfect, poor, ugly.

extant *adj* existent, existing, present, surviving, undestroyed, visible.

adj antonyms dead, extinct, non-existent.

extempore *adj* extemporaneous, extemporary, impromptu, improvised. • *adv* offhand, suddenly, unpremeditatedly, unpreparedly.

extend *vb* **1** reach, stretch. **2** continue, elongate, lengthen, prolong, protract, widen. **3** augment, broaden, dilate, distend, enlarge, expand, increase. **4** diffuse, spread. **5** give, impart, offer, yield. **6** lie, range.

vb antonym shorten.

extensible *adj* ductile, elastic, extendible, extensile, protractible, protractile.

extension *n* augmentation, continuation, delay, dilatation, dilation, distension, enlargement, expansion, increase, prolongation, protraction.

extensive *adj* broad, capacious, comprehensive, expanded, extended, far-reaching, large, wide, widespread.

adj antonyms narrow, restricted.

extent *n* **1** amplitude, expanse, expansion. **2** amount, bulk, content, degree, magnitude, size, volume. **3** compass, measure, length, proportions, reach, stretch. **4** area, field, latitude, range, scope. **5** breadth, depth, height, width.

extenuate *vb* **1** diminish, lessen, reduce, soften, weaken. **2** excuse, mitigate, palliate, qualify.

exterior *adj* **1** external, outer, outlying, outside, outward, superficial, surface. **2** extrinsic, foreign. • *n* **1** outside, surface. **2** appearance.

n antonym interior.

adj antonym interior.

exterminate *vb* abolish, annihilate, destroy, eliminate, eradicate, extirpate, uproot.

external *adj* **1** exterior, outer, outside, outward, superficial. **2** extrinsic, foreign. **3** apparent, visible.

adj antonym internal.

extinct *adj* **1** extinguished, quenched. **2** closed, dead, ended, lapsed, terminated, vanished.

adj antonyms extant, living.

extinction *n* **1** death, extinguishment. **2** abolishment, abolition, annihilation, destruction, excision, extermination, extirpation.

extinguish *vb* **1** choke, douse, put out, quell, smother, stifle, suffocate, suppress. **2** destroy, nullify, subdue. **3** eclipse, obscure.

extirpate *vb* abolish, annihilate, deracinate, destroy, eradicate, exterminate, uproot, weed.

extol *vb* **1** celebrate, exalt, glorify, laud, magnify, praise. **2** applaud, commend, eulogize.

vb antonyms blame, denigrate.

extort *vb* elicit, exact, extract, force, squeeze, wrench, wrest, wring.

extortion *n* **1** blackmail, compulsion, demand, exaction, oppression, overcharge, rapacity, tribute. **2** exorbitance.

extortionate *adj* **1** bloodsucking, exacting, hard, harsh, oppressive, rapacious, rigorous, severe. **2** exorbitant, unreasonable.

extra *adj* **1** accessory, additional, auxiliary, collateral. **2** another, farther, fresh, further, more, new, other, plus, ulterior. **3** side, spare, supernumerary, supplemental, supplementary, surplus. **4** extraordinary, extreme, unusual. • *adv* additionally, also, beyond, farthermore, furthermore, more, moreover, plus. • *n* **1** accessory, appendage, collateral, nonessential, special, supernumerary, supplement. **2** bonus, premium. **3** balance, leftover, remainder, spare, surplus.

adj antonym integral.

extract *vb* **1** extort, pull out, remove, withdraw. **2** derive, distil, draw, express, squeeze. **3** cite, determine, derive, quote, select. • *n* **1** citation, excerpt, passage, quotation, selection. **2** decoction, distillation, essence, infusion, juice.

vb antonym insert.

extraction *n* **1** drawing out, derivation, distillation, elicitation, essence, pulling out. **2** birth, descent, genealogy, lineage, origin, parentage.

extraneous *adj* **1** external, extrinsic, foreign. **2** additional, adventitious, external, superfluous, supplementary, unessential.

extraordinary *adj* abnormal, amazing, distinguished, egregious, exceptional, marvellous, monstrous, particular, peculiar, phenomenal, prodigious, rare, remarkable, signal, singular, special, strange, uncommon, unprecedented, unusual, unwonted, wonderful.

adj antonyms commonplace, ordinary.

extravagance *n* **1** excess, enormity, exorbitance, preposterousness, unreasonableness. **2** absurdity, excess, folly, irregularity, wildness. **3** lavishness, prodigality, profuseness, profusion, superabundance. **4** waste.

extravagant *adj* **1** excessive, exorbitant, inordinate, preposterous, unreasonable. **2** absurd, foolish, irregular, wild. **3** lavish, prodigal, profuse, spendthrift.

adj antonyms moderate, thrifty.

extreme *adj* **1** farthest, outermost, remotest, utmost, uttermost. **2** greatest, highest. **3** final, last, ultimate. **4** drastic, egregious,

excessive, extravagant, immoderate, intense, outrageous, radical, unreasonable. • *n* **1** end, extremity, limit. **2** acme, climax, degree, height, pink. **3** danger, distress.

adj antonyms mild, moderate.

extremity *n* border, edge, end, extreme, limb, termination, verge.

extricate *vb* clear, deliver, disembarrass, disengage, disentangle, liberate, release, relieve.

vb antonym involve.

extrinsic *adj* external, extraneous, foreign, outside, outward, superabundance, superfluity.

exuberance *n* **1** abundance, copiousness, flood, luxuriance, plenitude. **2** excess, lavishness, overabundance, overflow, overgrowth, over-luxuriance, profusion, rankness, redundancy, superabundance, superfluity.

exuberant *adj* **1** abounding, abundant, copious, fertile, flowing, luxuriant, prolific, rich. **2** excessive, lavish, overabundant, overflowing, over-luxuriant, profuse, rank, redundant, superabounding, superabundant, wanton.

adj antonyms apathetic, lifeless, scant.

exude *vb* **1** discharge, excrete, secrete, sweat. **2** infiltrate, ooze, percolate.

exult *vb* gloat, glory, jubilate, rejoice, transport, triumph, taunt, vault.

exultation *n* delight, elation, joy, jubilation, transport, triumph.

eye *vb* contemplate, inspect, ogle, scrutinize, survey, view, watch. • *n* **1** estimate, judgement, look, sight, vision, view. **2** inspection, notice, observation, scrutiny, sight, vigilance, watch. **3** aperture, eyelet, peephole, perforation. **4** bud, shoot.

F

fable *n* **1** allegory, legend, myth, parable, story, tale. **2** fabrication, falsehood, fiction, figment, forgery, untruth.

fabric *n* **1** building, edifice, pile, structure. **2** conformation, make, texture, workmanship. **3** cloth, material, stuff, textile, tissue, web.

fabricate *vb* **1** build, construct, erect, frame. **2** compose, devise, fashion, make, manufacture. **3** coin, fake, feign, forge, invent.

fabrication *n* **1** building, construction, erection. **2** manufacture. **3** fable, fake, falsehood, fiction, figment, forgery, invention, lie.
n antonym truth.

fabulous *adj* amazing, apocryphal, coined, fabricated, feigned, fictitious, forged, imaginary, invented, legendary, marvellous, mythical, romancing, unbelievable, unreal.
adj antonyms moderate, real, small.

façade *n* elevation, face, front.

face *vb* **1** confront. **2** beard, buck, brave, dare, defy, front, oppose. **3** dress, level, polish, smooth. **4** cover, incrust, veneer. • *n* **1** cover, facet, surface. **2** breast, escarpment, front. **3** countenance, features, grimace, physiognomy, visage. **4** appearance, expression, look, semblance. **5** assurance, audacity, boldness, brass, confidence, effrontery, impudence.

facet *n* cut, face, lozenge, surface.

facetious *adj* **1** amusing, comical, droll, funny, humorous, jocose, jocular, pleasant, waggish, witty. **2** entertaining, gay, lively, merry, sportive, sprightly.
adj antonym serious.

facile *adj* **1** easy. **2** affable, approachable, complaisant, conversable, courteous, mild. **3** compliant, ductile, flexible, fluent, manageable, pliable, pliant, tractable, yielding. **4** dextrous, ready, skilful.
adj antonyms clumsy, implausible, profound.

facilitate *vb* expedite, help.

facility *n* **1** ease, easiness. **2** ability, dexterity, expertness, knack, quickness, readiness. **3** ductility, flexibility, pliancy. **4** advantage, appliance, convenience, means, resource. **5** affability, civility, complaisance, politeness.

facsimile *n* copy, duplicate, fax, reproduction.

fact *n* **1** act, circumstance, deed, event, incident, occurrence, performance. **2** actuality, certainty, existence, reality, truth.

faction *n* **1** cabal, clique, combination, division, junta, party, side. **2** disagreement, discord, disorder, dissension, recalcitrance, recalcitrancy, refractoriness, sedition, seditiousness, tumult, turbulence, turbulency.
n antonyms agreement, peace.

factious *adj* litigious, malcontent, rebellious, recalcitrant, refractory, seditious. turbulent.

factitious *adj* artful, artificial, conventional, false, unnatural, unreal.
adj antonym genuine.

factor *n* **1** agent, bailiff, broker, consignee, go-between, steward, component, element, ingredient. **2** influence, reason.

factory *n* manufactory, mill, work, workshop.

faculty *n* **1** ability, capability, capacity, endowment, power, property, quality. **2** ableness, address, adroitness, aptitude, aptness, clearness, competency, dexterity, efficiency, expertness, facility, forte, ingenuity, knack, qualification, quickness, readiness, skill, skilfulness, talent, turn. **3** body, department, profession. **4** authority, prerogative, license, privilege, right.

fade *vb* **1** disappear, die, evanesce, fall, faint, perish, vanish. **2** decay, decline, droop, fall, languish, wither. **3** bleach, blanch, pale. **4** disperse, dissolve.

faeces *npl* **1** dregs, lees, sediment, settlings. **2** dung, excrement, ordure, settlings.

fag *vb* **1** droop, flag, sink. **2** drudge, toil. **3** fatigue, jade, tire, weary. • *n* **1** drudgery, fatigue, work. **2** drudge, grub, hack. **3** cigarette, smoke. **4** (*off, sl*) homosexual, queer.

fail *vb* **1** break, collapse, decay, decline, fade, sicken, sink, wane. **2** cease, disappear. **3** fall, miscarry, miss. **4** neglect, omit. **5** bankrupt, break.
vb antonyms gain, improve, prosper, succeed.

failing *adj* **1** deficient, lacking, needing,

120

wanting. **2** declining, deteriorating, fading, flagging, languishing, sinking, waning, wilting. **3** unsuccessful. • *prep* lacking, needing, wanting. • *n* **1** decay, decline. **2** failure, miscarriage. **3** defect, deficiency, fault, foible, frailty, imperfection, infirmity, shortcoming, vice, weakness. **4** error, lapse, slip. **5** bankruptcy, insolvency.
n antonyms advantage, strength.
adj antonyms thriving, vigorous.

failure *n* **1** defectiveness, deficiency, delinquency, shortcoming. **2** fail, miscarriage, negligence, neglect, nonobservance, nonperformance, omission, slip. **3** abortion, botch, breakdown, collapse, fiasco, fizzle. **4** bankruptcy, crash, downfall, insolvency, ruin. **5** decay, declension, decline, loss.
n antonym success.

fain *adj* anxious, glad, inclined, pleased, rejoiced, well-pleased. • *adv* cheerfully, eagerly, gladly, joyfully, willingly.

faint *vb* **1** swoon. **2** decline, fade, fail, languish, weaken. • *adj* **1** swooning. **2** drooping, exhausted, feeble, languid, listless, sickly, weak. **3** gentle, inconsiderable, little, slight, small, soft, thin. **4** dim, dull, indistinct, perceptible, scarce, slight. **5** cowardly, dastardly, faint-hearted, fearful, timid, timorous. **6** dejected, depressed, discouraged, disheartened, dispirited. • *n* blackout, swoon.
adj antonyms clear, strong.

faint-hearted *adj* cowardly, dastardly, faint, fearful, timid, timorous.

fair[1] *adj* **1** spotless, unblemished, unspotted, unstained, untarnished. **2** blond, light, white. **3** beautiful, comely, handsome, shapely. **4** clear, cloudless, pleasant, unclouded. **5** favourable, prosperous. **6** hopeful, promising, propitious. **7** clear, distinct, open, plain, unencumbered, unobstructed. **8** candid, frank, honest, honourable, impartial, ingenuous, just, unbiased, upright. **9** equitable, proper. **10** average, decent, indifferent, mediocre, moderate, ordinary, passable, reasonable, respectful, tolerable.
adj antonyms cloudy, inclement, poor, unfair.
adj antonym dark.

fair[2] *n* bazaar, carnival, exposition, festival, fete, funfair, gala.

fairy *n* brownie, elf, demon, fay, sprite.

faith *n* **1** assurance, belief, confidence, credence, credit, dependence, reliance,

trust. **2** creed, doctrine, dogma, persuasion, religion, tenet. **3** constancy, faithfulness, fidelity, loyalty, truth, truthfulness.
n antonyms mistrust, treachery, unfaithfulness.

faithful *adj* **1** constant, devoted, loyal, staunch, steadfast, true. **2** honest, upright, reliable, trustworthy, trusty. **3** reliable, truthful. **4** accurate, close, conscientiousness, exact, nice, strict.
adj antonyms disloyal, inaccurate, treacherous.

faithless *adj* **1** unbelieving. **2** dishonest, disloyal, false, fickle, fluctuating, inconstant, mercurial, mutable, perfidious, shifting, treacherous, truthless, unsteady, untruthful, vacillating, variable, wavering.
adj antonyms believing, faithful.

fall *vb* **1** collapse, depend, descend, drop, sink, topple, tumble. **2** abate, decline, decrease, depreciate, ebb, subside. **3** err, lapse, sin, stumble, transgress, trespass, trip. **4** die, perish. **5** befall, chance, come, happen, occur, pass. **6** become, get. **7** come, pass. • *n* **1** collapse, comedown, descent, downcome, dropping, falling, flop, plop, tumble. **2** cascade, cataract, waterfall. **3** death, destruction, downfall, overthrow, ruin, surrender. **4** comeuppance, degradation. **5** apostasy, declension, failure, lapse, slip. **6** decline, decrease, depreciation, diminution, ebb, sinking, subsidence. **7** cadence, close. **8** declivity, inclination, slope.
vb antonym rise.
n antonym rise.

fallacious *adj* **1** absurd, deceptive, deceiving, delusive, disappointing, erroneous, false, illusive, illusory, misleading. **2** paralogistic, sophistical, worthless.
adj antonyms correct, true.

fallacy *n* **1** aberration, deceit, deception, delusion, error, falsehood, illusion, misapprehension, misconception, mistake, untruth. **2** non sequitur, paralogism, sophism, sophistry.
n antonym truth.

fallibility *n* frailty, imperfection, uncertainty.

fallible *adj* erring, frail, ignorant, imperfect, uncertain, weak.

fallow *adj* **1** left, neglected, uncultivated, unsowed, untilled. **2** dormant, inactive, inert.

false *adj* **1** lying, mendacious, truthless, untrue, unveracious. **2** dishonest, dishonourable, disingenuous, disloyal, double-faced, double-tongued, faithless, false-hearted, perfidious, treacherous, unfaithful. **3** fictitious, forged, made-up, unreliable, untrustworthy. **4** artificial, bastard, bogus, counterfeit, factitious, feigned, forged, hollow, hypocritical, make-believe, pretended, pseudo, sham, spurious, supposititious. **5** erroneous, improper, incorrect, unfounded, wrong. **6** deceitful, deceiving, deceptive, disappointing, fallacious, misleading.

adj antonyms honest, reliable, true.

false-hearted *adj* dishonourable, disloyal, double, double-tongued, faithless, false, perfidious, treacherous.

falsehood *n* **1** falsity. **2** fabrication, fib, fiction, lie, untruth. **3** cheat, counterfeit, imposture, mendacity, treachery.

n antonyms truth, truthfulness.

falsify *vb* **1** alter, adulterate, belie, cook, counterfeit, doctor, fake, falsely, garble, misrepresent, represent. **2** disprove. **3** violate.

falsity *n* falsehood, untruth, untruthfulness.

falter *vb* **1** halt, hesitate, lisp, quaver, stammer, stutter. **2** fail, stagger, stumble, totter, tremble, waver. **3** dodder.

fame *n* **1** bruit, hearsay, report, rumour. **2** celebrity, credit, eminence, glory, greatness, honour, illustriousness, kudos, lustre, notoriety, renown, reputation, repute.

familiar *adj* **1** acquainted, aware, conversant, well-versed. **2** amicable, close, cordial, domestic, fraternal, friendly, homely, intimate, near. **3** affable, accessible, companionable, conversable, courteous, civil, friendly, kindly, sociable, social. **4** easy, free and easy, unceremonious, unconstrained. **5** common, frequent, well-known. • *n* acquaintance, associate, companion, friend, intimate.

adj antonyms formal, reserved, unfamiliar, unversed.

familiarity *n* **1** acquaintance, knowledge, understanding. **2** fellowship, friendship, intimacy. **3** closeness, friendliness, sociability. **4** freedom, informality, liberty. **5** disrespect, overfreedom, presumption. **6** intercourse.

n antonyms formality, reservation, unfamiliarity.

familiarize *vb* accustom, habituate, inure, train, use.

family *n* **1** brood, household, people. **2** ancestors, blood, breed, clan, dynasty, kindred, house, lineage, race, stock, strain, tribe. **3** class, genus, group, kind, subdivision.

famine *n* dearth, destitution, hunger, scarcity, starvation.

n antonym plenty.

famish *vb* distress, exhaust, pinch, starve.

famous *adj* celebrated, conspicuous, distinguished, eminent, excellent, fabled, famed, far-famed, great, glorious, heroic, honoured, illustrious, immortal, notable, noted, notorious, remarkable, renowned, signal.

adj antonym unknown.

fan[1] *vb* **1** agitate, beat, move, winnow. **2** blow, cool, refresh, ventilate. **3** excite, fire, increase, rouse, stimulate. • *n* blower, cooler, punkah, ventilator.

fan[2] *n* admirer, buff, devotee, enthusiast, fancier, follower, pursuer, supporter.

fanatic *n* bigot, devotee, enthusiast, visionary, zealot.

fanatical *adj* bigoted, enthusiastic, frenzied, mad, rabid, visionary, wild, zealous.

fanciful *adj* **1** capricious, crotchety, imaginary, visionary, whimsical. **2** chimerical, fantastical, ideal, imaginary, wild.

fancy *vb* **1** apprehend, believe, conjecture, imagine, suppose, think. **2** conceive, imagine. • *adj* **1** elegant, fine, nice, ornamented. **2** extravagant, fanciful, whimsical. • *n* **1** imagination. **2** apprehension, conceit, conception, impression, idea, image, notion, thought. **3** approval, fondness, inclination, judgement, liking, penchant, taste. **4** caprice, crotchet, fantasy, freak, humour, maggot, quirk, vagary, whim, whimsy. **5** apparition, chimera, daydream, delusion, hallucination, megrim, phantasm, reverie, vision.

vb antonym dislike.

n antonyms dislike, fact, reality.

adj antonym plain.

fang *n* **1** claw, nail, talon, tooth. **2** tusk.

fantastic *adj* **1** chimerical, fanciful, imaginary, romantic, unreal, visionary. **2** bizarre, capricious, grotesque, odd, quaint, queer, strange, whimsical, wild.

adj antonyms ordinary, plain, poor.

far *adj* **1** distant, long, protracted, remote.

2 farther, remoter. **3** alienated, estranged, hostile. • *adv* **1** considerably, extremely, greatly, very much. **2** afar, distantly, far away, remotely.
adv antonym near.
adj antonyms close, nearby.

farce *n* **1** burlesque, caricature, parody, travesty. **2** forcemeat, stuffing.

farcical *adj* absurd, comic, droll, funny, laughable, ludicrous, ridiculous.

fardel *n* **1** bundle, burden, load, pack. **2** annoyance, burden, ill, trouble.

fare *vb* **1** go, journey, pass, travel. **2** happen, prosper, prove. **3** feed, live, manage, subsist. • *n* **1** charge, price, ticket money. **2** passenger, traveller. **3** board, commons, food, table, victuals, provisions. **4** condition, experience, fortune, luck, outcome.

farewell *n* **1** adieu, leave-taking, valediction. **2** departure, leave, parting, valedictory.
n antonym hello.

far-fetched *adj* abstruse, forced, recondite, strained.

farrago *n* gallimaufry, hodgepodge, hotchpotch, jumble, medley, miscellany, mixture, potpourri, salmagundi.

farther *adj* **1** additional. **2** further, remoter, ulterior. • *adv* **1** beyond, further. **2** besides, furthermore, moreover.

fascinate *vb* **1** affect, bewitch, overpower, spellbind, stupefy, transfix. **2** absorb, captivate, catch, charm, delight, enamour, enchant, enrapture, entrance.
vb antonym bore.

fascination *n* absorption, charm, enchantment, magic, sorcery, spell, witchcraft, witchery.

fash *vb* harass, perplex, plague, torment, trouble, vex, worry. • *n* anxiety, care, trouble, vexation.

fashion *vb* **1** contrive, create, design, forge, form, make, mould, pattern, shape. **2** accommodate, adapt, adjust, fit, suit. • *n* **1** appearance, cast, configuration, conformation, cut, figure, form, make, model, mould, pattern, shape, stamp. **2** manner, method, sort, wake. **3** conventionalism, conventionality, custom, fad, mode, style, usage, vogue. **4** breeding, gentility. **5** quality.

fashionable *adj* **1** modish, stylish. **2** current, modern, prevailing, up-to-date. **3** customary, usual. **4** genteel, well-bred.
adj antonym unfashionable.

fast¹ *adj* **1** close, fastened, firm, fixed, immovable, tenacious, tight. **2** constant, faithful, permanent, resolute, staunch, steadfast, unswerving, unwavering. **3** fortified, impregnable, strong. **4** deep, profound, sound. **5** fleet, quick, rapid, swift. **6** dissipated, dissolute, extravagant, giddy, reckless, thoughtless, thriftless, wild. • *adv* **1** firmly, immovably, tightly. **2** quickly, rapidly, swiftly. **3** extravagantly, prodigally, reckless, wildly.
adj antonym slow.
adv antonym slowly.

fast² *vb* abstain, go hungry, starve. • *n* abstention, abstinence, diet, fasting, starvation.

fasten *vb* **1** attach, bind, bolt, catch, chain, cleat, fix, gird, lace, lock, pin, secure, strap, tether, tie. **2** belay, bend. **3** connect, hold, join, unite.
vb antonym unfasten.

fastidious *adj* critical, dainty, delicate, difficult, exquisite, finical, hypercritical, meticulous, overdelicate, overnice, particular, precise, precious, punctilious, queasy, squeamish.
adj antonym undemanding.

fat *adj* **1** adipose, fatty, greasy, oily, oleaginous, unctuous. **2** corpulent, fleshy, gross, obese, paunchy, portly, plump, pudgy, pursy. **3** coarse, dull, heavy, sluggish, stupid. **4** lucrative, profitable, rich. **5** fertile, fruitful, productive, rich. • *n* **1** adipose tissue, ester, grease, oil. **2** best part, cream, flower. **3** corpulence, fatness, fleshiness, obesity, plumpness, stoutness.
adj antonyms thin, unproductive.

fatal *adj* **1** deadly, lethal, mortal. **2** baleful, baneful, calamitous, catastrophic, destructive, mischievous, pernicious, ruinous. **3** destined, doomed, foreordained, inevitable, predestined.
adj antonym harmless.

fatality *n* **1** destiny, fate. **2** mortality. **3** calamity, disaster.

fate *n* **1** destination, destiny, fate. **2** cup, die, doom, experience, lot, fortune, portion, weird. **3** death, destruction, ruin.

fated *adj* appointed, destined, doomed, foredoomed, predetermined, predestinated, predestined, preordained.

fatherly *adj* benign, kind, paternal, protecting, tender.
adj antonyms cold, harsh, unkind.

fathom *vb* **1** comprehend, divine, penetrate, reach, understand. **2** estimate, gauge, measure, plumb, probe, sound.

fathomless *adj* **1** abysmal, bottomless, deep, immeasurable, profound. **2** impenetrable, incomprehensible, obscure.

fatigue *vb* exhaust, fag, jade, tire, weaken, weary. • *n* **1** exhaustion, lassitude, tiredness, weariness. **2** hardship, labour, toil.
vb antonym refresh.
n antonyms energy, freshness.

fatuity *n* **1** foolishness, idiocy, imbecility, stupidity. **2** absurdity, folly, inanity, infatuation, madness.

fatuous *adj* **1** dense, drivelling, dull, foolish, idiotic, stupid, witless. **2** infatuated, mad, senseless, silly, weak.

fault *n* **1** blemish, defect, flaw, foible, frailty, imperfection, infirmity, negligence, obliquity, offence, shortcoming, spot, weakness. **2** delinquency, error, indiscretion, lapse, misdeed, misdemeanour, offence, peccadillo, slip, transgression, trespass, vice, wrong. **3** blame, culpability.
n antonyms advantage, strength.
vb antonym praise.

faultless *adj* **1** blameless, guiltless, immaculate, innocent, sinless, spotless, stainless. **2** accurate, correct, perfect, unblemished.

faulty *adj* **1** bad, defective, imperfect, incorrect. **2** blamable, blameworthy, censurable, culpable, reprehensible.

faux pas *n* blunder, indiscretion, mistake.

favour *vb* **1** befriend, countenance, encourage, patronize. **2** approve. **3** ease, facilitate. **4** aid, assist, help, oblige, support. **5** extenuate, humour, indulge, palliate, spare. • *n* **1** approval, benignity, countenance, esteem, friendless, goodwill, grace, kindness. **2** benefaction, benefit, boon, dispensation, kindness. **3** championship, patronage, popularity, support. **4** gift, present, token. **5** badge, decoration, knot, rosette. **6** leave, pardon, permission. **7** advantage, cover, indulgence, protection. **8** bias, partiality, prejudice.

favourable *adj* **1** auspicious, friendly, kind, propitious, well-disposed, willing. **2** conductive, contributing, propitious. **3** adapted, advantage, beneficial, benign, convenient, fair, fit, good, helpful, suitable.

favourite *adj* **1** beloved, darling, dear. **2** choice, fancied, esteemed, pet, preferred.

fawn *vb* bootlick, bow, creep, cringe, crouch, dangle, kneel, stoop, toady, truckle.

fealty *n* **1** allegiance, homage, loyalty, obeisance, submission. **2** devotion, faithfulness, fidelity, honour, loyalty.

fear *vb* **1** apprehend, dread. **2** revere, reverence, venerate. • *n* **1** affright, alarm, apprehension, consternation, dismay, dread, fright, horror, panic, phobia, scare, terror. **2** disquietude, flutter, perturbation, palpitation, quaking, quivering, trembling, tremor, trepidation. **3** anxiety, apprehension, concern, misdoubt, misgiving, qualm, solicitude. **4** awe, dread, reverence, veneration.
n antonyms courage, fortitude.

fearful *adj* **1** afraid, apprehensive, haunted. **2** chicken-hearted, chicken-livered, cowardly, faint-hearted, lily-livered, nervous, pusillanimous, timid, timorous. **3** dire, direful, dreadful, frightful, ghastly, horrible, shocking, terrible.

fearless *adj* bold, brave, courageous, daring, dauntless, doughty, gallant, heroic, intrepid, valiant, valorous.
adj antonyms afraid, timid.

feasible *adj* achievable, attainable, possible, practicable, suitable.

feast *vb* delight, gladden, gratify, rejoice. • *n* **1** banquet, carousal, entertainment, regale, repast, revels, symposium, treat. **2** celebration, festival, fete, holiday. **3** delight, enjoyment, pleasure.

feat *n* accomplishment, achievement, act, deed, exploit, performance, stunt, trick.

feather *n* **1** plume. **2** kind, nature, species.

featly *adv* adroitly, dextrously, nimbly, skilfully.

feature *vb* **1** envisage, envision, picture, visualize. **2** imagine. **3** specialize. **4** appear in, headline, star. • *n* **1** appearance, aspect, component. **2** conformation, fashion, make. **3** characteristic, item, mark, particularity, peculiarity, property, point, trait. **4** leader, lead item, special. **5** favour, expression, lineament. **6** article, film, motion picture, movie, story. **7** highlight, high spot.

fecund *adj* fruitful, impregnated, productive, prolific, rich.

fecundity *n* fertility, fruitfulness, productiveness.

federation *n* **1** alliance, allying, confederation, federating, federation, leaguing, union, uniting. **2** affiliation, coalition, combination, compact, confederacy, entente, federacy, league, copartnership.

fee *vb* pay, recompense, reward. • *n* **1** account, bill, charge, compensation, honorarium, remuneration, reward, tip. **2** benefice, fief, feud.

feeble *adj* **1** anaemic, debilitated, declining, drooping, enervated, exhausted, frail, infirm, languid, languishing, sickly. **2** dim, faint, imperfect, indistinct.
adj antonyms strong, worthy.

feed *vb* **1** contribute, provide, supply. **2** cherish, eat, nourish, subsist, sustain. • *n* fodder, food, foodstuff, forage, provender.

feel *vb* **1** apprehend, intuit, perceive, sense. **2** examine, handle, probe, touch. **3** enjoy, experience, suffer. **4** prove, sound, test, try. **5** appear, look, seem. **6** believe, conceive, deem, fancy, infer, opine, suppose, think. • *n* **1** atmosphere, feeling, quality. **2** finish, surface, texture.

feeling *n* **1** consciousness, impression, notion, perception, sensation. **2** atmosphere, sense, sentience, touch. **3** affecting, emotion, heartstrings, impression, passion, soul, sympathy. **4** sensibility, sentiment, susceptibility, tenderness. **5** attitude, impression, opinion.

feign *vb* **1** devise, fabricate, forge, imagine, invent. **2** affect, assume, counterfeit, imitate, pretend, sham, simulate.

feint *n* artifice, blind, expedient, make-believe, pretence, stratagem, trick.

felicitate *vb* **1** complicate, congratulate. **2** beatify, bless, delight.

felicitous *adj* **1** appropriate, apt, fit, happy, ingenious, inspired, opportune, pertinent, seasonable, skilful, well-timed. **2** auspicious, fortunate, prosperous, propitious, successful.

felicity *n* **1** blessedness, bliss, blissfulness, gladness, happiness, joy. **2** appropriateness, aptitude, aptness, felicitousness, fitness, grace, propriety, readiness, suitableness. **3** fortune, luck, success.

fell[1] *vb* **1** beat, knock down, level, prostrate. **2** cut, demolish, hew.

fell[2] *adj* **1** barbarous, bloodthirsty, bloody, cruel, ferocious, fierce, implacable, inhuman, malicious, malign, malignant, pitiless, relentless, ruthless, sanguinary, savage, unrelenting, vandalistic. **2** deadly, destructive.

fellow *adj* affiliated, associated, joint, like, mutual, similar, twin. • *n* **1** associate, companion, comrade. **2** compeer, equal, peer. **3** counterpart, mate, match, partner. **4** member. **5** boy, character, individual, man, person.

fellowship *n* **1** brotherhood, companionship, comradeship, familiarity, intimacy. **2** participation. **3** partnership. **4** communion, converse, intercourse. **5** affability, kindliness, sociability, sociableness.

felon *n* **1** convict, criminal, culprit, delinquent, malefactor, outlaw. **2** inflammation, whitlow.

felonious *adj* atrocious, cruel, felon, heinous, infamous, malicious, malign, malignant, nefarious, perfidious, vicious, villainous.

female *adj* **1** delicate, gentle, ladylike, soft. **2** fertile, pistil-bearing, pistillate.

feminine *adj* **1** affectionate, delicate, gentle, graceful, modest, soft, tender. **2** female, ladylike, maidenly, womanish, womanly. **3** effeminateness, effeminacy, softness, unmanliness, weakness, womanliness.
adj antonym masculine.

fen *n* bog, marsh, moor, morass, quagmire, slough, swamp.

fence *vb* **1** defend, enclose, fortify, guard, protect, surround. **2** circumscribe, evade, equivocate, hedge, prevaricate. **3** guard, parry. • *n* **1** barrier, hedge, hoarding, palings, palisade, stockade, wall. **2** defence, protection, guard, security, shield. **3** fencing, swordplay, swordsmanship. **4** receiver.

fenny *adj* boggy, fennish, swampy, marshy.

feral, ferine *adj* ferocious, fierce, rapacious, ravenous, savage, untamed, wild.

ferment *vb* **1** agitate, excite, heat. **2** boil, brew, bubble, concoct, heat, seethe. • *n* **1** barm, leaven, yeast. **2** agitation, commotion, fever, glow, heat, tumult.

ferocious *adj* **1** feral, fierce, rapacious, ravenous, savage, untamed, wild. **2** barbarous, bloody, bloodthirsty, brutal, cruel, fell, inhuman, merciless, murderous, pitiless, remorseless, ruthless, sanguinary, truculent, vandalistic, violent.
adj antonyms gentle, mild.

ferocity *n* **1** ferociousness, ferocity, fierceness, rapacity, savageness, wildness. **2** barbarity, cruelty, inhumanity.

fertile *adj* **1** bearing, breeding, fecund, prolific. **2** exuberant, fruitful, luxuriant,

plenteous, productive, rich, teeming. **3** female, fruit-bearing, pistillate.
adj antonyms arid, barren.

fertility *n* **1** fertileness, fèrtility. **2** abundance, exuberant, fruitfulness, luxuriance, plenteousness, productiveness, richness.

fervent *adj* **1** burning, hot, glowing, melting, seething. **2** animated, ardent, earnest, enthusiastic, fervid, fierce, fiery, glowing, impassioned, intense, passionate, vehement, warm, zealous.

fervour *n* **1** heat, warmth. **2** animation, ardour, eagerness, earnestness, excitement, fervency, intensity, vehemence, zeal.

fester *vb* **1** corrupt, rankle, suppurate, ulcerate. **2** putrefy, rot. • *n* **1** abscess, canker, gathering, pustule, sore, suppination. **2** festering, rankling.

festival *n* **1** anniversary, carnival, feast, fete, gala, holiday, jubilee. **2** banquet, carousal, celebration, entertainment, treat.

festive *adj* carnival, convivial, festal, festival, gay, jolly, jovial, joyful, merry, mirthful, uproarious.
adj antonyms gloomy, sober, somber.

festivity *n* conviviality, festival, gaiety, jollity, joviality, joyfulness, joyousness, merrymaking, mirth.

festoon *vb* adorn, decorate, embellish, garland, hoop, ornament. • *n* decoration, embellishment, garland, hoop, ornament, ornamentation.

fetch *vb* **1** bring, elicit, get. **2** accomplish, achieve, effect, perform. **3** attain, reach. • *n* artifice, dodge, ruse, stratagem, trick.

fetid *adj* foul, malodorous, mephitic, noisome, offensive, rancid, rank, rank-smelling, stinking, strong-smelling.

fetish *n* charm, medicine, talisman.

fetter *vb* **1** clog, hamper, shackle, trammel. **2** bind, chain, confine, encumber, hamper, restrain, tie, trammel. • *n* bond, chain, clog, hamper, shackle.

feud *vb* argue, bicker, clash, contend, dispute, quarrel. • *n* affray, argument, bickering, broil, clashing, contention, contest, discord, dissension, enmity, fray, grudge, hostility, jarring, quarrel, rupture, strife, vendetta.
n antonyms agreement, peace.
vb antonym agree.

fever *n* agitation, excitement, ferment, fire, flush, heat, passion.

fey *adj* **1** clairvoyant, ethereal, strange, unusual, whimsical. **2** death-smitten, doomed.

fiasco *n* failure, fizzle.

fiat *n* command, decree, order, ordinance.

fibre *n* **1** filament, pile, staple, strand, texture, thread. **2** stamina, strength, toughness.

fickle *adj* capricious, changeable, faithless, fitful, inconstant, irresolute, mercurial, mutable, shifting, unsettled, unstable, unsteady, vacillating, variable, veering, violate, volatile, wavering.
adj antonym constant.

fiction *n* **1** fancy, fantasy, imagination, invention. **2** novel, romance. **3** fable, fabrication, falsehood, figment, forgery, invention, lie.
n antonym truth.

fictitious *adj* **1** assumed, fabulous, fanciful, feigned, imaginary, invented, mythical, unreal. **2** artificial, counterfeit, dummy, false, spurious, suppositious.
adj antonyms genuine, real.

fiddle *vb* **1** dawdle, fidget, interfere, tinker, trifle. **2** cheat, swindle, tamper. • *n* **1** fraud, swindle. **2** fiddler, violin, violinist.

fidelity *n* **1** constancy, devotedness, devotion, dutifulness, faithfulness, fealty, loyalty, true-heartedness, truth. **2** accuracy, closeness, exactness, faithfulness, precision.
n antonyms inaccuracy, inconstancy, treachery.

fidget *vb* chafe, fret, hitch, twitch, worry. • *n* fidgetiness, impatience, restlessness, uneasiness.

fiduciary *adj* **1** confident, fiducial, firm, steadfast, trustful, undoubting, unwavering. **2** reliable, trustworthy. • *n* depositary, trustee.

field *n* **1** clearing, glebe, meadow. **2** expanse, extent, opportunity, range, room, scope, surface. **3** department, domain, province, realm, region.

fiendish *adj* atrocious, cruel, demoniac, devilish, diabolical, hellish, implacable, infernal, malevolent, malicious, malign, malignant.

fierce *adj* **1** barbarous, brutal, cruel, fell, ferocious, furious, infuriate, ravenous, savage. **2** fiery, impetuous, murderous, passionate, tearing, tigerish, truculent, turbulent, uncurbed, untamed, vehement, violent.
adj antonyms calm, gentle, kind.

fiery *adj* **1** fervent, fervid, flaming, heated, hot, glowing, lurid. **2** ardent, fierce, impassioned, impetuous, inflamed, passionate, vehement.

fight *vb* **1** battle, combat, war. **2** contend, contest, dispute, feud, oppose, strive, struggle, wrestle. **3** encounter, engage. **4** handle, manage, manoeuvre. • *n* **1** affair, affray, action, battle, brush, combat, conflict, confrontation, contest, duel, encounter, engagement, melée, quarrel, struggle, war. **2** brawl, broil, riot, row, skirmish. **3** fighting, pluck, pugnacity, resistance, spirit, temper.

figment *n* fable, fabrication, falsehood, fiction, invention.

figurative *adj* **1** emblematical, representative, symbolic, representative, typical. **2** metaphorical, tropical. **3** florid, flowery, ornate, poetical.

figure *vb* **1** adorn, diversify, ornament, variegate. **2** delineate, depict, represent, signify, symbolize, typify. **3** conceive, image, imagine, picture. **4** calculate, cipher, compute. **5** act, appear, perform. • *n* **1** configuration, conformation, form, outline, shape. **2** effigy, image, likeness, representative. **3** design, diagram, drawing, pattern. **4** image, metaphor, trope. **5** emblem, symbol, type. **6** character, digit, number, numeral.

filament *n* cirrus, fibre, fibril, gossamer, hair, strand, tendril, thread.

filch *vb* crib, nick, pilfer, purloin, rob, snitch, seal, thieve.

file¹ *vb* order, pigeonhole, record, tidy. • *n* **1** data, dossier, folder, portfolio. **2** column, line, list, range, rank, row, series, tier.

file² *vb* burnish, furbish, polish, rasp, refine, smooth.

filibuster *vb* delay, frustrate, obstruct, play for time, stall, temporize. • *n* **1** frustrater, obstructionist, thwarter. **2** adventurer, buccaneer, corsair, freebooter, pirate.

fill *vb* **1** occupy, pervade. **2** dilate, distend, expand, stretch, trim. **3** furnish, replenish, stock, store, supply. **4** cloy, congest, content, cram, glut, gorge, line, pack, pall, sate, satiate, satisfy, saturate, stuff, suffuse, swell. **5** engage, fulfil, hold, occupy, officiate, perform.

vb antonyms clear, empty.

film *vb* **1** becloud, cloud, coat, cover, darken, fog, mist, obfuscate, obscure, veil. **2** photograph, shoot, take. • *n* **1** cloud, coating, gauze, membrane, nebula, pellicle, scum, skin, veil. **2** thread.

filter *vb* **1** filtrate, strain. **2** exude, ooze, percolate, transude. • *n* diffuser, colander, riddle, sieve, sifter, strainer.

filth *n* **1** dirt, nastiness, ordure. **2** corruption, defilement, foulness, grossness, impurity, obscenity, pollution, squalor, uncleanness, vileness.

n antonyms cleanliness, decency, purity.

filthy *adj* **1** defiled, dirty, foul, licentious, nasty, obscene, pornographic, squalid, unclean. **2** corrupt, gross, impure, unclean. **3** miry, mucky, muddy.

adj antonyms clean, decent, inoffensive, pure.

final *adj* **1** eventual, extreme, last, latest, terminal, ultimate. **2** conclusive, decisive, definitive, irrevocable.

finale *n* conclusion, end, termination.

finances *npl* **1** funds, resources, revenues, treasury. **2** income, property.

find *vb* **1** discover, fall upon. **2** gain, get, obtain, procure. **3** ascertain, notice, observe, perceive, remark. **4** catch, detect. **5** contribute, furnish, provide, supply. • *n* acquisition, catch, discovery, finding, plum, prize, strike.

fine¹ *vb* filter, purify, refine. • *adj* **1** comminuted, little, minute, small. **2** capillary, delicate, small. **3** choice, light. **4** exact, keen, sharp. **5** attenuated, subtle, tenuous, thin. **6** exquisite, fastidious, nice, refined, sensitive, subtle. **7** dandy, excellent, superb, superior. **8** beautiful, elegant, handsome, magnificent, splendid. **9** clean, pure, unadulterated.

fine² *vb* amerce, mulct, penalize, punish. • *n* amercement, forfeit, forfeiture, mulct, penalty, punishment.

finery *n* decorations, frippery, gewgaws, ornaments, splendour, showiness, trappings, trimmings, trinkets.

finesse *vb* manipulate, manoeuvre. • *n* artifice, contrivance, cunning, craft, manipulation, manoeuvre, manoeuvring, ruses, stratagems, strategy, wiles.

finger *vb* handle, manipulate, play, purloin.

finical *adj* critical, dainty, dapper, fastidious, foppish, jaunty, overnice, overparticular, scrupulous, spruce, squeamish, trim.

finish *vb* **1** accomplish, achieve, complete, consummate, execute, fulfil, perform. **2** elaborate, perfect, polish. **3** close, conclude, end, terminate. • *n* **1** elaboration, elegance, perfection, polish. **2** close, end, death, termination, wind-up.

finite *adj* bounded, circumscribed, conditioned, contracted, definable, limited, restricted, terminable.

fire *vb* **1** ignite, kindle, light. **2** animate, enliven, excite, inflame, inspirit, invigorate, rouse, stir up. **3** discharge, eject, expel, hurl. • *n* **1** combustion. **2** blaze, conflagration. **3** discharge, firing. **4** animation, ardour, enthusiasm, fervour, fervency, fever, force, heat, impetuosity, inflammation, intensity, passion, spirit, vigour, violence. **5** light, lustre, radiance, splendour. **6** imagination, imaginativeness, inspiration, vivacity. **7** affliction, persecution, torture, trouble.

firm¹ *adj* **1** established, coherent, confirmed, consistent, fast, fixed, immovable, inflexible, rooted, secure, settled, stable. **2** compact, compressed, dense, hard, solid. **3** constant, determined, resolute, staunch, steadfast, steady, unshaken. **4** loyal, robust, sinewy, stanch, stout, sturdy, strong.

adj antonyms infirm, soft, unsound.

firm² *n* association, business, company, concern, corporation, house, partnership.

firmament *n* heavens, sky, vault, welkin.

firmness *n* **1** compactness, fixedness, hardness, solidity. **2** stability, strength. **3** constancy, soundness, steadfastness, steadiness.

first *adj* **1** capital, chief, foremost, highest, leading, prime, principal. **2** earliest, eldest, original. **3** maiden. **4** elementary, primary, rudimentary. **5** aboriginal, primal, primeval, primitive, pristine. • *adv* **1** chiefly, firstly, initially, mainly, primarily, principally. **2** before, foremost, headmost. **3** before, rather, rather than, sooner, sooner than. • *n* alpha, initial, prime.

first-rate *adj* excellent, prime, superior.

fissure *n* breach, break, chasm, chink, cleft, crack, cranny, crevice, fracture, gap, hole, interstice, opening, rent, rift.

fit¹ *vb* **1** adapt, adjust, suit. **2** become, conform. **3** accommodate, equip, prepare, provide, qualify. • *adj* capacitated, competent, fitted. **4** adequate, appropriate, apt, becoming, befitting, consonant, convenient, fitting, good, meet, pertinent, proper, seemly, suitable.

adj antonym unfit.

fit² *n* **1** convulsion, fit, paroxysm, qualm, seizure, spasm, spell. **2** fancy, humour, whim. **3** mood, pet, tantrum. **4** interval, period, spell, turn.

fitful *adj* **1** capricious, changeable, convulsive, fanciful, fantastic, fickle, humoursome, impulsive, intermittent, irregular, odd, spasmodic, unstable, variable, whimsical. **2** checkered, eventful.

adj antonyms regular, steady.

fitness *n* **1** adaptation, appropriateness, aptitude, aptness, pertinence, propriety, suitableness. **2** preparation, qualification.

fix *vb* **1** establish, fasten, place, plant, set. **2** adjust, correct, mend, repair. **3** attach, bind, clinch, connect, fasten, lock, rivet, stay, tie. **4** appoint, decide, define, determine, limit, seal, settle. **5** consolidate, harden, solidify. **6** abide, remain, rest. **7** congeal, stiffen. • *n* difficulty, dilemma, quandary, pickle, plight, predicament.

flabbergast *vb* abash, amaze, astonish, astound, confound, confuse, disconcert, dumbfound, nonplus.

flabby *adj* feeble, flaccid, inelastic, limp, soft, week, yielding.

flaccid *adj* baggy, drooping, flabby, inelastic, lax, limber, limp, loose, pendulous, relaxed, soft, weak, yielding.

flag¹ *vb* **1** droop, hang, loose. **2** decline, droop, fail, faint, lag, languish, pine, sink, succumb, weaken, weary. **3** stale, pall.

flag² *vb* indicate, mark, semaphore, sign, signal. • *n* banner, colours, ensign, gonfalon, pennant, pennon, standard, streamer.

flagellate *vb* beat, castigate, chastise, cudgel, drub, flog, scourge, thrash, whip.

flagitious *adj* abandoned, atrocious, corrupt, flagrant, heinous, infamous, monstrous, nefarious, profligate, scandalous, villainous, wicked.

flagrant *adj* **1** burning, flaming, glowing, raging. **2** crying, enormous, flagitious, glaring, monstrous, nefarious, notorious, outrageous, shameful, wanton, wicked.

adj antonyms covert, secret.

flake *vb* desquamate, scale. • *n* lamina, layer, scale.

flamboyant *adj* bright, gorgeous, ornate, rococo.

adj antonyms modest, restrained.

flame *vb* **1** blaze, shine. **2** burn, flash, glow,

warm. • *n* **1** blaze, brightness, fire, flare, vapour. **2** affection, ardour, enthusiasm, fervency, fervour, keenness, warmth.

flaming *adj* **1** blazing. **2** burning, bursting, exciting, glowing, intense, lambent, vehement, violent.

flap *vb* **1** beat, flutter, shake, vibrate, wave. • *n* apron, fly, lap, lappet, tab. **2** beating, flapping, flop, flutter, slap, shaking, swinging, waving.

flare *vb* **1** blaze, flicker, flutter, waver. **2** dazzle, flame, glare. **3** splay, spread, widen. • *n* blaze, dazzle, flame, glare.

flash *vb* blaze, glance, glare, glisten, light, shimmer, scintillate, sparkle, twinkle. • *n* instant, moment, twinkling.

flashy *adj* flaunting, gaudy, gay, loud, ostentatious, pretentious, showy, tawdry, tinsel. *adj antonyms* plain, simple, tasteful.

flat *adj* **1** champaign, horizontal, level. **2** even, plane, smooth, unbroken. **3** low, prostrate, overthrow. **4** dull, frigid, jejune, lifeless, monotonous, pointless, prosaic, spiritless, tame, unanimated, uniform, uninteresting. **5** dead, flashy, insipid, mawkish, stale, tasteless, vapid. **6** absolute, clear, direct, downright, peremptory, positive. • *adv* flatly, flush, horizontally, level. • *n* **1** bar, sandbank, shallow, shoal, strand. **2** champaign, lowland, plain. **3** apartment, floor, lodging, storey. *adj antonym* equivocal.

flatter *vb* **1** compliment, gratify, praise. **2** blandish, blarney, butter up, cajole, coax, coddle, court, entice, fawn, humour, inveigle, wheedle.

flattery *n* adulation, blandishment, blarney, cajolery, fawning, obsequiousness, servility, sycophancy, toadyism. *n antonym* criticism.

flaunt *vb* **1** boast, display, disport, flourish, parade, sport, vaunt. **2** brandish.

flaunting *adj* flashy, garish, gaudy, ostentatious, showy, tawdry.

flavour *n* **1** gust, gusto, relish, savour, seasoning, smack, taste, zest. **2** admixture, lacing, seasoning. **3** aroma, essence, soul, spirit.

flaw *n* **1** break, breach, cleft, crack, fissure, fracture, gap, rent, rift. **2** blemish, defect, fault, fleck, imperfection, speck, spot.

flay *vb* **1** excoriate, flay. **2** criticize.

fleck *vb* dapple, mottle, speckle, spot, streak, variegate. • *n* speckle, spot, streak.

flecked *adj* dappled, mottled, piebald, spotted, straked, striped, variegated.

flee *vb* abscond, avoid, decamp, depart, escape, fly, leave, run, skedaddle. *vb antonyms* stand, stay.

fleece *vb* **1** clip, shear. **2** cheat, despoil, pluck, plunder, rifle, rob, steal, strip.

fleer *vb* mock, jeer, gibe, scoff, sneer.

fleet[1] *n* **1** armada, escadrille, flotilla, navy, squadron. **2** company, group.

fleet[2] *adj* fast, nimble, quick, rapid, speedy, swift. *adj antonym* slow.

fleeting *adj* brief, caducous, ephemeral, evanescent, flitting, flying, fugitive, passing, short-lived, temporary, transient, transitory. *adj antonym* lasting.

fleetness *n* celerity, nimbleness, quickness, rapidity, speed, swiftness, velocity.

flesh *n* **1** food, meat. **2** carnality, desires. **3** kindred, race, stock. **4** man, mankind, world.

fleshly *adj* animal, bodily, carnal, lascivious, lustful, lecherous, sensual.

fleshy *adj* corpulent, fat, obese, plump, stout. *adj antonym* thin.

flexibility *n* **1** flexibleness, limbersome, lithesome, pliability, pliancy, suppleness. **2** affability, complaisance, compliance, disposition, ductility, pliancy, tractableness, tractability, yielding.

flexible *adj* **1** flexible, limber, lithe, pliable, pliant, supple, willowy. **2** affable, complaisant, ductile, docile, gentle, tractable, tractile, yielding. *adj antonym* inflexible.

flexose, flexuous *adj* bending, crooked, serpentine, sinuate, sinuous, tortuous, waxy, winding.

flibbertigibbet *n* demon, imp, sprite.

flight[1] *n* **1** flying, mounting, soaring, volition. **2** shower, flight. **3** steps, stairs.

flight[2] *n* **1** departure, fleeing, flying, retreat, rout, stampede. **2** exodus, hegira.

flighty *adj* capricious, deranged, fickle, frivolous, giddy, light-headed, mercurial, unbalanced, volatile, wild, whimsical. *adj antonym* steady.

flimsy *adj* **1** slight, thin, unsubstantial. **2** feeble, foolish, frivolous, light, puerile, shallow, superficial, trashy, trifling, trivial, weak. **3** insubstantial, sleazy. *adj antonym* sturdy.

flinch vb blench, flee, recoil, retreat, shirk, shrink, swerve, wince, withdraw.

fling vb 1 cast, chuck, dart, emit, heave, hurl, pitch, shy, throw, toss. 2 flounce, wince. • n cast, throw, toss.

flippancy n 1 volubility. 2 assuredness, glibness, pertness.

flippant adj 1 fluent, glib, talkative, voluble. 2 bold, forward, frivolous, glib, impertinent, inconsiderate, irreverent, malapert, pert, saucy, trifling.
adj antonym earnest.

flirt vb 1 chuck, fling, hurl, pitch, shy, throw, toss. 2 flutter, twirl, whirl, whisk. 3 coquet, dally, philander. • n 1 coquette, jilt, philanderer. 2 jerk.

flirtation n coquetry, dalliance, philandering.

flit vb 1 flicker, flutter, hover. 2 depart, hasten, pass.

flitting adj brief, ephemeral, evanescent, fleeting, fugitive, passing, short, transient, transitory.

float vb 1 drift, glide, hang, ride, sail, soar, swim, waft. 2 launch, support.

flock vb collect, congregate, gather, group, herd, swarm, throng. • n 1 collection, group, multitude. 2 bevy, company, convoy, drove, flight, gaggle, herd, pack, swarm, team, troupe. 3 congregation.

flog vb beat, castigate, chastise, drub, flagellate, lash, scourge, thrash, whip.

flood vb deluge, inundate, overflow, submerge, swamp. • n 1 deluge, freshet, inundation, overflow, tide. 2 bore, downpour, eagre, flow, outburst, spate, rush. 3 abundance, excess.
n antonyms dearth, drought, trickle.

floor vb 1 deck, pave. 2 beat, confound, conquer, overthrow, prevail, prostrate, puzzle. 3 disconcert, nonplus. • n 1 storey. 2 bottom, deck, flooring, pavement, stage.

florid adj 1 bright-coloured, flushed, red-faced, rubicund. 2 embellished, figurative, luxuriant, ornate, rhetorical, rococo.
adj antonyms pale, plain.

flounce[1] vb fling, jerk, spring, throw, toss, wince. • n jerk, spring.

flounce[2] n frill, furbelow, ruffle.

flounder vb blunder, flop, flounce, plunge, struggle, toss, tumble, wallow.

flourish vb 1 grow, thrive. 2 boast, bluster, brag, gasconade, show off, vaunt, vapour. 3 brandish, flaunt, swing, wave. • n 1 dash, display, ostentation, parade, show. 2 bombast, fustian, grandiloquence. 3 brandishing, shake, waving. 4 blast, fanfare, tantivy.
vb antonyms fail, languish.

flout vb chaff, deride, fleer, gibe, insult, jeer, mock, ridicule, scoff, sneer, taunt. • n gibe, fling, insult, jeer, mock, mockery, mocking, scoff, scoffing, taunt.
vb antonym respect.

flow vb 1 pour, run, stream. 2 deliquesce, liquefy, melt. 3 arise, come, emanate, follow, grow, issue, proceed, result, spring. 4 glide. 5 float, undulate, wave, waver. 6 abound, run. • n 1 current, discharge, flood, flux, gush, rush, stream, trickle. 2 abundance, copiousness.

flower vb 1 bloom, blossom, effloresce. 2 develop. • n 1 bloom, blossom. 2 best, cream, elite, essence, pick. 3 freshness, prime, vigour.

flowery adj 1 bloomy, florid. 2 embellished, figurative, florid, ornate, overwrought.

flowing adj abundant, copious, fluent, smooth.

fluctuate vb 1 oscillate, swing, undulate, vibrate, wave. 2 change, vary. 3 vacillate, waver.

flue n 1 chimney, duct. 2 flew, fluff, nap, floss, fur.

fluency n 1 liquidness, smoothness. 2 affluence, copiousness. 3 ease, facility, readiness.

fluent adj 1 current, flowing, gliding, liquid. 2 smooth. 3 affluent, copious, easy, facile, glib, ready, talkative, voluble.
adj antonym tongue-tied.

fluff vb blunder, bungle, forget, fumble, mess up, miscue, misremember, muddle, muff. • n 1 down, flew, floss, flue, fur, lint, nap. 2 cobweb, feather, gossamer, thistledown. 3 blunder, bungle, fumble, muff.
vb antonym bring off.

flume n channel, chute, mill race, race.

flummery n 1 chaff, frivolity, froth, moonshine, nonsense, trash, trifling. 2 adulation, blandishment, blarney, flattery. 3 brose, porridge, sowens.

flunky, flunkey n 1 footman, lackey, livery servant, manservant, valet. 2 snob, toady.

flurry vb agitate, confuse, disconcert, disturb, excite, fluster, hurry, perturb. • n 1 gust, flaw, squall. 2 agitation, bustle, commotion, confusion, disturbance, excitement, flutter, haste, hurry, hurry-scurry, perturbation, ruffle, scurry.

flush¹ *vb* **1** flow, rush, start. **2** glow, mantle, redden. **3** animate, elate, elevate, erect, excite. **4** cleanse, drench. • *adj* **1** bright, fresh, glowing, vigorous. **2** abundant, affluent, exuberant, fecund, fertile, generous, lavish, liberal, prodigal, prolific, rich, wealthy, well-supplied. **3** even, flat, level, plane. • *adv* **1** evenly, flat, level. **2** full, point-blank, right, square, squarely, straight. • *n* **1** bloom, blush, glow, redness, rosiness, ruddiness. **2** impulse, shock, thrill.
vb antonym pale.

flush² *vb* disturb, rouse, start, uncover.

fluster *vb* **1** excite, flush, heat. **2** agitate, disturb, flurry, hurry, perturb, ruffle. **3** confound, confuse, discompose, disconcert. • *n* **1** glow, heat. **2** agitation, flurry, flutter, hurry, hurry-scurry, perturbation, ruffle.
vb antonym calm.
n antonym calm.

fluted *adj* channelled, corrugated, grooved.

flutter *vb* **1** flap, hover. **2** flirt, flit. **3** beat, palpitate, quiver, tremble. **4** fluctuate, oscillate, vacillate, waver. • *n* **1** agitation, tremor. **2** hurry, commotion, confusion, excitement, flurry, fluster, hurry-scurry, perturbation, quivering, tremble, tumult, twitter.

flux *n* **1** flow, flowing. **2** change, mutation, shifting, transition. **3** diarrhoea, dysentery, looseness. **4** fusing, melting, menstruum, solvent.

fly¹ *vb* **1** aviate, hover, mount, soar. **2** flap, float, flutter, play, sail, soar, undulate, vibrate, wave. **3** burst, explode. **4** abscond, decamp, depart, flee, vanish. **5** elapse, flit, glide, pass, slip.

fly² *adj* **1** alert, bright, sharp, smart, wideawake. **2** astute, cunning, knowing, sly. **3** agile, fleet, nimble, quick, spry.

foal *n* colt, filly.

foam *vb* **1** cream, froth, lather, spume. **2** boil, churn, ferment, fume, seethe, simmer, stew. • *n* bubbles, cream, froth, scum, spray, spume, suds.

fodder *n* feed, food, forage, provender, rations.

foe *n* adversary, antagonist, enemy, foeman, opponent.
n antonym friend.

fog *vb* **1** bedim, bemist, blear, blur, cloud, dim, enmist, mist. **2** addle, befuddle, confuse, fuddle, muddle. • *n* **1** blear, blur, dimness, film, fogginess, haze, haziness, mist, smog, vapour. **2** befuddlement, confusion, fuddle, maze, muddle.

foggy *adj* **1** blurred, cloudy, dim, dimmed, hazy, indistinct, misty, obscure. **2** befuddled, bewildered, confused, dazed, muddled, muddy, stupid.

foible *n* defect, failing, fault, frailty, imperfection, infirmity, penchant, weakness.

foil¹ *vb* baffle, balk, check, checkmate, circumvent, defeat, disappoint, frustrate, thwart.

foil² *n* **1** film, flake, lamina. **2** background, contrast.

foist *vb* impose, insert, interpolate, introduce, palm off, thrust.

fold¹ *vb* **1** bend, cover, double, envelop, wrap. **2** clasp, embrace, enfold, enwrap, gather, infold, interlace. **3** collapse, fail. • *n* double, doubling, gather, plait, plicature.

fold² *n* cot, enclosure, pen.

foliaceous *adj* **1** foliate, leafy. **2** flaky, foliated, lamellar, lamellate, lamellated, laminated, scaly, schistose.

folk *n* kindred, nation, people.

follow *vb* **1** ensue, succeed. **2** chase, dog, hound, pursue, run after, trail. **3** accompany, attend. **4** conform, heed, obey, observe. **5** cherish, cultivate, seek. **6** practise, pursue. **7** adopt, copy, imitate. **8** arise, come, flow, issue, proceed, result, spring.
vb antonyms desert, precede.

follower *n* **1** acolyte, attendant, associate, companion, dependant, retainer, supporter. **2** adherent, admirer, disciple, partisan, pupil. **3** copier, imitator.
n antonyms leader, opponent.

folly *n* **1** doltishness, dullness, imbecility, levity, shallowness. **2** absurdity, extravagance, fatuity, foolishness, imprudence, inanity, indiscretion, ineptitude, nonsense, senselessness. **3** blunder, faux pas, indiscretion, unwisdom.
n antonym prudence.
n antonyms hostile, realistic.

foment *vb* **1** bathe, embrocate, stupe. **2** abet, brew, encourage, excite, foster, instigate, promote, stimulate.

fond *adj* **1** absurd, baseless, empty, foolish, senseless, silly, vain, weak. **2** affectionate, amorous, doting, loving, overaffectionate, tender.

fondle *vb* blandish, caress, coddle, cosset, dandle, pet.

fondness n **1** absurdity, delusion, folly, silliness, weakness. **2** liking, partiality, predilection, preference, propensity. **3** appetite, relish, taste.

n antonym aversion.

food n **1** aliment, board, bread, cheer, commons, diet, fare, meat, nourishment, nutriment, nutrition, pabulum, provisions, rations, regimen, subsistence, sustenance, viands, victuals. **2** feed, fodder, forage, provender.

fool vb **1** jest, play, toy, trifle. **2** beguile, cheat, circumvent, cozen, deceive, delude, dupe, gull, hoodwink, overreach, trick. • n **1** blockhead, dolt, driveller, idiot, imbecile, nincompoop, ninny, nitwit, simpleton. **2** antic, buffoon, clown, droll, harlequin, jester, merry-andrew, punch, scaramouch. **3** butt, dupe.

foolery n **1** absurdity, folly, foolishness, nonsense. **2** buffoonery, mummery, tomfoolery.

foolhardy adj adventurous, bold, desperate, harebrained, headlong, hot-headed, incautious, precipitate, rash, reckless, venturesome, venturous.

foolish adj **1** brainless, daft, fatuous, idiotic, inane, inept, insensate, irrational, senseless, shallow, silly, simple, thick-skulled, vain, weak, witless. **2** absurd, ill-judged, imprudent, indiscreet, nonsensical, preposterous, ridiculous, unreasonable, unwise. **3** childish, contemptible, idle, puerile, trifling, trivial, vain.

adj antonym wise.

foolishness n **1** doltishness, dullness, fatuity, folly, imbecility, shallowness, silliness, stupidity. **2** absurdity, extravagance, imprudence, indiscretion, nonsense. **3** childishness, puerility, triviality.

footing n **1** foothold, purchase. **2** basis, foundation, groundwork, installation. **3** condition, grade, rank, standing, state, status. **4** settlement, establishment.

footman n footboy, menial, lackey, runner, servant.

footpad n bandit, brigand, freebooter, highwayman, robber.

footpath n footway, path, trail.

footprint n footfall, footmark, footstep, trace, track.

footstep n **1** footmark, footprint, trace, track. **2** footfall, step, tread. **3** mark, sign, token, trace, vestige.

fop n beau, coxcomb, dandy, dude, exquisite, macaroni, popinjay, prig, swell.

foppish adj coxcombical, dandified, dandyish, dressy, finical, spruce, vain.

forage vb **1** feed, graze, provender, provision, victual. **2** hunt for, range, rummage, search, seek. **3** maraud, plunder, raid. • n **1** feed, fodder, food, pasturage, provender. **2** hunt, rummage, search.

foray n descent, incursion, invasion, inroad, irruption, raid.

forbear vb **1** cease, desist, hold, pause, stop, stay. **2** abstain, refrain. **3** endure, tolerate. **4** avoid, decline, shun. **5** abstain, omit, withhold.

forbearance n **1** abstinence, avoidance, forbearing, self-restraint, shunning, refraining. **2** indulgence, leniency, long-suffering, mildness, moderation, patience.

n antonym intolerance.

forbid vb ban, debar, disallow, embargo, enjoin, hinder, inhibit, interdict, prohibit, proscribe, taboo, veto.

vb antonym allow.

forbidding adj abhorrent, disagreeable, displeasing, odious, offensive, repellant, repulsive, threatening, unpleasant.

adj antonyms approachable, congenial.

force vb **1** coerce, compel, constrain, necessitate, oblige. **2** drive, impel, overcome, press, urge. **3** ravish, violate. • n **1** emphasis, energy, head, might, pith, power, strength, stress, vigour, vim. **2** agency, efficacy, efficiency, cogency, potency, validity, virtue. **3** coercion, compulsion, constraint, enforcement, vehemence, violence. **4** army, array, battalion, host, legion, phalanx, posse, soldiery, squadron, troop.

forcible adj **1** all-powerful, cogent, impressive, irresistible, mighty, potent, powerful, strong, weighty. **2** impetuous, vehement, violent, unrestrained. **3** coerced, coercive, compulsory. **4** convincing, energetic, effective, efficacious, telling, vigorous.

adj antonym feeble.

forcibly adv **1** mightily, powerfully. **2** coercively, compulsorily, perforce, violently. **3** effectively, energetically, vigorously.

ford n **1** current, flood, stream. **2** crossing, wading place.

fore adj **1** anterior, antecedent, first, foregoing, former, forward, preceding, previous, prior. **2** advanced, foremost, head, leading.

forebode vb augur, betoken, foreshow, foretell, indicate, portend, predict, prefigure, presage, prognosticate, promise, signify.

foreboding *n* augury, omen, prediction, premonition, presage, presentiment, prognostication.

forecast *vb* **1** anticipate, foresee, predict. **2** calculate, contrive, devise, plan, project, scheme. • *n* anticipation, foresight, forethought, planning, prevision, prophecy, provident.

foreclose *vb* debar, hinder, preclude, prevent, stop.

foredoom *vb* foreordain, predestine, preordain.

forego *see* **forgo**.

foregoing *adj* antecedent, anterior, fore, former, preceding, previous, prior.

foregone *adj* bygone, former, past, previous.

foreign *adj* **1** alien, distant, exotic, exterior, external, outward, outlandish, remote, strange, unnative. **2** adventitious, exterior, extraneous, extrinsic, inappropriate, irrelevant, outside, unnatural, unrelated.
adj antonym native.

foreknowledge *n* foresight, prescience, prognostication.

foremost *adj* first, front, highest, leading, main, principal.

foreordain *vb* appoint, foredoom, predestinate, predetermine, preordain.

forerunner *n* **1** avant-courier, foregoer, harbinger, herald, precursor, predecessor. **2** omen, precursor, prelude, premonition, prognosticate, sign.
n antonyms aftermath, result.

foresee *vb* anticipate, forebode, forecast, foreknow, foretell, prognosticate, prophesy.

foreshadow *vb* forebode, predict, prefigure, presage, presignify, prognosticate, prophesy.

foresight *n* **1** foreknowledge, prescience, prevision. **2** anticipation, care, caution, forecast, forethought, precaution, providence, prudence.
n antonym improvidence.

forest *n* wood, woods, woodland.

forestall *vb* **1** hinder, frustrate, intercept, preclude, prevent, thwart. **2** antedate, anticipate, foretaste. **3** engross, monopolize, regrate.
vb antonyms encourage, facilitate.

foretaste *n* anticipation, forestalling, prelibation.

foretell *vb* **1** predict, prophesy. **2** augur, betoken, forebode, forecast, foreshadow, foreshow, portend, presage, presignify, prognosticate, prophesy.

forethought *n* anticipation, forecast, foresight, precaution, providence, prudence.

forever *adv* always, constantly, continually, endlessly, eternally, ever, evermore, everlastingly, perpetually, unceasingly.

forewarn *vb* admonish, advise, caution, dissuade.

forfeit *vb* alienate, lose. • *n* amercement, damages, fine, forfeiture, mulct, penalty.

forfend *vb* avert, forbid, hinder, prevent, protect.

forge *vb* **1** beat, fabricate, form, frame, hammer. **2** coin, devise, frame, invent. **3** counterfeit, falsify, feign. • *n* furnace, ironworks, smithy.

forgery *n* counterfeit, fake, falsification, imitation.

forgetful *adj* careless, heedless, inattentive, mindless, neglectful, negligent, oblivious, unmindful.
adj antonyms attentive, heedful.

forgive *vb* absolve, acquit, condone, excuse, exonerate, pardon, remit.
vb antonym censure.

forgiveness *n* absolution, acquittal, amnesty, condoning. exoneration, pardon, remission, reprieve.

forgiving *adj* absolutory, absolvatory, acquitting, clearing, excusing, pardoning, placable, releasing.
adj antonym censorious.

forgo *vb* abandon, cede, relinquish, renounce, resign, surrender, yield.
vb antonyms claim, indulge in, insist on.

fork *vb* bifurcate, branch, divaricate, divide. • *n* bifurcation, branch, branching, crotch, divarication, division.

forked *adj* bifurcated, branching, divaricated, furcate, furcated.

forlorn *adj* **1** abandoned, deserted, forsaken, friendless, helpless, lost, solitary. **2** abject, comfortless, dejected, desolate, destitute, disconsolate, helpless, hopeless, lamentable, pitiable, miserable, woebegone, wretched.
adj antonym hopeful.

form *vb* **1** fashion model, mould, shape. **2** build, conceive, construct, create, fabricate, make, produce. **3** contrive, devise, frame, invent. **4** compose, constitute, develop, organize. **5** discipline, educate, teach, train. • *n* **1** body, build, cast, configuration, conformation, contour, cut, fashion, figure, format, mould, outline, pattern, shape. **2** formula, formulary, method, mode, practice, ritual. **3** class, kind, manner, model, order, sort, system, type. **4** arrangement, order, regularity, shapeliness. **5** ceremonial, ceremony, conventionality, etiquette, formality, observance, ordinance, punctilio, rite, ritual. **6** bench, seat. **7** class, rank. **8** arrangement, combination, organization.

formal *adj* **1** explicit, express, official, positive, strict. **2** fixed, methodical, regular, rigid, set, stiff. **3** affected, ceremonious, exact, precise, prim, punctilious, starchy. starched. **4** constitutive, essential. **5** external, outward, perfunctory. **6** formative, innate, organic, primordial.
adj antonym informal.

formality *n* ceremonial, ceremony, conventionality, etiquette, punctilio, rite, ritual.
n antonym informality.

formation *n* **1** creation, genesis, production. **2** composition, constitution. **3** arrangement, combination, disposal, disposition.

formative *adj* **1** creative, determinative, plastic, shaping. **2** derivative, inflectional, nonradical.

former *adj* **1** antecedent, anterior, earlier, foregoing, preceding, previous, prior. **2** late, old-time, quondam. **3** by, bygone, foregone, gone, past.
adj antonyms current, future, later, present, prospective, subsequent.

formidable *adj* appalling, dangerous, difficult, dreadful, fearful, frightful, horrible, menacing, redoubtable, shocking, terrible, terrific, threatening, tremendous.
adj antonyms easy, genial.

forsake *vb* **1** abandon, desert, leave, quit. **2** drop, forgo, forswear, relinquish, renounce, surrender, yield.
vb antonyms resume, revert to.

forsooth *adv* certainly, indeed, really, surely, truly.

forswear *vb* **1** abandon, desert, drop, forsake, leave, quit, reject, renounce. **2** abjure, deny, eschew, perjure, recant, repudiate, retract.

fort *n* bulwark, castle, citadel, defence, fastness, fortification, fortress, stronghold.

forthwith *adv* directly, immediately, instantly, quickly, straightaway.

fortification *n* breastwork, bulwark, castle, citadel, defence, earthwork, fastness, fort, keep, rampart, redoubt, stronghold, tower.

fortify *vb* **1** brace, encourage, entrench, garrison, protect, reinforce, stiffen, strengthen. **2** confirm, corroborate.
vb antonyms dilute, weaken.

fortitude *n* braveness, bravery, courage, determination, endurance, firmness, hardiness, patience, pluck, resolution, strength, valour.

fortuitous *adj* accidental, casual, chance, contingent, incidental.
adj antonym intentional.

fortunate *adj* **1** favoured, happy, lucky, prosperous, providential, successful. **2** advantageous, auspicious, favourable, happy, lucky, propitious, timely.
adj antonym unfortunate.

fortune *n* **1** accident, casualty, chance, contingency, fortuity, hap, luck. **2** estate, possessions, property, substance. **3** affluence, felicity, opulence, prosperity, riches, wealth. **4** destination, destiny, doom, fate, lot, star. **5** event, issue, result. **6** favour, success.

forward *vb* **1** advance, aid, encourage, favour, foster, further, help, promote, support. **2** accelerate, dispatch, expedite, hasten, hurry, quicken, speed. **3** dispatch, post, send, ship, transmit. • *adj* ahead, advanced, onward. **4** anterior, front, fore, head. **5** prompt, eager, earnest, hasty, impulsive, quick, ready, willing, zealous. **6** assuming, bold, brazen, brazen-faced, confident, flippant, impertinent, pert, presumptuous, presuming. **7** advanced, early, premature.

foster *vb* **1** cosset, feed, nurse, nourish, support, sustain. **2** advance, aid, breed, cherish, cultivate, encourage, favour, foment, forward, further, harbour, patronize, promote, rear, stimulate.

foul *vb* **1** besmirch, defile, dirty, pollute, soil, stain, sully. **2** clog, collide, entangle, jam. • **1** *adj* dirty, fetid, filthy, impure, nasty, polluted, putrid, soiled, stained, squalid, sullied, rank, tarnished, unclean. **2** disgusting, hateful, loathsome, noisome, odious, offensive. **3** dishonourable, underhand, unfair, sinister. **4** abominable, base, dark, detestable, disgraceful, infamous,

scandalous, scurvy, shameful, wile, wicked. **5** coarse, low, obscene, vulgar. **6** abusive, foul-mouthed, foul-spoken, insulting, scurrilous. **7** cloudy, rainy, rough, stormy, wet. **8** feculent, muddy, thick, turbid. **9** entangled, tangled.
vb antonyms clean, clear, disentangle.
adj antonyms clean, fair, pure, worthy.

foul-mouthed *adj* abusive, blackguardy, blasphemous, filthy, foul, indecent, insolent, insulting, obscene, scurrilous.

found *vb* **1** base, fix, ground, place, rest, set. **2** build, construct, erect, raise. **3** colonize, establish, institute, originate, plant. **4** cast, mould.

foundation *n* **1** base, basis, bed, bottom, footing, ground, groundwork, substructure, support. **2** endowment, establishment, settlement.

founder[1] *n* author, builder, establisher, father, institutor, originator, organizer, planter.

founder[2] *n* caster, moulder.

founder[3] *vb* **1** sink, swamp, welter. **2** collapse, fail, miscarry. **3** fall, stumble, trip.

fountain *n* **1** fount, reservoir, spring, well. **2** jet, upswelling. **3** cause, fountainhead, origin, original, source.

foxy *adj* artful, crafty, cunning, sly, subtle, wily.
adj antonyms naïve, open.

fracas *n* affray, brawl, disturbance, outbreak, quarrel, riot, row, uproar, tumult.

fractious *adj* captious, cross, fretful, irritable, peevish, pettish, perverse, petulant, querulous, snappish, splenetic, touchy, testy, waspish.
adj antonyms complaisant, placid.

fracture *vb* break, crack, split. • *n* **1** breaking, rupture. **2** breach, break, cleft, crack, fissure, flaw, opening, rift, rent.
vb antonym join.

fragile *adj* **1** breakable, brittle, delicate, frangible. **2** feeble, frail, infirm, weak.
adj antonyms durable, robust, tough.

fragility *n* **1** breakability, breakableness, brittleness, frangibility, frangibleness. **2** feebleness, frailty, infirmity, weakness.

fragment *vb* atomize, break, fracture, pulverize, splinter. • *n* bit, chip, fraction, fracture, morsel, part, piece, remnant, scrap.
vb antonyms hold together, join.
n antonyms whole.

fragrance *n* aroma, balminess, bouquet, odour, perfume, redolence, scent, smell.

fragrant *adj* ambrosial, aromatic, balmy, odoriferous, odorous, perfumed, redolent, spicy, sweet, sweet-scented, sweet-smelling.
adj antonyms smelly, unscented.

frail *adj* **1** breakable, brittle, delicate, fragile, frangible, slight. **2** feeble, infirm, weak.
adj antonyms firm, robust, strong, tough.

frailty *n* **1** feebleness, frailness, infirmity, weakness. **2** blemish, defect, failing, fault, foible, imperfection, peccability, shortcoming.

frame *vb* **1** build, compose, constitute, construct, erect, form, make, mould, plan, shape. **2** contrive, devise, fabricate, fashion, forge, invest, plan. • *n* **1** body, carcass, framework, framing, shell, skeleton. **2** constitution, fabric, form, structure, scheme, system. **3** condition, humour, mood, state, temper.

franchise *n* **1** privilege, right. **2** suffrage, vote. **3** exemption, immunity.

frangible *adj* breakable, brittle, fragile.

frank *adj* artless, candid, direct, downright, frank-hearted, free, genuine, guileless, ingenuous, naïve, open, outspoken, outright, plain, plain-spoken, point-blank, sincere, straightforward, truthful, unequivocal, unreserved, unrestricted.

frankness *n* candour, ingenuousness, openness, outspokenness, plain speaking, truth, straightforwardness.

frantic *adj* crazy, distracted, distraught, frenzied, furious, infuriate, mad. outrageous, phrenetic, rabid, raging, raving, transported, wild.
adj antonym calm.

fraternity *n* **1** association, brotherhood, circle, clan, club, company, fellowship, league, set, society, sodality. **2** brotherliness.

fraternize *vb* associate, coalesce, concur, consort, cooperate, harmonize, sympathize, unite.
vb antonyms ignore, shun.

fraud *n* artifice, cheat, craft, deception, deceit, duplicity, guile, hoax, humbug, imposition, imposture, sham, stratagem, treachery, trick, trickery, wile.

fraudulent *adj* crafty, deceitful, deceptive, dishonest, false, knavish, treacherous, trickish, tricky, wily.
adj antonyms genuine, honest.

fraught *adj* abounding, big, burdened, charged, filled, freighted, laden, pregnant, stored, weighted.

fray[1] *n* affray, battle, brawl, broil, combat, fight, quarrel, riot.

fray[2] *vb* 1 chafe, fret, rub, wear. 2 ravel, shred.

freak *adj* bizarre, freakish, grotesque, monstrous, odd, unexpected, unforeseen. • *n* 1 caprice, crotchet, fancy, humour, maggot, quirk, vagary, whim, whimsey. 2 antic, caper, gambol. 3 abnormality, abortion, monstrosity.
adj antonyms common, expected.

freakish *adj* capricious, changeable, eccentric, erratic, fanciful, humoursome, odd, queer, whimsical.

free *vb* 1 deliver, discharge, disenthral, emancipate, enfranchise, enlarge, liberate, manumit, ransom, release, redeem, rescue, save. 2 clear, disencumber, disengage, extricate, rid, unbind, unchain, unfetter, unlock. 3 exempt, immunize, privilege. • *adj* 1 bondless, independent, loose, unattached, unconfined, unentangled, unimpeded, unrestrained, untrammelled. 2 autonomous, delivered, emancipated, freeborn, liberated, manumitted, ransomed, released, self-governing. 3 clear, exempt, immune, privileged. 4 allowed, permitted. 5 devoid, empty, open, unimpeded, unobstructed, unrestricted. 6 affable, artless, candid, frank, ingenuous, sincere, unreserved. 7 bountiful, charitable, freehearted, generous, hospitable, liberal, munificent, openhanded. 8 immoderate, lavish, prodigal. 9 eager, prompt, ready, willing. 10 available, gratuitous, spontaneous. 11 careless, lax, loose. 12 bold, easy, familiar, informal, overfamiliar, unconstrained. • *adv* 1 openly, outright, unreservedly, unrestrainedly, unstintingly. 2 freely, gratis, gratuitously.
vb antonyms confine, enslave, imprison.
adj antonyms attached, confined, costly, formal, mean, niggardly, restricted, tied.
adv antonym meanly.

freebooter *n* 1 bandit, brigand, despoiler, footpad, gangster, highwayman, marauder, pillager, plunderer, robber. 2 buccaneer, pirate, rover.

freedom *n* 1 emancipation, independence, liberation, liberty, release. 2 elbowroom, margin, play, range, scope, swing. 3 franchise, immunity, privilege. 4 familiarity, laxity, license, looseness.
n antonyms confinement, reserve, restriction.

freethinker *n* agnostic, deist, doubter, infidel, sceptic, unbeliever.

freeze *vb* 1 congeal, glaciate, harden, stiffen. 2 benumb, chill.

freight *vb* burden, charge, lade, load. • *n* burden, cargo, lading, load.

frenzy *n* aberration, delirium, derangement, distraction, fury, insanity, lunacy, madness, mania, paroxysm, rage, raving, transport.
n antonyms calm, placidness.

frequent *vb* attend, haunt, resort, visit. • *adj* 1 iterating, oft-repeated. 2 common, customary, everyday, familiar, habitual, persistent, usual. 3 constant, continual, incessant.
adj antonym infrequent.

fresh *adj* 1 new, novel, recent. 2 renewed, revived. 3 blooming, flourishing, green, undecayed, unimpaired, unfaded, unobliterated, unwilted, unwithered, well-preserved. 4 sweet. 5 delicate, fair, fresh-coloured, ruddy, rosy. 6 florid, hardy, healthy, vigorous, strong. 7 active, energetic, unexhausted, unfatigued, unwearied, vigorous. 8 keen, lively, unabated, undecayed, unimpaired, vivid. 9 additional, further. 10 uncured, undried, unsalted, unsmoked. 11 bracing, health-giving, invigorating, refreshing, sweet. 12 brink, stiff, strong. 13 inexperienced, raw, uncultivated, unpractised, unskilled, untrained, unused.
adj antonyms experienced, faded, old hat, polite, stale, tired.

freshen *vb* quicken, receive, refresh, revive.

fret[1] *vb* 1 abrade, chafe, fray, gall, rub, wear. 2 affront, agitate, annoy, gall, harass, irritate, nettle, provoke, ruffle, tease, vex, wear, worry. 3 ripple, roughen. 4 corrode. 5 fume, peeve, rage, stew. • *n* agitation, fretfulness, fretting, irritation, peevishness, vexation.
vb antonym calm.

fret[2] *vb* diversify, interlace, ornament, variegate. • *n* 1 fretwork, interlacing, ornament. 2 ridge, wale, whelk.

fretful *adj* captious, cross, fractious, ill-humoured, ill-tempered, irritable, peevish, pettish, petulant, querulous, short-tempered, snappish, spleeny, splenetic, testy, touchy, uneasy, waspish.
adj antonym calm.

friable *adj* brittle, crisp, crumbling, powdery, pulverable.

friction *n* **1** abrasion, attrition, grating, rubbing. **2** bickering, disagreement, dissension, wrangling.

friend *adj* **1** benefactor, chum, companion, comrade, crony, confidant, intimate. **2** adherent, ally, associate, confrere, partisan. **3** advocate, defender, encourager, patron, supporter, well-wisher.
n antonym enemy.

friendly *adj* **1** affectionate, amiable, benevolent, favourable, kind, kind-hearted, kindly, well-disposed. **2** amicable, cordial, fraternal, neighbourly. **3** conciliatory, peaceable, unhostile.
adj antonyms cold, unsociable.

friendship *n* **1** affection, attachment, benevolence, fondness, goodness, love, regard. **2** fellowship, intimacy. **3** amicability, amicableness, amity, cordiality, familiarity, fraternization, friendliness, harmony.
n antonym enmity.

fright *n* affright, alarm, consternation, dismay, funk, horror, panic, scare, terror.

frighten *vb* affright, alarm, appal, daunt, dismay, intimidate, scare, stampede, terrify.
vb antonyms calm, reassure.

frightful *adj* **1** alarming, awful, dire, direful, dread, dreadful, fearful, horrible, horrid, shocking, terrible, terrific. **2** ghastly, grim, grisly, gruesome, hideous.

frigid *adj* **1** cold, cool, gelid. **2** dull, lifeless, spiritless, tame, unanimated, uninterested, uninteresting. **3** chilling, distant, forbidding, formal, freezing, prim, repellent, repelling, repulsive, rigid, stiff.
adj antonyms responsive, warm.

frill *n* **1** edging, frilling, furbelow, gathering, ruche, ruching, ruffle. **2** affectation, mannerism.

fringe *vb* border, bound, edge, hem, march, rim, skirt, verge. • *n* border, edge, edging, tassel, trimming. • *adj* edging, extra, unofficial.

frisk *vb* caper, dance, frolic, gambol, hop, jump, play, leap, romp, skip, sport, wanton.

frisky *adj* frolicsome, coltish, gay, lively, playful, sportive.
adj antonym quiet.

frivolity *n* flummery, folly, frippery, frivolousness, levity, puerility, trifling, triviality.

frivolous *adj* childish, empty, flighty, flimsy, flippant, foolish, giddy, idle, light, paltry. petty, puerile, silly, trashy, trifling, trivial, unimportant, vain, worthless.

frolic *vb* caper, frisk, gambol, lark, play, romp, sport. • *n* **1** escapade, gambol, lark, romp, skylark, spree, trick. **2** drollery, fun, play, pleasantry, sport.

frolicsome *adj* coltish, fresh, frolic, gamesome, gay, lively, playful, sportive.

front *vb* confront, encounter, face, oppose. • *adj* **1** anterior, forward. **2** foremost, frontal, headmost. • *n* brow, face, forehead. **3** assurance, boldness, brass, effrontery, impudence. **4** breast, head, van, vanguard. **5** anterior, face, forepart, obverse. **6** facade, frontage.
vb antonym support.
adj antonyms back, last, least, posterior.
n antonym back.

frontier *n* border, boundary, coast, confine, limits, marches.

frosty *adj* **1** chill, chilly, cold, icy, stinging, wintry. **2** cold, cold-hearted, frigid, indifferent, unaffectionate, uncordial, unimpassioned, unloving. **3** dull-hearted, lifeless, spiritless, unanimated. **4** frosted, grey-haired, hoary, white.

froth *vb* bubble, cream, foam, lather, spume. • *n* **1** bubbles, foam, lather, spume. **2** balderdash, flummery, nonsense, trash, triviality.

frothy *adj* **1** foamy, spumy. **2** empty, frivolous, light, trifling, trivial, unsubstantial, vain.

froward *adj* captious, contrary, contumacious, cross, defiant, disobedient, fractious, impudent, intractable, obstinate, peevish, perverse, petulant, refractory, stubborn, ungovernable, untoward, unyielding, wayward, wilful.

frown *vb* glower, lower, scowl.

frowzy, frowsy *adj* **1** fetid, musty, noisome, rancid, rank, stale. **2** disordered, disorderly, dowdy, slatternly, slovenly.

frugal *adj* abstemious, careful, chary, choice, economical, provident, saving, sparing, temperate, thrifty, unwasteful.
adj antonym wasteful.

fruit *n* **1** crop, harvest, produce, production. **2** advantage, consequence, effect, good, outcome, product, profit, result. **3** issue, offspring, young.

fruitful *adj* **1** abounding, productive. **2** fecund, fertile, prolific. **3** abundant, exuber-

ant, plenteous, plentiful, rich, teeming.
adj antonyms barren, fruitless.

fruition *n* **1** completion, fulfilment, perfection. **2** enjoyment.

fruitless *adj* **1** acarpous, barren, sterile, infecund, unfertile, unfruitful, unproductive, unprolific. **2** abortive, bootless, futile, idle, ineffectual, profitless, unavailing, unprofitable, useless, vain.
adj antonyms fruitful, successful.

frumpy *adj* cross, cross-grained, cross-tempered, dowdy, grumpy, irritable, shabby, slatternly, snappish.

frustrate *vb* **1** baffle, balk, check, circumvent, defeat, disappoint, disconcert, foil, thwart. **2** cross, hinder, outwit.
vb antonyms fulfil, further, promote.

frustrated *adj* **1** balked, blighted, dashed, defeated, foiled, thwarted. **2** ineffectual, null, useless, vain.

fuddled *adj* befuddled, boozy, corned, crapulous, drunk, groggy, high, inebriated, intoxicated, muddled, slewed, tight, tipsy.
adj antonyms clear, sober.

fugacious *adj* evanescent, fleeting, fugitive, transient, transitory.

fugitive *adj* **1** escaping, fleeing, flying. **2** brief, ephemeral, evanescent, fleeting, flitting, fugacious, momentary, short, short-lived, temporal, temporary, transient, transitory, uncertain, unstable, volatile. • *n* émigré, escapee, evacuee, fleer, outlaw, refugee, runaway.
n antonym permanent.

fulfil *vb* **1** accomplish, complete, consummate, effect, effectuate, execute, realize. **2** adhere, discharge, do, keep, obey, observe, perform. **3** answer, fill, meet, satisfy.
vb antonyms break, defect, fail, frustrate.

full *adj* **1** brimful, filled, flush, replete. **2** abounding, replete, well-stocked. **3** bagging, flowing, loose, voluminous. **4** chockfull, cloyed, crammed, glutted, gorged, overflowing, packed, sated, satiated, saturated, soaked, stuffed, swollen. **5** adequate, complete, entire, mature, perfect. **6** abundant, ample, copious, plenteous, plentiful, sufficient. **7** clear, deep, distinct, loud, rounded, strong. **8** broad, large, capacious, comprehensive, extensive, plump. **9** circumstantial, detailed, exhaustive. • *adv* **1** completely, fully. **2** directly, exactly, precisely.
adj antonyms empty, incomplete.

fullness *n* **1** abundance, affluence, copiousness, plenitude, plenty, profusion. **2** glut, satiety, sating, repletion. **3** completeness, completion, entireness, perfection. **4** clearness, loudness, resonance, strength. **5** dilation, distension, enlargement, plumpness, rotundity, roundness, swelling.
n antonyms emptiness, incompleteness.

fully *adv* abundantly, amply, completely, copiously, entirely, largely, plentifully, sufficiently.

fully-fledged *adj* experienced, full-blown, graduate, mature, professional, qualified, trained.

fulminate *vb* **1** detonate, explode. **2** curse, denounce, hurl, menace, threaten, thunder.
vb antonym praise.

fulmination *n* condemnation, deunciation, detonation, diatribe, invective, obloquy, tirade.

fulsome *adj* **1** excessive, extravagant, fawning. **2** disgusting, nauseous, nauseating, offensive, repulsive. **3** coarse, gross, lustful, questionable.
adj antonym sincere.

fumble *vb* **1** bungle, grope, mismanage, stumble. **2** mumble, stammer, stutter.

fume *vb* reek, smoke, vaporize. • *n* **1** effluvium exhalation, reek, smell, smoke, steam, vapour. **2** agitation, fret, fry, fury, passion, pet, rage, storm.

fun *adj* amusing, diverting, droll, entertaining. • *n* amusement, diversion, drollery, frolic, gaiety, humour, jesting, jocularity, jollity, joy, merriment, mirth, play, pranks, sport, pleasantry, waggishness.

function *vb* act, discharge, go, operate, officiate, perform, run, serve, work. • *n* **1** discharge, execution, exercise, operation, performance, purpose, use. **2** activity, business, capacity, duty, employment, occupation, office, part, province, role. **3** ceremony, rite. **4** dependant, derivative.

fund *vb* **1** afford, endow, finance, invest, provide, subsidise, support. **2** garner, hoard, stock, store. • *n* **1** accumulation, capital, endowment, reserve, stock. **2** store, supply. **3** foundation.

fundament *n* bottom, buttocks, seat.

fundamental *adj* basal, basic, bottom, cardinal, constitutional, elementary, essential, indispensable, organic, principal, primary, radical. • *n* essential, principal, rule.

adj antonym advanced.

funeral *n* burial, cremation, exequies, internment, obsequies.

funereal *adj* dark, dismal, gloomy, lugubrious, melancholy, mournful, sad, sepulchral, sombre, woeful.

adj antonyms happy, lively.

funk *vb* blanch, shrink, quail. • *n* stench, 1 stink. 2 fear, fright, panic.

funky *adj* 1 earthy, fusty, mouldy, musty, offensive smelling. 2 unusual, unconventional. 3 (*mus, fashion*) cool, exciting, jazzy, stylish. 4 cowardly, fearful, panicky.

funny *adj* 1 amusing, comic, comical, diverting, droll, entertaining, facetious, hilarious, humorous, jocose, jocular, witty. 2 farcical, laughable, ludicrous. 3 bizarre, curious, odd, peculiar, strange. • *n* 1 jest, joke. 2 cartoon, comic.

adj antonyms sad, solemn, unamusing, unfunny.

furious *adj* 1 angry, fierce, frantic, frenzied, fuming, infuriated, mad, raging, violent, wild. 2 boisterous, fierce, impetuous, stormy, tempestuous, tumultuous, turbulent, vehement.

adj antonyms calm, pleased.

furnish *vb* 1 appoint, endow, provide, supply. 2 decorate, equip, fit. 3 afford, bestow, contribute, give, offer, present, produce, yield.

vb antonym divest.

furniture *n* 1 chattels, effects, household goods, movables. 2 apparatus, appendages, appliances, equipment, fittings, furnishings. 3 decorations, embellishments, ornaments.

furore *n* commotion, craze, enthusiasm, excitement, fad, fury, madness, mania, rage, vogue.

n antonym calm.

furrow *vb* 1 chamfer, channel, cleave, corrugate, cut, flute, groove, hollow. 2 pucker, seam, wrinkle. • *n* chamfer, channel, cut, depression, fluting, groove, hollow, line, seam, track, trench, rot, wrinkle.

further *vb* advance, aid, assist, encourage, help, forward, promote, succour, strengthen. • *adj* additional. • *adv* also, besides, farther, furthermore, moreover.

furtive *adj* clandestine, hidden, secret, sly, skulking, sneaking, sneaky, stealthy, stolen, surreptitious.

adj antonym open.

fury *n* 1 anger, frenzy, fit, furore, ire, madness, passion, rage. 2 fierceness, impetuosity, turbulence, turbulency, vehemence. 3 bacchant, bacchante, bedlam, hag, shrew, termagant, virago, vixen.

n antonym calm.

fuse *vb* 1 dissolve, melt, liquefy, smelt. 2 amalgamate, blend, coalesce, combine, commingle, intermingle, intermix, merge, unite. • *n* match.

fusion *n* 1 liquefaction, melting. 2 amalgamation, blending, commingling, commixture, intermingling, intermixture, union. 3 coalition, merging.

fuss *vb* 1 bustle, fidget. 2 fret, fume, worry. • *n* ado, agitation, bother, bustle, commotion, disturbance, excitement, fidget, flurry, fluster, fret, hurry, pother, stir, worry.

n antonym calm.

fustian *n* 1 bombast, claptrap, rant, rodomontade. 2 balderdash, inanity, nonsense, stuff, trash, twaddle.

fusty *adj* ill-smelling, malodorous, mildewed, mouldy, musty, rank.

futile *adj* 1 frivolous, trifling, trivial. 2 bootless, fruitless, idle, ineffectual, profitless, unavailing, unprofitable, useless, vain, valueless, worthless.

adj antonyms fruitful, profitable.

futility *n* 1 frivolousness, triviality. 2 bootlessness, fruitlessness, uselessness, vanity, worthlessness.

n antonyms fruitfulness, profitability.

future *adj* coming, eventual, forthcoming, hereafter, prospective, subsequent. • *n* hereafter, outlook, prospect.

n antonym past.

adj antonym past.

G

gabble *vb* babble, chatter, clack, gibber, gossip, prate, prattle. • *n* babble, chatter, clack, gap, gossip, jabber, palaver, prate, prattle, twaddle.

gadabout *n* **1** idler, loafer, rambler, rover, vagrant. **2** gossip, talebearer, vagrant.

gaffer *n* boss, foreman, overseer, supervisor.

gag[1] *n* jape, jest, joke, stunt, wisecrack.

gag[2] *vb* **1** muffle, muzzle, shackle, silence, stifle, throttle. **2** regurgitate, retch, throw up, vomit. **3** choke, gasp, pant. • *n* muzzle.

gage *n* **1** pawn, pledge, security, surety. **2** challenge, defiance, gauntlet, glove.

gaiety *n* animation, cheerfulness, glee, hilarity, jollity, joviality, merriment, mirth, vivacity.

n antonyms drabness, dreariness, sadness.

gain *vb* **1** achieve, acquire, earn, get, obtain, procure, reap, secure. **2** conciliate, enlist, persuade, prevail, win. **3** arrive, attain, reach. **4** clear, net, profit. • *n* **1** accretion, addition, gainings, profits, winnings. **2** acquisition, earnings, emolument, lucre. **3** advantage, benefit, blessing, good, profit.

vb antonym lose.

n antonyms loss, losses.

gainful *adj* **1** advantageous, beneficial, profitable. **2** lucrative, paying, productive, remunerative.

adj antonym useless.

gainsay *vb* contradict, controvert, deny, dispute, forbid.

vb antonym agree.

gait *n* carriage, pace, step, stride, walk.

galaxy *n* assemblage, assembly, cluster, collection, constellation, group.

gale *n* blast, hurricane, squall, storm, tempest, tornado, typhoon.

gall[1] *n* **1** effrontery, impudence. **2** bile. **3** acerbity, bitterness, malice, maliciousness, malignity, rancour, spite.

n antonyms friendliness, modesty, reserve.

gall[2] *vb* **1** chafe, excoriate, fret, hurt. **2** affront, annoy, exasperate, harass, incense, irritate, plague, provoke, sting, tease, vex.

gallant *adj* **1** fine, magnificent, showy, splendid, well-dressed. **2** bold, brave, chivalrous, courageous, daring, fearless, heroic, high-spirited, intrepid, valiant, valorous. **3** chivalrous, fine, honourable, high-minded, lofty, magnanimous, noble. • *n* **1** beau, blade, spark. **2** lover, suitor, wooer.

adj antonyms cowardly, craven, ungentlemanly.

gallantry *n* **1** boldness, bravery, chivalry, courage, courageousness, fearlessness, heroism, intrepidity, prowess, valour. **2** courtesy, courteousness, elegance, politeness.

n antonyms cowardice, ungentlemanliness.

galling *adj* chafing, irritating, vexing.

adj antonym pleasing.

gallop *vb* fly, hurry, run, rush, scamper, speed.

gamble *vb* bet, dice, game, hazard, plunge, speculate, wager. • *n* **1** chance, risk, speculation. **2** bet, punt, wager.

gambol *vb* caper, cut, frisk, frolic, hop, jump, leap, romp, skip. • *n* frolic, hop, jump, skip.

game[1] *vb* gamble, sport, stake. • *n* **1** amusement, contest, diversion, pastime, play, sport. **2** adventure, enterprise, measure, plan, project, scheme, stratagem, undertaking. **3** prey, quarry, victim.

game[2] *adj* **1** brave, courageous, dauntless, fearless, gallant, heroic, intrepid, plucky, unflinching, valorous. **2** enduring, persevering, resolute, undaunted. **3** ready, eager, willing.

game[3] *adj* crippled, disabled, halt, injured, lame.

adj antonyms cowardly, unwilling.

gameness *n* bravery, courage, grit, heart, mettle, nerve, pith, pluck, pluckiness, spirit, stamina.

gamesome *adj* frisky, frolicsome, lively, merry, playful, sportive, sprightly, vivacious.

gammon *vb* bamboozle, beguile, cheat, circumvent, deceive, delude, dupe, gull, hoax, humbug, inveigle, mislead, overreach, outwit. • *n* bosh, hoax, humbug, imposition, nonsense.

gang *n* band, cabal, clique, company, coterie, crew, horde, party, set, troop.

gaol *see* jail.

gap *n* breach, break, cavity, chasm, chink, cleft, crack, cranny, crevice, hiatus, hollow, interval, interstice, lacuna, opening, pass, ravine, rift, space, vacancy.

gape *vb* burst open, open, stare, yawn.

garb *vb* attire, clothe, dress. • *n* apparel, attire, clothes, costume, dress, garments, habiliment, habit, raiment, robes, uniform, vestment.

garbage *n* filth, offal, refuse, remains, rubbish, trash, waste.

garble *vb* corrupt, distort, falsify, misquote, misrepresent, mutilate, pervert.

vb antonym decipher.

gargantuan *adj* big, Brobdingnagian, colossal, enormous, gigantic, huge, prodigious, tremendous.

adj antonym small.

garish *adj* bright, dazzling, flashy, flaunting, gaudy, glaring, loud, showy, staring, tawdry.

garland *vb* adorn, festoon, wreathe. • *n* chaplet, coronal, crown, festoon, wreath.

garment *n* clothes, clothing, dress, habit, vestment.

garner *vb* accumulate, collect, deposit, gather, hoard, husband, reserve, save, store, treasure.

garnish *vb* adorn, beautify, bedeck, decorate, deck, embellish, grace, ornament, prank, trim. • *n* decoration, enhancement, ornament, trimming.

vb antonym divest.

garrulous *adj* babbling, loquacious, prating, prattling, talkative.

adj antonyms taciturn, terse.

gasconade *n* bluster, boast, brag, bravado, swagger, vaunt, vapouring.

gasp *vb* blow, choke, pant, puff. • *n* blow, exclamation, gulp, puff.

gather *vb* **1** assemble, cluster, collect, convene, group, muster, rally. **2** accumulate, amass, garner, hoard, huddle, lump. **3** bunch, crop, cull, glean, pick, pluck, rake, reap, shock, stack. **4** acquire, gain, get, win. **5** conclude, deduce, derive, infer. **6** fold, plait, pucker, shirr, tuck. **7** condense, grow, increase, thicken.

vb antonyms dissipate, scatter.

gathering *n* **1** acquisition, collecting, earning, gain, heap, pile, procuring. **2** assemblage, assembly, collection, company, concourse, congregation, meeting, muster. **3** abscess, boil, fester, pimple, pustule, sore, suppuration, tumour, ulcer.

n antonym scattering.

gauche *adj* awkward, blundering, bungling, clumsy, inept, tactless, uncouth.

gaudy *adj* bespangled, brilliant, brummagem, cheap, flashy, flaunting, garish, gimcrack, glittering, loud, ostentatious, over-decorated, sham, showy, spurious, tawdry, tinsel.

adj antonyms drab, plain, quiet.

gauge *vb* **1** calculate, check, determine, weigh. **2** assess, estimate, guess, reckon. • *n* **1** criterion, example, indicator, measure, meter, touchstone, yardstick. **2** bore, depth, height, magnitude, size, thickness, width.

gaunt *adj* angular, attenuated, emaciated, haggard, lank, lean, meagre, scraggy, skinny, slender, spare, thin.

adj antonyms hale, plump.

gawky *adj* awkward, boorish, clownish, clumsy, green, loutish, raw, rustic, uncouth, ungainly.

gay *adj* **1** homosexual, lesbian, (*inf*) camp, (*off*) queer, same-sex. **2** bright, brilliant, dashing, fine, showy. **3** flashy, flaunting, garish, gaudy, glittering, loud. **4** airy, blithe, blithesome, cheerful, festive, frivolous, frolicsome, gladsome, gleeful, hilarious, jaunty, jolly, jovial, light-hearted, lively, merry, mirthful, sportive, sprightly, vivacious.

gear *vb* adapt, equip, fit, suit, tailor. • *n* **1** apparel, array, clothes, clothing, dress, garb. **2** accoutrements, appliances, appointments, appurtenances, array, harness, goods, movables, subsidiaries. **3** harness, rigging, tackle, trappings. **4** apparatus, machinery, mechanics.

gelid *adj* chill, chilly, cold, freezing, frigid, icy.

gem *n* jewel, stone, treasure.

genealogy *n* ancestry, descent, lineage, pedigree, stock.

general *adj* **1** broad, collective, generic, popular, universal, widespread. **2** catholic, ecumenical. **3** common, current, ordinary, usual. **4** inaccurate, indefinite, inexact, vague.

adj antonyms limited, novel, particular.

generally *adv* commonly, extensively, universally, usually.

adv antonym rarely.

generate *vb* **1** beget, breed, engender, procreate, propagate, reproduce, spawn. **2** cause, form, make, produce.

vb antonym prevent.

generation *n* **1** creation, engendering, formation, procreation, production. **2** age, epoch, era, period, time. **3** breed, children, family, kind, offspring, progeny, race, stock.

generosity *n* **1** disinterestedness, high-mindedness, magnanimity, nobleness. **2** bounteousness, bountifulness, bounty, charity, liberality, openhandedness.
n antonyms meanness, selfishness.

generous *adj* **1** high-minded, honourable, magnanimous, noble. **2** beneficent, bountiful, charitable, free, hospitable, liberal, munificent, open-handed. **3** abundant, ample, copious, plentiful, rich.
adj antonyms mean, selfish.

genial *adj* **1** cheering, encouraging, enlivening, fostering, inspiring, mild, warm. **2** agreeable, cheerful, cordial, friendly, hearty, jovial, kindly, merry, mirthful, pleasant.

genius *n* **1** aptitude, aptness, bent, capacity, endowment, faculty, flair, gift, talent, turn. **2** brains, creative power, ingenuity, inspiration, intellect, invention, parts, sagacity, wit. **3** adeptness, master, master hand, proficiency. **4** character, disposition, naturalness, nature. **5** deity, demon, spirit.

genteel *adj* **1** aristocratic, courteous, gentlemanly, lady-like, polished, polite, refined, well-bred. **2** elegant, fashionable, graceful, stylish.
adj antonyms crude, rough, unpolished.

gentility *n* civility, courtesy, good breeding, politeness, refinement, urbanity.

gentle *adj* **1** amiable, bland, clement, compassionate, humane, indulgent, kind, kindly, lenient, meek, merciful, mild, moderate, soft, tender, tender-hearted. **2** docile, pacific, peaceable, placid, quiet, tame, temperate, tractable. **3** bland, easy, gradual, light, slight. **4** soft. **5** high-born, noble, well-born. **6** chivalrous, courteous, cultivated, knightly, polished, refined, well-bred.
adj antonyms cruel, crude, rough, unkind.

gentlemanly *adj* civil, complaisant, courteous, cultivated, delicate, genteel, honourable, polite, refined, urbane, well-bred.

genuine *adj* **1** authentic, honest, proper, pure, real, right, true, unadulterated, unalloyed, uncorrupted, veritable. **2** frank, native, sincere, unaffected.
adj antonyms artificial, insincere.

genus *n* class, group, kind, order, race, sort, type.

germ *n* **1** embryo, nucleus, ovule, ovum, seed, seed-bud. **2** bacterium, microbe, microorganism. **3** beginning, cause, origin, rudiment, source.

germane *adj* **1** akin, allied, cognate, related. **2** apposite, appropriate, fitting, pertinent, relevant, suitable.

germinate *vb* bud, burgeon, develop, generate, grow, pollinate, push, shoot, sprout, vegetate.

gesture *vb* indicate, motion, signal, wave. • *n* action, attitude, gesticulation, gesturing, posture, sign, signal.

get *vb* **1** achieve, acquire, attain, earn, gain, obtain, procure, receive, relieve, secure, win. **2** finish, master, prepare. **3** beget, breed, engender, generate, procreate.
vb antonyms lose, misunderstand, pacify.

ghastly *adj* **1** cadaverous, corpse-like, death-like, deathly, ghostly, lurid, pale, pallid, wan. **2** dismal, dreadful, fearful, frightful, grim, grisly, gruesome, hideous, horrible, shocking, terrible.
adj antonym delightful.

ghost *n* **1** soul, spirit. **2** apparition, phantom, revenant, shade, spectre, spook, sprite, wraith.

giant *adj* colossal, enormous, Herculean, huge, large, monstrous, prodigious, vast. • *n* colossus, cyclops, Hercules, monster.

gibberish *n* babble, balderdash, drivel, gabble, gobbledygook, jabber, nonsense, prate, prating.

gibe, jibe *vb* deride, fleer, flout, jeer, mock, ridicule, scoff, sneer, taunt. • *n* ridicule, sneer, taunt.

giddiness *n* dizziness, head-spinning, vertigo.

giddy *adj* **1** dizzy, head-spinning, vertiginous. **2** careless, changeable, fickle, flighty, frivolous, hare-brained, headlong, heedless, inconstant, irresolute, light-headed, thoughtless, unsteady, vacillating, wild.
adj antonyms sensible, sober.

gift *n* **1** alms, allowance, benefaction, bequest, bonus, boon, bounty, contribution, donation, dowry, endowment, favour, grant, gratuity, honorarium, largesse, legacy, offering, premium, present, prize, subscription, subsidy, tip. **2** faculty, talent.

gifted *adj* able, capable, clever, ingenious, intelligent, inventive, sagacious, talented.

gigantic *adj* colossal, Cyclopean, enormous, giant, herculean, huge, immense, prodigious, titanic, tremendous, vast.
adj antonym small.

giggle *vb*, *n* cackle, grin, laugh, snigger, snicker, titter.

gild *vb* adorn, beautify, bedeck, brighten, decorate, embellish, grace, illuminate.

gird *vb* **1** belt, girdle. **2** begird, encircle, enclose, encompass, engird, environ, surround. **3** brace, support. • *n* band, belt, cincture, girdle, girth, sash, waistband.

gist *n* basis, core, essence, force, ground, marrow, meaning, pith, point, substance.

give *vb* **1** accord, bequeath, bestow, confer, devise, entrust, present. **2** afford, contribute, donate, furnish, grant, proffer, spare, supply. **3** communicate, impart. **4** deliver, exchange, pay, requite. **5** allow, permit, vouchsafe. **6** emit, pronounce, render, utter. **7** produce, yield. **8** cause, occasion. **9** apply, devote, surrender. **10** bend, sink, recede, retire, retreat, yield.
vb antonyms hold out, take, withstand.

glad *adj* **1** delighted, gratified, happy, pleased, rejoicing, well-contented. **2** animated, blithe, cheerful, cheery, elated, gladsome, jocund, joyful, joyous, light, light-hearted, merry, playful, radiant. **3** animating, bright, cheering, exhilarating, gladdening, gratifying, pleasing.
adj antonym sad.

gladden *vb* bless, cheer, delight, elate, enliven, exhilarate, gratify, please, rejoice.

gladiator *n* prize-fighter, sword-player, swordsman.

gladness *n* animation, cheerfulness, delight, gratification, happiness, joy, joyfulness, joyousness, pleasure.
n antonym sadness.

gladsome *adj* airy, blithe, blithesome, cheerful,

delighted, frolicsome, glad, gleeful, jocund, jolly, jovial, joyful, joyous, light-hearted, lively, merry, pleased, sportive, sprightly, vivacious.

glamour *n* bewitchment, charm, enchantment, fascination, spell, witchery.

glance *vb* **1** coruscate, gleam, glisten, glister, glitter, scintillate, shine. **2** dart, flit. **3** gaze, glimpse, look, view. • *n* **1** gleam, glitter. **2** gleam, look, view.

glare *vb* **1** dazzle, flame, flare, gleam, glisten,

glitter, sparkle. **2** frown, gaze, glower. • *n* flare, glitter.

glaring *adj* **1** dazzling, gleaming, glistening, glittering. **2** barefaced, conspicuous, extreme, manifest, notorious, open.
adj antonyms dull, hidden, minor.

glassy *adj* brilliant, crystal, crystalline, gleaming, lucent, shining, transparent.

glaze *vb* burnish, calender, furbish, gloss, polish. • *n* coat, enamel, finish, glazing, polish, varnish.

gleam *vb* beam, coruscate, flash, glance, glimmer, glitter, shine, sparkle. • *n* **1** beam, flash, glance, glimmer, glimmering, glow, ray. **2** brightness, coruscation, flashing, gleaming, glitter, glittering, lustre, splendour.

glean *vb* collect, cull, gather, get, harvest, pick, select.

glee *n* exhilaration, fun, gaiety, hilarity, jocularity, jollity, joviality, joy, liveliness, merriment, mirth, sportiveness, verve.

glib *adj* **1** slippery, smooth. **2** artful, facile, flippant, fluent, ready, talkative, voluble.
adj antonyms implausible, tongue-tied.

glide *vb* **1** float, glissade, roll on, skate, skim, slide, slip. **2** flow, lapse, run, roll. • *n* gliding, lapse, sliding, slip.

glimmer *vb* flash, flicker, gleam, glitter, shine, twinkle. • *n* **1** beam, gleam, glimmering, ray. **2** glance, glimpse.

glimpse *vb* espy, look, spot, view. • *n* flash, glance, glimmering, glint, look, sight.

glitter *vb* coruscate, flare, flash, glance, glare, gleam, glisten, glister, scintillate, shine, sparkle. • *n* beam, beaming, brightness, brilliancy, coruscation, gleam, glister, lustre, radiance, scintillation, shine, sparkle, splendour.

gloaming *n* dusk, eventide, nightfall, twilight.

gloat *vb* exult, gaze, rejoice, stare, triumph.

globe *n* ball, earth, orb, sphere.

globular *adj* globate, globated, globe-shaped, globose, globous, round, spheral, spheric, spherical.

globule *n* bead, drop, particle, spherule.

gloom *n* **1** cloud, darkness, dimness, gloominess, obscurity, shade, shadow. **2** cheerlessness, dejection, depression, despondency, downheartedness, dullness, melancholy, sadness.
n antonym brightness.

gloomy *adj* **1** dark, dim, dusky, obscure.

2 cheerless, dismal, lowering, lurid. **3** crestfallen, dejected, depressed, despondent, disheartened, dispirited, downcast, downhearted, glum, melancholy, morose, sad, sullen. **4** depressing, disheartening, dispiriting, heavy, saddening.
adj antonym bright.

glorify *vb* **1** adore, bless, celebrate, exalt, extol, honour, laud, magnify, worship. **2** adorn, brighten, elevate, ennoble, make bright.
vb antonyms denounce, vilify.

glorious *adj* **1** celebrated, conspicuous, distinguished, eminent, excellent, famed, famous, illustrious, pre-eminent, renowned. **2** brilliant, bright, grand, magnificent, radiant, resplendent, splendid. **3** consummate, exalted, high, lofty, noble, supreme.
adj antonyms dreadful, inglorious, plain, unknown.

glory *vb* boast, exult, vaunt. • *n* **1** celebrity, distinction, eminence, fame, honour, illustriousness, praise, renown. **2** brightness, brilliancy, effulgence, lustre, pride, resplendence, splendour. **3** exaltation, exceeding, gloriousness, greatness, grandeur, nobleness. **4** bliss, happiness.
n antonyms blame, restraint.

gloss¹ *vb* coat, colour, disguise, extenuate, glaze, palliate, varnish, veneer, veil. • *n* **1** coating, lustre, polish, sheen, varnish, veneer. **2** pretence, pretext.

gloss² *vb* annotate, comment, elucidate, explain, interpret. • *n* annotation, comment, commentary, elucidation, explanation, interpretation, note.

glove *n* **1** gantlet, gauntlet, handwear, mitt, mitten. **2** challenge.

glow *vb* **1** incandesce, radiate, shine. **2** blush, burn, flush, redden. • *n* **1** blaze, brightness, brilliance, burning, incandescence, luminosity, reddening. **2** ardour, bloom, enthusiasm, fervency, fervour, flush, impetuosity, vehemence, warmth.

glower *vb* frown, glare, lower, scowl, stare. • *n* frown, glare, scowl.

glum *adj* churlish, crabbed, crestfallen, cross-grained, crusty, depressed, frowning, gloomy, glowering, moody, morose, sour, sulky, sullen, surly.
adj antonyms ecstatic, happy.

glut *vb* block up, cloy, cram, gorge, satiate, stuff. • *n* excess, saturation, surfeit, surplus.
n antonyms lack, scarcity.

glutinous *adj* adhesive, clammy, cohesive, gluey, gummy, sticky, tenacious, viscid, viscous.

glutton *n* gobbler, gorger, gourmand, gormandizer, greedy-guts, lurcher, pig.
n antonym ascetic.

gnarled *adj* contorted, cross-grained, gnarly, knotted, knotty, snaggy, twisted.

go *vb* **1** advance, move, pass, proceed, progress repair. **2** act, operate. **3** be about, fare, journey, roam, rove, travel, walk, wend. **4** depart, disappear, cease: **5** elapse, extend, lead, reach, run. **6** avail, concur, contribute, tend, serve. **7** eventuate, fare, turn out. **8** afford, bet, risk, wager. • *n* **1** action, business, case, chance, circumstance, doings, turn. **2** custom, fad, fashion, mode, vogue. **3** energy, endurance, power, stamina, verve, vivacity.

goad *vb* **1** annoy, badger, harass, irritate, sting, worry. **2** arouse, impel, incite, instigate, prod, spur, stimulate, urge. • *n* incentive, incitement, pressure, stimulation.

goal *n* **1** bound, home, limit, mark, mete, post. **2** end, object. **3** aim, design, destination.

gobble *vb* bolt, devour, gorge, gulp, swallow.

goblin *n* apparition, elf, bogey, demon, gnome, hobgoblin, phantom, spectre, sprite.

god *n* almighty, creator, deity, divinity, idol, Jehovah, omnipotence, providence.

godless *adj* atheistic, impious, irreligious, profane, ungodly, wicked.

godlike *adj* celestial, divine, heavenly, supernal.

godly *adj* devout, holy, pious, religious, righteous, saint-like, saintly.
adj antonyms godless, impious.

godsend *n* fortune, gift, luck, present, windfall.

golden *adj* **1** aureate, brilliant, bright, gilded, resplendent, shining, splendid. **2** excellent, precious. **3** auspicious, favourable, opportune, propitious. **4** blessed, delightful, glorious, halcyon, happy.

good *adj* **1** advantageous, beneficial, favourable, profitable, serviceable, useful. **2** adequate, appropriate, becoming, convenient, fit, proper, satisfactory, suitable, well-adapted. **3** decorous, dutiful, honest, just, pious, reliable, religious, righteous, true, upright, virtuous, well-behaved, worthy. **4** admirable, capable, excellent, genuine, healthy, precious, sincere, sound, sterling, valid, valuable. **5** benevolent, favourable, friendly, gracious, humane, kind, merciful, obliging, well-disposed. **6** fair, honourable, immaculate, unblemished, unimpeachable, unimpeached, unsullied, untarnished. **7** cheerful, companionable, lively, genial, social. **8** able, competent, dextrous, expert, qualified, ready, skilful, thorough, well-qualified. **9** credit-worthy. **10** agreeable, cheering, gratifying, pleasant. • *n* **1** advantage, benefit, boon, favour, gain, profit, utility. **2** interest, prosperity, welfare, weal. **3** excellence, righteousness, virtue, worth.

good breeding *n* affability, civility, courtesy, good manners, polish, politeness, urbanity.

goodbye *n* adieu, farewell, parting.

goodly *adj* **1** beautiful, comely, good-looking, graceful. **2** agreeable, considerate, desirable, happy, pleasant.

good-natured *adj* amiable, benevolent, friendly, kind, kind-hearted, kindly.
adj antonym ill-natured.

goodness *n* **1** excellence, quality, value, worth. **2** honesty, integrity, morality, principle, probity, righteousness, uprightness, virtue. **3** benevolence, beneficence, benignity, good-will, humaneness, humanity, kindness.
n antonyms badness, inferiority, wickedness.

goods *npl* **1** belongings, chattels, effects, furniture, movables. **2** commodities, merchandise, stock, wares.

goodwill *n* **1** benevolence, kindness, good nature. **2** ardour, earnestness, heartiness, willingness, zeal. **3** custom, patronage.
n antonym ill-will.

gore *vb* horn, pierce, stab, wound.

gorge[1] *vb* **1** bolt, devour, eat, feed, swallow. **2** cram, fill, glut, gormandize, sate, satiate, stuff, surfeit. • *n* craw, crop, gullet, throat.
vb antonym abstain.

gorge[2] *n* canyon, defile, fissure, notch, ravine.

gorgeous *adj* bright, brilliant, dazzling, fine, glittering, grand, magnificent, resplendent, rich, shining, showy, splendid, superb.
adj antonyms dull, plain, seedy.

Gorgon *n* bugaboo, fright, hobgoblin, hydra, ogre, spectre.

gory *adj* bloody, ensanguined, sanguinary.

gospel *n* creed, doctrine, message, news, revelation, tidings.

gossip *vb* chat, cackle, clack, gabble, prate, prattle, tattle. • *n* **1** babbler, busybody, chatterer, gossip monger, newsmonger, quidnunc, tale-bearer, tattler, tell-tale. **2** cackle, chat, chit-chat, prate, prattle, tattle.

gourmand *n* **1** glutton. **2** epicure, gourmet.
n antonym ascetic.

gourmet *n* connoisseur, epicure, epicurean.
n antonym omnivore.

govern *vb* **1** administer, conduct, direct, manage, regulate, reign, rule, superintend, supervise. **2** guide, pilot, steer. **3** bridle, check, command, control, curb, restrain, rule, sway.

government *n* **1** autonomy, command, conduct, control, direction, discipline, dominion, guidance, management, regulation, restraint, rule, sway. **2** administration, cabinet, commonwealth, polity, sovereignty, state.

governor *n* **1** commander, comptroller, director, head, headmaster, manager, overseer, ruler, superintendent, supervisor. **2** chief magistrate, executive. **3** guardian, instructor, tutor.

grab *vb* capture, clutch, seize, snatch.

grace *vb* **1** adorn, beautify, deck, decorate, embellish. **2** dignify, honour. • *n* **1** benignity, condescension, favour, good-will, kindness, love. **2** devotion, efficacy, holiness, love, piety, religion, sanctity, virtue. **3** forgiveness, mercy, pardon, reprieve. **4** accomplishment, attractiveness, charm, elegance, polish, propriety, refinement. **5** beauty, comeliness, ease, gracefulness, symmetry. **6** blessing, petition, thanks.
vb antonyms deface, detract from, spoil.

graceful *adj* **1** beautiful, becoming, comely, easy, elegant. **2** flowing, natural, rounded, unlaboured. **3** appropriate. **4** felicitous, happy, tactful.
adj antonym graceless.

graceless *adj* abandoned, corrupt, depraved, dissolute, hardened, incorrigible, irreclaimable, lost, obdurate, profligate, reprobate, repugnant, shameless,

gracious *adj* **1** beneficent, benevolent, benign, benignant, compassionate, condescending, favourable, friendly, gentle, good-natured, kind, kindly, lenient, merciful, mild, tender. **2** affable, civil, courteous, easy, familiar, polite.
adj antonym ungracious.

grade *vb* arrange, classify, group, order, rank, sort. • *n* **1** brand, degree, intensity, stage, step, rank. **2** gradient, incline, slope.

gradual *adj* approximate, continuous, gentle, progressive, regular, slow, successive.
adj antonyms precipitate, sudden.

graduate *vb* adapt, adjust, proportion, regulate. • *n* alumna, alumnus, laureate, postgraduate.

graft *vb* ingraft, inoculate, insert, transplant. • *n* **1** bud, scion, shoot, slip, sprout. **2** corruption, favouritism, influence, nepotism.

grain *n* **1** kernel, ovule, seed. **2** cereals, corn, grist. **3** atom, bit, glimmer, jot, particle, scintilla, scrap, shadow, spark, tittle, trace, whit. **4** disposition, fibre, humour, temper, texture. **5** colour, dye, hue, shade, stain, texture, tincture, tinge.

granary *n* corn-house, garner, grange, storehouse.

grand *adj* **1** august, dignified, elevated, eminent, exalted, great, illustrious, lordly, majestic, princely, stately, sublime. **2** fine, glorious, gorgeous, magnificent, pompous, lofty, noble, splendid, superb. **3** chief, leading, main, pre-eminent, principal, superior.

grandee *n* lord, noble, nobleman.

grandeur *n* **1** elevation, greatness, immensity, impressiveness, loftiness, vastness. **2** augustness, dignity, eminence, glory, magnificence, majesty, nobility, pomp, splendour, state, stateliness.
n antonyms humbleness, simplicity.

grandiloquent *adj* bombastic, declamatory, high-minded, high-sounding, inflated, pompous, rhetorical, stilted, swelling, tumid, turgid.

grant *vb* **1** accord, admit, allow, sanction. **2** cede, concede, give, impart, indulge. **3** bestow, confer, deign, invest, vouchsafe. **4** convey, transfer, yield. • *n* **1** admission, allowance, benefaction, bestowal, boon, bounty, concession, donation, endowment, gift, indulgence, largesse, present. **2** conveyance, cession.
vb antonyms deny, refuse.

graphic *adj* descriptive, diagrammatic, figural, figurative, forcible, lively, pictorial, picturesque, striking, telling, vivid, well-delineated, well-drawn.
adj antonyms impressionistic, vague.

grapple *vb* catch, clutch, grasp, grip, hold, hug, seize, tackle, wrestle.
vb antonyms avoid, evade.

grasp *vb* **1** catch, clasp, clinch, clutch, grapple, grip, seize. **2** comprehend, understand. • *n* **1** clasp, grip, hold. **2** comprehension, power, reach, scope, understanding.

grasping *adj* acquisitive, avaricious, covetous, exacting, greedy, rapacious, sordid, tight-fisted.
adj antonym generous.

grate *vb* **1** abrade, rub, scrape, triturate. **2** comminute, rasp. **3** creak, fret, grind, jar, vex. • *n* **1** bars, grating, latticework, screen. **2** basket, fire bed.

grateful *adj* **1** appreciative, beholden, indebted, obliged, sensible, thankful. **2** pleasant, welcome.
adj antonym ungrateful.

gratification *n* **1** gratifying, indulgence, indulging, pleasing, satisfaction, satisfying. **2** delight, enjoyment, fruition, pleasure, reward.

gratify *vb* **1** delight, gladden, please. **2** humour, fulfil, grant, indulge, requite, satisfy.
vb antonyms frustrate, thwart.

gratifying *adj* agreeable, delightful, grateful, pleasing, welcome.

grating *adj* disagreeable, displeasing, harsh, irritating, offensive. • *n* grate, partition.
adj antonyms harmonious, pleasing.

gratis *adv* freely, gratuitously.

gratitude *n* goodwill, gratitude, indebtedness, thankfulness.
n antonym ingratitude.

gratuitous *adj* **1** free, spontaneous, unrewarded, voluntary. **2** assumed, baseless, groundless, unfounded, unwarranted, wanton.

gratuity *n* benefaction, bounty, charity, donation, endowment, gift, grant, largesse, present.

grave[1] *n* crypt, mausoleum, ossuary, pit, sepulchre, sepulture, tomb, vault.

grave[2] *adj* **1** cogent, heavy, important, momentous, ponderous, pressing, serious, weighty. **2** dignified, sage, sedate, serious, slow, solemn, staid, thoughtful. **3** dull, grim, plain, quiet, sober, sombre, subdued. **4** cruel, hard, harsh, severe. **5** despicable, dire, dismal, gross, heinous, infamous, outrageous, scandalous, shameful, shocking. **6** heavy, hollow, low, low-pitched, sepulchral.
adj antonyms cheerful, light, slight, trivial.

grave[3] *vb* **1** engrave, impress, imprint, infix. **2** carve, chisel, cut, sculpt.

gravel *vb* bewilder, embarrass, nonplus, perplex, pose, puzzle, stagger. • *n* ballast, grit, sand, shingle.

graveyard *n* burial ground, cemetery, churchyard, god's acre, mortuary, necropolis.

gravity *n* **1** heaviness, weight. **2** demureness, sedateness, seriousness, sobriety, thoughtfulness. **3** importance, moment, momentousness, weightiness.

n antonyms gaiety, levity, triviality.

graze *vb* **1** brush, glance, scrape, scratch. **2** abrade, shave, skim. **3** browse, crop, feed, pasture. • *n* abrasion, bruise, scrape, scratch.

great *adj* **1** ample, big, bulky, Cyclopean, enormous, gigantic, Herculean, huge, immense, large, pregnant, vast. **2** decided, excessive, high, much, pronounced. **3** countless, numerous. **4** chief, considerable, grand, important, leading, main, pre-eminent, principal, superior, weighty. **5** celebrated, distinguished, eminent, exalted, excellent, famed, famous, far-famed, illustrious, noted, prominent, renowned. **6** august, dignified, elevated, grand, lofty, majestic, noble, sublime. **7** chivalrous, generous, high-minded, magnanimous. **8** fine, magnificent, rich, sumptuous.

adj antonyms insignificant, pusillanimous, small, unimportant.

greatness *n* **1** bulk, dimensions, largeness, magnitude, size. **2** distinction, elevation, eminence, fame, importance, renown. **3** augustness, dignity, grandeur, majesty, loftiness, nobility, nobleness, sublimity. **4** chivalry, generosity, magnanimity, spirit.

greed, greediness *n* **1** gluttony, hunger, ravenousness, voracity. **2** avidity, covetousness, desire, eagerness, longing. **3** avarice, cupidity, graspingness, grasping, rapacity, selfishness.

n antonym abstemiousness.

greedy *adj* **1** devouring, gluttonous, insatiable, insatiate, rapacious, ravenous, voracious. **2** desirous, eager. **3** avaricious, grasping, selfish.

adj antonym abstemious.

green *adj* **1** aquamarine, emerald, olive, verdant, verdure, viridescent, viridian. **2** blooming, flourishing, fresh, undecayed. **3** fresh, new, recent. **4** immature, unfledged, unripe. **5** callow, crude, inexpert, ignorant, inexperienced, raw, unskilful, untrained, verdant, young. **6** unseasoned. **7** conservationist, ecological, environmentalist. • *n* common, grass plot, lawn, sward, turf, verdure.

greenhorn *n* beginner, novice, tyro.

n antonyms old hand, veteran.

greet *vb* accost, address, complement, hail, receive, salute, welcome.

vb antonym ignore.

greeting *n* compliment, salutation, salute, welcome.

grief *n* **1** affliction, agony, anguish, bitterness, distress, dole, heartbreak, misery, regret, sadness, sorrow, suffering, tribulation, mourning, woe. **2** grievance, trial. **3** disaster, failure, mishap.

n antonym happiness.

grievance *n* **1** burden, complaint, hardship, injury, oppression, wrong. **2** affliction, distress, grief, sorrow, trial, woe.

grieve *vb* **1** afflict, aggrieve, agonize, discomfort, distress, hurt, oppress, pain, sadden, wound. **2** bewail, deplore, mourn, lament, regret, sorrow, suffer.

grievous *adj* **1** afflicting, afflictive, burdensome, deplorable, distressing, heavy, lamentable, oppressive, painful, sad, sorrowful. **2** baleful, baneful, calamitous, destructive, detrimental, hurtful, injurious, mischievous, noxious, troublesome. **3** aggravated, atrocious, dreadful, flagitious, flagrant, gross, heinous, iniquitous, intense, intolerable, severe, outrageous, wicked.

grill *vb* **1** broil, griddle, roast, toast. **2** sweat. **3** cross-examine, interrogate, question. **4** torment, torture. • *n* **1** grating, gridiron. **2** cross-examination, cross-questioning.

grim *adj* **1** cruel, ferocious, fierce, harsh, relentless, ruthless, savage, stern, unyielding. **2** appalling, dire, dreadful, fearful, frightful, grisly, hideous, horrid, horrible, terrific.

adj antonyms benign, congenial, pleasant.

grimace *vb, n* frown, scowl, smirk, sneer.

grime *n* dirt, filth, foulness, smut.

grimy *adj* begrimed, defiled, dirty, filthy, foul, soiled, sullied, unclean.

adj antonyms clean, pure.

grind *vb* **1** bruise, crunch, crush, grate, grit, pulverize, rub, triturate. **2** sharpen, whet. **3** afflict, harass, oppress, persecute, plague, trouble. • *n* chore, drudgery, labour, toil.

grip *vb* clasp, clutch, grasp, hold, seize. • *n* clasp, clutch, control, domination, grasp, hold.

grisly *adj* appalling, frightful, dreadful, ghastly, grim, grey, hideous, horrible, horrid, terrible, terrific.

grit *vb* clench, grate, grind. • *n* **1** bran, gravel, pebbles, sand. **2** courage, decision, determination, firmness, perseverance, pluck, resolution, spirit.

groan *vb* **1** complain, lament, moan, whine. **2** creak. • *n* **1** cry, moan, whine. **2** complaint. **3** grouse, grumble.
n antonym cheer.
vb antonym cheer.

groom *vb* **1** clean, dress, tidy. **2** brush, tend. **3** coach, educate, nurture, train. • *n* equerry, hostler, manservant, ostler, servant, stable-hand, valet, waiter.

groove *n* **1** channel, cut, furrow, rabbet, rebate, recess, rut, scoring. **2** routine.
n antonym ridge.

gross *vb* accumulate, earn, make. • *adj* **1** big, bulky, burly, fat, great, large. **2** dense, dull, stupid, thick. **3** beastly, broad, carnal, coarse, crass, earthy, impure, indelicate, licentious, low, obscene, unbecoming, unrefined, unseemly, vulgar, rough, sensual. **4** aggravated, brutal, enormous, flagrant, glaring, grievous, manifest, obvious, palpable, plain, outrageous, shameful. **5** aggregate, entire, total, whole. • *n* aggregate, bulk, total, whole.
adj antonyms delicate, fine, seemly, slight.

grossness *n* **1** bigness, bulkiness, greatness. **2** density, thickness. **3** coarseness, ill-breeding, rudeness, vulgarity. **4** bestiality, brutality, carnality, coarseness, impurity, indelicacy, licentiousness, sensuality.

grotesque *adj* **1** bizarre, extravagant, fanciful, fantastic, incongruous, odd, strange, unnatural, whimsical, wild. **2** absurd, antic, burlesque, ludicrous, ridiculous.

ground *vb* **1** fell, place. **2** base, establish, fix, found, set. **3** instruct, train. • *n* **1** area, clod, distance, earth, loam, mould, sod, soil, turf. **2** country, domain, land, region, territory. **3** acres, estate, field, property. **4** base, basis, foundation, groundwork, support. **5** account, consideration, excuse, gist, motive, opinion, reason.

groundless *adj* baseless, causeless, false, gratuitous, idle, unauthorized, unfounded, unjustifiable, unsolicited, unsought, unwarranted.
adj antonyms justified, reasonable.

grounds *npl* **1** deposit, dregs, grouts, lees, precipitate, sediment, settlings. **2** accounts, arguments, considerations, reasons, support. **3** campus, gardens, lawns, premises, yard.

group *vb* arrange, assemble, dispose, order. • *n* aggregation, assemblage, assembly, body, combination, class, clump, cluster, collection, order.

grove *n* copse, glade, spinney, thicket, wood, woodland.

grovel *vb* cower, crawl, creep, cringe, fawn, flatter, sneak.

grovelling *adj* **1** creeping, crouching, squat. **2** abject, base, beggarly, cringing, fawning, low, mean, servile, slavish, sneaking, undignified, unworthy, vile.

grow *vb* **1** enlarge, expand, extend, increase, swell. **2** arise, burgeon, develop, germinate, shoot, sprout, vegetate. **3** advance, extend, improve, progress, thrive, wax. **4** cultivate, produce, raise.
vb antonyms decrease, fail, halt.

growl *vb* complain, croak, find fault, gnarl, groan, grumble, lament, murmur, snarl. • *n* **1** croak, grown, snarl. **2** complaint.

growth *n* **1** augmentation, development, expansion, extension, growing, increase. **2** burgeoning, excrescence, formation, germination, pollution, shooting, sprouting, vegetation. **3** cultivation, produce, product, production. **4** advance, advancement, development, improvement, progress. **5** adulthood, maturity.
n antonyms decrease, failure, stagnation, stoppage.

grub *vb* clear, dig, eradicate, root. • *n* **1** caterpillar, larvae, maggot. **2** drudge, plodder.

grudge *vb* **1** begrudge, envy, repine. **2** complain, grieve, murmur. • *n* aversion, dislike, enmity, grievance, hate, hatred, ill-will, malevolence, malice, pique, rancour, resentment, spite, venom.
n antonyms favour, regard.
vb antonyms applaud, approve.

gruff *adj* bluff, blunt, brusque, churlish, discourteous, grumpy, harsh, impolite, rough, rude, rugged, surly, uncivil, ungracious.
adj antonyms clear, courteous, sweet.

grumble *vb* **1** croak, complain, murmur, repine. **2** gnarl, growl, snarl. **3** roar, rumble. • *n* growl, murmur, complaint, roar, rumble.
vb antonym acquiesce.

grumpy *adj* crabbed, cross, glum, moody, morose, sour, sullen, surly.
adj antonyms civil, contented.

guarantee *vb* assure, insure, pledge, secure, warrant. • *n* assurance, pledge, security, surety, warrant, warranty.

guard *vb* defend, keep, patrol, protect, safeguard, save, secure, shelter, shield, watch. • *n* 1 aegis, bulwark, custody, defence, palladium, protection, rampart, safeguard, security, shield. 2 keeper, guardian, patrol, sentinel, sentry, warden, watch, watchman. 3 conduct, convoy, escort. 4 attention, care, caution, circumspection, heed, watchfulness.

guarded *adj* careful, cautious, circumspect, reserved, reticent, wary, watchful.
adj antonyms frank, wholehearted.

guardian *n* custodian, defender, guard, keeper, preserver, protector, trustee, warden.

guerdon *n* recompense, remuneration, requital, reward.

guess *vb* 1 conjecture, divine, mistrust, surmise, suspect. 2 fathom, find out, penetrate, solve. 3 believe, fancy, hazard, imagine, reckon, suppose, think. • *n* conjecture, divination, notion, supposition, surmise.

guest *n* caller, company, visitant.

guidance *n* conduct, control, direction, escort, government, lead, leadership, pilotage, steering.

guide *vb* 1 conduct, escort, lead, pilot. 2 control, direct, govern, manage, preside, regulate, rule, steer, superintend, supervise. • *n* 1 cicerone, conductor, director, monitor, pilot. 2 adviser, counsellor, instructor, mentor. 3 clew, directory, index, key, thread. 4 guidebook, itinerary, landmark.

guild *n* association, brotherhood, company, corporation, fellowship, fraternity, society, union.

guile *n* art, artfulness, artifice, craft, cunning, deceit, deception, duplicity, fraud, knavery, ruse, subtlety, treachery, trickery, wiles, wiliness.
n antonyms artlessness, guilelessness.

guileless *adj* artless, candid, frank, honest, ingenuous, innocent, open, pure, simpleminded, sincere, straightforward, truthful, undesigning, unsophisticated.
adj antonyms artful, guileful.

guilt *n* 1 blame, criminality, culpability, guiltless. 2 ill-desert, iniquity, offensiveness, wickedness, wrong. 3 crime, offence, sin.
n antonyms innocence, shamelessness.

guiltless *adj* blameless, immaculate, innocent, pure, sinless, spotless, unpolluted, unspotted, unsullied, untarnished.

guilty *adj* criminal, culpable, evil, sinful, wicked, wrong.
adj antonyms guiltless, innocent.

guise *n* 1 appearance, aspect, costume, dress, fashion, figure, form, garb, manner, mode, shape. 2 air, behaviour, demeanour, mien. 3 cover, custom, disguise, habit, pretence, pretext, practice.

gulf *n* 1 abyss, chasm, opening. 2 bay, inlet. 3 whirlpool.

gull *vb* beguile, cheat, circumvent, cozen, deceive, dupe, hoax, overreach, swindle, trick. • *n* 1 cheat, deception, hoax, imposition, fraud, trick. 2 cat's paw, dupe.

gullibility *n* credulity, naiveness, naivety, overtrustfulness, simplicity, unsophistication.

gullible *adj* confiding, credulous, naive, over-trustful, simple, unsophisticated, unsuspicious.
adj antonym astute.

gumption *n* 1 ability, astuteness, cleverness, capacity, common sense, discernment, penetration, power, sagacity, shrewdness, skill. 2 courage, guts, spirit.

gun *n* blunderbuss, cannon, carbine, firearm, musket, pistol, revolver, rifle, shotgun.

gurgle *vb* babble, bubble, murmur, purl, ripple. • *n* babbling, murmur, ripple.

gush *vb* 1 burst, flood, flow, pour, rush, spout, stream. 2 emotionalize, sentimentalize. • *n* 1 flow, jet, onrush, rush, spurt, surge. 2 effusion, effusiveness, loquacity, loquaciousness, talkativeness.

gushing *adj* 1 flowing, issuing, rushing. 2 demonstrative, effusive, sentimental.

gust *vb* blast, blow, puff. • *n* 1 blast, blow, squall. 2 burst, fit, outburst, paroxysm.

gusto *n* enjoyment, gust, liking, pleasure, relish, zest.

gusty *adj* blustering, blustery, puffy, squally, stormy, tempestuous, unsteady, windy.

gut *vb* destroy, disembowel, embowel, eviscerate, paunch. • *n* bowels, entrails, intestines, inwards, viscera.

gutter *n* channel, conduit, kennel, pipe, tube.

guttural *adj* deep, gruff, hoarse, thick, throaty.

guy *vb* caricature, mimic, ridicule. • *n* 1 boy, man, person. 2 dowdy, eccentric, fright, scarecrow.

guzzle *vb* carouse, drink, gorge, gormandize, quaff, swill, tipple, tope.

gyrate *vb* revolve, rotate, spin, whirl.

H

habiliment *n* apparel, attire, clothes, costume, dress, garb, garment, habit, raiment, robes, uniform, vesture, vestment.

habit *vb* accoutre, array, attire, clothe, dress, equip, robe. • *n* **1** condition, constitution, temperament. **2** addiction, custom, habitude, manner, practice, rule, usage, way, wont. **3** apparel, costume, dress, garb, habiliment.

habitation *n* abode, domicile, dwelling, headquarters, home, house, lodging, quarters, residence.

habitual *adj* accustomed, common, confirmed, customary, everyday, familiar, inveterate, ordinary, regular, routine, settled, usual, wonted.
adj antonym occasional.

habituate *vb* accustom, familiarize, harden, inure, train, use.

habitude *n* custom, practice, usage, wont.

hack¹ *vb* **1** chop, cut, hew, mangle, mutilate, notch. **2** cough, rasp. • *n* **1** cut, cleft, incision, notch. **2** cough, rasp.

hack² *vb* ride. • *adj* **1** hired, mercenary. **2** banal, hackneyed, pedestrian, uninspired, unoriginal. • *n* **1** horse, nag, pony. **2** hireling, mercenary. **3** journalist, scribbler, writer.

hackneyed *adj* banal, common, commonplace, overworked, pedestrian, stale, threadbare, trite.
adj antonyms arresting, new.

hag *n* beldame, crone, fury, harridan, jezebel, she-monster, shrew, termagant, virago, vixen, witch.

haggard *adj* **1** intractable, refractory, unruly, untamed, wild, wayward. **2** careworn, emaciated, gaunt, ghastly, lank, lean, meagre, raw, spare, thin, wasted, worn.
adj antonym hale.

haggle *vb* **1** argue, bargain, cavil, chaffer, dispute, higgle, stickle. **2** annoy, badger, bait, fret, harass, tease, worry.

hail¹ *vb* **1** acclaim, greet, salute, welcome. **2** accost, address, call, hallo, signal. • *n* greeting, salute.

hail² *vb* assail, bombard, rain, shower, storm, volley. • *n* bombardment, rain, shower, storm, volley.

halcyon *adj* calm, golden, happy, palmy, placid, peaceful, quiet, serene, still, tranquil, unruffled, undisturbed.

hale *adj* hardy, healthy, hearty, robust, sound, strong, vigorous, well.
adj antonym ill.

halfwit *n* blockhead, dunce, moron, simpleton.

halfwitted *adj* doltish, dull, dull-witted, feeble-minded, foolish, sappy, shallow, silly, simple, soft, stolid, stupid, thick.

hall *n* **1** chamber, corridor, entrance, entry, hallway, lobby, passage, vestibule. **2** manor, manor-house. **3** auditorium, lecture-room.

hallow *vb* **1** consecrate, dedicate, devote, revere, sanctify, solemnize. **2** enshrine, honour, respect, reverence, venerate.

hallowed *adj* blessed, holy, honoured, revered, sacred.

hallucination *n* **1** blunder, error, fallacy, mistake. **2** aberration, delusion, illusion, phantasm, phantasy, self-deception, vision.

halo *n* aura, aureole, glory, nimbus.

halt¹ *vb* cease, desist, hold, rest, stand, stop. • *n* end, impasse, pause, standstill, stop.
vb antonyms assist, continue, start.
n antonyms continuation, start.

halt² *vb* **1** hesitate, pause, stammer, waver. **2** falter, hobble, limp. • *adj* crippled, disabled, lame. • *n* hobble, limp.

hammer *vb* **1** beat, forge, form, shape. **2** excogitate, contrive, invent.

hammer and tongs *adv* earnestly, energetically, resolutely, strenuously, vigorously, zealously.

hamper *vb* bind, clog, confine, curb, embarrass, encumber, entangle, fetter, hinder, impede, obstruct, prevent, restrain, restrict, shackle, trammel. • *n* **1** basket, box, crate, picnic basket. **2** embarrassment, encumbrance, fetter, handicap, impediment, obstruction, restraint, trammel.
vb antonyms aid, expedite.

hand *vb* **1** deliver, give, present, transmit. **2** conduct, guide, lead. • *n* **1** direction, part, side. **2** ability, dexterity, faculty, skill, talent. **3** course, inning, management, turn. **4** agency, intervention, participation, share. **5** control, possession, power. **6** artificer, artisan, craftsman, employee, labourer, operative, workman. **7** index, indicator, pointer. **8** chirography, handwriting.

handbook *n* guidebook, manual.

handcuff *vb* bind, fetter, manacle, shackle. • *n* fetter, manacle, shackle.

handful *n* fistful, maniple, smattering.

handicap *vb* encumber, hamper, hinder, restrict. • *n* disadvantage, encumbrance, hampering, hindrance, restriction.
n antonyms assistance, benefit.
vb antonyms assist, further.

handicraft *n* hand manufacture, handwork, workmanship.

handle *vb* **1** feel, finger, manhandle, paw, touch. **2** direct, manage, manipulate, use, wield. **3** discourse, discuss, treat. • *n* haft, helve, hilt, stock.

handsome *adj* **1** admirable, comely, fine-looking, stately, well-formed, well-proportioned. **2** appropriate, suitable, becoming, easy, graceful. **3** generous, gracious, liberal, magnanimous, noble. **4** ample, large, plentiful, sufficient.
adj antonyms mean, stingy, ugly.

handy *adj* **1** adroit, clever, dextrous, expert, ready, skilful, skilled. **2** close, convenient, near.
adj antonyms clumsy, inconvenient, unwieldy.

hang *vb* **1** attach, swing. **2** execute, truss. **3** decline, drop, droop, incline. **4** adorn, drape. **5** dangle, depend, impend, suspend. **6** rely. **7** cling, loiter, rest, stick. **8** float, hover, pay.

hangdog *adj* ashamed, base, blackguard, low, villainous, scurvy, sneaking.

hanger-on *n* dependant, minion, parasite, vassal.

hanker *vb* covet, crave, desire, hunger, long, lust, want, yearn.

hap *n* accident, chance, fate, fortune, lot.

haphazard *adj* aimless, chance, random.
adj antonyms deliberate, planned.

hapless *adj* ill-fated, ill-starred, luckless, miserable, unfortunate, unhappy, unlucky, wretched.
adj antonym lucky.

happen *vb* befall, betide, chance, come, occur.

happily *adv* **1** fortunately, luckily. **2** agreeably, delightfully, prosperously, successfully.

happiness *n* **1** brightness, cheerfulness, delight, gaiety, joy, light-heartedness, merriment, pleasure. **2** beatitude, blessedness, bliss, felicity, enjoyment, welfare, well-being.
n antonym unhappiness.

happy *adj* **1** blessed, blest, blissful, cheerful, contented, joyful, joyous, light-hearted, merry. **2** charmed, delighted, glad, gladdened, gratified, pleased. **3** fortunate, lucky, prosperous, successful. **4** able, adroit, apt, dextrous, expert, ready, skilful. **5** befitting, felicitous, opportune, pertinent, seasonable, well-timed. **6** auspicious, bright, favourable, propitious.
adj antonym unhappy.

harangue *vb* address, declaim, spout. • *n* address, bombast, declamation, oration, rant, screed, speech, tirade.

harass *vb* **1** exhaust, fag, fatigue, jade, tire, weary. **2** annoy, badger, distress, gall, heckle, disturb, harry, molest, pester, plague, tantalize, tease, torment, trouble, vex, worry.
vb antonym assist.

harbour *vb* **1** protect, lodge, shelter. **2** cherish, entertain, foster, indulge. • *n* **1** asylum, cover, refuge, resting place, retreat, sanctuary, shelter. **2** anchorage, destination, haven, port.

hard *adj* **1** adamantine, compact, firm, flinty, impenetrable, marble, rigid, solid, resistant, stony, stubborn, unyielding. **2** difficult, intricate, knotty, perplexing, puzzling. **3** arduous, exacting, fatiguing, laborious, toilsome, wearying. **4** austere, callous, cruel, exacting, hard-hearted, incorrigible, inflexible, insensible, insensitive, obdurate, oppressive, reprobate, rigorous, severe, unfeeling, unkind, unsusceptible, unsympathetic, unyielding, untender. **5** calamitous, disagreeable, distressing, grievous, painful, unpleasant. **6** acid, alcoholic, harsh, rough, sour. **7** excessive, intemperate. • *adv* **1** close, near. **2** diligently, earnestly, energetically, incessantly, laboriously. **3** distressfully, painfully, rigorously, severely. **4** forcibly, vehemently, violently.
adj antonyms harmless, kind, mild, non-

alcoholic, pleasant, pleasing, soft, yielding. *adv antonyms* gently, mildly, moderately, softly, unenthusiastically.

harden *vb* **1** accustom, discipline, form, habituate, inure, season, train. **2** brace, fortify, indurate, nerve, steel, stiffen, strengthen.
vb antonym soften.

hardened *adj* **1** annealed, case-hardened, tempered, indurated. **2** abandoned, accustomed, benumbed, callous, confirmed, deadened, depraved, habituated, impenitent, incorrigible, inured, insensible, irreclaimable, lost, obdurate, reprobate, seared, seasoned, steeled, trained, unfeeling.

hard-headed *adj* astute, collected, cool, intelligent, sagacious, shrewd, well-balanced, wise.
adj antonym unrealistic.

hardhearted *adj* cruel, fell, implacable, inexorable, merciless, pitiless, relentless, ruthless, unfeeling, uncompassionate, unmerciful, unpitying, unrelenting.
adj antonyms kind, merciful.

hardihood *n* **1** audacity, boldness, bravery, courage, decision, firmness, fortitude, intrepidity, manhood, mettle, pluck, resolution, stoutness. **2** assurance, audacity, brass, effrontery, impudence.

hardly *adv* **1** barely, scarcely. **2** cruelly, harshly, rigorously, roughly, severely, unkindly.
adv antonyms easily, very.

hardship *n* **1** fatigue, toil, weariness. **2** affliction, burden, calamity, grievance, hardness, injury, misfortune, privation, suffering, trial, trouble.
n antonym ease.

hardy *adj* **1** enduring, firm, hale, healthy, hearty, inured, lusty, rigorous, robust, rugged, sound, stout, strong, sturdy, tough. **2** bold, brave, courageous, daring, heroic, intrepid, manly, resolute, stout-hearted, valiant.
adj antonyms unhealthy, weak.

harebrained *adj* careless, changeable, flighty, giddy, harum-scarum, headlong, heedless, rash, reckless, unsteady, volatile, wild.

hark *interj* attend, hear, hearken, listen.

harlequin *n* antic, buffoon, clown, droll, fool, jester, punch, fool.

harm *vb* **1** damage, hurt, injure, scathe.

2 abuse, desecrate, ill-use, ill-treat, maltreat, molest. • *n* damage, detriment, disadvantage, hurt, injury, mischief, misfortune, prejudice, wrong.
n antonyms benefit, service.
vb antonyms benefit, improve.

harmful *adj* baneful, detrimental, disadvantageous, hurtful, injurious, mischievous, noxious, pernicious, prejudicial.
adj antonym harmless.

harmless *adj* **1** innocent, innocuous, innoxious. **2** inoffensive, safe, unoffending.
adj antonym harmful.

harmonious *adj* **1** concordant, consonant, harmonic. **2** dulcet, euphonious, mellifluous, melodious, musical, smooth, tuneful. **3** comfortable, congruent, consistent, correspondent, orderly, symmetrical. **4** agreeable, amicable, brotherly, cordial, fraternal, friendly, neighbourly.
adj antonym inharmonious.

harmonize *vb* **1** adapt, attune, reconcile, unite. **2** accord, agree, blend, chime, comport, conform, correspond, square, sympathize, tally, tune.

harmony *n* **1** euphony, melodiousness, melody. **2** accord, accordance, agreement, chime, concord, concordance, consonance, order, unison. **3** adaptation, congruence, congruity, consistency, correspondence, fairness, smoothness, suitableness. **4** amity, friendship, peace.
n antonym discord.

harness *vb* hitch, tackle. • *n* **1** equipment, gear, tackle, tackling. **2** accoutrements, armour, array, mail, mounting.

harp *vb* dwell, iterate, reiterate, renew, repeat.

harping *n* dwelling, iteration, reiteration, repetition.

harrow *vb* harass, lacerate, rend, tear, torment, torture, wound.

harry *vb* **1** devastate, pillage, plunder, raid, ravage, rob. **2** annoy, chafe, disturb, fret, gall, harass, harrow, incommode, pester, plague, molest, tease, torment, trouble, vex, worry.
vb antonyms aid, calm.

harsh *adj* **1** acid, acrid, astringent, biting, caustic, corrosive, crabbed, rough, sharp, sour, tart. **2** cacophonous, discordant, grating, jarring, metallic, raucous, strident, unmelodious. **3** abusive, austere, crabbed, crabby, cruel, disagreeable, hard, ill-natured, ill-tempered, morose, rigorous, severe, stern, unfeeling. **4** bearish, bluff, blunt, brutal, gruff, rude, uncivil, ungracious.

adj antonyms mild, smooth, soft.

harshness *n* **1** roughness. **2** acerbity, asperity, austerity, churlishness, crabbedness, hardness, ill-nature, ill-temper, moroseness, rigour, severity, sternness, unkindness. **3** bluffness, bluntness, churlishness, gruffness, incivility, ungraciousness, rudeness.

harum-scarum *adj* hare-brained, precipitate, rash, reckless, volatile, wild.

harvest *vb* gather, glean, reap. • *n* **1** crops, produce, yield. **2** consequence, effect, issue, outcome, produce, result.

haste *n* **1** alacrity, celerity, dispatch, expedition, nimbleness, promptitude, quickness, rapidity, speed, urgency, velocity. **2** flurry, hurry, hustle, impetuosity, precipitateness, precipitation, press, rashness, rush, vehemence.

n antonyms care, deliberation, slowness.

hasten *vb* **1** haste, hurry. **2** accelerate, dispatch, expedite, precipitate, press, push, quicken, speed, urge.

vb antonym dawdle.

hasty *adj* **1** brisk, fast, fleet, quick, rapid, speedy, swift. **2** cursory, hurried, passing, slight, superficial. **3** ill-advised, rash, reckless. **4** headlong, helter-skelter, pell-mell, precipitate. **5** abrupt, choleric, excitable, fiery, fretful, hot-headed, irascible, irritable, passionate, peevish, peppery, pettish, petulant, testy, touchy, waspish.

adj antonyms careful, deliberate, slow.

hatch *vb* **1** brew, concoct, contrive, excogitate, design, devise, plan, plot, project, scheme. **2** breed, incubate.

hate *vb* abhor, abominate, detest, dislike, execrate, loathe, nauseate. • *n* abomination, animosity, antipathy, detestation, dislike, enmity, execration, hatred, hostility, loathing.

vb antonym like.

n antonym like.

hateful *adj* **1** malevolent, malicious, malign, malignant, rancorous, spiteful. **2** abhorrent, abominable, accursed, damnable, detestable, execrable, horrid, odious, shocking. **3** disgusting, foul, loathsome, nauseous, obnoxious, offensive, repellent, repugnant, repulsive, revolting, vile.

adj antonym pleasing.

hatred *n* **1** animosity, enmity, hate, hostility, ill-will, malevolence, malice, malignity, odium, rancour. **2** abhorrence, abomination, antipathy, aversion, detestation, disgust, execration, horror, loathing, repugnance, revulsion.

n antonym like.

haughtiness *n* arrogance, contempt, contemptuousness, disdain, hauteur, insolence, loftiness, pride, self-importance, snobbishness, stateliness, superciliousness.

n antonyms friendliness, humility.

haughty *adj* arrogant, assuming, contemptuous, disdainful, imperious, insolent, lofty, lordly, overbearing, overweening, proud, scornful, snobbish, supercilious.

adj antonyms friendly, humble.

haul *vb* drag, draw, lug, pull, tow, trail, tug. • *n* **1** heaving, pull, tug. **2** booty, harvest, takings, yield.

haunt *vb* **1** frequent, resort. **2** follow, importune. **3** hover, inhabit, obsess. • *n* den, resort, retreat.

hauteur *n* arrogance, contempt, contemptuousness, disdain, haughtiness, insolence, loftiness, pride, self-importance, stateliness, superciliousness.

have *vb* **1** cherish, exercise, experience, keep, hold, occupy, own, possess. **2** acquire, gain, get, obtain, receive. **3** accept, take.

haven *n* **1** asylum, refuge, retreat, shelter. **2** anchorage, harbour, port.

havoc *n* carnage, damage, desolation, destruction, devastation, ravage, ruin, slaughter, waste, wreck.

hawk-eyed *adj* eagle-eyed, sharp-sighted.

hazard *vb* **1** adventure, risk, venture. **2** endanger, imperil, jeopardize. • *n* **1** accident, casualty, chance, contingency, event, fortuity, stake. **2** danger, jeopardy, peril, risk, venture.

n antonym safety.

hazardous *adj* dangerous, insecure, perilous, precarious, risky, uncertain, unsafe.

adj antonyms safe, secure.

haze *n* **1** fog, har, mist, smog. **2** cloud, dimness, fume, miasma, obscurity, pall.

hazy *adj* **1** foggy, misty. **2** cloudy, dim, nebulous, obscure. **3** confused, indefinite, indistinct, uncertain, vague.

adj antonyms clear, definite.

head *vb* **1** command, control, direct, govern, guide, lead, rule. **2** aim, point, tend. **3** beat, excel, outdo, precede, surpass. • *adj* **1** chief, first, grand, highest, leading, main, principal. **2** adverse, contrary. • *n* **1** acme, summit, top. **2** beginning, commencement, origin, rise, source. **3** chief, chieftain, commander, director, leader, master, principal, superintendent, superior. **4** intellect, mind, thought, understanding. **5** branch, category, class, department, division, section, subject, topic. **6** brain, crown, headpiece, intellect, mind, thought, understanding. **7** cape, headland, point, promontory.

n antonyms foot, subordinate, tail.

headiness *n* **1** hurry, precipitation, rashness. **2** obstinacy, stubbornness.

headless *adj* **1** acephalous, beheaded. **2** leaderless, undirected. **3** headstrong, heady, imprudent, obstinate, rash, senseless, stubborn.

headlong *adj* **1** dangerous, hasty, heady, impulsive, inconsiderate, perilous, precipitate, rash, reckless, ruinous, thoughtless. **2** perpendicular, precipitous, sheer, steep. • *adv* hastily, headfirst, helter-skelter, hurriedly, precipitately, rashly, thoughtlessly.

headstone *n* cornerstone, gravestone.

headstrong *adj* cantankerous, crossgrained, dogged, forward, headless, heady, intractable, obstinate, self-willed, stubborn, ungovernable, unruly, violent, wayward.

adj antonyms biddable, docile, obedient.

heady *adj* **1** hasty, headlong, impetuous, impulsive, inconsiderate, precipitate, rash, reckless, rushing, stubborn, thoughtless. **2** exciting, inebriating, inflaming, intoxicating, spirituous, strong.

heal *vb* **1** amend, cure, remedy, repair, restore. **2** compose, harmonize, reconcile, settle, soothe.

healing *adj* **1** curative, palliative, remedial, restoring, restorative. **2** assuaging, assuasive, comforting, composing, gentle, lenitive, mild, soothing.

health *n* healthfulness, robustness, salubrity, sanity, soundness, strength, tone, vigour.

healthy *adj* **1** active, hale, hearty, lusty, sound, vigorous, well. **2** bracing, healthful, health-giving, hygienic, invigorating, nourishing, salubrious, salutary, wholesome.

adj antonyms diseased, ill, infirm, sick, unhealthy.

heap *vb* accumulate, augment, amass, collect, overfill, pile up, store. • *n* accumulation, collection, cumulus, huddle, lot, mass, mound, pile, stack.

hear *vb* **1** eavesdrop, hearken, heed, listen, overhear. **2** ascertain, discover, gather, learn, understand. **3** examine, judge.

heart *n* **1** bosom, breast. **2** centre, core, essence, interior, kernel, marrow, meaning, pith. **3** affection, benevolence, character, disposition, feeling, inclination, love, mind, passion, purpose, will. **4** affections, ardour, emotion, feeling, love. **5** boldness, courage, fortitude, resolution, spirit.

heartache *n* affliction, anguish, bitterness, distress, dole, grief, heartbreak, sorrow, woe.

heartbroken *adj* broken-hearted, cheerless, comfortless, desolate, disconsolate, forlorn, inconsolable, miserable, woebegone, wretched.

adj antonyms delighted, elated.

hearten *vb* animate, assure, cheer, comfort, console, embolden, encourage, enhearten, incite, inspire, inspirit, reassure, stimulate.

vb antonym dishearten.

heartfelt *adj* cordial, deep, deep-felt, hearty, profound, sincere, warm.

hearth *n* fireplace, fireside, forge, hearthstone.

heartily *adv* abundantly, completely, cordially, earnestly, freely, largely, sincerely, vigorously.

heartless *adj* **1** brutal, cold, cruel, hard, harsh, merciless, pitiless, unfeeling, unsympathetic. **2** spiritless, timid, timorous, uncourageous.

adj antonyms considerate, kind, merciful, sympathetic.

heart-rending *adj* affecting, afflicting, anguishing, crushing, distressing.

hearty *adj* **1** cordial, deep, earnest, fervent, heartfelt, profound, sincere, true, unfeigned, warm. **2** active, animated, energetic, fit, vigorous, zealous. **3** convivial, hale, healthy, robust, sound, strong, warm. **4** abundant, full, heavy. **5** nourishing, nutritious, rich.

adj antonyms cold, emotionless.

heat *vb* **1** excite, flush, inflame. **2** animate, rouse, stimulate, stir. • *n* **1** calorie, caloricity, torridity, warmth. **2** excitement, fever, flush, impetuosity, passion, vehemence, violence. **3** ardour, earnestness, fervency, fervour, glow, intensity, zeal. **4** exasperation, fierceness, frenzy, rage. *n antonyms* cold(ness), coolness. *vb antonyms* chill, cool.

heath *n* field, moor, wasteland, plain.

heathen *adj* **1** animist, animistic. **2** pagan, paganical, paganish, paganistic, unconverted. **3** agnostic, atheist, atheistic, gentile, idolatrous, infidel, irreligious. **4** barbarous, cruel, inhuman, savage. • *n* **1** atheist, gentile, idolater, idolatress, infidel, pagan, unbeliever. **2** barbarian, philistine, savage.

heave *vb* **1** elevate, hoist, lift, raise. **2** breathe, exhale. **3** cast, fling, hurl, send, throw, toss. **4** dilate, expand, pant, rise, swell. **5** retch, throw up. **6** strive, struggle.

heaven *n* **1** empyrean, firmament, sky, welkin. **2** bliss, ecstasy, elysium, felicity, happiness, paradise, rapture, transport. *n antonym* hell.

heavenly *adj* **1** celestial, empyreal, ethereal. **2** angelic, beatific, beatified, cherubic, divine, elysian, glorious, god-like, sainted, saintly, seraphic. **3** blissful, delightful, divine, ecstatic, enrapturing, enravishing, exquisite, golden, rapturous, ravishing, exquisite, transporting. *adj antonym* hellish.

heaviness *n* **1** gravity, heft, ponderousness, weight. **2** grievousness, oppressiveness, severity. **3** dullness, languor, lassitude, sluggishness, stupidity. **4** dejection, depression, despondency, gloom, melancholy, sadness, seriousness.

heavy *adj* **1** grave, hard, onerous, ponderous, weighty. **2** afflictive, burdensome, crushing, cumbersome, grievous, oppressive, severe, serious. **3** dilatory, dull, inactive, inanimate, indolent, inert, lifeless, listless, sleepy, slow, sluggish, stupid, torpid. **4** crestfallen, crushed, depressed, dejected, despondent, disconsolate, downhearted, gloomy, low-spirited, melancholy, sad, sobered, sorrowful. **5** difficult, laborious. **6** tedious, tiresome, wearisome, weary. **7** burdened, encumbered, loaded. **8** clammy, clayey, cloggy, ill-raised, miry, muddy, soggy. **9** boisterous, deep, energetic, loud, roaring, severe, stormy, strong, tempestuous, violent. **10** cloudy, dark, dense, gloomy, lowering, overcast.

adj antonyms airy, insignificant, light.

hectic *adj* animated, excited, fevered, feverish, flushed, heated, hot.

hector *vb* **1** bluster, boast, bully, menace, threaten. **2** annoy, fret, harass, harry, irritate, provoke, tease, vex, worry. • *n* blusterer, bully, swaggerer.

hedge *vb* **1** block, encumber, hinder, obstruct, surround. **2** enclose, fence, fortify, guard, protect. **3** disappear, dodge, evade, hide, skulk, temporize. • *n* barrier, hedgerow, fence, limit.

heed *vb* attend, consider, mark, mind, note, notice, observe, regard. • *n* (usage: give, pay or take heed) attention, care, carefulness, caution, circumspection, consideration, heedfulness, mindfulness, notice, observation, regard, wariness, vigilance, watchfulness. *vb antonyms* disregard, ignore. *n antonyms* inattention, indifference, unconcern.

heedful *adj* attentive, careful, cautious, circumspect, mindful, observant, observing, provident, regardful, watchful, wary.

heedless *adj* careless, inattentive, neglectful, negligent, precipitate, rash, reckless, thoughtless, unmindful, unminding, unobserving, unobservant. *adj antonym* heedful.

heft *n* **1** handle, haft, helve. **2** bulk, weight.

hegemony *n* ascendancy, authority, headship, leadership, predominance, preponderance, rule.

height *n* **1** altitude, elevation, tallness. **2** acme, apex, climax, eminence, head, meridian, pinnacle, summit, top, vertex, zenith. **3** eminence, hill, mountain. **4** dignity, exaltation, grandeur, loftiness, perfection. *n antonym* depth.

heighten *vb* **1** elevate, raise. **2** ennoble, exalt, magnify, make greater. **3** augment, enhance, improve, increase, strengthen. **4** aggravate, intensify. *vb antonyms* decrease, diminish.

heinous *adj* aggravated, atrocious, crying, enormous, excessive, flagitious, flagrant, hateful, infamous, monstrous, nefarious, odious, villainous.

heir *n* child, inheritor, offspring, product.

helical *adj* screw-shaped, spiral, winding.

hellish *adj* abominable, accursed, atrocious, curst, damnable, damned, demoniacal, detestable, devilish, diabolical, execrable, fiendish, infernal, monstrous, nefarious, satanic.

helm *n* 1 rudder, steering-gear, tiller, wheel. 2 command, control, direction, rein, rule.

help *vb* 1 relieve, save, succour. 2 abet, aid, assist, back, cooperate, second, serve, support, sustain, wait. 3 alleviate, ameliorate, better, cure, heal, improve, remedy, restore. 4 control, hinder, prevent, repress, resist, withstand. 6 avoid, forbear, control. • *n* 1 aid, assistance, succour, support. 2 relief, remedy. 3 assistant, helper, servant.

vb antonym hindrance.

helper *adj* aider, abettor, ally, assistant, auxiliary, coadjutor, colleague, helpmate, partner, supporter.

helpful *adj* advantageous, assistant, auxiliary, beneficial, contributory, convenient, favourable, kind, profitable, serviceable, useful.

adj antonyms futile, useless, worthless.

helpless *adj* 1 disabled, feeble, imbecile, impotent, infirm, powerless, prostrate, resourceless, weak. 2 abandoned, defenceless, exposed, unprotected. 3 desperate, irremediable, remediless.

adj antonyms competent, enterprising, independent, resourceful, strong.

helpmate *n* 1 companion, consort, husband, partner, wife. 2 aider, assistant, associate, helper.

helter-skelter *adj* disorderly, headlong, irregular, pell-mell, precipitate. • *adv* confusedly, hastily, headlong, higgledy-piggledy, pell-mell, precipitately, wildly.

hem *vb* 1 border, edge, skirt. 2 beset, confine, enclose, environ, surround, sew. 3 hesitate. • *n* border, edge, trim.

henchman *n* attendant, follower, retainer, servant, supporter.

herald *vb* announce, proclaim, publish. • *n* 1 announcer, crier, publisher. 2 harbinger, precursor, proclaimer.

heraldry *n* blazonry, emblazonry.

herculean *adj* 1 able-bodied, athletic, brawny, mighty, muscular, powerful, puissant, sinewy, stalwart, strong, sturdy, vigorous. 2 dangerous, difficult, hard, laborious, perilous, toilsome, troublesome. 3 colossal, Cyclopean, gigantic, great, large, strapping.

herd *vb* 1 drive, gather, lead, tend. 2 assemble, associate, flock. • *n* 1 drover, herder, herdsman, shepherd. 2 crowd, multitude, populace, rabble. 3 assemblage, assembly, collection, drove, flock, pack.

hereditary *adj* ancestral, inheritable, inherited, patrimonial, transmitted.

heresy *n* dissent, error, heterodoxy, impiety, recusancy, unorthodoxy.

heretic *n* dissenter, dissident, nonconformist, recusant, schismatic, sectarian, sectary, separatist, unbeliever.

n antonym conformist.

heretical *adj* heterodox, impious, schismatic, schismatical, sectarian, unorthodox.

heritage *n* estate, inheritance, legacy, patrimony, portion.

hermetic *adj* 1 airtight, impervious. 2 cabbalistic, emblematic, emblematical, magical, mysterious, mystic, mystical, occult, secret, symbolic, symbolical.

hermit *n* anchoress, anchoret, anchorite, ascetic, eremite, monk, recluse, solitaire, solitary.

heroic *adj* 1 bold, brave, courageous, daring, dauntless, fearless, gallant, illustrious, intrepid, magnanimous, noble, valiant. 2 desperate, extravagant, extreme, violent.

adj antonyms cowardly, pusillanimous, timid.

heroism *n* boldness, bravery, courage, daring, endurance, fearlessness, fortitude, gallantry, intrepidity, prowess, valour.

n antonyms cowardice, pusillanimity, timidity.

hesitate *vb* 1 boggle, delay, demur, doubt, pause, scruple, shilly-shally, stickle, vacillate, waver. 2 falter, stammer, stutter.

hesitation *n* 1 halting, misgiving, reluctance. 2 delay, doubt, indecision, suspense, uncertainty, vacillation. 3 faltering, stammering, stuttering.

n antonyms alacrity, assurance, eagerness.

heterodox *adj* 1 heretical, recusant, schismatic, unorthodox, unsound. 2 apocryphal, uncanonical.

heterogeneous *adj* contrasted, contrary, different, dissimilar, diverse, incongruous, indiscriminate, miscellaneous, mixed, opposed, unhomogeneous, unlike.

hew *vb* 1 chop, cut, fell, hack. 2 fashion, form, shape, smooth.

hiatus *n* blank, break, chasm, gap, interval, lacuna, opening, rift.

hidden *adj* 1 blind, clandestine, cloaked, close, concealed, covered, covert, enshrouded, latent, masked, occult, private, secluded, secret, suppressed, undiscovered, veiled. **2** abstruse, cabbalistic, cryptic, dark, esoteric, hermetic, inward, mysterious, mystic, mystical, obscure, oracular, recondite.

adj antonyms open, showing.

hide *vb* **1** bury, conceal, cover, secrete, suppress, withhold. **2** cloak, disguise, eclipse, hoard, mask, screen, shelter, veil.

vb antonyms display, reveal, show.

hideous *adj* abominable, appalling, awful, dreadful, frightful, ghastly, ghoulish, grim, grisly, horrible, horrid, repulsive, revolting, shocking, terrible, terrifying.

adj antonym beautiful.

hie *vb* hasten, speed.

hieratic *adj* consecrated, devoted, priestly, sacred, sacerdotal.

hieroglyph *n* picture-writing, rebus, sign, symbol.

hieroglyphic *adj* emblematic, emblematical, figurative, obscure, symbolic, symbolical.

higgle *vb* **1** hawk, peddle. **2** bargain, chaffer, haggle, negotiate.

higgledy-piggledy *adj* chaotic, confused, disorderly, jumbled. • *adv* confusedly, in disorder, helter-skelter, pell-mell.

high *adj* **1** elevated, high-reaching, lofty, soaring, tall, towering. **2** distinguished, eminent, pre-eminent, prominent, superior. **3** admirable, dignified, exalted, great, noble. **4** arrogant, haughty, lordly, proud, supercilious. **5** boisterous, strong, tumultuous, turbulent, violent. **6** costly, dear, pricey. **7** acute, high-pitched, high-toned, piercing, sharp, shrill. **8** tainted, malodorous. • *adv* **1** powerfully, profoundly. **2** eminently, loftily. **3** luxuriously, richly.

adj antonyms deep, low, lowly, short.

n antonyms low, nadir.

high-flown *adj* **1** elevated, presumptuous, proud, lofty, swollen. **2** extravagant, high-coloured, lofty, overdrawn. **3** bombastic, inflated, pompous, pretentious, strained, swollen, turgid.

high-handed *adj* arbitrary, despotic, dictatorial, domineering, oppressive, overbearing, self-willed, violent, wilful.

highly strung *adj* **1** ardent, excitable, irascible, nervous, quick, tense. **2** high-spirited, sensitive.

high-minded *adj* **1** arrogant, haughty, lofty, proud. **2** elevated, high-toned. **3** generous

honourable, magnanimous, noble, spiritual.

adj antonyms immoral, unscrupulous.

highwayman *n* bandit, brigand, footpad, freebooter, marauder, outlaw, robber.

hilarious *adj* boisterous, cheerful, comical, convivial, funny, riotous, uproarious, jovial, joyful, merry, mirthful, noisy.

adj antonyms grave, serious.

hilarity *n* cheerfulness, conviviality, exhilarated, gaiety, glee, jollity, joviality, joyousness, merriment, mirth.

hill *n* ascent, ben, elevation, eminence, hillock, knoll, mount, mountain, rise, tor.

hind *adj* back, hinder, hindmost, posterior, rear, rearward.

hinder *vb* bar, check, clog, delay, embarrass, encumber, impede, interrupt, obstruct, oppose, prevent, restrain, retard, stop, thwart.

vb antonyms aid, assist, help.

hindrance *n* check, deterrent, encumbrance, hitch, impediment, interruption, obstacle, obstruction, restraint, stop, stoppage.

n antonyms aid, assistance, help.

hinge *vb* depend, hang, rest, turn.

hint *vb* allude, glance, imply, insinuate, intimate, mention, refer, suggest. • *n* allusion, clue, implication, indication, innuendo, insinuation, intimation, mention, reminder, suggestion, taste, trace.

hire *vb* **1** buy, rent, secure. **2** charter, employ, engage, lease, let. • *n* allowance, bribe, compensation, pay, remuneration, rent, reward, salary, stipend, wages.

vb antonyms dismiss, fire.

hirsute *adj* **1** bristled, bristly, hairy, shaggy. **2** boorish, course, ill-bred, loutish, rough, rude, rustic, uncouth, unmannerly.

hiss *vb* **1** shrill, sibilate, whistle, whir, whiz. **2** condemn, damn, ridicule. • *n* fizzle, hissing, sibilant, sibilation, sizzle.

historian *n* annalist, autobiographer, biographer, chronicler, narrator, recorder.

history *n* account, autobiography, annals, biography, chronicle, genealogy, memoirs, narration, narrative, recital, record, relation, story.

hit *vb* **1** discomfit, hurt, knock, strike. **2** accomplish, achieve, attain, gain, reach, secure, succeed, win. **3** accord, fit, suit. **4** beat, clash, collide, contact, smite. • *n* **1** blow, collision, strike, stroke. **2** chance, fortune, hazard, success, venture.

hitch *vb* **1** catch, impede, stick, stop. **2** attach, connect, fasten, harness, join, tether, tie, unite, yoke. • *n* **1** catch, check, hindrance, impediment, interruption, obstacle. **2** knot, noose.
vb antonyms unfasten, unhitch.

hoar *adj* ancient, grey, hoary, old, white.

hoard *vb* accumulate, amass, collect, deposit, garner, hive, husband, save, store, treasure. • *n* accumulation, collection, deposit, fund, mass, reserve, savings, stockpile, store.
n antonyms spend, squander, use.

hoarse *adj* discordant, grating, gruff, guttural, harsh, husky, low, raucous, rough.
adj antonyms clear, smooth.

hoary *adj* **1** grey, hoar, silvery, white. **2** ancient, old, venerable.

hoax *vb* deceive, dupe, fool, gammon, gull, hoodwink, swindle, trick. • *n* canard, cheat, deception, fraud, humbug, imposition, imposture, joke, trick, swindle.

hobble *vb* **1** falter, halt, hop, limp. **2** fasten, fetter, hopple, shackle, tie. • *n* **1** halt, limp. **2** clog, fetter, shackle. **3** embarrassment, difficulty, perplexity, pickle, strait.

hobgoblin *n* apparition, bogey, bugbear, goblin, imp, spectre, spirit, sprite.

hobnail *n* bumpkin, churl, clodhopper, clown, lout, rustic.

hocus-pocus *n* **1** cheater, impostor, juggler, sharper, swindler, trickster. **2** artifice, cheat, deceit, deception, delusion, hoax, imposition, juggle, trick.

hodgepodge *n* farrago, hash, hotchpotch, jumble, medley, miscellany, mixture, ragout, stew.

hog *n* **1** beast, glutton, pig. **2** grunter, porker, swine.

hoggish *adj* **1** brutish, filthy, gluttonish, piggish, swinish. **2** grasping, greedy, mean, selfish, sordid.

hoist *vb* elevate, heave, lift, raise, rear. • *n* elevator, lift.

hold *vb* **1** clasp, clinch, clutch, grasp, grip, seize. **2** have, keep, occupy, possess, retain. **3** bind, confine, control, detain, imprison, restrain, restrict. **4** connect, fasten, fix, lock. **5** arrest, check, stay, stop, suspend, withhold. **6** continue, keep up, maintain, manage, prosecute, support, sustain. **7** cherish, embrace, entertain. **8** account, believe, consider, count, deem, entertain, esteem, judge, reckon, regard,

think. **9** accommodate, admit, carry, contain, receive, stow. **10** assemble, conduct, convene. **11** endure, last, persist, remain. **12** adhere, cleave, cling, cohere, stick. • *n* **1** anchor, bite, clasp, control, embrace, foothold, grasp, grip, possession, retention, seizure. **2** prop, stay, support. **3** claim, footing, vantage point. **4** castle, fort, fortification, fortress, stronghold, tower. **5** locker, storage, storehouse.

hole *n* **1** aperture, opening, perforation. **2** abyss, bore, cave, cavern, cavity, chasm, depression, excavation, eye, hollow, pit, pore, void. **3** burrow, cover, lair, retreat. **4** den, hovel, kennel.

holiday *n* anniversary, celebration, feast, festival, festivity, fete, gala, recess, vacation.

holiness *n* blessedness, consecration, devotion, devoutness, godliness, piety, purity, religiousness, righteousness, sacredness, saintliness, sanctity, sinlessness.

hollow *vb* dig, excavate, groove, scoop. • *adj* **1** cavernous, concave, depressed, empty, sunken, vacant, void. **2** deceitful, faithless, false, false-hearted, hollow-hearted, hypocritical, insincere, pharisaical, treacherous, unfeeling. **3** deep, low, muffled, reverberating, rumbling, sepulchral. • *n* **1** basin, bowl, depression. **2** cave, cavern, cavity, concavity, dent, dimple, dint, depression, excavation, hole, pit. **3** canal, channel, cup, dimple, dig, groove, pocket, sag.

holocaust *n* carnage, destruction, devastation, genocide, massacre.

holy *adj* **1** blessed, consecrated, dedicated, devoted, hallowed, sacred, sanctified. **2** devout, godly, pious, pure, religious, righteous, saintlike, saintly, sinless, spiritual.
adj antonyms impious, unsanctified, wicked.

homage *n* **1** allegiance, devotion, fealty, fidelity, loyalty. **2** court, deference, duty, honour, obeisance, respect, reverence, service. **3** adoration, devotion, worship.

home *adj* **1** domestic, family. **2** close, direct, effective, penetrating, pointed. • *n* abode, dwelling, seat, quarters, residence.

homely *adj* **1** domestic, familiar, house-like. **2** coarse, commonplace, homespun, inelegant, plain, simple, unattractive, uncomely, unpolished, unpretentious.
adj antonyms formal, unfamiliar.

homespun *adj* coarse, homely, inelegant, plain, rude, rustic, unpolished.

homicide *n* manslaughter, murder.

homily *n* address, discourse, lecture, sermon.

homogeneous *adj* akin, alike, cognate, kindred, similar, uniform.

honest *adj* 1 equitable, fair, faithful, honourable, open, straight, straightforward. 2 conscientious, equitable, reliable, sound, square, true, trustworthy, trusty, uncorrupted, upright, virtuous. 3 above-board, faithful, genuine, thorough, unadulterated. 4 creditable, decent, proper, reputable, respectable, suitable. 5 chaste, decent. 6 candid, direct, frank, ingenuous, sincere, unreserved.

adj antonyms covert, devious, dishonest, dishonourable.

honesty *n* 1 equity, fairness, faithfulness, fidelity, honour, integrity, justice, probity, trustiness, trustworthiness, uprightness. 2 truth, truthfulness, veracity. 3 genuineness, thoroughness. 4 candour, frankness, ingenuousness, openness, sincerity, straightforwardness, unreserve.

n antonyms deviousness, dishonesty.

honorary *adj* formal, nominal, titular, unofficial, unpaid.

adj antonyms gainful, paid, salaried, waged.

honour *vb* 1 dignify, exalt, glorify, grace. 2 respect, revere, reverence, venerate. 3 adore, hallow, worship. 4 celebrate, commemorate, keep, observe. • *n* 1 civility, deference, esteem, homage, respect, reverence, veneration. 2 dignity, distinction, elevation, nobleness. 3 consideration, credit, fame, glory, reputation. 4 highmindedness, honesty, integrity, magnanimity, probity, uprightness. 5 chastity, purity, virtue. 6 boast, credit, ornament, pride.

honourable *adj* 1 elevated, famous, great, illustrious, noble. 2 admirable, conscientious, fair, honest, just, magnanimous, true, trustworthy, upright, virtuous, worshipful. 3 creditable, esteemed, estimable, equitable, proper, respected, reputable, right.

honours *npl* 1 dignities, distinctions, privilege, titles. 2 adornments, beauties, decorations, glories. 3 civilities.

hood *n* capuche, coif, cover, cowl, head.

hoodwink *vb* 1 blind, blindfold. 2 cloak, conceal, cover, hide. 3 cheat, circumvent, cozen, deceive, delete, dupe, fool, gull, impose, overreach, trick.

hook *vb* 1 catch, ensnare, entrap, hasp, snare. 2 bend, curve. • *n* 1 catch, clasp, fastener, hasp. 2 snare, trap. 3 cutter, grass-hook, reaper, reaping-hook, sickle.

hooked *adj* aquiline, bent, crooked, curved, hamate.

hoop *vb* clasp, encircle, enclose, surround. • *n* 1 band, circlet, girdle, ring. 2 crinoline, farthingale.

hoot *vb* 1 boo, cry, jeer, shout, yell. 2 condemn, decry, denounce, execrate, hiss. • *n* boo, cry, jeer, shout, yell.

hop *vb* 1 bound, caper, frisk, jump, leap, skip, spring. 2 dance, trip. 3 halt, hobble, limp. • *n* bound, caper, dance, jump, leap, skip, spring.

hope *vb* 1 anticipate, await, desire, expect, long. 2 believe, rely, trust. • *n* 1 confidence, belief, faith, reliance, sanguineness, sanguinity, trust. 2 anticipation, desire, expectancy, expectation.

vb antonym despair.

n antonyms apathy, despair, pessimism.

hopeful *adj* 1 anticipatory, confident, expectant, fond, optimistic, sanguine. 2 cheerful, encouraging, promising.

adj antonyms despairing, discouraging, pessimistic.

hopeless *adj* 1 abject, crushed, depressed, despondent, despairing, desperate, disconsolate, downcast, forlorn, pessimistic, woebegone. 2 abandoned, helpless, incurable, remediless. 3 impossible, impracticable, unachievable, unattainable.

adj antonyms curable, hopeful, optimistic.

horde *n* 1 clan, crew, gang, troop. 2 crowd, multitude, pack, throng.

horn *vb* gore, pierce. • *n* 1 trumpet, wind instrument. 2 beaker, drinking cup, cornucopia. 3 spike, spur. 4 cusp, prong, wing.

horrid *adj* 1 alarming, awful, bristling, dire, dreadful, fearful, frightful, harrowing, hideous, horrible, horrific, horrifying, rough, terrible, terrific. 2 abominable, disagreeable, disgusting, odious, offensive, repulsive, revolting, shocking, unpleasant, vile.

adj antonyms agreeable, lovely, pleasant.

horrify *vb* affright, alarm, frighten, shock, terrify, terrorise.

horror *n* 1 alarm, awe, consternation, dismay, dread, fear, fright, panic. 2 abhorrence, abomination, antipathy, aversion, detestation, disgust, hatred, loathing, repugnance, revulsion. **3** shuddering.

horse *n* **1** charger, cob, colt, courser, filly, gelding, mare, nag, pad, palfrey, pony, stallion, steed. **2** cavalry, horseman. **3** buck, clotheshorse, frame, sawhorse, stand, support.

horseman *n* **1** cavalier, equestrian, rider. **2** cavalryman, chasseur, dragoon, horse-soldier.

hospitable *adj* **1** attentive, bountiful, kind. **2** bountiful, cordial, generous, liberal, open, receptive, sociable, unconstrained, unreserved.

adj antonyms hostile, inhospitable.

host[1] *n* entertainer, innkeeper, landlord, master of ceremonies, presenter, proprietor, owner, receptionist.

host[2] *n* **1** array, army, legion. **2** assemblage, assembly, horde, multitude, throng.

host[3] *n* altar bread, bread, consecrated bread, loaf, wafer.

hostile *adj* **1** inimical, unfriendly, warlike. **2** adverse, antagonistic, contrary, opposed, opposite, repugnant.

adj antonyms friendly, sympathetic.

hostilities *npl* conflict, fighting, war, warfare.

hostility *n* **1** animosity, antagonism, enmity, hatred, ill-will, unfriendliness. **2** contrariness, opposition, repugnance, variance.

n antonyms friendliness, sympathy.

hot *adj* **1** burning, fiery, scalding. **2** boiling, flaming, heated, incandescent, parching, roasting, torrid. **3** heated, oppressive, sweltering, warm. **4** angry, choleric, excitable, furious, hasty, impatient, impetuous, irascible, lustful, passionate, touchy, urgent, violent. **5** animated, ardent, eager, fervent, fervid, glowing, passionate, vehement. **6** acrid, biting, highly flavoured, highly seasoned, peppery, piquant, pungent, sharp, stinging.

adj antonyms calm, cold, mild, moderate.

hotchpotch *n* farrago, jumble, hodgepodge, medley, miscellany, stew.

hotel *n* inn, public house, tavern.

hot-headed *adj* furious, headlong, headstrong, hot-brained, impetuous, inconsiderate, passionate, precipitate, rash, reckless, vehement, violent.

adj antonyms calm, cool.

hound *vb* **1** drive, incite, spur, urge. **2** bate, chase, goad, harass, harry, hunt, pursue.

house *vb* harbour, lodge, protect, shelter.

• *n* **1** abode, dwelling, habitation, home, mansion, residence. **2** building, edifice. **3** family, household. **4** kindred, race, lineage, tribe. **5** company, concern, firm, partnership. **6** hotel, inn, public house, tavern.

housing *n* **1** accommodation, dwellings, houses. **2** casing, container, covering, protection, shelter.

hovel *n* cabin, cot, den, hole, hut, shed.

hover *vb* **1** flutter. **2** hang. **3** vacillate, waver.

however *adv* but, however, nevertheless, notwithstanding, still, though, yet.

howl *vb* bawl, cry, lament, ululate, weep, yell, yowl. • *n* cry, yell, ululation.

hubbub *n* clamour, confusion, din, disorder, disturbance, hullaballoo, racket, riot, outcry, tumult, uproar.

n antonym calm.

huckster *n* hawker, peddler, retailer.

huddle *vb* **1** cluster, crowd, gather. **2** crouch, curl up, nestle, snuggle. • *n* confusion, crowd, disorder, disturbance, jumble, tumult.

vb antonym disperse.

hue *n* cast, colour, complexion, dye, shade, tinge, tint, tone.

huff *vb* blow, breathe, exhale, pant, puff. • *n* anger, fume, miff, passion, pet, quarrel, rage, temper, tiff.

hug *vb* **1** clasp, cling, cuddle, embrace, grasp, grip, squeeze. **2** cherish, nurse, retain. • *n* clasp, cuddle, embrace, grasp, squeeze.

huge *adj* bulky, colossal, Cyclopean, elephantine, enormous, gigantic, herculean, immense, stupendous, vast,

adj antonyms dainty, tiny.

huggermugger *adj* **1** clandestine, secret, sly. **2** base, contemptible, mean, unfair. **3** confused, disorderly, slovenly.

hull *vb* husk, peel, shell. • *n* covering, husk, rind, shell.

hullabaloo *n* clamour, confusion, din, disturbance, hubbub, outcry, racket, vociferation, uproar.

hum *vb* **1** buzz, drone, murmur. **2** croon, sing.

humane *adj* **1** accommodating, benevolent, benign, charitable, clement, compassionate, gentle, good-hearted, kind, kind-hearted, lenient, merciful, obliging, tender, sympathetic. **2** cultivating, elevating, humanizing, refining, rational, spiritual.

adj antonym inhumane.

humanity *n* **1** benevolence, benignity, charity, fellow-feeling, humaneness, kindheartedness, kindness, philanthropy, sympathy, tenderness. **2** humankind, mankind, mortality.
n antonym inhumanity.

humanize *vb* civilize, cultivate, educate, enlighten, improve, polish, reclaim, refine, soften.

humble *vb* abase, abash, break, crush, debase, degrade, disgrace, humiliate, lower, mortify, reduce, sink, subdue. • *adj* **1** meek, modest, lowly, simple, submissive, unambitious, unassuming, unobtrusive, unostentatious, unpretending. **2** low, obscure, mean, plain, poor, small, undistinguished, unpretentious.
vb antonyms exalt, raise.
adj antonyms assertive, important, pretentious, proud.

humbug *vb* cheat, cozen, deceive, hoax, swindle, trick. • *n* **1** cheat, dodge, gammon, hoax, imposition, imposture, deception, fraud, trick. **2** cant, charlatanism, charlatanry, hypocrisy, mummery, quackery. **3** charlatan, impostor, fake, quack.

humdrum *adj* boring, dronish, dreary, dry, dull, monotonous, prosy, stupid, tedious, tiresome, wearisome.
adj antonyms exceptional, unusual.

humid *adj* damp, dank, moist, wet.
adj antonym dry.

humiliate *vb* abase, abash, debase, degrade, depress, humble, mortify, shame.
vb antonyms boost, dignify, exalt, vindicate.

humiliation *n* abasement, affront, condescension, crushing, degradation, disgrace, dishonouring, humbling, indignity, mortification, self-abasement, submissiveness, resignation.
n antonyms gratification, triumph.

humility *n* diffidence, humbleness, lowliness, meekness, modesty, self-abasement, submissiveness.

humorist *n* comic, comedian, droll, jester, joker, wag, wit.

humorous *adj* comic, comical, droll, facetious, funny, humorous, jocose, jocular, laughable, ludicrous, merry, playful, pleasant, sportive, whimsical, witty.
adj antonym humourless.

humour *vb* favour, gratify, indulge. • *n* **1** bent, bias, disposition, predilection, prosperity, temper, vein. **2** mood, state. **3** caprice, crotchet, fancy, freak, vagary, whim, whimsy, wrinkle. **4** drollery, facetiousness, fun, jocoseness, jocularity, pleasantry, wit. **5** fluid, moisture, vapour.

hunch *vb* arch, jostle, nudge, punch, push, shove. • *n* **1** bunch, hump, knob, protuberance. **2** nudge, punch, push, shove. **3** feeling, idea, intuition, premonition.

hungry *adj* **1** covetous, craving, desirous, greedy. **2** famished, starved, starving. **3** barren, poor, unfertile, unproductive.
adj antonyms full, replete, satisfied.

hunk *n* chunk, hunch, lump, slice.

hunt *vb* **1** chase, drive, follow, hound, pursue, stalk, trap, trail. **2** poach, shoot. **3** search, seek. • *n* chase, field-sport, hunting, pursuit.

hurl *vb* cast, dart, fling, pitch, project, send, sling, throw, toss.

hurly-burly *n* bustle, commotion, confusion, disturbance, hurl, hurly, uproar, tumult, turmoil.

hurricane *n* cyclone, gale, storm, tempest, tornado, typhoon.

hurried *adj* cursory, hasty, slight, superficial.
adj antonym leisurely.

hurry *vb* **1** drive, precipitate. **2** dispatch, expedite, hasten, quicken, speed. **3** haste, scurry. • *n* **1** agitation, bustle, confusion, flurry, flutter, perturbation, precipitation. **2** celerity, haste, dispatch, expedition, promptitude, promptness, quickness.
vb antonyms dally, delay.
n antonyms calm, leisureliness.

hurt *vb* **1** damage, disable, disadvantage, harm, impair, injure, mar. **2** bruise, pain, wound. **3** afflict, grieve, offend. **4** ache, smart, throb. • *n* **1** damage, detriment, disadvantage, harm, injury, mischief. **2** ache, bruise, pain, suffering, wound.

hurtful *adj* baleful, baneful, deleterious, destructive, detrimental, disadvantageous, harmful, injurious, mischievous, noxious, pernicious, prejudicial, unwholesome.
adj antonyms helpful, kind.

husband *vb* economize, hoard, save, store.

husbandry *n* **1** agriculture, cultivation, farming, geoponics, tillage. **2** economy, frugality, thrift.

hush *vb* **1** quiet, repress, silence, still, suppress. **2** appease, assuage, calm, console, quiet, still. • *n* quiet, quietness, silence, stillness.

vb antonyms disturb, rouse.

n antonyms clamour, uproar.

hypocrite *n* deceiver, dissembler, impostor, pretender.

hypocritical *adj* deceiving, dissembling, false, insincere, spurious, two-faced.

adj antonyms genuine, humble, sincere.

hypothesis *n* assumption, proposition, supposition, theory.

hypothetical *adj* assumed, imaginary, supposed, theoretical.

adj antonyms actual, real.

hysterical *adj* **1** frantic, frenzied, overwrought, uncontrollable. **2** comical, uproarious.

I

ice *vb* chill, congeal, freeze. • *n* **1** crystal. **2** frosting, sugar.

icy *adj* **1** glacial. **2** chilling, cold, frosty. **3** cold-hearted, distant, frigid, indifferent, unemotional.

idea *n* **1** archetype, essence, exemplar, ideal, model, pattern, plan, model. **2** fantasy, fiction, image, imagination. **3** apprehension, conceit, conception, fancy, illusion, impression, thought. **4** belief, judgement, notion, opinion, sentiment, supposition.

ideal *adj* **1** intellectual, mental. **2** chimerical, fancied, fanciful, fantastic, illusory, imaginary, unreal, visionary, shadowy. **3** complete, consummate, excellent, perfect. **4** impractical, unattainable, utopian. • *n* criterion, example, model, standard.

identical *adj* equivalent, same, selfsame, tantamount.

identity *n* existence, individuality, personality, sameness.

ideology *n* belief, creed, dogma, philosophy, principle.

idiocy *n* fatuity, feebleness, foolishness, imbecility, insanity.

idiosyncrasy *n* caprice, eccentricity, fad, peculiarity, singularity.

idiot *n* blockhead, booby, dunce, fool, ignoramus, imbecile, simpleton.

idiotic *adj* fatuous, foolish, imbecile, irrational, senseless, sottish, stupid.
adj antonyms sane, sensible.

idle *adj* **1** inactive, unemployed, unoccupied, vacant. **2** indolent, inert, lazy, slothful, sluggish. **3** abortive, bootless, fruitless, futile, groundless, ineffectual, unavailing, useless, vain. **4** foolish, frivolous, trashy, trifling, trivial, unimportant, unprofitable.
• *vb* **1** dally, dawdle, laze, loiter, potter, waste. **2** drift, shirk, slack.
adj antonyms active, effective, purposeful.
vb antonyms act, work.

idler *n* dawdler, doodle, drone, laggard, lazybones, loafer, lounger, slacker, slowcoach, sluggard, trifler.

idol *n* **1** deity, god, icon, image, pagan, simulacrum, symbol. **2** delusion, falsity, pretender, sham. **3** beloved, darling, favourite, pet.

idolater *n* **1** heathen, pagan. **2** admirer, adorer, worshipper.

idolize *vb* **1** canonize, deify. **2** adore, honour, love, reverence, venerate.
vb antonym vilify.

idyll *n* **1** ideal, paradise, Utopia. **2** (*mus*) opus, pastorale, piece. **3** (*poet*) bucolic, eclogue, pastoral.

idyllic *adj* charming, picturesque, romantic.

if *conj* admitting, allowing, granting, provided, supposing, though, whether. • *n* condition, hesitation, uncertainty.

igneous *adj* combustible, combustive, conflagrative, fiery, molten.

ignite *vb* burn, inflame, kindle, light, torch.

ignoble *adj* **1** base-born, low, low-born, mean, peasant, plebeian, rustic, vulgar. **2** contemptible, degraded, insignificant, mean, worthless. **3** disgraceful, dishonourable, infamous, low, unworthy.
adj antonyms honourable, noble.

ignominious *adj* **1** discreditable, disgraceful, dishonourable, disreputable, infamous, opprobrious, scandalous, shameful. **2** base, contemptible, despicable.
adj antonyms honourable, triumphant.

ignominy *n* abasement, contempt, discredit, disgrace, dishonour disrepute, infamy, obloquy, odium, opprobrium, scandal, shame.

ignoramus *n* blockhead, duffer, dunce, fool, greenhorn, novice, numskull, simpleton.

ignorance *n* **1** benightedness, darkness, illiteracy, nescience, rusticity. **2** blindness, unawareness.

ignorant *adj* blind, illiterate, nescient, unaware, unconversant, uneducated, unenlightened, uninformed, uninstructed, unlearned, unread, untaught, untutored, unwitting.
adj antonyms knowlegeable, wise.

ignore *vb* disregard, neglect, overlook, reject, skip.
v antonym note.

ill *adj* **1** bad, evil, faulty, harmful, iniquitous, naughty, unfavourable, unfortunate, unjust, wicked. **2** ailing, diseased, disordered, indisposed, sick, unwell, wrong. **3** crabbed, cross, hateful, malicious, malevolent, peevish, surly, unkind, ill-bred. **4** ill-favoured, ugly, unprepossessing. • *adv* badly, poorly, unfortunately. • *n* **1** badness, depravity, evil, mischief, misfortune, wickedness. **2** affliction, ailment, calamity, harm, misery, pain, trouble.

adj antonyms beneficial, fortunate, good, kind; well.

adv antonym well.

n antonym benefit.

ill-advised *adj* foolish, ill-judged, imprudent, injudicious, unwise.

adj antonym sensible.

ill-bred *adj* discourteous, ill-behaved, ill-mannered, impolite, rude, uncivil, uncourteous, uncourtly, uncouth.

illegal *adj* contraband, forbidden, illegitimate, illicit, prohibited, unauthorized, unlawful, unlicensed.

adj antonym legal.

illegible *adj* indecipherable, obscure, undecipherable, unreadable.

illegitimate *adj* bastard, misbegotten, natural.

ill-fated *adj* ill-starred, luckless, unfortunate, unlucky.

adj antonym lucky.

ill-favoured *adj* homely, ugly, offensive, plain, unpleasant.

ill humour *n* fretfulness, ill-temper, peevishness, petulance, testiness.

illiberal *adj* **1** close, close-fisted, covetous, mean, miserly, narrow, niggardly, parsimonious, penurious, selfish, sordid, stingy, ungenerous. **2** bigoted, narrow-minded, uncharitable, ungentlemanly, vulgar.

adj antonym liberal.

illicit *adj* **1** illegal, illegitimate, unauthorized, unlawful, unlegalized, unlicensed. **2** criminal, guilty, forbidden, improper, wrong.

adj antonyms legal.

illimitable *adj* boundless, endless, immeasurable, immense, infinite, unbounded, unlimited, vast.

illiterate *adj* ignorant, uneducated, uninstructed, unlearned, unlettered, untaught, untutored.

adj antonym literate.

ill-judged *adj* foolish, ill-advised, imprudent, injudicious, unwise.

ill-mannered *adj* discourteous, ill-behaved, ill-bred, impolite, rude, uncivil, uncourteous, uncourtly, uncouth, unpolished.

ill-natured *adj* **1** disobliging, hateful, malevolent, unamiable, unfriendly, unkind. **2** acrimonious, bitter, churlish, crabbed, cross, cross-grained, crusty, ill-tempered, morose, perverse, petulant, sour, spiteful, sulky, sullen, wayward.

adj antonym good-natured.

illness *n* ailing, ailment, complaint, disease, disorder, distemper, indisposition, malady, sickness.

n antonym health.

illogical *adj* absurd, fallacious, inconsistent, inconclusive, inconsequent, incorrect, invalid, unreasonable, unsound.

adj antonym logical.

ill-proportioned *adj* awkward, ill-made, ill-shaped, misshapen, misproportioned, shapeless.

ill-starred *adj* ill-fated, luckless, unfortunate, unhappy, unlucky.

ill temper *n* bad temper, crabbedness, crossness, grouchiness, ill nature, moroseness, sulkiness, sullenness.

ill-tempered *adj* acrimonious, bad-tempered, crabbed, cross, grouchy, ill-natured, morose, sour, sulky, surly.

adj antonym good-tempered.

ill-timed *adj* inapposite, inopportune, irrelevant, unseasonable, untimely.

ill-treat *vb* abuse, ill-use, injure, maltreat, mishandle, misuse.

illude *vb* cheat, deceive, delude, disappoint, mock, swindle, trick.

illuminate *vb* **1** illume, illumine, light. **2** adorn, brighten, decorate, depict, edify, enlighten, inform, inspire, instruct, make wise.

vb antonyms darken, deface, divest.

illusion *n* chimera, deception, delusion, error, fallacy, false appearance, fantasy, hallucination, mockery, phantasm.

n antonym reality.

illusive, illusory *adj* deceitful, deceptive, delusive, fallacious, imaginary, make-believe, mock, sham, unsatisfying, unreal, unsubstantial, visionary, tantalizing.

adj antonym real.

illustrate *vb* **1** clarify, demonstrate, elucidate, enlighten, exemplify, explain. **2** adorn, depict, draw.

illustration *n* **1** demonstration, elucidation, enlightenment, exemplification, explanation, interpretation. **2** adornment, decoration, picture.

illustrative *adj* elucidative, elucidatory, exemplifying.

illustrious *adj* **1** bright, brilliant, glorious, radiant, splendid. **2** celebrated, conspicuous, distinguished, eminent, famed, famous, noble, noted, remarkable, renowned, signal.
adj antonyms inglorious, shameful.

ill will *n* animosity, dislike, enmity, envy, grudge, hate, hatred, hostility, ill nature, malevolence, malice, malignity, rancour, spleen, spite, uncharitableness, unkindness, venom.

image *n* **1** idol, statue. **2** copy, effigy, figure, form, imago, likeness, picture, resemblance, representation, shape, similitude, simulacrum, statue, symbol. **3** conception, counterpart, embodiment, idea, reflection.

imagery *n* dream, phantasm, phantom, vision.

imaginable *adj* assumable, cogitable, conceivable, conjecturable, plausible, possible, supposable, thinkable.

imaginary *adj* **1** chimerical, dreamy, fancied, fanciful, fantastic, fictitious, ideal, illusive, illusory, invented, quixotic, shadowy, unreal, utopian, visionary, wild. **2** assumed, conceivable, hypothetical, supposed.
adj antonym real.

imagination *n* **1** chimera, conception, fancy, fantasy, invention, unreality. **2** position. **3** contrivance, device, plot, scheme.
n antonyms reality, unimaginativeness.

imaginative *adj* creative, dreamy, fanciful, inventive, poetical, plastic, visionary.
adj antonym unimaginative.

imagine *vb* **1** conceive, dream, fancy, imagine, picture, pretend. **2** contrive, create, devise, frame, invent, mould, project. **3** assume, suppose, hypothesize. **4** apprehend, assume, believe, deem, guess, opine, suppose, think.

imbecile *adj* cretinous, drivelling, fatuous, feeble, feeble-minded, foolish, helpless, idiotic, imbecilic, inane, infirm, witless. • *n* dotard, driveller.
adj antonyms intelligent, sensible.

imbecility *n* **1** debility, feebleness, helplessness, infirmity, weakness. **2** foolishness, idiocy, silliness, stupidity, weak-mindedness.

imbibe *vb* **1** absorb, assimilate, drink, suck, swallow. **2** acquire, gain, gather, get, receive.

imbroglio *n* complexity, complication, embarrassment, entanglement, misunderstanding.

imbrue *vb* drench, embrue, gain, moisten, soak, stain, steep, wet.

imbue *vb* **1** colour, dye, stain, tincture, tinge, tint. **2** bathe, impregnate, infuse, inoculate, permeate, pervade, provide, saturate, steep.

imitate *vb* **1** copy, counterfeit, duplicate, echo, emulate, follow, forge, mirror, reproduce, simulate. **2** ape, impersonate, mimic, mock, personate. **3** burlesque, parody, travesty.

imitation *adj* artificial, fake, man-made, mock, reproduction, synthetic. • *n* **1** aping, copying, imitation, mimicking, parroting. **2** copy, duplicate, likeness, resemblance. **3** mimicry, mocking. **4** burlesque, parody, travesty.
adj antonym genuine.

imitative *adj* **1** copying, emulative, imitating, mimetic, simulative. **2** apeish, aping, mimicking.

imitator *n* copier, copycat, copyist, echo, impersonator, mimic, mimicker, parrot.

immaculate *adj* **1** clean, pure, spotless, stainless, unblemished, uncontaminated, undefiled, unpolluted, unspotted, unsullied, untainted, untarnished. **2** faultless, guiltless, holy, innocent, pure, saintly, sinless, stainless.
adj antonyms contaminated, spoiled.

immanent *adj* congenital, inborn, indwelling, inherent, innate, internal, intrinsic, subjective.

immaterial *adj* **1** bodiless, ethereal, extramundane, impalpable, incorporeal, mental, metaphysical, spiritual, unbodied, unfleshly, unsubstantial. **2** inconsequential, insignificant, nonessential, unessential, unimportant.

immature *adj* **1** crude, green, imperfect, raw, rudimental, rudimentary, unfinished, unformed, unprepared, unripe, unripened, youthful. **2** hasty, premature, unseasonable, untimely.
adj antonym mature.

immaturity *n* crudeness, crudity, greenness, imperfection, rawness, unpreparedness, unripeness.

immeasurable *adj* bottomless, boundless,

illimitable, immense, infinite, limitless, measureless, unbounded, vast.
adj antonym limited.

immediate *adj* 1 close, contiguous, near, next, proximate. 2 intuitive, primary, unmeditated. 3 direct, instant, instantaneous, present, pressing, prompt.
adj antonym distant.

immediately *adv* 1 closely, proximately. 2 directly, forthwith, instantly, presently, presto, pronto.
adv antonyms eventually, never.

immemorial *adj* ancient, hoary, olden.

immense *adj* 1 boundless, illimitable, infinite, interminable, measureless, unbounded, unlimited. 2 colossal, elephantine, enormous, gigantic, huge, large, monstrous, mountainous, prodigious, stupendous, titanic, tremendous, vast.
adj antonym minute.

immensity *n* 1 boundlessness, endlessness, limitlessness, infiniteness, infinitude, infinity. 2 amplitude, enormity, greatness, hugeness, magnitude, vastness.
n antonym minuteness.

immerse *vb* 1 baptize, bathe, dip, douse, duck, overwhelm, plunge, sink, souse, submerge. 2 absorb, engage, engross, involve.

immersion *n* 1 dipping, immersing, plunging. 2 absorption, engagement. 3 disappearance. 4 baptism.

imminent *adj* 1 close, impending, near, overhanging, threatening. 2 alarming, dangerous, perilous.
adj antonym far-off.

immobile *adj* 1 fixed, immovable, inflexible, motionless, quiescent, stable, static, stationary, steadfast. 2 dull, expressionless, impassive, rigid, stiff, stolid.

immobility *n* 1 fixedness, fixity, immovability, immovableness, motionlessness, stability, steadfastness. 2 dullness, expressionlessness, inflexibility, rigidity, stiffness, stolidity.

immoderate *adj* excessive, exorbitant, extravagant, extreme, inordinate, intemperate, unreasonable.

immodest *adj* 1 coarse, gross, indecorous, indelicate, lewd, shameless. 2 bold, brazen, forward, impudent, indecent. 3 broad, filthy, impure, indecent, obscene, smutty, unchaste.

immodesty *n* 1 coarseness, grossness, indecorum, indelicacy, shamelessness. 2 impurity, lewdness, obscenity, smuttiness, unchastity. 3 boldness, brass, forwardness, impatience.

immolate *vb* kill, sacrifice.

immoral *adj* 1 antisocial, corrupt, loose, sinful, unethical, vicious, wicked, wrong. 2 bad, depraved, dissolute, profligate, unprincipled. 3 abandoned, indecent, licentious.
adj antonym moral.

immorality *n* 1 corruption, corruptness, criminality, demoralization, depravity, impurity, profligacy, sin, sinfulness, vice, wickedness. 2 wrong.
adj antonym morality.

immortal *adj* 1 deathless, ever-living, imperishable, incorruptible, indestructible, indissoluble, never-dying, undying, unfading. 2 ceaseless, continuing, eternal, endless, everlasting, never-ending, perpetual, sempiternal. 3 abiding, enduring, lasting, permanent. • *n* 1 god, goddess. 2 genius, hero.
adj antonym mortal.

immortality *n* 1 deathlessness, incorruptibility, incorruptibleness, indestructibility. 2 perpetuity.

immortalize *vb* apotheosize, enshrine, glorify, perpetuate.

immovable *adj* 1 firm, fixed, immobile, stable, stationary. 2 impassive, steadfast, unalterable, unchangeable, unshaken, unyielding.

immunity *n* 1 exemption, exoneration, freedom, release. 2 charter, franchise, liberty, license, prerogative, privilege, right.

immure *vb* confine, entomb, imprison, incarcerate.

immutability *n* constancy, inflexibility, invariability, invariableness, permanence, stability, unalterableness, unchangeableness.

immutable *adj* constant, fixed, inflexible, invariable, permanent, stable, unalterable, unchangeable, undeviating.
adj antonym mutable.

imp *n* 1 demon, devil, elf, flibbertigibbet, hobgoblin, scamp, sprite. 2 graft, scion, shoot.

impact *vb* collide, crash, strike. • *n* brunt, 1 impression, impulse, shock, stroke, touch. 2 collision, contact, impinging, striking.

impair *vb* 1 blemish, damage, deface, deteriorate, injure, mar, ruin, spoil, vitiate.

2 decrease, diminish, lessen, reduce. **3** enervate, enfeeble, weaken.

vb antonym enhance.

impale *vb* hole, pierce, puncture, spear, spike, stab, transfix.

impalpable *adj* **1** attenuated, delicate, fine, intangible. **2** imperceptible, inapprehensible, incorporeal, indistinct, shadowy, unsubstantial.

impart *vb* **1** bestow, confer, give, grant. **2** communicate, disclose, discover, divulge, relate, reveal, share, tell.

impartial *adj* candid, disinterested, dispassionate, equal, equitable, even-handed, fair, honourable, just, unbiased, unprejudiced, unwarped.

adj antonym biased.

impassable *adj* blocked, closed, impenetrable, impermeable, impervious, inaccessible, pathless, unattainable, unnavigable, unreachable.

impassioned *adj* animated, ardent, burning, excited, fervent, fervid, fiery, glowing, impetuous, intense, passionate, vehement, warm, zealous.

adj antonyms apathetic, mild.

impassive *adj* **1** calm, passionless. **2** apathetic, callous, indifferent, insensible, insusceptible, unfeeling, unimpressible, unsusceptible.

adj antonyms moved, responsive, warm.

impassivity *n* calmness, composure, indifference, insensibility, insusceptibility, passionlessness, stolidity.

impatience *n* **1** disquietude, restlessness, uneasiness. **2** eagerness, haste, impetuosity, precipitation, vehemence. **3** heat, irritableness, irritability, violence.

impatient *adj* **1** restless, uneasy, unquiet. **2** eager, hasty, impetuous, precipitate, vehement. **3** abrupt, brusque, choleric, fretful, hot, intolerant, irritable, peevish, sudden, testy, violent.

impeach *vb* **1** accuse, arraign, charge, indict. **2** asperse, censure, denounce, disparage, discredit, impair, impute, incriminate, lessen.

impeachment *n* **1** accusation, arraignment, indictment. **2** aspersion, censure, disparagement, imputation, incrimination, reproach.

impeccable *adj* faultless, immaculate, incorrupt, innocent, perfect, pure, sinless, stainless, uncorrupt.

impede *vb* bar, block, check, clog, curb, delay, encumber, hinder, interrupt, obstruct, restrain, retard, stop, thwart.

vb antonym aid.

impediment *n* bar, barrier, block, check, curb, difficulty, encumbrance, hindrance, obstacle, obstruction, stumbling block.

n antonym aid.

impel *vb* **1** drive, push, send, urge. **2** actuate, animate, compel, constrain, embolden, incite, induce, influence, instigate, move, persuade, stimulate.

vb antonym dissuade.

impend *vb* approach, menace, near, threaten.

impending *adj* approaching, imminent, menacing, near, threatening.

adj antonym remote.

impenetrable *adj* **1** impermeable, impervious, inaccessible. **2** cold, dull, impassive, indifferent, obtuse, senseless, stolid, unsympathetic. **3** dense, proof.

adj antonyms intelligible, penetrable.

impenitence *n* hardheartedness, impenitency, impenitentness, obduracy, stubbornness.

impenitent *adj* hardened, hard-hearted, incorrigible, irreclaimable, obdurate, recusant, relentless, seared, stubborn, uncontrite, unconverted, unrepentant.

imperative *adj* **1** authoritative, commanding, despotic, domineering, imperious, overbearing, peremptory, urgent. **2** binding, obligatory.

adj antonyms humble, optional.

imperceptible *adj* **1** inaudible, indiscernible, indistinguishable, invisible. **2** fine, impalpable, inappreciable, gradual, minute.

adj antonym perceptible.

imperfect *adj* **1** abortive, crude, deficient, garbled, incomplete, poor. **2** defective, faulty, impaired.

imperfection *n* **1** defectiveness, deficiency, faultiness, incompleteness. **2** blemish, defect, fault, flaw, lack, stain, taint. **3** failing, foible, frailty, limitation, vice, weakness.

n antonyms asset, perfection.

imperial *adj* **1** kingly, regal, royal, sovereign. **2** august, consummate, exalted, grand, great, kingly, magnificent, majestic, noble, regal, royal, queenly, supreme, sovereign, supreme, consummate.

imperil *vb* endanger, expose, hazard, jeopardize, risk.

imperious *adj* arrogant, authoritative, commanding, compelling, despotic, dictatorial, domineering, haughty, imperative, lordly, magisterial, overbearing, tyrannical, urgent, compelling.

imperishable *adj* eternal, everlasting, immortal, incorruptible, indestructible, never-ending, perennial, unfading.

impermeable *adj* impenetrable, impervious.

impermissible *adj* deniable, insufferable, objectionable, unallowable, unallowed, unlawful.

impersonate *vb* **1** act, ape, enact, imitate, mimic, mock, personate. **2** embody, incarnate, personify, typify.

impersonation *n* **1** incarnation, manifestation, personification. **2** enacting, imitation, impersonating, mimicking, personating, representation.

impertinence *n* **1** irrelevance, irrelevancy, unfitness, impropriety. **2** assurance, boldness, brass, brazenness, effrontery, face, forwardness, impudence, incivility, insolence, intrusiveness, presumption, rudeness, sauciness, pertness.

impertinent *adj* **1** inapplicable, inapposite, irrelevant. **2** bold, forward, impudent, insolent, intrusive, malapert, meddling, officious, pert, rude, saucy, unmannerly.
adj antonym polite.

imperturbability *n* calmness, collectedness, composure, dispassion, placidity, placidness, sedateness, serenity, steadiness, tranquility.

imperturbable *adj* calm, collected, composed, cool, placid, sedate, serene, tranquil, unmoved, undisturbed, unexcitable, unmoved, unruffled.

impervious *adj* impassable, impenetrable, impermeable.

impetuosity *n* force, fury, haste, precipitancy, vehemence, violence.

impetuous *adj* ardent, boisterous, brash, breakneck, fierce, fiery, furious, hasty, headlong, hot, hot-headed, impulsive, overzealous, passionate, precipitate, vehement, violent.
adj antonym circumspect.

impetus *n* energy, force, momentum, propulsion.

impiety *n* **1** irreverence, profanity, ungodliness. **2** iniquity, sacreligiousness, sin, sinfulness, ungodliness, unholiness, unrighteousness, wickedness.

impinge *vb* clash, dash, encroach, hit, infringe, strike, touch.

impious *adj* blasphemous, godless, iniquitous, irreligious, irreverent, profane, sinful, ungodly, unholy, unrighteous, wicked.

implacable *adj* deadly, inexorable, merciless, pitiless, rancorous, relentless, unappeasable, unforgiving, unpropitiating, unrelenting.
adj antonym forgiving, relenting.

implant *vb* ingraft, infix, insert, introduce, place.

implement *vb* effect, execute, fulfil. • *n* appliance, instrument, tool, utensil.

implicate *vb* **1** entangle, enfold. **2** compromise, concern, entangle, include, involve.
vb antonyms absolve, exonerate.

implication *n* **1** entanglement, involvement, involution. **2** connotation, hint, inference, innuendo, intimation. **3** conclusion, meaning, significance.

implicit *adj* **1** implied, inferred, understood. **2** absolute, constant, firm, steadfast, unhesitating, unquestioning, unreserved, unshaken.
adj antonym explicit.

implicitly *adv* by implication, silently, tacitly, virtually, wordlessly.

implore *vb* adjure, ask, beg, beseech, entreat, petition, pray, solicit, supplicate.

imply *vb* betoken, connote, denote, import, include, infer, insinuate, involve, mean, presuppose, signify.
vb antonym state.

impolicy *n* folly, imprudence, ill-judgement, indiscretion, inexpediency.

impolite *adj* bearish, boorish, discourteous, disrespectful, ill-bred, insolent, rough, rude, uncivil, uncourteous, ungentle, ungentlemanly, ungracious, unmannerly, unpolished, unrefined.
adj antonym polite.

impoliteness *n* boorishness, discourteousness, discourtesy, disrespect, ill-breeding, incivility, insolence, rudeness, unmannerliness.

impolitic *adj* ill-advised, imprudent, indiscreet, inexpedient, injudicious, unwise.

import *vb* **1** bring in, introduce, transport. **2** betoken, denote, imply, mean, purport, signify. • *n* **1** goods, importation, merchandise. **2** bearing, drift, gist, intention, interpretation, matter, meaning, purpose, sense, signification, spirit, tenor. **3** consequence, importance, significance, weight.

importance *n* **1** concern, consequence, gravity, import, moment, momentousness, significance, weight, weightiness. **2** consequence, pomposity, self-importance.

important *adj* **1** considerable, grave, material, momentous, notable, pompous, ponderous, serious, significant, urgent, valuable, weighty. **2** esteemed, influential, prominent, substantial. **3** consequential, pompous, self-important.

adj antonym unimportant.

importunate *adj* busy, earnest, persistent, pertinacious, pressing, teasing, troublesome, urgent.

importune *vb* ask, beset, dun, ply, press, solicit, urge.

importunity *n* **1** appeal, beseechment, entreaty, petition, plying, prayer, pressing, suit, supplication, urging. **2** contention, insistence. **3** urgency.

impose *vb* **1** lay, place, put, set. **2** appoint, charge, dictate, enjoin, force, inflict, obtrude, prescribe, tax. **3** (*with* **on, upon**) abuse, cheat, circumvent, deceive, delude, dupe, exploit, hoax, trick, victimize.

imposing *adj* august, commanding, dignified, exalted, grand, grandiose, impressive, lofty, magnificent, majestic, noble, stately, striking.

adj antonyms modest, unimposing.

imposition *n* **1** imposing, laying, placing, putting. **2** burden, charge, constraint, injunction, levy, oppression, tax. **3** artifice, cheating, deception, dupery, fraud, imposture, trickery.

impossibility *n* **1** hopelessness, impracticability, inability, infeasibility, unattainability. **2** inconceivability.

impossible *adj* **1** hopeless, impracticable, infeasible, unachievable, unattainable. **2** inconceivable, self-contradictory, unthinkable.

adj antonym possible.

impost *n* custom, duty, excise, rate, tax, toil, tribute.

impostor *n* charlatan, cheat, counterfeiter, deceiver, double-dealer, humbug, hypocrite, knave, mountebank, pretender, quack, rogue, trickster.

imposture *n* artifice, cheat, deceit, deception, delusion, dodge, fraud, hoax, imposition, ruse, stratagem, trick, wile.

impotence *n* disability, feebleness, frailty, helplessness, inability, incapability, incapacity, incompetence, inefficaciousness, inefficacy, inefficiency, infirmity, powerlessness, weakness.

impotent *adj* **1** disabled, enfeebled, feeble, frail, helpless, incapable, incapacitated, incompetent, inefficient, infirm, nerveless, powerless, unable, weak. **2** barren, sterile.

impound *vb* confine, coop, engage, imprison.

impoverish *vb* **1** beggar, make poor, make destitute, pauperize. **2** deplete, exhaust, ruin.

impracticability *n* impossibility, impracticableness, impracticality, infeasibility, unpracticability.

impracticable *adj* **1** impossible, infeasible. **2** intractable, obstinate, recalcitrant, stubborn, thorny, unmanageable. **3** impassable, insurmountable.

impracticality *n* **1** impossibility, impracticableness, impractibility, infeasibility, unpracticability. **2** irrationality, unpracticalness, unrealism, unreality, unreasonableness.

imprecate *vb* anathematize, curse, execrate, invoke, maledict.

imprecation *n* anathema, curse, denunciation, execration, invocation, malediction.

imprecatory *adj* **1** appealing, beseeching, entreating, imploratory, imploring, imprecatory, pleading. **2** cursing, damnatory, execrating, maledictory.

impregnable *adj* immovable, impenetrable, indestructible, invincible, inviolable, invulnerable, irrefrangible, secure, unconquerable, unassailable, unyielding.

adj antonym vulnerable.

impregnate *vb* **1** fecundate, fertilize, fructify. **2** dye, fill, imbrue, imbue, infuse, permeate, pervade, saturate, soak, tincture, tinge.

impress *vb* **1** engrave, imprint, print, stamp. **2** affect, move, strike. **3** fix, inculcate. **4** draft, enlist, levy, press, requisition. • *n* **1** impression, imprint, mark, print, seal, stamp. **2** cognizance, device, emblem, motto, symbol.

impressibility *n* affectibility, impressionability, pliancy, receptiveness, responsiveness, sensibility, sensitiveness, susceptibility.

impressible *adj* affectible, excitable, impressionable, pliant, receptive, responsive, sensitive, soft, susceptible, tender.

impression *n* **1** edition, imprinting, printing, stamping. **2** brand, dent, impress, mark, stamp. **3** effect, influence, sensation. **4** fancy, idea, instinct, notion, opinion, recollection.

impressive *adj* affecting, effective, emphatic, exciting, forcible, moving, overpowering, powerful, solemn, speaking, splendid, stirring, striking, telling, touching.
adj antonym unimpressive.

imprint *vb* **1** engrave, mark, print, stamp. **2** impress, inculcate. • *n* impression, mark, print, sign, stamp.

imprison *vb* confine, jail, immure, incarcerate, shut up.

imprisonment *n* captivity, commitment, confinement, constraint, durance, duress, incarceration, restraint.

improbability *n* doubt, uncertainty, unlikelihood.

improbable *adj* doubtful, uncertain, unlikely, unplausible.

improbity *n* dishonesty, faithlessness, fraud, fraudulence, knavery, unfairness.

impromptu *adj* extempore, improvised, offhand, spontaneous, unpremeditated, unprepared, unrehearsed. • *adv* extemporaneously, extemporarily, extempore, offhand, ad-lib.
adj antonyms planned, rehearsed.

improper *adj* **1** immodest, inapposite, inappropriate, irregular, unadapted, unfit, unsuitable, unsuited. **2** indecent, indecorous, indelicate, unbecoming, unseemly. **3** erroneous, inaccurate, incorrect, wrong.
adj antonym proper.

impropriety *n* **1** inappropriateness, unfitness, unsuitability, unsuitableness. **2** indecorousness, indecorum, unseemliness.

improve *vb* **1** ameliorate, amend, better, correct, edify, meliorate, mend, rectify, reform. **2** cultivate. **3** gain, mend, progress. **4** enhance, increase, rise.
vb antonyms decline, diminish.

improvement *n* **1** ameliorating, amelioration, amendment, bettering, improving, meliorating, melioration. **2** advancement, proficiency, progress.

improvidence *n* imprudence, thriftlessness, unthriftiness.

improvident *adj* careless, heedless, imprudent, incautious, inconsiderate, negligent,

prodigal, rash, reckless, shiftless, thoughtless, thriftless, unthrifty, wasteful.
adj antonym thrifty.

improvisation *n* **1** ad-libbing, contrivance, extemporaneousness, extemporariness, extemporization, fabrication, invention. **2** (*mus*) extempore, impromptu.

improvise *vb* ad-lib, contrive, extemporize, fabricate, imagine, invent.

imprudence *n* carelessness, heedlessness, improvidence, incautiousness, inconsideration, indiscretion, rashness.

imprudent *adj* careless, heedless, ill-advised, ill-judged, improvident, incautious, inconsiderate, indiscreet, rash, unadvised, unwise.
adj antonym prudent.

impudence *n* assurance, audacity, boldness, brashness, brass, bumptiousness, cheek, cheekiness, effrontery, face, flippancy, forwardness, front, gall, impertinence, insolence, jaw, lip, nerve, pertness, presumption, rudeness, sauciness, shamelessness.
n antonym politeness.

impudent *adj* bold, bold-faced, brazen, brazen-faced, cool, flippant, forward, immodest, impertinent, insolent, insulting, pert, presumptuous, rude, saucy, shameless.
adj antonym polite.

impugn *vb* assail, attack, challenge, contradict, dispute, gainsay, oppose, question, resist.

impulse *n* **1** force, impetus, impelling, momentum, push, thrust. **2** appetite, inclination, instinct, passion, proclivity. **3** incentive, incitement, influence, instigation, motive, instigation.

impulsive *adj* **1** impelling, moving, propulsive. **2** emotional, hasty, heedless, hot, impetuous, mad-cap, passionate, quick, rash, vehement, violent.
adj antonym cautious.

impunity *n* exemption, immunity, liberty, licence, permission, security.

impure *adj* **1** defiled, dirty, feculent, filthy, foul, polluted, unclean. **2** bawdy, coarse, immodest, gross, immoral, indelicate, indecent, lewd, licentious, loose, obscene, ribald, smutty, unchaste. **3** adulterated, corrupt, mixed.
adj antonyms chaste, pure.

impurity *n* **1** defilement, feculence, filth, foulness, pollution, uncleanness. **2** admixture, coarseness, grossness, immodesty, indecency, indelicacy, lewdness, licentiousness, looseness, obscenity, ribaldry, smut, smuttiness, unchastity, vulgarity.

imputable *adj* ascribable, attributable, chargeable, owing, referable, traceable, owing.

imputation *n* **1** attributing, charging, imputing. **2** accusation, blame, censure, charge, reproach.

impute *vb* ascribe, attribute, charge, consider, imply, insinuate, refer.

inability *n* **1** impotence, incapacity, incapability, incompetence, incompetency, inefficiency. **2** disability, disqualification.
n antonym ability.

inaccessible *adj* unapproachable, unattainable.

inaccuracy *n* **1** erroneousness, impropriety, incorrectness, inexactness. **2** blunder, defect, error, fault, mistake.

inaccurate *adj* defective, erroneous, faulty, incorrect, inexact, mistaken, wrong.
adj antonym accurate.

inaccurately *adv* carelessly, cursorily, imprecisely, incorrectly, inexactly, mistakenly, unprecisely, wrongly.

inactive *adj* **1** inactive. **2** dormant, inert, inoperative, peaceful, quiet, quiescent. **3** dilatory, drowsy, dull, idle, inanimate, indolent, inert, lazy, lifeless, lumpish, passive, slothful, sleepy, stagnant, supine.
adj antonym active.

inactivity *n* dilatoriness, idleness, inaction, indolence, inertness, laziness, sloth, sluggishness, supineness, torpidity, torpor.
n antonym activeness.

inadequacy *n* **1** inadequateness, insufficiency. **2** defectiveness, imperfection, incompetence, incompetency, incompleteness, insufficiency, unfitness, unsuitableness.

inadequate *adj* **1** disproportionate, incapable, insufficient, unequal. **2** defective, imperfect, inapt, incompetent, incomplete.
adj antonym adequate.

inadmissible *adj* improper, incompetent, unacceptable, unallowable, unqualified, unreasonable.

inadvertence, inadvertency *n* **1** carelessness, heedlessness, inattention, inconsiderateness, negligence, thoughtlessness. **2** blunder, error, oversight, slip.

inadvertent *adj* careless, heedless, inattentive, inconsiderate, negligent, thoughtless, unobservant.

adj antonym deliberate.

inadvertently *adv* accidently, carelessly, heedlessly, inconsiderately, negligently, thoughtlessly, unintentionally.

inalienable *adj* undeprivable, unforfeitable, untransferable.

inane *adj* **1** empty, fatuous, vacuous, void. **2** foolish, frivolous, idiotic, puerile, senseless, silly, stupid, trifling, vain, worthless.
adj antonym sensible.

inanimate *adj* **1** breathless, dead, extinct. **2** dead, dull, inert, lifeless, soulless, spiritless.
adj antonyms alive, animate, lively, living.

inanition *n* **1** emptiness, inanity, vacuity. **2** exhaustion, hunger, malnutrition, starvation, want.

inanity *n* **1** emptiness, foolishness, vacuity. **2** folly, frivolousness, puerility, vanity, worthlessness.

inapplicable *adj* inapposite, inappropriate, inapt, irrelevant, unfit, unsuitable, unsuited.

inapposite *adj* **1** inapplicable, irrelevant, nonpertinent. **2** inappropriate, unfit, unsuitable.

inappreciable *adj* impalpable, imperceptible, inconsiderable, inconspicuous, indiscernible, infinitesimal, insignificant, negligible, undiscernible, unnoticed.

inappropriate *adj* inapposite, unadapted, unbecoming, unfit, unsuitable, unsullied.
adj antonym appropriate.

inapt *adj* **1** inapposite, unapt, unfit, unsuitable. **2** awkward, clumsy, dull, slow, stolid, stupid.

inaptitude *n* awkwardness, inapplicability, inappropriateness, inaptness, unfitness, unsuitableness.

inarticulate *adj* **1** blurred, indistinct, thick. **2** dumb, mute.
adj antonym articulate.

inartificial *adj* artless, direct, guileless, ingenuous, naive, simple, simple-minded, sincere, single-minded.

inattention *n* absent-mindedness, carelessness, disregard, heedlessness, inadvertence, inapplication, inconsiderateness, neglect, remissness, slip, thoughtlessness.

inattentive *adj* absent-minded, careless, disregarding, heedless, inadvertent, inconsiderate, neglectful, remiss, thoughtless, unmindful, unobservant.
adj antonym attentive.

inaudible *adj* **1** faint, indistinct, muffled. **2** mute, noiseless, silent, still.

inaugurate *vb* **1** induct, install, introduce, invest. **2** begin, commence, initiate, institute, originate.

inauguration *n* beginning, commencement, initiation, institution, investiture, installation, opening, origination.

inauspicious *adj* bad, discouraging, ill-omened, ill-starred, ominous, unfavourable, unfortunate, unlucky, unpromising, unpropitious, untoward.

inborn *adj* congenital, inbred, ingrained, inherent, innate, instinctive, native, natural.

incalculable *adj* countless, enormous, immense, incalculable, inestimable, innumerable, sumless, unknown, untold.

incandescence *n* candescence, glow, gleam, luminousness, luminosity.

incandescent *adj* aglow, candent, candescent, gleaming, glowing, luminous, luminant, radiant.

incantation *n* charm, conjuration, enchantment, magic, necromancy, sorcery, spell, witchcraft, witchery.

incapability *n* disability, inability, incapacity, incompetence.

incapable *adj* feeble, impotent, incompetent, insufficient, unable, unfit, unfitted, unqualified, weak.
adj antonyms capable, sober.

incapacious *adj* cramped, deficient, incommodious, narrow, scant.

incapacitate *vb* **1** cripple, disable. **2** disqualify, make unfit.

incapacity *n* **1** disability, inability, incapability, incompetence. **2** disqualification, unfitness.

incarcerate *vb* commit, confine, immure, imprison, jail, restrain, restrict.
vb antonym free.

incarnate *vb* body, embody, incorporate, personify. • *adj* bodied, embodied, incorporated, personified.

incarnation *n* embodiment, exemplification, impersonation, manifestation, personification.

incautious *adj* **1** impolitic, imprudent, indiscreet, uncircumspect, unwary. **2** careless, headlong, heedless, inconsiderate, negligent, rash, reckless, thoughtless.

incendiary *adj* dissentious, factious, inflammatory, seditious. • *n* agitator, firebrand, fire-raiser.

incense[1] *vb* anger, chafe, enkindle, enrage, exasperate, excite, heat, inflame, irritate, madden, provoke.
vb antonym calm.

incense[2] *n* **1** aroma, fragrance, perfume, scent. **2** admiration, adulation, applause, laudation.

incentive *n* cause, encouragement, goad, impulse, incitement, inducement, instigation, mainspring, motive, provocation, spur, stimulus.
n antonym disincentive.

inception *n* beginning, commencement, inauguration, initiation, origin, rise, start.
n antonym end.

incertitude *n* ambiguity, doubt, doubtfulness, indecision, uncertainty.

incessant *adj* ceaseless, constant, continual, continuous, eternal, everlasting, never-ending, perpetual, unceasing, unending, uninterrupted, unremitting.
adj antonym intermittent.

inchoate *adj* beginning, commencing, inceptive, incipient, initial.

incident *n* **1** circumstance, episode, event, fact, happening, occurrence. • *adj* happening. **2** belonging, pertaining, appertaining, accessory, relating, natural. **3** falling, impinging.

incidental *adj* **1** accidental, casual, chance, concomitant, contingent, fortuitous, subordinate. **2** adventitious, extraneous, nonessential, occasional.
adj antonym essential.

incinerate *vb* burn, char, conflagrate, cremate, incremate.

incipient *adj* beginning, commencing, inchoate, inceptive, originating, starting.

incised *adj* carved, cut, engraved, gashed, graved, graven.

incision *n* cut, gash, notch, opening, penetration.

incisive *adj* **1** cutting. **2** acute, biting, sarcastic, satirical, sharp. **3** acute, clear, distinct, penetrating, sharp-cut, trenchant.
adj antonym woolly.

incite *vb* actuate, animate, arouse, drive, encourage, excite, foment, goad, hound, impel, instigate, prod, prompt, provoke, push, rouse, spur, stimulate, urge.
vb antonym restrain.

incitement *n* encouragement, goad, impulse, incentive, inducement, motive, provocative, spur, stimulus.
n antonyms check, discouragement.

incivility *n* discourteousness, discourtesy, disrespect, ill-breeding, ill-manners, impoliteness, impudence, inurbanity, rudeness, uncourtliness, unmannerliness.

inclemency *n* boisterousness, cruelty, harshness, rigour, roughness, severity, storminess, tempestuousness, tyranny.

inclement *adj* **1** boisterous, harsh, rigorous, rough, severe, stormy. **2** cruel, unmerciful.

inclination *n* **1** inclining, leaning, slant, slope. **2** trending, verging. **3** aptitude, bent, bias, disposition, penchant, predilection, predisposition, proclivity, proneness, propensity, tendency, turn, twist. **4** desire, fondness, liking, taste, partiality, predilection, wish. **5** bow, nod, obeisance.

incline *vb* **1** lean, slant, slope. **2** bend, nod, verge. **3** tend. **4** bias, dispose, predispose, turn. **5** bow. • *n* ascent, descent, grade, gradient, rise, slope.

inclose *see* **enclose**.

include *vb* **1** contain, hold. **2** comprehend, comprise, contain, cover, embody, embrace, incorporate, involve, take in.
vb antonyms exclude, ignore.

inclusive *adj* comprehending, embracing, encircling, enclosing, including, taking in.

incognito, incognita *adj* camouflaged, concealed, disguised, unknown. • *n* camouflage, concealment, disguise.

incoherent *adj* **1** detached, loose, nonadhesive, noncohesive. **2** disconnected, incongruous, inconsequential, inconsistent, uncoordinated. **3** confused, illogical, irrational, rambling, unintelligible, wild.
adj antonym coherent.

income *n* earnings, emolument, gains, interest, pay, perquisite, proceeds, profits, receipts, rents, return, revenue, salary, wages.
n antonym expenses.

incommensurate *adj* disproportionate, inadequate, insufficient, unequal.

incommode *vb* annoy, discommode, disquiet, disturb, embarrass, hinder, inconvenience, molest, plague, trouble, upset, vex.

incommodious *adj* **1** awkward, cumbersome, cumbrous, inconvenient, unhandy, unmanageable, unsuitable, unwieldy. **2** annoying, disadvantageous, harassing, irritating, vexatious.

incommunicative *adj* exclusive, unsociable, unsocial, reserved.

incomparable *adj* matchless, inimitable, peerless, surpassing, transcendent, unequalled, unparalleled, unrivalled.
adj antonyms poor, run-of-the-mill.

incompatibility *n* contrariety, contradictoriness, discrepancy, incongruity, inconsistency, irreconcilability, unsuitability, unsuitableness

incompatible *adj* contradictory, incongruous, inconsistent, inharmonious, irreconcilable, unadapted, unsuitable.

incompetence *n* **1** inability, incapability, incapacity, incompetency. **2** inadequacy, insufficiency. **3** disqualification, unfitness.
n antonym competence.

incompetent *adj* **1** incapable, unable. **2** inadequate, insufficient. **3** disqualified, incapacitated, unconstitutional, unfit, unfitted.

incomplete *adj* **1** defective, deficient, imperfect, partial. **2** inexhaustive, unaccompanied, uncompleted, unexecuted, unfinished.

incomprehensible *adj* **1** inconceivable, inexhaustible, unfathomable, unimaginable. **2** inconceivable, unintelligible, unthinkable.
adj antonym comprehensible.

incomputable *adj* enormous, immense, incalculable, innumerable, prodigious.

inconceivable *adj* incomprehensible, incredible, unbelievable, unimaginable, unthinkable.
adj antonym conceivable.

inconclusive *adj* inconsequent, inconsequential, indecisive, unconvincing. illogical, unproved, unproven.

incongruity *n* absurdity, contradiction, contradictoriness, contrariety, discordance, discordancy, discrepancy, impropriety, inappropriateness, incoherence, incompatibility, inconsistency, unfitness, unsuitableness.

incongruous *adj* absurd, contradictory, contrary, disagreeing, discrepant, inappropriate, incoherent, incompatible, inconsistent, inharmonious, unfit, unsuitable.
adj antonyms consistent, harmonious.

inconsequent *adj* desultory, disconnected, fragmentary, illogical, inconclusive, inconsistent, irrelevant, loose.

inconsiderable *adj* immaterial, insignificant, petty, slight, small, trifling, trivial, unimportant.

inconsiderate *adj* **1** intolerant, uncharitable,

unthoughtful. **2** careless, heedless, giddy, hare-brained, hasty, headlong, imprudent, inadvertent, inattentive, indifferent, indiscreet, light-headed, negligent, rash, thoughtless.
adj antonym considerate.

inconsistency *n* **1** incoherence, incompatibility, incongruity, unsuitableness. **2** contradiction, contrariety. **3** changeableness, inconstancy, instability, vacillation, unsteadiness.
n antonym consistency, constancy, stability.

inconsistent *adj* **1** different, discrepant, illogical, incoherent, incompatible, incongruous, inconsequent, inconsonant, irreconcilable, unsuitable. **2** contradictory, contrary. **3** changeable, fickle, inconstant, unstable, unsteady, vacillating, variable.
adj antonym constant.

inconsolable *adj* comfortless, crushed, disconsolate, forlorn, heartbroken, hopeless, woebegone.

inconstancy *n* changeableness, mutability, variability, variation, fluctuation, faithlessness, fickleness, capriciousness, vacillation, uncertainty, unsteadiness, volatility.

inconstant *adj* **1** capricious, changeable, faithless, fickle, fluctuating, mercurial, mutable, unsettled, unsteady, vacillating, variable, varying, volatile, wavering. **2** mutable, uncertain, unstable.
adj antonym constant.

incontestable *adj* certain, incontrovertible, indisputable, indubitable, irrefrangible, sure, undeniable, unquestionable.

incontinence *n* excess, extravagance, indulgence, intemperance, irrepressibility, lasciviousness, lewdness, licentiousness, prodigality, profligacy, riotousness, unrestraint, wantonness, wildness.

incontinent *adj* debauched, lascivious, lewd, licentious, lustful, prodigal, unchaste, uncontrolled, unrestrained.

incontrovertible *adj* certain, incontestable, indisputable, indubitable, irrefutable, sure, undeniable, unquestionable.

inconvenience *vb* **1** discommode. **2** annoy, disturb, molest, trouble, vex. • *n* **1** annoyance, disadvantage, disturbance, molestation, trouble, vexation. **2** awkwardness, cumbersomeness, incommodiousness, unwieldiness. **3** unfitness, unseasonableness, unsuitableness.

inconvenient *adj* annoying, awkward, cumbersome, cumbrous, disadvantageous, incommodious, inopportune, troublesome, uncomfortable, unfit, unhandy, unmanageable, unseasonable, unsuitable, untimely, unwieldy, vexatious.
adj antonym convenient.

incorporate *vb* **1** affiliate, amalgamate, associate, blend, combine, consolidate, include, merge, mix, unite. **2** embody, incarnate. • *adj* **1** incorporeal, immaterial, spiritual, supernatural. **2** blended, consolidated, merged, united.

incorporation *n* affiliation, alignment, amalgamation, association, blend, blending, combination, consolidation, fusion, inclusion, merger, mixture, unification, union, embodiment, incarnation, personification.

incorporeal *adj* bodiless, immaterial, impalpable, incorporate, spiritual, supernatural, unsubstantial.

incorrect *adj* **1** erroneous, false, inaccurate, inexact, untrue, wrong. **2** faulty, improper, mistaken, ungrammatical, unbecoming, unsound.
adj antonym correct.

incorrectness *n* error, inaccuracy, inexactness, mistake.

incorrigible *adj* **1** abandoned, graceless, hardened, irreclaimable, lost, obdurate, recreant, reprobate, shameless. **2** helpless, hopeless, irremediable, irrecoverable, irreparable, irretrievable, irreversible, remediless.

incorruptibility *n* **1** unpurchasableness. **2** deathlessness, immortality, imperishableness, incorruptibleness, incorruption, indestructibility.

incorruptible *adj* **1** honest, unbribable. **2** imperishable, indestructible, immortal, undying, deathless, everlasting.
adj antonym corruptible.

increase *vb* **1** accrue, advance, augment, enlarge, extend, grow, intensify, mount, wax. **2** multiply. **3** enhance, greaten, heighten, raise, reinforce. **4** aggravate, prolong. • *n* **1** accession, accretion, accumulation, addition, augmentation, crescendo, development, enlargement, expansion, extension, growth, heightening, increment, intensification, multiplication, swelling. **2** gain, produce, product, profit. **3** descendants, issue, offspring, progeny.
vb antonym decrease.
n antonym decrease.

incredible *adj* absurd, inadmissible, nonsensical, unbelievable.
adj antonyms believable, run-of-the-mill.

incredulity *n* distrust, doubt, incredulousness, scepticism, unbelief.

incredulous *adj* distrustful, doubtful, dubious, sceptical, unbelieving.

increment *n* addition, augmentation, enlargement, increase.

incriminate *vb* accuse, blame, charge, criminate, impeach.
vb antonym exonerate.

incubate *vb* brood, develop, hatch, sit.

inculcate *vb* enforce, implant, impress, infix, infuse, ingraft, inspire, instil.

inculpable *adj* blameless, faultless, innocent, irreprehensible, irreproachable, irreprovable, sinless, unblameable.

inculpate *vb* accuse, blame, censure, charge, incriminate, impeach, incriminate.

inculpatory *adj* criminatory, incriminating.

incumbent *adj* 1 binding, devolved, devolving, laid, obligatory. 2 leaning, prone, reclining, resting. • *n* holder, occupant.

incur *vb* acquire, bring, contract.

incurable *adj* 1 cureless, hopeless, irrecoverable, remediless. 2 helpless, incorrigible, irremediable, irreparable, irretrievable, remediless.

incurious *adj* careless, heedless, inattentive, indifferent, uninquisitive, unobservant, uninterested.
adj antonym curious.

incursion *n* descent, foray, raid, inroad, irruption.

incursive *adj* aggressive, hostile, invasive, predatory, raiding.

incurvate *vb* bend, bow, crook, curve. • *adj* (*bot*) aduncous, arcuate, bowed, crooked, curved, hooked.

indebted *adj* beholden, obliged, owing.

indecency *n* 1 impropriety, indecorum, offensiveness, outrageousness, unseemliness. 2 coarseness, filthiness, foulness, grossness, immodesty, impurity, obscenity, vileness.
n antonyms decency, modesty.

indecent *adj* 1 bold, improper, indecorous, offensive, outrageous, unbecoming, unseemly. 2 coarse, dirty, filthy, gross, immodest, impure, indelicate, lewd, nasty, obscene, pornographic, salacious, shameless, smutty, unchaste.
adj antonyms decent, modest.

indecipherable *adj* illegible, undecipherable, undiscoverable, inexplicable, obscure, unintelligible, unreadable.

indecision *n* changeableness, fickleness, hesitation, inconstancy, irresolution, unsteadiness, vacillation.

indecisive *adj* dubious, hesitating, inconclusive, irresolute, undecided, unsettled, vacillating, wavering.
adj antonym decisive.

indecorous *adj* coarse, gross, ill-bred, impolite, improper, indecent, rude, unbecoming, uncivil, unseemly.

indecorum *n* grossness, ill-breeding, ill manners, impoliteness, impropriety, incivility, indecency, indecorousness.

indeed *adv* absolutely, actually, certainly, in fact, in truth, in reality, positively, really, strictly, truly, verily, veritably. • *interj* really! you don't say so! is it possible?

indefatigable *adj* assiduous, never-tiring, persevering, persistent, sedulous, tireless, unflagging, unremitting, untiring, unwearied.

indefeasible *adj* immutable, inalienable, irreversible, irrevocable, unalterable.

indefensible *adj* 1 censurable, defenceless, faulty, unpardonable, untenable. 2 inexcusable, insupportable, unjustifiable, unwarrantable, wrong.

indefinite *adj* confused, doubtful, equivocal, general, imprecise, indefinable, indecisive, indeterminate, indistinct, inexact, inexplicit, lax, loose, nondescript, obscure, uncertain, undefined, undetermined, unfixed, unsettled, vague.
adj antonyms clear, definite, finite, limited.

indelible *adj* fast, fixed, ineffaceable, ingrained, permanent.

indelicacy *n* 1 coarseness, grossness, indecorousness, indecorum, impropriety, offensiveness, unseemliness, vulgarity. 2 immodesty, indecency, lewdness, unchastity. 3 foulness, obscenity.

indelicate *adj* 1 broad, coarse, gross, indecorous, intrusive, rude, unbecoming, unseemly. 2 foul, immodest, indecent, lewd, obscene, unchaste, vulgar.
adj antonym delicate.

indemnification *n* compensation, reimbursement, remuneration, security.

indemnify *vb* compensate, reimburse, remunerate, requite, secure.

indent *vb* 1 bruise, jag, notch, pink, scallop, serrate. 2 bind, indenture.

indentation *n* bruise, dent, depression, jag, notch.

indenture *vb* bind, indent. • *n* **1** contract, instrument. **2** indentation.

independence *n* **1** freedom, liberty, self-direction. **2** distinctness, nondependence, separation. **3** competence, ease.

independent *adj* **1** absolute, autonomous, free, self-directing, uncoerced, unrestrained, unrestricted, voluntary. **2** (*person*) self-reliant, unconstrained, unconventional.
adj antonyms conventional, dependent, timid.

indescribable *adj* ineffable, inexpressible, nameless, unutterable.

indestructible *adj* abiding, endless, enduring, everlasting, fadeless, imperishable, incorruptible, undecaying.
adj antonyms breakable, mortal.

indeterminate *adj* indefinite, uncertain, undetermined, unfixed.

index *vb* alphabetize, catalogue, codify, earmark, file, list, mark, tabulate. • *n* **1** catalogue, list, register, tally. **2** indicator, lead, mark, pointer, sign, signal, token. **3** contents, table of contents. **4** forefinger. **5** exponent.

indicate *vb* **1** betoken, denote, designate, evince, exhibit, foreshadow, manifest, mark, point out, prefigure, presage, register, show, signify, specify, tell. **2** hint, imply, intimate, sketch, suggest.

indication *n* hint, index, manifestation, mark, note, sign, suggestion, symptom, token.

indicative *adj* **1** significant, suggestive, symptomatic. **2** (*gram*) affirmative, declarative.

indict *vb* (*law*) accuse, charge, present.
vb antonym exonerate.

indictment *n* (*law*) **1** indicting, presentment. **2** accusation, arraignment, charge, crimination, impeachment.
n antonym exoneration.

indifference *n* **1** apathy, carelessness, coldness, coolness, heedlessness, inattention, insignificance, negligence, unconcern, unconcernedness, uninterestedness. **2** disinterestedness, impartiality, neutrality.
n antonyms bias, interest.

indifferent *adj* **1** apathetic, cold, cool, dead, distant, dull, easy-going, frigid, heedless, inattentive, incurious, insensible, insouci-

ant, listless, lukewarm, nonchalant, perfunctory, regardless, stoical, unconcerned, uninterested, unmindful, unmoved. **2** equal. **3** fair, medium, middling, moderate, ordinary, passable, tolerable. **4** mediocre, so-so. **5** immaterial, unimportant. **6** disinterested, impartial, neutral, unbiased.
adj antonyms biased, interested.

indigence *n* destitution, distress, necessity, need, neediness, pauperism, penury, poverty, privation, want.
n antonym affluence.

indigenous *adj* aboriginal, home-grown, inborn, inherent, native.
adj antonym foreign.

indigent *adj* destitute, distressed, insolvent, moneyless, necessitous, needy, penniless, pinched, poor, reduced.
adj antonym affluent, rich.

indigested *adj* **1** unconcocted, undigested. **2** crude, ill-advised, ill-considered, ill-judged. **3** confused, disorderly, ill-arranged, unmethodical.

indigestion *n* dyspepsia.

indignant *adj* angry, exasperated, incensed, irate, ireful, provoked, roused, wrathful, wroth.
adj antonym calm, pleased.

indignation *n* anger, choler, displeasure, exasperation, fury, ire, rage, resentment, wrath.
n antonym calmness, pleasure.

indignity *n* abuse, affront, contumely, dishonour, disrespect, ignominy, insult, obloquy, opprobrium, outrage, reproach, slight.
n antonym honour.

indirect *adj* **1** circuitous, circumlocutory, collateral, devious, oblique, roundabout, sidelong, tortuous. **2** deceitful, dishonest, dishonorable, unfair. **3** mediate, remote, secondary, subordinate.
adj antonym direct.

indiscernible *adj* imperceptible, indistinguishable, invisible, undiscernible, undiscoverable.

indiscipline *n* laxity, insubordination.

indiscreet *adj* foolish, hasty, headlong, heedless, imprudent, incautious, inconsiderate, injudicious, rash, reckless, unwise.

indiscretion *n* **1** folly, imprudence, inconsiderateness, rashness. **2** blunder, faux pas, lapse, mistake, misstep.
n antonym discretion.

indiscriminate *adj* confused, heterogeneous, indistinct, mingled, miscellaneous, mixed, promiscuous, undiscriminating, undistinguishable, undistinguishing.

indispensable *adj* essential, expedient, necessary, needed, needful, requisite.
adj antonym unnecessary.

indisputable *adj* certain, incontestable, indubitable, infallible, sure, undeniable, undoubted,
unmistakable, unquestionable.

indisposed *adj* **1** ailing, ill, sick, unwell. **2** averse, backward, disinclined, loath, reluctant, unfriendly, unwilling.

indisposition *n* **1** ailment, illness, sickness. **2** aversion, backwardness, dislike, disinclination, reluctance, unwillingness.

indisputable *adj* certain, incontestable, indutitable, infallible, sure, undeniable, undoubted, unmistakable, unquestionable.

indissoluble *adj* abiding, enduring, firm, imperishable, incorruptible, indestructible, lasting, stable, unbreakable.

indistinct *adj* **1** ambiguous, doubtful, uncertain. **2** blurred, dim, dull, faint, hazy, misty, nebulous, obscure, shadowy, vague. **3** confused, inarticulate, indefinite, indistinguishable, undefined, undistinguishable.
adj antonym distinct.

indistinguishable *adj* **1** imperceptible, indiscernible, unnoticeable, unobservable. **2** chaotic, confused, dim, indistinct, obscure, vague.
adj antonyms distinguishable, unalike.

indite *vb* compose, pen, write.

individual *adj* **1** characteristic, distinct, identical, idiosyncratic, marked, one, particular, personal, respective, separate, single, singular, special, unique. **2** peculiar, proper. **3** decided, definite, independent, positive, self-guided, unconventional. • *n* **1** being, character, party, person, personage, somebody, someone. **2** type, unit.

individuality *n* **1** definiteness, indentity, personality. **2** originality, self-direction, self-determination, singularity, uniqueness.
n antonym sameness.

individualize *vb* individuate, particularize, singularize, specify.

indivisible *adj* incommensurable, indissoluble, inseparable, unbreakable, unpartiable.

indocile *adj* cantankerous, contumacious, dogged, froward, inapt, headstrong, intractable, mulish, obstinate, perverse, refractory, stubborn, ungovernable, unmanageable, unruly, unteachable.

indoctrinate *vb* brainwash, imbue, initiate, instruct, rehabilitate, teach.

indoctrination *n* grounding, initiation, instruction, rehabilitation.

indolence *n* idleness, inactivity, inertia, inertness, laziness, listlessness, sloth, slothfulness, sluggishness.

indolent *adj* easy, easy-going, inactive, inert, lazy, listless, lumpish, otiose, slothful, sluggish, supine.
adj antonyms active, enthusiastic, industrious.

indomitable *adj* invincible, unconquerable, unyielding.
adj antonyms compliant, timid.

indorse *see* **endorse**.

indubitable *adj* certain, evident, incontestable, incontrovertible, indisputable, sure, undeniable, unquestionable.

induce *vb* **1** actuate, allure, bring, draw, drive, entice, impel, incite, influence, instigate, move, persuade, prevail, prompt, spur, urge. **2** bring on, cause, effect, motivate, lead, occasion, produce.

inducement *n* **1** allurement, draw, enticement, instigation, persuasion. **2** cause, consideration, impulse, incentive, incitement, influence, motive, reason, spur, stimulus.
n antonym disincentive.

induct *vb* inaugurate, initiate, install, institute, introduce, invest.

induction *n* **1** inauguration, initiation, institution, installation, introduction. **2** conclusion, generalization, inference.

indue *vb* assume, endow, clothe, endue, invest, supply.

indulge *vb* **1** gratify, license, revel, satisfy, wallow, yield to. **2** coddle, cosset, favour, humour, pamper, pet, spoil. **3** allow, cherish, foster, harbour, permit, suffer.

indulgence *n* **1** gratification, humouring, pampering. **2** favour, kindness, lenience, lenity, liberality, tenderness. **3** (*theol*) absolution, remission.

indulgent *adj* clement, easy, favouring, forbearing, gentle, humouring, kind, lenient, mild, pampering, tender, tolerant.
adj antonyms moderate, strict.

indurate *vb* harden, inure, sear, strengthen.

induration *n* hardening, obduracy.

industrious *adj* **1** assiduous, diligent,

hard-working, laborious, notable, operose, sedulous. **2** brisk, busy, persevering, persistent.

adj antonym indolent, lazy.

industry *n* **1** activity, application, assiduousness, assiduity, diligence. **2** perseverance, persistence, sedulousness, vigour. **3** effort, labour, toil.

inebriated *adj* drunk, intoxicated, stupefied.

adj antonym sober.

ineffable *adj* indescribable, inexpressible, unspeakable, unutterable.

ineffaceable *adj* indelible, indestructible, inexpungeable, ingrained.

ineffectual *adj* **1** abortive, bootless, fruitless, futile, inadequate, inefficacious, ineffective, inoperative, useless, unavailing, vain. **2** feeble, inefficient, powerless, impotent, weak.

adj antonyms effective, fruitful.

inefficacy *n* ineffectualness, inefficiency.

inefficient *adj* feeble, incapable, ineffectual, ineffective, inefficacious, weak.

adj antonym efficient.

inelastic *adj* flabby, flaccid, inductile, inflexible, irresilient.

inelegant *adj* abrupt, awkward, clumsy, coarse, constrained, cramped, crude, graceless, harsh, homely, homespun, rough, rude, stiff, tasteless, uncourtly, uncouth, ungainly, ungraceful, unpolished, unrefined.

ineligible *adj* **1** disqualified, unqualified. **2** inexpedient, objectionable, unadvisable, undesirable.

adj antonym eligible.

inept *adj* **1** awkward, improper, inapposite, inappropriate, unapt, unfit, unsuitable. **2** null, useless, void, worthless. **3** foolish, nonsensical, pointless, senseless, silly, stupid.

adj antonyms adroit, apt.

ineptitude *n* **1** inappositeness, inappropriateness, inaptitude, unfitness, unsuitability, unsuitableness. **2** emptiness, nullity, uselessness, worthlessness. **3** folly, foolishness, nonsense, pointlessness, senselessness, silliness, stupidity.

inequality *n* **1** disproportion, inequitableness, injustice, unfairness. **2** difference, disparity, dissimilarity, diversity, imparity, irregularity, roughness, unevenness. **3** inadequacy, incompetency, insufficiency.

inequitable *adj* unfair, unjust.

inert *adj* **1** comatose, dead, inactive, lifeless, motionless, quiescent, passive. **2** apathetic, dronish, dull, idle, indolent, lazy, lethargic, lumpish, phlegmatic, slothful, sluggish, supine, torpid.

adj antonyms alive, animated.

inertia *n* apathy, inertness, lethargy, passiveness, passivity, slothfulness, sluggishness.

n antonyms activity, liveliness.

inestimable *adj* incalculable, invaluable, precious, priceless, valuable.

inevitable *adj* certain, necessary, unavoidable, undoubted.

adj antonyms alterable, avoidable, uncertain.

inexact *adj* **1** imprecise, inaccurate, incorrect. **2** careless, crude, loose.

inexcusable *adj* indefensible, irremissible, unallowable, unjustifiable, unpardonable.

inexhaustible *adj* boundless, exhaustless, indefatigable, unfailing, unlimited.

inexorable *adj* cruel, firm, hard, immovable, implacable, inflexible, merciless, pitiless, relentless, severe, steadfast, unbending, uncompassionate, unmerciful, unrelenting, unyielding.

adj antonyms flexible, lenient, yielding.

inexpedient *adj* disadvantageous, ill-judged, impolitic, imprudent, indiscreet, injudicious, inopportune, unadvisable, unprofitable, unwise.

inexperience *n* greenness, ignorance, rawness.

inexperienced *adj* callow, green, raw, strange, unacquainted, unconversant, undisciplined, uninitiated, unpractised, unschooled, unskilled, untrained, untried, unversed, young.

adj antonym experienced.

inexpert *adj* awkward, bungling, clumsy, inapt, maladroit, unhandy, unskilful, unskilled.

inexpiable *adj* **1** implacable, inexorable, irreconcilable, unappeasable. **2** irremissible, unatonable, unpardonable.

inexplicable *adj* enigmatic, enigmatical, incomprehensible, inscrutable, mysterious, strange, unaccountable, unintelligible.

adj antonym explicable.

inexpressible *adj* **1** indescribable, ineffable, unspeakable, unutterable. **2** boundless, infinite, surpassing.

inexpressive *adj* blank, characterless, dull, unexpressive.

inextinguishable *adj* unquenchable.

in extremis *adv* moribund.

inextricable *adj* entangled, intricate, perplexed, unsolvable.

infallibility *n* certainty, infallibleness, perfection.

n antonym fallibility.

infallible *adj* certain, indubitable, oracular, sure, unerring, unfailing.

infamous *adj* abominable, atrocious, base, damnable, dark, detestable, discreditable, disgraceful, dishonourable, disreputable, heinous, ignominious, nefarious, odious, opprobrious, outrageous, scandalous, shameful, shameless, vile, villainous, wicked.

adj antonym glorious.

infamy *n* 1 abasement, discredit, disgrace, dishonour, disrepute, ignominy, obloquy, odium, opprobrium, scandal, shame. 2 atrocity, detestableness, disgracefulness, dishonourableness, odiousness, scandalousness, shamefulness, villainy, wickedness.

infancy *n* 1 beginning, commencement. 2 babyhood, childhood, minority, nonage, pupillage.

infant *n* babe, baby, bairn, bantling, brat, chit, minor, nursling, papoose, suckling, tot.

infantile *adj* 1 childish, newborn, tender, young. 2 babyish, childish, weak. 3 babylike, childlike.

adj antonyms adult, mature.

infatuate *vb* befool, captivate, delude, prepossess, stultify.

infatuation *n* absorption, adoration, besottedness, folly, foolishness, prepossession, stupefaction.

n antonyms disenchantment, indifference.

infeasible *adj* impractical, unfeasible.

infect *vb* affect, contaminate, corrupt, defile, poison, pollute, taint, vitiate.

infection *n* affection, bane, contagion, contamination, corruption, defilement, pest, poison, pollution, taint, virus, vitiation.

infectious *adj* catching, communicable, contagious, contaminating, corrupting, defiling, demoralizing, pestiferous, pestilential, poisoning, polluting, sympathetic, vitiating.

infecund *adj* barren, infertile, sterile, unfruitful, unproductive, unprolific.

infecundity *n* unfruitfulness.

infelicitous *adj* 1 calamitous, miserable, unfortunate, unhappy, wretched. 2 inauspicious, unfavourable, unpropitious. 3 ill-chosen, inappropriate, unfitting.

infer *vb* collect, conclude, deduce, derive, draw, gather, glean, guess, presume, reason.

inference *n* conclusion, consequence, corollary, deduction, generalization, guess, illation, implication, induction, presumption.

inferior *adj* 1 lower, nether. 2 junior, minor, secondary, subordinate. 3 bad, base, deficient, humble, imperfect, indifferent, mean, mediocre, paltry, poor, second-rate, shabby.

adj antonym superior.

inferiority *n* 1 subjection, subordination, mediocrity. 2 deficiency, imperfection, inadequacy, shortcoming.

n antonym superiority.

infernal *adj* abominable, accursed, atrocious, damnable, dark, demoniacal, devilish, diabolical, fiendish, fiendlike, hellish, malicious, nefarious, satanic, Stygian.

adj antonym heavenly.

infertility *n* barrenness, infecundity, sterility, unfruitfulness, unproductivity.

infest *vb* 1 annoy, disturb, harass, haunt, molest, plague, tease, torment, trouble, vex, worry. 2 beset, overrun, possess, swarm, throng.

infidel *n* agnostic, atheist, disbeliever, heathen, heretic, sceptic, unbeliever.

infidelity *n* 1 adultery, disloyalty, faithlessness, treachery, unfaithfulness. 2 disbelief, scepticism, unbelief.

infiltrate *vb* absorb, pervade, soak.

infinite *adj* 1 boundless, endless, illimitable, immeasurable, inexhaustible, interminable, limitless, measureless, perfect, unbounded, unlimited. 2 enormous, immense, stupendous, vast. 3 absolute, eternal, self-determined, self-existent, unconditioned.

adj antonym finite.

infinitesimal *adj* 1 infinitely small. 2 microscopic, miniscule.

adj antonyms significant, substantial.

infinity *n* absoluteness, boundlessness, endlessness, eternity, immensity, infiniteness, infinitude, interminateness, self-determination, self-existence, vastness.

infirm *adj* 1 ailing, debilitated, enfeebled, feeble, frail, weak, weakened. 2 faltering,

irresolute, vacillating, wavering. **3** insecure, precarious, unsound, unstable.
adj antonyms healthy, strong.

infirmity *n* **1** ailment, debility, feebleness, frailness, frailty, weakness. **2** defect, failing, fault, foible, weakness.
n antonyms health, strength.

infix *vb* **1** fasten, fix, plant, set. **2** implant, inculcate, infuse, ingraft, instil.

inflame *vb* **1** animate, arouse, excite, enkindle, fire, heat, incite, inspirit, intensify, rouse, stimulate. **2** aggravate, anger, chafe, embitter, enrage, exasperate, incense, infuriate, irritate, madden, nettle, provoke.
vb antonyms cool, quench.

inflammability *n* combustibility, combustibleness, inflammableness.

inflammable *adj* **1** combustible, ignitible. **2** excitable.

inflammation *n* **1** burning, conflagration. **2** anger, animosity, excitement, heat, rage, turbulence, violence.

inflammatory *adj* **1** fiery, inflaming. **2** dissentious, incendiary, seditious.
adj antonyms calming, pacific.

inflate *vb* **1** bloat, blow up, distend, expand, swell, sufflate. **2** elate, puff up. **3** enlarge, increase.
vb antonym deflate.

inflated *adj* **1** bloated, distended, puffed-up, swollen. **2** bombastic, declamatory, grandiloquent, high-flown, magniloquent, overblown, pompous, rhetorical, stilted, tumid, turgid.

inflation *n* **1** enlargement, increase, overenlargement, overissue. **2** bloatedness, distension, expansion, sufflation. **3** bombast, conceit, conceitedness, self-conceit, self-complacency, self-importance, self-sufficiency, vaingloriousness, vainglory.

inflect *vb* **1** bend, bow, curve, turn. **2** (*gram*) conjugate, decline, vary.

inflection *n* **1** bend, bending, crook, curvature, curvity, flexure. **2** (*gram*) accidence, conjugation, declension, variation. **3** (*mus*) modulation.

inflexibility *n* **1** inflexibleness, rigidity, stiffness. **2** doggedness, obstinacy, perinacity, stubbornness. **3** firmness, perseverance, resolution, tenacity.

inflexible *adj* **1** rigid, rigorous, stiff, unbending. **2** cantankerous, cross-grained, dogged, headstrong, heady, inexorable, intractable, obdurate, obstinate, pertina-

cious, refractory, stubborn, unyielding, wilful. **3** firm, immovable, persevering, resolute, steadfast, unbending.
adj antonym flexible.

inflict *vb* bring, impose, lay on.

infliction *n* **1** imposition, inflicting. **2** judgment, punishment.

inflorescence *n* blooming, blossoming, flowering.

influence *vb* **1** affect, bias, control, direct, lead, modify, prejudice, prepossess, sway. **2** actuate, arouse, impel, incite, induce, instigate, move, persuade, prevail upon, rouse. • *n* **1** ascendancy, authority, control, mastery, potency, predominance, pull, rule, sway. **2** credit, reputation, weight. **3** inflow, inflowing, influx. **4** magnetism, power, spell.

influential *adj* **1** controlling, effective, effectual, potent, powerful, strong. **2** authoritative, momentous, substantial, weighty.
adj antonym ineffectual.

influx *n* flowing in, introduction.

infold *see* **enfold**.

inform *vb* **1** animate, inspire, quicken. **2** acquaint, advise, apprise, enlighten, instruct, notify, teach, tell, tip, warn.

informal *adj* **1** unceremonious, unconventional, unofficial. **2** easy, familiar, natural, simple. **3** irregular, nonconformist, unusual.
adj antonym formal.

informality *n* **1** unceremoniousness. **2** unconventionality. **3** ease, familiarity, naturalness, simplicity. **4** noncomformity, irregularity, unusualness.
n antonym formality.

informant *n* **1** advertiser, adviser, informer, intelligencer, newsmonger, notifier, relator. **2** accuser, complainant, informer.

information *n* **1** advice, data, intelligence, knowledge, notice. **2** advertisement, enlightenment, instruction, message, tip, word, warning. **3** accusation, complaint, denunciation.

informer *n* accuser, complainant, informant, snitch.

infraction *n* breach, breaking, disobedience, encroachment, infringement, nonobservance, transgression, violation.

infrangible *adj* inseparable, inviolable, unbreakable.

infrequency *n* rareness, rarity, uncommonness, unusualness.

infrequent *adj* **1** rare, uncommon, unfrequent, unusual. **2** occasional, scant, scarce, sporadic.

adj antonym frequent.

infringe *vb* break, contravene, disobey, intrude, invade, transgress, violate.

infringement *n* breach, breaking, disobedience, infraction, nonobservance, transgression, violation.

infuriated *adj* angry, enraged, furious, incensed, maddened, raging, wild.

infuse *vb* **1** breathe into, implant, inculcate, ingraft, insinuate, inspire, instil, introduce. **2** macerate, steep.

infusion *n* **1** inculcation, instillation, introduction. **2** infusing, macerating, steeping.

ingathering *n* harvest.

ingenious *adj* able, adroit, artful, bright, clever, fertile, gifted, inventive, ready, sagacious, shrewd, witty.

adj antonyms clumsy, unimaginative.

ingenuity *n* ability, acuteness, aptitude, aptness, capacity, capableness, cleverness, faculty, genius, gift, ingeniousness, inventiveness, knack, readiness, skill, turn.

n antonyms clumsiness, dullness, stupidity.

ingenuous *adj* artless, candid, childlike, downright, frank, generous, guileless, honest, innocent, naive, open, open-hearted, plain, simple-minded, sincere, single-minded, straightforward, transparent, truthful, unreserved.

adj antonyms artful, sly.

ingenuousness *n* artlessness, candour, childlikeness, frankness, guilelessness, honesty, naivety, open-heartedness, openness, sincerity, single-mindedness, truthfulness.

inglorious *adj* **1** humble, lowly, mean, nameless, obscure, undistinguished, unhonoured, unknown, unmarked, unnoted. **2** discreditable, disgraceful, humiliating, ignominious, scandalous, shameful.

ingloriousness *n* **1** humbleness, lowliness, meanness, namelessness, obscurity. **2** abasement, discredit, disgrace, dishonour, disrepute, humiliation, infamy, ignominousness, ignominy, shame.

ingraft *vb* graft, implant, inculcate, infix, infuse, instil.

ingrain *vb* dye, imbue, impregnate.

ingratiate *vb* insinuate.

ingratitude *n* thanklessness, ungratefulness, unthankfulness.

n antonym gratitude.

ingredient *n* component, constituent, element.

ingress *n* entrance, entré, entry, introgression.

ingulf *see* **engulf**.

inhabit *vb* abide, dwell, live, occupy, people, reside, sojourn.

inhabitable *adj* habitable, livable.

inhabitant *n* citizen, denizen, dweller, inhabiter, resident.

inhalation *n* **1** breath, inhaling, inspiration. **2** sniff, snuff.

inhale *vb* breathe in, draw in, inbreathe, inspire.

inharmonious *adj* discordant, inharmonic, out of tune, unharmonious, unmusical.

inhere *vb* **1** cleave to, stick, stick fast. **2** abide, belong, exist, lie, pertain, reside.

inherent *adj* **1** essential, immanent, inborn, inbred, indwelling, ingrained, innate, inseparable, intrinsic, native, natural, proper. **2** adhering, sticking.

inherit *vb* get, receive.

inheritance *n* **1** heritage, legacy, patrimony. **2** inheriting.

inheritor *n* heir, (*law*) parcener.

inhibit *vb* **1** bar, check, debar, hinder, obstruct, prevent, repress, restrain, stop. **2** forbid, interdict, prohibit.

inhibition *n* **1** check, hindrance, impediment, obstacle, obstruction, restraint. **2** disallowance, embargo, interdict, interdiction, prevention, prohibition.

inhospitable *adj* **1** cool, forbidding, unfriendly, unkind. **2** bigoted, illiberal, intolerant, narrow, prejudiced, ungenerous, unreceptive. **3** barren, wild.

inhospitality *n* **1** inhospitableness, unkindness. **2** illiberality, narrowness.

inhuman *adj* **1** barbarous, brutal, cruel, fell, ferocious, merciless, pitiless, remorseless, ruthless, savage, unfeeling. **2** nonhuman.

adj antonym human.

inhumanity *n* **1** barbarity, brutality, cruelty, ferocity, savageness. **2** hard-heartedness, unkindness.

inhume *vb* bury, entomb, inter.

inimical *adj* **1** antagonistic, hostile, unfriendly. **2** adverse, contrary, harmful, hurtful, noxious, opposed, pernicious, repugnant, unfavourable.

adj antonyms favourable, friendly, sympathetic.

inimitable *adj* incomparable, matchless, peerless, unequalled, unexampled, unmatched, unparagoned, unparalleled, un-rivalled, unsurpassed.

iniquitous *adj* atrocious, criminal, heinous, inequitable, nefarious, sinful, wicked, wrong, unfair, unjust, unrighteous.
adj antonym virtuous.

iniquity *n* **1** injustice, sin, sinfulness, unrighteousness, wickedness, wrong. **2** crime, misdeed, offence.
n antonym virtue.

initial *adj* **1** first. **2** beginning, commencing, incipient, initiatory, introductory, opening, original. **3** elementary, inchoate, rudimentary.
adj antonym final.

initiate *vb* **1** begin, commence, enter upon, inaugurate, introduce, open. **2** ground, indoctrinate, instruct, prime, teach.

initiation *n* **1** beginning, commencement, inauguration, opening. **2** admission, entrance, introduction. **3** indoctrinate, instruction.

initiative *n* **1** beginning. **2** energy, enterprise.

initiatory *adj* inceptive, initiative.

inject *vb* force in, interject, insert, introduce, intromit.

injudicious *adj* foolish, hasty, ill-advised, ill-judged, imprudent, incautious, inconsiderate, indiscreet, rash, unwise.

injunction *n* admonition, bidding, command, mandate, order, precept.

injure *vb* **1** damage, disfigure, harm, hurt, impair, mar, spoil, sully, wound. **2** abuse, aggrieve, wrong. **3** affront, dishonour, insult.

injurious *adj* **1** baneful, damaging, deadly, deleterious, destructive, detrimental, disadvantageous, evil, fatal, hurtful, mischievous, noxious, pernicious, prejudicial, ruinous. **2** inequitable, iniquitous, unjust, wrongful. **3** contumelious, detractory, libellous, slanderous.
adj antonyms beneficial, favourable.

injury *n* **1** evil, ill, injustice, wrong. **2** damage, detriment, harm, hurt, impairment, loss, mischief, prejudice.

injustice *n* **1** inequity, unfairness. **2** grievance, iniquity, injury, wrong.
n antonym justice.

inkhorn *n* inkbottle, inkstand.

inkling *n* hint, intimation, suggestion, whisper.

inky *adj* atramentous, black, murky.

inland *adj* **1** domestic, hinterland, home, upcountry. **2** interior, internal.

inlet *n* **1** arm, bay, bight, cove, creek. **2** entrance, ingress, passage.

inmate *n* denizen, dweller, guest, intern, occupant.

inmost *adj* deepest, innermost.

inn *n* hostel, hostelry, hotel, pub, public house, tavern.

innate *adj* congenital, constitutional, inborn, inbred, indigenous, inherent, inherited, instinctive, native, natural, organic.

inner *adj* interior, internal.

innermost *adj* deepest, inmost.

innkeeper *n* host, innholder, landlady, landlord, tavernkeeper.

innocence *n* **1** blamelessness, chastity, guilelessness, guiltlessness, purity, simplicity, sinlessness, stainlessness. **2** harmlessness, innocuousness, inoffensiveness.

innocent *adj* **1** blameless, clean, clear, faultless, guiltless, immaculate, pure, sinless, spotless, unfallen, upright. **2** harmless, innocuous, innoxious, inoffensive. **3** lawful, legitimate, permitted. **4** artless, guileless, ignorant, ingenuous, simple. • *n* babe, child, ingénue, naif, naive, unsophisticate.
adj antonyms experienced, guilty, knowing.
n antonyms connoisseur, expert.

innocuous *adj* harmless, innocent, inoffensive, safe.
adj antonym harmful.

innovate *vb* change, introduce.

innovation *n* **1** change, introduction. **2** departure, novelty.

innuendo *n* allusion, hint, insinuation, intimation, suggestion.

innumerable *adj* countless, numberless.

inoculate *vb* infect, vaccinate.

inoffensive *adj* harmless, innocent, innocuous, innoxious, unobjectionable, unoffending.

inoperative *adj* inactive, ineffectual, inefficacious, not in force.
adj antonym operative.

inopportune *adj* ill-timed, inexpedient, infelicitous, mistimed, unfortunate, unhappy, unseasonable, untimely.
adj antonym opportune, timely.

inordinate *adj* excessive, extravagant, immoderate, intemperate, irregular.

inorganic *adj* **1** inanimate, unorganized. **2** mineral.

inquest *n* inquiry, inquisition, investigation, quest, search.

inquietude *n* anxiety, disquiet, disquietude, disturbance, restlessness, uneasiness.

inquire, enquire *vb* ask, catechize, interpellate, interrogate, investigate, query, question, quiz.

inquiry, enquiry *n* 1 examination, exploration, investigation, research, scrutiny, study. 2 interrogation, query, question, quiz.

inquisition *n* examination, inquest, inquiry, investigation, search.

inquisitive *adj* 1 curious, inquiring, scrutinizing. 2 curious, meddlesome, peeping, peering, prying.
adj antonym incurious.

inroad *n* encroachment, foray, incursion, invasion, irruption, raid.

insalubrious *adj* noxious, unhealthful, unhealthy, unwholesome.

insane *adj* abnormal, crazed, crazy, delirious, demented, deranged, distracted, lunatic, mad, maniacal, unhealthy, unsound.
adj antonym sane.

insanity *n* craziness, delirium, dementia, derangement, lunacy, madness, mania, mental aberration, mental alienation.
n antonym sanity.

insatiable *adj* 1 greedy, rapacious, voracious. 2 insatiate, unappeasable.
adj antonym moderate.

inscribe *vb* 1 emblaze, endorse, engrave, enroll, impress, imprint, letter, mark, write. 2 address, dedicate.

inscrutable *adj* hidden, impenetrable, incomprehensible, inexplicable, mysterious, undiscoverable, unfathomable, unsearchable.
adj antonyms clear, comprehensible, expressive.

inscrutableness *n* impenetrability, incomprehensibility, incomprehensibleness, inexplicability, inscrutability, mysteriousness, mystery, unfathomableness, unsearchableness.

insecure *adj* 1 risky, uncertain, unconfident, unsure. 2 exposed, ill-protected, unprotected, unsafe. 3 dangerous, hazardous, perilous. 4 infirm, shaking, shaky, tottering, unstable, weak, wobbly.
adj antonyms confident, safe, secure.

insecurity *n* 1 riskiness, uncertainty. 2 danger, hazardousness, peril. 3 instability, shakiness, weakness, wobbliness.

insensate *adj* 1 dull, indifferent, insensible, torpid. 2 brutal, foolish, senseless, unwise. 3 inanimate, insensible, insentient, unconscious, unperceiving.

insensibility *n* 1 dullness, insentience, lethargy, torpor. 2 apathy, indifference, insusceptibility, unfeelingness, dullness, stupidity. 3 anaesthesia, coma, stupor, unconsciousness.

insensible *adj* 1 imperceivable, imperceptible, undiscoverable. 2 blunted, brutish, deaf, dull, insensate, numb, obtuse, senseless, sluggish, stolid, stupid, torpid, unconscious. 3 apathetic, callous, phlegmatic, impassive, indifferent, insensitive, insentient, unfeeling, unimpressible, unsusceptible.

insensibly *adv* imperceptibly.

insentient *adj* 1 inert, nonsentient, senseless. 2 inanimate, insensible, insensate, nonpercipient, unconscious, unperceiving.

inseparable *adj* 1 close, friendly, intimate, together. 2 indissoluble, indivisible, inseverable.

insert *vb* infix, inject, intercalate, interpolate, introduce, inweave, parenthesize, place, put, set.

inside *adj* 1 inner, interior, internal. 2 confidential, exclusive, internal, private, secret. • *adv* indoors, within. • *n* 1 inner part, interior. 2 nature.

insidious *adj* 1 creeping, deceptive, gradual, secretive. 2 arch, artful, crafty, crooked, cunning, deceitful, designing, diplomatic, foxy, guileful, intriguing, Machiavellian, sly, sneaky, subtle, treacherous, trickish, tricky, wily.

insight *n* discernment, intuition, penetration, perception, perspicuity, understanding.

insignia *npl* badges, marks.

insignificance *n* emptiness, nothingness, paltriness, triviality, unimportance.

insignificant *adj* contemptible, empty, immaterial, inconsequential, inconsiderable, inferior, meaningless, paltry, petty, small, sorry, trifling, trivial, unessential, unimportant.
adj antonym significant.

insincere *adj* deceitful, dishonest, disingenuous, dissembling, dissimulating, double-faced, double-tongued, duplicitous, empty, faithless, false, hollow, hypocritical, pharisaical, truthless, uncandid, untrue.
adj antonym sincere.

insincerity *n* bad faith, deceitfulness, dishonesty, disingenuousness, dissimulation, duplicity, falseness, faithlessness, hypocrisy.

insinuate *vb* hint, inculcate, infuse, ingratiate, instil, intimate, introduce, suggest.

insipid *adj* **1** dead, dull, flat, heavy, inanimate, jejune, lifeless, monotonous, pointless, prosaic, prosy, spiritless, stupid, tame, unentertaining, uninteresting. **2** mawkish, savourless, stale, tasteless, vapid, zestless. *adj antonyms* appetizing, piquant, punchy, tasty.

insipidity, insipidness *n* **1** dullness, heaviness, lifelessness, prosiness, stupidity, tameness. **2** flatness, mawkishness, staleness, tastlessness, unsavouriness, vapidness, zestlessness.

insist *vb* demand, maintain, urge.

insistence *n* importunity, solicitousness, urging, urgency.

insnare *see* **ensnare**.

insolence *n* **1** impertinence, impudence, malapertness, pertness, rudeness, sauciness. **2** contempt, contumacy, contumely, disrespect, frowardness, insubordination. *n antonyms* politeness, respect.

insolent *adj* **1** abusive, contemptuous, contumelious, disrespectful, domineering, insulting, offensive, overbearing, rude, supercilious. **2** cheeky, impertinent, impudent, malapert, pert, saucy. **3** contumacious, disobedient, froward, insubordinate. *adj antonyms* polite, respectful.

insoluble *adj* **1** indissoluble, indissolvable, irreducible. **2** inexplicable, insolvable. *adj antonym* explicable.

insolvable *adj* inexplicable.

insolvent *adj* bankrupt, broken, failed, ruined. *adj antonym* solvent.

insomnia *n* sleeplessness, wakefulness.

inspect *vb* **1** examine, investigate, look into, pry into, scrutinize. **2** oversee, superintend, supervise.

inspection *n* **1** examination, investigation, scrutiny. **2** oversight, superintendence, supervision.

inspector *n* **1** censor, critic, examiner, visitor. **2** boss, overseer, superintendent, supervisor.

inspiration *n* **1** breathing, inhalation. **2** afflatus, fire, inflatus. **3** elevation, exaltation. **4** enthusiasm.

inspire *vb* **1** breathe, inhale. **2** infuse, instil. **3** animate, cheer, enliven, inspirit. **4** elevate, exalt, stimulate. **5** fill, imbue, impart, inform, quicken.

inspirit *vb* animate, arouse, cheer, comfort, embolden, encourage, enhearten, enliven, fire, hearten, incite, invigorate, quicken, rouse, stimulate.

instable *see* **unstable**.

instability *n* changeableness, fickleness, inconstancy, insecurity, mutability.

install, instal *vb* **1** inaugurate, induct, introduce. **2** establish, place, set up.

installation *n* inauguration, induction, instalment, investiture.

instalment *n* earnest, payment, portion.

instance *vb* adduce, cite, mention, specify. • *n* **1** case, example, exemplification, illustration, occasion. **2** impulse, incitement, instigation, motive, prompting, request, solicitation.

instant *adj* **1** direct, immediate, instantaneous, prompt, quick. **2** current, present. **3** earnest, fast, imperative, importunate, pressing, urgent. **4** ready cooked. • *n* **1** flash, jiffy, moment, second, trice, twinkling. **2** hour, time.

instantaneous *adj* abrupt, immediate, instant, quick, sudden. *adj antonym* eventual.

instantaneously *adv* forthwith, immediately, presto, quickly, right away.

instauration *n* reconstitution, reconstruction, redintegration, re-establishment, rehabilitation, reinstatement, renewal, renovation, restoration.

instead *adv* in lieu, in place, rather.

instigate *vb* actuate, agitate, encourage, impel, incite, influence, initiate, move, persuade, prompt, provoke, rouse, set on, spur on, stimulate, stir up, tempt, urge.

instigation *n* encouragement, incitement, influence, instance, prompting, solicitation, urgency.

instil, instill *vb* **1** enforce, implant, impress, inculcate, ingraft. **2** impart, infuse, insinuate.

instillation *n* infusion, insinuation, introduction.

instinct *n* natural impulse.

instinctive *adj* **1** automatic, inherent, innate, intuitive, involuntary, natural, spontaneous. **2** impulsive, unreflecting. *adj antonyms* conscious, deliberate, voluntary.

institute[1] *n* **1** academy, college, foundation, guild, institution, school. **2** custom, doctrine, dogma, law, maxim, precedent, principle, rule, tenet.

institute[2] *vb* begin, commence, constitute, establish, found, initial, install, introduce, organize, originate, start.

vb antonyms abolish, cancel, discontinue.

institution *n* **1** enactment, establishment, foundation, institute, society. **2** investiture. **3** custom, law, practice.

instruct *vb* **1** discipline, educate, enlighten, exercise, guide, indoctrinate, inform, initiate, school, teach, train. **2** apprise, bid, command, direct, enjoin, order, prescribe to.

instruction *n* **1** breeding, discipline, education, indoctrination, information, nurture, schooling, teaching, training, tuition. **2** advice, counsel, precept. **3** command, direction, mandate, order.

instructor *n* educator, master, preceptor, schoolteacher, teacher, tutor.

instrument *n* **1** appliance, apparatus, contrivance, device, implement, musical instrument, tool, utensil. **2** agent, means, medium. **3** charter, deed, document, indenture, writing.

instrumental *adj* ancillary, assisting, auxiliary, conducive, contributory, helpful, helping, ministerial, ministrant, serviceable, subservient, subsidiary.

instrumentality *n* **1** agency, intermediary. **2** intervention, means, mediation.

insubordinate *adj* disobedient, disorderly, mutinous, refractory, riotous, seditious, turbulent, ungovernable, unruly.

adj antonyms docile, obedient.

insubordination *n* **1** disobedience, insurrection, mutiny, revolt, riotousness, sedition. **2** indiscipline, laxity.

insufferable *adj* **1** intolerable, unbearable, unendurable, insupportable. **2** abominable, detestable, disgusting, execrable, outrageous.

insufficiency *n* dearth, defectiveness, deficiency, lack, inadequacy, inadequateness, incapability, incompetence, paucity, shortage.

insufficient *adj* **1** deficient, inadequate, incommensurate, incompetent, scanty. **2** incapable, incompetent, unfitted, unqualified, unsuited, unsatisfactory.

adj antonyms excessive, sufficient.

insular *adj* **1** contracted, illiberal, limited, narrow, petty, prejudiced, restricted. **2** isolated, remote.

insulate *vb* detach, disconnect, disengage, disunite, isolate, separate.

insulation *n* disconnection, disengagement, isolation, separation.

insult *vb* abuse, affront, injure, offend, outrage, slander, slight. • *n* abuse, affront, cheek, contumely, indignity, insolence, offence, outrage, sauce, slight.

vb antonyms compliment, honour.

n antonyms compliment, honour.

insulting *adj* abusive, arrogant, contumelious, impertinent, impolite, insolent, rude, vituperative.

adj antonyms complimentary, respectful.

insuperable *adj* impassable, insurmountable.

insupportable *adj* insufferable, intolerable, unbearable, unendurable.

insuppressible *adj* irrepressible, uncontrollable.

insurance *n* assurance, security.

insure *vb* assure, guarantee, indemnify, secure, underwrite.

insurgent *adj* disobedient, insubordinate, mutinous, rebellious, revolting, revolutionary, seditious. • *n* mutineer, rebel, revolter, revolutionary.

insurmountable *adj* impassable, insuperable.

insurrection *n* insurgence, mutiny, rebellion, revolt, revolution, rising, sedition, uprising.

intact *adj* **1** unharmed, unhurt, unimpaired, uninjured, untouched. **2** complete, entire, integral, sound, unbroken, undiminished, whole.

adj antonyms broken, damaged, harmed.

intangible *adj* **1** dim, imperceptible, indefinite, insubstantial, intactile, shadowy, vague. **2** aerial, phantom, spiritous.

intangibility *n* imperceptibility, insubstantiality, intangibleness, shadowiness, vagueness.

integral *adj* complete, component, entire, integrant, total, whole.

integrity *n* **1** goodness, honesty, principle, probity, purity, rectitude, soundness, uprightness, virtue. **2** completeness, entireness, entirety, wholeness.

n antonyms dishonesty, incompleteness, unreliability.

integument *n* coat, covering, envelope, skin, tegument.

intellect *n* brains, cognitive faculty, intelligence, mind, rational faculty, reason, reasoning, faculty, sense, thought, understanding, wit.
n antonym dunce.

intellectual *adj* cerebral, intelligent, mental, scholarly, thoughtful. • *n* academic, highbrow, pundit, savant, scholar.
adj antonym low-brow.
n antonym low-brow.

intelligence *n* **1** acumen, apprehension, brightness, discernment, imagination, insight, penetration, quickness, sagacity, shrewdness, understanding, wits. **2** information, knowledge. **3** advice, instruction, news, notice, notification, tidings. **4** brains, intellect, mentality, sense, spirit.
n antonym foolishness.

intelligent *adj* acute, alert, apt, astute, brainy, bright, clear-headed, clear-sighted, clever, discerning, keen-eyed, keen-sighted, knowing, long-headed, quick, quick-sighted, sagacious, sensible, sharp-sighted, sharp-witted, shrewd, understanding.
adj antonyms foolish, unintelligent.

intelligibility *n* clarity, comprehensibility, intelligibleness, perspicuity.

intelligible *adj* clear, comprehensible, distinct, evident, lucid, manifest, obvious, patent, perspicuous, plain, transparent, understandable.

intemperate *adj* **1** drunken. **2** excessive, extravagant, extreme, immoderate, inordinate, unbridled, uncontrolled, unrestrained. **3** self-indulgent.

intend *vb* aim at, contemplate, design, determine, drive at, mean, meditate, propose, purpose, think of.

intendant *n* inspector, overseer, superintendent, supervisor.

intense *adj* **1** ardent, earnest, fervid, passionate, vehement. **2** close, intent, severe, strained, stretched, strict. **3** energetic, forcible, keen, potent, powerful, sharp, strong, vigorous, violent. **4** acute, deep, extreme, exquisite, grievous, poignant.
adj antonyms apathetic, mild.

intensify *vb* aggravate, concentrate, deepen, enhance, heighten, quicken, strengthen, whet.
vb antonyms damp down, die down.

intensity *n* **1** closeness, intenseness, severity, strictness. **2** excess, extremity, violence. **3** activity, energy, force, power, strength, vigour. **4** ardour, earnestness, vehemence.

intensive *adj* emphatic, intensifying.

intent *adj* **1** absorbed, attentive, close, eager, earnest, engrossed, occupied, preoccupied, zealous. **2** bent, determined, decided, resolved, set. • *n* aim, design, drift, end, import, intention, mark, meaning, object, plan, purport, purpose, purview, scope, view.
adj antonyms absent-minded, distracted.

intention *n* aim, design, drift, end, import, intent, mark, meaning, object, plan, purport, purpose, purview, scope, view.

intentional *adj* contemplated, deliberate, designed, intended, preconcerted, predetermined, premeditated, purposed, studied, voluntary, wilful.
adj antonym accidental.

inter *vb* bury, commit to the earth, entomb, inhume, inurn.

intercede *vb* **1** arbitrate, interpose, mediate. **2** entreat, plead, supplicate.

intercept *vb* cut off, interrupt, obstruct, seize.

intercession *n* **1** interposition, intervention, mediation. **2** entreaty, pleading, prayer, supplication.

intercessor *n* interceder, mediator.

interchange *vb* alternate, change, exchange, vary. • *n* alternation.

interchangeableness *n* interchangeability.

interchangeably *adv* alternately.

intercourse *n* **1** commerce, communication, communion, connection, converse, correspondence, dealings, fellowship, truck. **2** acquaintance, intimacy.

interdict *vb* debar, forbid, inhibit, prohibit, prescribe, proscribe, restrain from. • *n* ban, decree, interdiction, prohibition.

interest *vb* **1** affect, concern, touch. **2** absorb, attract, engage, enlist, excite, grip, hold, occupy. • *n* **1** advantage, benefit, good, profit, weal. **2** attention, concern, regard, sympathy. **3** part, participation, portion, share, stake. **4** discount, premium, profit.
vb antonym bore.
n antonyms boredom, irrelevance.

interested *adj* **1** attentive, concerned, involved, occupied. **2** biassed, partial, prejudiced. **3** selfish, self-seeking.
adj antonyms apathetic, indifferent, unaffected.

interesting *adj* attractive, engaging, entertaining, pleasing.
adj antonym boring.

interfere *vb* **1** intermeddle, interpose, meddle. **2** clash, collide, conflict.
vb antonyms assist, forbear.

interference *n* **1** intermeddling, interposition. **2** clashing, collision, interfering, opposition.
n antonyms assistance, forbearance.

interim *n* intermediate time, interval, meantime.

interior *adj* **1** inmost, inner, internal, inward. **2** inland, remote. **3** domestic, home. • *n* inner part, inland, inside.
adj antonyms exterior, external.

interjacent *adj* intermediate, interposed, intervening, parenthetical.

interject *vb* comment, inject, insert, interpose.

interjection *n* exclamation.

interlace *vb* bind, complicate, entwine, intersperse, intertwine, interweave, inweave, knit, mix, plait, twine, twist, unite.

interline *vb* insert, write between.

interlineal *adj* interlinear, interlined.

interlink, interlock *vb* connect, interchain, interrelate, join.

interlocution *n* colloquy, conference, dialogue, interchange.

interlocutor *n* respondent, speaker.

interloper *n* intruder, meddler.

intermeddle *vb* interfere, interpose, meddle.

intermediary *n* go-between, mediator.

intermediate *adj* interposed, intervening, mean, median, middle, transitional.
adj antonym extreme.

interment *n* burial, entombment, inhumation, sepulture.

interminable *adj* **1** boundless, endless, illimitable, immeasurable, infinite, limitless, unbounded, unlimited. **2** long-drawn-out, tedious, wearisome.
adj antonym limited.

intermingle *vb* blend, commingle, commix, intermix, mingle, mix.

intermission *n* cessation, interruption, interval, lull, pause, remission, respite, rest, stop, stoppage, suspension.

intermit *vb* **1** interrupt, intervene, stop, suspend. **2** discontinue, give over, leave off. **3** abate, subside.

intermittent *adj* broken, capricious, dis-continuous, fitful, flickering, intermitting, periodic, recurrent, remittent, spasmodic.
adj antonym continuous.

intermix *vb* blend, commingle, commix, intermingle, mingle, mix.

internal *adj* **1** inner, inside, interior, inward. **2** incorporeal, mental, spiritual. **3** deeper, emblematic, hidden, higher, metaphorical, secret, symbolical, under. **4** genuine, inherent, intrinsic, real, true. **5** domestic, home, inland, inside.
adj antonym external.

international *adj* cosmopolitan, universal.

internecine *adj* deadly, destructive, exterminating, exterminatory, interneciary, internecinal, internecive, mortal.

interpellate *vb* interrogate, question.

interpellation *n* **1** interruption. **2** intercession, interposition. **3** interrogation, questioning.

interplay *n* interaction.

interpolate *vb* **1** add, foist, insert, interpose. **2** (*math*) intercalate, introduce.

interpose *vb* **1** arbitrate, intercede, intervene, mediate. **2** interfere, intermeddle, interrupt, meddle, tamper. **3** insert, interject, put in, remark, sandwich, set between. **4** intrude, thrust in.
vb antonym forbear.

interposition *n* intercession, interpellation, intervention, mediation.

interpret *vb* **1** decipher, decode, define, elucidate, explain, expound, solve, unfold, unravel. **2** construe, render, translate.

interpretation *n* **1** meaning, sense, signification. **2** elucidation, explanation, explication, exposition. **3** construction, rendering, rendition, translation, version.

interpreter *n* expositor, expounder, translator.

interrogate *vb* ask, catechize, examine, inquire of, interpellate, question.

interrogation *n* **1** catechizing, examination, examining, interpellation, interrogating, questioning. **2** inquiry, query, question.

interrogative *adj* interrogatory, questioning.

interrupt *vb* **1** break, check, disturb, hinder, intercept, interfere with, obstruct, pretermit, stop. **2** break, cut, disconnect, disjoin, dissever, dissolve, disunite, divide, separate, sever, sunder. **3** break off, cease, discontinue, intermit, leave off, suspend.
vb antonym forbear.

interruption *n* **1** hindrance, impediment,

obstacle, obstruction, stop, stoppage. **2** cessation, discontinuance, intermission, pause, suspension. **3** break, breaking, disconnecting, disconnection, disjunction, dissolution, disunion, disuniting, division, separation, severing, sundering.

intersect *vb* cross, cut, decussate, divide, interrupt.

intersection *n* crossing.

interspace *n* interlude, interstice, interval.

intersperse *vb* **1** intermingle, scatter, sprinkle. **2** diversify, interlard, mix.

interstice *n* **1** interspace, interval, space. **2** chink, crevice.

interstitial *adj* intermediate, intervening.

intertwine *vb* interlace, intertwine, interweave, inweave, twine.

interval *n* **1** interim, interlude, interregnum, pause, period, recess, season, space, spell, term. **2** interstice, skip.

intervene *vb* **1** come between, interfere, mediate. **2** befall, happen, occur.

intervening *adj* **1** interjacent, intermediate. **2** interstitial.

intervention *n* **1** interference, interposition. **2** agency, mediation.

interview *n* **1** conference, consultation, parley. **2** meeting.

interweave *vb* **1** interlace, intertwine, inweave, weave. **2** intermingle, intermix, mingle, mix.

intestinal *adj* domestic, interior, internal.

intestines *npl* bowels, entrails, guts, insides, inwards, viscera.

intimacy *n* **1** close acquaintance, familiarity, fellowship, friendship. **2** closeness, nearness.

intimate[1] *adj* **1** close, near. **2** familiar, friendly. **3** bosom, chummy, close, dear, homelike, special. **4** confidential, personal, private, secret. **5** detailed, exhaustive, firsthand, immediate, penetrating, profound. **6** cosy, warm. • *n* chum, confidant, companion, crony, friend.
adj antonyms cold, distant, unfriendly.
n antonym stranger.

intimate[2] *vb* allude to, express, hint, impart, indicate, insinuate, signify, suggest, tell.

intimately *adv* closely, confidentially, familiarly, nearly, thoroughly.

intimation *n* allusion, hint, innuendo, insinuation, suggestion.

intimidate *vb* abash, affright, alarm, appal, browbeat, bully, cow, daunt, dishearten, dismay, frighten, overawe, scare, subdue, terrify, terrorize.
vb antonym persuade.

intimidation *n* fear, intimidating, terror, terrorism.

intolerable *adj* insufferable, insupportable, unbearable, unendurable.

intolerance *n* **1** bigotry, narrowness. **2** impatience, rejection.

intolerant *adj* **1** bigoted, narrow, proscriptive. **2** dictatorial, impatient, imperious, overbearing, supercilious.
adj antonym tolerant.

intonation *n* **1** cadence, modulation, tone. **2** musical recitation.

in toto *adv* entirely, wholly.

intoxicate *vb* fuddle, inebriate, muddle.

intoxicated *adj* boozy, drunk, drunken, fuddled, inebriated, maudlin, mellow, muddled, stewed, tight, tipsy.
adj antonym sober.

intoxication *n* **1** drunkenness, ebriety, inebriation, inebriety. **2** excitement, exhilaration, infatuation.

intractability *n* cantankerousness, contrariety, inflexibility, intractableness, obduracy, obstinacy, perverseness, perversity, pigheadedness, stubbornness, wilfulness.

intractable *adj* cantankerous, contrary, contumacious, cross-grained, dogged, headstrong, indocile, inflexible, mulish, obdurate, obstinate, perverse, pig-headed, refractory, restive, stubborn, tough, uncontrollable, ungovernable, unmanageable, unruly, unyielding, wilful.

intrench *see* **entrench**.

intrenchment *see* **entrenchment**.

intrepid *adj* bold, brave, chivalrous, courageous, daring, dauntless, doughty, fearless, gallant, heroic, undaunted, undismayed, valiant, valorous.
adj antonyms cowardly, timid.

intrepidity *n* boldness, bravery, courage, daring, dauntlessness, fearlessness, gallantry, heroism, intrepidness, prowess, spirit, valour.

intricacy *n* complexity, complication, difficulty, entanglement, intricateness, involution, obscurity, perplexity.

intricate *adj* complicated, difficult, entangled, involved, mazy, obscure, perplexed.
adj antonym simple.

intrigue *vb* **1** connive, conspire, machinate, plot, scheme. **2** beguile, bewitch, captivate, charm, fascinate. • *n* **1** artifice, cabal, conspiracy, deception, finesse, Machiavelianism, machination, manoeuvre, plot, ruse, scheme, stratagem, wile. **2** amour, liaison, love affair.

intriguing *adj* arch, artful, crafty, crooked, cunning, deceitful, designing, diplomatic, foxy, Machiavelian, insidious, politic, sly, sneaky, subtle, tortuous, tricky, wily.

intrinsic *adj* **1** essential, genuine, real, sterling, true. **2** inborn, inbred, ingrained, inherent, internal, inward, native, natural.
adj antonym extrinsic.

intrinsically *adv* **1** essentially, really, truly. **2** inherently, naturally.

introduce *vb* **1** bring in, conduct, import, induct, inject, insert, lead in, usher in. **2** present. **3** begin, broach, commence, inaugurate, initiate, institute, start.
vb antonym take away.

introduction *n* **1** preface, prelude. **2** introducing, ushering in. **3** presentation.
n antonym withdrawal.

introductory *adj* precursory, preliminary.

introspection *n* introversion, self-contemplation.

intrude *vb* encroach, impose, infringe, interfere, interlope, obtrude, trespass.
vb antonyms stand back, withdraw.

intruder *n* interloper, intermeddler, meddler, stranger.

intrusion *n* encroachment, infringement, intruding, obtrusion.

intrusive *adj* obtrusive, trespassing.

intuition *n* **1** apprehension, cognition, insight, instinct. **2** clairvoyance, divination, presentiment.
n antonym reasoning.

intuitive *adj* **1** instinctive, intuitional, natural. **2** clear, distinct, full, immediate.

intumesce *vb* bubble up, dilate, expand, swell.

intumescence *n* inturgescence, swelling, tumefaction, turgescence.

inundate *vb* deluge, drown, flood, glut, overflow, overwhelm, submerge.

inundation *n* cataclysm, deluge, flood, glut, overflow, superfluity.

inure *vb* accustom, discipline, familiarize, habituate, harden, toughen, train, use.

inutile *adj* bootless, ineffectual, inoperative, unavailing, unprofitable, useless.

invade *vb* **1** encroach upon, infringe, violate. **2** attack, enter in, march into.
vb antonym withdraw.

invalid[1] *adj* **1** baseless, fallacious, false, inoperative, nugatory, unfounded, unsound, untrue, worthless. **2** (*law*) null, void.
adj antonym healthy.

invalid[2] *adj* ailing, bedridden, feeble, frail, ill, infirm, sick, sickly, valetudinary, weak, weakly. • *n* convalescent, patient, valetudinarian.
adj antonym valid.

invalidate *vb* abrogate, annul, cancel, nullify, overthrow, quash, repeal, reverse, undo, unmake, vitiate.
vb antonym validate.

invalidity *n* baselessness, fallaciousness, fallacy, falsity, unsoundness.

invaluable *adj* inestimable, priceless.
adj antonym worthless.

invariable *adj* **1** changeless, constant, unchanging, uniform, unvarying. **2** changeless, immutable, unalterable, unchangeable.
adj antonym variable.

invariableness *n* **1** changelessness, constancy, uniformity, unvaryingness. **2** changelessness, immutability, unchangeableness, invariability.

invasion *n* **1** encroachment, incursion, infringement, inroad. **2** aggression, assault, attack, foray, raid.
n antonym withdrawal.

invective *n* abuse, censure, contumely, denunciation, diatribe, railing, reproach, sarcasm, satire, vituperation.
n antonym praise.

inveigh *vb* blame, censure, condemn, declaim against, denounce, exclaim against, rail at, reproach, vituperate.

inveigle *vb* **1** contrive, devise. **2** concoct, conceive, create, design, excogitate, frame, imagine, originate. **3** coin, fabricate, forge, spin.

invent *vb* concoct, contrive, design, devise, discover, fabricate, find out, frame, originate.

invention *n* **1** creation, discovery, ingenuity, inventing, origination. **2** contrivance, design, device. **3** coinage, fabrication, fiction, forgery.
n antonym truth.

inventive *adj* creative, fertile, ingenious.
adj antonym uninventive.

inventor *n* author, contriver, creator, originator.

inventory *n* account, catalogue, list, record, roll, register, schedule.

inverse *adj* indirect, inverted, opposite, re-versed.

inversion *n* inverting, reversing, transposal, transposition.

invert *vb* **1** capsize, overturn. **2** reverse, transpose.
vb antonym right.

invertebrate *adj* **1** invertebral. **2** spineless.

invest *vb* **1** put money into. **2** confer, endow, endue. **3** (*mil*) beset, besiege, enclose, sur-round. **4** array, clothe, dress.
vb antonym divest.

investigate *vb* canvass, consider, dissect, ex-amine, explore, follow up, inquire into, look into, overhaul, probe, question, research, scrutinize, search into, search out, sift, study.

investigation *n* examination, exploration, inquiry, inquisition, overhauling, research, scrutiny, search, sifting, study.

investiture *n* habilitation, induction, instal-lation, ordination.

investment *n* **1** money invested. **2** endow-ment. **3** (*mil*) siege. **4** clothes, dress, gar-ments, habiliments, robe, vestment.

inveteracy *n* inveterateness, obstinacy.

inveterate *adj* accustomed, besetting, chronic, confirmed, deep-seated, habitual, habituated, hardened, ingrained, long-established, obstinate.

invidious *adj* disagreeable, envious, hateful, odious, offensive, unfair.
adj antonym desirable.

invigorate *vb* animate, brace, energize, for-tify, harden, nerve, quicken, refresh, stim-ulate, strengthen, vivify.

invincible *adj* impregnable, indomitable, in-eradicable, insuperable, insurmountable, irrepressible, unconquerable, unsubdu-able, unyielding.
adj antonym beatable.

inviolable *adj* hallowed, holy, inviolate, sac-ramental, sacred, sacrosanct, stainless.

inviolate *adj* **1** unbroken, unviolated. **2** pure, stainless, unblemished, undefiled, unhurt, uninjured, unpolluted, unstained. **3** invio-lable, sacred.

invisibility *n* imperceptibility, indistinct-ness, invisibleness, obscurity.

invisible *adj* impalpable, imperceptible, in-distinguishable, intangible, unapparent, undiscernable, unseen.
adj antonym visible.

invitation *n* bidding, call, challenge, solicita-tion, summons.

invite *vb* **1** ask, bid, call, challenge, request, solicit, summon. **2** allure, attract, draw on, entice, lead, persuade, prevail upon.
vb antonyms force, order.

inviting *adj* **1** alluring, attractive, bewitch-ing, captivating, engaging, fascinating, pleasing, winning. **2** prepossessing, prom-ising.
adj antonym uninviting.

invocation *n* conjuration, orison, petition, prayer, summoning, supplication.

invoice *vb* bill, list. • *n* bill, inventory, list, schedule.

invoke *vb* adjure, appeal to, beseech, beg, call upon, conjure, entreat, implore, im-portune, pray, pray to, solicit, summon, supplicate.

involuntary *adj* **1** automatic, blind, instinc-tive, mechanical, reflex, spontaneous, unintentional. **2** compulsory, reluctant, unwilling.
adj antonym voluntary.

involve *vb* **1** comprise, contain, embrace, imply, include, lead to. **2** complicate, com-promise, embarrass, entangle, implicate, incriminate, inculpate. **3** cover, envelop, enwrap, surround, wrap. **4** blend, conjoin, connect, join, mingle. **5** entwine, interlace, intertwine, inweave, inweave.

invulnerability *n* invincibility, invulnerable-ness.

invulnerable *adj* incontrovertible, invinci-ble, unassailable, irrefragable.
adj antonym vulnerable.

inward[1] *adj* **1** incoming, inner, interior, in-ternal. **2** essential, hidden, mental, spir-itual. **3** private, secret.

inward[2], **inwards** *adv* inwardly, towards the inside, within.

inweave *vb* entwine, interlace, intertwine, interweave, weave together.

iota *n* atom, bit, glimmer, grain, jot, mite, particle, scintilla, scrap, shadow, spark, tit-tle, trace, whit.

irascibility *n* hastiness, hot-headedness, impatience, irascibleness, irritability, pee-vishness, petulance, quickness, spleen, testiness, touchiness.

irascible *adj* choleric, cranky, hasty, hot, hot-headed, impatient, irritable, nettle-some, peevish, peppery, pettish, petulant, quick, splenetic, snappish, testy, touchy, waspish.

irate *adj* angry, incensed, ireful, irritated, piqued.
adj antonym calm.

ire *n* anger, choler, exasperation, fury, indignation, passion, rage, resentment, wrath.
n antonym calmness.

ireful *adj* angry, furious, incensed, irate, raging, passionate.

iridescent *adj* opalescent, prismatic, rainbow-like.

iris *n* **1** rainbow. **2** (*bot*) fleur-de-lis, flower-de-luce. **3** diaphragm of the eye.

irksome *adj* annoying, burdensome, humdrum, monotonous, tedious, tiresome, wearisome, weary, wearying.
adj antonym pleasing.

iron *adj* ferric, ferrous.

ironic, ironical *adj* mocking, sarcastic.

irons *npl* chains, fetters, gyves, hampers, manacles, shackles.

irony *n* mockery, raillery, ridicule, sarcasm, satire.

irradiate *vb* brighten, illume, illuminate, illumine, light up, shine upon.

irrational *adj* **1** absurd, extravagant, foolish, injudicious, preposterous, ridiculous, silly, unwise. **2** unreasonable, unreasoning, unthinking. **3** brute, brutish. **4** aberrant, alienated, brainless, crazy, demented, fantastic, idiotic, imbecilic, insane, lunatic.
adj antonym rational.

irrationality *n* **1** absurdity, folly, foolishness, unreasonableness. **2** brutishness.

irreclaimable *adj* **1** hopeless, incurable, irrecoverable, irreparable, irretrievable, irreversible. **2** abandoned, graceless, hardened, impenitent, incorrigible, lost, obdurate, profligate, recreant, reprobate, shameless, unrepentant.

irreconcilable *adj* **1** implacable, inexorable, inexpiable, unappeasable. **2** incompatible, incongruous, inconsistent.
adj antonym reconcilable.

irrecoverable *adj* hopeless, incurable, irremediable, irreparable, irretrievable.

irrefragable *adj* impregnable, incontestable, incontrovertible, indisputable, invincible, irrefutable, irresistible, unanswerable, unassailable, undeniable.

irrefutable *adj* impregnable, incontestable, incontrovertible, indisputable, invincible, irrefragable, irresistible, unanswerable, unassailable, undeniable.

irregular *adj* **1** aberrant, abnormal, anomalistic, anomalous, crooked, devious, eccentric, erratic, exceptional, heteromorphous, raged, tortuous, unconformable, unusual. **2** capricious, changeable, desultory, fitful, spasmodic, uncertain, unpunctual, unsettled, variable. **3** disordered, disorderly, improper, uncanonical, unparliamentary, unsystematic. **4** asymmetric, uneven, unsymmetrical. **5** disorderly, dissolute, immoral, loose, wild. • *n* casual, freelance, hireling, mercenary.
adj antonyms conventional, regular, smooth.

irregularity *n* **1** aberration, abnormality, anomaly, anomalousness, singularity. **2** capriciousness, changeableness, uncertainty, variableness. **3** asymmetry. **4** disorderliness, dissoluteness, immorality, laxity, looseness, wildness.
n antonyms conventionality, regularity, smoothness.

irrelevance, irrelevancy *n* impertinency, inapplicability, nonpertinency.

irrelevant *adj* extraneous, foreign, illogical, impertinent, inapplicable, inapposite, inappropriate, inconsequent, unessential, unrelated.
adj antonym relevant.

irreligion *n* atheism, godlessness, impiety, ungodliness.

irreligious *adj* **1** godless, ungodly, undevout. **2** blasphemous, disrespectful, impious, irreverent, profane, ribald, wicked.

irremediable *adj* hopeless, incurable, immedicable, irrecoverable, irreparable, remediless.

irremissible *adj* binding, inexpiable, obligatory, unatonable, unpardonable.

irreparable *adj* irrecoverable, irremediable, irretrievable, remediless.

irreprehensible *adj* blameless, faultless, inculpable, innocent, irreproachable, irreprovable, unblamable.

irrepressible *adj* insuppressible, uncontrollable, unquenchable, unsmotherable.
adj antonyms depressed, depressive, despondent, resistible.

irreproachable *adj* blameless, faultless, inculpable, innocent, irreprehensible, irreprovable, unblamable.

irresistible *adj* irrefragable, irrepressible, overpowering, overwhelming, resistless.
adj antonyms avoidable, resistible.

irresolute *adj* changeable, faltering, fickle,

hesitant, hesitating, inconstant, mutable, spineless, uncertain, undecided, undetermined, unsettled, unstable, unsteady, vacillating, wavering.

adj antonym resolute.

irrespective *adj* independent, regardless.

irresponsible *adj* **1** unaccountable. **2** untrustworthy.

adj antonym responsible.

irretrievable *adj* incurable, irrecoverable, irremediable, irreparable, remediless.

irreverence *n* **1** blasphemy, impiety, profaneness, profanity. **2** disesteem, disrespect.

irreverent *adj* **1** blasphemous, impious, irreligious, profane. **2** disrespectful, slighting.

adj antonym respectful, reverent.

irreversible *adj* **1** irrepealable, irrevocable, unalterable, unchangeable. **2** changeless, immutable, invariable.

irrevocable *adj* irrepealable, irreversible, unalterable, unchangeable.

adj antonyms alterable, flexible, mutable, reversible.

irrigate *vb* moisten, wash, water, wet.

irrigation *n* watering.

irritability *n* excitability, fretfulness, irascibility, peevishness, petulance, snappishness, susceptibility, testiness.

irritable *adj* captious, choleric, excitable, fiery, fretful, hasty, hot, irascible, passionate, peppery, peevish, pettish, petulant, snappish, splenetic, susceptible, testy, touchy, waspish.

adj antonyms cheerful, complacent.

irritate *vb* **1** anger, annoy, chafe, enrage, exacerbate, exasperate, fret, incense, jar, nag, nettle, offend, provoke, rasp, rile, ruffle, vex. **2** gall, tease. **3** (*med*) excite, inflame, stimulate.

vb antonyms gratify, mollify, placate, please.

irritation *n* **1** irritating. **2** anger, exacerbation, exasperation, excitement, indignation, ire, passion, provocation, resentment, wrath. **3** (*med*) excitation, inflammation, stimulation. **4** burn, itch.

n antonyms pleasure, satisfaction.

irruption *n* **1** breaking in, bursting in. **2** foray, incursion, inroad, invasion, raid.

island *n* atoll, isle, islet, reef.

isochronal *adj* isochronous, uniform.

isolate *vb* detach, dissociate, insulate, quarantine, segregate, separate, set apart.

vb antonyms assimilate, incorporate.

isolated *adj* detached, separate, single, solitary.

adj antonyms populous, typical.

isolation *n* **1** detachment, disconnection, insulation, quarantine, segregation, separation. **2** loneliness, solitariness, solitude.

issue *vb* **1** come out, flow out, flow forth, gush, run, rush out, spout, spring, spurt, well. **2** arise, come, emanate, ensue, flow, follow, originate, proceed, spring. **3** end, eventuate, result, terminate. **4** appear, come out, deliver, depart, debouch, discharge, emerge, emit, put forth, send out. **5** distribute, give out. **6** publish, utter. • *n* **1** conclusion, consequence, consummation, denouement, end, effect, event, finale, outcome, result, termination, upshot. **2** antagonism, contest, controversy. **3** debouchment, delivering, delivery, discharge, emergence, emigration, emission, issuance. **4** flux, outflow, outpouring, stream. **5** copy, edition, number. **6** egress, exit, outlet, passage out, vent, way out. **7** escape, sally, sortie. **8** children, offspring, posterity, progeny.

itch *vb* tingle. • *n* **1** itching. **2** burning, coveting, importunate craving, teasing desire, uneasy hankering.

itching *n* **1** itch. **2** craving, longing, importunate craving, desire, appetite, hankering.

item *adv* also, in like manner. • *n* article, detail, entry, particular, point.

iterate *vb* reiterate, repeat.

itinerant *adj* nomadic, peripatetic, roaming, roving, travelling, unsettled, wandering.

adj antonyms settled, stationary.

itinerary *n* **1** guide, guidebook. **2** circuit, route.

J

jabber *vb* chatter, gabble, prate, prattle.

jacket *n* **1** casing, cover, sheath. **2** anorak, blazer coat, doublet, jerkin.

jaded *adj* dull, exhausted, fatigued, satiated, tired, weary.
adj antonyms fresh, refreshed.

jagged *adj* cleft, divided, indented, notched, serrated, ragged, uneven.
adj antonyms smooth.

jail, gaol *n* bridewell, (*sl*) clink, dungeon, lockup, (*sl*) nick, penitentiary, prison.

jam *vb* block, crowd, crush, press. • *n* block, crowd, crush, mass, pack, press.

jangle *vb* bicker, chatter, dispute, gossip, jar, quarrel, spar, spat, squabble, tiff, wrangle. • *n* clang, clangour, clash, din, dissonance.
n antonyms euphony, harmony.

jar¹ *vb* **1** clash, grate, interfere, shake. **2** bicker, contend, jangle, quarrel, spar, spat, squabble, tiff, wrangle. **3** agitate, jolt, jounce, shake. • *n* **1** clash, conflict, disaccord, discord, jangle, dissonance. **2** agitation, jolt, jostle, shake, shaking, shock, start.

jar² *n* can, crock, cruse, ewer, flagon.

jarring *adj* conflicting, discordant, inconsistent, inconsonant, wrangling.

jargon *n* **1** gabble, gibberish, nonsense, rigmarole. **2** argot, cant, lingo, slang. **3** chaos, confusion, disarray, disorder, jumble.

jaundiced *adj* biased, envious, prejudiced.
adj antonyms fresh, naïve, optimistic.

jaunt *n* excursion, ramble, tour, trip.

jaunty *adj* airy, cheery, garish, gay, fine, fluttering, showy, sprightly, unconcerned.
adj antonyms anxious, depressed, dowdy, seedy.

jealous *adj* **1** distrustful, envious, suspicious. **2** anxious, apprehensive, intolerant, solicitous, zealous.

jealousy *n* envy, suspicion, watchfulness.

jeer *vb* deride, despise, flout, gibe, jape, jest, mock, scoff, sneer, spurn, rail, ridicule, taunt. • *n* abuse, derision, mockery, sneer, ridicule, taunt.

jeopardize *vb* endanger, hazard, imperil, risk, venture.
vb antonyms protect, safeguard.

jeopardy *n* danger, hazard, peril, risk, venture.

jerk *vb, n* flip, hitch, pluck, tweak, twitch, yank.

jest *vb* banter, joke, quiz. • *n* fun, joke, pleasantry, raillery, sport.

jester *n* **1** humorist, joker, wag. **2** buffoon, clown, droll, fool, harlequin, punch.

jibe *see* **gibe**.

jiffy *n* instant, moment, second, twinkling, trice.

jilt *vb* break with, deceive, disappoint, discard. • *n* coquette, flirt, light-o'-love.
vb antonym cleave to.

jingle *vb* chink, clink, jangle, rattle, tinkle. • *n* **1** chink, clink, jangle, rattle, tinkle. **2** chorus, ditty, melody, song.

jocose *adj* comical, droll, facetious, funny, humorous, jesting, jocular, merry, sportive, waggish, witty.

jocund *adj* airy, blithe, cheerful, debonair, frolicsome, jolly, joyful, joyous, lively, merry, playful.

jog *vb* **1** jostle, notify, nudge, push, remind, warn. **2** canter, run, trot. • *n* push, reminder.

join *vb* **1** add, annex, append, attach. **2** cement, combine, conjoin, connect, couple, dovetail, link, unite, yoke. **3** amalgamate, assemble, associate, confederate, consolidate.
vb antonyms leave, separate.

joint *vb* fit, join, unite. • *adj* combined, concerted, concurrent, conjoint. • *n* connection, junction, juncture, hinge, splice.

joke *vb* banter, jest, frolic, rally. • *n* crank, jest, quip, quirk, witticism.

jolly *adj* **1** airy, blithe, cheerful, frolicsome, gamesome, facetious, funny, gay, jovial, joyous, merry, mirthful, jocular, jocund, playful, sportive, sprightly, waggish. **2** bouncing, chubby, lusty, plump, portly, stout.
adj antonym sad.

jolt *vb* jar, shake, shock. • *n* jar, jolting, jounce, shaking.

jostle *vb* collide, elbow, hustle, joggle, shake, shoulder, shove.

jot *n* ace, atom, bit, corpuscle, iota, grain, mite, particle, scrap, whit.

journal *n* **1** daybook, diary, log. **2** gazette, magazine, newspapers, periodical.

journey *vb* **1** ramble, roam, rove, travel. **2** fare, go, proceed. • *n* excursion, expedition, jaunt, passage, pilgrimage, tour, travel, trip, voyage.

jovial *adj* airy, convivial, festive, jolly, joyous, merry, mirthful.
adj antonyms morose, sad, saturnine.

joy *n* **1** beatification, beatitude, delight, ecstasy, exultation, gladness, glee, mirth, pleasure, rapture, ravishment, transport. **2** bliss, felicity, happiness.
n antonyms mourning, sorrow.

joyful *adj* blithe, blithesome, buoyant, delighted, elate, elated, exultant, glad, happy, jocund, jolly, joyous, merry, rejoicing.
adj antonyms mournful, sorrowful.

jubilant *adj* exultant, exulting, rejoicing, triumphant.
adj antonyms defeated, depressed.

judge *vb* **1** conclude, decide, decree, determine, pronounce. **2** adjudicate, arbitrate, condemn, doom, sentence, try, umpire. **3** account, apprehend, believe, consider, deem, esteem, guess, hold, imagine, measure, reckon, regard, suppose, think. **4** appreciate, estimate. • *n* adjudicator, arbiter, arbitrator, bencher, justice, magistrate, moderator, referee, umpire, connoisseur, critic.

judgment, judgement *n* **1** brains, ballast, circumspection, depth, discernment, discretion, discrimination, intelligence, judiciousness, penetration, prudence, sagacity, sense, sensibility, taste, understanding, wisdom, wit. **2** conclusion, consideration, decision, determination, estimation, notion, opinion, thought. **3** adjudication, arbitration, award, censure, condemnation, decree, doom, sentence.

judicious *adj* cautious, considerate, cool, critical, discriminating, discreet, enlightened, provident, politic, prudent, rational, reasonable, sagacious, sensible, sober, solid, sound, staid, wise.
adj antonym injudicious.

jug *n* cruse, ewer, flagon, pitcher, vessel.

juicy *adj* **1** lush, moist, sappy, succulent, watery. **2** entertaining, exciting, interesting, lively, racy, spicy.

jumble *vb* confound, confuse, disarrange, disorder, mix, muddle. • *n* confusion, disarrangement, disorder, medley, mess, mixture, muddle.
vb antonym order.

jump *vb* bound, caper, clear, hop, leap, skip, spring, vault. • *n* **1** bound, caper, hop, leak, skip, spring, vault. **2** fence, hurdle, obstacle. **3** break, gap, interruption, space. **4** advance, boost, increase, rise. **5** jar, jolt, shock, start, twitch.

junction *n* **1** combination, connection, coupling, hook-up, joining, linking, seam, union. **2** conjunction, joint, juncture.

junta *n* cabal, clique, combination, confederacy, coterie, faction, gang, league, party, set.

just *adj* **1** equitable, lawful, legitimate, reasonable, right, rightful. **2** candid, even-handed, fair, fair-minded, impartial. **3** blameless, conscientious, good, honest, honourable, pure, square, straightforward, virtuous. **4** accurate, correct, exact, normal, proper, regular, true. **5** condign, deserved, due, merited, suitable.
adj antonym unjust.

justice *n* **1** accuracy, equitableness, equity, fairness, honesty, impartiality, justness, right. **2** judge, justiciary.

justifiable *adj* defensible, fit, proper, right, vindicable, warrantable.
adj antonyms culpable, illicit, unjustifiable.

justification *n* defence, exculpation, excuse, exoneration, reason, vindication, warrant.

justify *vb* approve, defend, exculpate, excuse, exonerate, maintain, vindicate, support, warrant.

justness *n* accuracy, correctness, fitness, justice, precision, propriety.

juvenile *adj* childish, immature, puerile, young, youthful. • *n* boy, child, girl, youth.
adj antonym mature.
n antonym adult.

juxtaposition *n* adjacency, contiguity, contact, proximity.

K

keen¹ *adj* **1** ardent, eager, earnest, fervid, intense, vehement, vivid. **2** acute, sharp. **3** cutting. **4** acrimonious, biting, bitter, caustic, poignant, pungent, sarcastic, severe. **5** astute, discerning, intelligent, quick, sagacious, sharp-sighted, shrewd.
adj antonyms apathetic, blunt, dull.

keen² *vb* bemoan, bewail, deplore, grieve, lament, mourn, sorrow, weep. • *n* coronach, dirge, elegy, lament, lamentation, monody, plaint, requiem, threnody.

keenness *n* **1** ardour, eagerness, fervour, vehemence, zest. **2** acuteness, sharpness. **3** rigour, severity, sternness. **4** acrimony, asperity, bitterness, causticity, causticness, pungency. **5** astuteness, sagacity, shrewdness.

keep *vb* **1** detain, hold, retain. **2** continue, preserve. **3** confine, detain, reserve, restrain, withhold. **4** attend, guard, preserve, protect. **5** adhere to, fulfil. **6** celebrate, commemorate, honour, observe, perform, solemnize. **7** maintain, support, sustain. **8** husband, save, store. **9** abide, dwell, lodge, stay, remain. **10** endure, last. • *n* **1** board, maintenance, subsistence, support. **2** donjon, dungeon, stronghold, tower.

keeper *n* caretaker, conservator, curator, custodian, defender, gaoler, governor, guardian, jailer, superintendent, warden, warder, watchman.

keeping *n* **1** care, charge, custody, guard, possession. **2** feed, maintenance, support. **3** agreement, conformity, congruity, consistency, harmony.

keepsake *n* memento, souvenir, token.

ken *n* cognizance, sight, view.

key *adj* basic, crucial, essential, important, major, principal. • *n* **1** lock-opener, opener. **2** clue, elucidation, explanation, guide, solution, translation. **3** (*mus*) keynote, tonic. **2** clamp, lever, wedge.

kick *vb* **1** boot, punt. **2** oppose, rebel, resist, spurn. • *n* **1** force, intensity, power, punch, vitality. **2** excitement, pleasure, thrill.

kidnap *vb* abduct, capture, carry off, remove, steal away.

kill *vb* assassinate, butcher, dispatch, destroy, massacre, murder, slaughter, slay.

kin *adj* akin, allied, cognate, kindred, related. • *n* **1** affinity, consanguinity, relationship. **2** connections, family, kindred, kinsfolk, relations, relatives, siblings.

kind¹ *adj* accommodating, amiable, beneficent, benevolent, benign, bland, bounteous, brotherly, charitable, clement, compassionate, complaisant, gentle, good, good-natured, forbearing, friendly, generous, gracious, humane, indulgent, lenient, mild, obliging, sympathetic, tender, tender-hearted.
adj antonyms cruel, inconsiderate, unhelpful.

kind² *n* **1** breed, class, family, genus, race, set, species, type. **2** brand, character, colour, denomination, description, form, make, manner, nature, persuasion, sort, stamp, strain, style.

kindle *vb* **1** fire, ignite, inflame, light. **2** animate, awaken, bestir, exasperate, excite, foment, incite, provoke, rouse, stimulate, stir, thrill, warm.

kindliness *n* **1** amiability, benevolence, benignity, charity, compassion, friendliness, humanity, kindness, sympathy. **2** gentleness, mildness, softness.

kindly *adj* **1** appropriate, congenial, kindred, natural, proper. **2** benevolent, considerate, friendly, gracious, humane, sympathetic, well-disposed. • *adv* agreeably, graciously, humanely, politely, thoughtfully.
adv antonyms cruel, inconsiderate, uncharitable, unpleasant.

kindness *n* **1** benefaction, charity, favour. **2** amiability, beneficence, benevolence, benignity, clemency, generosity, goodness, grace, humanity, kindliness, mildness, philanthropy, sympathy, tenderness.

kindred *adj* akin, allied, congenial, connected, related, sympathetic. • *n* **1** affinity, consanguinity, flesh, relationship. **2** folks, kin, kinsfolk, kinsmen, relations, relatives.

king *n* majesty, monarch, sovereign.

kingdom *n* **1** dominion, empire, monarchy, rule, sovereignty, supremacy. **2** region, tract. **3** division, department, domain, province, realm.

kingly *adj* **1** imperial, kinglike, monarchical, regal, royal, sovereign. **2** august, glorious, grand, imperial, imposing, magnificent, majestic, noble, splendid.

kink *n* **1** cramp, crick, curl, entanglement, knot, loop, twist. **2** crochet, whim, wrinkle.

kinsfolk *n* kin, kindred, kinsmen, relations, relatives.

kit *n* equipment, implements, outfit, set, working.

knack *n* ability, address, adroitness, aptitude, aptness, dexterity, dextrousness, expertness, facility, quickness, readiness, skill.

knave *n* caitiff, cheat, miscreant, rascal, rogue, scamp, scapegrace, scoundrel, sharper, swindler, trickster, villain.

knavery *n* criminality, dishonesty, fraud, knavishness, rascality, scoundrelism, trickery, villainy.

knavish *adj* dishonest, fraudulent, rascally, scoundrelly, unprincipled, roguish, trickish, tricky, villainous.

knell *vb* announce, peal, ring, toll. • *n* chime, peal, ring, toll.

knife *vb* cut, slash, stab. • *n* blade, jackknife, lance.

knit *vb* connect, interlace, join, unite, weave.

knob *n* boss, bunch, hunch, lump, protuberance, stud.

knock *vb* **1** clap, cuff, hit, rap, rattle, slap, strike, thump. **2** beat, blow, box. • *n* **1** blow, slap, smack, thump. **2** blame, criticism, rejection, setback.

knoll *n* hill, hillock, mound.

knot *vb* complicate, entangle, gnarl, kink, tie, weave. • *n* **1** complication, entanglement. **2** connection, tie. **3** joint, node, knag. **4** bunch, rosette, tuft. **5** band, cluster, clique, crew, gang, group, pack, set, squad.

knotty *adj* **1** gnarled, hard, knaggy, knurled, knotted, rough, rugged. **2** complex, difficult, harassing, intricate, involved, perplexing, troublesome.

know *vb* **1** apprehend, comprehend, cognize, discern, perceive, recognize, see, understand. **2** discriminate, distinguish.

knowing *adj* **1** accomplished, competent, experienced, intelligent, proficient, qualified, skilful, well-informed. **2** aware, conscious, percipient, sensible, thinking. **3** cunning, expressive, significant.
adj antonyms ignorant, obtuse.

knowingly *adv* consciously, intentionally, purposely, wittingly.

knowledge *n* **1** apprehension, command, comprehension, discernment, judgment, perception, understanding, wit. **2** acquaintance, acquirement, attainments, enlightenment, erudition, information, learning, lore, mastery, scholarship, science. **3** cognition, cognizance, consciousness, ken, notice, prescience, recognition.
n antonym ignorance.

knowledgeable *adj* **1** aware, conscious, experienced, well-informed. **2** educated, intelligent, learned, scholarly.
adj antonym ignorant.

knuckle *vb* cringe, crouch, stoop, submit, yield

L

laborious *adj* 1 assiduous, diligent, hardworking, indefatigable, industrious, painstaking, sedulous, toiling. 2 arduous, difficult, fatiguing, hard, Herculean, irksome, onerous, tiresome, toilsome, wearisome.
adj antonyms easy, effortless, relaxing, simple.

labour *vb* 1 drudge, endeavour, exert, strive, toil, travail, work. • *n* drudgery, effort, exertion, industry, pains, toil, work. 2 childbirth, delivery, parturition.

labyrinth *n* entanglement, intricacy, maze, perplexity, windings.

labyrinthine *adj* confused, convoluted, intricate, involved, labyrinthian, labyrinthic, perplexing, winding.

lace *vb* attach, bind, fasten, intertwine, tie, twine. • *n* filigree, lattice, mesh, net, netting, network, openwork, web.

lacerate *vb* 1 claw, cut, lancinate, mangle, rend, rip, sever, slash, tear, wound. 2 afflict, harrow, rend, torture, wound.

lack *vb* need, want. • *n* dearth, default, defectiveness, deficiency, deficit, destitution, insufficiency, need, scantiness, scarcity, shortcoming, shortness, want.
n antonyms abundance, profusion.

lackadaisical *adj* languishing, sentimental, pensive.

laconic *adj* brief, compact, concise, pithy, sententious, short, succinct, terse.
adj antonyms garrulous, verbose, wordy.

lad *n* boy, schoolboy, youngster, youth.

lady *n* 1 woman, female, girl. 1 aristocrat, baroness, countess, dame, duchess, noblewoman.

ladylike *adj* courtly, genteel, refined, well-bred.

lag *vb* dawdle, delay, idle, linger, loiter, saunter, tarry.
vb antonym lead.

lair *n* burrow, couch, den, form, resting place.

lame *vb* cripple, disable, hobble. • *adj* 1 crippled, defective, disabled, halt, hobbling, limping. 2 feeble, insufficient, poor, unsatisfactory, weak.

lament *vb* 1 complain, grieve, keen, moan, mourn, sorrow, wail, weep. 2 bemoan, bewail, deplore, regret. • *n* 1 complaint, lamentation, moan, moaning, plaint, wailing. 2 coronach, dirge, elegy, keen, monody, requiem, threnody.
vb antonyms celebrate, rejoice.

lamentable *adj* 1 deplorable, doleful, grievous, lamented, melancholy, woeful. 2 contemptible, miserable, pitiful, poor, wretched.

lamentation *n* dirge, grief, lament, moan, moaning, mourning, plaint, ululation, sorrow, wailing.

lampoon *vb* calumniate, defame, lash, libel, parody, ridicule, satirize, slander. • *n* calumny, defamation, libel, parody, pasquinade, parody, satire, slander.

land *vb* arrive, debark, disembark. • *n* 1 earth, ground, soil. 2 country, district, province, region, reservation, territory, tract, weald.

landlord *n* 1 owner, proprietor. 2 host, hotelier, innkeeper.
n antonym tenant.

landscape *n* prospect, scene, view.

language *n* 1 dialect, speech, tongue, vernacular. 2 conversation. 3 expression, idiom, jargon, parlance, phraseology, slang, style, terminology. 4 utterance, voice.

languid *adj* 1 drooping, exhausted, faint, feeble, flagging, languishing, pining, weak. 2 dull, heartless, heavy, inactive, listless, lukewarm, slow, sluggish, spiritless, torpid.
adj antonyms alert, lively, vivacious.

languish *vb* decline, droop, fade, fail, faint, pine, sicken, sink, wither.
vb antonym flourish.

languor *n* 1 debility, faintness, feebleness, languidness, languishment, weakness. 2 apathy, ennui, heartlessness, heaviness, lethargy, listlessness, torpidness, torpor, weariness.
n antonyms alacrity, gusto.

lank *adj* attenuated, emaciated, gaunt, lean, meagre, scraggy, slender, skinny, slim, starveling, thin.

lap¹ *vb* 1 drink, lick, mouth, tongue. 2 plash, ripple, splash, wash. 3 quaff, sip, sup, swizzle, tipple. • *n* 1 draught, dram, drench, drink, gulp, lick, swig, swill, quaff, sip, sup, suck. **2** plash, splash, wash.

lap² *vb* **1** cover, enfold, fold, turn, twist, swaddle, wrap. **2** distance, pass, outdistance, overlap. • *n* **1** fold, flap, lappet, lapel, ply, plait. **2** ambit, beat, circle, circuit, cycle, loop, orbit, revolution, round, tour, turn, walk.

lapse *vb* **1** glide, sink, slide, slip. **2** err, fail, fall. • *n* **1** course, flow, gliding. **2** declension, decline, fall. **3** error, fault, indiscretion, misstep, shortcoming, slip.

larceny *n* pilfering, robbery, stealing, theft, thievery.

large *adj* **1** big, broad, bulky, colossal, elephantine, enormous, heroic, great, huge, immense, vast. **2** broad, expanded, extensive, spacious, wide. **3** abundant, ample, copious, full, liberal, plentiful. **4** capacious, comprehensive.
adj antonyms diminutive, little, slight, small, tiny.

lascivious *adj* concupiscent, immodest, incontinent, goatish, lecherous, lewd, libidinous, loose, lubricious, lustful, prurient, salacious, sensual, unchaste, voluptuous, wanton.

lash¹ *vb* **1** belay, bind, strap, tie. **2** fasten, join, moor, pinion, secure.

lash² *vb* **1** beat, castigate, chastise, flagellate, flail, flay, flog, goad, scourge, swinge, thrash, whip. **2** assail, censure, excoriate, lampoon, satirize, trounce. • *n* **1** scourge, strap, thong, whip. **2** cut, slap, smack, stroke, stripe.

lass *n* damsel, girl, lassie, maiden, miss.

lassitude *n* dullness, exhaustion, fatigue, languor, languidness, prostration, tiredness, weariness.

last¹ *vb* abide, carry on, continue, dwell, endure, extend, maintain, persist, prevail, remain, stand, stay, survive.

last² *adj* **1** hindermost, hindmost, latest. **2** conclusive, final, terminal, ultimate. **3** eventual, endmost, extreme, farthest, ultimate. **4** greatest, highest, maximal, maximum, most, supreme, superlative, utmost. **5** latest, newest. **6** aforegoing, foregoing, latter, preceding. **7** departing, farewell, final, leaving, parting, valedictory. • *n* conclusion, consummation, culmination, end, ending, finale, finis, finish, termination.
adj antonyms first, initial.
n antonyms beginning, start.

last³ *n* cast, form, matrix, mould, shape, template.

lasting *adj* abiding, durable, enduring, fixed, perennial, permanent, perpetual, stable.

lastly *adv* conclusively, eventually, finally, ultimately.

late *adj* **1** delayed, overdue, slow, tardy. **2** deceased, former. **3** recent. • *adv* **1** lately, recently, sometime. **2** tardily.
adj antonyms early, punctual.
adv antonyms early, punctually.

latent *adj* abeyant, concealed, hidden, invisible, occult, secret, unseen, veiled.
adj antonyms active, live, patent.

latitude *n* **1** amplitude, breadth, compass, extent, range, room, scope. **2** freedom, indulgence, liberty. **3** laxity.

latter *adj* last, latest, modern, recent.
adj antonym former.

lattice *n* grating, latticework, trellis.

laud *vb* approve, celebrate, extol, glorify, magnify, praise.
vb antonyms blame, condemn, curse, damn.

laudable *adj* commendable, meritorious, praiseworthy.
adj antonyms damnable, execrable.

laugh *vb* cackle, chortle, chuckle, giggle, guffaw, snicker, snigger, titter. • *n* chortle, chuckle, giggle, guffaw, laughter, titter.
vb antonym cry.

laughable *adj* amusing, comical, diverting, droll, farcical, funny, ludicrous, mirthful, ridiculous.
adj antonyms impressive, serious, solemn.

laughter *n* cackle, chortle, chuckle, glee, giggle, guffaw, laugh, laughing.

launch *vb* **1** cast, dart, dispatch, hurl, lance, project, throw. **2** descant, dilate, enlarge, expiate. **3** begin, commence, inaugurate, open, start.

lavish *vb* dissipate, expend, spend, squander, waste. • *adj* excessive, extravagant, generous, immoderate, overliberal, prodigal, profuse, thriftless, unrestrained, unstinted, unthrifty, wasteful.
adj antonyms economical, frugal, parsimonious, scanty, sparing, thrifty.

law *n* **1** act, code, canon, command, commandment, covenant, decree, edict, enactment, order, precept, principle, statute, regulation, rule. **2** jurisprudence. **3** litigation, process, suit.
n antonym chance.

lawful *adj* **1** constitutional, constituted, legal, legalized, legitimate. **2** allowable, authorized, permissible, warrantable. **3** equitable, rightful, just, proper, valid.

adj antonyms illegal, illicit, lawless, unlawful.

lawless *adj* anarchic, anarchical, chaotic, disorderly, insubordinate, rebellious, reckless, riotous, seditious, wild.

adj antonym lawful.

lawyer *n* advocate, attorney, barrister, counsel, counsellor, solicitor.

lax *adj* **1** loose, relaxed, slow. **2** drooping, flabby, soft. **3** neglectful, negligent, remiss. **4** dissolute, immoral, licentious, seditious, wild.

adj antonyms rigid, strict, stringent.

lay¹ *vb* **1** deposit, establish, leave, place, plant, posit, put, set, settle, spread. **2** arrange, dispose, locate, organize, position. **3** bear, produce. **4** advance, lodge, offer, submit. **5** allocate, allot, ascribe, assign, attribute, charge, impute. **6** concoct, contrive, design, plan, plot, prepare. **7** apply, burden, encumber, impose, saddle, tax. **8** bet, gamble, hazard, risk, stake, wager. **9** allay, alleviate, appease, assuage, calm, relieve, soothe, still, suppress. **10** disclose, divulge, explain, reveal, show, unveil. **11** acquire, grab, grasp, seize. **12** assault, attack, beat up. **13** discover, find, unearth. **14** bless, confirm, consecrate, ordain. • *n* **1** arrangement, array, form, formation. **2** attitude, aspect, bearing, demeanour, direction, lie, pose, position, posture, set.

lay² *adj* **1** amateur, inexpert, nonprofessional. **2** civil, laic, laical, nonclerical, nonecclesiastical, nonreligious, secular, temporal, unclerical.

lay³ *n* ballad, carol, ditty, lied, lyric, ode, poem, rhyme, round, song, verse.

layer *n* bed, course, lay, seam, stratum.

laziness *n* idleness, inactivity, indolence, slackness, sloth, sluggishness, tardiness.

lazy *adj* idle, inactive, indolent, inert, slack, slothful, slow, sluggish, supine, torpid.

adj antonyms active, diligent, energetic, industrious.

lead *vb* **1** conduct, deliver, direct, draw, escort, guide. **2** front, head, precede. **3** advance, excel, outstrip, pass. **4** allure, entice, induce, persuade, prevail. **5** conduce, contribute, serve, tend. • *adj* chief, first, foremost, main, primary, prime, principal.

• *n* **1** direction, guidance, leadership. **2** advance. **3** precedence, priority.

vb antonym follow.

leader *n* **1** conductor, director, guide. **2** captain, chief, chieftain, commander, head. **3** superior, dominator, victor.

n antonym follower.

leading *adj* **1** governing, ruling. **2** capital, chief, first, foremost, highest, principal, superior.

adj antonyms subordinate.

league *vb* ally, associate, band, combine, confederate, unite. • *n* alliance, association, coalition, combination, combine, confederacy, confederation, consortium, union.

leak *vb* drip, escape, exude, ooze, pass, percolate, spill. • *n* **1** chink, crack, crevice, hole, fissure, oozing, opening. **2** drip, leakage, leaking, percolation.

lean¹ *adj* **1** bony, emaciated, gaunt, lank, meagre, poor, skinny, thin. **2** dull, barren, jejune, meagre, tame. **3** inadequate, pitiful, scanty, slender. **4** bare, barren, infertile, unproductive.

adj antonyms fat, fleshy.

lean² *vb* **1** incline, slope. **2** bear, recline, repose, rest. **3** confide, depend, rely, trust.

leaning *n* aptitude, bent, bias, disposition, inclination, liking, predilection, proneness, propensity, tendency.

leap *vb* **1** bound, clear, jump, spring, vault. **2** caper, frisk, gambol, hop, skip. • *n* **1** bound, jump, spring, vault. **2** caper, frisk, gambol, hop, skip.

vb antonyms drop, fall, sink.

learn *vb* acquire, ascertain, attain, collect, gain, gather, hear, memorize.

learned *adj* **1** erudite, lettered, literate, scholarly, well-read. **2** expert, experienced, knowing, skilled, versed, well-informed.

adj antonyms ignorant, illiterate, uneducated.

learner *n* beginner, novice, pupil, student, tyro.

learning *n* acquirements, attainments, culture, education, information, knowledge, lore, scholarship, tuition.

least *adj* meanest, minutest, smallest, tiniest.

adj antonym most.

leave¹ *vb* **1** abandon, decamp, go, quit, vacate, withdraw. **2** desert, forsake, relinquish, renounce. **3** commit, consign, refer.

4 cease, desist from, discontinue, refrain, stop. **5** allow, let, let alone, permit. **6** bequeath, demise, desist, will.

vb antonyms arrive.

leave² *n* **1** allowance, liberty, permission, licence, sufferance. **2** departure, retirement, withdrawal. **3** adieu, farewell, goodbye.

n antonyms refusal, rejection.

leaven *vb* **1** ferment, lighten, raise. **2** colour, elevate, imbue, inspire, lift, permeate, tinge. **3** infect, vitiate. • *n* **1** barm, ferment, yeast. **2** influence, inspiration.

leavings *npl* bits, dregs, fragments, leftovers, pieces, relics, remains, remnants, scraps.

lecherous *adj* carnal, concupiscent, incontinent, lascivious, lewd, libidinous, lubricious, lustful, wanton, salacious, unchaste.

lechery *n*, lasciviousness, lewdness, lubriciousness, lubricity, lust, salaciousness, salacity.

lecture *vb* **1** censure, chide, reprimand, reprove, scold, sermonize. **2** address, harangue, teach. • *n* **1** censure, lecturing, lesson, reprimand, reproof, scolding. **2** address, discourse, prelection.

ledge *n* projection, ridge, shelf.

lees *npl* dregs, precipitate, refuse, sediment, settlings.

leg *n* limb, prop.

legacy *n* **1** bequest, gift, heirloom. **2** heritage, inheritance, tradition.

legal *adj* allowable, authorized, constitutional, lawful, legalized, legitimate, proper, sanctioned.

adj antonym illegal.

legalize *vb* authorize, legitimate, legitimatize, legitimize, permit, sanction.

legend *n* fable, fiction, myth, narrative, romance, story, tale.

legendary *adj* fabulous, fictitious, mythical, romantic.

legible *adj* **1** clear, decipherable, fair, distinct, plain, readable. **2** apparent, discoverable, recognizable, manifest.

adj antonym illegible.

legion *n* **1** army, body, cohort, column, corps, detachment, detail, division, force, maniple, phalanx, platoon. **2** squad. **3** army, horde, host, multitude, number, swarm, throng. • *adj* many, multitudinous, myriad, numerous.

legislate *vb* enact, ordain.

legitimacy *n* **1** lawfulness, legality. **2** genuineness.

legitimate *adj* **1** authorized, lawful, legal, sanctioned. **2** genuine, valid. **3** correct, justifiable, logical, reasonable, warrantable, warranted.

adj antonym illegitimate.

leisure *n* convenience, ease, freedom, liberty, opportunity, recreation, retirement, vacation.

n antonyms toil, work.

lend *vb* advance, afford, bestow, confer, furnish, give, grant, impart, loan, supply.

vb antonym borrow.

lengthen *vb* **1** elongate, extend, produce, prolong, stretch. **2** continue, protract.

vb antonym shorten.

lengthy *adj* diffuse, lengthened, long, long-drawn-out, prolix, prolonged, protracted.

lenience, leniency *n* clemency, compassion, forbearance, gentleness, lenity, mercy, mildness, tenderness.

n antonym severity.

lenient *adj* **1** assuasive, lenitive, mitigating, mitigative, softening, soothing. **2** clement, easy, forbearing, gentle, humouring, indulgent, long-suffering, merciful, mild, tender, tolerant.

adj antonym severe.

lesion *n* derangement, disorder, hurt, injury.

less *adj* **1** baser, inferior, lower, smaller. **2** decreased, fewer, lesser, reduced, smaller, shorter. • *adv* **1** barely, below, least, under. **2** decreasingly. • *prep* excepting, lacking, minus, sans, short of, without.

lessen *vb* **1** abate, abridge, contract, curtail, decrease, diminish, narrow, reduce, shrink. **2** degrade, lower. **3** dwindle, weaken.

vb antonym increase.

lesson *n* **1** exercise, task. **2** instruction, precept. **3** censure, chiding, lecture, lecturing, rebuke, reproof, scolding.

let¹ *vb* **1** admit, allow, authorize, permit, suffer. **2** charter, hire, lease, rent.

vb antonym forbid.

let² *vb* hinder, impede, instruct, prevent. • *n* hindrance, impediment, interference, obstacle, obstruction, restriction.

n antonym assistance.

lethal *adj* deadly, destructive, fatal, mortal, murderous.

adj antonym harmless.

lethargic *adj* apathetic, comatose, drowsy, dull, heavy, inactive, inert, sleepy, stupid, stupefied, torpid.

adj antonym lively.

lethargy *n* apathy, coma, drowsiness, dullness, hypnotism, inactiveness, inactivity, inertia, sleepiness, sluggishness, stupefaction, stupidity, stupor, torpor.
n antonym liveliness.

letter *n* epistle, missive, note.

lettered *adj* bookish, educated, erudite, learned, literary, versed, well-read.

levee *n* **1** ceremony, entertainment, reception, party, soiree. **2** embankment.

level *vb* **1** equalize, flatten, smooth. **2** demolish, destroy, raze. **3** aim, direct, point. • *adj* equal, even, flat, flush, horizontal, plain, plane, smooth. • *n* **1** altitude, degree, equality, evenness, plain, plane, smoothness. **2** deck, floor, layer, stage, storey, tier.
adj antonyms behind, uneven, unstable.
vb antonym prevaricate.

levity *n* buoyancy, facetiousness, fickleness, flightiness, flippancy, frivolity, giddiness, inconstancy, levity, volatility.
n antonyms seriousness, sobriety.

levy *vb* **1** collect, exact, gather, tax. **2** call, muster, raise, summon. • *n* duty, tax.

lewd *adj* despicable, impure, lascivious, libidinous, licentious, loose, lustful, profligate, unchaste, vile, wanton, wicked.
adj antonyms chaste, polite.

liability *n* **1** accountableness, accountability, duty, obligation, responsibility, tendency. **2** exposedness. **3** debt, indebtedness, obligation.
n antonyms asset(s), unaccountability.

liable *adj* **1** accountable, amenable, answerable, bound, responsible. **2** exposed, likely, obnoxious, subject.
adj antonyms unaccountable, unlikely.

liaison *n* **1** amour, intimacy, intrigue. **2** connection, relation, union.

libel *vb* calumniate, defame, lampoon, satirize, slander, vilify. • *n* calumny, defamation, lampoon, satire, slander, vilification, vituperation.
vb antonym praise.
n antonym praise.

liberal *adj* **1** beneficent, bountiful, charitable, disinterested, free, generous, munificent, open-hearted, princely, unselfish. **2** broad-minded, catholic, chivalrous, enlarged, high-minded, honourable, magnanimous, tolerant, unbiased, unbigoted. **3** abundant, ample, bounteous, full, large, plentiful, unstinted. **4** humanizing, liberalizing, refined, refining.

adj antonyms conservative, illiberal, mean, narrow-minded.

liberality *n* **1** beneficence, bountifulness, bounty, charity, disinterestedness, generosity, kindness, munificence. **2** benefaction, donation, gift, gratuity, present. **3** broad-mindedness, catholicity, candour, impartiality, large-mindedness, magnanimity, toleration.
n antonyms illiberality, meanness.

liberate *vb* deliver, discharge, disenthral, emancipate, free, manumit, ransom, release.
vb antonyms enslave, imprison, restrict.

libertine *adj* corrupt, depraved, dissolute, licentious, profligate, rakish. • *n* debauchee, lecher, profligate, rake, roue, voluptuary.

liberty *n* **1** emancipation, freedom, independence, liberation, self-direction, self-government. **2** franchise, immunity, privilege. **3** leave, licence, permission.
n antonyms imprisonment, restriction, slavery.

libidinous *adj* carnal, concupiscent, debauched, impure, incontinent, lascivious, lecherous, lewd, loose, lubricious, lustful, salacious, sensual, unchaste, wanton, wicked.

licence *n* **1** authorization, leave, permission, privilege, right. **2** certificate, charter, dispensation, imprimatur, permit, warrant. **3** anarchy, disorder, freedom, lawlessness, laxity, liberty.
n antonyms banning, dependence, restriction.

license *vb* **1** allow, authorize, grant, permit, warrant. **2** suffer, tolerate.
vb antonym ban.

licentious *adj* **1** disorderly, riotous, uncontrolled, uncurbed, ungovernable, unrestrained, unruly, wanton. **2** debauched, dissolute, lax, libertine, loose, profligate, rakish. **3** immoral, impure, lascivious, lecherous, lewd, libertine, libidinous, lustful, sensual, unchaste, wicked.

lick *vb* **1** beat, flog, spank, thrash. **2** lap, taste. • *n* **1** blow, slap, stroke. **2** salt-spring.

lie[1] *vb* **1** couch, recline, remain, repose, rest. **2** consist, pertain.

lie[2] *vb* equivocate, falsify, fib, prevaricate, romance. • *n* **1** equivocation, falsehood, falsification, fib, misrepresentation, prevarication, untruth. **2** delusion, illusion.
n antonym truth.

lief *adv* freely, gladly, willingly.

life *n* **1** activity, alertness, animation, briskness, energy, sparkle, spirit, sprightliness, verve, vigour, vivacity. **2** behaviour, conduct, deportment. **3** being, duration, existence, lifetime. **4** autobiography, biography, curriculum vitae, memoirs, story.

lifeless *adj* **1** dead, deceased, defunct, extinct, inanimate. **2** cold, dull, flat, frigid, inert, lethargic, passive, pulseless, slow, sluggish, tame, torpid.

lift *vb* **1** elevate, exalt, hoist, raise, uplift. • *n* aid, assistance, help. **2** elevator.

light¹ *vb* alight, land, perch, settle. • *adj* **1** porous, sandy, spongy, well-leavened. **2** loose, sandy. **3** free, portable, unburdened, unencumbered. **4** inconsiderable, moderate, negligible, slight, small, trifling, trivial, unimportant. **5** ethereal, feathery, flimsy, gossamer, insubstantial, weightless. **6** easy, effortless, facile. **7** fickle, frivolous, unsettled, unsteady, volatile. **8** airy, buoyant, carefree, light-hearted, lightsome. **9** unaccented, unstressed, weak.
adj antonyms clumsy, harsh, heavy, important, sad, severe, sober, solid, stiff.

light² *vb* **1** conflagrate, fire, ignite, inflame, kindle. **2** brighten, illume, illuminate, illumine, luminate, irradiate, lighten. • *adj* bright, clear, fair, lightsome, luminous, pale, pearly, whitish. • *n* **1** dawn, day, daybreak, sunrise. **2** blaze, brightness, effulgence, gleam, illumination, luminosity, phosphorescence, radiance, ray. **3** candle, lamp, lantern, lighthouse, taper, torch. **4** comprehension, enlightenment, information, insight, instruction, knowledge. **5** elucidation, explanation, illustration. **6** attitude, construction, interpretation, observation, reference, regard, respect, view.
vb antonyms darken, extinguish.
adj antonym dark.
n antonym darkness.

lighten¹ *vb* **1** allay, alleviate, ease, mitigate, palliate. **2** disburden, disencumber, relieve, unburden, unload.
vb antonyms burden, depress, oppress.

lighten² *vb* **1** brighten, gleam, shine. **2** light, illume, illuminate, illumine, irradiate. **3** enlighten, inform. **4** emit, flash.
vb antonym darken.

light-headed *adj* **1** dizzy, giddy, vertiginous. **2** confused, delirious, wandering. **3** frivolous, giddy, heedless, indiscreet, light, rattle-brained, thoughtless, volatile.

light-hearted *adj* blithe, blithesome, carefree, cheerful, frolicsome, gay, glad, gladsome, gleeful, happy, jocund, jovial, joyful, lightsome, merry.
adj antonym sad.

lightness *n* **1** flightiness, frivolity, giddiness, levity, volatility. **2** agility, buoyancy, facility.

like¹ *vb* **1** approve, please. **2** cherish, enjoy, love, relish. **3** esteem, fancy, regard. **4** choose, desire, elect, list, prefer, select, wish. • *n* liking, partiality, preference.
vb antonym dislike.
n antonym dislike.

like² *adj* **1** alike, allied, analogous, cognate, corresponding, parallel, resembling, similar. **2** equal, same. **3** likely, probable. • *adv* likely, probably. • *n* counterpart, equal, match, peer, twin.
adj antonym unlike.

likelihood *n* probability, verisimilitude.

likely *adj* **1** credible, liable, possible, probable. **2** agreeable, appropriate, convenient, likable, pleasing, suitable, well-adapted, well-suited. • *adv* doubtlessly, presumably, probably.
adj antonyms unlikely, unsuitable.

likeness *n* **1** appearance, form, parallel, resemblance, semblance, similarity, similitude. **2** copy, counterpart, effigy, facsimile, image, picture, portrait, representation.
n antonym unlikeness.

liking *n* **1** desire, fondness, partiality, wish. **2** appearance, bent, bias, disposition, inclination, leaning, penchant, predisposition, proneness, propensity, tendency, turn.
n antonym dislike.

limb *n* **1** arm, extremity, leg, member. **2** bough, branch, offshoot.

limit *vb* **1** bound, circumscribe, define. **2** check, condition, hinder, restrain, restrict. • *n* **1** bound, boundary, bourn, confine, frontier, march, precinct, term, termination, terminus. **2** check, hindrance, obstruction, restraint, restriction.
vb antonyms extend, free.

limitation *n* check, constraint, restraint, restriction.

limitless *adj* boundless, endless, eternal, illimitable, immeasurable, infinite, never-ending, unbounded, undefined, unending, unlimited.

limp¹ *vb* halt, hitch, hobble, totter. • *n* hitch, hobble, shamble, shuffle, totter.

limp² *adj* **1** drooping, droopy, floppy, sagging, weak. **2** flabby, flaccid, flexible, limber, pliable, relaxed, slack, soft.
adj antonym strong.

limpid *adj* bright, clear, crystal, crystalline, lucid, pellucid, pure, translucent, transparent.
adj antonyms muddy, ripply, turbid, unintelligible.

line *vb* **1** align, line up, range, rank, regiment. **2** border, bound, edge, fringe, hem, interline, march, rim, verge. **3** seam, stripe, streak, striate, trace. **4** carve, chisel, crease, cut, crosshatch. **5** define, delineate, describe. • *n* mark, **1** streak, stripe. **2** cable, cord, rope, string, thread. **3** rank, row. **4** ancestry, family, lineage, race, succession. **5** course, method. **6** business, calling, employment, job, occupation, post, pursuit.

lineage *n* ancestry, birth, breed, descendants, descent, extraction, family, forebears, forefathers, genealogy, house, line, offspring, progeny, race.

linen *n* cloth, fabric, flax, lingerie.

linger *vb* dally, dawdle, delay, idle, lag, loiter, remain, saunter, stay, tarry, wait.
vb antonyms leave, rush.

link *vb* bind, conjoin, connect, fasten, join, tie, unite. • *n* **1** bond, connection, connective, copula, coupler, joint, juncture. **2** division, member, part, piece.
vb antonyms separate, unfasten.

liquefy *vb* dissolve, fuse, melt, thaw.

liquid *adj* **1** fluid. **2** clear, dulcet, flowing, mellifluous, mellifluent, melting, soft. • *n* fluid, liquor.
adj antonyms harsh, solid.

list¹ *vb* **1** alphabetize, catalogue, chronicle, codify, docket, enumerate, file, index, inventory, record, register, tabulate, tally. **2** enlist, enrol. **3** choose, desire, elect, like, please, prefer, wish. • *n* **1** catalogue, enumeration, index, inventory, invoice, register, roll, schedule, scroll, series, table, tally. **2** border, bound, limit. **3** border, edge, selvedge, strip, stripe. **4** fillet, listel.

list² *vb* cant, heel, incline, keel, lean, pitch, tilt, tip. • *n* cant, inclination, incline, leaning, pitch, slope, tilt, tip.

listen *vb* attend, eavesdrop, hark, hear, hearken, heed, obey, observe.

listless *adj* apathetic, careless, heedless, impassive, inattentive, indifferent, indolent, languid, torpid, vacant, supine, thoughtless, vacant.
adj antonym lively.

listlessness *n* apathy, carelessness, heedlessness, impassivity, inattention, indifference, indolence, languidness, languor, supineness, torpor, torpidity, vacancy.

literally *adv* **1** actually, really. **2** exactly, precisely, rigorously, strictly.
adv antonym loosely.

literary *adj* bookish, book-learned, erudite, instructed, learned, lettered, literate, scholarly, well-read.
adj antonym illiterate.

literature *n* erudition, learning, letters, lore, writings.

lithe *adj* flexible, flexile, limber, pliable, pliant, supple.
adj antonym stiff.

litigation *n* contending, contest, disputing, lawsuit.

litigious *adj* **1** contentious, disputatious, quarrelsome. **2** controvertible, disputable.
adj antonym easy-going.

litter *vb* **1** derange, disarrange, disorder, scatter, strew. **2** bear. • *n* **1** bedding, couch, palanquin, sedan, stretcher. **2** confusion, disarray, disorder, mess, untidiness. **3** fragments, rubbish, shreds, trash.
vb antonym tidy.

little *adj* **1** diminutive, infinitesimal, minute, small, tiny, wee. **2** brief, short, small. **3** feeble, inconsiderable, insignificant, moderate, petty, scanty, slender, slight, trivial, unimportant, weak. **4** contemptible, illiberal, mean, narrow, niggardly, paltry, selfish, stingy. • *n* handful, jot, modicum, pinch, pittance, trifle, whit.
adj antonyms important, large, long.
n antonym lot.

live¹ *vb* **1** be, exist. **2** continue, endure, last, remain, survive. **3** abide, dwell, reside. **4** fare, feed, nourish, subsist, support. **5** continue, lead, pass.
vb antonyms cease, die.

live² *adj* **1** alive, animate, living, quick. **2** burning, hot, ignited. **3** bright, brilliant, glowing, lively, vivid. **4** active, animated, earnest, glowing, wide-awake.
adj antonyms apathetic, dead, out.

livelihood *n* living, maintenance, subsistence, support, sustenance.

liveliness *n* activity, animation, briskness, gaiety, spirit, sprightliness, vivacity.

lively *adj* **1** active, agile, alert, brisk, energetic, nimble, quick, smart, stirring, supple, vigorous, vivacious. **2** airy, animated, blithe, blithesome, buoyant, frolicsome, gleeful, jocund, jolly, merry, spirited, sportive, sprightly, spry. **3** bright, brilliant, clear, fresh, glowing, strong, vivid. **4** dynamic, forcible, glowing, impassioned, intense, keen, nervous, piquant, racy, sparkling, strenuous, vigorous.
adj antonyms apathetic, inactive.

living *adj* **1** alive, breathing, existing, live, organic, quick. **2** active, lively, quickening. • *n* **1** livelihood, maintenance, subsistence, support. **2** estate, keeping. **3** benefice.
adj antonyms dead, sluggish.

load *vb* **1** freight, lade. **2** burden, cumber, encumber, oppress, weigh. • *n* **1** burden, freightage, pack, weight. **2** cargo, freight, lading. **3** clog, deadweight, encumbrance, incubus, oppression, pressure.

loafer *n* (*sl*) bum, idler, lounger, vagabond, vagrant.
n antonym worker.

loath *adj* averse, backward, disinclined, indisposed, reluctant, unwilling.
adj antonym willing.

loathe *vb* abhor, abominate, detest, dislike, hate, recoil.
vb antonym like.

loathing *n* abhorrence, abomination, antipathy, aversion, detestation, disgust, hatred, horror, repugnance, revulsion.

loathsome *adj* **1** disgusting, nauseating, nauseous, offensive, palling, repulsive, revolting, sickening. **2** abominable, abhorrent, detestable, execrable, hateful, odious, shocking.
adj antonym likeable.

local *adj* limited, neighbouring, provincial, regional, restricted, sectional, territorial, topical.
adj antonym far-away.
n antonym incomer.

locality *n* location, neighbourhood, place, position, site, situation, spot.

locate *vb* determine, establish, fix, place, set, settle.

lock¹ *vb* **1** bolt, fasten, padlock, seal. **2** confine. **3** clog, impede, restrain, stop. **4** clasp, embrace, encircle, enclose, grapple, hug, join, press. • *n* **1** bolt, fastening, padlock. **2** embrace, grapple, hug.

lock² *n* curl, ringlet, tress, tuft.

lodge *vb* **1** deposit, fix, settle. **2** fix, place, plant. **3** accommodate, cover, entertain, harbour, quarter, shelter. **4** abide, dwell, inhabit, live, reside, rest. **5** remain, rest, sojourn, stay, stop. • *n* **1** cabin, cottage, hovel, hut, shed. **2** cave, den, haunt, lair. **3** assemblage, assembly, group, society.

lodging *n* **1** abode, apartment, dwelling, habitation, quarters, residence. **2** cover, harbour, protection, refuge, shelter.

loftiness *n* **1** altitude, elevation, height. **2** arrogance, haughtiness, pride, vanity. **3** dignity, grandeur, sublimity.

lofty *adj* **1** elevated, high, tall, towering. **2** arrogant, haughty, proud. **3** eminent, exalted, sublime. **4** dignified, imposing, majestic, stately.
adj antonyms humble, low(ly), modest.

logical *adj* **1** close, coherent, consistent, dialectical, sound, valid. **2** discriminating, rational, reasoned.

loiter *vb* dally, dawdle, delay, dilly-dally, idle, lag, linger, saunter, stroll, tarry.

loneliness *n* **1** isolation, retirement, seclusion, solitariness, solitude. **2** desolation, dreariness, forlornness.

lonely *adj* **1** apart, dreary, isolated, lonesome, remote, retired, secluded, separate, sequestrated, solitary. **2** alone, lone, companionless, friendless, unaccompanied. **3** deserted, desolate, forlorn, forsaken, withdrawn.

lonesome *adj* cheerless, deserted, desolate, dreary, gloomy, lone, lonely.

long¹ *vb* **1** anticipate, await, expect. **2** aspire, covet, crave, desire, hanker, lust, pine, wish, yearn.

long² *adj* **1** drawn-out, extended, extensive, far-reaching, lengthy, prolonged, protracted, stretched. **2** diffuse, long-winded, prolix, tedious, wearisome. **3** backward, behindhand, dilatory, lingering, slack, slow, tardy.

longing *n* aspiration, coveting, craving, desire, hankering, hunger, pining, yearning.

long-suffering *adj* enduring, forbearing, patient. • *n* clemency, endurance, forbearing.

look *vb* **1** behold, examine, notice, see, search. **2** consider, inspect, investigate, observe, study, contemplate, gaze, regard, scan, survey, view. **3** anticipate, await, expect. **4** heed, mind, watch. **5** face, front.

6 appear, seem. • *n* **1** examination, gaze, glance, peep, peer, search. **2** appearance, aspect, complexion. **3** air, aspect, manner, mien.

loophole *n* **1** aperture, crenellation, loop, opening. **2** excuse, plea, pretence, pretext, subterfuge.

loose *vb* **1** free, liberate, release, unbind, undo, unfasten, unlash, unlock, untie. **2** ease, loosen, relax, slacken. **3** detach, disconnect, disengage. • *adj* **1** unbound, unconfined, unfastened, unsewn, untied. **2** disengaged, free, unattached. **3** relaxed. **4** diffuse, diffusive, prolix, rambling, unconnected. **5** ill-defined, indefinite, indeterminate, indistinct, vague. **6** careless, heedless, negligent, lax, slack. **7** debauched, dissolute, immoral, licentious, unchaste, wanton.

vb antonyms bind, fasten, fix, secure.

adj antonyms close, compact, precise, strict, taut, tense, tight; strict, stringent, tight.

loosen *vb* liberate, relax, release, separate, slacken, unbind, unloose, untie.

vb antonym tighten.

looseness *n* **1** easiness, slackness. **2** laxity, levity. **2** lewdness, unchastity, wantonness, wickedness. **3** diarrhoea, flux.

loot *vb* pillage, plunder, ransack, rifle, rob, sack. • *n* booty, plunder, spoil.

lop *vb* **1** cut, truncate. **2** crop, curtail, dock, prune. **3** detach, dissever, sever.

loquacious *adj* **1** garrulous, talkative, voluble, wordy. **2** noisy, speaking, talking. **3** babbling, blabbing, tattling, tell-tale.

adj antonyms succinct, taciturn, terse.

loquacity *n* babbling, chattering, gabbling, garrulity, loquaciousness, talkativeness, volubility.

lord *n* **1** earl, noble, nobleman, peer, viscount. **2** governor, king, liege, master, monarch, prince, ruler, seigneur, seignior, sovereign, superior. **3** husband, spouse.

lordly *adj* **1** aristocratic, dignified, exalted, grand, lofty, majestic, noble. **2** arrogant, despotic, domineering, haughty, imperious, insolent, masterful, overbearing, proud, tyrannical. **3** large, liberal.

lordship *n* **1** authority, command, control, direction, domination, dominion, empire, government, rule, sovereignty, sway. **2** manor, domain, seigneury, seigniory.

lore *n* **1** erudition, knowledge, learning, letters, scholarship. **2** admonition, advice, counsel, doctrine, instruction, lesson, teaching, wisdom.

lose *vb* **1** deprive, dispossess, forfeit, miss. **2** dislodge, displace, mislay, misspend, squander, waste. **3** decline, fall, succumb, yield.

vb antonyms gain, make, win.

loss *n* **1** deprivation, failure, forfeiture, privation. **2** casualty, damage, defeat, destruction, detriment, disadvantage, injury, overthrow, ruin. **3** squandering, waste.

n antonyms benefit, gain.

lost *adj* **1** astray, missing. **2** forfeited, missed, unredeemed. **3** dissipated, misspent, squandered, wasted. **4** bewildered, confused, distracted, perplexed, puzzled. **5** absent, absent-minded, abstracted, dreamy, napping, preoccupied. **6** abandoned, corrupt, debauched, depraved, dissolute, graceless, hardened, incorrigible, irreclaimable, licentious, profligate, reprobate, shameless, unchaste, wanton. **7** destroyed, ruined.

adj antonym found.

lot *n* **1** allotment, apportionment, destiny, doom, fate. **2** accident, chance, fate, fortune, hap, haphazard, hazard. **3** division, parcel, part, portion.

loth *adj* averse, disinclined, disliking, reluctant, unwilling

loud *adj* **1** high-sounding, noisy, resounding, sonorous. **2** deafening, strong, stunning. **3** boisterous, clamorous, noisy, obstreperous, tumultuous, turbulent, uproarious, vociferous. **4** emphatic, impressive, positive, vehement. **5** flashy, gaudy, glaring, loud, ostentatious, showy, vulgar.

adj antonyms low, quiet, soft.

lounge *vb* **1** loll, recline, sprawl. **2** dawdle, idle, loaf, loiter.

love *vb* adore, like, worship. • *n* **1** accord, affection, amity, courtship, delight, fondness, friendship, kindness, regard, tenderness, warmth. **2** adoration, amour, ardour, attachment, passion. **3** devotion, inclination, liking. **4** benevolence, charity, goodwill.

vb antonyms detest, hate, loathe.

n antonyms detestation, hate, loathing.

lovely *adj* **1** beautiful, charming, delectable, delightful, enchanting, exquisite, graceful, pleasing, sweet, winning. **2** admirable, adorable, amiable.

adj antonyms hideous, ugly, unlovely.

loving *adj* affectionate, dear, fond, kind, tender.

low¹ *vb* bellow, moo.

low² *adj* **1** basal, depressed, profound. **2** gentle, grave, soft, subdued. **3** cheap, humble, mean, plebeian, vulgar. **4** abject, base, base-minded, degraded, dirty, grovelling, ignoble, low-minded, menial, scurvy, servile, shabby, slavish, vile. **5** derogatory, disgraceful, dishonourable, disreputable, unbecoming, undignified, ungentlemanly, unhandsome, unmanly. **6** exhausted, feeble, reduced, weak. **7** frugal, plain, poor, simple, spare. **8** lowly, reverent, submissive. **9** dejected, depressed, dispirited.

adj antonyms elevated, high, lofty, noble.

lower¹ *vb* **1** depress, drop, sink, subside. **2** debase, degrade, disgrace, humble, humiliate, reduce. **3** abate, decrease, diminish, lessen. • *adj* **1** baser, inferior, less, lesser, shorter, smaller. **2** subjacent, under.

vb antonyms elevate, increase, raise, rise.

adj antonyms better, higher, superior.

lower² *vb* blacken, darken, frown, glower, threaten.

lowering *adj* dark, clouded, cloudy, lurid, murky, overcast, threatening.

lowliness *n* humbleness, humility, meekness, self-abasement, submissiveness.

lowly *adj* **1** gentle, humble, meek, mild, modest, plain, poor, simple, unassuming, unpretending, unpretentious. **2** low-born, mean, servile.

adj antonyms lofty, noble.

loyal *adj* constant, devoted, faithful, patriotic, true.

adj antonyms disloyal, traitorous.

loyalty *n* allegiance, constancy, devotion, faithfulness, fealty, fidelity, patriotism.

n antonyms disloyalty, treachery.

lubricious *adj* **1** slippery, smooth. **2** uncertain, unstable, wavering. **3** impure, incontinent, lascivious, lecherous, lewd, libidinous, licentious, lustful, salacious, unchaste, wanton.

lucid *adj* **1** beaming, bright, brilliant, luminous, radiant, resplendent, shining, clear, crystalline, diaphanous, limpid, lucent, pellucid, pure, transparent. **2** clear, distinct, evident, intelligible, obvious, perspicuous, plain. **3** reasonable, sane, sober, sound.

adj antonyms dark, murky, unclear.

luck *n* accident, casualty, chance, fate, fortune, hap, haphazard, hazard, serendipity, success.

n antonym misfortune.

luckless *adj* ill-fated, ill-starred, unfortunate, unhappy, unlucky, unpropitious, unprosperous, unsuccessful.

lucky *adj* **1** blessed, favoured, fortunate, happy, successful. **2** auspicious, favourable, propitious, prosperous.

adj antonyms luckless, unlucky.

lucrative *adj* advantageous, gainful, paying, profitable, remunerative.

adj antonym unprofitable.

ludicrous *adj* absurd, burlesque, comic, comical, droll, farcical, funny, laughable, odd, ridiculous, sportive.

lugubrious *adj* complaining, doleful, gloomy, melancholy, mournful, sad, serious, sombre, sorrowful.

adj antonyms cheerful, jovial, merry.

lukewarm *adj* **1** blood-warm, tepid, thermal. **2** apathetic, cold, dull, indifferent, listless, unconcerned, torpid.

lull *vb* **1** calm, compose, hush, quiet, still. **2** abate, cease, decrease, diminish, subside. • *n* calm, calmness, cessation.

vb antonym agitate.

n antonym agitation, liveliness.

lumber¹ *vb* rumble, shamble, trudge.

lumber² *n* **1** refuse, rubbish, trash, trumpery. **2** wood.

luminous *adj* **1** effulgent, incandescent, radiant, refulgent, resplendent, shining. **2** bright, brilliant, clear. **3** clear, lucid, lucent, perspicuous, plain.

lunacy *n* aberration, craziness, dementia, derangement, insanity, madness, mania.

n antonym sanity.

lunatic *adj* crazy, demented, deranged, insane, mad, psychopathic. • *n* madman, maniac, psychopath.

lurch *vb* **1** appropriate, filch, pilfer, purloin, steal. **2** deceive, defeat, disappoint, evade. **3** ambush, lurk, skulk. **4** contrive, dodge, shift, trick. **5** pitch, sway.

lure *vb* allure, attract, decoy, entice, inveigle, seduce, tempt. • *n* allurement, attraction, bait, decoy, enticement, temptation.

lurid *adj* **1** dismal, ghastly, gloomy, lowering, murky, pale, wan. **2** glaring, sensational, startling, unrestrained.

lurk *vb* hide, prowl, skulk, slink, sneak, snoop.

luscious *adj* delicious, delightful, grateful, palatable, pleasing, savoury, sweet.
adj antonym austere.

lush *adj* fresh, juicy, luxuriant, moist, sappy, succulent, watery.

lust *vb* covet, crave, desire, hanker, need, want, yearn. • *n* **1** cupidity, desire, longing. **2** carnality, concupiscence, lasciviousness, lechery, lewdness, lubricity, salaciousness, salacity, wantonness.

lustful *adj* carnal, concupiscent, hankering, lascivious, lecherous, licentious, libidinous, lubricious, salacious.

lustily *adv* strongly, vigorously.

lustiness *n* hardihood, power, robustness, stoutness, strength, sturdiness, vigour.

lustre *n* brightness, brilliance, brilliancy, splendour.

lusty *adj* **1** healthful, lively, robust, stout, strong, sturdy, vigorous. **2** bulky, burly, corpulent, fat, large, stout.
adj antonyms effete, weak.

luxuriance *n* exuberance, profusion, superabundance.

luxuriant *adj* exuberant, plenteous, plentiful, profuse, superabundant.
adj antonyms barren, infertile.

luxuriate *vb* abound, delight, enjoy, flourish, indulge, revel.

luxurious *adj* epicurean, opulent, pampered, self-indulgent, sensual, sybaritic, voluptuous.
adj antonyms ascetic, austere, economical, frugal, scant(y), spartan.

luxury *n* **1** epicureanism, epicurism, luxuriousness, opulence, sensuality, voluptuousness. **2** delight, enjoyment, gratification, indulgence, pleasure. **3** dainty, delicacy, treat.
n antonym economy, poverty, spareness.

lying *adj* equivocating, false, mendacious, untruthful, untrue.
adj antonyms honest, truthful.

lyric *adj* dulcet, euphonious, lyrical, mellifluous, mellifluent, melodic, melodious, musical, poetic, silvery, tuneful.

lyrical *adj* **1** ecstatic, enthusiastic, expressive, impassion. **2** dulcet, lyric, mellifluous, mellifluent, melodic, melodious, musical, poetic.

M

macabre *adj* cadaverous, deathlike, deathly, dreadful, eerie, frightening, frightful, ghoulish, grim, grisly, gruesome, hideous, horrid, morbid, unearthly, weird.

mace *n* baton, staff, truncheon.

macerate *vb* 1 harass, mortify, torture. 2 digest, soak, soften, steep.

Machiavellian *adj* arch, artful, astute, crafty, crooked, cunning, deceitful, designing, diplomatic, insidious, intriguing, shrewd, sly, subtle, tricky, wily.

machination *n* artifice, cabal, conspiracy, contrivance, design, intrigue, plot, scheme, stratagem, trick.

machine *n* 1 instrument, puppet, tool. 2 machinery, organization, system. 3 engine.

mad *adj* 1 crazed, crazy, delirious, demented, deranged, distracted, insane, irrational, lunatic, maniac, maniacal. 2 enraged, furious, rabid, raging, violent. 3 angry, enraged, exasperated, furious, incensed, provoked, wrathful. 4 distracted, infatuated, wild. 5 frantic, frenzied, raving.
adj antonyms lucid, rational, sane.

madden *vb* annoy, craze, enrage, exasperate, inflame, infuriate, irritate, provoke.
vb antonyms calm, pacify, please.

madness *n* 1 aberration, craziness, dementia, derangement, insanity, lunacy, mania. 2 delirium, frenzy, fury, rage.
n antonym sanity.

magazine *n* 1 depository, depot, entrepot, receptacle, repository, storehouse, warehouse. 2 pamphlet, paper, periodical.

magic *adj* bewitching, charming, enchanting, fascinating, magical, miraculous, spellbinding. • *n* 1 conjuring, enchantment, necromancy, sorcery, thaumaturgy, voodoo, witchcraft. 2 char, fascination, witchery.

magician *n* conjurer, enchanter, juggler, magus, necromancer, shaman, sorcerer, wizard.

magisterial *adj* 1 august, dignified, majestic, pompous. 2 authoritative, despotic, domineering, imperious, dictatorial.

magnanimity *n* chivalry, disinterestedness, forbearance, high-mindedness, generosity, nobility.

magnificence *n* brilliance, éclat, grandeur, luxuriousness, luxury, majesty, pomp, splendour.
n antonyms modesty, plainness, simplicity.

magnificent *adj* 1 elegant, grand, majestic, noble, splendid, superb. 2 brilliant, gorgeous, imposing, lavish, luxurious, pompous, showy, stately.
adj antonyms humble, modest, plain, simple.

magnify *vb* 1 amplify, augment, enlarge. 2 bless, celebrate, elevate, exalt, extol, glorify, laud, praise. 3 exaggerate.
vb antonyms belittle, play down.

magnitude *n* 1 bulk, dimension, extent, mass, size, volume. 2 consequence, greatness, importance. 3 grandeur, loftiness, sublimity.
n antonym smallness.

maid *n* 1 damsel, girl, lass, lassie, maiden, virgin. 2 maidservant, servant.

maiden *adj* 1 chaste, pure, undefiled, virgin. 2 fresh, new, unused. • *n* girl, maid, virgin.

maidenly *adj* demure, gentle, modest, maidenlike, reserved.

maim *vb* cripple, disable, disfigure, mangle, mar, mutilate. • *n* 1 crippling, disfigurement, mutilation. 2 harm, hurt, injury, mischief.
vb antonyms heal, repair.

main¹ *adj* 1 capital, cardinal, chief, leading, principal. 2 essential, important, indispensable, necessary, requisite, vital. 3 enormous, huge, mighty, vast. 4 pure, sheer. 5 absolute, direct, entire, mere. • *n* 1 channel, pipe. 2 force, might, power, strength, violence.
adj antonyms minor, unimportant.
n antonym weakness.

main² *n* 1 high seas, ocean. 2 continent, mainland.

maintain *vb* 1 keep, preserve, support, sustain, uphold. 2 hold, possess. 3 defend, vindicate, justify. 4 carry on, continue, keep up. 5 feed, provide, supply. 6 allege, assert, declare. 7 affirm, contend, hold, say.
vb antonyms deny, neglect, oppose.

maintenance *n* 1 defence, justification, preservation, support, sustenance, vindication.

2 bread, food, livelihood, provisions, subsistence, sustenance, victuals.
n antonym neglect.

majestic *adj* **1** august, dignified, imperial, imposing, lofty, noble, pompous, princely, stately, regal, royal. **2** grand, magnificent, splendid, sublime.
adj antonyms unimportant, unimpressive.

majesty *n* augustness, dignity, elevation, grandeur, loftiness, stateliness.
n antonyms unimportance, unimpressiveness.

majority *n* **1** bulk, greater, mass, more, most, plurality, preponderance, superiority. **2** adulthood, manhood.

make *vb* **1** create. **2** fashion, figure, form, frame, mould, shape. **3** cause, construct, effect, establish, fabricate, produce. **4** do, execute, perform, practice. **5** acquire, gain, get, raise, secure. **6** cause, compel, constrain, force, occasion. **7** compose, constitute. **8** go, journey, move, proceed, tend, travel. **9** conduce, contribute, effect, favour, operate. **10** estimate, judge, reckon, suppose, think. • *n* brand, build, constitution, construction, form, shape, structure.
vb antonyms dismantle, lose, persuade.

maker *n* **1** creator, god. **2** builder, constructor, fabricator, framer, manufacturer. **3** author, composer, poet, writer.
n antonym dismantler.

maladministration *n* malversation, misgovernment, misrule.

maladroit *adj* awkward, bungling, clumsy, inept, inexpert, unhandy, unskilful, unskilled.
adj antonyms adroit, tactful.

malady *n* affliction, ailment, complaint, disease, disorder, illness, indisposition, sickness.
n antonym health.

malcontent *adj* discontented, dissatisfied, insurgent, rebellious, resentful, uneasy, unsatisfied. • *n* agitator, complainer, faultfinder, grumbler, spoilsport.
adj antonym contented.

malediction *n* anathema, ban, curse, cursing, denunciation, execration, imprecation.

malefactor *n* convict, criminal, culprit, delinquent, evildoer, felon, offender, outlaw.

malevolence *n* hate, hatred, ill-will, malice, malignity, rancour, spite, spitefulness, vindictiveness.
n antonym benevolence.

malevolent *adj* evil-minded, hateful, hostile, ill-natured, malicious, malignant, mischievous, rancorous, spiteful, venomous. vindictive.

malice *n* animosity, bitterness, enmity, grudge, hate, ill-will, malevolence, maliciousness, malignity, pique, rancour, spite, spitefulness, venom, vindictiveness.
n antonym kindness.

malicious *adj* bitter, envious, evil-minded, ill-disposed, ill-natured, invidious, malevolent, malignant, mischievous, rancorous, resentful, spiteful, vicious.
adj antonyms kind, thoughtful.

malign *vb* abuse, asperse, blacken, calumniate, defame, disparage, revile, scandalize, slander, traduce, vilify. • *adj* **1** malevolent, malicious, malignant, ill-disposed. **2** baneful, injurious, pernicious, unfavourable, unpropitious.
vb antonym praise.
adj antonym benign.

malignant *adj* **1** bitter, envious, hostile, inimical, malevolent, malicious, malign, spiteful, rancorous, resentful, virulent. **2** heinous, pernicious. **3** ill-boding, unfavourable, unpropitious. **4** dangerous, fatal.
adj antonyms harmless, kind.

malignity *n* **1** animosity, hatred, ill-will, malice, malevolence, maliciousness, rancour, spite. **2** deadliness, destructiveness, fatality, harmfulness, malignancy, perniciousness, virulence. **3** enormity, evilness, heinousness.

malpractice *n* dereliction, malversation, misbehaviour, misconduct, misdeed, misdoing, sin, transgression.

maltreat *vb* abuse, harm, hurt, ill-treat, illuse, injure.
vb antonym care for.

mammoth *adj* colossal, enormous, gigantic, huge, immense, vast.
adj antonym small.

man *vb* **1** crew, garrison, furnish. **2** fortify, reinforce, strengthen. • *n* **1** adult, being, body, human, individual, one, person, personage, somebody, soul. **2** humanity, humankind, mankind. **3** attendant, butler, dependant, liege, servant, subject, valet, vassal. **4** employee, workman.

manacle *vb* bind, chain, fetter, handcuff, restrain, shackle, tie. • *n* bond, chain, handcuff, gyve, hand-fetter, shackle.
vb antonym unshackle.

manage *vb* **1** administer, conduct, direct, guide, handle, operate, order, regulate, superintend, supervise, transact, treat. **2** control, govern, rule. **3** handle, manipulate, train, wield. **4** contrive, economize, husband, save.
vb antonym fail.

manageable *adj* controllable, docile, easy, governable, tamable, tractable.
adj antonym unmanageable.

management *n* administration, care, charge, conduct, control, direction, disposal, economy, government, guidance, superintendence, supervision, surveillance, treatment.

manager *n* comptroller, conductor, director, executive, governor, impresario, overseer, superintendent, supervisor.

mandate *n* charge, command, commission, edict, injunction, order, precept, requirement.

manful *adj* bold, brave, courageous, daring, heroic, honourable, intrepid, noble, stout, strong, undaunted, vigorous.

mangily *adv* basely, foully, meanly, scabbily, scurvily, vilely.

mangle[1] *vb* **1** hack, lacerate, mutilate, rend, tear. **2** cripple, crush, destroy, maim, mar, spoil.

mangle[2] *vb* calender, polish, press, smooth.

manhood *n* **1** virility. **2** bravery, courage, firmness, fortitude, hardihood, manfulness, manliness, resolution. **3** human nature, humanity. **4** adulthood, maturity.
n antonym womanhood.

mania *n* **1** aberration, craziness, delirium, dementia, derangement, frenzy, insanity, lunacy, madness. **2** craze, desire, enthusiasm, fad, fanaticism.

manifest *vb* declare, demonstrate, disclose, discover, display, evidence, evince, exhibit, express, reveal, show. • *adj* apparent, clear, conspicuous, distinct, evident, glaring, indubitable, obvious, open, palpable, patent, plain, unmistakable, visible.
vb antonym hide.
adj antonym unclear.

manifestation *n* disclosure, display, exhibition, exposure, expression, revelation.

manifold *adj* complex, diverse, many, multifarious, multiplied, multitudinous, numerous, several, sundry, varied, various.
adj antonym simple.

manipulate *vb* handle, operate, work.

manliness *n* boldness, bravery, courage,

dignity, fearlessness, firmness, heroism, intrepidity, nobleness, resolution, valour.

manly *adj* **1** bold, brave, courageous, daring, dignified, firm, heroic, intrepid, manful, noble, stout, strong, undaunted, vigorous. **2** male, masculine, virile.
adj antonym womanly.

manner *n* **1** fashion, form, method, mode, style, way. **2** custom, habit, practice. **3** degree, extent, measure. **4** kind, kinds, sort, sorts. **5** air, appearance, aspect, behaviour, carriage, demeanour, deportment, look, mien. **6** mannerism, peculiarity. **7** behaviour, conduct, habits, morals. **8** civility, deportment.

mannerly *adj* ceremonious, civil, complaisant, courteous, polite, refined, respectful, urbane, well-behaved, well-bred.
adj antonym unmannerly.

manners *npl* **1** conduct, habits, morals. **2** air, bearing, behaviour, breeding, carriage, comportment, deportment, etiquette.

manoeuvre *vb* contrive, finesse, intrigue, manage, plan, plot, scheme. • *n* **1** evolution, exercise, movement, operation. **2** artifice, finesse, intrigue, plan, plot, ruse, scheme, stratagem, trick.

mansion *n* abode, dwelling, dwelling house, habitation, hall, residence, seat.

mantle *vb* **1** cloak, cover, discover, obscure. **2** expand, spread. **3** bubble, cream, effervesce, foam, froth, sparkle. • *n* chasuble, cloak, toga. **4** cover, covering, hood.

manufacture *vb* build, compose, construct, create, fabricate, forge, form, make, mould, produce, shape. • *n* constructing, fabrication, making, production.

manumission *n* deliverance, emancipation, enfranchisement, freedom, liberation, release.

manumit *vb* deliver, emancipate, enfranchise, free, liberate, release.

manure *vb* enrich, fertilize. • *n* compost, dressing, fertilizer, guano, muck.

many *adj* abundant, diverse, frequent, innumerable, manifold, multifarious, multifold, multiplied, multitudinous, numerous, sundry, varied, various. • *n* crowd, multitude, people.
adj antonym few.

map *vb* chart, draw up, plan, plot, set out, sketch. • *n* chart, diagram, outline, plot, sketch.

mar *vb* **1** blot, damage, harm, hurt, impair,

injure, ruin, spoil, stain. **2** deface, deform, disfigure, maim, mutilate.
vb antonym enhance.

marauder *n* bandit, brigand, desperado, filibuster, freebooter, outlaw, pillager, plunderer, ravager, robber, rover.

march *vb* go, pace, parade, step, tramp, walk. • *n* **1** hike, tramp, walk. **2** parade, procession. **3** gait, step, stride. **4** advance, evolution, progress.

marches *npl* borders, boundaries, confines, frontiers, limits, precincts.

margin *n* **1** border, brim, brink, confine, edge, limit, rim, skirt, verge. **2** latitude, room, space, surplus.
n antonyms centre, core.

marine *adj* **1** oceanic, pelagic, saltwater, sea. **2** maritime, naval, nautical. • *n* **1** navy, shipping. **2** sea-dog, sea soldier, soldier. **3** sea piece, seascape.

mariner *n* navigator, sailor, salt, seafarer, seaman, tar.

marital *adj* connubial, conjugal, matrimonial.

maritime *adj* **1** marine, naval, nautical, oceanic, sea, seafaring, seagoing. **2** coastal, seaside.

mark *vb* **1** distinguish, earmark, label. **2** betoken, brand, characterize, denote, designate, engrave, impress, imprint, indicate, print, stamp. **3** evince, heed, note, notice, observe, regard, remark, show, spot. • *n* **1** brand, character, characteristic, impression, impress, line, note, print, sign, stamp, symbol, token, race. **2** evidence, indication, proof, symptom, trace, track, vestige. **3** badge. **4** footprint. **5** bull's-eye, butt, object, target. **6** consequence, distinction, eminence, fame, importance, notability, position, preeminence, reputation, significance.

marked *adj* conspicuous, distinguished, eminent, notable, noted, outstanding, prominent, remarkable.
adj antonyms slight, unnoticeable.

marriage *n* **1** espousals, nuptials, spousals, wedding. **2** matrimony, wedlock. **3** union. **4** alliance, association, confederation.
n antonym divorce.

marrow *n* **1** medulla, pith. **2** cream, essence, quintessence, substance.

marsh *n* bog, fen, mire, morass, quagmire, slough, swamp.

marshal *vb* **1** arrange, array, dispose, gather,

muster, range, order, rank. **2** guide, herald, lead. • *n* **1** conductor, director, master of ceremonies, regulator. **2** harbinger, herald, pursuivant.

marshy *adj* boggy, miry, mossy, swampy, wet.

martial *adj* brave, heroic, military, soldierlike, warlike.
adj antonym pacific.

marvel *vb* gape, gaze, goggle, wonder. • *n* **1** miracle, prodigy, wonder. **2** admiration, amazement, astonishment, surprise.

marvellous *adj* **1** amazing, astonishing, extraordinary, miraculous, prodigious, strange, stupendous, wonderful, wondrous. **2** improbable, incredible, surprising, unbelievable.
adj antonyms ordinary, plausible, run-of-the-mill.

masculine *adj* **1** bold, hardy, manful, manlike, manly, mannish, virile. **2** potent, powerful, robust, strong, vigorous. **3** bold, coarse, forward.
adj antonym feminine.

mask *vb* cloak, conceal, cover, disguise, hide, screen, shroud, veil. • *n* **1** blind, cloak, disguise, screen, veil. **2** evasion, pretence, plea, pretext, ruse, shift, subterfuge, trick. **3** masquerade. **4** bustle, mummery.
vb antonym uncover.

masquerade *vb* cover, disguise, hide, mask, revel, veil. • *n* mask, mummery, revel, revelry.

Mass *n* communion, Eucharist.

mass *vb* accumulate, amass, assemble, collect, gather, rally, throng. • *adj* extensive, general, large-scale, widespread. • *n* **1** cake, clot, lump. **2** assemblage, collection, combination, congeries, heap. **3** bulk, dimension, magnitude, size. **4** accumulation, aggregate, body, sum, total, totality, whole.
vb antonym separate.
adj antonym limited.

massacre *vb* annihilate, butcher, exterminate, kill, murder, slaughter, slay. • *n* annihilation, butchery, carnage, extermination, killing, murder, pogrom, slaughter.

massive *adj* big, bulky, colossal, enormous, heavy, huge, immense, ponderous, solid, substantial, vast, weighty.
adj antonyms slight, small.

master *vb* **1** conquer, defeat, direct, govern, overcome, overpower, rule, subdue, subjugate, vanquish. **2** acquire, learn. • *adj*

1 cardinal, chief, especial, grand, great, main, leading, prime, principal. **2** adept, expert, proficient. • *n* **1** director, governor, lord, manager, overseer, superintendent, ruler. **2** captain, commander. **3** instructor, pedagogue, preceptor, schoolteacher, teacher, tutor. **4** holder, owner, possessor, proprietor. **5** chief, head, leader, principal.
vb antonyms fail.
adj antonyms copy, subordinate, unskilled.
n antonyms amateur, learner, pupil, servant, slave.

masterly *adj* **1** adroit, clever, dextrous, excellent, expert, finished, skilful, skilled. **2** arbitrary, despotic, despotical, domineering, imperious.
adj antonyms clumsy, poor, unskilled.

mastery *n* **1** command, dominion, mastership, power, rule, supremacy, sway. **2** ascendancy, conquest, leadership, preeminence, superiority, upper-hand, victory. **3** acquisition, acquirement, attainment. **4** ability, cleverness, dexterity, proficiency, skill.
n antonyms clumsiness, unfamiliarity.

masticate *vb* chew, eat, munch.

match *vb* **1** equal, rival. **2** adapt, fit, harmonize, proportion, suit. **3** marry, mate. **4** combine, couple, join, sort. **5** oppose, pit. **6** correspond, suit, tally. • *n* **1** companion, equal, mate, tally. **2** competition, contest, game, trial. **3** marriage, union.
vb antonyms clash, separate.
n antonym opposite.

matchless *adj* consummate, excellent, exquisite, incomparable, inimitable, peerless, perfect, surpassing, unequalled, unmatched, unparalleled, unrivalled.
adj antonyms commonplace, poor.

mate *vb* **1** marry, match, wed. **2** compete, equal, vie. **3** appal, confound, crush, enervate, subdue, stupefy. • *n* **1** associate, companion, compeer, consort, crony, friend, fellow, intimate. **2** companion, equal, match. **3** assistant, subordinate. **4** husband, spouse, wife.

material *adj* **1** bodily, corporeal, nonspiritual, physical, temporal. **2** essential, important, momentous, relevant, vital, weighty. • *n* body, element, stuff, substance.
adj antonyms ethereal, immaterial.

maternal *adj* motherlike, motherly.
adj antonym paternal.

matrimonial *adj* conjugal, connubial,

espousal, hymeneal, marital, nuptial, spousal.

matrimony *n* marriage, wedlock.

matter *vb* import, signify, weigh. • *n* **1** body, content, sense, substance. **2** difficulty, distress, trouble. **3** material, stuff. **4** question, subject, subject matter, topic. **5** affair, business, concern, event. **6** consequence, import, importance, moment, significance. **7** discharge, purulence, pus.
n antonym insignificance.

mature *vb* develop, perfect, ripen. • *adj* **1** complete, fit, full-grown, perfect, ripe. **2** completed, prepared, ready, well-considered, well-digested.
adj antonym immature.

maturity *n* completeness, completion, matureness, perfection, ripeness.

mawkish *adj* **1** disgusting, flat, insipid, nauseous, sickly, stale, tasteless, vapid. **2** emotional, feeble, maudlin, sentimental.
adj antonyms matter-of-fact, pleasant.

maxim *n* adage, aphorism, apothegm, axiom, byword, dictum, proverb, saw, saying, truism.

maze *vb* amaze, bewilder, confound, confuse, perplex. • *n* **1** intricacy, labyrinth, meander. **2** bewilderment, embarrassment, intricacy, perplexity, puzzle, uncertainty.

mazy *adj* confused, confusing, intricate, labyrinthian, labyrinthic, labyrinthine, perplexing, winding.

meagre *adj* **1** emaciated, gaunt, lank, lean, poor, skinny, starved, spare, thin. **2** barren, poor, sterile, unproductive. **3** bald, barren, dry, dull, mean, poor, prosy, feeble, insignificant, jejune, scanty, small, tame, uninteresting, vapid.

mean[1] *vb* **1** contemplate, design, intend, purpose. **2** connote, denote, express, imply, import, indicate, purport, signify, symbolize.

mean[2] *adj* **1** average, medium, middle. **2** intermediate, intervening. • *n* **1** measure, mediocrity, medium, moderation. **2** average. **3** agency, instrument, instrumentality, means, measure, method, mode, way.
adj antonym generous, kind, noble, superior, extreme.
n antonym extreme.

mean[3] *adj* **1** coarse, common, humble, ignoble, low, ordinary, plebeian, vulgar. **2** abject, base, base-minded, beggarly,

contemptible, degraded, dirty, dishonourable, disingenuous, grovelling, low-minded, pitiful, rascally, scurvy, servile, shabby, sneaking, sorry, spiritless, unfair, vile. **3** illiberal, mercenary, miserly, narrow, narrow-minded, niggardly, parsimonious, penurious, selfish, sordid, stingy, ungenerous, unhandsome. **4** contemptible, despicable, diminutive, insignificant, paltry, petty, poor, small, wretched.
adj antonyms generous, kind, noble, superior.

meaning *n* acceptation, drift, import, intention, purport, purpose, sense, signification.

means *npl* **1** instrument, method, mode, way. **2** appliance, expedient, measure, resource, shift, step. **3** estate, income, property, resources, revenue, substance, wealth, wherewithal.

measure *vb* **1** mete. **2** adjust, gauge, proportion. **3** appraise, appreciate, estimate, gauge, value. • *n* **1** gauge, meter, rule, standard. **2** degree, extent, length, limit. **3** allotment, share, proportion. **4** means, step. **5** foot, metre, rhythm, tune, verse.

measureless *adj* boundless, endless, immeasurable, immense, limitless, unbounded, unlimited, vast.
adj antonym measurable.

meat *n* aliment, cheer, diet, fare, feed, flesh, food, nourishment, nutriment, provision, rations, regimen, subsistence, sustenance, viands, victuals.

mechanic *n* artificer, artisan, craftsman, hand, handicraftsman, machinist, operative, workman.

meddle *vb* interfere, intermeddle, interpose, intrude.

meddlesome *adj* interfering, intermeddling, intrusive, officious, prying.

mediate *vb* arbitrate, intercede, interpose, intervene, settle. • *adj* interposed, intervening, middle.

mediation *n* arbitration, intercession, interposition, intervention.

mediator *n* advocate, arbitrator, interceder, intercessor, propitiator, umpire.

medicine *n* **1** drug, medicament, medication, physic. **2** therapy.

mediocre *adj* average, commonplace, indifferent, mean, medium, middling, ordinary.
adj antonyms excellent, exceptional, extraordinary.

meditate *vb* **1** concoct, contrive, design, devise, intend, plan, purpose, scheme.

2 chew, contemplate, ruminate, study. **3** cogitate, muse, ponder, think.

meditation *n* cogitation, contemplation, musing, pondering, reflection, ruminating, study, thought.

meditative *adj* contemplative, pensive, reflective, studious, thoughtful.

medium *adj* average, mean, mediocre, middle. • *n* **1** agency, channel, intermediary, instrument, instrumentality, means, organ. **2** conditions, environment, influences. **3** average, means.

medley *n* confusion, farrago, hodgepodge, hotchpotch, jumble, mass, melange, miscellany, mishmash, mixture.

meed *n* award, guerdon, premium, prize, recompense, remuneration, reward.

meek *adj* gentle, humble, lowly, mild, modest, pacific, soft, submissive, unassuming, yielding.
adj antonyms arrogant, rebellious.

meekness *n* gentleness, humbleness, humility, lowliness, mildness, modesty, submission, submissiveness.

meet *vb* **1** cross, intersect, transact. **2** confront, encounter, engage. **3** answer, comply, fulfil, gratify, satisfy. **4** converge, join, unite. **5** assemble, collect, convene, congregate, forgather, muster, rally. • *adj* adapted, appropriate, befitting, convenient, fit, fitting, proper, qualified, suitable, suited.

meeting *n* **1** encounter, interview. **2** assemblage, assembly, audience, company, concourse, conference, congregation, convention, gathering. **3** assignation, encounter, introduction, rendezvous. **4** confluence, conflux, intersection, joining, junction, union. **5** collision.

melancholy *adj* **1** blue, dejected, depressed, despondent, desponding, disconsolate, dismal, dispirited, doleful, down, downcast, downhearted, gloomy, glum, hypochondriac, low-spirited, lugubrious, moody, mopish, sad, sombre, sorrowful, unhappy. **2** afflictive, calamitous, unfortunate, unlucky. **3** dark, gloomy, grave, quiet. • *n* blues, dejection, depression, despondency, dismals, dumps, gloom, gloominess, hypochondria, sadness, vapours.
adj antonyms cheerful, gay, happy, joyful.
n antonym exhilaration.

melee *n* affray, brawl, broil, contest, fight, fray, scuffle.

mellifluous, mellifluent *adj* dulcet,

euphonic, euphonical, euphonious, mellow, silver-toned, silvery, smooth, soft, sweet.

mellow *vb* 1 mature, ripen. 2 improve, smooth, soften, tone. 3 pulverize. 4 perfect. • *adj* 1 mature, ripe. 2 dulcet, mellifluous, mellifluent, rich, silver-toned, silvery, smooth, soft. 3 delicate. 4 genial, good-humoured, jolly, jovial, matured, softened. 5 mellowy, loamy, unctuous. 6 perfected, well-prepared. 7 disguised, fuddled, intoxicated, tipsy.

adj antonyms immature, unripe.

melodious *adj* arioso, concordant, dulcet, euphonious, harmonious, mellifluous, mellifluent, musical, silvery, sweet, tuneful.

adj antonyms discordant, grating, harsh.

melody *n* air, descant, music, plainsong, song, theme, tune.

melt *vb* 1 dissolve, fuse, liquefy, thaw. 2 mollify, relax, soften, subdue. 3 dissipate, waste. 4 blend, pass, shade.

vb antonyms freeze, harden, solidify.

member *n* 1 arm, leg, limb, organ. 2 component, constituent, element, part, portion. 3 branch, clause, division, head.

memento *n* memorial, remembrance, reminder, souvenir.

memoir *n* account, autobiography, biography, journal, narrative, record, register.

memorable *adj* celebrated, distinguished, extraordinary, famous, great, illustrious, important, notable, noteworthy, remarkable, signal, significant.

adj antonym forgettable.

memorandum *n* minute, note, record.

memorial *adj* commemorative, monumental. • *n* 1 cairn, commemoration, memento, monument, plaque, record, souvenir. 2 memorandum, remembrance.

memory *n* 1 recollection, remembrance, reminiscence. 2 celebrity, fame, renown, reputation. 3 commemoration, memorial.

n antonym forgetfulness.

menace *vb* alarm, frighten, intimidate, threaten. • *n* 1 danger, hazard, peril, threat, warning. 2 nuisance, pest, troublemaker.

menage *n* household, housekeeping, management.

mend *vb* 1 darn, patch, rectify, refit, repair, restore, retouch. 2 ameliorate, amend, better, correct, emend, improve, meliorate,

reconcile, rectify, reform. 3 advance, help. 4 augment, increase.

vb antonyms break, destroy, deteriorate.

mendacious *adj* deceitful, deceptive, fallacious, false, lying, untrue, untruthful.

adj antonyms honest, truthful.

mendacity *n* deceit, deceitfulness, deception, duplicity, falsehood, lie, untruth.

mendicant *n* beggar, pauper, tramp.

menial *adj* base, low, mean, servile, vile. • *n* attendant, bondsman, domestic, flunkey, footman, lackey, serf, servant, slave, underling, valet, waiter.

mensuration *n* 1 measurement, measuring. 2 survey, surveying.

mental *adj* ideal, immaterial, intellectual, psychiatric, subjective.

adj antonym physical, balanced, sane.

mention *vb* acquaint, allude, cite, communicate, declare, disclose, divulge, impart, inform, name, report, reveal, state, tell. • *n* allusion, citation, designation, notice, noting, reference.

mentor *n* adviser, counsellor, guide, instructor, monitor.

mephitic *adj* baleful, baneful, fetid, foul, mephitical, noisome, noxious, poisonous, pestilential.

mercantile *adj* commercial, marketable, trading.

mercenary *adj* 1 hired, paid, purchased, venal. 2 avaricious, covetous, grasping, mean, niggardly, parsimonious, penurious, sordid, stingy. • *n* hireling, soldier.

merchandise *n* commodities, goods, wares.

merchant *n* dealer, retailer, shopkeeper, trader, tradesman.

merciful *adj* 1 clement, compassionate, forgiving, gracious, lenient, pitiful. 2 benignant, forbearing, gentle, humane, kind, mild, tender, tender-hearted.

adj antonyms cruel, merciless.

merciless *adj* barbarous, callous, cruel, fell, hard-hearted, inexorable, pitiless, relentless, remorseless, ruthless, savage, severe, uncompassionate, unfeeling, unmerciful, unrelenting, unrepenting, unsparing.

adj antonym merciful.

mercurial *adj* 1 active, lively, nimble, prompt, quick, sprightly. 2 cheerful, light-hearted. 3 changeable, fickle, flighty, inconstant, mobile, volatile.

adj antonym saturnine.

mercy *n* 1 benevolence, clemency,

compassion, gentleness, kindness, lenience, leniency, lenity, mildness, pity, tenderness. **2** blessing, favour, grace. **3** discretion, disposal. **4** forgiveness, pardon.
n antonyms cruelty, revenge.

mere *adj* **1** bald, bare, naked, plain, sole, simple. **2** absolute, entire, pure, sheer, unmixed. • *n* lake, pond, pool.

meretricious *adj* deceitful, brummagem, false, gaudy, make-believe, sham, showy, spurious, tawdry.

merge *vb* bury, dip, immerse, involve, lose, plunge, sink, submerge.

meridian *n* **1** acme, apex, climax, culmination, summit, zenith. **2** midday, noon, noontide.

merit *vb* **1** deserve, earn, incur. **2** acquire, gain, profit, value. • *n* **1** claim, right. **2** credit, desert, excellence, goodness, worth, worthiness.
n antonyms demerit, fault.

meritorious *adj* commendable, deserving, excellent, good, worthy.
adj antonym unworthy.

merriment *n* amusement, frolic, gaiety, hilarity, jocularity, jollity, joviality, laughter, liveliness, mirth, sport, sportiveness.

merry *adj* **1** agreeable, brisk, delightful, exhilarating, lively, pleasant, stirring. **2** airy, blithe, blithesome, buxom, cheerful, comical, droll, facetious, frolicsome, gladsome, gleeful, hilarious, jocund, jolly, jovial, joyous, light-hearted, lively, mirthful, sportive, sprightly, vivacious.
adj antonyms gloomy, glum, grave, melancholy, serious, sober, sombre.

mess *n* **1** company, set. **2** farrago, hodgepodge, hotchpotch, jumble, medley, mass, melange, miscellany, mishmash, mixture. **3** confusion, muddle, perplexity, pickle, plight, predicament.
n antonyms order, tidiness.
vb antonyms order, tidy.

message *n* communication, dispatch, intimation, letter, missive, notice, telegram, wire, word.

messenger *n* **1** carrier, courier, emissary, envoy, express, mercury, nuncio. **2** forerunner, harbinger, herald, precursor.

metamorphic *adj* changeable, mutable, variable.

metamorphose *vb* change, mutate, transfigure, transform, transmute.

metamorphosis *n* change, mutation,

transfiguration, transformation, transmutation.

metaphorical *adj* allegorical, figurative, symbolic, symbolical.

metaphysical *adj* abstract, allegorical, figurative, general, intellectual, parabolic, subjective, unreal.

mete *vb* dispense, distribute, divide, measure, ration, share. • *n* bound, boundary, butt, limit, measure, term, terminus.

meteor *n* aerolite, falling star, shooting star.

method *n* **1** course, manner, means, mode, procedure, process, rule, way. **2** arrangement, classification, disposition, order, plan, regularity, scheme, system.

methodical *adj* exact, orderly, regular, systematic, systematical.
adj antonyms confused, desultory, irregular.

metropolis *n* capital, city, conurbation.

mettle *n* **1** constitution, element, material, stuff. **2** character, disposition, spirit, temper. **3** ardour, courage, fire, hardihood, life, nerve, pluck, sprightliness, vigour.

mettlesome *adj* ardent, brisk, courageous, fiery, frisky, high-spirited, lively, spirited, sprightly.

mew *vb* **1** confine, coop, encase, enclose, imprison. **2** cast, change, mould, shed.

microscopic *adj* infinitesimal, minute, tiny.
adj antonyms huge, vast.

middle *adj* **1** central, halfway, mean, medial, mid. **2** intermediate, intervening. • *n* centre, halfway, mean, midst.
n antonyms beginning, border, edge, end, extreme.

middleman *n* agent, broker, factor, go-between, intermediary.

mien *n* air, appearance, aspect, bearing, behaviour, carriage, countenance, demeanour, deportment, look, manner.

might *n* ability, capacity, efficacy, efficiency, force, main, power, prowess, puissance, strength.

mighty *adj* **1** able, bold, courageous, potent, powerful, puissant, robust, strong, sturdy, valiant, valorous, vigorous. **2** bulky, enormous, huge, immense, monstrous, stupendous, vast.
adj antonyms frail, weak.

migratory *adj* nomadic, roving, shifting, strolling, unsettled, wandering, vagrant.

mild *adj* **1** amiable, clement, compassionate, gentle, good-natured, indulgent,

kind, lenient, meek, merciful, pacific, tender. **2** bland, pleasant, soft, suave. **3** calm, kind, placid, temperate, tranquil. **4** assuasive, compliant, demulcent, emollient, lenitive, mollifying, soothing.
adj antonyms fierce, harsh, stormy, strong, violent.

mildness *n* amiability, clemency, gentleness, indulgence, kindness, meekness, moderation, softness, tenderness, warmth.

mildew *n* blight, blast, mould, must, mustiness, smut, rust.

milieu *n* background, environment, sphere, surroundings.

militant *adj* belligerent, combative, contending, fighting.

military *adj* martial, soldier, soldierly, warlike. • *n* army, militia, soldiers.

mill *vb* comminute, crush, grate, grind, levigate, powder, pulverize. • *n* **1** factory, manufactory. **2** grinder. **3** crowd, throng.

mimic *vb* ape, counterfeit, imitate, impersonate, mime, mock, parody. • *adj* imitative, mock, simulated. • *n* imitator, impersonator, mime, mocker, parodist, parrot.

mince¹ *vb* chop, cut, hash, shatter. • *n* forcemeat, hash, mash, mincemeat.

mince² *vb* **1** attenuate, diminish, extenuate, mitigate, palliate, soften. **2** pose, sashay, simper, smirk.

mind¹ *vb* **1** attend, heed, mark, note, notice, regard, tend, watch. **2** obey, observe, submit. **3** design, incline, intend, mean. **4** recall, recollect, remember, remind. **5** beware, look out, watch out. • *n* **1** soul, spirit. **2** brains, common sense, intellect, reason, sense, understanding. **3** belief, consideration, contemplation, judgement, opinion, reflection, sentiment, thought. **4** memory, recollection, remembrance. **5** bent, desire, disposition, inclination, intention, leaning, purpose, tendency, will.

mind² *vb* balk, begrudge, grudge, object, resent.

mindful *adj* attentive, careful, heedful, observant, regardful, thoughtful.
adj antonyms heedless, inattentive, mindless.

mindless *adj* **1** dull, heavy, insensible, senseless, sluggish, stupid, unthinking. **2** careless, forgetful, heedless, neglectful, negligent, regardless.

mine *vb* **1** dig, excavate, quarry, unearth. **2** sap, undermine, weaken. **3** destroy, ruin. • *n* colliery, deposit, lode, pit, shaft.

mingle *vb* blend, combine, commingle, compound, intermingle, intermix, join, mix, unite.

miniature *adj* bantam, diminutive, little, small, tiny.
adj antonym giant.

minion *n* **1** creature, dependant, favourite, hanger-on, parasite, sycophant. **2** darling, favourite, flatterer, pet.

minister *vb* **1** administer, afford, furnish, give, supply. **2** aid, assist, contribute, help, succour. • *n* **1** agent, assistant, servant, subordinate, underling. **2** administrator, executive. **3** ambassador, delegate, envoy, plenipotentiary. **4** chaplain, churchman, clergyman, cleric, curate, divine, ecclesiastic, parson, pastor, preacher, priest, rector, vicar.

ministry *n* **1** agency, aid, help, instrumentality, interposition, intervention, ministration, service, support. **2** administration, cabinet, council, government.

minor *adj* **1** less, smaller. **2** inferior, junior, secondary, subordinate, younger. **3** inconsiderable, petty, unimportant, small.
adj antonym major.

minstrel *n* bard, musician, singer, troubadour.

mint *vb* **1** coin, stamp. **2** fabricate, fashion, forge, invent, make, produce. • *adj* fresh, new, perfect, undamaged. • *n* **1** die, punch, seal, stamp. **2** fortune, (*inf*) heap, million, pile, wad.

minute¹ *adj* **1** diminutive, fine, little, microscopic, miniature, slender, slight, small, tiny. **2** circumstantial, critical, detailed, exact, fussy, meticulous, nice, particular, precise.
adj antonyms gigantic, huge, immense.

minute² *n* **1** account, entry, item, memorandum, note, proceedings, record. **2** instant, moment, second, trice, twinkling.

miracle *n* marvel, prodigy, wonder.

miraculous *adj* **1** supernatural, thaumaturgic, thaumaturgical. **2** amazing, extraordinary, incredible, marvellous, unaccountable, unbelievable, wondrous.
adj antonyms natural, normal.

mirror *vb* copy, echo, emulate, reflect, show. • *n* **1** looking-glass, reflector, speculum. **2** archetype, exemplar, example, model, paragon, pattern, prototype.

mirth *n* cheerfulness, festivity, frolic, fun, gaiety, gladness, glee, hilarity, festivity, jollity, joviality, joyousness, laughter, merriment, merry-making, rejoicing, sport.
n antonyms gloom, gloominess, melancholy.

mirthful *adj* **1** cheery, festive, frolicsome, hilarious, jocund, jolly, merry, jovial, joyous, lively, playful, sportive, vivacious. **2** comic, droll, humorous, facetious, funny, jocose, jocular, ludicrous, merry, waggish, witty.

misadventure *n* accident, calamity, catastrophe, cross, disaster, failure, ill-luck, infelicity, mischance, misfortune, mishap, reverse.

misanthrope *n* cynic, egoist, egotist, man-hater, misanthropist.

misapply *vb* abuse, misuse, pervert.

misapprehend *vb* misconceive, mistake, misunderstand.

misbehaviour *n* ill-behaviour, ill-conduct, incivility, miscarriage, misconduct, misdemeanour, naughtiness, rudeness.

miscarriage *n* **1** calamity, defeat, disaster, failure, mischance, mishap. **2** misbehaviour, misconduct, ill-behaviour.
n antonym success.

miscellaneous *adj* confused, diverse, diversified, heterogeneous, indiscriminate, jumbled, many, mingled, mixed, promiscuous, stromatic, stromatous, various.

miscellany *n* collection, diversity, farrago, gallimaufry, hodgepodge, hotchpotch, jumble, medley, mishmash, melange, miscellaneous, mixture, variety.

mischance *n* accident, calamity, disaster, ill-fortune, ill-luck, infelicity, misadventure, misfortune, mishap.

mischief *n* **1** damage, detriment, disadvantage, evil, harm, hurt, ill, injury, prejudice. **2** ill-consequence, misfortune, trouble. **3** devilry, wrong-doing.
n antonym authority, fortune, goodness, virtue.

mischievous *adj* **1** destructive, detrimental, harmful, hurtful, injurious, noxious, pernicious. **2** malicious, sinful, vicious, wicked. **3** annoying, impish, naughty, troublesome, vexatious.
adj antonyms good, well-behaved.

misconceive *vb* misapprehend, misjudge, mistake, misunderstand.

misconduct *vb* botch, bungle, misdirect, mismanage. • *n* **1** bad conduct, ill-conduct, misbehaviour, misdemeanour, rudeness, transgression. **2** ill-management, mismanagement.

misconstrue *vb* **1** misread, mistranslate. **2** misapprehend, misinterpret, mistake, misunderstand.

miscreant *adj* corrupt, criminal, evil, rascally, unprincipled, vicious, villainous, wicked. • *n* knave, ragamuffin, rascal, rogue, ruffian, scamp, scoundrel, vagabond, villain.
adj antonym good, principled, worthy.
n antonym angel.

misdemeanour *n* fault, ill-behaviour, misbehaviour, misconduct, misdeed, offence, transgression, trespass.

miser *n* churl, curmudgeon, lickpenny, money-grabber, niggard, penny-pincher, pinch-fist, screw, scrimp, skinflint.
n antonym spendthrift, profligate.

miserable *adj* **1** afflicted, broken-hearted, comfortless, disconsolate, distressed, forlorn, heartbroken, unhappy, wretched. **2** calamitous, hapless, ill-starred, pitiable, unfortunate, unlucky. **3** poor, valueless, worthless. **4** abject, contemptible, despicable, low, mean, worthless.
adj antonyms cheerful, comfortable, generous, honourable, noble.

miserly *adj* avaricious, beggarly, close, close-fisted, covetous, grasping, mean, niggardly, parsimonious, penurious, sordid, stingy, tight-fisted.
adj antonyms generous, lavish, prodigal, spendthrift, profligate.

misery *n* affliction, agony, anguish, calamity, desolation, distress, grief, heartache, heavy-heartedness, misfortune, sorrow, suffering, torment, torture, tribulation, unhappiness, woe, wretchedness.

misfortune *n* adversity, affliction, bad luck, blow, calamity, casualty, catastrophe, disaster, distress, hardship, harm, ill, infliction, misadventure, mischance, mishap, reverse, scourge, stroke, trial, trouble, visitation.
n antonyms luck, success.

misgiving *n* apprehension, distrust, doubt, hesitation, suspicion, uncertainty.
n antonym certainty, confidence, trust.

mishap *n* accident, calamity, disaster, ill luck, misadventure, mischance, misfortune.

misinterpret *vb* distort, falsify, misapprehend, misconceive, misconstrue, misjudge.

mislead *vb* beguile, deceive, delude, misdirect, misguide.

mismanage *vb* botch, fumble, misconduct, mishandle, misrule.

misprize *vb* slight, underestimate, underrate, undervalue.

misrepresent *vb* belie, caricature, distort, falsify, misinterpret, misstate, pervert.

misrule *n* anarchy, confusion, disorder, maladministration, misgovernment, mismanagement.

miss[1] *vb* 1 blunder, err, fail, fall short, forgo, lack, lose, miscarry, mistake, omit, overlook, trip. 2 avoid, escape, evade, skip, slip. 3 feel the loss of, need, want, wish. • *n* 1 blunder, error, failure, fault, mistake, omission, oversight, slip, trip. 2 loss, want.

miss[2] *n* damsel, girl, lass, maid, maiden.

misshapen *adj* deformed, ill-formed, ill-shaped, ill-proportioned, misformed, ugly, ungainly.

adj antonyms regular, shapely.

missile *n* projectile, weapon.

mission *n* 1 commission, legation. 2 business, charge, duty, errand, office, trust. 3 delegation, deputation, embassy.

missive *n* communication, epistle, letter, message, note.

mist *vb* cloud, drizzle, mizzle, smog. • *n* 1 cloud, fog, haze. 2 bewilderment, obscurity, perplexity.

vb antonym clear.

mistake *vb* 1 misapprehend, miscalculate, misconceive, misjudge, misunderstand. 2 confound, take. 3 blunder, err. • *n* 1 misapprehension, miscalculation, misconception, mistaking, misunderstanding. 2 blunder, error, fault, inaccuracy, oversight, slip, trip.

mistaken *adj* erroneous, inaccurate, incorrect, misinformed, wrong.

adj antonyms correct, justified.

mistrust *vb* 1 distrust, doubt, suspect. 2 apprehend, fear, surmise, suspect. • *n* doubt, distrust, misgiving, suspicion.

vb antonym trust.

n antonym trust.

misty *adj* cloudy, clouded, dark, dim, foggy, obscure, overcast.

misunderstand *vb* misapprehend, misconceive, misconstrue, mistake.

vb antonyms grasp, understand.

misunderstanding *n* 1 error, misapprehension, misconception, mistake. 2 difference, difficulty, disagreement, discord, dissension, quarrel.

n antonyms agreement, reconciliation, understanding.

misuse *vb* 1 desecrate, misapply, misemploy, pervert, profane. 2 abuse, ill-treat, maltreat, ill-use. 3 fritter, squander, waste. • *n* 1 abuse, perversion, profanation, prostitution. 2 ill-treatment, ill-use, ill-usage, misusage. 3 misapplication, solecism.

mitigate *vb* 1 abate, alleviate, assuage, diminish, extenuate, lessen, moderate, palliate, relieve. 2 allay, appease, calm, mollify, pacify, quell, quiet, reduce, soften, soothe. 3 moderate, temper.

vb antonyms aggravate, exacerbate, increase.

mitigation *n* abatement, allaying, alleviation, assuagement, diminution, moderation, palliation, relief.

mix *vb* 1 alloy, amalgamate, blend, commingle, combine, compound, incorporate, interfuse, interlard, mingle, unite. 2 associate, join. • *n* alloy, amalgam, blend, combination, compound, mixture.

vb antonym separate.

mixture *n* 1 admixture, association, intermixture, union. 2 compound, farrago, hash, hodgepodge, hotchpotch, jumble, medley, melange, mishmash. 3 diversity, miscellany, variety.

moan *vb* bemoan, bewail, deplore, grieve, groan, lament, mourn, sigh, weep. • *n* groan, lament, lamentation, sigh, wail.

vb antonym congratulate, rejoice.

mob *vb* crowd, jostle, surround, swarm, pack, throng. • *n* 1 assemblage, crowd, rabble, multitude, throng, tumult. 2 dregs, canaille, populace, rabble, riffraff, scum.

vb antonym shun.

mobile *adj* changeable, fickle, expressive, inconstant, sensitive, variable, volatile.

adj antonym immobile.

mock *vb* 1 ape, counterfeit, imitate, mimic, take off. 2 deride, flout, gibe, insult, jeer, ridicule, taunt. 3 balk, cheat, deceive, defeat, disappoint, dupe, elude, illude, mislead. • *adj* assumed, clap-trap, counterfeit, fake, false, feigned, make-believe, pretended, spurious. • *n* 1 fake, imitation, phoney, sham. 2 gibe, insult, jeer, scoff, taunt.

vb antonyms flatter, praise.

mockery *n* contumely, counterfeit, deception, derision, imitation, jeering, mimicry, ridicule, scoffing, scorn, sham, travesty.

mode *n* 1 fashion, manner, method, style, way. 2 accident, affection, degree, graduation, modification, quality, variety.

model *vb* design, fashion, form, mould, plan, shape. • *adj* admirable, archetypal, estimable, exemplary, ideal, meritorious, paradigmatic, perfect, praiseworthy, worthy. • *n* 1 archetype, design, mould, original, pattern, protoplast, prototype, type. 2 dummy, example, form. 3 copy, facsimile, image, imitation, representation.

moderate *vb* 1 abate, allay, appease, assuage, blunt, dull, lessen, soothe, mitigate, mollify, pacify, quell, quiet, reduce, repress, soften, still, subdue. 2 diminish, qualify, slacken, temper. 3 control, govern, regulate. • *adj* 1 abstinent, frugal, sparing, temperate. 2 limited, mediocre. 3 abstemious, sober. 4 calm, cool, judicious, reasonable, steady. 5 gentle, mild, temperate, tolerable.

moderation *n* 1 abstemiousness, forbearance, frugality, restraint, sobriety, temperance. 2 calmness, composure, coolness, deliberateness, equanimity, mildness, sedateness.

n antonyms increase, intemperance.

modern *adj* fresh, late, latest, new, novel, present, recent, up-to-date.

adj antonyms antiquated, old.

modest *adj* 1 bashful, coy, diffident, humble, meek, reserved, retiring, shy, unassuming, unobtrusive, unostentatious, unpretending, unpretentious. 2 chaste, proper, pure, virtuous. 3 becoming, decent, moderate.

adj antonyms conceited, immodest, pretentious, vain.

modesty *n* 1 bashfulness, coyness, diffidence, humility, meekness, propriety, prudishness, reserve, shyness, unobtrusiveness. 2 chastity, purity, virtue. 3 decency, moderation.

n antonyms conceit, immodesty, vanity.

modification *n* 1 alteration, change, qualification, reformation, variation. 2 form, manner, mode, state.

modify *vb* 1 alter, change, qualify, reform, shape, vary. 2 lower, moderate, qualify, soften.

modish *adj* 1 fashionable, stylish.

2 ceremonious, conventional, courtly, genteel.

adj antonyms dowdy, old-fashioned.

modulate *vb* 1 attune, harmonize, tune. 2 inflect, vary. 3 adapt, adjust, proportion.

vb antonyms increase, raise.

moiety *n* 1 half. 2 part, portion, share.

moil *vb* 1 drudge, labour, toil. 2 bespatter, daub, defile, soil, splash, spot, stain. 3 fatigue, weary, tire.

moist *adj* damp, dank, humid, marshy, muggy, swampy, wet.

adj antonyms arid, dry.

moisture *n* dampness, dankness, humidity, wetness.

n antonym dryness.

mole *n* breakwater, dike, dyke, jetty, mound, pier, quay.

molecule *n* atom, monad, particle.

molest *vb* annoy, badger, bore, bother, chafe, discommode, disquiet, disturb, harass, harry, fret, gull, hector, incommode, inconvenience, irritate, oppress, pester, plague, tease, torment, trouble, vex, worry.

mollify *vb* 1 soften. 2 appease, calm, compose, pacify, quiet, soothe, tranquillize. 3 abate, allay, assuage, blunt, dull, ease, lessen, mitigate, moderate, relieve, temper. 4 qualify, tone down.

vb antonyms aggravate, anger.

moment *n* 1 flash, instant, jiffy, second, trice, twinkling, wink. 2 avail, consequence, consideration, force, gravity, importance, significance, signification, value, weight. 3 drive, force, impetus, momentum.

n antonym insignificance.

momentous *adj* grave, important, serious, significant, vital, weighty.

adj antonym insignificant.

momentum *n* impetus, moment.

monarch *n* 1 autocrat, despot. 2 chief, dictator, emperor, king, potentate, prince, queen, ruler, sovereign.

monastery *n* abbey, cloister, convent, lamasery, nunnery, priory.

monastic *adj* austere, celibate, cloistered, cenobitic, cloistral, conventual, eremitic, hermit-like, monastical, monkish, reclusive, secluded, unworldly.

money *n* banknotes, bread (*inf*), bucks (*inf*), capital, cash, coin, currency, funds, legal tender, lolly (*inf*), riches, silver, wealth.

moneyed, monied *adj* affluent, opulent, rich, well-off, well-to-do.

monitor *vb* check, observe, oversee, supervise, watch. • *n* admonisher, admonitor, adviser, counsellor, instructor, mentor, overseer.

monomania *n* delusion, hallucination, illusion, insanity, self-deception.

monopolize *vb* control, dominate, engross, forestall.

monotonous *adj* boring, dull, tedious, tiresome, undiversified, uniform, unvaried, unvarying, wearisome.
adj antonyms colourful, lively, varied.

monotony *n* boredom, dullness, sameness, tedium, tiresomeness, uniformity, wearisomeness.

monster *adj* enormous, gigantic, huge, immense, mammoth, monstrous. • *n* 1 enormity, marvel, prodigy, wonder. 2 brute, demon, fiend, miscreant, ruffian, villain, wretch.
adj antonym minute, tiny.

monstrous *adj* 1 abnormal, preternatural, prodigious, unnatural. 2 colossal, enormous, extraordinary, huge, immense, stupendous, vast. 3 marvellous, strange, wonderful. 4 bad, base, dreadful, flagrant, frightful, hateful, hideous, horrible, shocking, terrible.

monument *n* 1 memorial, record, remembrance, testimonial. 2 cairn, cenotaph, gravestone, mausoleum, memorial, pillar, tomb, tombstone.

mood *n* disposition, humour, temper, vein.

moody *adj* 1 capricious, variable. 2 angry, crabbed, crusty, fretful, ill-tempered, irascible, irritable, passionate, peevish, petulant, snappish, snarling, sour, testy. 3 dogged, frowning, glowering, glum, intractable, morose, perverse, stubborn, sulky, sullen, wayward. 4 abstracted, gloomy, melancholy, pensive, sad, saturnine.
adj antonyms cheerful, equable.

moonshine *n* balderdash, fiction, flummery, fudge, fustian, nonsense, pretence, stuff, trash, twaddle, vanity.

moor[1] *vb* anchor, berth, fasten, fix, secure, tie.
vb antonym loose.

moor[2] *n* bog, common, heath, moorland, morass, moss, wasteland.

moot *vb* agitate, argue, debate, discuss, dispute. • *adj* arguable, debatable, doubtful, unsettled.

mopish *adj* dejected, depressed, desponding, downcast, down-hearted, gloomy, glum, sad.

moral *adj* 1 ethical, good, honest, honourable, just, upright, virtuous. 2 abstract, ideal, intellectual, mental. • *n* intent, meaning, significance.
adj antonym immoral.

morals *npl* 1 ethics, morality. 2 behaviour, conduct, habits, manners.

morass *n* bog, fen, marsh, quagmire, slough, swamp.

morbid *adj* 1 ailing, corrupted, diseased, sick, sickly, tainted, unhealthy, unsound, vitiated. 2 depressed, downcast, gloomy, pessimistic, sensitive.

mordacious *adj* 1 acrid, biting, cutting, mordant, pungent, sharp, stinging. 2 caustic, poignant, satirical, sarcastic, scathing, severe.

mordant *adj* biting, caustic, keen, mordacious, nipping, sarcastic.

moreover *adv, conj* also, besides, further, furthermore, likewise, too.

morning *n* aurora, daybreak, dawn, morn, morningtide, sunrise.

morose *adj* austere, churlish, crabbed, crusty, dejected, desponding, downcast, downhearted, gloomy, glum, melancholy, moody, sad, severe, sour, sullen, surly.
adj antonyms cheerful, communicative.

morsel *n* 1 bite, mouthful, titbit. 2 bit, fragment, part, piece, scrap.

mortal *adj* deadly, destructive, fatal, final, human, lethal, perishable, vital. • *n* being, earthling, human, man, person, woman.
adj antonym immortal.
n antonyms god, immortal.

mortality *n* corruption, death, destruction, fatality.

mortification *n* 1 chagrin, disappointment, discontent, dissatisfaction, displeasure, humiliation, trouble, shame, vexation. 2 humility, penance, self-abasement, self-denial. 3 gangrene, necrosis.

mortify *vb* 1 annoy, chagrin, depress, disappoint, displease, disquiet, dissatisfy, harass, humble, plague, vex, worry. 2 abase, abash, confound, humiliate, restrain, shame, subdue. 3 corrupt, fester, gangrene, putrefy.

mortuary *n* 1 burial place, cemetery, churchyard, graveyard, necropolis. 2 morgue.

mostly *adv* chiefly, customarily, especially,

generally, mainly, particularly, principally.

mote *n* atom, corpuscle, flaw, mite, particle, speck, spot.

motherly *adj* affectionate, kind, maternal, paternal, tender.

motion *vb* beckon, direct, gesture, signal. • *n* **1** action, change, drift, flux, movement, passage, stir, transit. **2** air, gait, port. **3** gesture, impulse, prompting, suggestion. **4** proposal, proposition.

motionless *adj* fixed, immobile, quiescent, stable, stagnant, standing, stationary, still, torpid, unmoved.

adj antonym active.

motive *n* cause, consideration, ground, impulse, incentive, incitement, inducement, influence, occasion, prompting, purpose, reason, spur, stimulus.

n antonyms deterrent, discouragement, disincentive; inhibitory, preventive.

motley *adj* **1** coloured, dappled, mottled, speckled, spotted, variegated. **2** composite, diversified, heterogeneous, mingled, mixed.

adj antonyms homogeneous, monochrome, uniform.

mottled *adj* dappled, motley, piebald, speckled, spotted, variegated.

adj antonyms monochrome, plain, uniform.

mould[1] *vb* carve, cast, fashion, form, make, model, shape. • *n* **1** cast, character, fashion, form, matrix, pattern, shape. **2** material, matter, substance.

mould[2] *n* **1** blight, mildew, mouldiness, must, mustiness, rot. **2** fungus, lichen, mushroom, puffball, rust, smut, toadstool. **3** earth, loam, soil.

moulder *vb* crumble, decay, perish, waste.

mouldy *adj* decaying, fusty, mildewed, musty.

mound *n* **1** bank, barrow, hill, hillock, knoll, tumulus. **2** bulwark, defence, rampart.

mount[1] *n* hill, mountain, peak.

mount[2] *vb* **1** arise, ascend, climb, rise, soar, tower. **2** escalate, scale. **3** embellish, ornament. **4** bestride, get upon. • *n* charger, horse, ride, steed.

mountain *n* **1** alp, height, hill, mount, peak. **2** abundance, heap, mound, stack.

mountebank *n* charlatan, cheat, impostor, pretender, quack.

mourn *vb* bemoan, bewail, deplore, grieve, lament, sorrow, wail.

vb antonyms bless, rejoice.

mournful *adj* **1** afflicting, afflictive, calamitous, deplorable, distressed, grievous, lamentable, sad, woeful. **2** doleful, heavy, heavy-hearted, lugubrious, melancholy, sorrowful, tearful.

adj antonyms cheerful, joyful.

mouth *vb* clamour, declaim, rant, roar, vociferate. • *n* **1** chaps, jaws. **2** aperture, opening, orifice. **3** entrance, inlet. **4** oracle, mouthpiece, speaker, spokesman.

movables *npl* chattels, effects, furniture, goods, property, wares.

move *vb* **1** dislodge, drive, impel, propel, push, shift, start, stir. **2** actuate, incite, instigate, rouse. **3** determine, incline, induce, influence, persuade, prompt. **4** affect, impress, touch, trouble. **5** agitate, awaken, excite, incense, irritate. **6** propose, recommend, suggest. **7** go, march, proceed, walk. **8** act, live. **9** flit, remove. • *n* action, motion, movement.

movement *n* **1** change, move, motion, passage. **2** emotion. **3** crusade, drive.

moving *adj* **1** impelling, influencing, instigating, persuading, persuasive. **2** affecting, impressive, pathetic, touching.

adj antonyms fixed, stationary, unemotional.

mucous *adj* glutinous, gummy, mucilaginous, ropy, slimy, viscid.

mud *n* dirt, mire, muck, slime.

muddle *vb* **1** confuse, disarrange, disorder. **2** fuddle, inebriate, stupefy. **3** muff, mull, spoil. • *n* confusion, disorder, mess, plight, predicament.

muddy *vb* **1** dirty, foul, smear, soil. **2** confuse, obscure. • *adj* **1** dirty, foul, impure, slimy, soiled, turbid. **2** bothered, confused, dull, heavy, stupid. **3** incoherent, obscure, vague.

muffle *vb* **1** cover, envelop, shroud, wrap. **2** conceal, disguise, involve. **3** deaden, soften, stifle, suppress.

vb antonym amplify.

mulish *adj* cross-grained, headstrong, intractable, obstinate, stubborn.

multifarious *adj* different, divers, diverse, diversified, manifold, multiform, multitudinous, various.

multiloquence *n* garrulity, loquacity, loquaciousness, talkativeness.

multiply *vb* augment, extend, increase, spread.

vb antonyms decrease, lessen.

multitude *n* 1 numerousness. 2 host, legion. 3 army, assemblage, assembly, collection, concourse, congregation, crowd, horde, mob, swarm, throng. 4 commonality, herd, mass, mob, pack, populace, rabble.

n antonyms handful, scattering.

mundane *adj* earthly, secular, sublunary, temporal, terrene, terrestrial, worldly.

adj antonyms cosmic, extraordinary, supernatural.

munificence *n* benefice, bounteousness, bountifulness, bounty, generosity, liberality.

munificent *adj* beneficent, bounteous, bountiful, free, generous, liberal, princely.

adj antonym mean.

murder *vb* 1 assassinate, butcher, destroy, dispatch, kill, massacre, slaughter, slay. 2 abuse, mar, spoil. • *n* assassination, butchery, destruction, homicide, killing, manslaughter, massacre.

murderer *n* assassin, butcher, cut-throat, killer, manslaughterer, slaughterer, slayer.

murderous *adj* barbarous, bloodthirsty, bloody, cruel, fell, sanguinary, savage.

murky *adj* cheerless, cloudy, dark, dim, dusky, gloomy, hazy, lowering, lurid, obscure, overcast.

adj antonyms bright, clear.

murmur *vb* 1 croak, grumble, mumble, mutter. 2 hum, whisper. • *n* 1 complaint, grumble, mutter, plaint, whimper. 2 hum, undertone, whisper.

muscular *adj* 1 sinewy. 2 athletic, brawny, powerful, lusty, stalwart, stout, strong, sturdy, vigorous.

muse *vb* brood, cogitate, consider, contemplate, deliberate, dream, meditate, ponder, reflect, ruminate, speculate, think. • *n* abstraction, musing, reverie.

music *n* harmony, melody, symphony.

musical *adj* dulcet, harmonious, melodious, sweet, sweet-sounding, symphonious, tuneful.

adj antonym unmusical.

musing *adj* absent-minded, meditative, preoccupied. • *n* absent-mindedness, abstraction, contemplation, daydreaming, meditation, muse, reflection, reverie, rumination.

muster *vb* assemble, collect, congregate, convene, convoke, gather, marshal, meet, rally, summon. • *n* assemblage, assembly, collection, congregation, convention, convocation, gathering, meeting, rally.

musty *adj* 1 fetid, foul, fusty, mouldy, rank, sour, spoiled. 2 hackneyed, old, stale, threadbare, trite. 3 ill-favoured, insipid, vapid. 4 dull, heavy, rusty, spiritless.

mutable *adj* 1 alterable, changeable. 2 changeful, fickle, inconstant, irresolute, mutational, unsettled, unstable, unsteady, vacillating, variable, wavering.

mutation *n* alteration, change, variation.

mute *vb* dampen, lower, moderate, muffle, soften. • *adj* 1 dumb, voiceless. 2 silent, speechless, still, taciturn.

adj antonyms articulate, vocal, voluble.

mutilate *vb* cripple, damage, disable, disfigure, hamstring, injure, maim, mangle, mar.

mutinous *adj* 1 contumacious, insubordinate, rebellious, refractory, riotous, tumultuous, turbulent, unruly. 2 insurgent, seditious.

adj antonyms compliant, dutiful, obedient.

mutiny *vb* rebel, revolt, rise, resist. • *n* insubordination, insurrection, rebellion, revolt, revolution, riot, rising, sedition, uprising.

mutter *vb* grumble, muffle, mumble, murmur.

mutual *adj* alternate, common, correlative, interchangeable, interchanged, reciprocal, requited.

myopic *adj* near-sighted, purblind, shortsighted.

adj antonym far-sighted.

myriad *adj* innumerable, manifold, multitudinous, uncounted. • *n* host, million(s), multitude, score(s), sea, swarm, thousand(s).

mysterious *adj* abstruse, cabbalistic, concealed, cryptic, dark, dim, enigmatic, enigmatical, hidden, incomprehensible, inexplicable, inscrutable, mystic, mystical, obscure, occult, puzzling, recondite, secret, sphinx-like, unaccountable, unfathomable, unintelligible, unknown.

adj antonyms comprehensible, frank, straightforward.

mystery *n* 1 enigma, puzzle, riddle, secret. 2 art, business, calling, trade.

mystical *adj* 1 abstruse, cabbalistic, dark, enigmatical, esoteric, hidden, inscrutable, mysterious, obscure, occult, recondite, transcendental. **2** allegorical, emblematic, emblematical, symbolic, symbolical.

mystify *vb* befog, bewilder, confound, confuse, dumbfound, embarrass, obfuscate, perplex, pose, puzzle.

myth *n* **1** fable, legend, tradition. **2** allegory, fiction, invention, parable, story. **3** falsehood, fancy, figment, lie, untruth.

mythical *adj* allegorical, fabled, fabulous, fanciful, fictitious, imaginary, legendary, mythological.

N

nab *vb* catch, clutch, grasp, seize.

nag[1] *vb* carp, fuss, hector, henpeck, pester, torment, worry. • *n* nagger, scold, shrew, tartar.

nag[2] *n* bronco, crock, hack, horse, pony, scrag.

naive *adj* artless, candid, ingenuous, natural, plain, simple, unaffected, unsophisticated.

naked *adj* **1** bare, nude, uncovered. **2** denuded, unclad, unclothed, undressed. **3** defenceless, exposed, open, unarmed, unguarded, unprotected. **4** evident, manifest, plain, stark, unconcealed, undisguised. **5** mere, sheer, simple. **6** bare, destitute, rough, rude, unfurnished, unprovided. **7** uncoloured, unexaggerated, unvarnished.

adj antonyms clothed, concealed, covered.

name *vb* **1** call, christen, denounce, dub, entitle, phrase, style, term. **2** mention. **3** denominate, designate, indicate, nominate, specify. • *n* **1** appellation, cognomen, denomination, designation, epithet, nickname, surname, sobriquet, title. **2** character, credit, reputation, repute. **3** celebrity, distinction, eminence, fame, honour, note, praise, renown.

narcotic *adj* stupefacient, stupefactive, stupefying. • *n* anaesthetic, anodyne, dope, opiate, sedative, stupefacient, tranquillizer.

narrate *vb* chronicle, describe, detail, enumerate, recite, recount, rehearse, relate, tell.

narration *n* account, description, chronicle, history, narrative, recital, rehearsal, relation, story, tale.

narrow *vb* confine, contract, cramp, limit, restrict, straiten. • *adj* **1** circumscribed, confined, contracted, cramped, incapacious, limited, pinched, scanty, straitened. **2** bigoted, hidebound, illiberal, ungenerous. **3** close, near.

adj antonyms broad, liberal, tolerant, wide.

vb antonyms broaden, increase, loosen, widen.

nastiness *n* **1** defilement, dirtiness, filth, filthiness, foulness, impurity, pollution, squalor, uncleanness. **2** indecency, grossness, obscenity, pornography, ribaldry, smut, smuttiness.

nasty *adj* **1** defiled, dirty, filthy, foul, impure, loathsome, polluted, squalid, unclean. **2** gross, indecent, indelicate, lewd, loose, obscene, smutty, vile. **3** disagreeable, disgusting, nauseous, odious, offensive, repulsive, sickening. **4** aggravating, annoying, pesky, pestering, troublesome.

adj antonyms agreeable, clean, decent, pleasant.

nation *n* **1** commonwealth, realm, state. **2** community, people, population, race, stock, tribe.

native *adj* **1** aboriginal, autochthonal, autochthonous, domestic, home, indigenous, vernacular. **2** genuine, intrinsic, natural, original, real. **3** congenital, inborn, inbred, inherent, innate, natal. • *n* aborigine, autochthon, inhabitant, national, resident.

n antonyms foreigner, outsider, stranger.

natty *adj* dandyish, fine, foppish, jaunty, neat, nice, spruce, tidy.

natural *adj* **1** indigenous, innate, native, original. **2** characteristic, essential. **3** legitimate, normal, regular. **4** artless, authentic, genuine, ingenious, unreal, simple, spontaneous, unaffected. **5** bastard, illegitimate.

adj antonyms abnormal, affected, alien, artificial, pretended, unnatural.

nature *n* **1** universe, world. **2** character, constitution, essence. **3** kind, quality, species, sort. **4** disposition, grain, humour, mood, temper. **5** being, intellect, intelligence, mind.

naughty *adj* bad, corrupt, mischievous, perverse, worthless.

adj antonyms good, polite, well-behaved.

nausea *n* **1** queasiness, seasickness. **2** loathing, qualm. **3** aversion, disgust, repugnance.

nauseous *adj* abhorrent, disgusting, distasteful, loathsome, offensive, repulsive, revolting, sickening.

naval *adj* marine, maritime, nautical.

navigate *vb* cruise, direct, guide, pilot, plan, sail, steer.

navy *n* fleet, shipping, vessels.

near *vb* approach, draw close. • *adj* **1** adjacent, approximate, close, contiguous, neighbouring, nigh. **2** approaching, forthcoming, imminent, impending. **3** dear, familiar, friendly, intimate. **4** direct, immediate, short, straight. **5** accurate, literal. **6** narrow, parsimonious.
adj antonyms distant, far, remote.

nearly *adv* **1** almost, approximately, wellnigh. **2** closely, intimately, pressingly. **3** meanly, parsimoniously, penuriously, stingily.

neat *adj* **1** clean, cleanly, orderly, tidy, trim, unsoiled. **2** nice, smart, spruce. **3** chaste, pure, simple. **4** excellent, pure, unadulterated. **5** adroit, clever, exact, finished. **6** dainty, nice.
adj antonyms disordered, disorderly, messy, untidy.

nebulous *adj* cloudy, hazy, misty.
adj antonym clear.

necessary *adj* **1** inevitable, unavoidable. **2** essential, expedient, indispensable, needful, requisite. **3** compelling, compulsory, involuntary. • *n* essential, necessity, requirement, requisite.
adj antonyms inessential, unimportant, unnecessary.

necessitate *vb* compel, constrain, demand, force, impel, oblige.

necessitous *adj* **1** destitute, distressed, indigent, moneyless, needy, penniless, pinched, poor, poverty-stricken. **2** narrow, pinching.

necessity *n* **1** inevitability, inevitableness, unavoidability, unavoidableness. **2** compulsion, destiny, fatality, fate. **3** emergency, urgency. **4** exigency, indigence, indispensability, indispensableness, need, needfulness, poverty, want. **5** essentiality, essentialness, requirement, requisite.

necromancy *n* conjuration, divination, enchantment, magic, sorcery, witchcraft, wizardry.

necropolis *n* burial ground, cemetery, churchyard, crematorium, graveyard, mortuary.

need *vb* demand, lack, require, want. • *n* **1** emergency, exigency, extremity, necessity, strait, urgency, want. **2** destitution, distress, indigence, neediness, penury, poverty, privation.
n antonym sufficiency.

needful *adj* **1** distressful, necessitous, necessary. **2** essential, indispensable, requisite.

needless *adj* superfluous, unnecessary, useless.
adj antonyms necessary, needful.

needy *adj* destitute, indigent, necessitous, poor.
adj antonyms affluent, wealthy, well-off.

nefarious *adj* abominable, atrocious, detestable, dreadful, execrable, flagitious, heinous, horrible, infamous, iniquitous, scandalous, vile, wicked.
adj antonym exemplary.

negation *n* denial, disavowal, disclaimer, rejection, renunciation.

neglect *vb* condemn, despise, disregard, forget, ignore, omit, overlook, slight. • *n* **1** carelessness, default, failure, heedlessness, inattention, omission, remissness. **2** disregard, disrespect, slight. **3** indifference, negligence.
vb antonyms cherish, nurture, treasure.

negligence *n* **1** carelessness, disregard, heedlessness, inadvertency, inattention, indifference, neglect, remissness, slackness, thoughtlessness. **2** defect, fault, inadvertence, omission, shortcoming.

negligent *adj* careless, heedless, inattentive, indifferent, neglectful, regardless, thoughtless.
adj antonyms attentive, careful, heedful, scrupulous.

negotiate *vb* arrange, bargain, deal, debate, sell, settle, transact, treat.

neighbourhood *n* **1** district, environs, locality, vicinage, vicinity. **2** adjacency, nearness, propinquity, proximity.

neighbourly *adj* attentive, civil, friendly, kind, obliging, social.

neophyte *n* beginner, catechumen, convert, novice, pupil, tyro.

nerve *vb* brace, energize, fortify, invigorate, strengthen. • *n* **1** force, might, power, strength, vigour. **2** coolness, courage, endurance, firmness, fortitude, hardihood, manhood, pluck, resolution, self-command, steadiness.
vb antonym unnerve.
n antonyms cowardice, weakness.

nervous *adj* **1** forcible, powerful, robust, strong, vigorous. **2** irritable, fearful, shaky, timid, timorous, weak, weakly.
adj antonyms bold, calm, confident, cool, relaxed.

nestle *vb* cuddle, harbour, lodge, nuzzle, snug, snuggle.

nettle *vb* chafe, exasperate, fret, harass, incense, irritate, provoke, ruffle, sting, tease, vex.

neutral *adj* **1** impartial, indifferent. **2** colourless, mediocre.

adj antonyms biased, prejudiced.

neutralize *vb* cancel, counterbalance, counterpoise, invalidate, offset.

nevertheless *adv* however, nonetheless, notwithstanding, yet.

new *adj* **1** fresh, latest, modern, novel, recent, unused. **2** additional, another, further. **3** reinvigorated, renovated, repaired.

adj antonyms hackneyed, old, outdated, out-of-date, usual.

news *n* advice, information, intelligence, report, tidings, word.

nice *adj* **1** accurate, correct, critical, definite, delicate, exact, exquisite, precise, rigorous, strict. **2** dainty, difficult, exacting, fastidious, finical, punctilious, squeamish. **3** discerning, discriminating, particular, precise, scrupulous. **4** neat, tidy, trim. **5** fine, minute, refined, subtle. **6** delicate, delicious, luscious, palatable, savoury, soft, tender. **7** agreeable, delightful, good, pleasant.

adj antonyms careless, disagreeable, haphazard, nasty, unpleasant.

nicety *n* **1** accuracy, exactness, niceness, precision, truth, daintiness, fastidiousness, squeamishness. **2** discrimination, subtlety.

niggard *n* churl, curmudgeon, miser, screw, scrimp, skinflint.

niggardly *adj* avaricious, close, close-fisted, illiberal, mean, mercenary, miserly, parsimonious, penurious, skinflint, sordid, stingy.

adj antonyms bountiful, generous.

nigh *adj* **1** adjacent, adjoining, contiguous, near. **2** present, proximate. • *adv* almost, near, nearly.

nimble *adj* active, agile, alert, brisk, lively, prompt, quick, speedy, sprightly, spry, swift, tripping.

adj antonyms awkward, clumsy.

nobility *n* aristocracy, dignity, elevation, eminence, grandeur, greatness, loftiness, magnanimity, nobleness, peerage, superiority, worthiness.

noble *adj* **1** dignified, elevated, eminent, exalted, generous, great, honourable, illustrious, magnanimous, superior, worthy. **2** choice, excellent. **3** aristocratic, gentle, high-born, patrician. **4** grand, lofty,

lordly, magnificent, splendid, stately. • *n* aristocrat, grandee, lord, nobleman, peer.

adj antonyms base, ignoble, low-born.

n antonyms pleb, prole.

noctambulist *n* sleepwalker, somnambulist.

noise *vb* bruit, gossip, repeat, report, rumour. • *n* ado, blare, clamour, clatter, cry, din, fuss, hubbub, hullabaloo, outcry, pandemonium, racket, row, sound, tumult, uproar, vociferation.

n antonyms quiet, silence.

noiseless *adj* inaudible, quiet, silent, soundless.

noisome *adj* bad, baneful, deleterious, disgusting, fetid, foul, hurtful, injurious, mischievous, nocuous, noxious, offensive, pernicious, pestiferous, pestilential, poisonous, unhealthy, unwholesome.

adj antonyms balmy, pleasant, wholesome.

noisy *adj* blatant, blustering, boisterous, brawling, clamorous, loud, uproarious, riotous, tumultuous, vociferous.

adj antonyms peaceful, quiet, silent.

nomadic *adj* migratory, pastoral, vagrant, wandering.

nominal *adj* formal, inconsiderable, minimal, ostensible, pretended, professed, so-called, titular.

nominate *vb* appoint, choose, designate, name, present, propose.

nonchalant *adj* apathetic, careless, cool, indifferent, unconcerned.

adj antonyms anxious, careful, concerned, worried.

nondescript *adj* amorphous, characterless, commonplace, dull, indescribable, odd, ordinary, unclassifiable, uninteresting, unremarkable.

nonentity *n* cipher, futility, inexistence, inexistency, insignificance, nobody, nonexistence, nothingness.

nonplus *vb* astonish, bewilder, confound, confuse, discomfit, disconcert, embarrass, floor, gravel, perplex, pose, puzzle.

nonsensical *adj* absurd, foolish, irrational, senseless, silly, stupid.

adj antonyms logical, sensible.

norm *n* model, pattern, rule, standard.

normal *adj* **1** analogical, legitimate, natural, ordinary, regular, usual. **2** erect, perpendicular, vertical.

adj antonyms abnormal, irregular, odd, peculiar.

notable *adj* **1** distinguished, extraordinary,

memorable, noted, remarkable, signal. **2** conspicuous, evident, noticeable, observable, plain, prominent, striking. **3** notorious, rare, well-known. • *n* celebrity, dignitary, notability, worthy.

adj antonyms commonplace, ordinary, usual.

n antonyms nobody, nonentity.

note *vb* **1** heed, mark, notice, observe, regard, remark. **2** record, register. **3** denote, designate. • *n* **1** memorandum, minute, record. **2** annotation, comment, remark. **3** indication, mark, sign, symbol, token. **4** account, bill, catalogue, reckoning. **5** billet, epistle, letter. **6** consideration, heed, notice, observation. **7** celebrity, consequence, credit, distinction, eminence, fame, notability, notedness, renown, reputation, respectability. **8** banknote, bill, promissory note. **9** song, strain, tune, voice.

noted *adj* celebrated, conspicuous, distinguished, eminent, famed, famous, illustrious, notable, notorious, remarkable, renowned, well-known.

adj antonyms commonplace, ordinary, unexceptional, usual

nothing *n* **1** inexistence, nonentity, nonexistence, nothingness, nullity. **2** bagatelle, trifle.

notice *vb* **1** mark, note, observe, perceive, regard, see. **2** comment on, mention, remark. **3** attend to, heed. • *n* **1** cognizance, heed, note, observation, regard. **2** advice, announcement, information, intelligence, mention, news, notification. **3** communication, intimation, premonition, warning. **4** attention, civility, consideration, respect. **5** comments, remarks.

vb antonyms ignore, overlook.

notify *vb* **1** advertise, announce, declare, publish, promulgate. **2** acquaint, apprise, inform.

notion *n* **1** concept, conception, idea. **2** apprehension, belief, conceit, conviction, expectation, estimation, impression, judgement, opinion, sentiment, view.

notoriety *n* celebrity, fame, figure, name, note, publicity, reputation, repute, vogue.

notorious *adj* **1** apparent, egregious, evident, notable, obvious, open, overt, manifest, patent, well-known. **2** celebrated, conspicuous, distinguished,

famed, famous, flagrant, infamous, noted, remarkable, renowned.

notwithstanding *conj* despite, however, nevertheless, yet. • *prep* despite.

nourish *vb* **1** feed, nurse, nurture. **2** maintain, supply, support. **3** breed, educate, instruct, train. **4** cherish, encourage, foment, foster, promote, succour.

nourishment *n* aliment, diet, food, nutriment, nutrition, sustenance.

novel *adj* fresh, modern, new, rare, recent, strange, uncommon, unusual. • *n* fiction, romance, story, tale.

adj antonyms familiar, ordinary.

novice *n* **1** convert, proselyte. **2** initiate, neophyte, novitiate, probationer. **3** apprentice, beginner, learner, tyro.

n antonyms doyen, expert, professional.

noxious *adj* baneful, deadly, deleterious, destructive, detrimental, hurtful, injurious, insalubrious, mischievous, noisome, pernicious, pestilent, poisonous, unfavourable, unwholesome.

adj antonyms innocuous, wholesome.

nude *adj* bare, denuded, exposed, naked, uncovered, unclothed, undressed.

adj antonyms clothed, covered, dressed.

nugatory *adj* **1** frivolous, insignificant, trifling, trivial, vain, worthless. **2** bootless, ineffectual, inefficacious, inoperative, null, unavailing, useless.

nuisance *n* annoyance, bore, bother, infliction, offence, pest, plague, trouble.

null *adj* **1** ineffectual, invalid, nugatory, useless, void. **2** characterless, colourless.

nullify *vb* abolish, abrogate, annul, cancel, invalidate, negate, quash, repeal, revoke.

vb antonym validate.

numb *vb* benumb, deaden, stupefy. • *adj* benumbed, deadened, dulled, insensible, paralysed.

vb antonym sensitize.

adj antonym sensitive.

number *vb* **1** calculate, compute, count, enumerate, numerate, reckon, tell. **2** account, reckon. • *n* **1** digit, figure, numeral. **2** horde, multitude, numerousness, throng. **3** aggregate, collection, sum, total.

numerous *adj* abundant, many, numberless.

adj antonyms few, scanty.

nuncio *n* ambassador, legate, messenger.

nunnery *n* abbey, cloister, convent, monastery.

nuptial *adj* bridal, conjugal, connubial, hymeneal, matrimonial.

nuptials npl espousal, marriage, wedding.

nurse *vb* **1** nourish, nurture. **2** rear, suckle. **3** cherish, encourage, feed, foment, foster, pamper, promote, succour. **4** economize, manage. **5** caress, dandle, fondle. • *n* **1** auxiliary, orderly, sister. **2** amah, au pair, babysitter, nanny, nursemaid, nurserymaid,

nurture *vb* **1** feed, nourish, nurse, tend. **2** breed, discipline, educate, instruct, rear, school, train. • *n* **1** diet, food, nourishment. **2** breeding, discipline, education, instruction, schooling, training, tuition. **3** attention, nourishing, nursing.

nutriment *n* aliment, food, nourishment, nutrition, pabulum, subsistence, sustenance.

nutrition *n* diet, food, nourishment, nutriment.

nutritious *adj* invigorating, nourishing, strengthening, supporting, sustaining.

nymph *n* damsel, dryad, lass, girl, maid, maiden, naiad.

O

oaf *n* blockhead, dolt, dunce, fool, idiot, simpleton.

oath *n* **1** blasphemy, curse, expletive, imprecation, malediction. **2** affirmation, pledge, promise, vow.

obduracy *n* **1** contumacy, doggedness, obstinacy, stubbornness, tenacity. **2** depravity, impenitence.

obdurate *adj* **1** hard, harsh, rough, rugged. **2** callous, cantankerous, dogged, firm, hardened, inflexible, insensible, obstinate, pigheaded, unfeeling, stubborn, unbending, unyielding. **3** depraved, graceless, lost, reprobate, shameless, impenitent, incorrigible, irreclaimable.
adj antonyms submissive, tender.

obedience *n* acquiescence, agreement, compliance, duty, respect, reverence, submission, submissiveness, subservience.
n antonym disobedience.

obedient *adj* acquiescent, compliant, deferential, duteous, dutiful, observant, regardful, respectful, submissive, subservient, yielding.
adj antonyms disobedient, rebellious, refractory, unruly, wilful.

obeisance *n* bow, courtesy, curtsy, homage, reverence, salutation.

obelisk *n* column, pillar.

obese *adj* corpulent, fat, fleshy, gross, plump, podgy, portly, stout.
adj antonyms skinny, slender, thin.

obesity *n* corpulence, corpulency, embonpoint, fatness, fleshiness, obeseness, plumpness.

obey *vb* comply, conform, heed, keep, mind, observe, submit, yield.
vb antonym disobey.

obfuscate *vb* **1** cloud, darken, obscure. **2** bewilder, confuse, muddle.

object[1] *vb* cavil, contravene, demur, deprecate, disapprove of, except to, impeach, oppose, protest, refuse.
vb antonyms accede, acquiesce, agree, assent.

object[2] *n* **1** particular, phenomenon, precept, reality, thing. **2** aim, butt, destination, end, mark, recipient, target. **3** design, drift, goal, intention, motive, purpose, use, view.

objection *n* censure, difficulty, doubt, exception, protest, remonstrance, scruple.
n antonyms agreement, assent.

objurgate *vb* chide, reprehend, reprove.

oblation *n* gift, offering, sacrifice.

obligation *n* **1** accountability, accountableness, responsibility. **2** agreement, bond, contract, covenant, engagement, stipulation. **3** debt, indebtedness, liability.
n antonyms choice, discretion.

obligatory *adj* binding, coercive, compulsory, enforced, necessary, unavoidable.
adj antonym optional.

oblige *vb* **1** bind, coerce, compel, constrain, force, necessitate, require. **2** accommodate, benefit, convenience, favour, gratify, please. **3** obligate, bind.

obliging *adj* accommodating, civil, complaisant, considerate, kind, friendly, polite.
adj antonyms inconsiderate, unhelpful, unkind.

oblique *adj* **1** aslant, inclined, sidelong, slanting. **2** indirect, obscure.

obliterate *vb* cancel, delete, destroy, efface, eradicate, erase, expunge.

oblivious *adj* careless, forgetful, heedless, inattentive, mindless, negligent, neglectful.
adj antonyms aware, conscious.

obloquy *n* aspersion, backbiting, blame, calumny, censure, contumely, defamation, detraction, disgrace, odium, reproach, reviling, slander, traducing.

obnoxious *adj* **1** blameworthy, censurable, faulty, reprehensible. **2** hateful, objectionable, obscene, odious, offensive, repellent, repugnant, repulsive, unpleasant, unpleasing.
adj antonyms agreeable, likable, pleasant.

obscene *adj* **1** broad, coarse, filthy, gross, immodest, impure, indecent, indelicate, ribald, unchaste, lewd, licentious, loose, offensive, pornographic, shameless, smutty. **2** disgusting, dirty, foul.
adj antonyms clean, decent, decorous.

obscure *vb* **1** becloud, befog, blur, cloud, darken, eclipse, dim, obfuscate, obnubilate, shade. **2** conceal, cover, equivocate, hide. • *adj* **1** dark, darksome, dim, dusky, gloomy, lurid, murky, rayless, shadowy, sombre, unenlightened, unilluminated. **2** abstruse, blind, cabbalistic, difficult, doubtful, enigmatic, high, incomprehensible, indefinite, indistinct, intricate, involved, mysterious, mystic, recondite, undefined, unintelligible, vague. **3** remote, secluded. **4** humble, inglorious, nameless, renownless, undistinguished, unhonoured, unknown, unnoted, unnoticed.

vb antonyms clarify, illuminate.

adj antonyms clear, definite, explicit, famous, lucid.

obsequious *adj* cringing, deferential, fawning, flattering, servile, slavish, supple, subservient, sycophantic, truckling.

adj antonym assertive.

observant *adj* attentive, heedful, mindful, perceptive, quick, regardful, vigilant, watchful.

adj antonyms inattentive, unobservant.

observation *n* **1** attention, cognition, notice, observance. **2** annotation, note, remark. **3** experience, knowledge.

observe *vb* **1** eye, mark, note, notice, remark, watch. **2** behold, detect, discover, perceive, see. **3** express, mention, remark, say, utter. **4** comply, conform, follow, fulfil, obey. **5** celebrate, keep, regard, solemnize.

vb antonyms break, miss, overlook, violate.

obsolete *adj* ancient, antiquated, antique, archaic, disused, neglected, old, old-fashioned, obsolescent, out-of-date, past, passé, unfashionable.

adj antonyms contemporary, current, modern, new, up-to-date.

obstacle *n* barrier, check, difficulty, hindrance, impediment, interference, interruption, obstruction, snag, stumbling block.

n antonyms advantage, help.

obstinacy *n* contumacy, doggedness, headiness, firmness, inflexibility, intractability, obduracy, persistence, perseverance, perversity, resoluteness, stubbornness, tenacity, wilfulness.

obstinate *adj* cross-grained, contumacious, dogged, firm, headstrong, inflexible, immovable, intractable, mulish, obdurate, opinionated, persistent, pertinacious, perverse, resolute, self-willed, stubborn, tenacious, unyielding, wilful.

adj antonyms co-operative, flexible, pliant, submissive.

obstreperous *adj* boisterous, clamorous, loud, noisy, riotous, tumultuous, turbulent, unruly, uproarious, vociferous.

obstruct *vb* **1** bar, barricade, block, blockade, block up, choke, clog, close, glut, jam, obturate, stop. **2** hinder, impede, oppose, prevent. **3** arrest, check, curb, delay, embrace, interrupt, retard, slow.

vb antonym help.

obstruction *n* **1** bar, barrier, block, blocking, check, difficulty, hindrance, impediment, obstacle, stoppage. **2** check, clog, embarrassment, interruption, obturation.

n antonym help.

obtain *vb* **1** achieve, acquire, attain, bring, contrive, earn, elicit, gain, get, induce, procure, secure. **2** hold, prevail, stand, subsist.

obtrusive *adj* forward, interfering, intrusive, meddling, officious.

adj antonym unobtrusive.

obtuse *adj* **1** blunt. **2** blockish, doltish, dull, dull-witted, heavy, stockish, stolid, stupid, slow, unintellectual, unintelligent.

adj antonyms bright, sharp.

obviate *vb* anticipate, avert, counteract, preclude, prevent, remove.

obvious *adj* **1** exposed, liable, open, subject. **2** apparent, clear, distinct, evident, manifest, palatable, patent, perceptible, plain, self-evident, unmistakable, visible.

adj antonyms obscure, unclear.

occasion *vb* **1** breed, cause, create, originate, produce. **2** induce, influence, move, persuade. • *n* **1** casualty, event, incident, occurrence. **2** conjuncture, convenience, juncture, opening, opportunity. **3** condition, necessity, need, exigency, requirement, want. **4** cause, ground, reason. **5** inducement, influence. **6** circumstance, exigency.

occasional *adj* **1** accidental, casual, incidental, infrequent, irregular, uncommon. **2** causative, causing.

adj antonym frequent.

occasionally *adv* casually, sometimes.

adv antonym frequently.

occult *adj* abstruse, cabbalistic, hidden, latent, secret, invisible, mysterious, mystic, mystical, recondite, shrouded, undetected, undiscovered, unknown, unrevealed, veiled. • *n* magic, sorcery, witchcraft.

v antonym reveal.

occupation *n* **1** holding, occupancy, possession, tenure, use. **2** avocation, business, calling, craft, employment, engagement, job, post, profession, trade, vocation.

occupy *vb* 1 capture, hold, keep, possess. 2 cover, fill, garrison, inhabit, take up, tenant. 3 engage, employ, use.

occur *vb* 1 appear, arise, offer. 2 befall, chance, eventuate, happen, result, supervene.

occurrence *n* accident, adventure, affair, casualty, event, happening, incident, proceeding, transaction.

odd *adj* 1 additional, redundant, remaining. 2 casual, incidental. 3 inappropriate, queer, unsuitable. 4 comical, droll, erratic, extravagant, extraordinary, fantastic, grotesque, irregular, peculiar, quaint, singular, strange, uncommon, uncouth, unique, unusual, whimsical.
adj antonym normal.

odds *npl* 1 difference, disparity, inequality. 2 advantage, superiority, supremacy.

odious *adj* 1 abominable, detestable, execrable, hateful, shocking. 2 hated, obnoxious, unpopular. 3 disagreeable, forbidding, loathsome, offensive.
adj antonym pleasant.

odium *n* 1 abhorrence, detestation, dislike, enmity, hate, hatred. 2 odiousness, repulsiveness. 3 obloquy, opprobrium, reproach, shame.

odorous *adj* aromatic, balmy, fragrant, perfumed, redolent, scented, sweet-scented, sweet-smelling.

odour *n* aroma, fragrance, perfume, redolence, scent, smell.

offal *n* carrion, dregs, garbage, refuse, rubbish, waste.

offence *n* 1 aggression, attack, assault. 2 anger, displeasure, indignation, pique, resentment, umbrage, wrath. 3 affront, harm, injury, injustice, insult, outrage, wrong. 4 crime, delinquency, fault, misdeed, misdemeanour, sin, transgression, trespass.

offend *vb* 1 affront, annoy, chafe, displease, fret, gall, irritate, mortify, nettle, provoke, vex. 2 molest, pain, shock, wound. 3 fall, sin, stumble, transgress.
vb antonym compliment, please.

offender *n* convict, criminal, culprit, delinquent, felon, malefactor, sinner, transgressor, trespasser.

offensive *adj* 1 aggressive, attacking, invading. 2 disgusting, loathsome, nauseating, nauseous, repulsive, sickening. 3 abominable, detestable, disagreeable, displeasing, execrable, hateful, obnoxious, repugnant, revolting, shocking, unpalatable, unpleasant. 4 abusive, disagreeable, impertinent, insolent, insulting, irritating, opprobrious, rude, saucy, unpleasant. • *n* attack, onslaught.
adj antonyms defensive, pleasing.

offer *vb* 1 present, proffer, tender. 2 exhibit. 3 furnish, propose, propound, show. 4 volunteer. 5 dare, essay, endeavour, venture. • *n* 1 overture, proffering, proposal, proposition, tender, overture. 2 attempt, bid, endeavour, essay.

offhand *adj* abrupt, brusque, casual, curt, extempore, impromptu, informal, unpremeditated, unstudied. • *adv* 1 carelessly, casually, clumsily, haphazardly, informally, slapdash. 2 ad-lib, extemporaneously, extemporarily, extempore, impromptu.
adj antonyms calculated, planned.

office *n* 1 duty, function, service, work. 2 berth, place, position, post, situation. 3 business, capacity, charge, employment, trust. 4 bureau, room.

officiate *vb* act, perform, preside, serve.

officious *adj* busy, dictatorial, forward, impertinent, interfering, intermeddling, meddlesome, meddling, obtrusive, pushing, pushy.

offset *vb* balance, counteract, counterbalance, counterpoise. • *n* 1 branch, offshoot, scion, shoot, slip, sprout, twig. 2 counterbalance, counterpoise, set-off, equivalent.

offspring *n* 1 brood, children, descendants, issue, litter, posterity, progeny. 2 cadet, child, scion.
n antonym parent(s).

often *adv* frequently, generally, oftentimes, repeatedly.
adv antonym seldom.

ogre *n* bugbear, demon, devil, goblin, hobgoblin, monster, spectre.

old *adj* 1 aged, ancient, antiquated, antique, archaic, elderly, obsolete, olden, old-fashioned, superannuated. 2 decayed, done, senile, worn-out. 3 original, primitive, pristine. 4 former, preceding, pre-existing.
adj antonym young.

oleaginous *adj* adipose, fat, fatty, greasy, oily, sebaceous, unctuous.

omen *n* augury, auspice, foreboding, portent, presage, prognosis, sign, warning.

ominous *adj* inauspicious, monitory, portentous, premonitory, threatening, unpropitious.
adj antonym auspicious.

omission *n* default, failure, forgetfulness, neglect, oversight.
n antonyms addition, inclusion.

omit *vb* disregard, drop, eliminate, exclude, miss, neglect, overlook, skip.
vb antonyms add, include.

omnipotent *adj* almighty, all-powerful.
adj antonym impotent.

omniscient *adj* all-knowing, all-seeing, all-wise.

oneness *n* individuality, singleness, unity.

onerous *adj* burdensome, difficult, hard, heavy, laborious, oppressive, responsible, weighty.
adj antonyms easy, light.

one-sided *adj* partial, prejudiced, unfair, unilateral, unjust.
adj antonym impartial.

only *adj* alone, single, sole, solitary. • *adv* barely, merely, simply.

onset *n* assault, attack, charge, onslaught, storm, storming.
n antonyms end, finish.

onus *n* burden, liability, load, responsibility.

ooze *vb* 1 distil, drip, drop, shed. 2 drain, exude, filter, leak, percolate, stain, transude. • *n* mire, mud, slime.

opaque *adj* 1 dark, dim, hazy, muddy. 2 abstruse, cryptic, enigmatic, enigmatical, obscure, unclear.
adj antonym transparent.

open *vb* 1 expand, spread. 2 begin, commence, initiate. 2 disclose, exhibit, reveal, show. 3 unbar, unclose, uncover, unlock, unseal, untie. • *adj* 1 expanded, extended, unclosed, spread wide. 2 aboveboard, artless, candid, cordial, fair, frank, guileless, hearty, honest, sincere, openhearted, single-minded, undesigning, undisguised, undissembling, unreserved. 3 bounteous, bountiful, free, generous, liberal, munificent. 4 ajar, uncovered. 5 exposed, undefended, unprotected. 6 clear, unobstructed. 7 accessible, public, unenclosed, unrestricted. 8 mild, moderate. 9 apparent, debatable, evident, obvious, patent, plain, undetermined.
vb antonyms close, shut.
adj antonyms closed, shut.

opening *adj* commencing, first, inaugural, initiatory, introductory. • *n* 1 aperture, breach, chasm, cleft, fissure, flaw, gap, gulf, hole, interspace, loophole, orifice, perforation, rent, rift. 2 beginning, commencement, dawn. 3 chance, opportunity, vacancy.
n antonyms closing, closure.
adj antonym closing.

openly *adv* candidly, frankly, honestly, plainly, publicly.
adv antonyms secretly, slyly.

openness *n* candour, frankness, honesty, ingenuousness, plainness, unreservedness.

operate *vb* 1 act, function, work. 2 cause, effect, occasion, produce. 3 manipulate, use, run.

operation *n* 1 manipulation, performance, procedure, proceeding, process. 2 action, affair, manoeuvre, motion, movement.

operative *adj* 1 active, effective, effectual, efficient, serviceable, vigorous. 2 important, indicative, influential, significant. • *n* artisan, employee, labourer, mechanic, worker, workman.
adj antonym inoperative.

opiate *adj* narcotic, sedative, soporiferous, soporific. • *n* anodyne, drug, narcotic, sedative, tranquillizer.

opine *vb* apprehend, believe, conceive, fancy, judge, suppose, presume, surmise, think.

opinion *n* 1 conception, idea, impression, judgment, notion, sentiment, view. 2 belief, persuasion, tenet. 3 esteem, estimation, judgment.

opinionated *adj* biased, bigoted, cocksure, conceited, dictatorial, dogmatic, opinionative, prejudiced, stubborn.
adj antonym open-minded.

opponent *adj* adverse, antagonistic, contrary, opposing, opposite, repugnant. • *n* adversary, antagonist, competitor, contestant, counteragent, enemy, foe, opposite, opposer, party, rival.
n antonyms ally, proponent.

opportune *adj* appropriate, auspicious, convenient, favourable, felicitous, fit, fitting, fortunate, lucky, propitious, seasonable, suitable, timely, well-timed.
adj antonym inopportune.

opportunity *n* chance, convenience, moment, occasion.

oppose *vb* 1 combat, contravene, counteract, dispute, obstruct, oppugn, resist, thwart, withstand. **2** check, prevent. **3** confront, counterpoise.

vb antonyms favour, support.

opposite *adj* **1** facing, fronting. **2** conflicting, contradictory, contrary, different, diverse, incompatible, inconsistent, irreconcilable. **3** adverse, antagonistic, hostile, inimical, opposed, opposing, repugnant. • *n* contradiction, contrary, converse, reverse.

adj antonym same.

n antonym same.

opposition *n* **1** antagonism, antinomy, contrariety, inconsistency, repugnance. **2** counteraction, counter-influence, hostility, resistance. **3** hindrance, obstacle, obstruction, oppression, prevention.

n antonyms co-operation, support.

oppress *vb* burden, crush, depress, harass, load, maltreat, overburden, overpower, overwhelm, persecute, subdue, suppress, tyrannize, wrong.

oppression *n* **1** abuse, calamity, cruelty, hardship, injury, injustice, misery, persecution, severity, suffering, tyranny. **2** depression, dullness, heaviness, lassitude.

oppressive *adj* close, muggy, stifling, suffocating, sultry.

adj antonym gentle.

opprobrious *adj* **1** abusive, condemnatory, contemptuous, damnatory, insolent, insulting, offensive, reproachable, scandalous, scurrilous, vituperative. **2** despised, dishonourable, disreputable, hateful, infamous, shameful.

opprobrium *n* **1** contumely, scurrility. **2** calumny, disgrace, ignominy, infamy, obloquy, odium, reproach.

oppugn *vb* assail, argue, attack, combat, contravene, oppose, resist, thwart, withstand.

option *n* choice, discretion, election, preference, selection.

optional *adj* discretionary, elective, nonobligatory, voluntary.

adj antonym compulsory.

opulence *n* affluence, fortune, independence, luxury, riches, wealth.

n antonyms penury, poverty.

opulent *adj* affluent, flush, luxurious, moneyed, plentiful, rich, sumptuous, wealthy.

adj antonyms penurious, poor.

oracular *adj* **1** ominous, portentous, prophetic. **2** authoritative, dogmatic, magisterial, positive. **3** aged, grave, wise.

4 ambiguous, blind, dark, equivocal, obscure.

oral *adj* spoken, verbal, vocal.

adj antonym written.

oration *n* address, declamation, discourse, harangue, speech.

orb *n* **1** ball, globe, sphere. **2** circle, circuit, orbit, ring. **3** disk, wheel.

orbit *vb* circle, encircle, revolve around. • *n* course, path, revolution, track.

ordain *vb* **1** appoint, call, consecrate, elect, experiment, constitute, establish, institute, regulate. **2** decree, enjoin, enact, order, prescribe.

order *vb* **1** adjust, arrange, methodize, regulate, systematize. **2** carry on, conduct, manage. **3** bid, command, direct, instruct, require. • *n* **1** arrangement, disposition, method, regularity, symmetry, system. **2** law, regulation, rule. **3** discipline, peace, quiet. **4** command, commission, direction, injunction, instruction, mandate, prescription. **5** class, degree, grade, kind, rank. **6** family, tribe. **7** brotherhood, community, fraternity, society. **8** sequence, succession.

vb antonym disorder.

n antonym disorder.

orderly *adj* **1** methodical, regular, systematic. **2** peaceable, quiet, well-behaved. **3** neat, shipshape, tidy.

adj antonym disorderly.

ordinance *n* **1** appointment, command, decree, edict, enactment, law, order, prescript, regulation, rule, statute. **2** ceremony, observance, sacrament, rite, ritual.

ordinary *adj* **1** accustomed, customary, established, everyday, normal, regular, settled, wonted, everyday, regular. **2** common, frequent, habitual, usual. **3** average, commonplace, indifferent, inferior, mean, mediocre, second-rate, undistinguished. **4** homely, plain.

adj antonyms extraordinary, special, unusual.

organization *n* business, construction, constitution, organism, structure, system.

n antonym disorganization.

organize *vb* **1** adjust, constitute, construct, form, make, shape. **2** arrange, coordinate, correlate, establish, systematize.

vb antonym disorganize.

orgy *n* carousal, debauch, debauchery, revel, saturnalia.

orifice *n* aperture, hole, mouth, perforation, pore, vent.

origin *n* **1** beginning, birth, commencement, cradle, derivation, foundation, fountain, fountainhead, original, rise, root, source, spring, starting point. **2** cause, occasion. **3** heritage, lineage, parentage.
n antonyms end, termination.

original *adj* **1** aboriginal, first, primary, primeval, primitive, primordial, pristine. **2** fresh, inventive, novel. **3** eccentric, odd, peculiar. • *n* **1** cause, commencement, origin, source, spring. **2** archetype, exemplar, model, pattern, prototype, protoplast, type.
adj antonym unoriginal.

originate *vb* **1** arise, begin, emanate, flow, proceed, rise, spring. **2** create, discover, form, invent, produce.
vb antonyms end, terminate.

originator *n* author, creator, former, inventor, maker, parent.

orison *n* petition, prayer, solicitation, supplication.

ornament *vb* adorn, beautify, bedeck, bedizen, decorate, deck, emblazon, garnish, grace. • *n* adornment, bedizenment, decoration, design, embellishment, garnish, ornamentation.

ornate *adj* beautiful, bedecked, decorated, elaborate, elegant, embellished, florid, flowery, ornamental, ornamented.
adj antonyms austere, plain.

orthodox *adj* conventional, correct, sound, true.
adj antonym unorthodox.

oscillate *vb* fluctuate, sway, swing, vacillate, vary, vibrate.

ostensible *adj* **1** apparent, assigned, avowed, declared, exhibited, manifest, presented, visible. **2** plausible, professed, specious.

ostentation *n* **1** dash, display, flourish, pageantry, parade, pomp, pomposity, pompousness, show, vaunting. **2** appearance, semblance, showiness.
n antonym unpretentiousness.

ostentatious *adj* **1** boastful, dashing, flaunting, pompous, pretentious, showy, vain, vainglorious. **2** gaudy.
adj antonyms quiet, restrained.

ostracize *vb* banish, boycott, exclude, excommunicate, exile, expatriate, expel, evict.
vb antonyms accept, receive, reinstate, welcome.

oust *vb* dislodge, dispossess, eject, evict, expel.
vb antonyms ensconce, install, reinstate, settle.

outbreak *n* **1** ebullition, eruption, explosion, outburst. **2** affray, broil, conflict, commotion, fray, riot, row. **3** flare-up, manifestation.

outcast *n* **1** exile, expatriate. **2** castaway, pariah, reprobate, vagabond.
n antonyms favourite, idol.

outcome *n* conclusion, consequence, event, issue, result, upshot.

outcry *n* **1** cry, scream, screech, yell. **2** bruit, clamour, noise, tumult, vociferation.

outdo *vb* beat, exceed, excel, outgo, outstrip, outvie, surpass.

outlandish *adj* **1** alien, exotic, foreign, strange. **2** barbarous, bizarre, uncouth.
adj antonyms familiar, ordinary.

outlaw *vb* ban, banish, condemn, exclude, forbid, make illegal, prohibit. • *n* bandit, brigand, crook, freebooter, highwayman, lawbreaker, marauder, robber, thief.
vb antonyms allow, legalize.

outlay *n* disbursement, expenditure, outgoings.
n antonym income.

outline *vb* delineate, draft, draw, plan, silhouette, sketch. • *n* **1** contour, profile. **2** delineation, draft, drawing, plan, rough draft, silhouette, sketch.

outlive *vb* last, live longer, survive.

outlook *n* **1** future, prospect, sight, view. **2** lookout, watch-tower.

outrage *vb* abuse, injure, insult, maltreat, offend, shock, injure. • *n* abuse, affront, indignity, insult, offence.

outrageous *adj* **1** abusive, frantic, furious, frenzied, mad, raging, turbulent, violent, wild. **2** atrocious, enormous, flagrant, heinous, monstrous, nefarious, villainous. **3** enormous, excessive, extravagant, unwarrantable.
adj antonyms acceptable, irreproachable.

outré *adj* excessive, exorbitant, extravagant, immoderate, inordinate, overstrained, unconventional.

outrun *vb* beat, exceed, outdistance, outgo, outstrip, outspeed, surpass.

outset *n* beginning, commencement, entrance, opening, start, starting point.
n antonyms conclusion, end, finish.

outshine *vb* eclipse, outstrip, overshadow, surpass.

outspoken *adj* abrupt, blunt, candid, frank, plain, plainspoken, unceremonious, unreserved.

adj antonyms diplomatic, tactful.

outstanding *adj* **1** due, owing, uncollected, ungathered, unpaid, unsettled. **2** conspicuous, eminent, prominent, striking.

adj antonyms ordinary, unexceptional.

outward *adj* exterior, external, outer, outside.

adj antonyms inner, private.

outwit *vb* cheat, circumvent, deceive, defraud, diddle, dupe, gull, outmanoeuvre, overreach, swindle, victimize.

overawe *vb* affright, awe, browbeat, cow, daunt, frighten, intimidate, scare, terrify.

overbalance *vb* **1** capsize, overset, overturn, tumble, upset. **2** outweigh, preponderate.

overbearing *adj* **1** oppressive, overpowering. **2** arrogant, dictatorial, dogmatic, domineering, haughty, imperious, overweening, proud, supercilious.

adj antonyms modest, unassertive, unassuming.

overcast *vb* cloud, darken, overcloud, overshadow, shade, shadow. •*adj* cloudy, darkened, hazy, murky, obscure.

adj antonyms bright, clear, sunny.

overcharge *vb* **1** burden, oppress, overburden, overload, surcharge. **2** crowd, overfill. **3** exaggerate, overstate, overstrain.

overcome *vb* beat, choke, conquer, crush, defeat, discomfit, overbear, overmaster, overpower, overthrow, overturn, overwhelm, prevail, rout, subdue, subjugate, surmount, vanquish.

overflow *vb* **1** brim over, fall over, pour over, pour out, shower, spill. **2** deluge, inundate, submerge. • *n* deluge, inundation, profusion, superabundance.

overhaul *vb* **1** overtake. **2** check, examine, inspect, repair, survey. • *n* check, examination, inspection.

overlay *vb* **1** cover, spread over. **2** overlie, overpress, smother. **3** crush, overpower, overwhelm. **4** cloud, hide, obscure, overcast. • *n* appliqué, covering, decoration, veneer.

overlook *vb* **1** inspect, oversee, superintend, supervise. **2** disregard, miss, neglect, slight. **3** condone, excuse, forgive, pardon, pass over.

vb antonyms note, notice, record, remember.

overpower *vb* beat, conquer, crush, defeat, discomfit, overbear, overcome, overmaster, overturn, overwhelm, subdue, subjugate, vanquish.

overreach *vb* **1** exceed, outstrip, overshoot, pass, surpass. **2** cheat, circumvent, deceive, defraud.

override *vb* outride, outweigh, pass, quash, supersede, surpass.

overrule *vb* **1** control, govern, sway. **2** annul, cancel, nullify, recall, reject, repeal, repudiate, rescind, revoke, reject, set aside, supersede, suppress.

v antonyms allow, approve.

oversight *n* **1** care, charge, control, direction, inspection, management, superintendence, supervision, surveillance. **2** blunder, error, fault, inadvertence, inattention, lapse, miss, mistake, neglect, omission, slip, trip.

overt *adj* apparent, glaring, open, manifest, notorious, patent, public, unconcealed.

adj antonyms covert, secret.

overthrow *vb* **1** overturn, upset, subvert. **2** demolish, destroy, level. **3** beat, conquer, crush, defeat, discomfit, foil, master, overcome, overpower, overwhelm, rout, subjugate, vanquish, worst. • *n* **1** downfall, fall, prostration, subversion. **2** destruction, demolition, ruin. **3** defeat, discomfiture, dispersion, rout.

vb antonyms install, reinstate.

overturn *vb* invert, overthrow, reverse, subvert, upset.

overture *n* invitation, offer, proposal, proposition.

overweening *adj* arrogant, conceited, consequential, egotistical, haughty, opinionated, proud, supercilious, vain, vainglorious.

overwhelm *vb* **1** drown, engulf, inundate, overflow, submerge, swallow up, swamp. **2** conquer, crush, defeat, overbear, overcome, overpower, subdue, vanquish.

overwrought *adj* **1** overdone, overelaborate. **2** agitated, excited, overexcited, overworked, stirred.

adj antonyms calm, cool, impassive.

own[1] *vb* **1** have, hold, possess. **2** avow, confess. **3** acknowledge, admit, allow, concede.

own[2] *adj* particular, personal, private.

owner *n* freeholder, holder, landlord, possessor, proprietor.

P

pace *vb* go, hasten, hurry, move, step, walk.
• *n* amble, gait, step, walk.

pacific *adj* **1** appeasing, conciliatory, ironic, mollifying, placating, peacemaking, propitiatory. **2** calm, gentle, peaceable, peaceful, quiet, smooth, tranquil, unruffled.
adj antonyms aggressive, belligerent, contentious, pugnacious.

pacify *vb* **1** appease, conciliate, harmonize, tranquillize. **2** allay, appease, assuage, calm, compose, hush, lay, lull, moderate, mollify, placate, propitiate, quell, quiet, smooth, soften, soothe, still.
vb antonyms aggravate, anger.

pack *vb* **1** compact, compress, crowd, fill. **2** bundle, burden, load, stow. • *n* **1** bale, budget, bundle, package, packet, parcel. **2** burden, load. **3** assemblage, assembly, assortment, collection, set. **4** band, bevy, clan, company, crew, gang, knot, lot, party, squad.

pact *n* agreement, alliance, bargain, bond, compact, concordat, contract, convention, covenant, league, stipulation.
n antonyms breach, disagreement, quarrel.

pagan *adj* heathen, heathenish, idolatrous, irreligious, paganist, paganistic. • *n* gentile, heathen, idolater.

pageantry *n* display, flourish, magnificence, parade, pomp, show, splendour, state.

pain *vb* **1** agonize, bite, distress, hurt, rack, sting, torment, torture. **2** afflict, aggrieve, annoy, bore, chafe, displease, disquiet, fret, grieve, harass, incommode, plague, tease, trouble, vex, worry. **3** rankle, smart, shoot, sting, twinge. • *n* **1** ache, agony, anguish, discomfort, distress, gripe, hurt, pang, smart, soreness, sting, suffering, throe, torment, torture, twinge. **2** affliction, anguish, anxiety, bitterness, care, chagrin, disquiet, dolour, grief, heartache, misery, punishment, solicitude, sorrow, trouble, uneasiness, unhappiness, vexation, woe, wretchedness.
vb antonyms gratify, please.
n antonyms happiness, joy, pleasure.

painful *adj* **1** agonizing, distressful, excruciating, racking, sharp, tormenting, torturing. **2** afflicting, afflictive, annoying, baleful, disagreeable, displeasing, disquieting, distressing, dolorous, grievous, provoking, troublesome, unpleasant, vexatious. **3** arduous, careful, difficult, hard, severe, sore, toilsome.
adj antonyms easy, painless.

pains *npl* **1** care, effort, labour, task, toilsomeness, trouble. **2** childbirth, labour, travail.

painstaking *adj* assiduous, careful, conscientious, diligent, hardworking, industrious, laborious, persevering, plodding, sedulous, strenuous.
adj antonyms careless, negligent.

paint *vb* **1** delineate, depict, describe, draw, figure, pencil, portray, represent, sketch. **2** adorn, beautify, deck, embellish, ornament. • *n* **1** colouring, dye, pigment, stain. **2** cosmetics, greasepaint, make-up.

pair *vb* couple, marry, mate, match. • *n* brace, couple, double, duo, match, twosome.
vb antonyms dissever, sever.

pal *n* buddy, chum, companion, comrade, crony, friend, mate, mucker.
n antonym enemy.

palatable *adj* acceptable, agreeable, appetizing, delicate, delicious, enjoyable, flavourful, flavoursome, gustative, gustatory, luscious, nice, pleasant, pleasing, savoury, relishable, tasteful, tasty, toothsome.

palaver *vb* **1** chat, chatter, converse, patter, prattle, say, speak, talk. **2** confer, parley. **3** blandish, cajole, flatter, wheedle. • *n* **1** chat, chatter, conversation, discussion, language, prattle, speech, talk. **2** confab, confabulation, conference, conclave, parley, powwow. **3** balderdash, cajolery, flummery, gibberish.

pale *vb* blanch, lose colour, whiten. • *adj* **1** ashen, ashy, blanched, bloodless, pallid, sickly, wan, white. **2** blank, dim, obscure, spectral. • *n* **1** picket, stake. **2** circuit,

enclosure. **3** district, region, territory. **4** boundary, confine, fence, limit.
adj antonym ruddy.
vb antonyms blush, colour.

pall[1] *n* cloak, cover, curtain, mantle, pallium, shield, shroud, veil.

pall[2] *vb* **1** cloy, glut, gorge, satiate, surfeit. **2** deject, depress, discourage, dishearten, dispirit. **3** cloak, cover, drape, invest, overspread, shroud.

palliate *vb* **1** cloak, conceal, cover, excuse, extenuate, hide, gloss, lessen. **2** abate, allay, alleviate, assuage, blunt, diminish, dull, ease, mitigate, moderate, mollify, quell, quiet, relieve, soften, soothe, still.

pallid *adj* ashen, ashy, cadaverous, colourless, pale, sallow, wan, whitish.
adj antonyms high-complexioned, ruddy, vigorous.

palm[1] *vb* **1** foist, impose, obtrude, pass off. **2** handle, touch.

palm[2] *n* bays, crown, laurels, prize, trophy, victory.

palmy *adj* flourishing, fortunate, glorious, golden, halcyon, happy, joyous, prosperous, thriving, victorious.

palpable *adj* **1** corporeal, material, tactile, tangible. **2** evident, glaring, gross, intelligible, manifest, obvious, patent, plain, unmistakable.
adj antonyms elusive, impalpable, imperceptible, intangible.

palpitate *vb* **1** flutter, pulsate, throb. **2** quiver, shiver, tremble.

palter *vb* dodge, equivocate, evade, haggle, prevaricate, quibble, shift, shuffle, trifle.

paltry *adj* diminutive, feeble, inconsiderable, insignificant, little, miserable, petty, slender, slight, small, sorry, trifling, trivial, unimportant, wretched.
adj antonyms significant, substantial.

pamper *vb* baby, coddle, fondle, gratify, humour, spoil.
vb antonyms ill-treat, neglect.

panacea *n* catholicon, cure-all, medicine, remedy.

pang *n* agony, anguish, distress, gripe, pain, throe, twinge.

panic *vb* **1** affright, alarm, scare, startle, terrify. **2** become terrified, overreact. • *n* alarm, consternation, fear, fright, jitters, terror.
n antonyms assurance, confidence.
vb antonyms reassure, relax.

pant *vb* **1** blow, gasp, puff. **2** heave, palpitate, pulsate, throb. **3** languish. **4** desire, hunger, long, sigh, thirst, yearn. • *n* blow, gasp, puff.

parable *n* allegory, fable, story.

paraclete *n* advocate, comforter, consoler, intercessor, mediator.

parade *vb* display, flaunt, show, vaunt. • *n* **1** ceremony, display, flaunting, ostentation, pomp, show. **2** array, pageant, review, spectacle. **3** mall, promenade.

paradox *n* absurdity, contradiction, mystery.

paragon *n* flower, ideal, masterpiece, model, nonpareil, pattern, standard.

paragraph *n* clause, item, notice, passage, section, sentence, subdivision.

parallel *vb* be alike, compare, conform, correlate, match. • *adj* **1** abreast, concurrent. **2** allied, analogous, correspondent, equal, like, resembling, similar. • *n* **1** conformity, likeness, resemblance, similarity. **2** analogue, correlative, counterpart.
vb antonyms diverge, separate.
adj antonyms divergent, separate.

paramount *adj* chief, dominant, eminent, pre-eminent, principal, superior, supreme.
adj antonyms inferior, last, lowest.

paraphernalia *n* accoutrements, appendages, appurtenances, baggage, belongings, effects, equipage, equipment, ornaments, trappings.

parasite *n* bloodsucker, fawner, flatterer, flunky, hanger-on, leech, spaniel, sycophant, toady, wheedler.

parcel *vb* allot, apportion, dispense, distribute, divide. • *n* **1** budget, bundle, package. **2** batch, collection, group, lot, set. **3** division, part, patch, pierce, plot, portion, tract.

parched *adj* arid, dry, scorched, shrivelled, thirsty.

pardon *vb* **1** condone, forgive, overlook, remit. **2** absolve, acquit, clear, discharge, excuse, release. • *n* absolution, amnesty, condonation, discharge, excuse, forgiveness, grace, mercy, overlook, release.

parentage *n* ancestry, birth, descent, extraction, family, lineage, origin, parenthood, pedigree, stock.

pariah *n* outcast, wretch.

parish *n* **1** community, congregation, parishioners. **2** district, subdivision.

parity *n* analogy, correspondence, equality, equivalence, likeness, sameness, similarity.

parody *vb* burlesque, caricature, imitate, lampoon, mock, ridicule, satirize, travesty. • *n* burlesque, caricature, imitation, ridicule, satire, travesty.

paroxysm *n* attack, convulsion, exacerbation, fit, outburst, seizure, spasm, throe.

parsimonious *adj* avaricious, close, close-fisted, covetous, frugal, grasping, grudging, illiberal, mean, mercenary, miserly, near, niggardly, penurious, shabby, sordid, sparing, stingy, tightfisted.
adj antonyms generous, liberal, open-handed.

parson *n* churchman, clergyman, divine, ecclesiastic, incumbent, minister, pastor, priest, rector.

part *vb* 1 break, dismember, dissever, divide, sever, subdivide, sunder. 2 detach, disconnect, disjoin, dissociate, disunite, separate. 3 allot, apportion, distribute, divide, mete, share. 4 secrete. • *n* 1 crumb, division, fraction, fragment, moiety, parcel, piece, portion, remnant, scrap, section, segment, subdivision. 2 component, constituent, element, ingredient, member, organ. 3 lot, share. 4 concern, interest, participation. 5 allotment, apportionment, dividend. 6 business, charge, duty, function, office, work. 7 faction, party, side. 8 character, cue, lines, role. 9 clause, paragraph, passage.

partake *vb* 1 engage, participate, share. 2 consume, eat, take. 3 evince, evoke, show, suggest.

partial *adj* 1 component, fractional, imperfect, incomplete, limited. 2 biased, influential, interested, one-sided, prejudiced, prepossessed, unfair, unjust, warped. 3 fond, indulgent.
adj antonyms complete, exhaustive, total; disinterested, fair, unbiased.

participate *vb* engage in, partake, perform, share.

particle *n* atom, bit, corpuscle, crumb, drop, glimmer, grain, granule, iota, jot, mite, molecule, morsel, mote, scrap, shred, snip, spark, speck, whit.

particular *adj* 1 especial, special, specific. 2 distinct, individual, respective, separate, single. 3 characteristic, distinctive, peculiar. 4 individual, intimate, own, personal, private. 5 notable, noteworthy. 6 circumstantial, definite, detailed, exact, minute, narrow, precise. 7 careful, close, conscientious, critical, fastidious, nice, scrupulous, strict. 8 marked, odd, singular, strange, uncommon. • *n* case, circumstance, count, detail, feature, instance, item, particularity, point, regard, respect.
adj antonym general; casual.

parting *adj* 1 breaking, dividing, separating. 2 final, last, valedictory. 3 declining, departing. • *n* 1 breaking, disruption, rupture, severing. 2 detachment, division, separation. 3 death, departure, farewell, leave-taking.

partisan *adj* biased, factional, interested, partial, prejudiced. • *n* 1 adherent, backer, champion, disciple, follower, supporter, votary. 2 baton, halberd, pike, quarterstaff, truncheon, staff.

partition *vb* apportion, distribute, divide, portion, separate, share. • *n* 1 division, separation. 2 barrier, division, screen, wall. 3 allotment, apportionment, distribution.

partner *n* 1 associate, colleague, copartner, partaker, participant, participator. 2 accomplice, ally, coadjutor, confederate. 3 companion, consort, spouse.

partnership *n* 1 association, company, copartnership, firm, house, society. 2 connection, interest, participation, union.

parts *npl* 1 abilities, accomplishments, endowments, faculties, genius, gifts, intellect, intelligence, mind, qualities, powers, talents. 2 districts, regions.

party *n* 1 alliance, association, cabal, circle, clique, combination, confederacy, coterie, faction, group, junta, league, ring, set. 2 body, company, detachment, squad, troop. 3 assembly, gathering. 4 partaker, participant, participator, sharer. 5 defendant, litigant, plaintiff. 6 individual, one, person, somebody. 7 cause, division, interest, side.

pass¹ *vb* 1 devolve, fall, go, move, proceed. 2 change, elapse, flit, glide, lapse, slip. 3 cease, die, fade, expire, vanish. 4 happen, occur. 5 convey, deliver, send, transmit, transfer. 6 disregard, ignore, neglect. 7 exceed, excel, surpass. 8 approve, ratify, sanction. 9 answer, do, succeed, suffice, suit. 10 express, pronounce, utter. 11 beguile, wile.

pass² *n* 1 avenue, ford, road, route, way. 2 defile, gorge, passage, ravine. 3 authorization, licence, passport, permission, ticket. 4 condition, conjecture, plight, situation, state. **5** lunge, push, thrust, tilt. **6** transfer, trick.

passable *adj* **1** admissible, allowable, mediocre, middling, moderate, ordinary, so-so, tolerable. **2** acceptable, current, receivable. **3** navigable, traversable.

passage *n* **1** going, passing, progress, transit. **2** evacuation, journey, migration, transit, voyage. **3** avenue, channel, course, pass, path, road, route, thoroughfare, vennel, way. **4** access, currency, entry, reception. **5** act, deed, event, feat, incidence, occurrence, passion. **6** corridor, gallery, gate, hall. **7** clause, paragraph, sentence, text. **8** course, death, decease, departure, expiration, lapse. **9** affair, brush, change, collision, combat, conflict, contest, encounter, exchange, joust, skirmish, tilt.

passenger *n* fare, itinerant, tourist, traveller, voyager, wayfarer.

passionate *adj* **1** animated, ardent, burning, earnest, enthusiastic, excited, fervent, fiery, furious, glowing, hot-blooded, impassioned, impetuous, impulsive, intense, vehement, warm, zealous. **2** hot-headed, irascible, quick-tempered, tempestuous, violent.
adj antonyms frigid, laid-back, phlegmatic.

passive *adj* **1** inactive, inert, quiescent, receptive. **2** apathetic, enduring, long-suffering, nonresistant, patient, stoical, submissive, suffering, unresisting.
adj antonyms active, involved, lively.

past *adj* **1** accomplished, elapsed, ended, gone, spent. **2** ancient, bygone, former, obsolete, outworn. • *adv* above, extra, beyond, over. • *prep* above, after, beyond, exceeding. • *n* antiquity, heretofore, history, olden times, yesterday.

pastime *n* amusement, diversion, entertainment, hobby, play, recreation, sport.
n antonyms business, employment, occupation, vocation, work.

pastor *n* clergyman, churchman, divine, ecclesiastic, minister, parson, priest, vicar.

pat¹ *vb* **1** dab, hit, rap, tap. **2** caress, chuck, fondle, pet. • *n* **1** dab, hit, pad, rap, tap. **2** caress.
adv antonyms imprecisely, wrongly.

pat² *adj* appropriate, apt, fit, pertinent, suitable. • *adv* aptly, conveniently, opportunely, seasonably.
adj antonyms irrelevant, unsuitable.

patch *vb* mend, repair. • *n* **1** repair. **2** parcel, plot, tract.

patent *adj* **1** expanded, open, spreading. **2** apparent, clear, conspicuous, evident, glaring, indisputable, manifest, notorious, obvious, public, open, palpable, plain, unconcealed, unmistakable. • *n* copyright, privilege, right.
adj antonyms hidden, opaque.

paternity *n* derivation, descent, fatherhood, origin.

path *n* access, avenue, course, footway, passage, pathway, road, route, track, trail, way.

pathetic *adj* affecting, melting, moving, pitiable, plaintive, sad, tender, touching.
adj antonyms admirable, cheerful.

patience *n* **1** endurance, fortitude, long-sufferance, resignation, submission, sufferance. **2** calmness, composure, quietness. **3** forbearance, indulgence, leniency. **4** assiduity, constancy, diligence, indefatigability, indefatigableness, perseverance, persistence.
n antonyms impatience, intolerance.

patient *adj* **1** meek, passive, resigned, submissive, uncomplaining, unrepining. **2** calm, composed, contented, quiet. **3** indulgent, lenient, long-suffering. **4** assiduous, constant, diligent, indefatigable, persevering, persistent. • *n* case, invalid, subject, sufferer.
adj antonyms impatient, intolerant.

patrician *adj* aristocratic, blue-blooded, highborn, noble, senatorial, well-born. • *n* aristocrat, blue blood, nobleman.

patron *n* advocate, defender, favourer, guardian, helper, protector, supporter.

patronize *vb* **1** aid, assist, befriend, countenance, defend, favour, maintain, support. **2** condescend, disparage, scorn.

pattern *vb* copy, follow, imitate. • *n* **1** archetype, exemplar, last, model, original, paradigm, plan, prototype. **2** example, guide, sample, specimen. **3** mirror, paragon. **4** design, figure, shape, style, type.

paucity *n* deficiency, exiguity, insufficiency, lack, poverty, rarity, shortage.

paunch *n* abdomen, belly, gut, stomach.

pauperism *n* beggary, destitution, indigence, mendicancy, mendicity, need, poverty, penury, want.

pause *vb* **1** breathe, cease, delay, desist, rest, stay, stop, wait. **2** delay, forbear, intermit, stay, stop, tarry, wait. **3** deliberate, demur, hesitate, waver. • *n* **1** break, caesura, cessation, halt, intermission, interruption, interval, remission, rest, stop, stoppage, stopping, suspension. **2** hesitation, suspense, uncertainty. **3** paragraph.

pawn¹ *n* cat's-paw, dupe, plaything, puppet, stooge, tool, toy.

pawn² *vb* bet, hazard, lay, pledge, risk, stake, wager. • *n* assurance, bond, guarantee, pledge, security.

pay *vb* **1** defray, discharge, discount, foot, honour, liquidate, meet, quit, settle. **2** compensate, recompense, reimburse, requite, reward. **3** punish, revenge. **4** give, offer, render. • *n* allowance, commission, compensation, emolument, hire, recompense, reimbursement, remuneration, requital, reward, salary, wages.

peace *n* **1** calm, calmness, quiet, quietness, repose, stillness. **2** accord, amity, friendliness, harmony. **3** composure, equanimity, imperturbability, placidity, quietude, tranquillity. **4** agreement, armistice.
n antonyms disagreement, disturbance, war.

peaceable *adj* **1** pacific, peaceful. **2** amiable, amicable, friendly, gentle, inoffensive, mild. **3** placid, quiet, serene, still, tranquil, undisturbed, unmoved.
adj antonyms belligerent, offensive.

peaceful *adj* **1** quiet, undisturbed. **2** amicable, concordant, friendly, gentle, harmonious, mild, pacific, peaceable. **3** calm, composed, placid, serene, still.
adj antonyms disturbed, noisy, troubled.

peak *vb* **1** climax, culminate, top. **2** dwindle, thin. • *n* acme, apex, crest, crown, pinnacle, summit, top, zenith.
n antonyms nadir, trough.

peaked *adj* piked, pointed, thin.

peasant *n* boor, countryman, clown, hind, labourer, rustic, swain.

peculate *vb* appropriate, defraud, embezzle, misappropriate, pilfer, purloin, rob, steal.

peculiar *adj* **1** appropriate, idiosyncratic, individual, proper. **2** characteristic, eccentric, exceptional, extraordinary, odd, queer, rare, singular, strange, striking, uncommon, unusual. **3** individual, especial, particular, select, special, specific.
adj antonyms normal, ordinary; general, uncharacteristic.

peculiarity *n* **1** appropriateness, distinctiveness,

individuality, speciality. **2** characteristic, idiosyncrasy, oddity, peculiarity, singularity.

pedantic *adj* conceited, fussy, officious, ostentatious, over-learned, particular, pedagogical, pompous, precise, pretentious, priggish, stilted.
adj antonyms casual, imprecise, informal.

pedlar *n* chapman, costermonger, hawker, packman, vendor.

pedigree *adj* purebred, thoroughbred. • *n* ancestry, breed, descent, extraction, family, genealogy, house, line, lineage, race, stock, strain.

peer¹ *vb* **1** gaze, look, peek, peep, pry, squinny, squint. **2** appear, emerge.

peer² *n* **1** associate, co-equal, companion, compeer, equal, equivalent, fellow, like, mate, match. **2** aristocrat, baron, count, duke, earl, grandee, lord, marquis, noble, nobleman, viscount.

peerless *adj* excellent, incomparable, matchless, outstanding, superlative, unequalled, unique, unmatched, unsurpassed.

peevish *adj* **1** acrimonious, captious, churlish, complaining, crabbed, cross, crusty, discontented, fretful, ill-natured, ill-tempered, irascible, irritable, pettish, petulant, querulous, snappish, snarling, splenetic, spleeny, testy, waspish. **2** forward, headstrong, obstinate, self-willed, stubborn. **3** childish, silly, thoughtless, trifling.
adj antonym good-tempered.

pellucid *adj* bright, clear, crystalline, diaphanous, limpid, lucid, transparent.

pelt¹ *vb* **1** assail, batter, beat, belabour, bombard, pepper, stone, strike. **2** cast, hurl, throw. **3** hurry, rush, speed, tear.

pelt² *n* coat, hide, skin.

pen¹ *vb* compose, draft, indite, inscribe, write.

pen² *vb* confine, coop, encage, enclose, impound, imprison, incarcerate. • *n* cage, coop, corral, crib, hutch, enclosure, paddock, pound, stall, sty.

penalty *n* chastisement, fine, forfeiture, mulct, punishment, retribution.
n antonym reward.

penance *n* humiliation, maceration, mortification, penalty, punishment.

penchant *n* bent, bias, disposition, fondness, inclination, leaning, liking, predilection, predisposition, proclivity, proneness, propensity, taste, tendency, turn.
n antonym dislike.

penetrate *vb* **1** bore, burrow, cut, enter, invade, penetrate, percolate, perforate, pervade, pierce, soak, stab. **2** affect, sensitize, touch. **3** comprehend, discern, perceive, understand.

penetrating *adj* **1** penetrative, permeating, piercing, sharp, subtle. **2** acute, clear-sighted, discerning, intelligent, keen, quick, sagacious, sharp-witted, shrewd.
adj antonyms gentle, obtuse, soft.

penetration *n* acuteness, discernment, insight, sagacity.

penitence *n* compunction, contrition, qualms, regret, remorse, repentance, sorrow.

penitent *adj* compunctious, conscience-stricken, contrite, regretful, remorseful, repentant, sorrowing, sorrowful. • *n* penance-doer, penitentiary, repentant.
adj antonym unrepentant.

penniless *adj* broke (*inf*), destitute, distressed, impecunious, impoverished, indigent, moneyless, pinched, poor, necessitous, needy, pensive, poverty-stricken, reduced, skint (*sl*).
adj antonyms rich, wealthy.

pensive *adj* **1** contemplative, dreamy, meditative, reflective, sober, thoughtful. **2** grave, melancholic, melancholy, mournful, sad, serious, solemn.

penurious *adj* **1** inadequate, ill-provided, insufficient, meagre, niggardly, poor, scanty, stinted. **2** avaricious, close, close-fisted, covetous, illiberal, grasping, grudging, mean, mercenary, miserly, near, niggardly, parsimonious, sordid, stingy, tightfisted.
adj antonyms generous, wealthy.

penury *n* beggary, destitution, indigence, need, poverty, privation, want.
n antonym prosperity.

people *vb* colonize, inhabit, populate. • *n* **1** clan, country, family, nation, race, state, tribe. **2** folk, humankind, persons, population, public. **3** commons, community, democracy, populace, proletariat. **4** mob, multitude, rabble.

perceive *vb* **1** behold, descry, detect, discern, discover, discriminate, distinguish, note, notice, observe, recognize, remark, see, spot. **2** appreciate, comprehend, know, understand.

perceptible *adj* apparent, appreciable, cognizable, discernible, noticeable, perceivable, understandable, visible.
adj antonym imperceptible.

perception *n* **1** apprehension, cognition, discernment, perceiving, recognition, seeing. **2** comprehension, conception, consciousness, perceptiveness, perceptivity, understanding, feeling.

perchance *adv* haply, maybe, mayhap, peradventure, perhaps, possibly, probably.

percolate *vb* drain, drip, exude, filter, filtrate, ooze, penetrate, stain, transude.

percussion *n* collision, clash, concussion, crash, encounter, shock.

perdition *n* damnation, demolition, destruction, downfall, hell, overthrow, ruin, wreck.

peremptory *adj* **1** absolute, authoritative, categorical, commanding, decisive, express, imperative, imperious, positive. **2** determined, resolute, resolved. **3** arbitrary, dogmatic, incontrovertible.

perennial *adj* ceaseless, constant, continual, deathless, enduring, immortal, imperishable, lasting, never-failing, permanent, perpetual, unceasing, undying, unfailing, uninterrupted.

perfect *vb* accomplish, complete, consummate, elaborate, finish. • *adj* **1** completed, finished. **2** complete, entire, full, unqualified, utter, whole. **3** capital, consummate, excellent, exquisite, faultless, ideal. **4** accomplished, disciplined, expert, skilled. **5** blameless, faultless, holy, immaculate, pure, spotless, unblemished.
adj antonyms flawed, imperfect.

perfection *n* **1** completeness, completion, consummation, correctness, excellence, faultlessness, finish, maturity, perfection, perfectness, wholeness. **2** beauty, quality.
n antonyms flaw, imperfection.

perfidious *adj* deceitful, dishonest, disloyal, double-faced, faithless, false, false-hearted, traitorous, treacherous, unfaithful, untrustworthy, venal.

perfidy *n* defection, disloyalty, faithlessness, infidelity, perfidiousness, traitorousness, treachery, treason.

perforate *vb* bore, drill, penetrate, pierce, pink, prick, punch, riddle, trepan.

perform *vb* **1** accomplish, achieve, compass, consummate, do, effect, transact. **2** complete, discharge, execute, fulfil, meet, observe, satisfy. **3** act, play, represent.

performance *n* **1** accomplishment, achievement, completion, consummation, discharge, doing, execution, fulfilment. **2** act, action, deed, exploit, feat, work.

3 composition, production. **4** acting, entertainment, exhibition, play, representation, hold. **5** execution, playing.

perfume *n* aroma, balminess, bouquet, fragrance, incense, odour, redolence, scent, smell, sweetness.

perfunctory *adj* careless, formal, heedless, indifferent, mechanical, negligent, reckless, slight, slovenly, thoughtless, unmindful.

adj antonym cordial.

perhaps *adv* haply, peradventure, perchance, possibly.

peril *vb* endanger, imperil, jeopardize, risk. • *n* danger, hazard, insecurity, jeopardy, pitfall, risk, snare, uncertainty.

n antonyms safety, security.

perilous *adj* dangerous, hazardous, risky, unsafe.

adj antonyms safe, secure.

period *n* **1** aeon, age, cycle, date, eon, epoch, season, span, spell, stage, term, time. **2** continuance, duration. **3** bound, conclusion, determination, end, limit, term, termination. **4** clause, phrase, proposition, sentence.

periodical *adj* cyclical, incidental, intermittent, recurrent, recurring, regular, seasonal, systematic. • *n* magazine, paper, review, serial, weekly.

periphery *n* boundary, circumference, outside, perimeter, superficies, surface.

perish *vb* **1** decay, moulder, shrivel, waste, wither. **2** decease, die, expire, vanish.

perishable *adj* **1** decaying, decomposable, destructible. **2** dying, frail, mortal, temporary.

perjured *adj* false, forsworn, perfidious, traitorous, treacherous, untrue.

permanent *adj* abiding, constant, continuing, durable, enduring, fixed, immutable, invariable, lasting, perpetual, persistent, stable, standing, steadfast, unchangeable, unchanging, unfading, unmovable.

adj antonyms ephemeral, fleeting, temporary.

permissible *adj* admissible, allowable, free, lawful, legal, legitimate, proper, sufferable, unprohibited.

adj antonym prohibited.

permission *n* allowance, authorization, consent, dispensation, leave, liberty, licence, permit, sufferance, toleration, warrant.

n antonym prohibition.

permit *vb* **1** agree, allow, endure, let, suffer, tolerate. **2** admit, authorize, consent, empower, license, warrant. • *n* leave, liberty, licence, passport, permission, sanction, warrant.

vb antonym prohibit.

n antonym prohibition.

pernicious *adj* **1** baleful, baneful, damaging, deadly, deleterious, destructive, detrimental, disadvantageous, fatal, harmful, hurtful, injurious, malign, mischievous, noisome, noxious, prejudicial, ruinous. **2** evilhearted, malevolent, malicious, malignant, mischief-making, wicked.

perpetrate *vb* commit, do, execute, perform.

perpetual *adj* ceaseless, continual, constant, endless, enduring, eternal, ever-enduring, everlasting, incessant, interminable, never-ceasing, never-ending, perennial, permanent, sempiternal, unceasing, unending, unfailing, uninterrupted.

adj antonyms ephemeral, intermittent, transient.

perplex *vb* **1** complicate, encumber, entangle, involve, snarl, tangle. **2** beset, bewilder, confound, confuse, corner, distract, embarrass, fog, mystify, nonplus, pother, puzzle, set. **3** annoy, bother, disturb, harass, molest, pester, plague, tease, trouble, vex, worry.

persecute *vb* **1** afflict, distress, harass, molest, oppress, worry. **2** annoy, beset, importune, pester, solicit, tease.

vb antonyms accommodate, humour, indulge, pamper.

perseverance *n* constancy, continuance, doggedness, indefatigableness, persistence, persistency, pertinacity, resolution, steadfastness, steadiness, tenacity.

persevere *vb* continue, determine, endure, maintain, persist, remain, resolve, stick.

vb antonyms desist, discontinue, give up, stop.

persist *vb* **1** continue, endure, last, remain. **2** insist, persevere.

vb antonyms desist, stop.

persistent *adj* **1** constant, continuing, enduring, fixed, immovable, persevering, persisting, steady, tenacious. **2** contumacious, dogged, indefatigable, obdurate, obstinate, pertinacious, perverse, pigheaded, stubborn.

personable *adj* comely, good-looking, graceful, seemly, well-turned-out.

adj antonyms disagreeable, unattractive.

personal *adj* **1** individual, peculiar, private, special. **2** bodily, corporal, corporeal, exterior, material, physical.
adj antonyms general, public, universal.

personate *vb* **1** act, impersonate, personify, play, represent. **2** disguise, mast. **3** counterfeit, feign, simulate.

perspective *n* **1** panorama, prospect, view, vista. **2** proportion, relation.

perspicacious *adj* **1** keen-sighted, quick-sighted, sharp-sighted. **2** acute, clever, discerning, keen, penetrating, sagacious, sharp-witted, shrewd.

perspicacity *n* acumen, acuteness, astuteness, discernment, insight, penetration, perspicaciousness, sagacity, sharpness, shrewdness.

perspicuity *n* clearness, distinctness, explicitness, intelligibility, lucidity, lucidness, perspicuousness, plainness, transparency.

perspicuous *adj* clear, distinct, explicit, intelligible, lucid, obvious, plain, transparent, unequivocal.

perspire *vb* exhale, glow, sweat, swelter.

persuade *vb* **1** allure, actuate, entice, impel, incite, induce, influence, lead, move, prevail upon, urge. **2** advise, counsel. **3** convince, satisfy. **4** inculcate, teach.
vb antonyms discourage, dissuade.

persuasion *n* **1** exhortation, incitement, inducement, influence. **2** belief, conviction, opinion. **3** creed, doctrine, dogma, tenet. **4** kind, sort, variety.

persuasive *adj* cogent, convincing, inducing, inducible, logical, persuading, plausible, sound, valid, weighty.

pert *adj* **1** brisk, dapper, lively, nimble, smart, sprightly, perky. **2** bold, flippant, forward, free, impertinent, impudent, malapert, presuming, smart, saucy.

pertain *vb* appertain, befit, behove, belong, concern, refer, regard, relate.

pertinacious *adj* **1** constant, determined, firm, obdurate, persevering, resolute, staunch, steadfast, steady. **2** dogged, headstrong, inflexible, mulish, intractable, obstinate, perverse, stubborn, unyielding, wayward, wilful.

pertinent *adj* **1** adapted, applicable, apposite, appropriate, apropos, apt, fit, germane, pat, proper, relevant, suitable. **2** appurtenant, belonging, concerning, pertaining, regarding.
adj antonyms inappropriate, irrelevant, unsuitable.

perturb *vb* **1** agitate, disquiet, distress, disturb, excite, trouble, unsettle, upset, vex, worry. **2** confuse.

pervade *vb* affect, animate, diffuse, extend, fill, imbue, impregnate, infiltrate, penetrate, permeate.

perverse *adj* **1** bad, disturbed, oblique, perverted. **2** contrary, dogged, headstrong, mulish, obstinate, pertinacious, perversive, stubborn, ungovernable, intractable, unyielding, wayward, wilful. **3** cantankerous, churlish, crabbed, cross, cross-grained, crusty, cussed, morose, peevish, petulant, snappish, snarling, spiteful, spleeny, surly, testy, touchy, wicked, wrongheaded. **4** inconvenient, troublesome, untoward, vexatious.
adj antonyms normal, reasonable.

perversion *n* abasement, corruption, debasement, impairment, injury, prostitution, vitiation.

perverted *adj* corrupt, debased, distorted, evil, impaired, misguiding, vitiated, wicked.

pessimistic *adj* cynical, dark, dejected, depressed, despondent, downhearted, gloomy, glum, melancholy, melancholic, morose, sad.

pest *n* **1** disease, epidemic, infection, pestilence, plague. **2** annoyance, bane, curse, infliction, nuisance, scourge, trouble.

pestilent *adj* **1** contagious, infectious, malignant, pestilential. **2** deadly, evil, injurious, malign, mischievous, noxious, poisonous. **3** annoying, corrupt, pernicious, troublesome, vexatious.

petition *vb* ask, beg, crave, entreat, pray, solicit, sue, supplicate. • *n* address, appeal, application, entreaty, prayer, request, solicitation, supplication, suit.

petrify *vb* **1** calcify, fossilize, lapidify. **2** benumb, deaden. **3** amaze, appal, astonish, astound, confound, dumbfound, paralyse, stun, stupefy.

petty *adj* diminutive, frivolous, inconsiderable, inferior, insignificant, little, mean, slight, small, trifling, trivial, unimportant.
adj antonyms generous, important, large-hearted, significant, vital.

petulant *adj* acrimonious, captious, cavilling, censorious, choleric, crabbed, cross, crusty, forward, fretful, hasty, ill-humoured, ill-tempered, irascible, irritable, peevish, perverse, pettish, querulous, snappish, snarling, testy, touchy, waspish.

phantom n apparition, ghost, illusion, phantasm, spectre, vision, wraith.

pharisaism n cant, formalism, hypocrisy, phariseeism, piety, sanctimoniousness, self-righteousness.

phenomenal adj marvellous, miraculous, prodigious, wondrous.

philanthropy n alms-giving, altruism, benevolence, charity, grace, humanitarianism, humanity, kindness.

philosophical, philosophic adj 1 rational, reasonable, sound, wise. 2 calm, collected, composed, cool, imperturbable, sedate, serene, stoical, tranquil, unruffled.

phlegmatic adj apathetic, calm, cold, cold-blooded, dull, frigid, heavy, impassive, indifferent, inert, sluggish, stoical, tame, unfeeling.
adj antonyms demonstrative, passionate.

phobia n aversion, detestation, dislike, distaste, dread, fear, hatred.

phrase vb call, christen, denominate, designate, describe, dub, entitle, name, style. • n diction, expression, phraseology, style.

phraseology n diction, expression, language, phrasing, style.

physical adj 1 material, natural. 2 bodily, corporeal, external, substantial, tangible, sensible.
adj antonyms mental, spiritual.

physiognomy n configuration, countenance, face, look, visage.

picaroon n 1 adventurer, cheat, rogue. 2 buccaneer, corsair, freebooter, marauder, pirate, plunderer, sea-rover.

pick vb 1 peck, pierce, strike. 2 cut, detach, gather, pluck. 3 choose, cull, select. 4 acquire, collect, get. 5 pilfer, steal. • n pickaxe, pike, spike, toothpick.
vb antonym reject.

picture vb delineate, draw, imagine, paint, represent. • n 1 drawing, engraving, painting, print. 2 copy, counterpart, delineation, embodiment, illustration, image, likeness, portraiture, portrayal, semblance, representation, resemblance, similitude. 3 description.

picturesque adj beautiful, charming, colourful, graphic, scenic, striking, vivid.

piece vb 1 mend, patch, repair. 2 augment, complete, enlarge, increase. 3 cement, join, unite. • n 1 amount, bit, chunk, cut, fragment, hunk, part, quantity, scrap, shred, slice. 2 portion. 3 article, item,

object. 4 composition, lucubration, work, writing.

pied adj irregular, motley, mottled, particoloured, piebald, spotted, variegated.

pierce vb 1 gore, impale, pink, prick, stab, transfix. 2 bore, drill, excite, penetrate, perforate, puncture. 3 affect, move, rouse, strike, thrill, touch.

piety n devotion, devoutness, holiness, godliness, grace, religion, sanctity.

pile[1] vb 1 accumulate, amass. 2 collect, gather, heap, load. • n 1 accumulation, collection, heap, mass, stack. 2 fortune, wad. 3 building, edifice, erection, fabric, pyramid, skyscraper, structure, tower. 4 reactor, nuclear reactor.

pile[2] n beam, column, pier, pillar, pole, post.

pile[3] n down, feel, finish, fur, fluff, fuzz, grain, nap, pappus, shag, surface, texture.

pilfer vb filch, purloin, rob, steal, thieve.

pilgrim n 1 journeyer, sojourner, traveller, wanderer, wayfarer. 2 crusader, devotee, palmer.

pilgrimage n crusade, excursion, expedition, journey, tour, trip.

pillage vb despoil, loot, plunder, rifle, sack, spoil, strip. • n 1 depredation, destruction, devastation, plundering, rapine, spoliation. 2 despoliation, plunder, rifling, sack, spoils.

pillar n 1 column, pier, pilaster, post, shaft, stanchion. 2 maintainer, prop, support, supporter, upholder.

pilot vb conduct, control, direct, guide, navigate, steer. • adj experimental, model, trial. • n 1 helmsman, navigator, steersman. 2 airman, aviator, conductor, director, flier, guide.

pinch vb 1 compress, contract, cramp, gripe, nip, squeeze. 2 afflict, distress, famish, oppress, straiten, stint. 3 frost, nip. 4 apprehend, arrest. 5 economize, spare, stint. • n 1 gripe, nip. 2 pang, throe. 3 crisis, difficulty, emergency, exigency, oppression, pressure, push, strait, stress.

pine vb 1 decay, decline, droop, fade, flag, languish, waste, wilt, wither. 2 desire, long, yearn.

pinion vb bind, chain, fasten, fetter, maim, restrain, shackle. • n 1 pennon, wing. 2 feather, quill, pen, plume, wing. 3 fetter.

pinnacle n 1 minaret, turret. 2 acme, apex, height, peak, summit, top, zenith.

pious *adj* **1** filial. **2** devout, godly, holy, religious, reverential, righteous, saintly.
adj antonyms impious.

piquant *adj* **1** biting, highly flavoured, piercing, prickling, pungent, sharp, stinging. **2** interesting, lively, racy, sparkling, stimulating. **3** cutting, keen, pointed, severe, strong, tart.
adj antonyms banal, jejune.

pique *vb* **1** goad, incite, instigate, spur, stimulate, urge. **2** affront, chafe, displease, fret, incense, irritate, nettle, offend, provoke, sting, vex, wound. • *n* annoyance, displeasure, irritation, offence, resentment, vexation.

pirate *vb* copy, crib, plagiarize, reproduce, steal. • *n* buccaneer, corsair, freebooter, marauder, picaroon, privateer, seadog, searobber, sea-rover, sea wolf.

pit *vb* **1** match, oppose. **2** dent, gouge, hole, mark, nick, notch, scar. • *n* **1** cavity, hole, hollow. **2** crater, dent, depression, dint, excavation, well. **3** abyss, chasm, gulf. **4** pitfall, snare, trap. **5** auditorium, orchestra.

pitch *vb* **1** fall, lurch, plunge, reel. **2** light, settle, rest. **3** cast, dart, fling, heave, hurl, lance, launch, send, toss, throw. **4** erect, establish, fix, locate, place, plant, set, settle, station. • *n* **1** degree, extent, height, intensity, measure, modulation, rage, rate. **2** declivity, descent, inclination, slope. **3** cast, jerk, plunge, throw, toss. **4** place, position, spot. **5** field, ground. **6** line, patter.

piteous *adj* **1** affecting, distressing, doleful, grievous, mournful, pathetic, rueful, sorrowful, woeful. **2** deplorable, lamentable, miserable, pitiable, wretched. **3** compassionate, tender.

pith *n* **1** chief, core, essence, heart, gist, kernel, marrow, part, quintessence, soul, substance. **2** importance, moment, weight. **3** cogency, force, energy, strength, vigour.

pithy *adj* **1** cogent, energetic, forcible, powerful. **2** compact, concise, brief, laconic, meaty, pointed, short, sententious, substantial, terse. **3** corky, porous.

pitiable *adj* **1** deplorable, lamentable, miserable, pathetic, piteous, pitiable, woeful, wretched. **2** abject, base, contemptible, despicable, disreputable, insignificant, low, paltry, mean, rascally, sorry, vile, worthless.

pitiably *adv* deplorably, distressingly, grievously, lamentably, miserably, pathetically, piteously, woefully, wretchedly.

pitiful *adj* **1** compassionate, kind, lenient, merciful, mild, sympathetic, tender, tenderhearted. **2** deplorable, lamentable, miserable, pathetic, piteous, pitiable, wretched. **3** abject, base, contemptible, despicable, disreputable, insignificant, mean, paltry, rascally, sorry, vile, worthless.

pitiless *adj* cruel, hardhearted, implacable, inexorable, merciless, unmerciful, relentless, remorseless, unfeeling, unpitying, unrelenting, unsympathetic.
adj antonyms compassionate, gentle, kind, merciful.

pittance *n* **1** allowance, allotment, alms, charity, dole, gift. **2** driblet, drop, insufficiency, mite, modicum, trifle.

pity *vb* commiserate, condole, sympathize. • *n* clemency, commiseration, compassion, condolence, fellow-feeling, grace, humanity, leniency, mercy, quarter, sympathy, tenderheartedness.
n antonyms cruelty, disdain, scorn.

pivot *vb* depend, hinge, turn. • *n* axis, axle, centre, focus, hinge, joint.

place *vb* **1** arrange, bestow, commit, deposit, dispose, fix, install, lay, locate, lodge, orient, orientate, pitch, plant, pose, put, seat, set, settle, situate, stand, station, rest. **2** allocate, arrange, class, classify, identify, order, organize, recognize. **3** appoint, assign, commission, establish, induct, nominate. • *n* **1** area, courtyard, square. **2** bounds, district, division, locale, locality, location, part, position, premises, quarter, region, scene, site, situation, spot, station, tract, whereabouts. **3** calling, charge, employment, function, occupation, office, pitch, post. **4** calling, condition, grade, precedence, rank, sphere, stakes, standing. **5** abode, building, dwelling, habitation, mansion, residence, seat. **6** city, town, village. **7** fort, fortress, stronghold. **8** paragraph, part, passage, portion. **9** ground, occasion, opportunity, reason, room. **10** lieu, stead.

placid *adj* **1** calm, collected, composed, cool, equable, gentle, peaceful, quiet, serene, tranquil, undisturbed, unexcitable, unmoved, unruffled. **2** halcyon, mild, serene.
adj antonyms agitated, jumpy.

plague *vb* afflict, annoy, badger, bore, bother, pester, chafe, disquiet, distress, disturb, embarrass, harass, fret, gall, harry, hector, incommode, irritate, molest, perplex, tantalize, tease, torment, trouble, vex, worry. • *n* **1** disease, pestilence, pest. **2** affliction, annoyance, curse, molestation, nuisance, thorn, torment, trouble, vexation, worry.

plain *adj* **1** dull, even, flat, level, plane, smooth, uniform. **2** clear, open, unencumbered, uninterrupted. **3** apparent, certain, conspicuous, evident, distinct, glaring, manifest, notable, notorious, obvious, overt, palpable, patent, prominent, pronounced, staring, transparent, unmistakable, visible. **4** explicit, intelligible, perspicuous, unambiguous, unequivocal. **5** homely, ugly. **6** aboveboard, blunt, crude, candid, direct, downright, frank, honest, ingenuous, open, openhearted, sincere, single-minded, straightforward, undesigning, unreserved, unsophisticated. **7** artless, common, natural, simple, unaffected, unlearned. **8** absolute, mere, unmistakable. **9** clear, direct, easy. **10** audible, articulate, definite. **11** frugal, homely. **12** unadorned, unfigured, unornamented, unvariegated. • *n* expanse, flats, grassland, pampas, plateau, prairie, steppe, stretch.

adj antonyms abstruse, attractive, elaborate, exaggerated, ostentatious, rich, striking, unclear.

plaint *n* complaint, cry, lament, lamentation, moan, wail.

plaintiff *n* accuser, prosecutor.

plaintive *adj* dirge-like, doleful, grievous, melancholy, mournful, piteous, rueful, sad, sorrowful, woeful.

plan *vb* **1** arrange, calculate, concert, delineate, devise, diagram, figure, premeditate, project, represent, study. **2** concoct, conspire, contrive, design, digest, hatch, invent, manoeuvre, machinate, plot, prepare, scheme. • *n* **1** chart, delineation, diagram, draught, drawing, layout, map, plot, sketch. **2** arrangement, conception, contrivance, design, device, idea, method, programme, project, proposal, proposition, scheme, system. **3** cabal, conspiracy, intrigue, machination. **4** custom, process, way.

plane *vb* **1** even, flatten, level, smooth. **2** float, fly, glide, skate, skim, soar. • *adj* even, flat, horizontal, level, smooth. • *n* **1** degree, evenness, level, levelness, smoothness. **2** aeroplane, aircraft. **3** groover, jointer, rabbet, rebate, router, scraper.

plant *vb* **1** bed, sow. **2** breed, engender. **3** direct, point, set. **4** colonize, furnish, inhabit, settle. **5** establish, introduce. **6** deposit, establish, fix, found, hide. • *n* **1** herb, organism, vegetable. **2** establishment, equipment, factory, works.

plaster *vb* bedaub, coat, cover, smear, spread. • *n* cement, gypsum, mortar, stucco.

plastic *adj* ductile, flexible, formative, mouldable, pliable, pliant, soft.

adj antonyms inflexible, rigid.

platitude *n* **1** dullness, flatness, insipidity, mawkishness. **2** banality, commonplace, truism. **3** balderdash, chatter, flummery, fudge, jargon, moonshine, nonsense, palaver, stuff, trash, twaddle, verbiage.

plaudit *n* acclaim, acclamation, applause, approbation, clapping, commendation, encomium, praise.

plausible *adj* **1** believable, credible, probable, reasonable. **2** bland, fair-spoken, glib, smooth, suave.

adj antonyms implausible, improbable, unlikely.

play *vb* **1** caper, disport, frisk, frolic, gambol, revel, romp, skip, sport. **2** dally, flirt, idle, toy, trifle, wanton. **3** flutter, hover, wave. **4** act, impersonate, perform, personate, represent. **5** bet, gamble, stake, wager. • *n* **1** amusement, exercise, frolic, gambols, game, jest, pastime, prank, romp, sport. **2** gambling, gaming. **3** act, comedy, drama, farce, performance, tragedy. **4** action, motion, movement. **5** elbowroom, freedom, latitude, movement, opportunity, range, scope, sweep, swing, use.

vb antonym work.

n antonym work.

playful *adj* **1** frisky, frolicsome, gamesome, jolly, kittenish, merry, mirthful, rollicking, sportive. **2** amusing, arch, humorous, lively, mischievous, roguish, skittish, sprightly, vivacious.

adj antonyms serious, stern.

plead *vb* **1** answer, appeal, argue, reason. **2** argue, defend, discuss, reason, rejoin. **3** beg, beseech, entreat, implore, petition, sue, supplicate.

pleasant *adj* **1** acceptable, agreeable, delectable, delightful, enjoyable, grateful, gratifying, nice, pleasing, pleasurable, prepossessing, seemly, welcome. **2** cheerful, enlivening, good-humoured, gracious,

likable, lively, merry, sportive, sprightly, vivacious. **3** amusing, facetious, humorous, jocose, jocular, sportive, witty.
adj antonyms distasteful, nasty, repugnant, unpleasant.

please *vb* **1** charm, delight, elate, gladden, gratify, pleasure, rejoice. **2** content, oblige, satisfy. **3** choose, like, prefer.
vb antonyms anger, annoy, displease.

pleasure *n* **1** cheer, comfort, delight, delectation, elation, enjoyment, exhilaration, joy, gladness, gratifying, gusto, relish, satisfaction, solace. **2** amusement, diversion, entertainment, indulgence, refreshment, treat. **3** gratification, luxury, sensuality, voluptuousness. **4** choice, desire, preference, purpose, will, wish. **5** favour, kindness.
n antonyms displeasure, pain, sorrow, trouble.

plebeian *adj* base, common, ignoble, low, lowborn, mean, obscure, popular, vulgar. • *n* commoner, peasant, proletarian.

pledge *vb* **1** hypothecate, mortgage, pawn, plight. **2** affiance, bind, contract, engage, plight, promise. • *n* **1** collateral, deposit, gage, pawn. **2** earnest, guarantee, security. **3** hostage, security.

plenipotentiary *n* ambassador, envoy, legate, minister.

plenitude *n* abundance, completeness, fullness, plenteousness, plentifulness, plenty, plethora, profusion, repletion.

plentiful *adj* abundant, ample, copious, full, enough, exuberant, fruitful, luxuriant, plenteous, productive, sufficient.
adj antonyms rare, scanty, scarce.

plenty *n* abundance, adequacy, affluence, amplitude, copiousness, enough, exuberance, fertility, fruitfulness, fullness, overflow, plenteousness, plentifulness, plethora, profusion, sufficiency, supply.
n antonyms lack, need, scarcity, want.

pleonastic *adj* circumlocutory, diffuse, redundant, superfluous, tautological, verbose, wordy.

plethora *n* **1** fullness, plenitude, repletion. **2** excess, redundance, redundancy, superabundance, superfluity, surfeit.

pliable *adj* **1** flexible, limber, lithe, lithesome, pliable, pliant, supple. **2** adaptable, compliant, docile, ductile, facile, manageable, obsequious, tractable, yielding.
adj antonyms inflexible, rigid.

plight[1] *n* case, category, complication,

condition, dilemma, imbroglio, mess, muddle, pass, predicament, scrape, situation, state, strait.

plight[2] *vb* avow, contract, covenant, engage, honour, pledge, promise, propose, swear, vow. • *n* **1** avowal, contract, covenant, oath, pledge, promise, troth, vow, word. **2** affiancing, betrothal, engagement.

plod *vb* drudge, lumber, moil, persevere, persist, toil, trudge.

plot[1] *vb* **1** connive, conspire, intrigue, machinate, scheme. **2** brew, concoct, contrive, devise, frame, hatch, compass, plan, project. **3** chart, map. • *n* **1** blueprint, chart, diagram, draft, outline, plan, scenario, skeleton. **2** cabal, combination, complicity, connivance, conspiracy, intrigue, plan, project, scheme, stratagem. **3** script, story, subject, theme, thread, topic.

plot[2] *n* field, lot, parcel, patch, piece, plat, section, tract.

pluck[1] *vb* **1** cull, gather, pick. **2** jerk, pull, snatch, tear, tug, twitch.

pluck[2] *n* backbone, bravery, courage, daring, determination, energy, force, grit, hardihood, heroism, indomitability, indomitableness, manhood, mettle, nerve, resolution, spirit, valour.

plump[1] *adj* **1** bonny, bouncing, buxom, chubby, corpulent, fat, fleshy, full-figured, obese, portly, rotund, round, sleek, stout, well-rounded. **2** distended, full, swollen, tumid.
adj antonyms skinny, thin.

plump[2] *vb* **1** dive, drop, plank, plop, plunge, plunk, put. **2** choose, favour, support • *adj* blunt, complete, direct, downright, full, unqualified, unreserved.

plunder *vb* desolate, despoil, devastate, fleece, forage, harry, loot, maraud, pillage, raid, ransack, ravage, rifle, rob, sack, spoil, spoliate, plunge. • *n* **1** freebooting, devastation, harrying, marauding, rapine, robbery, sack. **2** booty, pillage, prey, spoil.

ply[1] *vb* **1** apply, employ, exert, manipulate, wield. **2** exercise, practise. **3** assail, belabour, beset, press. **4** importune, solicit, urge. **5** offer, present.

ply[2] *n* **1** fold, layer, plait, twist. **2** bent, bias, direction, turn.

pocket *vb* **1** appropriate, steal. **2** bear, endure, suffer, tolerate. • *n* cavity, cul-de-sac, hollow, pouch, receptacle.

poignant *adj* **1** bitter, intense, penetrating, pierce, severe, sharp. **2** acrid, biting, mordacious, piquant, prickling, pungent, sharp, stinging. **3** caustic, irritating, keen, mordant, pointed, satirical, severe.

point *vb* **1** acuminate, sharpen. **2** aim, direct, level. **3** designate indicate, show. **4** punctuate. • *n* **1** apex, needle, nib, pin, prong, spike, stylus, tip. **2** cape, headland, projection, promontory. **3** eve, instant, moment, period, verge. **4** place, site, spot, stage, station. **5** condition, degree, grade, state. **6** aim, design, end, intent, limit, object, purpose. **7** nicety, pique, punctilio, trifle. **8** position, proposition, question, text, theme, thesis. **9** aspect, matter, respect. **10** characteristic, peculiarity, trait. **11** character, mark, stop. **12** dot, jot, speck. **13** epigram, quip, quirk, sally, witticism. **14** poignancy, sting.

point-blank *adj* categorical, direct, downright, explicit, express, plain, straight. • *adv* categorically, directly, flush, full, plainly, right, straight.

pointless *adj* **1** blunt, obtuse. **2** aimless, dull, flat, fruitless, futile, meaningless, vague, vapid, stupid.

adj antonyms meaningful, profitable.

poise *vb* balance, float, hang, hover, support, suspend. • *n* aplomb, balance, composure, dignity, equanimity, equilibrium, equipoise, serenity.

poison *vb* adulterate, contaminate, corrupt, defile, embitter, envenom, impair, infect, intoxicate, pollute, taint, vitiate. • *adj* deadly, lethal, poisonous, toxic. • *n* bane, canker, contagion, pest, taint, toxin, venom, virulence, virus.

poisonous *adj* baneful, corruptive, deadly, fatal, noxious, pestiferous, pestilential, toxic, venomous.

poke *vb* **1** jab, jog, punch, push, shove, thrust. **2** interfere, meddle, pry, snoop. • *n* **1** jab, jog, punch, push, shove, thrust. **2** bag, pocket, pouch, sack.

pole[1] *n* **1** caber, mast, post, rod, spar, staff, stick. **2** bar, beam, pile, shaft. **3** oar, paddle, scull.

pole[2] *n* axis, axle, hub, pivot, spindle.

poles *npl* antipodes, antipoles, counterpoles, opposites.

policy *n* **1** administration, government, management, rule. **2** plan, plank, platform, role. **3** art, address, cunning, discretion, prudence, shrewdness, skill, stratagem,

strategy, tactics. **4** acumen, astuteness, wisdom, wit.

polish *vb* **1** brighten, buff, burnish, furbish, glaze, gloss, scour, shine, smooth. **2** civilize, refine. • *n* **1** brightness, brilliance, brilliancy, lustre, splendour. **2** accomplishment, elegance, finish, grace, refinement.

vb antonyms dull, tarnish.

n antonyms clumsiness, dullness, gaucherie.

polished *adj* **1** bright, burnished, glossed, glossy, lustrous, shining, smooth. **2** accomplished, cultivated, elegant, finished, graceful, polite, refined.

adj antonyms clumsy, dull, gauche, inexpert, tarnished.

polite *adj* attentive, accomplished, affable, chivalrous, civil, complaisant, courtly, courteous, cultivated, elegant, gallant, genteel, gentle, gentlemanly, gracious, mannerly, obliging, polished, refined, suave, urbane, well, well-bred, well-mannered.

adj antonyms impolite, uncultivated.

politic *adj* **1** civic, civil, political. **2** astute, discreet, judicious, long-headed, noncommittal, provident, prudent, prudential, sagacious, wary, wise. **3** artful, crafty, cunning, diplomatic, expedient, foxy, ingenious, intriguing, Machiavellian, shrewd, skilful, sly, subtle, strategic, timeserving, unscrupulous, wily. **4** well-adapted, well-devised.

adj antonym impolitic.

political *adj* civic, civil, national, politic, public.

pollute *vb* **1** defile, foul, soil, taint. **2** contaminate, corrupt, debase, demoralize, deprave, impair, infect, pervert, poison, stain, tarnish, vitiate. **3** desecrate, profane. **4** abuse, debauch, defile, deflower, dishonour, ravish, violate.

pollution *n* abomination, contamination, corruption, defilement, foulness, impurity, pollutedness, taint, uncleanness, vitiation.

poltroon *n* coward, crave, dastard, milksop, recreant, skulk, sneak.

pomp *n* display, flourish, grandeur, magnificence, ostentation, pageant, pageantry, parade, pompousness, pride, show, splendour, state, style.

n antonyms austerity, simplicity.

pompous *adj* august, boastful, bombastic, dignified, gorgeous, grand, inflated, lofty, magisterial, ostentatious, pretentious, showy, splendid, stately, sumptuous, superb, vainglorious.

adj antonyms economical, modest, simple, unaffected, unassuming.

ponder *vb* cogitate, consider, contemplate, deliberate, examine, meditate, muse, reflect, study, weigh.

ponderous *adj* **1** bulky, heavy, massive, weighty. **2** dull, laboured, slow-moving. **3** important, momentous. **4** forcible, mighty.
adj antonyms delicate, light, simple.

poniard *n* dagger, dirk, stiletto.

poor *adj* **1** indigent, necessitous, needy, pinched, straitened. **2** destitute, distressed, embarrassed, impecunious, impoverished, insolvent, moneyless, penniless, poverty-stricken, reduced, seedy, unprosperous. **3** emaciated, gaunt, spare, lank, lean, shrunk, skinny, spare, thin. **4** barren, fruitless, sterile, unfertile, unfruitful, unproductive, unprolific. **5** flimsy, inadequate, insignificant, insufficient, paltry, slender, slight, small, trifling, trivial, unimportant, valueless, worthless. **6** decrepit, delicate, feeble, frail, infirm, unsound, weak. **7** inferior, shabby, valueless, worthless. **8** bad, beggarly, contemptible, despicable, humble, inferior, low, mean, pitiful, sorry. **9** bald, cold, dry, dull, feeble, frigid, jejune, languid, meagre, prosaic, prosing, spiritless, tame, vapid, weak. **10** ill-fated, ill-starred, inauspicious, indifferent, luckless, miserable, pitiable, unfavourable, unfortunate, unhappy, unlucky, wretched. **11** deficient, imperfect, inadequate, insufficient, mediocre, scant, scanty. **12** faulty, unsatisfactory. **13** feeble.
adj antonyms affluent, opulent, rich, wealthy; superior; lucky.

populace *n* citizens, crowd, inhabitants, masses, people, public, throng.

popular *adj* **1** lay, plebeian, public. **2** comprehensible, easy, familiar, plain. **3** acceptable, accepted, accredited, admired, approved, favoured, liked, pleasing, praised, received. **4** common, current, prevailing, prevalent. **5** cheap, inexpensive.
adj antonyms exclusive, unpopular, unusual.

pore[1] *n* hole, opening, orifice, spiracle.

pore[2] *vb* brood, consider, dwell, examine, gaze, read, study.

porous *adj* honeycombed, light, loose, open, penetrable, perforated, permeable, pervious, sandy.

porridge *n* broth, gruel, mush, pap, pottage, soup.

port[1] *n* **1** anchorage, harbour, haven, shelter. **2** door, entrance, gate, passageway. **3** embrasure, porthole.

port[2] *n* air, appearance, bearing, behaviour, carriage, demeanour, deportment, mien, presence.

portable *adj* convenient, handy, light, manageable, movable, portative, transmissible.
adj antonyms fixed, immovable.

portend *vb* augur, betoken, bode, forebode, foreshadow, foretoken, indicate, presage, procrastinate, signify, threaten.

portent *n* **1** augury, omen, presage, prognosis, sign, warning. **2** marvel, phenomenon, wonder.

portion *vb* **1** allot, distribute, divide, parcel. **2** endow, supply. • *n* **1** bit, fragment, morsel, part, piece, scrap, section. **2** allotment, contingent, dividend, division, lot, measure, quantity, quota, ration, share. **3** inheritance.

portly *adj* **1** dignified, grand, imposing, magisterial, majestic, stately. **2** bulky, burly, corpulent, fleshy, large, plump, round, stout.
adj antonyms slight, slim.

portray *vb* act, draw, depict, delineate, describe, paint, picture, represent, pose, position, sketch.

pose *vb* **1** arrange, place, set. **2** bewilder, confound, dumbfound, embarrass, mystify, nonplus, perplex, place, puzzle, set, stagger. **3** affect, attitudinize. • *n* **1** attitude, posture. **2** affectation, air, facade, mannerism, pretence, role.

position *vb* arrange, array, fix, locate, place, put, set, site, stand. • *n* **1** locality, place, post, site, situation, spot, station. **2** relation. **3** attitude, bearing, posture. **4** affirmation, assertion, doctrine, predication, principle, proposition, thesis. **5** caste, dignity, honour, rank, standing, status. **6** circumstance, condition, phase, place, state. **7** berth, billet, incumbency, place, post, situation.

positive *adj* **1** categorical, clear, defined, definite, direct, determinate, explicit, express, expressed, precise, unequivocal, unmistakable, unqualified. **2** absolute, actual, real, substantial, true, veritable. **3** assured, certain, confident, convinced, sure. **4** decisive, incontrovertible, indisputable, indubitable, inescapable. **5** imperative, unconditional, undeniable. **6** decided, dogmatic, emphatic, obstinate, overbearing, overconfident, peremptory, stubborn, tenacious.

adj antonyms indecisive, indefinite, negative, uncertain.

possess *vb* control, have, hold, keep, obsess, obtain, occupy, own, seize.

possession *n* **1** monopoly, ownership, proprietorship. **2** control, occupation, occupancy, retention, tenancy, tenure. **3** bedevilment, lunacy, madness, obsession. **4** (*pl*) assets, effects, estate, property, wealth.

possessor *n* owner, proprietor.

possible *adj* **1** conceivable, contingent, imaginable, potential. **2** accessible, feasible, likely, practical, practicable, workable.

adj antonym impossible.

possibly *adv* haply, maybe, mayhap, peradventure, perchance, perhaps.

post[1] *vb* **1** advertise, announce, inform, placard, publish. **2** brand, defame, disgrace, vilify. **3** enter, slate, record, register. • *n* column, picket, pier, pillar, stake, support.

post[2] *vb* establish, fix, place, put, set, station. • *n* billet, employment, office, place, position, quarter, seat, situation, station.

post[3] *vb* drop, dispatch, mail. • *n* **1** carrier, courier, express, mercury, messenger, postman. **2** dispatch, haste, hurry, speed.

posterior *adj* after, ensuing, following, later, latter, postprandial, subsequent. • *n* back, buttocks, hind, hinder, rump.

posterity *n* **1** descendants, offspring, progeny, seed. **2** breed, brood, children, family, heirs, issue.

postpone *vb* adjourn, defer, delay, procrastinate, prorogue, retard.

vb antonyms advance, forward.

postscript *n* addition, afterthought, appendix, supplement.

postulate *vb* **1** assume, presuppose. **2** beseech, entreat, solicit, supplicate. • *n* assumption, axiom, conjecture, hypothesis, proposition, speculation, supposition, theory.

posture *vb* attitudinize, pose. • *n* **1** attitude, pose, position. **2** condition, disposition, mood, phase, state.

pot *n* **1** kettle, pan, saucepan, skillet. **2** can, cup, mug, tankard. **3** crock, jar, jug.

potency *n* **1** efficacy, energy, force, intensity, might, power, strength, vigour. **2** authority, control, influence, sway.

n antonyms impotence, weakness.

potent *adj* **1** efficacious, forceful, forcible, intense, powerful, strong, virile. **2** able, authoritative, capable, efficient, mighty, puissant, strong. **3** cogent, influential.

potentate *n* emperor, king, monarch, prince, sovereign, ruler.

potential *adj* able, capable, inherent, latent, possible. • *n* ability, capability, dynamic, possibility, potentiality, power.

pother *vb* beset, bewilder, confound, confuse, embarrass, harass, perplex, pose, puzzle, tease. • *n* bustle, commotion, confusion, disturbance, flutter, fuss, huddle, hurly-burly, rumpus, tumult, turbulence, turmoil.

pound[1] *vb* **1** beat, strike, thump. **2** bray, bruise, comminute, crush, levigate, pulverize, triturate. **3** confound, coop, enclose, impound.

pound[2] *n* enclosure, fold, pen.

pour *vb* cascade, emerge, flood, flow, gush, issue, rain, shower, stream.

pouting *adj* bad-tempered, cross, ill-humoured, moody, morose, sulky, sullen.

poverty *n* **1** destitution, difficulties, distress, impecuniosity, impecuniousness, indigence, necessity, need, neediness, penury, privation, straits, want. **2** beggary, mendicancy, pauperism, pennilessness. **3** dearth, jejuneness, lack, scantiness, sparingness, meagreness. **4** exiguity, paucity, poorness, smallness. **5** humbleness, inferiority, lowliness. **6** barrenness, sterility, unfruitfulness, unproductiveness.

n antonyms affluence, fertility, fruitfulness, riches, richness.

power *n* **1** ability, ableness, capability, cogency, competency, efficacy, faculty, might, potency, validity, talent. **2** energy, force, strength, virtue. **3** capacity, susceptibility. **4** endowment, faculty, gift, talent. **5** ascendancy, authoritativeness, authority, carte blanche, command, control, domination, dominion, government, influence, omnipotence, predominance, prerogative, pressure, proxy, puissance, rule, sovereignty, sway, warrant. **6** governor, monarch, potentate, ruler, sovereign. **7** army, host, troop.

n antonyms impotence, ineffectiveness, weakness.

powerful *adj* **1** mighty, potent, puissant. **2** able-bodied, herculean, muscular, nervous, robust, sinewy, strong, sturdy, vigorous, vivid. **3** able, commanding, dominating, forceful, forcible, overpowering. **4** cogent, effective, effectual, efficacious, efficient, energetic, influential, operative, valid.

adj antonyms impotent, ineffective, weak.

practicable *adj* **1** achievable, attainable, bearable, feasible, performable, possible, workable. **2** operative, passable, penetrable.

practical *adj* **1** hardheaded, matter-of-fact, pragmatic, pragmatical. **2** able, experienced, practised, proficient, qualified, trained, skilled, thoroughbred, versed. **3** effective, useful, virtual, workable.

adj antonym impractical.

practice *n* **1** custom, habit, manner, method, repetition. **2** procedure, usage, use. **3** application, drill, exercise, pursuit. **4** action, acts, behaviour, conduct, dealing, proceeding.

practise *vb* apply, do, exercise, follow, observe, perform, perpetrate, pursue.

practised *adj* able, accomplished, experienced, instructed, practical, proficient, qualified, skilled, thoroughbred, trained, versed.

pragmatic *adj* **1** impertinent, intermeddling, interfering, intrusive, meddlesome, meddling, obtrusive, officious, over-busy. **2** earthy, hard-headed, matter-of-fact, practical, pragmatical, realistic, sensible, stolid.

adj antonyms idealistic, romantic, unrealistic.

praise *vb* **1** approbate, acclaim, applaud, approve, commend. **2** celebrate, compliment, eulogize, extol, flatter, laud. **3** adore, bless, exalt, glorify, magnify, worship. • *n* **1** acclaim, approbation, approval, commendation. **2** encomium, eulogy, glorification, laud, laudation, panegyric. **3** exaltation, extolling, glorification, homage, tribute, worship. **4** celebrity, distinction, fame, glory, honour, renown. **5** desert, merit, praiseworthiness.

vb antonyms criticize, revile.

n antonyms criticism, revilement.

praiseworthy *adj* commendable, creditable, good, laudable, meritorious.

adj antonyms discreditable, dishonorable, ignoble.

prank *n* antic, caper, escapade, frolic, gambol, trick.

prate *vb* babble, chatter, gabble, jabber,

palaver, prattle, tattle. • *n* chatter, gabble, nonsense, palaver, prattle, twaddle.

pray *vb* ask, beg, beseech, conjure, entreat, implore, importune, invoke, petition, request, solicit, supplicate.

prayer *n* **1** beseeching, entreaty, imploration, petition, request, solicitation, suit, supplication. **2** adoration, devotion(s), litany, invocation, orison, praise, suffrage.

preach *vb* **1** declare, deliver, proclaim, pronounce, publish. **2** inculcate, press, teach, urge. **3** exhort, lecture, moralize, sermonize.

preamble *n* foreword, introduction, preface, prelude, prologue.

n antonyms epilogue, postscript.

precarious *adj* critical, doubtful, dubious, equivocal, hazardous, insecure, perilous, unassured, riskful, risky, uncertain, unsettled, unstable, unsteady.

adj antonyms certain, safe, secure.

precaution *n* **1** care, caution, circumspection, foresight, forethought, providence, prudence, safeguard, wariness. **2** anticipation, premonition, provision.

precautionary *adj* preservative, preventative, provident.

precede *vb* antedate, forerun, head, herald, introduce, lead, utter.

precedence *n* advantage, antecedence, lead, pre-eminence, preference, priority, superiority, supremacy.

precedent *n* antecedent, authority, custom, example, instance, model, pattern, procedure, standard, usage.

precept *n* **1** behest, bidding, canon, charge, command, commandment, decree, dictate, edict, injunction, instruction, law, mandate, ordinance, ordination, order, regulation. **2** direction, doctrine, maxim, principle, teaching, rubric, rule.

preceptor *n* instructor, lecturer, master, pedagogue, professor, schoolteacher, teacher, tutor.

precinct *n* **1** border, bound, boundary, confine, environs, frontier, enclosure, limit, list, march, neighbourhood, purlieus, term, terminus. **2** area, district.

precious *adj* **1** costly, inestimable, invaluable, priceless, prized, valuable. **2** adored, beloved, cherished, darling, dear, idolized, treasured. **3** fastidious, overnice, over-refined, precise.

precipice *n* bluff, cliff, crag, steep.

precipitate *vb* advance, accelerate, dispatch,

expedite, forward, further, hasten, hurry, plunge, press, quicken, speed. • *adj* **1** hasty, hurried, headlong, impetuous, indiscreet, overhasty, rash, reckless. **2** abrupt, sudden, violent.

vb antonym halt, stop.

adj antonym cautious.

precipitous *adj* abrupt, cliffy, craggy, perpendicular, uphill, sheer, steep.

precise *adj* **1** accurate, correct, definite, distinct, exact, explicit, express, nice, pointed, severe, strict, unequivocal, well-defined. **2** careful, scrupulous. **3** ceremonious, finical, formal, prim, punctilious, rigid, starched, stiff.

adj antonym imprecise.

precision *n* accuracy, correctness, definiteness, distinctness, exactitude, exactness, nicety, preciseness.

n antonym imprecision.

preclude *vb* bar, check, debar, hinder, inhibit, obviate, prevent, prohibit, restrain, stop.

vb antonyms incur, involve.

precocious *adj* advanced, forward, premature.

adj antonym backward.

preconcert *vb* concoct, prearrange, predetermine, premeditate, prepare.

precursor *n* **1** antecedent, cause, forerunner, predecessor. **2** harbinger, herald, messenger, pioneer. **3** omen, presage, sign.

precursory *adj* **1** antecedent, anterior, forerunning, precedent, preceding, previous, prior. **2** initiatory, introductory, precursive, prefatory, preliminary, prelusive, prelusory, premonitory, preparatory, prognosticative.

predatory *adj* greedy, pillaging, plundering, predacious, rapacious, ravaging, ravenous, voracious.

predestination *n* doom, fate, foredoom, foreordination, necessity, predetermination, preordination.

predicament *n* **1** attitude, case, condition, plight, position, posture, situation, state. **2** corner, dilemma, emergency, exigency, fix, hole, impasse, mess, pass, pinch, push, quandary, scrape.

predict *vb* augur, betoken, bode, divine, forebode, forecast, foredoom, foresee, forespeak, foretell, foretoken, forewarn, portend, prognosticate, prophesy, read, signify, soothsay.

predilection *n* bent, bias, desire, fondness,

inclination, leaning, liking, love, partiality, predisposition, preference, prejudice, prepossession.

n antonyms antipathy, disinclination.

predisposition *n* aptitude, bent, bias, disposition, inclination, leaning, proclivity, proneness, propensity, willingness.

predominant *adj* ascendant, controlling, dominant, overruling, prevailing, prevalent, reigning, ruling, sovereign, supreme.

adj antonyms ineffective, lesser, minor, weak.

predominate *vb* dominate, preponderate, prevail, rule.

pre-eminent *adj* chief, conspicuous, consummate, controlling, distinguished, excellent, excelling, paramount, peerless, predominant, renowned, superior, supreme, surpassing, transcendent, unequalled.

adj antonyms undistinguished, unknown.

preface *vb* begin, introduce, induct, launch, open, precede. • *n* exordium, foreword, induction, introduction, preamble, preliminary, prelude, prelusion, premise, proem, prologue, prolusion.

vb antonyms append, complete, finish.

n antonyms afterthought, epilogue, postscript.

prefatory *adj* antecedent, initiative, introductory, precursive, precursory, preliminary, prelusive, prelusory, preparatory, proemial.

prefer *vb* **1** adopt, choose, elect, fancy, pick, select, wish. **2** advance, elevate, promote, raise. **3** address, offer, present, proffer, tender.

vb antonym reject; demote.

preference *n* advancement, choice, election, estimation, precedence, priority, selection.

preferment *n* advancement, benefice, dignity, elevation, exaltation, promotion.

pregnant *adj* **1** fecund, fertile, fruitful, generative, potential, procreant, procreative, productive, prolific. **2** big, fraught, full, important, replete, significant, weighty.

adj antonym infertile.

prejudice *vb* **1** bias, incline, influence, turn, warp. **2** damage, diminish, hurt, impair, injure. • *n* **1** bias, intolerance, partiality, preconception, predilection, prejudgement, prepossession, unfairness. **2** damage, detriment, disadvantage, harm, hurt, impairment, injury, loss, mischief.

n antonyms fairness, tolerance; advantage, benefit; advance, benefit, help.

prejudiced *adj* biased, bigoted, influenced, one-sided, partial, partisan, unfair.

adj antonyms fair, tolerant.

preliminary *adj* antecedent, initiatory, introductory, precedent, precursive, precursory, prefatory, prelusive, prelusory, preparatory, previous, prior, proemial. • *n* beginning, initiation, introduction, opening, preamble, preface, prelude, start.

adj antonyms closing, final.

prelude *n* 1 introduction, opening, overture, prelusion, preparation, voluntary. 2 exordium, preamble, preface, preliminary, proem.

premature *adj* hasty, ill-considered, precipitate, unmatured, unprepared, unripe, unseasonable, untimely.

adj antonyms late, tardy.

premeditation *n* deliberation, design, forethought, intention, prearrangement, predetermination, purpose.

n antonyms impulse, spontaneity.

premise *vb* introduce, preamble, preface, prefix. • *n* affirmation, antecedent, argument, assertion, assumption, basis, foundation, ground, hypothesis, position, premiss, presupposition, proposition, support, thesis, theorem.

premium *n* 1 bonus, bounty, encouragement, fee, gift, guerdon, meed, payment, prize, recompense, remuneration, reward. 2 appreciation, enhancement.

premonition *n* caution, foreboding, foreshadowing, forewarning, indication, omen, portent, presage, presentiment, sign, warning.

preoccupied *adj* absent, absentminded, abstracted, dreaming, engrossed, inadvertent, inattentive, lost, musing, unobservant.

prepare *vb* 1 adapt, adjust, fit, qualify. 2 arrange, concoct, fabricate, make, order, plan, procure, provide.

preponderant *adj* outweighing, overbalancing, preponderating.

prepossessing *adj* alluring, amiable, attractive, bewitching, captivating, charming, engaging, fascinating, inviting, taking, winning.

adj antonyms unattractive, unprepossessing.

preposterous *adj* absurd, excessive, exorbitant, extravagant, foolish, improper, irrational, monstrous, nonsensical, perverted, ridiculous, unfit, unreasonable, wrong.

adj antonym reasonable.

prerogative *n* advantage, birthright, claim, franchise, immunity, liberty, privilege, right.

presage *vb* 1 divine, forebode. 2 augur, betoken, bode, foreshadow, foretell, foretoken, indicate, portend, predict, prognosticate, prophesy, signify, soothsay. • *n* 1 augury, auspice, boding, foreboding, foreshowing, indication, omen, portent, prognostication, sign, token. 2 foreknowledge, precognition, prediction, premonition, presentiment, prophecy.

prescribe *vb* advocate, appoint, command, decree, dictate, direct, enjoin, establish, institute, ordain, order.

presence *n* 1 attendance, company, inhabitance, inhabitancy, nearness, neighbourhood, occupancy, propinquity, proximity, residence, ubiquity, vicinity. 2 air, appearance, carriage, demeanour, mien, personality.

n antonym absence.

present¹ *adj* 1 near. 2 actual, current, existing, happening, immediate, instant, living. 3 available, quick, ready. 4 attentive, favourable. • *n* now, time being, today.

adj antonyms absent, out-of-date, past.

vb antonym take.

present² *n* benefaction, boon, donation, favour, gift, grant, gratuity, largesse, offering.

present³ *vb* 1 introduce, nominate. 2 exhibit, offer. 3 bestow, confer, give, grant. 4 deliver, hand. 5 advance, express, prefer, proffer, tender.

presentiment *n* anticipation, apprehension, foreboding, forecast, foretaste, forethought, prescience.

presently *adv* anon, directly, forthwith, immediately, shortly, soon.

preservation *n* 1 cherishing, conservation, curing, maintenance, protection, support. 2 safety, salvation, security. 3 integrity, keeping, soundness.

preserve *vb* 1 defend, guard, keep, protect, rescue, save, secure, shield. 2 maintain, uphold, sustain, support. 3 conserve, economize, husband, retain. • *n* 1 comfit, compote, confection, confiture, conserve, jam, jelly, marmalade, sweetmeat. 2 enclosure, warren.

vb antonyms destroy, ruin.

preside *vb* control, direct, govern, manage, officiate.

press *vb* **1** compress, crowd, crush, squeeze. **2** flatten, iron, smooth. **3** clasp, embrace, hug. **4** force, compel, constrain. **5** emphasize, enforce, enjoin, inculcate, stress, urge. **6** hasten, hurry, push, rush. **7** crowd, throng. **8** entreat, importune, solicit. • *n* **1** crowd, crush, multitude, throng. **2** hurry, pressure, urgency. **3** case, closet, cupboard, repository.
vb antonyms expand, hang back, lighten, relieve.

pressing *adj* constraining, critical, distressing, imperative, importunate, persistent, serious, urgent, vital.
adj antonyms trivial, unimportant.

pressure *n* **1** compressing, crushing, squeezing. **2** influence, force. **3** compulsion, exigency, hurry, persuasion, press, stress, urgency. **4** affliction, calamity, difficulty, distress, embarrassment, grievance, oppression, straits. **5** impression, stamp.

prestidigitation *n* conjuring, juggling, legerdemain, sleight-of-hand.

prestige *n* credit, distinction, importance, influence, reputation, weight.
n antonyms humbleness, unimportance.

presume *vb* **1** anticipate, apprehend, assume, believe, conjecture, deduce, expect, infer, surmise, suppose, think. **2** consider, presuppose. **3** dare, undertake, venture.

presumption *n* **1** anticipation, assumption, belief, concession, conclusion, condition, conjecture, deduction, guess, hypothesis, inference, opinion, supposition, understanding. **2** arrogance, assurance, audacity, boldness, brass, effrontery, forwardness, haughtiness, presumptuousness. **3** probability.
n antonyms humility, politeness.

presumptuous *adj* **1** arrogant, assuming, audacious, bold, brash, forward, irreverent, insolent, intrusive, presuming. **2** foolhardy, overconfident, rash.
adj antonym modest.

pretence *n* **1** affectation, cloak, colour, disguise, mask, semblance, show, simulation, veil, window-dressing. **2** excuse, evasion, fabrication, feigning, makeshift, pretext, sham, subterfuge. **3** claim, pretension.

pretend *vb* **1** affect, counterfeit, deem, dissemble, fake, falsify, feign, sham, simulate. **2** act, imagine, lie, profess. **3** aspire, claim.

pretension *n* **1** assertion, assumption, claim, demand, pretence. **2** affectation, airs,

conceit, ostentation, pertness, pretentiousness, priggishness, vanity.

pretentious *adj* affected, assuming, conceited, conspicuous, ostentatious, presuming, priggish, showy, tawdry, unnatural, vain.
adj antonyms humble, modest, simple, straightforward.

preternatural *adj* abnormal, anomalous, extraordinary, inexplicable, irregular, miraculous, mysterious, odd, peculiar, strange, unnatural.

pretext *n* **1** affectation, appearance, blind, cloak, colour, guise, mask, pretence, semblance, show, simulation, veil. **2** excuse, justification, plea, vindication.

pretty *adj* **1** attractive, beautiful, bonny, comely, elegant, fair, handsome, neat, pleasing, trim. **2** affected, foppish. • *adv* fairly, moderately, quite, rather, somewhat.
adj antonyms tasteless, ugly.

prevail *vb* **1** overcome, succeed, triumph, win. **2** obtain, predominate, preponderate, reign, rule.
vb antonym lose.

prevailing *adj* controlling, dominant, effectual, efficacious, general, influential, operative, overruling, persuading, predominant, preponderant, prevalent, ruling, successful.
adj antonyms minor, uncommon.

prevalent *adj* **1** ascendant, compelling, efficacious, governing, predominant, prevailing, successful, superior. **2** extensive, general, rife, widespread.
adj antonyms subordinate, uncommon.

prevaricate *vb* deviate, dodge, equivocate, evade, quibble, shift, shuffle.

prevent *vb* bar, check, debar, deter, forestall, help, hinder, impede, inhibit, intercept, interrupt, obstruct, obviate, preclude, prohibit, restrain, save, stop, thwart.
v antonyms cause, foster, help.

prevention *n* anticipation, determent, deterrence, deterrent, frustration, hindrance, interception, interruption, obstruction, preclusion, prohibition, restriction, stoppage.

previous *adj* antecedent, anterior, earlier, foregoing, foregone, former, precedent, preceding, prior.
adj antonyms later, timely.

prey *vb* **1** devour, eat, feed on, live off. **2** exploit, intimidate, terrorize. **3** burden, distress, haunt, oppress, trouble, worry.

• *n* **1** booty, loot, pillage, plunder, prize, rapine, spoil. **2** food, game, kill, quarry, victim. **3** depredation, ravage.

price *vb* assess, estimate, evaluate, rate, value. • *n* **1** amount, cost, expense, outlay, value. **2** appraisal, charge, estimation, excellence, figure, rate, quotation, valuation, value, worth. **3** compensation, guerdon, recompense, return, reward.

priceless *adj* **1** dear, expensive, precious, inestimable, invaluable, valuable. **2** amusing, comic, droll, funny, humorous, killing, rich.

adj antonyms cheap, run-of-the-mill.

prick *vb* **1** perforate, pierce, puncture, stick. **2** drive, goad, impel, incite, spur, urge. **3** cut, hurt, mark, pain, sting, wound. **4** hasten, post, ride. • *n* **1** mark, perforation, point, puncture. **2** prickle, sting, wound.

pride *vb* boast, brag, crow, preen, revel in. • *n* **1** conceit, egotism, self-complacency, self-esteem, self-exaltation, self-importance, self-sufficiency, vanity. **2** arrogance, assumption, disdain, haughtiness, hauteur, insolence, loftiness, lordliness, pomposity, presumption, superciliousness, vainglory. **3** decorum, dignity, elevation, self-respect. **4** decoration, glory, ornament, show, splendour.

n antonym humility.

priest *n* churchman, clergyman, divine, ecclesiastic, minister, pastor, presbyter.

prim *adj* demure, formal, nice, precise, prudish, starch, starched, stiff, strait-laced.

adj antonyms broad-minded, informal.

primary *adj* **1** aboriginal, earliest, first, initial, original, prime, primitive, primeval, primordial, pristine. **2** chief, main, principal. **3** basic, elementary, fundamental, preparatory. **4** radical.

adj antonym secondary.

prime¹ *adj* **1** aboriginal, basic, first, initial, original, primal, primary, primeval, primitive, primordial, pristine. **2** chief, foremost, highest, leading, main, paramount, principal. **3** blooming, early. **4** capital, cardinal, dominant, predominant. **5** excellent, first-class, first-rate, optimal, optimum, quintessential, superlative. **6** beginning, opening. • *n* **1** beginning, dawn, morning, opening. **2** spring, springtime, youth. **3** bloom, cream, flower, height,

heyday, optimum, perfection, quintessence, zenith.

adj antonyms minor, secondary, secondrate.

prime² *vb* **1** charge, load, prepare, undercoat. **2** coach, groom, train, tutor.

primeval *adj* original, primitive, primordial, pristine.

adj antonyms developed, later, modern.

primitive *adj* **1** aboriginal, first, fundamental, original, primal, primary, prime, primitive, primordial, pristine. **2** ancient, antiquated, crude, old-fashioned, quaint, simple, uncivilized, unsophisticated.

adj antonyms advanced, civilized, developed.

prince *n* **1** monarch, potentate, ruler, sovereign. **2** dauphin, heir apparent, infant. **3** chief, leader, potentate.

princely *adj* **1** imperial, regal, royal. **2** august, generous, grand, liberal, magnanimous, magnificent, majestic, munificent, noble, pompous, splendid, superb, titled. **3** dignified, elevated, high-minded, lofty, noble, stately.

principal *adj* capital, cardinal, chief, essential, first, foremost, highest, leading, main, pre-eminent, prime. • *n* **1** chief, head, leader. **2** head teacher, master.

adj antonyms least, lesser, minor.

principally *adv* chiefly, essentially, especially, mainly, particularly.

principle *n* **1** cause, fountain, fountainhead, groundwork, mainspring, nature, origin, source, spring. **2** basis, constituent, element, essence, substratum. **3** assumption, axiom, law, maxim, postulation. **4** doctrine, dogma, impulse, maxim, opinion, precept, rule, tenet, theory. **5** conviction, ground, motive, reason. **6** equity, goodness, honesty, honour, incorruptibility, integrity, justice, probity, rectitude, righteousness, trustiness, truth, uprightness, virtue, worth. **7** faculty, power.

n antonyms corruption, wickedness.

prink *vb* **1** adorn, deck, decorate. **2** preen, primp, spruce.

print *vb* **1** engrave, impress, imprint, mark, stamp. **2** issue, publish. • *n* **1** book, periodical, publication. **2** copy, engraving, photograph, picture. **3** characters, font, fount, lettering, type, typeface.

prior *adj* antecedent, anterior, earlier, foregoing, precedent, preceding, precursory, previous, superior.

adj antonym later.

priority *n* antecedence, anteriority, precedence, pre-eminence, pre-existence, superiority.

priory *n* abbey, cloister, convent, monastery, nunnery.

prison *n* **1** confinement, dungeon, gaol, jail, keep, lockup, penitentiary, reformatory. **2** can, clink, cooler, jug.

pristine *adj* ancient, earliest, first, former, old, original, primary, primeval, primitive, primordial.

adj antonyms developed, later, spoiled.

privacy *n* **1** concealment, secrecy. **2** retirement, retreat, seclusion, solitude.

private *adj* **1** retired, secluded, sequestrated, solitary. **2** individual, own, particular, peculiar, personal, special, unofficial. **3** confidential, privy. **4** clandestine, concealed, hidden, secret. • *n* GI, soldier, tommy.

adj antonyms open, public.

privation *n* **1** bereavement, deprivation, dispossession, loss. **2** destitution, distress, indigence, necessity, need, want. **3** absence, negation. **4** degradation.

n antonyms affluence, wealth.

privilege *n* advantage, charter, claim, exemption, favour, franchise, immunity, leave, liberty, licence, permission, prerogative, right.

n antonym disadvantage.

privy *adj* **1** individual, particular, peculiar, personal, private, special. **2** clandestine, secret. **3** retired, sequestrated.

prize[1] *vb* appreciate, cherish, esteem, treasure, value.

vb antonyms despise, undervalue.

adj antonym second-rate.

prize[2] *adj* best, champion, first-rate, outstanding, winning. • *n* **1** guerdon, honours, meed, premium, reward. **2** cup, decoration, medal, laurels, palm, trophy. **3** booty, capture, lot, plunder, spoil. **4** advantage, gain, privilege.

probability *n* **1** chance, prospect, likelihood, presumption. **2** appearance, credibility, credibleness, likeliness, verisimilitude.

probable *adj* apparent, credible, likely, presumable, reasonable.

adj antonym improbable.

probably *adv* apparently, likely, maybe, perchance, perhaps, presumably, possibly, seemingly.

probation *n* **1** essay, examination, ordeal, proof, test, trial. **2** novitiate.

probe *vb* examine, explore, fathom, investigate, measure, prove, scrutinize, search, sift, sound, test, verify. • *n* examination, exploration, inquiry, investigation, scrutiny, study.

probity *n* candour, conscientiousness, equity, fairness, faith, goodness, honesty, honour, incorruptibility, integrity, justice, loyalty, morality, principle, rectitude, righteousness, sincerity, soundness, trustworthiness, truth, truthfulness, uprightness, veracity, virtue, worth.

problem *adj* difficult, intractable, uncontrollable, unruly. • *n* dilemma, dispute, doubt, enigma, exercise, proposition, puzzle, riddle, theorem.

adj antonyms manageable, well-behaved.

problematic *adj* debatable, disputable, doubtful, dubious, enigmatic, problematical, puzzling, questionable, suspicious, uncertain, unsettled.

procedure *n* **1** conduct, course, custom, management, method, operation, policy, practice, process. **2** act, action, deed, measure, performance, proceeding, step, transaction.

proceed *vb* **1** advance, continue, go, pass, progress. **2** accrue, arise, come, emanate, ensue, flow, follow, issue, originate, result, spring.

vb antonyms retreat, stop.

proceeds *npl* balance, earnings, effects, gain, income, net, produce, products, profits, receipts, returns, yield.

n antonyms losses, outlay.

process *vb* **1** advance, deal with, fulfil, handle, progress. **2** alter, convert, refine, transform. • *n* **1** advance, course, progress, train. **2** action, conduct, management, measure, mode, operation, performance, practice, procedure, proceeding, step, transaction, way. **3** action, case, suit, trial. **4** outgrowth, projection, protuberance.

procession *n* cavalcade, cortege, file, march, parade, retinue, train.

proclaim *vb* **1** advertise, announce, blazon, broach, broadcast, circulate, cry, declare, herald, promulgate, publish, trumpet. **2** ban, outlaw, proscribe.

proclamation *n* 1 advertisement, announcement, blazon, declaration, promulgation, publication. 2 ban, decree, edict, manifesto, ordinance.

proclivity *n* 1 bearing, bent, bias, determination, direction, disposition, drift, inclination, leaning, predisposition, proneness, propensity, tendency, turn. 2 aptitude, facility, readiness.

procrastinate *vb* 1 adjourn, defer, delay, postpone, prolong, protract, retard. 2 neglect, omit. 3 lag, loiter.
vb antonyms advance, proceed.

procrastination *n* delay, dilatoriness, postponement, protraction, slowness, tardiness.

procreate *vb* beget, breed, engender, generate, produce, propagate.

procurable *adj* acquirable, compassable, obtainable.

procurator *n* agent, attorney, deputy, proctor, proxy, representative, solicitor.

procure *vb* 1 acquire, gain, get, obtain. 2 cause, compass, contrive, effect.
vb antonym lose.

procurer *n* bawd, pander, pimp.

prodigal *adj* abundant, dissipated, excessive, extravagant, generous, improvident, lavish, profuse, reckless, squandering, thriftless, unthrifty, wasteful. • *n* spendthrift, squanderer, waster, wastrel.

prodigality *n* excess, extravagance, lavishness, profusion, squandering, unthriftiness, waste, wastefulness.

prodigious *adj* 1 amazing, astonishing, astounding, extraordinary, marvellous, miraculous, portentous, remarkable, startling, strange, surprising, uncommon, wonderful, wondrous. 2 enormous, huge, immense, monstrous, vast.
adj antonyms commonplace, small, unremarkable.

prodigy *n* 1 marvel, miracle, phenomenon, portent, sign, wonder. 2 curiosity, monster, monstrosity.

produce *vb* 1 exhibit, show. 2 bear, beget, breed, conceive, engender, furnish, generate, hatch, procreate, yield. 3 accomplish, achieve, cause, create, effect, make, occasion, originate. 4 accrue, afford, give, impart, make, render. 5 extend, lengthen, prolong, protract. 6 fabricate, fashion, manufacture. • *n* crop, fruit, greengrocery, harvest, product, vegetables, yield.

vb antonyms consume, result from.

producer *n* 1 creator, inventor, maker, originator. 2 agriculturalist, farmer, greengrocer, husbandman, raiser.

product *n* 1 crops, fruits, harvest, outcome, proceeds, produce, production, returns, yield. 2 consequence, effect, fruit, issue, performance, production, result, work.
n antonym cause.

production *n* 1 fruit, produce, product. 2 construction, creation, erection, fabrication, making, performance. 3 completion, fruition. 4 birth, breeding, development, growth, propagation. 5 opus, publication, work. 6 continuation, extension, lengthening, prolongation.

productive *adj* 1 copious, fertile, fruitful, luxuriant, plenteous, prolific, teeming. 2 causative, constructive, creative, efficient, life-giving, producing.
adj antonyms fruitless, unproductive.

proem *n* exordium, foreword, introduction, preface, prelims, prelude, prolegomena.

profane *vb* 1 defile, desecrate, pollute, violate. 2 abuse, debase. • *adj* 1 blasphemous, godless, heathen, idolatrous, impious, impure, pagan, secular, temporal, unconsecrated, unhallowed, unholy, unsanctified, worldly, unspiritual. 2 impure, polluted, unholy.

profanity *n* blasphemy, impiety, irreverence, profaneness, sacrilege.
n antonyms politeness, reverence.

profess *vb* 1 acknowledge, affirm, allege, aver, avouch, avow, confess, declare, own, proclaim, state. 2 affect, feign, pretend.

profession *n* 1 acknowledgement, assertion, avowal, claim, declaration. 2 avocation, evasion, pretence, pretension, protestation, representation. 3 business, calling, employment, engagement, occupation, office, trade, vocation.

proffer *vb* offer, propose, propound, suggest, tender, volunteer. • *n* offer, proposal, suggestion, tender.

proficiency *n* 1 advancement, forwardness, improvement. 2 accomplishment, aptitude, competency, dexterity, mastery, skill.

proficient *adj* able, accomplished, adept, competent, conversant, dextrous, expert, finished, masterly, practised, skilled, skilful, thoroughbred, trained, qualified, well-versed. • *n* adept, expert, master, master-hand.

adj antonyms clumsy, incompetent.

profit *vb* advance, benefit, gain, improve. • *n* 1 aid, clearance, earnings, emolument, fruit, gain, lucre, produce, return. 2 advancement, advantage, benefit, interest, perquisite, service, use, utility, weal.
vb antonyms harm, hinder.
n antonym loss.

profitable *adj* 1 advantageous, beneficial, desirable, gainful, productive, useful. 2 lucrative, remunerative.
adj antonym unprofitable.

profitless *adj* bootless, fruitless, unprofitable, useless, valueless, worthless.

profligate *adj* abandoned, corrupt, corrupted, degenerate, depraved, dissipated, dissolute, graceless, immoral, shameless, vicious, vitiated, wicked. • *n* debauchee, libertine, rake, reprobate, roué.
adj antonyms moral, parsimonious, thrifty, upright.

profound *adj* 1 abysmal, deep, fathomless. 2 heavy, undisturbed. 3 erudite, learned, penetrating, sagacious, skilled. 4 deeply felt, far-reaching, heartfelt, intense, lively, strong, touching, vivid. 5 low, submissive. 6 abstruse, mysterious, obscure, occult, subtle, recondite. 7 complete, thorough.
adj antonyms mild, shallow, slight.

profundity *n* deepness, depth, profoundness.

profuse *adj* abundant, bountiful, copious, excessive, extravagant, exuberant, generous, improvident, lavish, overabundant, plentiful, prodigal, wasteful.
adj antonyms sparing, sparse.

profusion *n* abundance, bounty, copiousness, excess, exuberance, extravagance, lavishness, prodigality, profuseness, superabundance, waste.
n antonyms springiness, sparsity.

progenitor *n* ancestor, forebear, forefather.

progeny *n* breed, children, descendants, family, issue, lineage, offshoot, offspring, posterity, race, scion, stock, young.

prognostic *adj* foreshadowing, foreshowing, foretokening. • *n* 1 augury, foreboding, indication, omen, presage, prognostication, sign, symptom, token. 2 foretelling, prediction, prophecy.

prognosticate *vb* 1 foretell, predict, prophesy. 2 augur, betoken, forebode, foreshadow, foreshow, foretoken, indicate, portend, presage.

prognostication *n* 1 foreknowledge, foreshowing, foretelling, prediction, presage. 2 augury, foreboding, foretoken, indication, portent, prophecy.

progress *vb* 1 advance, continue, proceed. 2 better, gain, improve, increase. • *n* 1 advance, advancement, progression. 2 course, headway, ongoing, passage. 3 betterment, development, growth, improvement, increase, reform. 4 circuit, procession.
vb antonyms decline, deteriorate.
n antonyms decline, deterioration.

prohibit *vb* 1 debar, hamper, hinder, preclude, prevent. 2 ban, disallow, forbid, inhibit, interdict.
vb antonym permit.

prohibition *n* ban, bar, disallowance, embargo, forbiddance, inhibition, interdict, interdiction, obstruction, prevention, proscription, taboo, veto.
n antonym permission.

prohibitive *adj* forbidding, prohibiting, refraining, restrictive.
adj antonyms encouraging, reasonable.

project *vb* 1 cast, eject, fling, hurl, propel, shoot, throw. 2 brew, concoct, contrive, design, devise, intend, plan, plot, purpose, scheme. 3 delineate, draw, exhibit. 4 bulge, extend, jut, protrude. • *n* contrivance, design, device, intention, plan, proposal, purpose, scheme.

projectile *n* bullet, missile, shell.

projection *n* 1 delivery, ejection, emission, propulsion, throwing. 2 contriving, designing, planning, scheming. 3 bulge, extension, outshoot, process, prominence, protuberance, salience, saliency, salient, spur. 4 delineation, map, plan.

proletarian *adj* mean, plebeian, vile, vulgar. • *n* commoner, plebeian.

proletariat *n* commonality, hoi polloi, masses, mob, plebs, working class.

prolific *adj* abundant, fertile, fruitful, generative, productive, teeming.
adj antonyms infertile, scarce.

prolix *adj* boring, circumlocutory, discursive, diffuse, lengthy, long, long-winded, loose, prolonged, protracted, prosaic, rambling, tedious, tiresome, verbose, wordy.

prologue *n* foreword, introduction, preamble, preface, preliminary, prelude, proem.

prolong *vb* 1 continue, extend, lengthen,

protract, sustain. 2 defer, postpone.
vb antonym shorten.

promenade *vb* saunter, walk. • *n* 1 dance, stroll, walk. 2 boulevard, esplanade, parade, walkway.

prominent *adj* 1 convex, embossed, jutting, projecting, protuberant, raised, relieved. 2 celebrated, conspicuous, distinguished, eminent, famous, foremost, influential, leading, main, noticeable, outstanding. 3 conspicuous, distinctive, important, manifest, marked, principal, salient.
adj antonyms inconspicuous, unimportant.

promiscuous *adj* 1 confused, heterogeneous, indiscriminate, intermingled, mingled, miscellaneous, mixed. 2 abandoned, dissipated, dissolute, immoral, licentious, loose, unchaste, wanton.

promise *vb* 1 covenant, engage, pledge, subscribe, swear, underwrite, vow. 2 assure, attest, guarantee, warrant. 3 agree, bargain, engage, stipulate, undertake. • *n* agreement, assurance, contract, engagement, oath, parole, pledge, profession, undertaking, vow, word.

promising *adj* auspicious, encouraging, hopeful, likely, propitious.

promote *vb* 1 advance, aid, assist, cultivate, encourage, further, help, promote. 2 dignify, elevate, exalt, graduate, honour, pass, prefer, raise.
vb antonyms demote, disparage, obstruct.

promotion *n* 1 advancement, encouragement, furtherance. 2 elevation, exaltation, preferment.

prompt *vb* 1 actuate, dispose, impel, incite, incline, induce, instigate, stimulate, urge. 2 remind. 3 dictate, hint, influence, suggest. • *adj* 1 active, alert, apt, quick, ready. 2 forward, hasty. 3 disposed, inclined, prone. 4 early, exact, immediate, instant, precise, punctual, seasonable, timely. • *adv* apace, directly, forthwith, immediately, promptly. • *n* cue, hint, prompter, reminder, stimulus.

promptly *adv* apace, directly, expeditiously, forthwith, immediately, instantly, pronto, punctually, quickly, speedily, straightway, straightaway, summarily, swiftly.

promptness *n* activity, alertness, alacrity, promptitude, readiness, quickness.

promulgate *vb* advertise, announce, broadcast, bruit, circulate, declare, notify, proclaim, publish, spread, trumpet.

prone *adj* 1 flat, horizontal, prostrate, recumbent. 2 inclined, inclining, sloping. 3 apt, bent, disposed, inclined, predisposed, tending. 4 eager, prompt, ready.

pronounce *vb* 1 articulate, enunciate, frame, say, speak, utter. 2 affirm, announce, assert, declare, deliver, state.

proof *adj* firm, fixed, impenetrable, stable, steadfast. • *n* 1 essay, examination, ordeal, test, trial. 2 attestation, certification, conclusion, conclusiveness, confirmation, corroboration, demonstration, evidence, ratification, substantiation, testimony, verification.
adj antonyms permeable, untreated.

prop *vb* bolster, brace, buttress, maintain, shore, stay, support, sustain, truss, uphold. • *n* 1 support, stay. 2 buttress, fulcrum, pin, shore, strut.

propaganda *n* inculcation, indoctrination, promotion.

propagate *vb* 1 continue, increase, multiply. 2 circulate, diffuse, disseminate, extend, promote, promulgate, publish, spread, transmit. 3 beget, breed, engender, generate, originate, procreate.

propel *vb* 1 drive, force, impel, push, urge. 2 cast, fling, hurl, project, throw.
vb antonyms slow, stop.

propensity *n* aptitude, bent, bias, disposition, inclination, ply, proclivity, proneness, tendency.
n antonym disinclination.

proper *adj* 1 individual, inherent, natural, original, particular, peculiar, special, specific. 2 adapted, appropriate, becoming, befitting, convenient, decent, decorous, demure, fit, fitting, legitimate, meet, pertinent, respectable, right, seemly, suitable. 3 accurate, correct, exact, fair, fastidious, formal, just, precise. 4 actual, real.
adj antonyms common, general, improper.

property *n* 1 attribute, characteristic, disposition, mark, peculiarity, quality, trait, virtue. 2 appurtenance, assets, belongings, chattels, circumstances, effects, estate, goods, possessions, resources, wealth. 3 ownership, possession, proprietorship, tenure. 4 claim, copyright, interest, participation, right, title.

prophecy *n* 1 augury, divination, forecast, foretelling, portent, prediction, premonition, presage, prognostication. **2** exhortation, instruction, preaching.

prophesy *vb* augur, divine, foretell, predict, prognosticate.

propinquity *n* **1** adjacency, contiguity, nearness, neighbourhood, proximity, vicinity. **2** affinity, connection, consanguinity, kindred, relationship.

propitiate *vb* appease, atone, conciliate, intercede, mediate, pacify, reconcile, satisfy.

propitious *adj* **1** benevolent, benign, friendly, gracious, kind, merciful. **2** auspicious, encouraging, favourable, fortunate, happy, lucky, opportune, promising, prosperous, thriving, timely, well-disposed.

adj antonym inauspicious.

proportion *vb* **1** adjust, graduate, regulate. **2** form, shape. • *n* **1** arrangement, relation. **2** adjustment, commensuration, dimension, distribution, symmetry. **3** extent, lot, part, portion, quota, ratio, share.

n antonyms disproportion, imbalance.

proposal *n* design, motion, offer, overture, proffer, proposition, recommendation, scheme, statement, suggestion, tender.

propose *vb* **1** move, offer, pose, present, propound, proffer, put, recommend, state, submit, suggest, tender. **2** design, intend, mean, purpose.

vb antonyms oppose, withdraw.

proposition *vb* **1** accost, proffer, solicit. • *n* offer, overture, project, proposal, suggestion, tender, undertaking. **2** affirmation, assertion, axiom, declaration, dictum, doctrine, position, postulation, predication, statement, theorem, thesis.

proprietor *n* lord, master, owner, possessor, proprietary.

propriety *n* **1** accuracy, adaptation, appropriation, aptness, becomingness, consonance, correctness, fitness, justness, reasonableness, rightness, seemliness, suitableness. **2** conventionality, decency, decorum, demureness, fastidiousness, formality, modesty, properness, respectability.

prorogation *n* adjournment, continuance, postponement.

prosaic *adj* commonplace, dull, flat, humdrum, matter-of-fact, pedestrian, plain, prolix, prosing, sober, stupid, tame, tedious, tiresome, unentertaining, unimaginative, uninspired, uninteresting, unromantic, vapid.

adj antonyms imaginative, interesting.

proscribe *vb* **1** banish, doom, exile, expel, ostracize, outlaw. **2** exclude, forbid, interdict, prohibit. **3** censure, condemn, curse, denounce, reject.

vb antonyms admit, allow.

prosecute *vb* **1** conduct, continue, exercise, follow, persist, pursue. **2** arraign, indict, sue, summon.

vb antonym desist.

prospect *vb* explore, search, seek, survey. • *n* **1** display, field, landscape, outlook, perspective, scene, show, sight, spectacle, survey, view, vision, vista. **2** picture, scenery. **3** anticipation, calculation, contemplation, expectance, expectancy, expectation, foreseeing, foresight, hope, presumption, promise, trust. **4** likelihood, probability.

n antonym unlikelihood.

prospectus *n* announcement, conspectus, description, design, outline, plan, programme, sketch, syllabus.

prosper *vb* **1** aid, favour, forward, help. **2** advance, flourish, grow rich, thrive, succeed. **3** batten, increase.

vb antonym fail.

prosperity *n* **1** affluence, blessings, happiness, felicity, good luck, success, thrift, weal, welfare, well-being. **2** boom, heyday.

prosperous *adj* **1** blooming, flourishing, fortunate, golden, halcyon, rich, successful, thriving. **2** auspicious, booming, bright, favourable, good, golden, lucky, promising, propitious, providential, rosy.

adj antonym poor.

prostrate *vb* **1** demolish, destroy, fell, level, overthrow, overturn, ruin. **2** depress, exhaust, overcome, reduce. • *adj* **1** fallen, prostrated, prone, recumbent, supine. **2** helpless, powerless.

vb antonyms elate, exalt, strengthen.

adj antonyms elated, erect, hale, happy, strong, triumphant.

prostration *n* **1** demolition, destruction, overthrow. **2** dejection, depression, exhaustion.

prosy *adj* **1** prosaic, unpoetic, unpoetical. **2** dull, flat, jejune, stupid, tedious, tiresome, unentertaining, unimaginative, uninteresting.

protect *vb* **1** cover, defend, guard, shield. **2** fortify, harbour, house, preserve, save, screen, secure, shelter. **3** champion, countenance, foster, patronize.

vb antonyms attack, threaten.

protector *n* champion, custodian, defender, guardian, patron, warden.

protest *vb* 1 affirm, assert, asseverate, attest, aver, avow, declare, profess, testify. 2 demur, expostulate, object, remonstrate, repudiate. • *n* complaint, declaration, disapproval, objection, protestation.
vb antonym accept.
n antonym acceptance.

prototype *n* archetype, copy, exemplar, example, ideal, model, original, paradigm, precedent, protoplast, type.

protract *vb* 1 continue, extend, lengthen, prolong. 2 defer, delay, postpone.
vb antonym shorten.

protrude *vb* beetle, bulge, extend, jut, project.

protuberance *n* bulge, bump, elevation, excrescence, hump, lump, process, projection, prominence, roundness, swelling, tumour.

proud *adj* 1 assuming, conceited, contended, egotistical, overweening, self-conscious, self-satisfied, vain. 2 arrogant, boastful, haughty, high-spirited, highly strung, imperious, lofty, lordly, presumptuous, supercilious, uppish, vainglorious.
adj antonym humble.

prove *vb* 1 ascertain, conform, demonstrate, establish, evidence, evince, justify, manifest, show, substantiate, sustain, verify. 2 assay, check, examine, experiment, test, try.
vb antonyms discredit, disprove, falsify.

proverb *n* adage, aphorism, apothegm, byword, dictum, maxim, precept, saw, saying.

proverbial *adj* acknowledged, current, notorious, unquestioned.

provide *vb* 1 arrange, collect, plan, prepare, procure. 2 gather, keep, store. 3 afford, contribute, feed, furnish, produce, stock, supply, yield. 4 cater, purvey. 5 agree, bargain, condition, contract, covenant, engage, stipulate.
vb antonyms remove, take.

provided, providing *conj* granted, if, supposing.

provident *adj* 1 careful, cautious, considerate, discreet, farseeing, forecasting, forehanded, foreseeing, prudent. 2 economical, frugal, thrifty.
adj antonym improvident.

province *n* 1 district, domain, region, sec-

tion, territory, tract. 2 colony, dependency. 3 business, calling, capacity, charge, department, duty, employment, function, office, part, post, sphere. 4 department, division, jurisdiction.

provincial *adj* 1 annexed, appendant, outlying. 2 bucolic, countrified, rude, rural, rustic, unpolished, unrefined. 3 insular, local, narrow. • *n* peasant, rustic, yokel.

provision *n* 1 anticipation, providing. 2 arrangement, care, preparation, readiness. 3 equipment, fund, grist, hoard, reserve, resources, stock, store, supplies, supply. 4 clause, condition, prerequisite, proviso, reservation, stipulation.
n antonyms neglect, removal.

provisions *npl* eatables, fare, food, provender, supplies, viands, victuals.

proviso *n* clause, condition, provision, stipulation.

provocation *n* 1 incentive, incitement, provocativeness, stimulant, stimulus. 2 affront, indignity, insult, offence. 3 angering, vexation.

provoke *vb* 1 animate, arouse, awaken, excite, impel, incite, induce, inflame, instigate, kindle, move, rouse, stimulate. 2 affront, aggravate, anger, annoy, chafe, enrage, exacerbate, exasperate, incense, infuriate, irritate, nettle, offend, pique, vex. 3 cause, elicit, evoke, instigate, occasion, produce, promote.
vb antonyms pacify, please, result.

provoking *adj* aggravating, annoying, exasperating, irritating, offensive, tormenting, vexatious, vexing.

prowess *n* 1 bravery, courage, daring, fearlessness, gallantry, heroism, intrepidity, valour. 2 aptitude, dexterity, expertness, facility.
n antonyms clumsiness, mediocrity.

proximity *n* adjacency, contiguity, nearness, neighbourhood, propinquity, vicinage, vicinity.
n antonym remoteness.

proxy *n* agent, attorney, commissioner, delegate, deputy, lieutenant, representative, substitute.

prudence *n* carefulness, caution, circumspection, common sense, considerateness, discretion, forecast, foresight, judgment, judiciousness, policy, providence, sense, tact, wariness, wisdom.
n antonym imprudence.

prudent *adj* cautious, careful, circumspect, considerate, discreet, foreseeing, heedful, judicious, politic, provident, prudential, wary, wise.
adj antonym imprudent.

prudish *adj* coy, demure, modest, precise, prim, reserved, strait-laced.
adj antonyms easy-going, lax.

prune *vb* **1** abbreviate, clip, cut, dock, lop, thin, trim. **2** dress, preen.

prurient *adj* covetous, craving, desiring, hankering, itching, lascivious, libidinous, longing, lustful.

pry *vb* **1** examine, ferret, inspect, investigate, peep, peer, question, scrutinize, search. **2** force, lever, prise.
vb antonym mind one's own business.

public *adj* **1** civil, common, countrywide, general, national, political, state. **2** known, notorious, open, popular, published, well-known. • *n* **1** citizens, community, country, everyone, general public, masses, nation, people, population. **2** audience, buyers, following, supporters.
adj antonym private.

publication *n* **1** advertisement, announcement, disclosure, divulgence, proclamation, promulgation, report. **2** edition, issue, issuance, printing.

publicity *n* **1** daylight, currency, limelight, notoriety, spotlight. **2** outlet, vent.

publish *vb* advertise, air, bruit, announce, blaze, blazon, broach, communicate, declare, diffuse, disclose, disseminate, impart, placard, post, proclaim, promulgate, reveal, tell, utter, vent, ventilate.
vb antonym keep secret.

pucker *vb* cockle, contract, corrugate, crease, crinkle, furrow, gather, pinch, purse, shirr, wrinkle. • *n* crease, crinkle, fold, furrow, wrinkle.

puerile *adj* **1** boyish, childish, infantile, juvenile, youthful. **2** foolish, frivolous, idle, nonsensical, petty, senseless, silly, simple, trifling, trivial, weak.
adj antonym mature.

puffy *adj* **1** distended, swelled, swollen, tumid, turgid. **2** bombastic, extravagant, inflated, pompous.

pugnacious *adj* belligerent, bellicose, contentious, fighting, irascible, irritable, petulant, quarrelsome.
adj antonym easy-going.

puissant *adj* forcible, mighty, potent, powerful, strong.

pull *vb* **1** drag, draw, haul, row, tow, tug. **2** cull, extract, gather, pick, pluck. **3** detach, rend, tear, wrest. • *n* **1** pluck, shake, tug, twitch, wrench. **2** contest, struggle. **3** attraction, gravity, magnetism. **4** graft, influence, power.
vb antonyms deter, push, repel.
n antonyms deterring, push, repelling.

pulsate *vb* beat, palpitate, pant, throb, thump, vibrate.

pulverize *vb* bruise, comminute, grind, levigate, triturate.

pun *vb* assonate, alliterate, play on words. • *n* assonance, alliteration, clinch, conceit, double-meaning, play on words, quip, rhyme, witticism, wordplay.

punctilious *adj* careful, ceremonious, conscientious, exact, formal, nice, particular, precise, punctual, scrupulous, strict.
adj antonyms boorish, easy-going, informal.

punctual *adj* **1** exact, nice, precise, punctilious. **2** early, prompt, ready, regular, seasonable, timely.
adj antonym unpunctual.

puncture *vb* bore, penetrate, perforate, pierce, prick. • *n* bite, hole, sting, wound.

pungent *adj* **1** acid, acrid, biting, burning, caustic, hot, mordant, penetrating, peppery, piercing, piquant, prickling, racy, salty, seasoned, sharp, smart, sour, spicy, stimulating, stinging. **2** acute, acrimonious, cutting, distressing, irritating, keen, painful, peevish, poignant, pointed, satirical, severe, tart, trenchant, waspish.
adj antonyms feeble, mild, tasteless.

punish *vb* beat, castigate, chasten, chastise, correct, discipline, flog, lash, scourge, torture, whip.

punishment *n* **1** castigation, chastening, chastisement, correction, discipline, infliction, retribution, scourging, trial. **2** judgment, nemesis, penalty.

puny *adj* **1** feeble, inferior, weak. **2** dwarf, dwarfish, insignificant, diminutive, little, petty, pygmy, small, stunted, tiny, underdeveloped, undersized.
adj antonyms important, large, strong.

pupil *n* beginner, catechumen, disciple, learner, neophyte, novice, scholar, student, tyro.
n antonym teacher.

pupillage *n* minority, nonage, tutelage, wardship.

puppet *n* 1 doll, image, manikin, marionette. 2 cat's-paw, pawn, tool.

purchase *vb* 1 buy, gain, get, obtain, pay for, procure. 2 achieve, attain, earn, win. • *n* 1 acquisition, buy, gain, possession, property. 2 advantage, foothold, grasp, hold, influence, support.
vb antonym sell.
n antonym sale.

pure *adj* 1 clean, clear, fair, immaculate, spotless, stainless, unadulterated, unalloyed, unblemished, uncorrupted, undefiled, unpolluted, unspotted, unstained, unsullied, untainted, untarnished. 2 chaste, continent, guileless, guiltless, holy, honest, incorrupt, innocent, modest, sincere, true, uncorrupt, upright, virgin, virtuous. 3 genuine, perfect, real, simple, true, unadorned. 4 absolute, essential, mere, sheer, thorough. 5 classic, classical.
adj antonyms adulterated, applied, defiled, immoral, impure, polluted, tainted.

purge *vb* 1 cleanse, clear, purify. 2 clarify, defecate, evacuate. 3 deterge, scour. 4 absolve, pardon, shrive. • *n* 1 elimination, eradication, expulsion, removal, suppression. 2 cathartic, emetic, enema, laxative, physic.

purify *vb* 1 clean, cleanse, clear, depurate, expurgate, purge, refine, wash. 2 clarify, fine.
vb antonyms contaminate, defile, pollute.

puritanical *adj* ascetic, narrow-minded, overscrupulous, prim, prudish, rigid, severe, strait-laced, strict.
adj antonyms broad-minded, hedonistic, indulgent, liberal.

purity *n* 1 clearness, fineness. 2 cleanness, correctness, faultlessness, immaculacy, immaculateness. 3 guilelessness, guiltlessness, holiness, honesty, innocence, integrity, piety, simplicity, truth, uprightness, virtue. 4 excellence, genuineness. 5 homogeneity, simpleness. 6 chasteness, chastity, continence, modesty, pudency, virginity.
n antonyms immorality, impurity.

purlieus *npl* borders, bounds, confines, environs, limits, neighbourhood, outskirts, precincts, suburbs, vicinage, vicinity.

purloin *vb* abstract, crib, filch, pilfer, rob, steal, thieve.

purport *vb* 1 allege, assert, claim, maintain, pretend, profess. 2 denote, express, imply, indicate, mean, signify, suggest. • *n* bearing, current, design, drift, gist, import, intent, meaning, scope, sense, significance, signification, spirit, tendency, tenor.

purpose *vb* 1 contemplate, design, intend, mean, meditate. 2 determine, resolve. • *n* 1 aim, design, drift, end, intent, intention, object, resolution, resolve, view. 2 plan, project. 3 meaning, purport, sense. 4 consequence, effect.

pursue *vb* 1 chase, dog, follow, hound, hunt, shadow, track. 2 conduct, continue, cultivate, maintain, practise, prosecute. 3 seek, strive. 4 accompany, attend.
vb antonyms eschew, shun.

pursuit *n* 1 chase, hunt, race. 2 conduct, cultivation, practice, prosecution, pursuance. 3 avocation, calling, business, employment, fad, hobby, occupation, vocation.

pursy *adj* 1 corpulent, fat, fleshy, plump, podgy, pudgy, short, thick. 2 short-breathed, short-winded. 3 opulent, rich.

purview *n* body, compass, extent, limit, reach, scope, sphere, view.

push *vb* 1 elbow, crowd, hustle, impel, jostle, shoulder, shove, thrust. 2 advance, drive, hurry, propel, urge. 3 importune, persuade, tease. • *n* 1 pressure, thrust. 2 determination, perseverance. 3 emergency, exigency, extremity, pinch, strait, test, trial. 4 assault, attack, charge, endeavour, onset.

pusillanimous *adj* chicken, chicken-hearted, cowardly, dastardly, faint-hearted, feeble, lily-livered, mean-spirited, spiritless, timid, recreant, timorous, weak.
adj antonyms ambitious, courageous, forceful, strong.

pustule *n* abscess, blain, blister, blotch, boil, fester, gathering, pimple, sore, ulcer.

put *vb* 1 bring, collocate, deposit, impose, lay, locate, place, set. 2 enjoin, impose, inflict, levy. 3 offer, present, propose, state. 4 compel, constrain, force, oblige. 5 entice, incite, induce, urge. 6 express, utter.

putative *adj* deemed, reckoned, reported, reputed, supposed.

putrefy *vb* corrupt, decay, decompose, fester, rot, stink.

putrid *adj* corrupt, decayed, decomposed, fetid, rank, rotten, stinking.
adj antonyms fresh, wholesome.

puzzle *vb* 1 bewilder, confound, confuse, embarrass, gravel, mystify, nonplus, perplex, pose, stagger. 2 complicate, entangle. • *n* 1 conundrum, enigma, labyrinth, maze, paradox, poser, problem, riddle. 2 bewilderment, complication, confusion, difficulty, dilemma, embarrassment, mystification, perplexity, point, quandary, question.

pygmy *adj* diminutive, dwarf, dwarfish, Lilliputian, little, midget, stunted, tiny. • *n* dwarf, Lilliputian, midget.

Q

quack¹ *vb, n* cackle, cry, squeak.

quack² *adj* fake, false, sham. • *n* charlatan, empiric, humbug, impostor, mountebank, pretender.

adj antonym genuine.

n antonym genuine article, expert, maestro, professional.

quadruple *adj* fourfold, quadruplicate.

quagmire *n* **1** bog, fen, marsh, morass, slough, swamp. **2** difficulty, impasse, muddle, predicament.

quail *vb* blench, cower, droop, faint, flinch, shrink, tremble.

quaint *adj* **1** antiquated, antique, archaic, curious, droll, extraordinary, fanciful, odd, old-fashioned, queer, singular, uncommon, unique, unusual. **2** affected, fantastic, far-fetched, whimsical. **3** artful, ingenious.

quake *vb* **1** quiver, shake, shiver, shudder. **2** move, vibrate. • *n* earthquake, shake, shudder.

qualification *n* **1** ability, accomplishment, capability, competency, eligibility, fitness, suitability. **2** condition, exception, limitation, modification, proviso, restriction, stipulation. **3** abatement, allowance, diminution, mitigation.

qualified *adj* **1** accomplished, certificated, certified, competent, fitted, equipped, licensed, trained. **2** adapted, circumscribed, conditional, limited, modified, restricted.

qualify *vb* **1** adapt, capacitate, empower, entitle, equip, fit. **2** limit, modify, narrow, restrain, restrict. **3** abate, assuage, ease, mitigate, moderate, reduce, soften. **4** diminish, modulate, temper, regulate, vary.

quality *n* **1** affection, attribute, characteristic, colour, distinction, feature, flavour, mark, nature, peculiarity, property, singularity, timbre, tinge, trait. **2** character, condition, disposition, humour, mood, temper. **3** brand, calibre, capacity, class, description, excellence, grade, kind, rank, sort, stamp, standing, station, status, virtue. **4** aristocracy, gentility, gentry, noblesse, nobility.

qualm *n* **1** agony, pang, throe. **2** nausea,

queasiness, sickness. **3** compunction, remorse, uneasiness, twinge.

quandary *n* bewilderment, difficulty, dilemma, doubt, embarrassment, perplexity, pickle, plight, predicament, problem, puzzle, strait, uncertainty.

quantity *n* **1** content, extent, greatness, measure, number, portion, share, size. **2** aggregate, batch, amount, bulk, lot, mass, quantum, store, sum, volume. **3** duration, length.

quarrel *vb* altercate, bicker, brawl, carp, cavil, clash, contend, differ, dispute, fight, jangle, jar, scold, scuffle, spar, spat, squabble, strive, wrangle. • *n* altercation, affray, bickering, brawl, breach, breeze, broil, clash, contention, contest, controversy, difference, disagreement, discord, dispute, dissension, disturbance, feud, fight, fray, imbroglio, jar, miff, misunderstanding, quarrelling, row, rupture, spat, squabble, strife, tiff, tumult, variance, wrangle.

vb antonym agree.

n antonyms agreement, harmony.

quarrelsome *adj* argumentative, choleric, combative, contentious, cross, discordant, disputatious, fiery, irascible, irritable, petulant, pugnacious, ugly, wranglesome.

adj antonyms peaceable, placid.

quarter *vb* **1** billet, lodge, post, station. **2** allot, furnish, share. • *n* **1** abode, billet, dwelling, habitation, lodgings, posts, quarters, stations. **2** direction, district, locality, location, lodge, position, region, territory. **3** clemency, mercy, mildness.

quash *vb* **1** abate, abolish, annul, cancel, invalidate, nullify, overthrow. **2** crush, extinguish, repress, stop, subdue, suppress.

vb antonyms confirm, justify, reinstate, vindicate.

queasy *adj* nauseated, pukish, seasick, sick, squeamish.

queer *vb* botch, harm, impair, mar, spoil. • *adj* **1** curious, droll, extraordinary, fantastic, odd, peculiar, quaint, singular, strange, uncommon, unusual, whimsical. **2** (*sl, off*) gay, homosexual.

adj antonyms common, ordinary, straightforward, unexceptional, usual.

quell *vb* **1** conquer, crush, overcome, overpower, subdue. **2** bridle, check, curb, extinguish, lay, quench, rein in, repress, restrain, stifle. **3** allay, calm, compose, hush, lull, pacify, quiet, quieten, still, tranquillize. **4** alleviate, appease, blunt, deaden, dull, mitigate, mollify, soften, soothe.

quench *vb* **1** extinguish, put out. **2** check, destroy, repress, satiate, stifle, still, suppress. **3** allay, cool, dampen, extinguish, slake.

querulous *adj* bewailing, complaining, cross, discontented, dissatisfied, fretful, fretting, irritable, mourning, murmuring, peevish, petulant, plaintive, touchy, whining.

adj antonyms contented, equable, placid, uncomplaining.

query *vb* **1** ask, enquire, inquire, question. **2** dispute, doubt. • *n* enquiry, inquiry, interrogatory, issue, problem, question.

vb antonym accept.

quest *n* **1** expedition, journey, search, voyage. **2** pursuit, suit. **3** examination, enquiry, inquiry. **4** demand, desire, invitation, prayer, request, solicitation.

question *vb* **1** ask, catechize, enquire, examine, inquire, interrogate, quiz, sound out. **2** doubt, query. **3** challenge, dispute. • *n* **1** examination, enquiry, inquiry, interpellation, interrogation. **2** enquiry, inquiry, interrogatory, query. **3** debate, discussion, disquisition, examination, investigation, issue, trial. **4** controversy, dispute, doubt. **5** motion, mystery, point, poser, problem, proposition, puzzle, topic.

questionable *adj* ambiguous, controversial, controvertible, debatable, doubtful, disputable, equivocal, problematic, problematical, suspicious, uncertain, undecided.

adj antonyms certain, indisputable, straightforward.

quibble *vb* cavil, equivocate, evade, prevaricate, shuffle. • *n* equivocation, evasion, pretence, prevarication, quirk, shift, shuffle, sophism, subtlety, subterfuge.

quick *adj* **1** active, agile, alert, animated, brisk, lively, nimble, prompt, ready, smart, sprightly. **2** expeditious, fast, fleet, flying, hurried, rapid, speedy, swift. **3** adroit, apt, clever, dextrous, expert, skilful. **4** choleric, hasty, impetuous, irascible, irritable, passionate, peppery, petulant, precipitate,

sharp, unceremonious, testy, touchy, waspish. **5** alive, animate, live, living.

adj antonyms dull, slow.

quicken *vb* **1** animate, energize, resuscitate, revivify, vivify. **2** cheer, enliven, invigorate, reinvigorate, revive, whet. **3** accelerate, dispatch, expedite, hasten, hurry, speed. **4** actuate, excite, incite, kindle, refresh, sharpen, stimulate. **5** accelerate, live, take effect.

vb antonyms dull, retard.

quickly *adv* apace, fast, immediately, nimbly, quick, rapidly, readily, soon, speedily, swiftly.

adv antonyms slowly, tardily, thoroughly.

quickness *n* **1** dispatch, expedition, haste, rapidity, speed, swiftness, velocity. **2** agility, alertness, activity, briskness, liveliness, nimbleness, promptness, readiness, smartness. **3** adroitness, aptitude, aptness, dexterity, facility, knack. **4** acumen, acuteness, keenness, penetration, perspicacity, sagacity, sharpness, shrewdness.

n antonyms dullness, slowness, tardiness.

quiescent *adj* **1** at rest, hushed, motionless, quiet, resting, still. **2** calm, mute, placid, quiet, serene, still, tranquil, unagitated, undisturbed, unruffled.

adj antonym active.

quiet *adj* **1** hushed, motionless, quiescent, still, unmoved. **2** calm, contented, gentle, mild, meek, modest, peaceable, peaceful, placid, silent, smooth, tranquil, undemonstrative, unobtrusive, unruffled. **3** patient. **4** retired, secluded. • *n* calmness, peace, repose, rest, silence, stillness.

adj antonyms busy, noisy, obtrusive.

n antonyms bustle, disturbance, noise.

quieten *vb* **1** arrest, discontinue, intermit, interrupt, still, stop, suspend. **2** allay, appease, calm, compose, lull, pacify, sober, soothe, tranquillize. **3** hush, silence. **4** alleviate, assuage, blunt, dull, mitigate, moderate, mollify, soften.

quip *n* crank, flout, gibe, jeer, mock, quirk, repartee, retort, sarcasm, scoff, sneer, taunt, witticism.

quit *vb* **1** absolve, acquit, deliver, free, release. **2** clear, deliver, discharge from, free, liberate, relieve. **3** acquit, behave, conduct. **4** carry through, perform. **5** discharge, pay, repay, requite. **6** relinquish, renounce, resign, stop, surrender. **7** depart from, leave, withdraw from. **8** abandon, desert, forsake, forswear.

• *adj* absolved, acquitted, clear, discharged, free, released.

quite *adv* completely, entirely, exactly, perfectly, positively, precisely, totally, wholly.

quiver *vb* flicker, flutter, oscillate, palpitate, quake, play, shake, shiver, shudder, tremble, twitch, vibrate. • *n* shake, shiver, shudder, trembling.

quixotic *adj* absurd, chimerical, fanciful, fantastic, fantastical, freakish, imaginary, mad, romantic, utopian, visionary, wild.
adj antonyms hard-headed, practical, realistic.

quiz *vb* 1 examine, question, test. 2 peer at. 3 banter, hoax, puzzle, ridicule. • *n* 1 enigma, hoax, jest, joke, puzzle. 2 jester, joker, hoax.

quota *n* allocation, allotment, apportionment, contingent, portion, proportion, quantity, share.

quotation *n* 1 citation, clipping, cutting, extract, excerpt, reference, selection. 2 estimate, rate, tender.

quote *vb* 1 adduce, cite, excerpt, extract, illustrate, instance, name, repeat, take. 2 estimate, tender.

R

rabble *n* commonality, horde, mob, populace, riffraff, rout, scum, trash.
n antonyms aristocracy, elite, nobility.

rabid *adj* **1** frantic, furious, mad, raging, wild. **2** bigoted, fanatical, intolerant, irrational, narrow-minded, rampant.

race¹ *n* **1** ancestry, breed, family, generation, house, kindred, line, lineage, pedigree, stock, strain. **2** clan, folk, nation, people, tribe. **3** breed, children, descendants, issue, offspring, progeny, stock.

race² *vb* career, compete, contest, course, hasten, hurry, run, speed. • *n* **1** career, chase, competition, contest, course, dash, heat, match, pursuit, run, sprint. **2** flavour, quality, smack, strength, taste.

rack *vb* **1** agonize, distress, excruciate, rend, torment, torture, wring. **2** exhaust, force, harass, oppress, strain, stretch, wrest. • *n* **1** agony, anguish, pang, torment, torture. **2** crib, manger. **3** neck, crag. **4** dampness, mist, moisture, vapour.

racket *n* **1** clamour, clatter, din, dissipation, disturbance, fracas, frolic, hubbub, noise, outcry, tumult, uproar. **2** game, graft, scheme, understanding.

racy *adj* **1** flavoursome, palatable, piquant, pungent, rich, spicy, strong. **2** forcible, lively, pungent, smart, spirited, stimulating, vigorous, vivacious.
adj antonyms dull, ponderous.

radiance *n* brightness, brilliance, brilliancy, effluence, efflux, emission, glare, glitter, light, lustre, refulgence, resplendence, shine, splendour.

radiant *adj* **1** beaming, brilliant, effulgent, glittering, glorious, luminous, lustrous, resplendent, shining, sparkling, splendid. **2** ecstatic, happy, pleased.
adj antonym dull.

radiate *vb* **1** beam, gleam, glitter, shine. **2** emanate, emit. **3** diffuse, spread.

radical *adj* **1** constitutional, deep-seated, essential, fundamental, ingrained, inherent, innate, native, natural, organic, original, uncompromising. **2** original, primitive, simple, uncompounded, underived. **3** complete, entire, extreme, fanatic, insurgent, perfect, rebellious, thorough, total. • *n* fanatic, revolutionary.
adj antonym superficial.

rage *vb* bluster, boil, chafe, foam, fret, fume, ravage, rave. • *n* **1** excitement, frenzy, fury, madness, passion, rampage, raving, vehemence, wrath. **2** craze, fashion, mania, mode, style, vogue.

ragged *adj* **1** rent, tattered, torn. **2** contemptible, mean, poor, shabby. **3** jagged, rough, rugged, shaggy, uneven. **4** discordant, dissonant, inharmonious, unmusical.

raid *vb* assault, forage, invade, pillage, plunder. • *n* attack, foray, invasion, inroad, plunder.

rail *vb* abuse, censure, inveigh, scoff, scold, sneer, upbraid.

raillery *n* banter, chaff, irony, joke, pleasantry, ridicule, satire.

raiment *n* array, apparel, attire, clothes, clothing, costume, dress, garb, garments, habiliment, habit, vestments, vesture.

rain *vb* **1** drizzle, drop, fall, pour, shower, sprinkle, teem. **2** bestow, lavish. • *n* cloudburst, downpour, drizzle, mist, shower, sprinkling.

raise *vb* **1** boost, construct, erect, heave, hoist, lift, uplift, upraise, rear. **2** advance, elevate, ennoble, exalt, promote. **3** aggravate, amplify, augment, enhance, heighten, increase, invigorate. **4** arouse, awake, cause, effect, excite, originate, produce, rouse, stir up, occasion, start. **5** assemble, collect, get, levy, obtain. **6** breed, cultivate, grow, propagate, rear. **7** ferment, leaven, work.
vb antonyms debase, decrease, degrade, dismiss, lower, reduce, suppress.

rake¹ *vb* **1** collect, comb, gather, scratch. **2** ransack, scour.

rake² *n* debauchee, libertine, profligate, roué.

rakish *adj* **1** debauched, dissipated, dissolute, lewd, licentious. **2** cavalier, jaunty.

ramble *vb* digress, maunder, range, roam, rove, saunter, straggle, stray, stroll, wander. • *n* excursion, rambling, roving, tour, trip, stroll, wandering.

rambling *adj* **1** discursive, irregular. **2** straggling, strolling, wandering.
adj antonym direct.

ramification *n* **1** arborescence, branching, divarication, forking, radiation. **2** branch, division, offshoot, subdivision. **3** consequence, upshot.

ramify *vb* branch, divaricate, extend, separate.

rampant *adj* **1** excessive, exuberant, luxuriant, rank, wanton. **2** boisterous, dominant, headstrong, impetuous, predominant, raging, uncontrollable, unbridled, ungovernable, vehement, violent.

rampart *n* bulwark, defence, fence, fortification, guard, security, wall.

rancid *adj* bad, fetid, foul, fusty, musty, offensive, rank, sour, stinking, tainted.
adj antonym sweet.

rancorous *adj* bitter, implacable, malevolent, malicious, malign, malignant, resentful, spiteful, vindictive, virulent.

rancour *n* animosity, antipathy, bitterness, enmity, gall, grudge, hate, hatred, ill-will, malevolence, malice, malignity, spite, venom, vindictiveness.

random *adj* accidental, casual, chance, fortuitous, haphazard, irregular, stray, wandering.
adj antonyms deliberate, systematic.

range *vb* **1** course, cruise, extend, ramble, roam, rove, straggle, stray, stroll, wander. **2** bend, lie, run. **3** arrange, class, dispose, rank. • *n* **1** file, line, row, rank, tier. **2** class, kind, order, sort. **3** excursion, expedition, ramble, roving, wandering. **4** amplitude, bound, command, compass, distance, extent, latitude, reach, scope, sweep, view. **5** register.

rank[1] *vb* arrange, class, classify, range. • *n* **1** file, line, order, range, row, tier. **2** class, division, group, order, series. **3** birth, blood, caste, degree, estate, grade, position, quality, sphere, stakes, standing. **4** dignity, distinction, eminence, nobility.

rank[2] *adj* **1** dense, exuberant, luxuriant, overabundant, overgrown, vigorous, wild. **2** excessive, extreme, extravagant, flagrant, gross, rampant, sheer, unmitigated, utter, violent. **3** fetid, foul, fusty, musty, offensive, rancid. **4** fertile, productive, rich. **5** coarse, disgusting.
adj antonyms sparse, sweet.

ransack *vb* **1** pillage, plunder, ravage, rifle,
sack, strip. **2** explore, overhaul, rummage, search thoroughly.

ransom *vb* deliver, emancipate, free, liberate, redeem, rescue, unfetter. • *n* **1** money, payment pay-off, price. **2** deliverance, liberation, redemption, release.

rant *vb* declaim, mouth, spout, vociferate. • *n* bombast, cant, exaggeration, fustian.

rapacious *adj* **1** predacious, preying, raptorial. **2** avaricious, grasping, greedy, ravenous, voracious.

rapid *adj* **1** fast, fleet, quick, swift. **2** brisk, expeditious, hasty, hurried, quick, speedy.
adj antonyms leisurely, slow, sluggish.

rapine *n* depredation, pillage, plunder, robbery, spoliation.

rapt *adj* absorbed, charmed, delighted, ecstatic, engrossed, enraptured, entranced, fascinated, inspired, spellbound.

rapture *vb* enrapture, ravish, transport. • *n* **1** delight, exultation, enthusiasm, rhapsody. **2** beatification, beatitude, bliss, ecstasy, felicity, happiness, joy, spell, transport.

rare[1] *adj* **1** sparse, subtle, thin. **2** extraordinary, infrequent, scarce, singular, strange, uncommon, unique, unusual. **3** choice, excellent, exquisite, fine, incomparable, inimitable.
adj antonyms abundant, common, usual.

rare[2] *adj* bloody, underdone.

rarity *n* **1** attenuation, ethereality, etherealness, rarefaction, rareness, tenuity, tenuousness, thinness. **2** infrequency, scarcity, singularity, sparseness, uncommonness, unwontedness.

rascal *n* blackguard, caitiff, knave, miscreant, rogue, reprobate, scallywag, scapegrace, scamp, scoundrel, vagabond, villain.

rash[1] *adj* adventurous, audacious, careless, foolhardy, hasty, headlong, headstrong, heedless, incautious, inconsiderate, indiscreet, injudicious, impetuous, impulsive, incautious, precipitate, quick, rapid, reckless, thoughtless, unguarded, unwary, venturesome.
adj antonyms calculating, careful, considered, wary.

rash[2] *n* **1** breaking-out, efflorescence, eruption. **2** epidemic, flood, outbreak, plague, spate.

rashness *n* carelessness, foolhardiness, hastiness, heedlessness, inconsideration, indiscretion, precipitation, recklessness, temerity, venturesomeness.

n antonyms carefulness, cautiousness.

rate¹ *vb* appraise, compute, estimate, value. • *n* **1** cost, price. **2** class, degree, estimate, rank, value, valuation, worth. **3** proportion, ration. **4** assessment, charge, impost, tax.

rate² *vb* abuse, berate, censure, chide, criticize, find fault, reprimand, reprove, scold.

ratify *vb* **1** confirm, corroborate, endorse, establish, seal, settle, substantiate. **2** approve, bind, consent, sanction.

vb antonyms reject, repudiate.

ration *vb* apportion, deal, distribute, dole, restrict. • *n* allowance, portion, quota, share.

rational *adj* **1** intellectual, reasoning. **2** equitable, fair, fit, just, moderate, natural, normal, proper, reasonable, right. **3** discreet, enlightened, intelligent, judicious, sagacious, sensible, sound, wise.

adj antonyms crazy, illogical, irrational.

raucous *adj* harsh, hoarse, husky, rough.

ravage *vb* consume, desolate, despoil, destroy, devastate, harry, overrun, pillage, plunder, ransack, ruin, sack, spoil, strip, waste. • *n* desolation, despoilment, destruction, devastation, havoc, pillage, plunder, rapine, ruin, spoil, waste.

ravenous *adj* devouring, ferocious, gluttonous, greedy, insatiable, omnivorous, ravening, rapacious, voracious.

ravine *n* canyon, cleft, defile, gap, gorge, gulch, gully, pass.

raving *adj* delirious, deranged, distracted, frantic, frenzied, furious, infuriated, mad, phrenetic, raging. • *n* delirium, frenzy, fury, madness, rage.

ravish *vb* **1** abuse, debauch, defile, deflower, force, outrage, violate. **2** captivate, charm, delight, enchant, enrapture, entrance, overjoy, transport. **3** abduct, kidnap, seize, snatch, strip.

raw *adj* **1** fresh, inexperienced, unpractised, unprepared, unseasoned, untried, unskilled. **2** crude, green, immature, unfinished, unripe. **3** bare, chafed, excoriated, galled, sensitive, sore. **4** bleak, chilly, cold, cutting, damp, piercing, windswept. **5** uncooked.

adj antonyms cooked, experienced, refined.

ray *n* beam, emanation, gleam, moonbeam, radiance, shaft, streak, sunbeam.

raze *vb* **1** demolish, destroy, dismantle, extirpate, fell, level, overthrow, ruin, subvert.

2 efface, erase, obliterate.

reach *vb* **1** extend, stretch. **2** grasp, hit, strike, touch. **3** arrive at, attain, gain, get, obtain, win. • *n* capability, capacity, grasp.

readily *adv* **1** easily, promptly, quickly. **2** cheerfully, willingly.

readiness *n* **1** alacrity, alertness, expedition, quickness, promptitude, promptness. **2** aptitude, aptness, dexterity, easiness, expertness, facility, quickness, skill. **3** preparation, preparedness, ripeness. **4** cheerfulness, disposition, eagerness, ease, willingness.

ready *vb* arrange, equip, organize, prepare. • *adj* **1** alert, expeditious, prompt, quick, punctual, speedy. **2** adroit, apt, clever, dextrous, expert, facile, handy, keen, nimble, prepared, prompt, ripe, quick, sharp, skilful, smart. **3** cheerful, disposed, eager, free, inclined, willing. **4** accommodating, available, convenient, near, handy. **5** easy, facile, fluent, offhand, opportune, short, spontaneous.

adj antonyms unprepared, unready.

real *adj* **1** absolute, actual, certain, literal, positive, practical, substantial, substantive, veritable. **2** authentic, genuine, true. **3** essential, internal, intrinsic.

adj antonyms imaginary, unreal.

realize *vb* **1** accomplish, achieve, discharge, effect, effectuate, perfect, perform. **2** apprehend, comprehend, experience, recognize, understand. **3** externalize, substantiate. **4** acquire, earn, gain, get, net, obtain, produce, sell.

reality *n* actuality, certainty, fact, truth, verity.

really *adv* absolutely, actually, certainly, indeed, positively, truly, verily, veritably.

reap *vb* acquire, crop, gain, gather, get, harvest, obtain, receive.

rear¹ *adj* aft, back, following, hind, last. • *n* **1** background, reverse, setting. **2** heel, posterior, rear end, rump, stern, tail. **2** path, trail, train, wake.

adj antonym front.

n antonym front.

rear² *vb* **1** construct, elevate, erect, hoist, lift, raise. **2** cherish, educate, foster, instruct, nourish, nurse, nurture, train. **3** breed, grow. **4** rouse, stir up.

reason *vb* argue, conclude, debate, deduce, draw from, infer, intellectualize, syllogize, think, trace. • *n* **1** faculty, intellect, intelligence, judgement, mind, principle, sanity, sense, thinking, understanding. **2** account, argument, basis, cause, consideration, excuse, explanation, gist, ground, motive, occasion, pretence, proof. **3** aim, design, end, object, purpose. **4** argument, reasoning. **5** common sense, reasonableness, wisdom. **6** equity, fairness, justice, right. **7** exposition, rationale, theory.

reasonable *adj* **1** equitable, fair, fit, honest, just, proper, rational, right, suitable. **2** enlightened, intelligent, judicious, sagacious, sensible, wise. **3** considerable, fair, moderate, tolerable. **4** credible, intellectual, plausible, well-founded. **5** sane, sober, sound. **6** cheap, inexpensive, low-priced.

adj antonyms crazy, extravagant, irrational, outrageous, unreasonable.

rebate *vb* **1** abate, bate, blunt, deduct, diminish, lessen, reduce. **2** cut, pare, rabbet. • *n* **1** decrease, decrement, diminution, lessening. **2** allowance, deduction, discount, reduction.

rebel *vb* mutiny, resist, revolt, strike. • *adj* insubordinate, insurgent, mutinous, rebellious. • *n* insurgent, mutineer, traitor.

rebellion *n* anarchy, insubordination, insurrection, mutiny, resistance, revolt, revolution, uprising.

rebellious *adj* contumacious, defiant, disloyal, disobedient, insubordinate, intractable, obstinate, mutinous, rebel, refractory, seditious.

adj antonyms obedient, submissive.

rebuff *vb* check, chide, oppose, refuse, reject, repel, reprimand, resist, snub. • *n* check, defeat, discouragement, opposition, rejection, resistance, snub.

rebuke *vb* blame, censure, chide, lecture, upbraid, reprehend, reprimand, reprove, scold, silence. • *n* **1** blame, censure, chiding, expostulation, remonstrance, reprimand, reprehension, reproach, reproof, reproval. **2** affliction, chastisement, punishment.

vb antonyms compliment, praise.

n antonyms compliment, praise.

recall *vb* **1** abjure, abnegate, annul, cancel, countermand, deny, nullify, overrule, recant, repeal, repudiate, rescind, retract, revoke, swallow, withdraw. **2** commemorate, recollect, remember, retrace, review, revive. • *n* **1** abjuration, abnegation, annulment, cancellation, nullification,

recantation, repeal, repudiation, rescindment, retraction, revocation, withdrawal. **2** memory, recollection, remembrance, reminiscence.

recant *vb* abjure, annul, disavow, disown, recall, renounce, repudiate, retract, revoke, unsay.

recapitulate *vb* epitomize, recite, rehearse, reiterate, repeat, restate, review, summarize.

recede *vb* desist, ebb, retire, regress, retreat, retrograde, return, withdraw.

vb antonyms advance, proceed.

receive *vb* **1** accept, acquire, derive, gain, get, obtain, take. **2** admit, shelter, take in. **3** entertain, greet, welcome. **4** allow, permit, tolerate. **5** adopt, approve, believe, credit, embrace, follow, learn, understand. **6** accommodate, carry, contain, hold, include, retain. **7** bear, encounter, endure, experience, meet, suffer, sustain.

vb antonyms donate, give.

recent *adj* **1** fresh, new, novel. **2** latter, modern, young. **3** deceased, foregoing, late, preceding, retiring.

adj antonyms dated, old, out-of-date.

reception *n* **1** acceptance, receipt, receiving. **2** entertainment, greeting, welcome. **3** levee, soiree, party. **4** admission, credence. **5** belief, credence, recognition.

recess *n* **1** alcove, corner, depth, hollow, niche, nook, privacy, retreat, seclusion. **2** break, holiday, intermission, interval, respite, vacation. **3** recession, retirement, retreat, withdrawal.

reciprocal *adj* alternate, commutable, complementary, correlative, correspondent, mutual.

recital *n* **1** rehearsal, repetition, recitation. **2** account, description, detail, explanation, narration, relation, statement, telling.

recite *vb* **1** declaim, deliver, rehearse, repeat. **2** describe, mention, narrate, recount, relate, tell. **3** count, detail, enumerate, number, recapitulate.

reckless *adj* breakneck, careless, desperate, devil-may-care, flighty, foolhardy, giddy, harebrained, headlong, heedless, inattentive, improvident, imprudent, inconsiderate, indifferent, indiscreet, mindless, negligent, rash, regardless, remiss, thoughtless, unconcerned, unsteady, volatile, wild.

adj antonyms calculating, careful, cautious.

reckon *vb* **1** calculate, cast, compute, consider, count, enumerate, guess, number. **2** account, class, esteem, estimate, regard, repute, value.

reckoning *n* **1** calculation, computation, consideration, counting. **2** account, bill, charge, estimate, register, score. **3** arrangement, settlement.

reclaim *vb* **1** amend, correct, reform. **2** recover, redeem, regenerate, regain, reinstate, restore. **3** civilize, tame.

recline *vb* couch, lean, lie, lounge, repose, rest.

recluse *adj* cloistered, hermitic, hermitical, reclusive, solitary, unsocial, withdrawn. • *n* ascetic, hermit, loner, monk, solitary.

reclusive *adj* recluse, retired, secluded, sequestered, sequestrated, solitary.

recognition *n* **1** identification, memory, recollection, remembrance. **2** acknowledgement, appreciation, avowal, comprehension, confession, notice. **3** allowance, concession.

recognize *vb* **1** apprehend, identify, perceive, remember. **2** acknowledge, admit, avow, confess, own. **3** allow, concede, grant. **4** greet, salute.

recoil *vb* **1** react, rebound, reverberate. **2** retire, retreat, withdraw. **3** blench, fail, falter, quail, shrink. • *n* backstroke, boomerang, elasticity, kick, reaction, rebound, repercussion, resilience, revulsion, ricochet, shrinking.

recollect *vb* recall, remember, reminisce.

recollection *n* memory, remembrance, reminiscence.

recommend *vb* **1** approve, commend, endorse, praise, sanction. **2** commit. **3** advise, counsel, prescribe, suggest.

vb antonyms disapprove, veto.

recommendation *n* advocacy, approbation, approval, commendation, counsel, credential, praise, testimonial.

n antonyms disapproval, veto.

recompense *vb* **1** compensate, remunerate, repay, requite, reward, satisfy. **2** indemnify, redress, reimburse. • *n* **1** amends, compensation, indemnification, indemnity, remuneration, repayment, reward, satisfaction. **2** requital, retribution.

reconcilable *adj* **1** appeasable, forgiving, placable. **2** companionable, congruous, consistent.

reconcile *vb* **1** appease, conciliate, pacify,

placate, propitiate, reunite. **2** content, harmonize, regulate. **3** adjust, compose, heal, settle.

vb antonym estrange.

recondite *adj* concealed, dark, hidden, mystic, mystical, obscure, occult, secret, transcendental.

record *vb* chronicle, enter, note, register. • *n* **1** account, annals, archive, chronicle, diary, docket, enrolment, entry, file, list, minute, memoir, memorandum, memorial, note, proceedings, register, registry, report, roll, score. **2** mark, memorial, relic, trace, track, trail, vestige. **3** memory, remembrance. **4** achievement, career, history.

recount *vb* describe, detail, enumerate, mention, narrate, particularize, portray, recite, relate, rehearse, report, tell.

recover *vb* **1** recapture, reclaim, regain. **2** rally, recruit, repair, retrieve. **3** cure, heal, restore, revive. **4** redeem, rescue, salvage, save. **5** convalesce, recuperate.

vb antonyms forfeit, lose, worsen.

recreant *adj* **1** base, cowardly, craven, dastardly, faint-hearted, mean-spirited, pusillanimous, yielding. **2** apostate, backsliding, faithless, false, perfidious, treacherous, unfaithful, untrue. • *n* **1** coward, dastard. **2** apostate, backslider, renegade.

recreation *n* amusement, cheer, diversion, entertainment, fun, game, leisure, pastime, play, relaxation, sport.

recreational *adj* amusing, diverting, entertaining, refreshing, relaxing, relieving.

recruit *vb* **1** repair, replenish. **2** recover, refresh, regain, reinvigorate, renew, renovate, restore, retrieve, revive, strengthen, supply. • *n* auxiliary, beginner, helper, learner, novice, tyro.

rectify *vb* adjust, amend, better, correct, emend, improve, mend, redress, reform, regulate, straighten.

rectitude *n* conscientiousness, equity, goodness, honesty, integrity, justice, principle, probity, right, righteousness, straightforwardness, uprightness, virtue.

recumbent *adj* **1** leaning, lying, prone, prostrate, reclining. **2** idle, inactive, listless, reposing.

recur *vb* reappear, resort, return, revert.

recusancy *n* dissent, heresy, heterodoxy, nonconformity.

redeem *vb* **1** reform, regain, repurchase, retrieve. **2** free, liberate, ransom, rescue, save. **3** deliver, reclaim, recover, reinstate. **4** atone, compensate for, recompense. **5** discharge, fulfil, keep, perform, satisfy.

redemption *n* **1** buying, compensation, recovery, repurchase, retrieval. **2** deliverance, liberation, ransom, release, rescue, salvation. **3** discharge, fulfilment, performance.

redolent *adj* aromatic, balmy, fragrant, odoriferous, odorous, scented, sweet, sweet-smelling.

redoubtable *adj* awful, doughty, dreadful, formidable, terrible, valiant.

redound *vb* accrue, conduce, contribute, result, tend.

redress *vb* **1** amend, correct, order, rectify, remedy, repair. **2** compensate, ease, relieve. • *n* abatement, amends, atonement, compensation, correction, cure, indemnification, rectification, repair, righting, remedy, relief, reparation, satisfaction.

reduce *vb* **1** bring. **2** form, make, model, mould, remodel, render, resolve, shape. **3** abate, abbreviate, abridge, attenuate, contract, curtail, decimate, decrease, diminish, lessen, minimize, shorten, thin. **4** abase, debase, degrade, depress, dwarf, impair, lower, weaken. **5** capture, conquer, master, overpower, overthrow, subject, subdue, subjugate, vanquish. **6** impoverish, ruin. **7** resolve, solve.

vb antonyms boost, fatten, increase, upgrade.

redundant *adj* **1** copious, excessive, exuberant, fulsome, inordinate, lavish, needless, overflowing, overmuch, plentiful, prodigal, superabundant, replete, superfluous, unnecessary, useless. **2** diffuse, periphrastic, pleonastic, tautological, verbose, wordy.

adj antonyms concise, essential, necessary.

reel[1] *n* **1** capstan, winch, windlass. **2** bobbin, spool.

reel[2] *vb* **1** falter, flounder, heave, lurch, pitch, plunge, rear, rock, roll, stagger, sway, toss, totter, tumble, wallow, welter, vacillate. **2** spin, swing, turn, twirl, wheel, whirl. • *n* gyre, pirouette, spin, turn, twirl, wheel, whirl.

re-establish *vb* re-found, rehabilitate, reinstall, reinstate, renew, renovate, replace, restore.

refer *vb* **1** commit, consign, direct, leave, relegate, send, submit. **2** ascribe, assign, attribute, impute. **3** appertain, belong,

concern, pertain, point, relate, respect, touch. **4** appeal, apply, consult. **5** advert, allude, cite, quote.

referee *vb* arbitrate, judge, umpire. • *n* arbiter, arbitrator, judge, umpire.

reference *n* **1** concern, connection, regard, respect. **2** allusion, ascription, citation, hint, intimation, mark, reference, relegation.

refine *vb* **1** clarify, cleanse, defecate, fine, purify. **2** cultivate, humanize, improve, polish, rarefy, spiritualize.

refined *adj* **1** courtly, cultured, genteel, polished, polite. **2** discerning, discriminating, fastidious, sensitive. **3** filtered, processed, purified.

adj antonyms brutish, coarse, earthy, rude, vulgar.

refinement *n* **1** clarification, filtration, purification, sublimation. **2** betterment, improvement. **3** delicacy, cultivation, culture, elegance, elevation, finish, gentility, good breeding, polish, politeness, purity, spirituality, style.

n antonyms coarseness, earthiness, vulgarity.

reflect *vb* **1** copy, imitate, mirror, reproduce. **2** cogitate, consider, contemplate, deliberate, meditate, muse, ponder, ruminate, study, think.

reflection *n* **1** echo, shadow. **2** cogitation, consideration, contemplation, deliberation, idea, meditation, musing, opinion, remark, rumination, thinking, thought. **3** aspersion, blame, censure, criticism, disparagement, reproach, slur.

reflective *adj* **1** reflecting, reflexive. **2** cogitating, deliberating, musing, pondering, reasoning, thoughtful.

reform *vb* **1** amend, ameliorate, better, correct, improve, mend, meliorate, rectify, reclaim, redeem, regenerate, repair, restore. **2** reconstruct, remodel, reshape. • *n* amendment, correction, progress, reconstruction, rectification, reformation.

reformation *n* **1** amendment, emendation, improvement, reform. **2** adoption, conversion, redemption. **3** refashioning, regeneration, reproduction, reconstruction.

refractory *adj* cantankerous, contumacious, cross-grained, disobedient, dogged, headstrong, heady, incoercible, intractable, mulish, obstinate, perverse, recalcitrant, self-willed, stiff, stubborn, sullen, ungovernable, unmanageable, unruly, unyielding.

adj antonyms co-operative, malleable, obedient.

refrain[1] *vb* abstain, cease, desist, forbear, stop, withhold.

refrain[2] *n* chorus, music, song vocal, melody.

refresh *vb* air, brace, cheer, cool, enliven, exhilarate, freshen, invigorate, reanimate, recreate, recruit, reinvigorate, revive, regale, slake.

vb antonyms exhaust, tire.

refreshing *adj* comfortable, cooling, grateful, invigorating, pleasant, reanimating, restful, reviving.

adj antonyms exhausting, tiring.

refuge *n* asylum, covert, harbour, haven, protection, retreat, safety, sanction, security, shelter.

refulgent *adj* bright, brilliant, effulgent, lustrous, radiant, resplendent, shining.

refund *vb* reimburse, repay, restore, return. • *n* reimbursement, repayment.

refuse[1] *n* chaff, discard, draff, dross, dregs, garbage, junk, leavings, lees, litter, lumber, offal, recrement, remains, rubbish, scoria, scum, sediment, slag, sweepings, trash, waste.

vb antonyms accept, allow.

refuse[2] *vb* 1 decline, deny, withhold. 2 disallow, disavow, exclude, rebuff, reject, renege, renounce, repel, repudiate, repulse, revoke, veto.

refute *vb* confute, defeat, disprove, overcome, overthrow, rebut, repel, silence.

regain *vb* recapture, recover, re-obtain, repossess, retrieve.

regal *adj* imposing, imperial, kingly, noble, royal, sovereign.

regale *vb* 1 delight, entertain, gratify, refresh. 2 banquet, feast.

regard *vb* 1 behold, gaze, look, notice, mark, observe, remark, see, view, watch. 2 attend to, consider, heed, mind, respect. 3 esteem, honour, revere, reverence, value. 4 account, believe, estimate, deem, hold, imagine, reckon, suppose, think, treat, use. • *n* 1 aspect, gaze, look, view. 2 attention, attentiveness, care, concern, consideration, heed, notice, observance. 3 account, reference, relation, respect. 4 admiration, affection, attachment, deference, esteem, estimation, favour, honour, interest, liking, love, respect, rever-

ence, sympathy, value. 5 account, eminence, note, reputation, repute. 6 condition, matter, point.

vb antonyms despise, disregard.

n antonyms contempt, disapproval, disregard.

regardful *adj* attentive, careful, considerate, deferential, heedful, mindful, observing, thoughtful, watchful.

regarding *prep* concerning, respecting, touching.

regardless *adj* careless, disregarding, heedless, inattentive, indifferent, mindless, neglectful, negligent, unconcerned, unmindful, unobservant. • *adv* however, irrespectively, nevertheless, nonetheless, notwithstanding.

adj antonyms attentive, heedful, regardful.

regenerate *vb* 1 reproduce. 2 renovate, revive. 3 change, convert, renew, sanctify. • *adj* born-again, converted, reformed, regenerated.

regime *n* administration, government, rule.

region *n* 1 climate, clime, country, district, division, latitude, locale, locality, province, quarter, scene, territory, tract. 2 area, neighbourhood, part, place, portion, spot, space, sphere, terrain, vicinity.

register *vb* delineate, portray, record, show. • *n* 1 annals, archive, catalogue, chronicle, list, record, roll, schedule. 2 clerk, registrar, registry. 3 compass, range.

regret *vb* 1 bewail, deplore, grieve, lament, repine, sorrow. 2 bemoan, repent, mourn, rue. • *n* 1 concern, disappointment, grief, lamentation, rue, sorrow, trouble. 2 compunction, contrition, penitence, remorse, repentance, repining, self-condemnation, self-reproach.

regular *adj* 1 conventional, natural, normal, ordinary, typical. 2 correct, customary, cyclic, established, fixed, habitual, periodic, periodical, recurring, reasonable, rhythmic, seasonal, stated, usual. 3 steady, constant, uniform, even. 4 just, methodical, orderly, punctual, systematic, unvarying. 5 complete, genuine, indubitable, out-and-out, perfect, thorough. 6 balanced, consistent, symmetrical.

adj antonyms irregular, sporadic, unconventional.

regulate *vb* 1 adjust, arrange, dispose, order, organize, settle, standardize, time, systematize. 2 conduct, control, direct, govern, guide, manage, rule.

regulation *adj* customary, mandatory, official, required, standard. • *n* adjustment, arrangement, control, disposal, disposition, law, management, order, ordering, precept, rule, settlement.

rehabilitate *vb* 1 reinstate, re-establish, restore. 2 reconstruct, reconstitute, reintegrate, reinvigorate, renew, renovate.

rehearsal *n* 1 drill, practice, recital, recitation, repetition. 2 account, history, mention, narration, narrative, recounting, relation, statement, story, telling.

rehearse *vb* 1 recite, repeat. 2 delineate, depict, describe, detail, enumerate, narrate, portray, recapitulate, recount, relate, tell.

reign *vb* administer, command, govern, influence, predominate, prevail, rule. • *n* control, dominion, empire, influence, power, royalty, sovereignty, power, rule, sway.

reimburse *vb* 1 refund, repay, restore. 2 compensate, indemnify, requite, satisfy.

rein *vb* bridle, check, control, curb, guide, harness, hold, restrain, restrict. • *n* bridle, check, curb, harness, restraint, restriction.

reinforce *vb* augment, fortify, strengthen.

vb antonyms undermine, weaken.

reinstate *vb* re-establish, rehabilitate, reinstall, replace, restore.

reject *vb* 1 cashier, discard, dismiss, eject, exclude, pluck. 2 decline, deny, disallow, despise, disapprove, disbelieve, rebuff, refuse, renounce, repel, repudiate, scout, slight, spurn, veto. • *n* cast-off, discard, failure, refusal, repudiation.

vb antonyms accept, select.

rejoice *vb* 1 cheer, delight, enliven, enrapture, exhilarate, gladden, gratify, please, transport. 2 crow, exult, delight, gloat, glory, jubilate, triumph, vaunt.

rejoin *vb* answer, rebut, respond, retort.

relate *vb* 1 describe, detail, mention, narrate, recite, recount, rehearse, report, tell. 2 apply, connect, correlate.

relation *n* 1 account, chronicle, description, detail, explanation, history, mention, narration, narrative, recital, rehearsal, report, statement, story, tale. 2 affinity, application, bearing, connection, correlation, dependency, pertinence, relationship. 3 concern, reference, regard, respect. 4 alliance, nearness, propinquity, rapport. 5 blood, consanguinity, kin, kindred, kinship, relationship. 6 kinsman, kinswoman, relative.

relax *vb* 1 loose, loosen, slacken, unbrace. 2 debilitate, enervate, enfeeble, prostrate, unbrace, unstring, weaken. 3 abate, diminish, lessen, mitigate, reduce, remit. 4 amuse, divert, ease, entertain, recreate, unbend.

vb antonyms intensify, tighten.

release *vb* 1 deliver, discharge, disengage, exempt, extricate, free, liberate, loose, unloose. 2 acquit, discharge, quit, relinquish, remit. • *n* 1 deliverance, discharge, freedom, liberation. 2 absolution, dispensation, excuse, exemption, exoneration. 3 acquaintance, clearance.

vb antonyms check, detain.

n antonym detention.

relentless *adj* cruel, hard, impenitent, implacable, inexorable, merciless, obdurate, pitiless, rancorous, remorseless, ruthless, unappeasable, uncompassionate, unfeeling, unforgiving, unmerciful, unpitying, unrelenting, unyielding, vindictive.

adj antonyms submissive, yielding.

relevant *adj* applicable, appropriate, apposite, apt, apropos, fit, germane, pertinent, proper, relative, suitable.

adj antonym irrelevant.

reliable *adj* authentic, certain, constant, dependable, sure, trustworthy, trusty, unfailing.

adj antonyms doubtful, suspect, unreliable, untrustworthy.

reliance *n* assurance, confidence, credence, dependence, hope, trust.

relic *n* 1 keepsake, memento, memorial, remembrance, souvenir, token, trophy. 2 trace, vestige.

relics *npl* 1 fragments, leavings, remainder, remains, remnants, ruins, scraps. 2 body, cadaver, corpse, remains.

relict *n* dowager, widow.

relief *n* 1 aid, alleviation, amelioration, assistance, assuagement, comfort, deliverance, ease, easement, help, mitigation, reinforcement, respite, rest, succour, softening, support. 2 indemnification, redress, remedy. 3 embossment, projection, prominence, protrusion. 4 clearness, distinction, perspective, vividness.

relieve *vb* 1 aid, comfort, help, spell, succour, support, sustain. 2 abate, allay, alleviate, assuage, cure, diminish, ease, lessen, lighten, mitigate, remedy, remove, soothe.

3 indemnify, redress, right, repair. 4 disengage, free, release, remedy, rescue.
vb antonyms aggravate, intensify.

religious *adj* 1 devotional, devout, god-fearing, godly, holy, pious, prayerful, spiritual. 2 conscientious, exact, rigid, scrupulous, strict. 3 canonical, divine, theological.
adj antonyms irreligious, lax, ungodly.

relinquish *vb* 1 abandon, desert, forsake, forswear, leave, quit, renounce, resign, vacate. 2 abdicate, cede, forbear, forgo, give up, surrender, yield.
n antonyms keep, retain.

relish *vb* 1 appreciate, enjoy, like, prefer. 2 season, flavour, taste. • *n* 1 appetite, appreciation, enjoyment, fondness, gratification, gusto, inclination, liking, partiality, predilection, taste, zest. 2 cast, flavour, manner, quality, savour, seasoning, sort, tang, tinge, touch. 3 appetizer, condiment.

reluctance *n* aversion, backwardness, disinclination, dislike, loathing, repugnance, unwillingness.
n antonyms eagerness, willingness.

reluctant *adj* averse, backward, disinclined, hesitant, indisposed, loath, unwilling.
adj antonyms eager, willing.

rely *vb* confide, count, depend, hope, lean, reckon, repose, trust.

remain *vb* 1 abide, continue, endure, last. 2 exceed, persist, survive. 3 abide, continue, dwell, halt, inhabit, rest, sojourn, stay, stop, tarry, wait.
vb antonyms depart, go, leave.

remainder *n* balance, excess, leavings, remains, remnant, residue, rest, surplus.

remark *vb* 1 heed, notice, observe, regard. 2 comment, express, mention, observe, say, state, utter. • *n* 1 consideration, heed, notice, observation, regard. 2 annotation, comment, gloss, note, stricture. 3 assertion, averment, comment, declaration, saying, statement, utterance.

remarkable *adj* conspicuous, distinguished, eminent, extraordinary, famous, notable, noteworthy, noticeable, pre-eminent, rare, singular, strange, striking, uncommon, unusual, wonderful.
adj antonyms average, commonplace, ordinary.

remedy *vb* 1 cure, heal, help, palliate, relieve. 2 amend, correct, rectify, redress, repair, restore, retrieve. • *n* 1 antidote, antitoxin, corrective, counteractive, cure, help,

medicine, nostrum, panacea, restorative, specific. 2 redress, reparation, restitution, restoration. 3 aid, assistance, relief.

remembrance *n* 1 recollection, reminiscence, retrospection. 2 keepsake, memento, memorial, memory, reminder, souvenir, token. 3 consideration, regard, thought.

reminiscence *n* memory, recollection, remembrance, retrospective.

remiss *adj* 1 backward, behindhand, dilatory, indolent, languid, lax, lazy, slack, slow, tardy. 2 careless, dilatory, heedless, idle, inattentive, neglectful, negligent, shiftless, slothful, thoughtless.
adj antonyms careful, scrupulous.

remission *n* 1 abatement, decrease, diminution, lessening, mitigation, moderation, reduction, relaxation. 2 cancellation, discharge, release, relinquishment. 3 intermission, interruption, pause, rest, stop, stoppage, suspense, suspension. 4 absolution, acquittal, excuse, exoneration, forgiveness, indulgence, pardon.

remit *vb* 1 replace, restore, return. 2 abate, bate, diminish, relax. 3 release. 4 absolve, condone, excuse, forgive, overlook, pardon. 5 relinquish, resign, surrender. 6 consign, forward, refer, send, transmit. • *n* authorization, brief, instructions, orders.

remnant *n* 1 remainder, remains, residue, rest, trace. 2 fragment, piece, scrap.

remorse *n* compunction, contrition, penitence, qualm, regret, repentance, reproach, self-reproach, sorrow.

remorseless *adj* cruel, barbarous, hard, harsh, implacable, inexorable, merciless, pitiless, relentless, ruthless, savage, uncompassionate, unmerciful, unrelenting.
adj antonyms remorseful, sorry.

remote *adj* 1 distant, far, out-of-the-way. 2 alien, far-fetched, foreign, inappropriate, unconnected, unrelated. 3 abstracted, separated. 4 inconsiderable, slight. 5 isolated, removed, secluded, sequestrated.
adj antonyms adjacent, close, nearby, significant.

removal *n* 1 abstraction, departure, dislodgement, displacement, relegation, remove, shift, transference. 2 elimination, extraction, withdrawal. 3 abatement, destruction. 4 discharge, dismissal, ejection, expulsion.

remove *vb* 1 carry, dislodge, displace, shift, transfer, transport. 2 abstract, extract, withdraw. **3** abate, banish, destroy, suppress. **4** cashier, depose, discharge, dismiss, eject, expel, oust, retire. **5** depart, move.

remunerate *vb* compensate, indemnify, pay, recompense, reimburse, repay, requite, reward, satisfy.

remuneration *n* compensation, earnings, indemnity, pay, payment, recompense, reimbursement, reparation, repayment, reward, salary, wages.

remunerative *adj* **1** gainful, lucrative, paying, profitable. **2** compensatory, recompensing, remuneratory, reparative, requiting, rewarding.

rend *vb* break, burst, cleave, crack, destroy, dismember, dissever, disrupt, divide, fracture, lacerate, rive, rupture, sever, shiver, snap, split, sunder, tear.

render *vb* **1** restore, return, surrender. **2** assign, deliver, give, present. **3** afford, contribute, furnish, supply, yield. **4** construe, interpret, translate.

rendition *n* **1** restitution, return, surrender. **2** delineation, exhibition, interpretation, rendering, representation, reproduction. **3** translation, version.

renegade *adj* apostate, backsliding, disloyal, false, outlawed, rebellious, recreant, unfaithful. • *n* **1** apostate, backslider, recreant, turncoat. **2** deserter, outlaw, rebel, revolter, traitor. **3** vagabond, wretch.

n antonyms adherent, disciple, follower.

renew *vb* **1** rebuild, recreate, re-establish, refit, refresh, rejuvenate, renovate, repair, replenish, restore, resuscitate, revive. **2** continue, recommence, repeat. **3** iterate, reiterate. **4** regenerate, transform.

renounce *vb* **1** abjure, abnegate, decline, deny, disclaim, disown, forswear, neglect, recant, repudiate, reject, slight. **2** abandon, abdicate, drop, forgo, forsake, desert, leave, quit, relinquish, resign.

renovate *vb* **1** reconstitute, re-establish, refresh, refurbish, renew, restore, revamp. **2** reanimate, recreate, regenerate, reproduce, resuscitate, revive, revivify.

renown *n* celebrity, distinction, eminence, fame, figure, glory, honour, greatness, name, note, notability, notoriety, reputation, repute.

n antonyms anonymity, obscurity.

renowned *adj* celebrated, distinguished, eminent, famed, famous, honoured, illustrious, remarkable, wonderful.

adj antonyms anonymous, obscure, unknown.

rent[1] *n* **1** breach, break, crack, cleft, crevice, fissure, flaw, fracture, gap, laceration, opening, rift, rupture, separation, split, tear. **2** schism.

rent[2] *vb* hire, lease, let. • *n* income, rental, revenue.

repair[1] *vb* **1** mend, patch, piece, refit, retouch, tinker, vamp. **2** correct, recruit, restore, retrieve. • *n* mending, refitting, renewal, reparation, restoration.

repair[2] *vb* betake oneself, go, move, resort, turn.

repairable *adj* curable, recoverable, reparable, restorable, retrievable.

reparable *adj* curable, recoverable, repairable, restorable, retrievable.

reparation *n* **1** renewal, repair, restoration. **2** amends, atonement, compensation, correction, indemnification, recompense, redress, requital, restitution, satisfaction.

repay *vb* **1** refund, reimburse, restore, return. **2** compensate, recompense, remunerate, reward, satisfy. **3** avenge, retaliate, revenge.

repeal *vb* abolish, annul, cancel, recall, rescind, reverse, revoke. • *n* abolition, abrogation, annulment, cancellation, rescission, reversal, revocation.

vb antonyms enact, establish.

n antonyms enactment, establishment.

repeat *vb* **1** double, duplicate, iterate. **2** cite, narrate, quote, recapitulate, recite, rehearse. **3** echo, renew, reproduce. • *n* duplicate, duplication, echo, iteration, recapitulation, reiteration, repetition.

repel *vb* **1** beat, disperse, repulse, scatter. **2** check, confront, oppose, parry, rebuff, resist, withstand. **3** decline, refuse, reject. **4** disgust, revolt, sicken.

vb antonym attract.

repellent *adj* abhorrent, disgusting, forbidding, repelling, repugnant, repulsive, revolting, uninviting.

adj antonym attractive.

repent *vb* atone, regret, relent, rue, sorrow.

repentance *n* compunction, contriteness, contrition, penitence, regret, remorse, self-accusation, self-condemnation, self-reproach.

repentant *adj* contrite, penitent, regretful, remorseful, rueful, sorrowful, sorry.

adj antonym unrepentant.

repercussion *n* **1** rebound, recoil, reverberation. **2** backlash, consequence, result.

repetition *n* **1** harping, iteration, recapitulation, reiteration. **2** diffuseness, redundancy, tautology, verbosity. **3** narration, recital, rehearsal, relation, retailing. **4** recurrence, renewal.

repine *vb* croak, complain, fret, grumble, long, mope, murmur.

replace *vb* **1** re-establish, reinstate, reset. **2** refund, repay, restore. **3** succeed, supersede, supplant.

replenish *vb* **1** fill, refill, renew, re-supply. **2** enrich, furnish, provide, store, supply.

replete *adj* abounding, charged, exuberant, fraught, full, glutted, gorged, satiated, well-stocked.

repletion *n* abundance, exuberance, fullness, glut, profusion, satiation, satiety, surfeit.

replica *n* autograph, copy, duplicate, facsimile, reproduction.

reply *vb* answer, echo, rejoin, respond. • *n* acknowledgement, answer, rejoinder, repartee, replication, response, retort.

report *vb* **1** announce, annunciate, communicate, declare. **2** advertise, broadcast, bruit, describe, detail, herald, mention, narrate, noise, promulgate, publish, recite, relate, rumour, state, tell. **3** minute, record. • *n* **1** account, announcement, communication, declaration, statement. **2** advice, description, detail, narration, narrative, news, recital, story, tale, talk, tidings. **3** gossip, hearsay, rumour. **4** clap, detonation, discharge, explosion, noise, repercussion, sound. **5** fame, reputation, repute. **6** account, bulletin, minute, note, record, statement.

repose[1] *vb* **1** compose, recline, rest, settle. **2** couch, lie, recline, sleep, slumber. **3** confide, lean. • *n* **1** quiet, recumbence, recumbency, rest, sleep, slumber. **2** breathing time, inactivity, leisure, respite, relaxation. **3** calm, ease, peace, peacefulness, quietness, quietude, stillness, tranquillity.

repose[2] *vb* **1** place, put, stake. **2** deposit, lodge, reposit, store.

repository *n* conservatory, depository, depot, magazine, museum, receptacle, repertory, **storehouse**, storeroom, thesaurus, treasury, vault.

reprehend *vb* accuse, blame, censure, chide, rebuke, reprimand, reproach, reprove, upbraid.

reprehensible *adj* blameable, blameworthy, censurable, condemnable, culpable, reprovable.
adj antonyms creditable, good, praiseworthy.

reprehension *n* admonition, blame, censure, condemnation, rebuke, reprimand, reproof.

represent *vb* **1** exhibit, express, show. **2** delineate, depict, describe, draw, portray, sketch. **3** act, impersonate, mimic, personate, personify. **4** exemplify, illustrate, image, reproduce, symbolize, typify.

representation *n* **1** delineation, exhibition, show. **2** impersonation, personation, simulation. **3** account, description, narration, narrative, relation, statement. **4** image, likeness, model, portraiture, resemblance, semblance. **5** sight, spectacle. **6** expostulation, remonstrance.

representative *adj* **1** figurative, illustrative, symbolic, typical. **2** delegated, deputed, representing. • *n* agent, commissioner, delegate, deputy, emissary, envoy, legate, lieutenant, messenger, proxy, substitute.
adj antonyms atypical, unrepresentative.

repress *vb* **1** choke, crush, dull, overcome, overpower, silence, smother, subdue, suppress, quell. **2** bridle, chasten, chastise, check, control, curb, restrain. **3** appease, calm, quiet.

reprimand *vb* admonish, blame, censure, chide, rebuke, reprehend, reproach, reprove, upbraid. • *n* admonition, blame, censure, rebuke, reprehension, reproach, reprobation, reproof, reproval.

reprint *vb* republish. • *n* **1** reimpression, republication. **2** copy.

reproach[1] *vb* **1** blame, censure, rebuke, reprehend, reprimand, reprove, upbraid. **2** abuse, accuse, asperse, condemn, defame, discredit, disparage, revile, traduce, vilify. • *n* **1** abuse, blame, censure, condemnation, contempt, contumely, disapprobation, disapproval, expostulation, insolence, invective, railing, rebuke, remonstrance, reprobation, reproof, reviling, scorn, scurrility, upbraiding, vilification. **2** abasement, discredit, disgrace, dishonour, disrepute, indignity, ignominy, infamy, insult, obloquy, odium, offence, opprobrium, scandal, shame, slur, stigma.

reproachful *adj* **1** abusive, censorious, condemnatory, contemptuous, contumelious, damnatory, insolent, insulting, offensive, opprobrious, railing, reproving, sacrifice, scolding, scornful, scurrilous, upbraiding, vituperative. **2** base, discreditable, disgraceful, dishonourable, disreputable, infamous, scandalous, shameful, vile.

reprobate *vb* **1** censure, condemn, disapprove, discard, reject, reprehend. **2** disallow. **3** abandon, disown. • *adj* abandoned, base, castaway, corrupt, depraved, graceless, hardened, irredeemable, lost, profligate, shameless, vile, vitiated, wicked. • *n* caitiff, castaway, miscreant, outcast, rascal, scamp, scoundrel, sinner, villain.

reproduce *vb* **1** copy, duplicate, emulate, imitate, print, repeat, represent. **2** breed, generate, procreate, propagate.

reproof *n* admonition, animadversion, blame, castigation, censure, chiding, condemnation, correction, criticism, lecture, monition, objurgation, rating, rebuke, reprehension, reprimand, reproach, reproval, upbraiding.

n antonym praise.

reprove *vb* admonish, blame, castigate, censure, chide, condemn, correct, criticize, inculpate, lecture, objurgate, rate, rebuke, reprimand, reproach, scold, upbraid.

reptilian *adj* abject, crawling, creeping, grovelling, low, mean, treacherous, vile, vulgar.

repudiate *vb* abjure, deny, disavow, discard, disclaim, disown, nullify, reject, renounce.

repugnance *n* **1** contrariety, contrariness, incompatibility, inconsistency, irreconcilability, irreconcilableness, unsuitability, unsuitableness. **2** contest, opposition, resistance, struggle. **3** antipathy, aversion, detestation, dislike, hatred, hostility, reluctance, repulsion, unwillingness.

n antonyms liking, pleasure.

repugnant *adj* **1** incompatible, inconsistent, irreconcilable. **2** adverse, antagonistic, contrary, hostile, inimical, opposed, opposing, unfavourable. **3** detestable, distasteful, offensive, repellent, repulsive.

repulse *vb* check, defeat, refuse, reject, repel. • *n* **1** repelling, repulsion. **2** denial, refusal. **3** disappointment, failure.

repulsion *n* abhorrence, antagonism, anticipation, aversion, discard, disgust, dislike,

hatred, hostility, loathing, rebuff, rejection, repugnance, repulse, spurning.

repulsive *adj* abhorrent, cold, disagreeable, disgusting, forbidding, frigid, harsh, hateful, loathsome, nauseating, nauseous, odious, offensive, repellent, repugnant, reserved, revolting, sickening, ugly, unpleasant.

adj antonyms friendly, pleasant.

reputable *adj* creditable, estimable, excellent, good, honourable, respectable, worthy.

adj antonyms disreputable, infamous.

reputation *n* **1** account, character, fame, mark, name, repute. **2** celebrity, credit, distinction, eclat, esteem, estimation, glory, honour, prestige, regard, renown, report, respect. **3** notoriety.

repute *vb* account, consider, deem, esteem, estimate, hold, judge, reckon, regard, think.

n antonym infamy.

request *vb* ask, beg, beseech, call, claim, demand, desire, entreat, pray, solicit, supplicate. • *n* asking, entreaty, importunity, invitation, petition, prayer, requisition, solicitation, suit, supplication.

require *vb* **1** beg, beseech, bid, claim, crave, demand, dun, importune, invite, pray, requisition, request, sue, summon. **2** need, want. **3** direct, enjoin, exact, order, prescribe.

requirement *n* **1** claim, demand, exigency, market, need, needfulness, requisite, requisition, request, urgency, want. **2** behest, bidding, charge, command, decree, exaction, injunction, mandate, order, precept.

n antonym inessential.

requisite *adj* essential, imperative, indispensable, necessary, needful, needed, required. • *n* essential, necessity, need, requirement.

adj antonyms inessential, optional.

n antonym inessential.

requite *vb* **1** compensate, pay, remunerate, reciprocate, recompense, repay, reward, satisfy. **2** avenge, punish, retaliate, satisfy.

rescind *vb* abolish, abrogate, annul, cancel, countermand, quash, recall, repeal, reverse, revoke, vacate, void.

vb antonym enforce.

rescue *vb* deliver, extricate, free, liberate, preserve, ransom, recapture, recover, redeem, release, retake, save. • *n* deliverance, extrication, liberation, redemption, release, salvation.

vb antonym capture.

n antonym capture.

research *vb* analyse, examine, explore, inquire, investigate, probe, study. • *n* analysis, examination, exploration, inquiry, investigation, scrutiny, study.

resemblance *n* **1** affinity, agreement, analogy, likeness, semblance, similarity, similitude. **2** counterpart, facsimile, image, representation.

n antonym dissimilarity.

resemble *vb* **1** compare, liken. **2** copy, counterfeit, imitate.

vb antonym differ from.

resentful *adj* angry, bitter, choleric, huffy, hurt, irascible, irritable, malignant, revengeful, sore, touchy.

adj antonym contented.

resentment *n* acrimony, anger, annoyance, bitterness, choler, displeasure, dudgeon, fury, gall, grudge, heartburning, huff, indignation, ire, irritation, pique, rage, soreness, spleen, sulks, umbrage, vexation, wrath.

n antonym contentment.

reservation *n* **1** reserve, suppression. **2** appropriation, booking, exception, restriction, saving. **3** proviso, salvo. **4** custody, park, reserve, sanctuary.

reserve *vb* hold, husband, keep, retain, store. • *adj* alternate, auxiliary, spare, substitute. • *n* **1** reservation. **2** aloofness, backwardness, closeness, coldness, concealment, constraint, suppression, reservedness, retention, restraint, reticence, uncommunicativeness, unresponsiveness. **3** coyness, demureness, modesty, shyness, taciturnity. **4** park, reservation, sanctuary.

reserved *adj* **1** coy, demure, modest, shy, taciturn. **2** aloof, backward, cautious, cold, distant, incommunicative, restrained, reticent, self-controlled, unsociable, unsocial. **3** bespoken, booked, excepted, held, kept, retained, set apart, taken, withheld.

reside *vb* abide, domicile, domiciliate, dwell, inhabit, live, lodge, remain, room, sojourn, stay.

residence *n* **1** inhabitance, inhabitancy, sojourn, stay, stop, tarrying. **2** abode, domicile, dwelling, habitation, home, house, lodging, mansion.

residue *n* **1** leavings, remainder, remains, remnant, residuum, rest. **2** excess, overplus, surplus.

n antonym core.

resign *vb* abandon, abdicate, abjure, cede, commit, disclaim, forego, forsake, leave, quit, relinquish, renounce, surrender, yield.

vb antonyms join, maintain.

resignation *n* **1** abandonment, abdication, relinquishment, renunciation, retirement, surrender. **2** acquiescence, compliance, endurance, forbearance, fortitude, long-sufferance, patience, submission, sufferance.

n antonym resistance.

resist *vb* assail, attack, baffle, block, check, confront, counteract, disappoint, frustrate, hinder, impede, impugn, neutralize, obstruct, oppose, rebel, rebuff, stand against, stem, stop, strive, thwart, withstand.

vb antonyms accept, submit.

resolute *adj* bold, constant, decided, determined, earnest, firm, fixed, game, hardy, inflexible, persevering, pertinacious, relentless, resolved, staunch, steadfast, steady, stout, stouthearted, sturdy, tenacious, unalterable, unbending, undaunted, unflinching, unshaken, unwavering, unyielding.

adj antonym irresolute.

resolution *n* **1** boldness, disentanglement, explication, unravelling. **2** backbone, constancy, courage, decision, determination, earnestness, energy, firmness, fortitude, grit, hardihood, inflexibility, intention, manliness, pluck, perseverance, purpose, relentlessness, resolve, resoluteness, stamina, steadfastness, steadiness, tenacity.

n antonym indecision.

resolve *vb* **1** analyse, disperse, scatter, separate, reduce. **2** change, dissolve, liquefy, melt, reduce, transform. **3** decipher, disentangle, elucidate, explain, interpret, unfold, solve, unravel. **4** conclude, decide, determine, fix, intend, purpose, will. • *n* **1** conclusion, decision, determination, intention, will. **2** declaration, resolution.

vb antonyms blend, waver.

n antonym indecision.

resonant *adj* booming, clangorous, resounding, reverberating, ringing, roaring, sonorous, thundering, vibrant.

resort *vb* **1** frequent, haunt. **2** assemble,

congregate, convene, go, repair. • *n* **1** application, expedient, recourse. **2** haunt, refuge, rendezvous, retreat, spa. **3** assembling, confluence, concourse, meeting. **4** recourse, reference.
vb antonym avoid.

resound *vb* **1** echo, re-echo, reverberate, ring. **2** celebrate, extol, praise, sound.

resource *n* **1** dependence, resort. **2** appliance, contrivance, device, expedient, instrumentality, means, resort.
n antonym unimaginativeness.

resources *npl* capital, funds, income, money, property, reserve, supplies, wealth.

respect *vb* **1** admire, esteem, honour, prize, regard, revere, reverence, spare, value, venerate. **2** consider, heed, notice, observe. • *n* **1** attention, civility, courtesy, consideration, deference, estimation, homage, honour, notice, politeness, recognition, regard, reverence, veneration. **2** consideration, favour, goodwill, kind. **3** aspect, bearing, connection, feature, matter, particular, point, reference, regard, relation.
vb antonym scorn.
n antonym disrespect.

respects *npl* compliments, greetings, regards.

respectable *adj* **1** considerable, estimable, honourable, presentable, proper, upright, worthy. **2** adequate, moderate. **3** tolerable.
adj antonyms disreputable, miserly, unseemly.

respectful *adj* ceremonious, civil, complaisant, courteous, decorous, deferential, dutiful, formal, polite.
adj antonym disrespectful.

respire *vb* breathe, exhale, live.

respite *vb* delay, relieve, reprieve. • *n* **1** break, cessation, delay, intermission, interval, pause, recess, rest, stay, stop. **2** forbearance, postponement, reprieve.

resplendent *adj* beaming, bright, brilliant, effulgent, lucid, glittering, glorious, gorgeous, luminous, lustrous, radiant, shining, splendid.

respond *vb* **1** answer, reply, rejoin. **2** accord, correspond, suit.

response *n* answer, replication, rejoinder, reply, retort.
n antonym query.

responsible *adj* accountable, amenable, answerable, liable, trustworthy.
adj antonym irresponsible.

rest[1] *vb* **1** cease, desist, halt, hold, pause, repose, stop. **2** breathe, relax, unbend. **3** repose, sleep, slumber. **4** lean, lie, lounge, perch, recline, ride. **5** acquiesce, confide, trust. **6** confide, rely, trust. **7** calm, comfort, ease. • *n* **1** fixity, immobility, inactivity, motionlessness, quiescence, quiet, repose. **2** hush, peace, peacefulness, quietness, relief, security, stillness, tranquillity. **3** cessation, intermission, interval, lull, pause, relaxation, respite, stop, stay. **4** siesta, sleep, slumber. **5** death. **6** brace, stay, support. **7** axis, fulcrum, pivot.
vb antonyms change, continue, work.
n antonyms action, activity, restlessness.

rest[2] *vb* be left, remain. • *n* **1** balance, remainder, remnant, residuum. **2** overplus, surplus.

restaurant *n* bistro, café, cafeteria, chophouse, eatery, eating house, pizzeria, trattoria.

restitution *n* **1** restoration, return. **2** amends, compensation, indemnification, recompense, rehabilitation, remuneration, reparation, repayment, requital, satisfaction.

restive *adj* **1** mulish, obstinate, stopping, stubborn, unwilling. **2** impatient, recalcitrant, restless, uneasy, unquiet.
adj antonyms calm, relaxed.

restless *adj* **1** disquieted, disturbed, restive, sleepless, uneasy, unquiet, unresting. **2** changeable, inconstant, irresolute, unsteady, vacillating. **3** active, astatic, roving, transient, unsettled, unstable, wandering. **4** agitated, fidgety, fretful, turbulent.
adj antonyms calm, relaxed.

restoration *n* **1** recall, recovery, re-establishment, reinstatement, reparation, replacement, restitution, return. **2** reconsideration, redemption, reintegration, renewal, renovation, repair, resuscitation, revival. **3** convalescence, cure, recruitment, recuperation.

restorative *adj* curative, invigorating, recuperative, remedial, restoring, stimulating. • *n* corrective, curative, cure, healing, medicine, remedy, reparative, stimulant.

restore *vb* **1** refund, repay, return. **2** caulk, cobble, emend, heal, mend, patch, reintegrate, re-establish, rehabilitate, reinstate, renew, repair, replace, retrieve. **3** cure, heal, recover, revive. **4** resuscitate.
vb antonyms damage, remove, weaken.

restrain *vb* **1** bridle, check, coerce, confine, constrain, curb, debar, govern, hamper, hinder, hold, keep, muzzle, picket, prevent, repress, restrict, rule, subdue, tie, withhold. **2** abridge, circumscribe, narrow.

vb antonyms encourage, liberate.

restraint *n* **1** bridle, check, coercion, control, compulsion, constraint, curb, discipline, repression, suppression. **2** arrest, deterrence, hindrance, inhibition, limitation, prevention, prohibition, restriction, stay, stop. **3** confinement, detention, imprisonment, shackles. **4** constraint, stiffness, reserve, unnaturalness.

n antonym freedom.

restrict *vb* bound, circumscribe, confine, limit, qualify, restrain, straiten.

vb antonyms broaden, encourage, free.

restriction *n* ,1 confinement, limitation. **2** constraint, restraint. **3** reservation, reserve.

n antonyms broadening, encouragement, freedom.

result *vb* **1** accrue, arise, come, ensue, flow, follow, issue, originate, proceed, spring, rise. **2** end, eventuate, terminate. • *n* **1** conclusion, consequence, deduction, inference, outcome. **2** corollary, effect, end, event, eventuality, fruit, harvest, issue, product, sequel, termination. **3** decision, determination, finding, resolution, resolve, solution, verdict.

vb antonyms begin, cause.

n antonyms beginning, cause.

resume *vb* continue, recommence, renew, restart, summarize.

vb antonym cease.

résumé *n* abstract, curriculum vitae, epitome, recapitulation, summary, synopsis.

resuscitate *vb* quicken, reanimate, renew, resurrect, restore, revive, revivify.

retain *vb* **1** detain, hold, husband, keep, preserve, recall, recollect, remember, reserve, save, withhold. **2** engage, maintain.

vb antonyms release, spend.

retainer *n* adherent, attendant, dependant, follower, hanger-on, servant.

retaliate *vb* avenge, match, repay, requite, retort, return, turn.

vb antonyms accept, submit.

retaliation *n* boomerang, counterstroke, punishment, repayment, requital, retribution, revenge.

retard *vb* **1** check, clog, hinder, impede, obstruct, slacken. **2** adjourn, defer, delay, postpone, procrastinate.

vb antonym advance.

reticent *adj* close, reserved, secretive, silent, taciturn, uncommunicative.

adj antonyms communicative, forward, frank.

retinue *n* bodyguard, cortege, entourage, escort, followers, household, ménage, suite, tail, train.

adj antonyms communicative, forward, frank.

retire *vb* **1** discharge, shelve, superannuate, withdraw. **2** depart, leave, resign, retreat.

vb antonyms enter, join.

retired *adj* **1** abstracted, removed, withdrawn. **2** apart, private, secret, sequestrated, solitary.

retirement *n* isolation, loneliness, privacy, retreat, seclusion, solitude, withdrawal.

retiring *adj* coy, demure, diffident, modest, reserved, retreating, shy, withdrawing.

adj antonyms assertive, forward.

retort *vb* answer, rejoin, reply, respond. • *n* **1** answer, rejoinder, repartee, reply, response. **2** crucible, jar, vessel, vial.

retract *vb* **1** reverse, withdraw. **2** abjure, cancel, disavow, recall, recant, revoke, unsay.

retreat *vb* **1** recoil, retire, withdraw. **2** recede. • *n* **1** departure, recession, recoil, retirement, withdrawal. **2** privacy, seclusion, solitude. **3** asylum, cove, den, habitat, haunt, niche, recess, refuge, resort, shelter.

vb antonym advance.

n antonyms advance, company, limelight.

retrench *vb* **1** clip, curtail, cut, delete, dock, lop, mutilate, pare, prune. **2** abridge, decrease, diminish, lessen. **3** confine, limit. **4** economize, encroach.

vb antonym increase.

retribution *n* compensation, desert, judgement, nemesis, penalty, recompense, repayment, requital, retaliation, return, revenge, reward, vengeance.

retrieve *vb* recall, recover, recoup, recruit, re-establish, regain, repair, restore.

vb antonym lose.

retrograde *vb* decline, degenerate, recede, retire, retrocede. • *adj* backward, inverse, retrogressive, unprogressive.

adj antonym progressive.

retrospect *n* recollection, re-examination, reminiscence, re-survey, review, survey.

return *vb* **1** reappear, recoil, recur, revert. **2** answer, reply, respond. **3** recriminate, retort. **4** convey, give, communicate, reciprocate, recompense, refund, remit, repay, report, requite, send, tell, transmit. **5** elect. • *n* **1** payment, reimbursement, remittance, repayment. **2** recompense, recovery, recurrence, renewal, repayment, requital, restitution, restoration, reward. **3** advantage, benefit, interest, profit, rent, yield.
vb antonyms leave, take.
n antonyms disappearance, expense, loss, payment.

reunion *n* **1** assemblage, assembly, gathering, meeting, re-assembly. **2** rapprochement, reconciliation.

reveal *vb* announce, communicate, confess, declare, disclose, discover, display, divulge, expose, impart, open, publish, tell, uncover, unmask, unseal, unveil.
vb antonym hide.

revel *vb* **1** carouse, disport, riot, roister, tipple. **2** delight, indulge, luxuriate, wanton. • *n* carousal, feast, festival, saturnalia, spree.

revelry *n* bacchanal, carousal, carouse, debauch, festivity, jollification, jollity, orgy, revel, riot, rout, saturnalia, wassail.
n antonym sobriety.

revenge *vb* avenge, repay, requite, retaliate, vindicate. • *n* malevolence, rancour, reprisal, requital, retaliation, retribution, vengeance, vindictiveness.

revengeful *adj* implacable, malevolent, malicious, malignant, resentful, rancorous, spiteful, vengeful, vindictive.

revenue *n* fruits, income, produce, proceeds, receipts, return, reward, wealth.
n antonym expenditure.

reverberate *vb* echo, re-echo, resound, return.

revere *vb* adore, esteem, hallow, honour, reverence, venerate, worship.
vb antonyms despise, scorn.

reverence *vb* adore, esteem, hallow, honour, revere, venerate, worship. • *n* adoration, awe, deference, homage, honour, respect, veneration, worship.
vb antonyms despise, scorn.
n antonym scorn.

reverential *adj* deferential, humble, respectful, reverent, submissive.

reverse *vb* **1** invert, transpose. **2** overset, overthrow, overturn, quash, subvert, undo,

unmake. **3** annul, countermand, repeal, rescind, retract, revoke. **4** back, back up, retreat. • *adj* back, converse, contrary, opposite, verso. • *n* **1** back, calamity, check, comedown, contrary, counterpart, defeat, opposite, tail. **2** change, vicissitude. **3** adversity, affliction, hardship, misadventure, mischance, misfortune, mishap, trial.
vb antonym enforce.

revert *vb* **1** repel, reverse. **2** backslide, lapse, recur, relapse, return.
vb antonym progress.

review *vb* **1** inspect, overlook, reconsider, re-examine, retrace, revise, survey. **2** analyse, criticize, discuss, edit, judge, scrutinize, study. • *n* **1** reconsideration, re-examination, re-survey, retrospect, survey. **2** analysis, digest, synopsis. **3** commentary, critique, criticism, notice, review, scrutiny, study.

revile *vb* abuse, asperse, backbite, calumniate, defame, execrate, malign, reproach, slander, traduce, upbraid, vilify.
vb antonym praise.

revise *vb* **1** reconsider, re-examine, review. **2** alter, amend, correct, edit, overhaul, polish.

revive *vb* **1** reanimate, reinspire, reinvigorate, resuscitate, revitalize, revivify. **2** animate, cheer, comfort, invigorate, quicken, reawaken, recover, refresh, renew, renovate, rouse, strengthen. **3** reawake, recall.
vb antonyms suppress, weary.

revocation *n* abjuration, recall, recantation, repeal, retraction, reversal.

revoke *vb* abolish, abrogate, annul, cancel, countermand, invalidate, quash, recall, recant, repeal, repudiate, rescind, retract.
vb antonym enforce.

revolt *vb* **1** desert, mutiny, rebel, rise. **2** disgust, nauseate, repel, sicken. • *n* **1** defection, desertion, faithlessness, inconstancy. **2** disobedience, insurrection, mutiny, outbreak, rebellion, sedition, strike, uprising.

revolting *adj* **1** abhorrent, abominable, disgusting, hateful, monstrous, nauseating, nauseous, objectionable, obnoxious, offensive, repulsive, shocking, sickening. **2** insurgent, mutinous, rebellious.
adj antonym pleasant.

revolution *n* **1** coup, disobedience, insurrection, mutiny, outbreak, rebellion, sedition, strike, uprising. **2** change, innovation, reformation, transformation, upheaval.

3 circle, circuit, cycle, lap, orbit, rotation, spin, turn.

revolve *vb* **1** circle, circulate, rotate, swing, turn, wheel. **2** devolve, return. **3** consider, mediate, ponder, ruminate, study.

revulsion *n* **1** abstraction, shrinking, withdrawal. **2** change, reaction, reversal, transition. **3** abhorrence, disgust, loathing, repugnance.

n antonym pleasure.

reward *vb* compensate, gratify, indemnify, pay, punish, recompense, remember, remunerate, require. • *n* **1** compensation, gratification, guerdon, indemnification, pay, recompense, remuneration, requital. **2** bounty, bonus, fee, gratuity, honorarium, meed, perquisite, premium, remembrance, tip. **3** punishment, retribution.

vb antonym punish.

n antonym punishment.

rhythm *n* **1** cadence, lilt, pulsation, swing. **2** measure, metre, number.

ribald *adj* base, blue, coarse, filthy, gross, indecent, lewd, loose, low, mean, obscene, vile.

adj antonym polite.

rich *adj* **1** affluent, flush, moneyed, opulent, prosperous, wealthy. **2** costly, estimable, gorgeous, luxurious, precious, splendid, sumptuous, superb, valuable. **3** delicious, luscious, savoury. **4** abundant, ample, copious, enough, full, plentiful, plenteous, sufficient. **5** fertile, fruitful, luxuriant, productive, prolific. **6** bright, dark, deep, exuberant, vivid. **7** harmonious, mellow, melodious, soft, sweet. **8** comical, funny, humorous, laughable.

adj antonyms harsh, miserly, plain, poor, simple, tasteless, thin, unfertile.

riches *npl* abundance, affluence, fortune, money, opulence, plenty, richness, wealth, wealthiness.

rickety *adj* broken, imperfect, shaky, shattered, tottering, tumbledown, unsteady, weak.

adj antonyms stable, strong.

rid *vb* **1** deliver, free, release. **2** clear, disburden, disencumber, scour, sweep. **3** disinherit, dispatch, dissolve, divorce, finish, sever.

vb antonym burden.

riddance *n* deliverance, disencumberment, extrication, escape, freedom, release, relief.

riddle[1] *vb* explain, solve, unriddle. • *n* conundrum, enigma, mystery, puzzle, rebus.

riddle[2] *vb* sieve, sift, perforate, permeate, spread. • *n* colander, sieve, strainer.

ridge *n* chine, hogback, ledge, saddle, spine, rib, watershed, weal, wrinkle.

ridicule *vb* banter, burlesque, chaff, deride, disparage, jeer, mock, lampoon, rally, satirize, scout, taunt. • *n* badinage, banter, burlesque, chaff, derision, game, gibe, irony, jeer, mockery, persiflage, quip, raillery, sarcasm, satire, sneer, squib, wit.

vb antonym praise.

n antonym praise.

ridiculous *adj* absurd, amusing, comical, droll, eccentric, fantastic, farcical, funny, laughable, ludicrous, nonsensical, odd, outlandish, preposterous, queer, risible, waggish.

adj antonym sensible.

rife *adj* abundant, common, current, general, numerous, plentiful, prevailing, prevalent, replete.

adj antonym scarce.

riffraff *n* horde, mob, populace, rabble, scum, trash.

rifle *vb* despoil, fleece, pillage, plunder, ransack, rob, strip.

rift *vb* cleave, rive, split. • *n* breach, break, chink, cleft, crack, cranny, crevice, fissure, fracture, gap, opening, reft, rent.

n antonym unity.

rig *vb* accoutre, clothe, dress. • *n* **1** costume, dress, garb. **2** equipment, team.

right *vb* adjust, correct, regulate, settle, straighten, vindicate. • *adj* **1** direct, rectilinear, straight. **2** erect, perpendicular, plumb, upright. **3** equitable, even-handed, fair, just, justifiable, honest, lawful, legal, legitimate, rightful, square, unswerving. **4** appropriate, becoming, correct, conventional, fit, fitting, meet, orderly, proper, reasonable, seemly, suitable, well-done. **5** actual, genuine, real, true, unquestionable. **6** dexter, dextral, right-handed. • *adv* **1** equitably, fairly, justly, lawfully, rightfully, rightly. **2** correctly, fitly, properly, suitably, truly. **3** actually, exactly, just, really, truly, well. • *n* **1** authority, claim, liberty, permission, power, privilege, title. **2** equity, good, honour, justice, lawfulness, legality, propriety, reason, righteousness, truth.

adj antonyms left, left-wing, mad, unfit, wrong.

adv antonyms incorrectly, left, unfairly, wrongly.

n antonyms depravity, wrong.

righteous *adj* **1** devout, godly, good, holy, honest, incorrupt, just, pious, religious, saintly, uncorrupt, upright, virtuous. **2** equitable, fair, right, rightful.

adj antonym unrighteous.

n antonym unrighteous.

righteousness *n* equity, faithfulness, godliness, goodness, holiness, honesty, integrity, justice, piety, purity, right, rightfulness, sanctity, uprightness, virtue.

rightful *adj* **1** lawful, legitimate, true. **2** appropriate, correct, deserved, due, equitable, fair, fitting, honest, just, legal, merited, proper, reasonable, suitable.

rigid *adj* **1** firm, hard, inflexible, permanent, stiff, stiffened, unbending, unpliant, unyielding. **2** bristling, erect, precipitous, steep. **3** austere, conventional, correct, exact, formal, harsh, meticulous, precise, rigorous, severe, sharp, stern, strict, unmitigated. **4** cruel.

adj antonym flexible.

rigmarole *n* balderdash, flummery, gibberish, gobbledegook, jargon, nonsense, palaver, trash, twaddle, verbiage.

rigour *n* **1** hardness, inflexibility, rigidity, rigidness, stiffness. **2** asperity, austerity, harshness, severity, sternness. **3** evenness, strictness. **4** inclemency.

rile *vb* anger, annoy, irritate, upset, vex.

vb antonym soothe.

rim *n* brim, brink, border, confine, curb, edge, flange, girdle, margin, ring, skirt.

n antonym centre.

ring[1] *vb* circle, encircle, enclose, girdle, surround. • *n* **1** circle, circlet, girdle, hoop, round, whorl. **2** cabal, clique, combination, confederacy, coterie, gang, junta, league, set.

ring[2] *vb* **1** chime, clang, jingle, knell, peal, resound, reverberate, sound, tingle, toll. **2** call, phone, telephone. • *n* **1** chime, knell, peal, tinkle, toll. **2** call, phone call, telephone call.

riot *vb* carouse, luxuriate, revel. • *n* **1** affray, altercation, brawl, broil, commotion, disturbance, fray, outbreak, pandemonium, quarrel, squabble, tumult, uproar. **2** dissipation, excess, luxury, merrymaking, revelry.

n antonyms calm, order.

riotous *adj* **1** boisterous, luxurious, merry, revelling, unrestrained, wanton. **2** disorderly, insubordinate, lawless, mutinous, rebellious, refractory, seditious, tumultuous, turbulent, ungovernable, unruly, violent.

adj antonyms orderly, restrained.

ripe *adj* **1** advanced, grown, mature, mellow, seasoned, soft. **2** fit, prepared, ready. **3** accomplished, complete, consummate, finished, perfect, perfected.

adj antonyms inopportune, untimely.

ripen *vb* burgeon, develop, mature, prepare.

rise *vb* **1** arise, ascend, clamber, climb, levitate, mount. **2** excel, succeed. **3** enlarge, heighten, increase, swell, thrive. **4** revive. **5** grow, kindle, wax. **6** begin, flow, head, originate, proceed, spring, start. **7** mutiny, rebel, revolt. **8** happen, occur. • *n* **1** ascension, ascent, rising. **2** elevation, grade, hill, slope. **3** beginning, emergence, flow, origin, source, spring. **4** advance, augmentation, expansion, increase.

vb antonyms descend, fall.

n antonyms descent, fall.

risible *adj* amusing, comical, droll, farcical, funny, laughable, ludicrous, ridiculous.

risk *vb* bet, endanger, hazard, jeopardize, peril, speculate, stake, venture, wager. • *n* chance, danger, hazard, jeopardy, peril, venture.

n antonyms certainty, safety.

rite *n* ceremonial, ceremony, form, formulary, ministration, observance, ordinance, ritual, rubric, sacrament, solemnity.

ritual *adj* ceremonial, conventional, formal, habitual, routine, stereotyped. • *n* **1** ceremonial, ceremony, liturgy, observance, rite, sacrament, service. **2** convention, form, formality, habit, practice, protocol.

adj antonyms informal, unusual.

rival *vb* emulate, match, oppose. • *adj* competing, contending, emulating, emulous, opposing. • *n* antagonist, competitor, emulator, opponent.

vb antonym co-operate.

adj antonyms associate, co-operating.

n antonyms associate, colleague, co-worker.

rive *vb* cleave, rend, split.

river *n* affluent, current, reach, stream, tributary.

road *n* course, highway, lane, passage, path, pathway, roadway, route, street, thoroughfare, track, trail, turnpike, way.

roam *vb* jaunt, prowl, ramble, range, rove, straggle, stray, stroll, wander.
vb antonym stay.

roar *vb* **1** bawl, bellow, cry, howl, vociferate, yell. **2** boom, peal, rattle, resound, thunder. • *n* **1** bellow, roaring. **2** rage, resonance, storm, thunder. **3** cry, outcry, shout. **4** laugh, laughter, shout.
vb antonym whisper.
n antonym whisper.

rob *vb* **1** despoil, fleece, pilfer, pillage, plunder, rook, strip. **2** appropriate, deprive, embezzle, plagiarize.
vb antonyms give, provide.

robber *n* bandit, brigand, desperado, depredator, despoiler, footpad, freebooter, highwayman, marauder, pillager, pirate, plunderer, rifler, thief.

robbery *n* depredation, despoliation, embezzlement, freebooting, larceny, peculation, piracy, plagiarism, plundering, spoliation, theft.

robe *vb* array, clothe, dress, invest. • *n* **1** attire, costume, dress, garment, gown, habit, vestment. **2** bathrobe, dressing gown, housecoat.

robust *adj* able-bodied, athletic, brawny, energetic, firm, forceful, hale, hardy, hearty, iron, lusty, muscular, powerful, seasoned, self-assertive, sinewy, sound, stalwart, stout, strong, sturdy, vigorous.
adj antonyms mealy-mouthed, unhealthy, unrealistic, weak.

rock¹ *n* **1** boulder, cliff, crag, reef, stone. **2** asylum, defence, foundation, protection, refuge, strength, support. **3** gneiss, granite, marble, slate, etc.

rock² *vb* **1** calm, cradle, lull, quiet, soothe, still, tranquillize. **2** reel, shake, sway, teeter, totter, wobble.

rogue *n* **1** beggar, vagabond, vagrant. **2** caitiff, cheat, knave, rascal, scamp, scapegrace, scoundrel, sharper, swindler, trickster, villain.
n antonym saint.

roguish *adj* **1** dishonest, fraudulent, knavish, rascally, scoundrelly, tricky. **2** arch, sportive, mischievous, puckish, waggish, wanton.
adj antonyms honest, serious.

role *n* character, function, impersonation, part, task.

roll *vb* **1** gyrate, revolve, rotate, turn, wheel. **2** curl, muffle, swathe, wind. **3** bind, involve, enfold, envelop. **4** flatten, level, smooth,

spread. **5** bowl, drive. **6** trundle, wheel. **7** gybe, lean, lurch, stagger, sway, yaw. **8** billow, swell, undulate. **9** wallow, welter. **10** flow, glide, run. • *n* **1** document, scroll, volume. **2** annals, chronicle, history, record, rota. **3** catalogue, inventory, list, register, schedule. **4** booming, resonance, reverberation, thunder. **5** cylinder, roller.

rollicking *adj* frisky, frolicking, frolicsome, jolly, jovial, lively, swaggering.
adj antonyms restrained, serious.

romance *vb* exaggerate, fantasize. • *n* **1** fantasy, fiction, legend, novel, story, tale. **2** exaggeration, falsehood, lie. **3** ballad, idyll, song.

romantic *adj* **1** extravagant, fanciful, fantastic, ideal, imaginative, sentimental, wild. **2** chimerical, fabulous, fantastic, fictitious, imaginary, improbable, legendary, picturesque, quixotic, sentimental. • *n* dreamer, idealist, sentimentalist, visionary.
adj antonyms humdrum, practical, real, sober, unromantic.
n antonym realist.

romp *vb* caper, gambol, frisk, sport. • *n* caper, frolic, gambol.

room *n* **1** accommodation, capacity, compass, elbowroom, expanse, extent, field, latitude, leeway, play, scope, space, swing. **2** place, stead. **3** apartment, chamber, lodging. **4** chance, occasion, opportunity.

roomy *adj* ample, broad, capacious, comfortable, commodious, expansive, extensive, large, spacious, wide.
adj antonym cramped.

root¹ *vb* **1** anchor, embed, fasten, implant, place, settle. **2** confirm, establish. • *n* **1** base, bottom, foundation. **2** cause, occasion, motive, origin, reason, source. **3** etymon, radical, radix, stem.

root² *vb* **1** destroy, eradicate, extirpate, exterminate, remove, unearth, uproot. **2** burrow, dig, forage, grub, rummage. **3** applaud, cheer, encourage.

rooted *adj* chronic, confirmed, deep, established, fixed, radical.
adj antonyms superficial, temporary.

roseate *adj* **1** blooming, blushing, rose-coloured, rosy, rubicund. **2** hopeful.

rostrum *n* platform, stage, stand, tribune.

rosy *adj* auspicious, blooming, blushing, favourable, flushed, hopeful, roseate, ruddy, sanguine.
adj antonyms depressed, depressing, sad.

rot *vb* corrupt, decay, decompose, degenerate, putrefy, spoil, taint. • *n* corruption, decay, decomposition, putrefaction.

rotary *adj* circular, rotating, revolving, rotatory, turning, whirling.
adj antonym fixed.

rotten *adj* **1** carious, corrupt, decomposed, fetid, putrefied, putrescent, putrid, rank, stinking. **2** defective, unsound. **3** corrupt, deceitful, immoral, treacherous, unsound, untrustworthy.
adj antonyms good, honest, practical, sensible, well.

rotund *adj* **1** buxom, chubby, full, globular, obese, plump, round, stout. **2** fluent, grandiloquent.
adj antonyms flat, gaunt, slim.

roué *n* debauchee, libertine, profligate, rake.

rough *vb* **1** coarsen, roughen. **2** manhandle, mishandle, molest. • *adj* **1** bumpy, craggy, irregular, jagged, rugged, scabrous, scraggy, scratchy, stubby, uneven. **2** approximate, cross-grained, crude, formless, incomplete, knotty, rough-hewn, shapeless, sketchy, uncut, unfashioned, unfinished, unhewn, unpolished, unwrought, vague. **3** bristly, bushy, coarse, disordered, hairy, hirsute, ragged, shaggy, unkempt. **4** austere, bearish, bluff, blunt, brusque, burly, churlish, discourteous, gruff, harsh, impolite, indelicate, rude, surly, uncivil, uncourteous, ungracious, unpolished, unrefined. **5** harsh, severe, sharp, violent. **6** astringent, crabbed, hard, sour, tart. **7** discordant, grating, inharmonious, jarring, raucous, scabrous, unmusical. **8** boisterous, foul, inclement, severe, stormy, tempestuous, tumultuous, turbulent, untamed, violent, wild. **9** acrimonious, brutal, cruel, disorderly, riotous, rowdy, severe, uncivil, unfeeling, ungentle. • *n* **1** bully, rowdy, roughneck, ruffian. **2** draft, outline, sketch, suggestion. **3** unevenness.
adj antonyms accurate, calm, harmonious, mild, polite, smooth, well.

round *vb* **1** curve. **2** circuit, encircle, encompass, surround. • *adj* **1** bulbous, circular, cylindrical, globular, orbed, orbicular, rotund, spherical. **2** complete, considerable, entire, full, great, large, unbroken, whole. **3** chubby, corpulent, plump, stout, swelling. **4** continuous, flowing, harmonious, smooth. **5** brisk, quick. **6** blunt, candid, fair, frank, honest, open, plain, upright. • *adv* around, circularly, circuitously. • *prep* about, around. • *n* **1** bout, cycle, game, lap, revolution, rotation, succession, turn. **2** canon, catch, dance. **3** ball, circle, circumference, cylinder, globe, sphere. **4** circuit, compass, perambulation, routine, tour, watch.
adj antonyms evasive, niggardly, partial, thin.

roundabout *adj* **1** circuitous, circumlocutory, indirect, tortuous. **2** ample, broad, extensive. **3** encircling, encompassing.
adj antonyms direct, straight, straightforward.

rouse *vb* **1** arouse, awaken, raise, shake, wake, waken. **2** animate, bestir, brace, enkindle, excite, inspire, kindle, rally, stimulate, stir, whet. **3** startle, surprise.
vb antonym calm.

rout *vb* **1** beat, conquer, defeat, discomfit, overcome, overpower, overthrow, vanquish. **2** chase away, dispel, disperse, scatter. • *n* **1** defeat, discomfiture, flight, ruin. **2** concourse, multitude, rabble. **3** brawl, disturbance, noise, roar, uproar.
n antonyms calm, win.

route *vb* direct, forward, send, steer. • *n* course, circuit, direction, itinerary, journey, march, road, passage, path, way.

routine *adj* **1** conventional, familiar, habitual, ordinary, standard, typical, usual. **2** boring, dull, humdrum, predictable, tiresome. • *n* beat, custom, groove, method, order, path, practice, procedure, round, rut.
adj antonyms exciting, unusual.

rove *vb* prowl, ramble, range, roam, stray, struggle, stroll, wander.

row¹ *n* **1** file, line, queue, range, rank, series, string, tier. **2** alley, street, terrace.

row² *vb* argue, dispute, fight, quarrel, squabble. • *n* affray, altercation, brawl, broil, commotion, dispute, disturbance, noise, outbreak, quarrel, riot, squabble, tumult, uproar.
n antonym calm.

royal *adj* august, courtly, dignified, generous, grand, imperial, kingly, kinglike, magnanimous, magnificent, majestic, monarchical, noble, princely, regal, sovereign, splendid, superb.

rub *vb* **1** abrade, chafe, grate, graze, scrape. **2** burnish, clean, massage, polish, scour, wipe. **3** apply, put, smear, spread. • *n* **1** caress, massage, polish, scouring, shine, wipe. **2** catch, difficulty, drawback, impediment, obstacle, problem.

rubbish *n* **1** debris, detritus, fragments, refuse, ruins, waste. **2** dregs, dross, garbage, litter, scum, sweepings, trash. **3** baloney, bunk, claptrap, drivel, garbage, gibberish, nonsense.

n antonym find, gem, prize, treasure, valuable; discernment, sense, rationality, wisdom.

rubicund *adj* blushing, erubescent, florid, flushed, red, reddish, ruddy.

rude *adj* **1** coarse, crude, ill-formed, rough, rugged, shapeless, uneven, unfashioned, unformed, unwrought. **2** artless, barbarous, boorish, clownish, ignorant, illiterate, loutish, raw, savage, uncivilized, uncouth, uncultivated, undisciplined, unpolished, ungraceful, unskilful, unskilled, untaught, untrained, untutored, vulgar. **3** awkward, barbarous, bluff, blunt, boorish, brusque, brutal, churlish, gruff, ill-bred, impertinent, impolite, impudent, insolent, insulting, ribald, saucy, uncivil, uncourteous, unrefined. **4** boisterous, fierce, harsh, severe, tumultuous, turbulent, violent. **5** artless, inelegant, rustic, unpolished. **6** hearty, robust.

adj antonyms graceful, polished, polite, smooth.

rudimentary *adj* elementary, embryonic, fundamental, initial, primary, rudimental, undeveloped.

adj antonyms advanced, developed.

rue *vb* deplore, grieve, lament, regret, repent.

vb antonym rejoice.

rueful *adj* dismal, doleful, lamentable, lugubrious, melancholic, melancholy, mournful, penitent, regretful, sad, sorrowful, woeful.

ruffian *n* bully, caitiff, cutthroat, hoodlum, miscreant, monster, murderer, rascal, robber, roisterer, rowdy, scoundrel, villain, wretch.

ruffle *vb* **1** damage, derange, disarrange, dishevel, disorder, ripple, roughen, rumple. **2** agitate, confuse, discompose, disquiet, disturb, excite, harass, irritate, molest, plague, perturb, torment, trouble, vex, worry. **3** cockle, flounce, pucker, wrinkle. • *n* **1** edging, frill, ruff. **2** agitation, bustle, commotion, confusion, contention,

disturbance, excitement, fight, fluster, flutter, flurry, perturbation, tumult.

vb antonym smooth.

rugged *adj* **1** austere, bristly, coarse, crabbed, cragged, craggy, hard, hardy, irregular, ragged, robust, rough, rude, scraggy, severe, seamed, shaggy, uneven, unkempt, wrinkled. **2** boisterous, inclement, stormy, tempestuous, tumultuous, turbulent, violent. **3** grating, harsh, inharmonious, unmusical, scabrous.

adj antonyms easy, refined, smooth.

ruin *vb* **1** crush, damn, defeat, demolish, desolate, destroy, devastate, overthrow, overturn, overwhelm, seduce, shatter, smash, subvert, wreck. **2** beggar, impoverish. • *n* **1** damnation, decay, defeat, demolition, desolation, destruction, devastation, discomfiture, downfall, fall, loss, perdition, prostration, rack, ruination, shipwreck, subversion, undoing, wrack, wreck. **2** bane, mischief, pest.

vb antonyms develop, restore.

n antonyms development, reconstruction.

ruination *n* demolition, destruction, overthrow, ruin, subversion.

ruinous *adj* **1** decayed, demolished, dilapidated. **2** baneful, calamitous, damnatory, destructive, disastrous, mischievous, noisome, noxious, pernicious, subversive, wasteful.

adj antonym beneficial.

rule *vb* **1** bridle, command, conduct, control, direct, domineer, govern, judge, lead, manage, reign, restrain. **2** advise, guide, persuade. **3** adjudicate, decide, determine, establish, settle. **4** obtain, prevail, predominate. • *n* **1** authority, command, control, direction, domination, dominion, empire, government, jurisdiction, lordship, mastery, mastership, regency, reign, sway. **2** behaviour, conduct. **3** habit, method, order, regularity, routine, system. **4** aphorism, canon, convention, criterion, formula, guide, law, maxim, model, precedent, precept, standard, system, test, touchstone. **5** decision, order, prescription, regulation, ruling.

ruler *n* **1** chief, governor, king, lord, master, monarch, potentate, regent, sovereign. **2** director, head, manager, president. **3** controller, guide, rule. **4** straight-edge.

n antonym subject.

ruminate *vb* brood, chew, cogitate, consider,

contemplate, meditate, muse, ponder, reflect, think.

rumour *vb* bruit, circulate, report, tell. • *n* **1** bruit, gossip, hearsay, report, talk. **2** news, report, story, tidings. **3** celebrity, fame, reputation, repute.

rumple *vb* crease, crush, corrugate, crumple, disarrange, dishevel, pucker, ruffle, wrinkle. • *n* crease, corrugation, crumple, fold, pucker, wrinkle.
vb antonym smooth.

run *vb* **1** bolt, career, course, gallop, haste, hasten, hie, hurry, lope, post, race, scamper, scour, scud, scuttle, speed, trip. **2** flow, glide, go, move, proceed, stream. **3** fuse, liquefy, melt. **4** advance, pass, proceed, vanish. **5** extend, lie, spread, stretch. **6** circulate, pass, press. **7** average, incline, tend. **8** flee. **9** pierce, stab. **10** drive, force, propel, push, thrust, turn. **11** cast, form, mould, shape. **12** follow, perform, pursue, take. **13** discharge, emit. **14** direct, maintain, manage. • *n* race, running. **1** course, current, flow, motion, passage, progress, way, wont. **2** continuance, currency, popularity. **3** excursion, gallop, journey, trip, trot. **4** demand, pressure. **5** brook, burn, flow, rill, rivulet, runlet, runnel, streamlet.
vb antonyms stay, stop.

rupture *vb* break, burst, fracture, sever, split. • *n* **1** breach, break, burst, disruption, fracture, split. **2** contention, faction, feud, hostility, quarrel, schism.

rural *adj* agrarian, bucolic, country, pastoral, rustic, sylvan.

ruse *n* artifice, deception, deceit, fraud, hoax, imposture, manoeuvre, sham, stratagem, trick, wile.

rush *vb* attack, career, charge, dash, drive, gush, hurtle, precipitate, surge, sweep, tear. • *n* dash, onrush, onset, plunge, precipitance, precipitancy, rout, stampede, tear.

rust *vb* corrode, decay, degenerate. • *n* blight, corrosion, crust, mildew, must, mould, mustiness.

rustic *adj* **1** country, rural. **2** awkward, boorish, clownish, countrified, loutish, outlandish, rough, rude, uncouth, unpolished, untaught. **3** coarse, countrified, homely, plain, simple, unadorned. **4** artless, honest, unsophisticated. • *n* boor, bumpkin, clown, countryman, peasant, swain, yokel.

ruthless *adj* barbarous, cruel, ferocious, hardhearted, inexorable, inhuman, merciless, pitiless, relentless, remorseless, savage, truculent, uncompassionate, unmerciful, unpitying, unrelenting, unsparing.

S

sable *adj* black, dark, dusky, ebony, sombre.

sabotage *v* **1** damage, destroy, disable, disrupt, subvert, thwart, undermine, vandalize, wreck. **2** spoil, intrude, interrupt. • *n* **1** damage, destruction, disablement, disruption, subversion, vandalism. **2** interference, intrusion, interruption.

sack[1] *n* bag, pouch.

sack[2] *vb* despoil, devastate, pillage, plunder, ravage, spoil. • *n* **1** desolation, despoliation, destruction, devastation, havoc, ravage, sacking, spoliation, waste. **2** booty, plunder, spoil.

sacred *adj* **1** consecrated, dedicated, devoted, divine, hallowed, holy. **2** inviolable, inviolate. **3** sainted, venerable.

adj antonyms mundane, profane, temporal.

sacrifice *vb* forgo, immolate, surrender. • *n* **1** immolation, oblation, offering. **2** destruction, devotion, loss, surrender.

sacrilege *n* desecration, profanation, violation.

sacrilegious *adj* desecrating, impious, irreverent, profane.

sad *adj* blue, dejected, depressed, despondent, dismal, gloomy, grave, grieving, mournful, pensive, sedate, serious, sober, sombre, sorrowful, upset, woeful.

adj antonyms cheerful, fortunate, happy, lucky.

saddle *vb* burden, charge, clog, encumber, load.

sadly *adv* **1** grievously, miserable, mournfully, sorrowfully. **2** badly, calamitously. **3** darkly. **4** gravely, seriously, soberly.

sadness *n* **1** dejection, depression, despondency, melancholy, mournful, sorrow, sorrowfulness. **2** dolefulness, gloominess, grief, mournfulness, sorrow. **3** gravity, sedateness, seriousness.

safe *adj* **1** undamaged, unharmed, unhurt, unscathed. **2** guarded, protected, secure, snug, unexposed. **3** certain, dependable, reliable, sure, trustworthy. **4** good, harmless, sound, whole. • *n* chest, coffer, strongbox.

adj antonyms exposed, harmful, unsafe, vulnerable.

safeguard *vb* guard, protect. • *n* **1** defence, protection, security. **2** convoy, escort, guard, safe-conduct. **3** pass, passport.

vb antonyms endanger, jeopardize.

sagacious *adj* acute, apt, astute, clear-sighted, discerning, intelligent, judicious, keen, penetrating, perspicacious, rational, sage, sharp-witted, wise, shrewd.

sagacity *n* acuteness, astuteness, discernment, ingenuity, insight, penetration, perspicacity, quickness, readiness, sense, sharpness, shrewdness, wisdom.

n antonyms folly, foolishness, obtuseness.

sage *adj* **1** acute, discerning, intelligent, prudent, sagacious, sapient, sensible, shrewd, wise. **2** judicious, well-judged. **3** grave, serious, solemn. • *n* philosopher, pundit, savant.

adj antonym foolish.

n antonym ignoramus.

sailor *n* mariner, navigator, salt, seafarer, seaman, tar.

saintly *adj* devout, godly, holy, pious, religious.

adj antonyms godless, unholy, unrighteous, wicked.

sake *n* **1** end, cause, purpose, reason. **2** account, consideration, interest, regard, respect, score.

saleable *adj* marketable, merchantable, vendible.

salacious *adj* carnal, concupiscent, incontinent, lascivious, lecherous, lewd, libidinous, loose, lustful, prurient, unchaste, wanton.

salary *n* allowance, hire, pay, stipend, wages.

salient *adj* **1** bounding, jumping, leaping. **2** beating, springing, throbbing. **3** jutting, projecting, prominent. **4** conspicuous, remarkable, striking.

saline *adj* briny, salty.

sally *vb* issue, rush. • *n* **1** digression, excursion, sortie, run, trip. **2** escapade, frolic. **3** crank, fancy, jest, joke, quip, quirk, sprightly, witticism.

salt *adj* **1** saline, salted, salty. **2** bitter, pungent, sharp. • *n* **1** flavour, savour, seasoning, smack, relish, taste. **2** humour, piquancy, poignancy, sarcasm, smartness, wit, zest. **3** mariner, sailor, seaman, tar.

salty *adj* **1** briny, saline, salted. **2** colourful, dry, sarcastic, smart, witty.

salubrious *adj* beneficial, benign, healthful, healthy, salutary, sanitary, wholesome.
adj antonyms insalubrious, unwholesome.

salutary *adj* **1** healthy, healthful, helpful, safe, salubrious, wholesome. **2** advantageous, beneficial, good, profitable, serviceable, useful.

salute *vb* accost, address, congratulate, greet, hail, welcome. • *n* address, greeting, salutation.

salvation *n* deliverance, escape, preservation, redemption, rescue, saving.
n antonyms damnation, loss.

same *adj* **1** ditto, identical, selfsame. **2** corresponding, like, similar.
adj antonyms changeable, different, incompatible, inconsistent, variable.

sample *vb* **1** savour, sip, smack, sup, taste. **2** test, try. **3** demonstrate, exemplify, illustrate, instance. • *adj* exemplary, illustrative, representative. • *n* **1** demonstration, exemplification, illustration, instance, piece, specimen. **2** example, model, pattern.

sanctify *vb* **1** consecrate, hallow, purify. **2** justify, ratify, sanction.

sanctimonious *adj* affected, devout, holy, hypocritical, pharisaical, pious, self-righteous.

sanction *vb* **1** authorize, countenance, encourage, support. **2** confirm, ratify. • *n* **1** approval, authority, authorization, confirmation, countenance, endorsement, ratification, support, warranty. **2** ban, boycott, embargo, penalty.
vb antonyms disallow, disapprove, veto.
n antonyms disapproval, veto.

sanctity *n* devotion, godliness, goodness, grace, holiness, piety, purity, religiousness, saintliness.

sanctuary *n* **1** altar, church, shrine, temple. **2** asylum, protection, refuge, retreat, shelter.

sane *adj* healthy, lucid, rational, reasonable, sober, sound.

sang-froid *n* calmness, composure, coolness, imperturbability, indifference, nonchalance, phlegm, unconcern.

sanguinary *adj* **1** bloody, gory, murderous. **2** barbarous, bloodthirsty, cruel, fell, pitiless, savage, ruthless.

sanguine *adj* **1** crimson, florid, red.

2 animated, ardent, cheerful, lively, warm. **3** buoyant, confident, enthusiastic, hopeful, optimistic. **4** full-blooded.

sanitary *adj* clean, curative, healing, healthy, hygienic, remedial, therapeutic, wholesome.
adj antonyms insanitary, unwholesome.

sanity *n* normality, rationality, reason, saneness, soundness.

sapient *adj* acute, discerning, intelligent, knowing, sagacious, sage, sensible, shrewd, wise.

sarcastic *adj* acrimonious, biting, cutting, mordant, sardonic, satirical, sharp, severe, sneering, taunting.

sardonic *adj* bitter, derisive, ironical, malevolent, malicious, malignant, sarcastic.

satanic *adj* devilish, diabolical, evil, false, fiendish, hellish, infernal, malicious.
adj antonyms benevolent, benign, divine, godlike, godly, heavenly, holy.

satellite *adj* dependent, subordinate, tributary, vassal. • *n* attendant, dependant, follower, hanger-on, retainer, vassal.

satiate *vb* **1** fill, sate, satisfy, suffice. **2** cloy, glut, gorge, overfeed, overfill, pall, surfeit.
vb antonyms deprive, dissatisfy, underfeed.

satire *n* burlesque, diatribe, invective, fling, irony, lampoon, pasquinade, philippic, ridicule, sarcasm, skit, squib.

satirical *adj* abusive, biting, bitter, censorious, cutting, invective, ironical, keen, poignant, reproachful, sarcastic, severe, sharp, taunting.

satirize *vb* abuse, censure, lampoon, ridicule.

satisfaction *n* **1** comfort, complacency, contentment, ease, enjoyment, gratification, pleasure, satiety. **2** amends, appeasement, atonement, compensation, indemnification, recompense, redress, remuneration, reparation, requital, reward.
n antonyms discontent, displeasure, dissatisfaction, frustration.

satisfactory *adj* **1** adequate, conclusive, convincing, decisive, sufficient. **2** gratifying, pleasing.
adj antonyms inadequate, unacceptable, unsatisfactory.

satisfy *vb* **1** appease, content, fill, gratify, please, sate, satiate, suffice. **2** indemnify, compensate, liquidate, pay, recompense, remunerate, requite. **3** discharge, settle.

4 assure, convince, persuade. **5** answer, fulfil, meet.

vb antonyms disappoint, dissatisfy, fail, frustrate, thwart.

saturate *vb* drench, fill, fit, imbue, soak, steep, wet.

saturnine *adj* **1** dark, dull, gloomy, grave, heavy, leaden, morose, phlegmatic, sad, sedate, sombre. **2** melancholic, mournful, serious, unhappy. **3** mischievous, naughty, troublesome, vexatious, wicked.

sauce *n* **1** cheekiness, impudence, insolence. **2** appetizer, compound, condiment, relish, seasoning.

saucy *adj* bold, cavalier, disrespectful, flippant, forward, immodest, impertinent, impudent, insolent, pert, rude.

adj antonyms polite, respectful.

saunter *vb* amble, dawdle, delay, dilly-dally, lag, linger, loiter, lounge, stroll, tarry. • *n* amble, stroll, walk.

savage *vb* attack, lacerate, mangle, maul. • *adj* **1** rough, uncultivated, wild. **2** rude, uncivilized, unpolished, untaught. **3** bloodthirsty, feral, ferine, ferocious, fierce, rapacious, untamed, vicious. **4** beastly, bestial, brutal, brutish, inhuman. **5** atrocious, barbarous, barbaric, bloody, brutal, cruel, fell, fiendish, hardhearted, heathenish, merciless, murderous, pitiless, relentless, ruthless, sanguinary, truculent. **6** native, rough, rugged. • *n* barbarian, brute, heathen, vandal.

adj antonyms benign, civilized, humane.

save *vb* **1** keep, liberate, preserve, rescue. **2** salvage, recover, redeem. **3** economize, gather, hoard, husband, reserve, store. **4** hinder, obviate, prevent, spare. • *prep* but, deducting, except.

vb antonyms discard, spend, squander, waste.

saviour *n* defender, deliverer, guardian, protector, preserver, rescuer, saver.

savour *vb* **1** affect, appreciate, enjoy, like, partake, relish. **2** flavour, season. • *n* **1** flavour, gusto, relish, smack, taste. **2** fragrance, odour, smell, scent.

savoury *adj* agreeable, delicious, flavourful, luscious, nice, palatable, piquant, relishing.

saw *n* adage, aphorism, apothegm, axiom, byword, dictum, maxim, precept, proverb, sententious saying.

say *vb* **1** declare, express, pronounce, speak, tell, utter. **2** affirm, allege, argue. **3** recite, rehearse, repeat. **4** assume, presume, suppose. • *n* **1** affirmation, declaration, speech, statement. **2** decision, voice, vote.

saying *n* **1** declaration, expression, observation, remark, speech, statement. **2** adage, aphorism, byword, dictum, maxim, proverb, saw.

scale¹ *n* **1** basin, dish, pan. **2** balance.

scale² *n* flake, lamina, lamella, layer, plate.

scale³ *vb* ascend, climb, escalate, mount. • *n* graduation.

scamp *n* cheat, knave, rascal, rogue, scapegrace, scoundrel, swindler, trickster, villain.

scamper *vb* haste, hasten, hie, run, scud, speed, trip.

scan *vb* examine, investigate, scrutinize, search, sift.

scandal *vb* asperse, defame, libel, traduce. • *n* **1** aspersion, calumny, defamation, obloquy, reproach. **2** discredit, disgrace, dishonour, disrepute, ignominy, infamy, odium, opprobrium, offence, shame.

scandalize *vb* **1** offend. **2** asperse, backbite, calumniate, decry, defame, disgust, lampoon, libel, reproach, revile, satirize, slander, traduce, vilify.

scandalous *adj* **1** defamatory, libellous, opprobrious, slanderous. **2** atrocious, disgraceful, disreputable, infamous, inglorious, ignominious, odious, shameful.

scanty *adj* **1** insufficient, meagre, narrow, scant, small. **2** hardly, scarce, short, slender. **3** niggardly, parsimonious, penurious, scrimpy, skimpy, sparing.

adj antonyms ample, plentiful, substantial.

scar¹ *vb* hurt, mark, wound. • *n* **1** cicatrice, cicatrix, seam. **2** blemish, defect, disfigurement, flaw, injury, mark.

scar² *n* bluff, cliff, crag, precipice.

scarce *adj* **1** deficient, wanting. **2** infrequent, rare, uncommon. • *adv* barely, hardly, scantily.

adj antonyms common, copious, plentiful.

scarcely *adv* barely, hardly, scantily.

scarcity *n* **1** dearth, deficiency, insufficiency, lack, want. **2** infrequency, rareness, rarity, uncommonness.

n antonyms abundance, enough, glut, plenty, sufficiency.

scare *vb* affright, alarm, appal, daunt, fright, frighten, intimidate, shock, startle, terrify. • *n* alarm, fright, panic, shock, terror.

vb antonym reassure.

n antonym reassurance.

scathe *vb* blast, damage, destroy, injure, harm, haste. • *n* damage, harm, injury, mischief, waste.

scatter *vb* 1 broadcast, sprinkle, strew. 2 diffuse, disperse, disseminate, dissipate, distribute, separate, spread. 3 disappoint, dispel, frustrate, overthrow.

vb antonyms collect, concentrate.

scene *n* 1 display, exhibition, pageant, representation, show, sight, spectacle, view. 2 place, situation, spot. 3 arena, stage.

scent *vb* 1 breathe in, inhale, nose, smell, sniff. 2 detect, smell out, sniff out. 3 aromatize, perfume. • *n* aroma, balminess, fragrance, odour, perfume, smell, redolence.

n antonym stink.

sceptic *n* doubter, freethinker, questioner, unbeliever.

sceptical *adj* doubtful, doubting, dubious, hesitating, incredulous, questioning, unbelieving.

scepticism *n* doubt, dubiety, freethinking, incredulity, unbelief.

schedule *vb* line up, list, plan, programme, tabulate. • *n* 1 document, scroll. 2 catalogue, inventory, list, plan, record, register, roll, table, timetable.

scheme *vb* contrive, design, frame, imagine, plan, plot, project. • *n* 1 plan, system, theory. 2 cabal, conspiracy, contrivance, design, device, intrigue, machination, plan, plot, project, stratagem. 3 arrangement, draught, diagram, outline.

schism *n* 1 division, separation, split. 2 discord, disunion, division, faction, separation.

scholar *n* 1 disciple, learner, pupil, student. 2 don, fellow, intellectual, pedant, savant.

n antonyms dullard, dunce, ignoramus, illiterate, philistine.

scholarship *n* 1 accomplishments, acquirements, attainments, erudition, knowledge, learning. 2 bursary, exhibition, foundation, grant, maintenance.

scholastic *adj* 1 academic, bookish, lettered, literary. 2 formal, pedantic.

school *vb* 1 drill, educate, exercise, indoctrinate, instruct, teach, train. 2 admonish, control, chide, discipline, govern, reprove, tutor. • *adj* academic, collegiate, institutional, scholastic, schoolish. • *n*

1 academy, college, gymnasium, institute, institution, kindergarten, lyceum, manège, polytechnic, seminary, university. 2 adherents, camarilla, circle, clique, coterie, disciples, followers. 3 body, order, organization, party, sect.

schooling *n* discipline, education, instruction, nurture, teaching, training, tuition.

scintillate *vb* coruscate, flash, gleam, glisten, glitter, sparkle, twinkle.

scoff *vb* 1 deride, flout, jeer, mock, ridicule, taunt. 2 gibe, sneer. • *n* 1 flout, gibe, jeer, sneer, mockery, taunt. 2 derision, ridicule.

scold *vb* 1 berate, blame, censure, chide, rate, reprimand, reprove. 2 brawl, rail, rate, reprimand, upbraid, vituperate. • *n* shrew, termagant, virago, vixen.

vb antonyms commend, praise.

scope *n* 1 aim, design, drift, end, intent, intention, mark, object, purpose, tendency, view. 2 amplitude, field, latitude, liberty, margin, opportunity, purview, range, room, space, sphere, vent. 3 extent, length, span, stretch, sweep.

scorch *vb* blister, burn, char, parch, roast, sear, shrivel, singe.

score *vb* 1 cut, furrow, mark, notch, scratch. 2 charge, note, record. 3 impute, note. 4 enter, register. • *n* 1 incision, mark, notch. 2 account, bill, charge, debt, reckoning. 3 consideration, ground, motive, reason.

scorn *vb* condemn, despise, disregard, disdain, scout, slight, spurn. • *n* 1 contempt, derision, disdain, mockery, slight, sneer. 2 scoff.

vb antonyms admire, respect.

n antonyms admiration, respect.

scornful *adj* contemptuous, defiant, disdainful, contemptuous, regardless.

adj antonyms admiring, complimentary, respectful.

scot-free *adj* 1 untaxed. 2 clear, unhurt, uninjured, safe.

scoundrel *n* cheat, knave, miscreant, rascal, reprobate, rogue, scamp, swindler, trickster, villain.

scour[1] *vb* 1 brighten, buff, burnish, clean, cleanse, polish, purge, scrape, scrub, rub, wash, whiten. 2 rake. 3 efface, obliterate, overrun.

scour[2] *vb* 1 career, course, range, scamper, scud, scuttle. 2 comb, hunt, rake, ransack, rifle, rummage, search.

scourge *vb* **1** lash, whip. **2** afflict, chasten, chastise, correct, punish. **3** harass, torment. • *n* **1** cord, cowhide, lash, strap, thong, whip. **2** affliction, banc, curse, infliction, nuisance, pest, plague, punishment.
n antonyms benefit, blessing, boon, godsend.

scout *vb* **1** contemn, deride, disdain, despise, ridicule, scoff, scorn, sneer, spurn. **2** investigate, probe, search. • *n* escort, lookout, precursor, vanguard.

scowl *vb* frown, glower, lower. • *n* frown, glower, lower.
n antonyms beam, grin, smile.

scraggy *adj* **1** broken, craggy, rough, rugged, scabrous, scragged, uneven. **2** attenuated, bony, emaciated, gaunt, lank, lean, meagre, scrawny, skinny, thin.

scrap[1] *vb* discard, junk, trash. • *n* **1** bit, fragment, modicum, particle, piece, snippet. **2** bite, crumb, morsel, mouthful. **3** debris, junk, litter, rubbish, rubble, trash, waste.
vb antonyms reinstate, restore, resume.

scrap[2] *vb* altercate, bicker, dispute, clash, fight, hassle, quarrel, row, spat, squabble, tiff, tussle, wrangle. • *n* affray, altercation, bickering, clash, dispute, fight, fray, hassle, melee, quarrel, row, run-in, set-to, spat, squabble, tiff, tussle, wrangle.
vb antonym agree.
n antonyms agreement, peace.

scrape *vb* **1** bark, grind, rasp, scuff. **2** accumulate, acquire, collect, gather, save. **3** erase, remove. • *n* difficulty, distress, embarrassment, perplexity, predicament.

scream *vb* screech, shriek, squall, ululate. • *n* cry, outcry, screech, shriek, shrill, ululation.

screen *vb* cloak, conceal, cover, defend, fence, hide, mask, protect, shelter, shroud. • *n* **1** blind, curtain, lattice, partition. **2** defence, guard, protection, shield. **3** cloak, cover, veil, disguise. **4** riddle, sieve.

screw *vb* **1** force, press, pressurize, squeeze, tighten, twist, wrench. **2** oppress, rack. **3** distort. • *n* **1** extortioner, extortionist, miser, scrimp, skinflint. **2** prison guard. **3** sexual intercourse.

scrimmage *n* brawl, melee, riot, scuffle, skirmish.

scrimp *vb* contract, curtail, limit, pinch, reduce, scant, shorten, straiten.
vb antonym spend.

scrimpy *adj* contracted, deficient, narrow, scanty.

scroll *n* inventory, list, parchment, roll, schedule.

scrub[1] *adj* contemptible, inferior, mean, niggardly, scrubby, shabby, small, stunted. • *n* brushwood, underbrush, underwood.

scrub[2] *vb* clean, cleanse, rub, scour, scrape, wash.

scruple *vb* boggle, demur, falter, hesitate, object, pause, stickle, waver. • *n* delicacy, hesitancy, hesitation, nicety, perplexity, qualm.

scrupulous *adj* **1** conscientious, fastidious, nice, precise, punctilious, rigorous, strict. **2** careful, cautious, circumspect, exact, vigilant.
adj antonym careless.

scrutinize *vb* canvass, dissect, examine, explore, investigate, overhaul, probe, search, sift, study.

scrutiny *n* examination, exploration, inquisition, inspection, investigation, search, searching, sifting.

scud *vb* flee, fly, haste, hasten, hie, post, run, scamper, speed, trip.

scuffle *vb* contend, fight, strive, struggle. • *n* altercation, brawl, broil, contest, encounter, fight, fray, quarrel, squabble, struggle, wrangle.

sculpt *vb* **1** carve, chisel, cut, sculpture. **2** engrave, grave.

scurrilous *adj* **1** abusive, blackguardly, contumelious, foul, foul-mouthed, indecent, infamous, insolent, insulting, offensive, opprobrious, reproachful, ribald, vituperative. **2** coarse, gross, low, mean, obscene, vile, vulgar.
adj antonym polite.

scurry *vb* bustle, dash, hasten, hurry, scamper, scud, scutter. • *n* burst, bustle, dash, flurry, haste, hurry, scamper, scud, spurt.
vb antonym stroll.
n antonym calm.

scurvy *adj* **1** scabbed, scabby, scurfy. **2** abject, bad, base, contemptible, despicable, low, mean, pitiful, sorry, vile, vulgar, worthless. **3** malicious, mischievous, offensive.

scuttle[1] *vb* hurry, hustle, run, rush, scamper, scramble, scud, scurry. • *n* dash, drive, flurry, haste, hurry, hustle, race, rush, scamper, scramble, scud, scurry.

scuttle[2] *vb* capsize, founder, go down, sink, overturn, upset. • *n* **1** hatch, hatchway.

seal *vb* close, fasten, secure. **2** attest, authenticate, confirm, establish, ratify, sanction. **3** confine, enclose, imprison. • *n* **1** fastening, stamp, wafer, wax. **2** assurance, attestation, authentication, confirmation, pledge, ratification.

vb antonym unseal.

seamy *adj* disreputable, nasty, seedy, sordid, unpleasant.

sear *vb* blight, brand, cauterize, dry, scorch, wither. • *adj* dried up, dry, sere, withered.

search *vb* **1** examine, explore, ferret, inspect, investigate, overhaul, probe, ransack, scrutinize, sift. **2** delve, hunt, forage, inquire, look, rummage. • *n* examination, exploration, hunt, inquiry, inspection, investigation, pursuit, quest, research, seeking, scrutiny.

searching *adj* **1** close, keen, penetrating, trying. **2** examining, exploring, inquiring, investigating, probing, seeking.

adj antonyms superficial, vague.

seared *adj* callous, graceless, hardened, impenitent, incorrigible, obdurate, shameless, unrepentant.

season *vb* **1** acclimatize, accustom, form, habituate, harden, inure, mature, qualify, temper, train. **2** flavour, spice. • *n* interval, period, spell, term, time, while.

seasonable *adj* appropriate, convenient, fit, opportune, suitable, timely.

seasoning *n* condiment, flavouring, relish, salt, sauce.

seat *vb* establish, fix, locate, place, set, station. • *n* **1** place, site, situation, station. **2** abode, capital, dwelling, house, mansion, residence. **3** bottom, fundament. **4** bench, chair, pew, settle, stall, stool.

secede *vb* apostatize, resign, retire, withdraw.

vb antonyms join, unite with.

secluded *adj* close, covert, embowered, isolated, private, removed, retired, screened, sequestrated, withdrawn.

adj antonyms busy, public.

seclusion *n* obscurity, privacy, retirement, secrecy, separation, solitude, withdrawal.

second[1] *n* instant, jiffy, minute, moment, trice.

second[2] *vb* **1** abet, advance, aid, assist, back, encourage, forward, further, help, promote, support, sustain. **2** approve, favour. • *adj* **1** inferior, second-rate, secondary. **2** following, next, subsequent. **3** additional, extra, other. **4** double, duplicate. • *n* **1** an-

other, other. **2** assistant, backer, supporter.

secondary *adj* collateral, inferior, minor, subsidiary, subordinate. • *n* delegate, deputy, proxy.

adj antonym primary.

secrecy *n* clandestineness, concealment, furtiveness, stealth, surreptitiousness.

secret *adj* **1** close, concealed, covered, covert, cryptic, hid, hidden, mysterious, privy, shrouded, veiled, unknown, unrevealed, unseen. **2** cabbalistic, clandestine, furtive, privy, sly, stealthy, surreptitious, underhand. **3** confidential, private, retired, secluded, unseen. **4** abstruse, latent, mysterious, obscure, occult, recondite, unknown. • *n* confidence, enigma, key, mystery.

adj antonyms open, public.

secretary *n* **1** clerk, scribe, writer. **2** escritoire, writing-desk.

secrete[1] *vb* **1** bury, cache, conceal, disguise, hide, shroud, stash. **2** screen, separate.

vb antonym reveal.

secrete[2] *vb* discharge, emit, excrete, exude, release, secern.

secretive *adj* cautious, close, reserved, reticent, taciturn, uncommunicative, wary.

sect *n* denomination, faction, schism, school.

section *n* cutting, division, fraction, part, piece, portion, segment, slice.

n antonym whole.

secular *adj* civil, laic, laical, lay, profane, temporal, worldly.

adj antonym religious.

secure *vb* **1** guard, protect, safeguard. **2** assure, ensure, guarantee, insure. **3** fasten. **4** acquire, gain, get, obtain, procure. • *adj* **1** assured, certain, confident, sure. **2** insured, protected, safe. **3** fast, firm, fixed, immovable, stable. **4** careless, easy, undisturbed, unsuspecting. **5** heedless, inattentive, incautious, negligent, overconfident.

vb antonyms lose, unfasten.

adj antonyms insecure, uncertain.

security *n* **1** bulwark, defence, guard, palladium, protection, safeguard, safety, shelter. **2** bond, collateral, deposit, guarantee, pawn, pledge, stake, surety, warranty. **3** carelessness, heedlessness, overconfidence, negligence. **4** assurance, assuredness, certainty, confidence, ease.

n antonym insecurity.

sedate *adj* calm, collected, composed, contemplative, cool, demure, grave, placid, philosophical, quiet, serene, serious, sober, still, thoughtful, tranquil, undisturbed, unemotional, unruffled.

adj antonyms flippant, hasty, undignified.

sedative *adj* allaying, anodyne, assuasive, balmy, calming, composing, demulcent, lenient, lenitive, soothing, tranquillizing. • *n* anaesthetic, anodyne, hypnotic, narcotic, opiate.

sedentary *adj* inactive, motionless, sluggish, torpid.

sediment *n* dregs, grounds, lees, precipitate, residue, residuum, settlings.

sedition *n* insurgence, insurrection, mutiny, rebellion, revolt, riot, rising, treason, tumult, uprising, uproar.

seditious *adj* factious, incendiary, insurgent, mutinous, rebellious, refractory, riotous, tumultuous, turbulent.

seduce *vb* allure, attract, betray, corrupt, debauch, deceive, decoy, deprave, ensnare, entice, inveigle, lead, mislead.

seductive *adj* alluring, attractive, enticing, tempting.

adj antonym unattractive.

sedulous *adj* active, assiduous, busy, diligent, industrious, laborious, notable, painstaking, persevering, unremitting, untiring.

see *vb* 1 behold, contemplate, descry, glimpse, sight, spot, survey. 2 comprehend, conceive, distinguish, espy, know, notice, observe, perceive, recognize, remark, understand. 3 beware, consider, envisage, regard, visualize. 4 experience, feel, suffer. 5 examine, inspire, notice, observe. 6 discern, look. 7 call on, visit.

seed *n* 1 grain, kernel, matured ovule. 2 germ, original. 3 children, descendants, offspring, progeny. 4 semen, sperm.

seedy *adj* 1 faded, old, shabby, worn. 2 destitute, distressed, indigent, needy, penniless, pinched, poor.

seek *vb* 1 hunt, look, search. 2 court, follow, prosecute, pursue, solicit. 3 attempt, endeavour, strive, try.

seem *vb* appear, assume, look, pretend.

seeming *adj* apparent, appearing, ostensible, specious. • *n* appearance, colour, guise, look, semblance.

seemly *adj* 1 appropriate, becoming, befitting, congruous, convenient, decent, decorous, expedient, fit, fitting, meet, proper, right, suitable. 2 beautiful, comely,

fair, good-looking, graceful, handsome, pretty, well-favoured.

adj antonym unseemly.

seer *n* augur, diviner, foreteller, predictor, prophet, soothsayer.

segment *n* bit, division, part, piece, portion, section, sector.

n antonym whole.

segregate *vb* detach, disconnect, disperse, insulate, part, separate.

vb antonym unite.

segregation *n* apartheid, discrimination, insulation, separation.

seize *vb* 1 capture, catch, clutch, grab, grapple, grasp, grip, snatch. 2 confiscate, impress, impound. 3 apprehend, comprehend. 4 arrest, take.

vb antonym let go.

seldom *adv* infrequently, occasionally, rarely.

adv antonym often.

select *vb* choose, cull, pick, prefer. • *adj* choice, chosen, excellent, exquisite, good, picked, rare, selected.

adj antonyms general, second-rate.

selection *n* choice, election, pick, preference.

self-conscious *adj* awkward, diffident, embarrassed, insecure, nervous.

adj antonyms natural, unaffected.

self-control *n* restraint, willpower.

self-important *adj* assuming, consequential, proud, haughty, lordly, overbearing, overweening.

adj antonym humble.

selfish *adj* egoistic, egotistical, greedy, illiberal, mean, narrow, self-seeking, ungenerous.

adj antonym unselfish.

self-possessed *adj* calm, collected, composed, cool, placid, sedate, undisturbed, unexcited, unruffled.

adj antonym worried.

self-willed *adj* contumacious, dogged, headstrong, obstinate, pig-headed, stubborn, uncompliant, wilful.

sell *vb* barter, exchange, hawk, market, peddle, trade, vend.

vb antonym buy.

semblance *n* 1 likeness, resemblance, similarity. 2 air, appearance, aspect, bearing, exterior, figure, form, mien, seeming, show. 3 image, representation, similitude.

seminal *adj* 1 important, original. 2 germinal, radical, rudimental, rudimentary, unformed.

seminary *n* academy, college, gymnasium, high school, institute, school, university.

send *vb* 1 cast, drive, emit, fling, hurl, impel, lance, launch, project, propel, throw, toss. 2 delegate, depute, dispatch. 3 forward, transmit. 4 bestow, confer, give, grant.

senile *adj* 1 aged, doddering, superannuated. 2 doting, imbecile.

senior *adj* 1 elder, older. 2 higher.
adj antonym junior.

seniority *n* eldership, precedence, priority, superiority.

sensation *n* 1 feeling, sense, perception. 2 excitement, impression, thrill.

sensational *adj* exciting, melodramatic, startling, thrilling.
adj antonym run-of-the-mill.

sense *vb* appraise, appreciate, estimate, notice, observe, perceive, suspect, understand. • *n* 1 brains, intellect, intelligence, mind, reason, understanding. 2 appreciation, apprehension, discernment, feeling, perception, recognition, tact. 3 connotation, idea, implication, judgment, notion, opinion, sentiment, view. 4 import, interpretation, meaning, purport, significance. 5 sagacity, soundness, substance, wisdom.
n antonym foolishness.

senseless *adj* 1 apathetic, inert, insensate, unfeeling. 2 absurd, foolish, ill-judged, nonsensical, silly, unmeaning, unreasonable, unwise. 3 doltish, foolish, simple, stupid, witless, weak-minded.
adj antonym sensible.

sensible *adj* 1 apprehensible, perceptible. 2 aware, cognizant, conscious, convinced, persuaded, satisfied. 3 discreet, intelligent, judicious, rational, reasonable, sagacious, sage, sober, sound, wise. 4 observant, understanding. 5 impressionable, sensitive.
adj antonyms imperceptible, senseless.

sensitive *adj* 1 perceptive, sentient. 2 affected, impressible, impressionable, responsive, susceptible. 3 delicate, tender, touchy.
adj antonym insensitive.

sensual *adj* 1 animal, bodily, carnal, voluptuous. 2 gross, lascivious, lewd, licentious, unchaste.
adj antonyms ascetic, Puritan.

sentence *vb* condemn, doom, judge. • *n* 1 decision, determination, judgment, opinion, verdict. 2 doctrine, dogma, opinion, tenet. 3 condemnation, conviction, doom. 4 period, proposition.

sententious *adj* compendious, compact, concise, didactic, laconic, pithy, pointed, succinct, terse.

sentiment *n* 1 judgment, notion, opinion. 2 maxim, saying. 3 emotion, tenderness. 4 disposition, feeling, thought.
n antonyms hard-heartedness, straightforwardness.

sentimental *adj* impressible, impressionable, over-emotional, romantic, tender.
adj antonym unsentimental.

sentinel *n* guard, guardsman, patrol, picket, sentry, watchman.

separate *vb* 1 detach, disconnect, disjoin, disunite, dissever, divide, divorce, part, sever, sunder. 2 eliminate, remove, withdraw. 3 cleave, open. • *adj* 1 detached, disconnected, disjoined, disjointed, dissociated, disunited, divided, parted, severed. 2 discrete, distinct, divorced, unconnected. 3 alone, segregated, withdrawn.
vb antonyms join, unite.
adj antonyms attached, together.

separation *n* 1 disjunction, disjuncture, dissociation. 2 disconnection, disseverance, disseveration, disunion, division, divorce. 3 analysis, decomposition.
n antonyms togetherness, unification.

sepulchral *adj* deep, dismal, funereal, gloomy, grave, hollow, lugubrious, melancholy, mournful, sad, sombre, woeful.

sepulchre *n* burial place, charnel house, grave, ossuary, sepulture, tomb.

sequel *n* 1 close, conclusion, denouement, end, termination. 2 consequence, event, issue, result, upshot.

sequence *n* 1 following, graduation, progression, succession. 2 arrangement, series, train.

sequestrated *adj* 1 hidden, private, retired, secluded, unfrequented, withdrawn. 2 seized.

seraphic *adj* 1 angelic, celestial, heavenly, sublime. 2 holy, pure, refined.

serene *adj* 1 calm, collected, placid, peaceful, quiet, tranquil, sedate, undisturbed, unperturbed, unruffled. 2 bright, calm, clear, fair, unclouded.
adj antonym troubled.

serenity *n* 1 calm, calmness, collectedness, composure, coolness, imperturbability, peace, peacefulness, quiescence, sedateness, tranquillity. **2** brightness, calmness, clearness, fairness, peace, quietness, stillness.

n antonyms anxiety, disruption.

serf *n* bondman, servant, slave, thrall, villein.

serfdom *n* bondage, enslavement, enthralment, servitude, slavery, subjection, thraldom.

series *n* chain, concatenation, course, line, order, progression, sequence, succession, train.

serious *adj* **1** earnest, grave, demure, pious, resolute, sedate, sober, solemn, staid, thoughtful. **2** dangerous, great, important, momentous, weighty.

adj antonyms facetious, light, slight, smiling, trivial.

sermon *n* discourse, exhortation, homily, lecture.

serpentine *adj* anfractuous, convoluted, crooked, meandering, sinuous, spiral, tortuous, twisted, undulating, winding.

servant *n* **1** attendant, dependant, factotum, helper, henchman, retainer, servitor, subaltern, subordinate, underling. **2** domestic, drudge, flunky, lackey, menial, scullion, slave.

n antonyms master, mistress.

serve *vb* **1** aid, assist, attend, help, minister, oblige, succour. **2** advance, benefit, forward, promote. **3** content, satisfy, supply. **4** handle, officiate, manage, manipulate, work.

service *vb* check, maintain, overhaul, repair. • *n* **1** labour, ministration, work. **2** attendance, business, duty, employ, employment, office. **3** advantage, benefit, good, gain, profit. **4** avail, purpose, use, utility. **5** ceremony, function, observance, rite, worship.

serviceable *adj* advantageous, available, beneficial, convenient, functional, handy, helpful, operative, profitable, useful.

adj antonym unserviceable.

servile *adj* **1** dependent, menial. **2** abject, base, beggarly, cringing, fawning, grovelling, low, mean, obsequious, slavish, sneaking, sycophantic, truckling.

adj antonyms aggressive, bold.

servility *n* **1** bondage, dependence, slavery. **2** abjection, abjectness, baseness, fawning, meanness, obsequiousness, slavishness, sycophancy.

servitude *n* bondage, enslavement, enthralment, serfdom, service, slavery, thraldom.

n antonym freedom.

set[1] *vb* **1** lay, locate, mount, place, put, stand, station. **2** appoint, determine, establish, fix, settle. **3** risk, stake, wager. **4** adapt, adjust, regulate. **5** adorn, stud, variegate. **6** arrange, dispose, pose, post. **7** appoint, assign, predetermine, prescribe. **8** estimate, prize, rate, value. **9** embarrass, perplex, pose. **10** contrive, produce. **11** decline, sink. **12** congeal, concern, consolidate, harden, solidify. **13** flow, incline, run, tend. **14** (*with* **about**) begin, commence. **15** (*with* **apart**) appropriate, consecrate, dedicate, devote, reserve, set aside. **16** (*with* **aside**) abrogate, annul, omit, reject. **17** reserve, set apart. **18** (*with* **before**) display, exhibit. **19** (*with* **down**) chronicle, jot down, record, register, state, write down. **20** (*with* **forth**) display, exhibit, explain, expound, manifest, promulgate, publish, put forward, represent, show. **21** (*with* **forward**) advance, further, promote. **22** (*with* **free**) acquit, clear, emancipate, liberate, release. **23** (*with* **off**) adorn, decorate, embellish. **24** define, portion off. **25** (*with* **on**) actuate, encourage, impel, influence, incite, instigate, prompt, spur, urge. **26** attack, assault, set upon. **27** (*with* **out**) display, issue, publish, proclaim, prove, recommend, show. **28** (*with* **right**) correct, put in order. **29** (*with* **to rights**) adjust, regulate. **30** (*with* **up**) elevate, erect, exalt, raise. **31** establish, found, institute. **32** (*with* **upon**) assail, assault, attack, fly at, rush upon. • *adj* **1** appointed, established, formal, ordained, prescribed, regular, settled. **2** determined, fixed, firm, obstinate, positive, stiff, unyielding. **3** immovable, predetermined. **4** located, placed, put. • *n* **1** attitude, position, posture. **2** scene, scenery, setting.

adj antonyms free, movable, spontaneous, undecided.

set[2] *n* **1** assortment, collection, suit. **2** class, circle, clique, cluster, company, coterie, division, gang, group, knot, party, school, sect.

setback *n* **1** blow, hitch, hold-up, rebuff. **2** defeat, disappointment, reverse.

set-off *n* **1** adornment, decoration, embellishment, ornament. **2** counterbalance, counterclaim, equivalent.

settle *vb* **1** adjust, arrange, compose, regulate. **2** account, balance, close up, conclude, discharge, liquidate, pay, pay up, reckon, satisfy, square. **3** allay, calm, compose, pacify, quiet, repose, rest, still, tranquillize. **4** confirm, decide, determine, make clear. **5** establish, fix, set. **6** fall, gravitate, sink, subside. **7** abide, colonize, domicile, dwell, establish, inhabit, people, place, plant, reside. **8** (*with* **on**) determine on, fix on, fix upon. **9** establish. • *n* bench, seat, stool.

settled *adj* **1** established, fixed, stable. **2** decided, deep-rooted, steady, unchanging. **3** adjusted, arranged. **4** methodical, orderly, quiet. **5** common, customary, everyday, ordinary, usual, wonted.

set-to *n* combat, conflict, contest, fight.

sever *vb* **1** divide, part, rend, separate, sunder. **2** detach, disconnect, disjoin, disunite.
vb antonyms join, unite.

several *adj* **1** individual, single, particular. **2** distinct, exclusive, independent, separate. **3** different, divers, diverse, manifold, many, sundry, various.

severance *n* partition, separation.

severe *adj* **1** austere, bitter, dour, hard, harsh, inexorable, morose, painful, relentless, rigid, rigorous, rough, sharp, stern, stiff, strait-laced, unmitigated, unrelenting, unsparing. **2** accurate, exact, methodical, strict. **3** chaste, plain, restrained, simple, unadorned. **4** biting, caustic, cruel, cutting, harsh, keen, sarcastic, satirical, trenchant. **5** acute, afflictive, distressing, excruciating, extreme, intense, stringent, violent. **6** critical, exact.
adj antonyms compassionate, kind, lenient, mild, sympathetic.

severity *n* **1** austerity, gravity, harshness, rigour, seriousness, sternness, strictness. **2** accuracy, exactness, niceness. **3** chasteness, plainness, simplicity. **4** acrimony, causticity, keenness, sharpness. **5** afflictiveness, extremity, keenness, stringency, violence. **6** cruelty.

sew *vb* baste, bind, hem, stitch, tack.

sex *n* **1** gender, femininity, masculinity, sexuality. **2** coitus, copulation, fornication, love-making.

shabby *adj* **1** faded, mean, poor, ragged, seedy, threadbare, worn, worn-out. **2** beggarly, mean, paltry, penurious, stingy, ungentlemanly, unhandsome.
adj antonyms honorable, smart.

shackle *vb* **1** chain, fetter, gyve, hamper, manacle. **2** bind, clog, confine, cumber, embarrass, encumber, impede, obstruct, restrict, trammel. • *n* chain, fetter, gyve, hamper, manacle.

shade *vb* **1** cloud, darken, dim, eclipse, obfuscate, obscure. **2** cover, ensconce, hide, protect, screen, shelter. • *n* **1** darkness, dusk, duskiness, gloom, obscurity, shadow. **2** cover, protection, shelter. **3** awning, blind, curtain, screen, shutter, veil. **4** degree, difference, kind, variety. **5** cast, colour, complexion, dye, hue, tinge, tint, tone. **6** apparition, ghost, manes, phantom, shadow, spectre, spirit.

shadow *vb* **1** becloud, cloud, darken, obscure, shade. **2** adumbrate, foreshadow, symbolize, typify. **3** conceal, cover, hide, protect, screen, shroud. • *n* **1** penumbra, shade, umbra, umbrage. **2** darkness, gloom, obscurity. **3** cover, protection, security, shelter. **4** adumbration, foreshadowing, image, prefiguration, representation. **5** apparition, ghost, phantom, shade, spirit. **6** image, portrait, reflection, silhouette.

shadowy *adj* **1** shady, umbrageous. **2** dark, dim, gloomy, murky, obscure. **3** ghostly, imaginary, impalpable, insubstantial, intangible, spectral, unreal, unsubstantial, visionary.

shady *adj* **1** shadowy, umbrageous. **2** crooked.

shaft *n* **1** arrow, missile, weapon. **2** handle, helve. **3** pole, tongue. **4** axis, spindle. **5** pinnacle, spire. **6** stalk, stem, trunk.

shaggy *adj* rough, rugged.
adj antonyms bald, shorn.

shake *vb* **1** quake, quaver, quiver, shiver, shudder, totter, tremble. **2** agitate, convulse, jar, jolt, stagger. **3** daunt, frighten, intimidate. **4** endanger, move, weaken. **5** oscillate, vibrate, wave. **6** move, put away, remove, throw off. • *n* agitation, concussion, flutter, jar, jolt, quaking, shaking, shivering, shock, trembling, tremor.

shaky *adj* jiggly, quaky, shaking, tottering, trembling.
adj antonyms firm, strong.

shallow *adj* **1** flimsy, foolish, frivolous, puerile, trashy, trifling, trivial. **2** empty, ignorant, silly, slight, simple, superficial, unintelligent.
adj antonyms analytical, deep.

sham *vb* **1** ape, feign, imitate, pretend. **2** cheat, deceive, delude, dupe, impose, trick. • *adj* assumed, counterfeit, false, feigned, mock, make-believe, pretended, spurious. • *n* delusion, feint, fraud, humbug, imposition, imposture, pretence, trick.

adj antonym genuine.

shamble *vb* hobble, shuffle.

shambles *npl* **1** abattoir, slaughterhouse. **2** confusion, disorder, mess.

shame *vb* **1** debase, degrade, discredit, disgrace, dishonour, stain, sully, taint, tarnish. **2** abash, confound, confuse, discompose, disconcert, humble, humiliate. **3** deride, flout, jeer, mock, ridicule, sneer. • *n* **1** contempt, degradation, derision, discredit, disgrace, dishonour, disrepute, ignominy, infamy, obloquy, odium, opprobrium. **2** abashment, chagrin, confusion, embarrassment, humiliation, mortification. **3** reproach, scandal. **4** decency, decorousness, decorum, modesty, propriety, seemliness.

n antonyms distinction, honour, pride.

shamefaced *adj* bashful, diffident, overmodest.

shameful *adj* **1** atrocious, base, disgraceful, dishonourable, disreputable, heinous, ignominious, infamous, nefarious, opprobrious, outrageous, scandalous, vile, villainous, wicked. **2** degrading, indecent, unbecoming.

adj antonyms creditable, honourable.

shameless *adj* **1** assuming, audacious, bold-faced, brazen, brazen-faced, cool, immodest, impudent, indecent, indelicate, insolent, unabashed, unblushing. **2** abandoned, corrupt, depraved, dissolute, graceless, hardened, incorrigible, irreclaimable, lost, obdurate, profligate, reprobate, sinful, unprincipled, vicious.

adj antonyms ashamed, contrite, shamefaced.

shape *vb* **1** create, form, make, produce. **2** fashion, model, mould. **3** adjust, direct, frame, regulate. **4** conceive, conjure up, figure, image, imagine. • *n* **1** appearance, aspect, fashion, figure, form, guise, make. **2** build, cast, cut, model, mould, pattern. **3** apparition, image.

shapeless *adj* **1** amorphous, formless. **2** grotesque, irregular, rude, uncouth, unsymmetrical.

adj antonym shapely.

shapely *adj* comely, symmetrical, trim, well-formed.

adj antonym shapeless.

share *vb* **1** apportion, distribute, divide, parcel out, portion, split. **2** partake, participate. **3** experience, receive. • *n* **1** part, portion, quantum. **2** allotment, allowance, contingent, deal, dividend, division, interest, lot, proportion, quantity, quota.

sharer *n* communicant, partaker, participator.

sharp *adj* **1** acute, cutting, keen, keen-edged, knife-edged, razor-edged, trenchant. **2** acuminate, needle-shaped, peaked, pointed, ridged. **3** apt, astute, canny, clear-sighted, clever, cunning, discerning, discriminating, ingenious, inventive, keen-witted, penetrating, perspicacious, quick, ready, sagacious, sharp-witted, shrewd, smart, subtle, witty. **4** acid, acrid, biting, bitter, burning, high-flavoured, high-seasoned, hot, piquant, poignant, pungent, sour, stinging. **5** acrimonious, biting, caustic, cutting, harsh, mordant, sarcastic, severe, tart, trenchant. **6** cruel, hard, rigid. **7** afflicting, distressing, excruciating, intense, painful, piercing, shooting, sore, violent. **8** nipping, pinching. **9** ardent, eager, fervid, fierce, fiery, impetuous, strong. **10** high, screeching, shrill. **11** attentive, vigilant. **12** severe. **13** close, exacting, shrewd, cold, crisp, freezing, icy wintry. • *adv* **1** abruptly, sharply, suddenly. **2** exactly, precisely, punctually.

adj antonyms blunt, dull, mild, obtuse, slow, stupid.

sharp-cut *adj* clear, distinct, well-defined.

sharpen *vb* edge, intensify, point.

vb antonym blunt.

sharper *n* cheat, deceiver, defrauder, knave, rogue, shark, swindler, trickster.

sharply *adv* **1** rigorously, roughly, severely. **2** acutely, keenly. **3** vehemently, violently. **4** accurately, exactly, minutely, trenchantly, wittily. **5** abruptly, steeply.

sharpness *n* **1** acuteness, keenness, trenchancy. **2** acuity, spinosity. **3** acumen, cleverness, discernment, ingenuity, quickness, sagacity, shrewdness, smartness, wit. **4** acidity, acridity, piquancy, pungency, sting, tartness. **5** causticness, incisiveness, pungency, sarcasm, satire, severity. **6** afflictiveness, intensity, painfulness, poignancy. **7** ardour, fierceness, violence. **8** discordance, dissonance, highness, screechiness, squeakiness, shrillness.

sharp-sighted *adj* clear-sighted, keen, keen-eyed, keen-sighted.

sharp-witted *adj* acute, clear-sighted, cunning, discerning, ingenious, intelligent, keen, keen-sighted, long-headed, quick, sagacious, sharp, shrewd.

shatter *vb* 1 break, burst, crack, rend, shiver, smash, splinter, split. 2 break up, derange, disorder, overthrow.

shave *vb* 1 crop, cut off, mow, pare. 2 slice. 3 graze, skim, touch.

shaver *n* 1 boy, child, youngster. 2 bargainer, extortioner, sharper.

shear *vb* 1 clip, cut, fleece, strip. 2 divest. 3 break off.

sheath *n* case, casing, covering, envelope, scabbard, sheathing.

sheathe *vb* case, cover, encase, enclose.

shed[1] *n* cabin, cot, hovel, hut, outhouse, shack, shelter.

shed[2] *vb* 1 effuse, let fall, pour out, spill. 2 diffuse, emit, give out, scatter, spread. 3 cast, let fall, put off, slough, throw off.

sheen *n* brightness, gloss, glossiness, shine, splendour.

sheep *n* ewe, lamb, ram.

sheepish *adj* bashful, diffident, overmodest, shamefaced, timid, timorous.
adj antonym unabashed.

sheer[1] *adj* 1 perpendicular, precipitous, steep, vertical. 2 clear, downright, mere, pure, simple, unadulterated, unmingled, unmixed, unqualified, utter. 3 clear. 4 fine, transparent. • *adv* 1 outright. 2 perpendicularly, steeply.

sheer[2] *vb* decline, deviate, move aside, swerve. • *n* bow, curve.
n antonyms heavy, thick.

shelf *n* bracket, console, ledge, mantelpiece.

shell *vb* 1 exfoliate, fall off, peel off. 2 bombard. • *n* 1 carapace, case, covering, shard. 2 bomb, grenade, shrapnel. 3 framework.

shelter *vb* cover, defend, ensconce, harbour, hide, house, protect, screen, shield, shroud. • *n* 1 asylum, cover, covert, harbour, haven, hideaway, refuge, retreat, sanctuary. 2 defence, protection, safety, screen, security, shield. 3 guardian, protector.
vb antonym expose.
n antonym exposure.

shelve *vb* 1 dismiss, put aside. 2 incline, slope.

shepherd *vb* 1 escort, guide, marshal, usher. 2 direct, drive, drove, herd, lead.

3 guard, tend, watch over. • *n* 1 drover, grazier, herder, herdsman. 2 chaplain, churchman, clergyman, cleric, divine, ecclesiastic, minister, padre, parson, pastor. 3 chaperon, duenna, escort, guide, squire, usher.

shield *vb* 1 cover, defend, guard, protect, shelter. 2 repel, ward off. 3 avert, forbid, forfend. • *n* 1 aegis, buckler, escutcheon, scutcheon, targe. 2 bulwark, cover, defence, guard, palladium, protection, rampart, safeguard, security, shelter.
vb antonym expose.

shift *vb* 1 alter, change, fluctuate, move, vary. 2 chop, dodge, swerve, veer. 3 contrive, devise, manage, plan, scheme, shuffle. • *n* 1 change, substitution, turn. 2 contrivance, expedient, means, resort, resource. 3 artifice, craft, device, dodge, evasion, fraud, mask, ruse, stratagem, subterfuge, trick, wile. 4 chemise, smock.

shiftless *adj* improvident, imprudent, negligent, slack, thriftless, unresourceful.

shifty *adj* tricky, undependable, wily.
adj antonyms honest, open.

shillyshally *vb* hesitate, waver. • *n* hesitation, irresolute, wavering.

shimmer *vb* flash, glimmer, glisten, shine. • *n* blink, glimmer, glitter, twinkle.

shin *vb* climb, swarm. • *n* shinbone, tibia.

shindy *n* disturbance, riot, roughhouse, row, spree, uproar.

shine *vb* 1 beam, blaze, coruscate, flare, give light, glare, gleam, glimmer, glisten, glitter, glow, lighten, radiate, sparkle. 2 excel. • *n* brightness, brilliancy, glaze, gloss, polish, sheen.

shining *adj* 1 beaming, bright, brilliant, effulgent, gleaming, glowing, glistening, glittering, luminous, lustrous, radiant, resplendent, splendid. 2 conspicuous, distinguished, illustrious.

shiny *adj* 1 bright, clear, luminous, sunshiny, unclouded. 2 brilliant, burnished, glassy, glossy, polished.
adj antonyms dark, dull.

ship *n* boat, craft, steamer, vessel.

shipshape *adj* neat, orderly, tidy, trim, well-arranged.
adj antonyms disorderly, untidy.

shipwreck *vb* cast away, maroon, strand, wreck. • *n* demolition, destruction, miscarriage, overthrow, perdition, ruin, subversion, wreck.

shirk *vb* **1** avoid, dodge, evade, malinger, quit, slack. **2** cheat, shark, trick.

shiver[1] *vb* break, shatter, splinter. • *n* bit, fragment, piece, slice, sliver, splinter.

shiver[2] *vb* quake, quiver, shake, shudder, tremble. • *n* shaking, shivering, shuddering, tremor.

shivery[1] *adj* brittle, crumbly, frangible, friable, shatterable, splintery.

shivery[2] *adj* **1** quaking, quavering, quivering, shaky, trembly, tremulous. **2** chilly, shivering.

shoal[1] *vb* crowd, throng. • *n* crowd, horde, multitude, swarm, throng.

shoal[2] *n* **1** sandbank, shallows. **2** danger.

shock *vb* **1** appal, horrify. **2** disgust, disquiet, disturb, nauseate, offend, outrage, revolt, scandalize, sicken. **3** astound, stagger, stun. **4** collide with, jar, jolt, shake, strike against. **5** encounter, meet. • *n* **1** agitation, blow, offence, stroke, trauma. **2** assault, brunt, conflict. **3** clash, collision, concussion, impact, percussion.

vb antonyms delight, gratify, please, reassure.

n antonyms delight, pleasure.

shocking *adj* **1** abominable, detestable, disgraceful, disgusting, execrable, foul, hateful, loathsome, obnoxious, odious, offensive, repugnant, repulsive, revolting. **2** appalling, awful, dire, dreadful, fearful, frightful, ghastly, hideous, horrible, horrid, horrific, monstrous, terrible.

adj antonyms acceptable, delightful, pleasant, satisfactory.

shoot *vb* **1** catapult, expel, hurl, let fly, propel. **2** discharge, fire, let off. **3** dart, fly, pass, pelt. **4** extend, jut, project, protrude, protuberate, push, put forth, send forth, stretch. **5** bud, germinate, sprout. **6** (*with* **up**) grow increase, spring up, run up, start up. • *n* branch, offshoot, scion, sprout, twig.

shop *n* **1** emporium, market, mart, store. **2** workshop.

shore[1] *n* beach, brim, coast, seabord, seaside, strand, waterside.

shore[2] *vb* brace, buttress, prop, stay, support. • *n* beam, brace, buttress, prop, stay, support.

shorn *adj* **1** cut-off. **2** deprived.

short *adj* **1** brief, curtailed. **2** direct, near, straight. **3** compendious, concise, condensed, laconic, pithy, terse, sententious, succinct, summary. **4** abrupt, curt, petulant, pointed, sharp, snappish, uncivil. **5** defective, deficient, inadequate, insufficient, niggardly, scanty, scrimpy. **6** contracted, lacking, limited, minus, wanting. **7** dwarfish, squat, undersized. **8** brittle, crisp, crumbling, friable. • *adv* abruptly, at once, forthwith, suddenly.

adj antonyms adequate, ample, expansive, large, lasting, long, long-lived, polite, tall.

shortcoming *n* defect, deficiency, delinquency, error, failing, failure, fault, imperfection, inadequacy, remissness, slip, weakness.

shorten *vb* **1** abbreviate, abridge, curtail, cut short. **2** abridge, contract, diminish, lessen, retrench, reduce. **3** cut off, dock, lop, trim. **4** confine, hinder, restrain, restrict.

vb antonyms amplify, enlarge, lengthen.

shortening *n* abbreviation, abridgment, contraction, curtailment, diminution, retrenchment, reduction.

shorthand *n* brachygraphy, stenography, tachygraphy.

short-lived *adj* emphemeral, transient, transitory.

adj antonyms abiding, enduring, lasting, long-lived.

shortly *adv* **1** quickly, soon. **2** briefly, concisely, succinctly, tersely.

short-sighted *adj* **1** myopic, nearsighted, purblind. **2** imprudent, indiscreet.

adj antonyms far-sighted, hypermetropic, long-sighted.

shot[1] *n* **1** discharge. **2** ball, bullet, missile, projectile. **3** marksman, shooter.

shot[2] *adj* **1** chatoyant, iridescent, irisated, moiré, watered. **2** intermingled, interspersed, interwoven.

shoulder *vb* **1** bear, bolster, carry, hump, maintain, pack, support, sustain, tote. **2** crowd, elbow, jostle, press forward, push, thrust. • *n* projection, protuberance.

shoulder blade *n* blade bone, omoplate, scapula, shoulder bone.

shout *vb* bawl, cheer, clamour, exclaim, halloo, roar, vociferate, whoop, yell. • *n* cheer, clamour, exclamation, halloo, hoot, huzza, outcry, roar, vociferation, whoop, yell.

shove *vb* **1** jostle, press against, propel, push, push aside. **2** (*with* **off**) push away, thrust away.

show *vb* **1** blazon, display, exhibit, flaunt, parade, present. **2** indicate, mark, point out. **3** disclose, discover, divulge, explain, make clear, make known, proclaim, publish, reveal, unfold. **4** demonstrate, evidence, manifest, prove, verify. **5** conduct, guide, usher. **6** direct, inform, instruct, teach. **7** expound, elucidate, interpret. **8** (*with* **off**) display, exhibit, make a show, set off. **9** (*with* **up**) expose. • *n* **1** array, exhibition, representation, sight, spectacle. **2** blazonry, bravery, ceremony, dash, demonstration, display, flourish, ostentation, pageant, pageantry, parade, pomp, splendour, splurge. **3** likeness, resemblance, semblance. **4** affectation, appearance, colour, illusion, mask, plausibility, pose, pretence, pretext, simulation, speciousness. **5** entertainment, production.

showy *adj* **1** dressy, fine, flashy, flaunting, garish, gaudy, glaring, gorgeous, loud, ornate, smart, swanky, splendid. **2** grand, magnificent, ostentatious, pompous, pretentious, stately, sumptuous.

adj antonyms quiet, restrained.

shred *vb* tear. • *n* bit, fragment, piece, rag, scrap, strip, tatter.

shrew *n* brawler, fury, scold, spitfire, termagant, virago, vixen.

shrewd *adj* **1** arch, artful, astute, crafty, cunning, Machiavellian, sly, subtle, wily. **2** acute, astute, canny, discerning, discriminating, ingenious, keen, knowing, penetrating, sagacious, sharp, sharp-sighted.

adj antonyms naïve, obtuse, unwise.

shrewdness *n* **1** address, archness, art, artfulness, astuteness, craft, cunning, policy, skill, slyness, subtlety. **2** acumen, acuteness, discernment, ingenuity, keenness, penetration, perspicacity, sagacity, sharpness, wit.

shrewish *adj* brawling, clamorous, froward, peevish, petulant, scolding, vixenish.

shriek *vb* scream, screech, squeal, yell, yelp. • *n* cry, scream, screech, yell.

shrill *adj* acute, high, high-toned, high-pitched, piercing, piping, sharp.

adj antonyms gentle, low, soft.

shrine *n* **1** reliquary, sacred tomb. **2** altar, hallowed place, sacred place.

shrink *vb* **1** contract, decrease, dwindle, shrivel, wither. **2** balk, blench, draw back, flinch, give way, quail, recoil, retire, swerve, wince, withdraw.

vb antonyms embrace, expand, stretch, warm to.

shrivel *vb* **1** dry, dry up, parch. **2** contract, decrease, dwindle, shrink, wither, wrinkle.

shroud *vb* bury, cloak, conceal, cover, hide, mask, muffle, protect, screen, shelter, veil. • *n* **1** covering, garment. **2** grave clothes, winding sheet.

shrub *n* bush, dwarf tree, low tree.

shrubby *adj* bushy.

shudder *vb* quake, quiver, shake, shiver, tremble. • *n* shaking, shuddering, trembling, tremor.

shuffle *vb* **1** confuse, disorder, intermix, jumble, mix, shift. **2** cavil, dodge, equivocate, evade, prevaricate, quibble, vacillate. **3** struggle. • *n* artifice, cavil, evasion, fraud, pretence, pretext, prevarication, quibble, ruse, shuffling, sophism, subterfuge, trick.

shun *vb* avoid, elude, eschew, escape, evade, get clear of.

vb antonyms accept, embrace.

shut *vb* **1** close, close up, stop. **2** confine, coop up, enclose, imprison, lock up, shut up. **3** (*with* **in**) confine, enclose. **4** (*with* **off**) bar, exclude, intercept. **5** (*with* **up**) close up, shut. **6** confine, enclose, fasten in, imprison, lock in, lock up.

vb antonym open.

shy *vb* **1** cast, chuck, fling, hurl, jerk, pitch, sling, throw, toss. **2** boggle, sheer, start aside. • *adj* **1** bashful, coy, diffident, reserved, retiring, sheepish, shrinking, timid. **2** cautious, chary, distrustful, heedful, wary. • *n* **1** start. **2** fling, throw.

adj antonyms bold, confident.

sibilant *adj* buzzing, hissing, sibilous.

sick *adj* **1** ailing, ill, indisposed, laid-up, unwell, weak. **2** nauseated, queasy. **3** disgusted, revolted, tired, weary. **4** diseased, distempered, disordered, feeble, morbid, unhealthy, unsound, weak. **5** languishing, longing, pining.

adj antonyms healthy, well.

sicken *vb* **1** ail, disease, fall sick, make sick. **2** nauseate. **3** disgust, weary. **4** decay, droop, languish, pine.

sickening *adj* **1** nauseating, nauseous, palling, sickish. **2** disgusting, distasteful, loathsome, offensive, repulsive, revolting.

sickly *adj* ailing, diseased, faint, feeble, infirm, languid, languishing, morbid, unhealthy, valetudinary, weak, weakly.

sickness *n* **1** ail, ailment, complaint, disease, disorder, distemper, illness, indisposition, invalidism, malady, morbidity. **2** nausea, qualmishness, queasiness.

n antonym health.

side *vb* **1** border, bound, edge, flank, frontier, march, rim, skirt, verge. **2** avert, turn aside. **3** (*with* **with**) befriend, favour, flock to, join with, second, support. • *adj* **1** flanking, later, skirting. **2** indirect, oblique. **3** extra, odd, off, spare. • *n* **1** border, edge, flank, margin, verge. **2** cause, faction, interest, party, sect.

sideboard *n* buffet, dresser.

side by side abreast, alongside, by the side.

sidelong *adj* **1** lateral, oblique. • *adv* laterally, obliquely. **2** on the side.

sidewalk *n* footpath, footway, pavement.

sideways, **sidewise** *adv* laterally. • *adv* athwart, crossways, crosswise, laterally, obliquely, sidelong, sidewards.

siesta *n* doze, nap.

sift *vb* **1** part, separate. **2** bolt, screen, winnow. **3** analyse, canvass, discuss, examine, fathom, follow up, enquire into, investigate, probe, scrutinize, sound, try.

sigh *vb* complain, grieve, lament, mourn. • *n* long breath, sough, suspiration.

sight *vb* get sight of, perceive, see. • *n* **1** cognizance, ken, perception, view. **2** beholding, eyesight, seeing, vision. **3** exhibition, prospect, representation, scene, show, spectacle, wonder. **4** consideration, estimation, knowledge. **5** examination, inspection.

sightless *adj* blind, eyeless, unseeing.

sightly *adj* beautiful, comely, handsome.

sign *vb* **1** indicate, signal, signify. **2** countersign, endorse, subscribe. • *n* **1** emblem, index, indication, manifestation, mark, note, proof, signal, signification, symbol, symptom, token. **2** beacon. **3** augury, auspice, foreboding, miracle, omen, portent, presage, prodigy, prognostic, wonder. **4** type. **5** countersign, password.

signal *vb* flag, glance, hail, nod, nudge, salute, sign, signalize, sound, speak, touch, wave, wink. • *adj* conspicuous, eminent, extraordinary, memorable, notable, noteworthy, remarkable. • *n* cue, indication, mark, sign, token.

signalize *vb* celebrate, distinguish, make memorable.

signature *n* **1** mark, sign, stamp. **2** autograph, hand.

significance *n* **1** implication, import, meaning, purport, sense. **2** consequence, importance, moment, portent, weight. **3** emphasis, energy, expressiveness, force, impressiveness.

n antonym unimportance.

significant *adj* **1** betokening, expressive, indicative, significative, signifying. **2** important, material, momentous, portentous, weighty. **3** forcible, emphatic, expressive, telling.

adj antonyms meaningless, unimportant.

signification *n* **1** expression. **2** acceptation, import, meaning, purport, sense.

signify *vb* **1** betoken, communication, express, indicate, intimate. **2** denote, imply, import, mean, purport, suggest. **3** announce, declare, give notice of, impart, make known, manifest, proclaim, utter. **4** augur, foreshadow, indicate, portend, represent. **5** matter, weigh.

silence *vb* **1** hush, muzzle, still. **2** allay, calm, quiet. • *interj* be silent, be still, hush, soft, tush, tut, whist. • *n* **1** calm, hush, lull, noiselessness, peace, quiet, quietude, soundlessness, stillness. **2** dumbness, mumness, muteness, reticence, speechlessness, taciturnity.

silent *adj* **1** calm, hushed, noiseless, quiet, soundless, still. **2** dumb, inarticulate, mum, mute, nonvocal, speechless, tacit. **3** reticent, taciturn, uncommunicative.

adj antonyms loud, noisy, talkative.

silken *adj* flossy, silky, soft.

silkiness *n* smoothness, softness.

silly *adj* **1** brainless, childish, foolish, inept, senseless, shallow, simple, stupid, weak-minded, witless. **2** absurd, extravagant, frivolous, imprudent, indiscreet, nonsensical, preposterous, trifling, unwise. • *n* ass, duffer, goose, idiot, simpleton.

adj antonyms collected, mature, sane, sensible, wise.

silt *n* alluvium, deposit, deposition, residue, settlement, settlings, sediment.

silver *adj* **1** argent, silvery. **2** bright, silvery, white. **3** clear, mellifluous, soft.

similar *adj* **1** analogous, duplicate, like, resembling, twin. **2** homogeneous, uniform.

adj antonym different.

similarity *n* agreement, analogy, correspondence, likeness, parallelism, parity, resemblance, sameness, semblance, similitude.

n antonym difference.

simile *n* comparison, metaphor, similitude.

similitude *n* **1** image, likeness, resemblance. **2** comparison, metaphor, simile.

simmer *vb* boil, bubble, seethe, stew.

simper *vb* smile, smirk.

simple *adj* **1** bare, elementary, homogeneous, incomplex, mere, single, unalloyed, unblended, uncombined, uncompounded, unmingled, unmixed. **2** chaste, plain, homespun, natural, neat, unadorned, unaffected, unembellished, unpretentious, unstudied, unvarnished. **3** artless, downright, frank, guileless, ingenuous, naive, open, simple-hearted, simple-minded, sincere, single-minded, straightforward, true, unconstrained, undesigning, unsophisticated. **4** credulous, fatuous, foolish, shallow, silly, unwise, weak. **5** clear, intelligible, understandable, uninvolved, unmistakable.
adj antonyms artful, clever, complicated, difficult, fancy, intricate.

simpleton *n* blockhead, dunce, fool, greenhorn, moron, nincompoop, ninny.
n antonym brain.

simplicity *n* **1** chasteness, homeliness, naturalness, neatness, plainness. **2** artlessness, frankness, naivety, openness, simplesse, sincerity. **3** clearness. **4** gullibility, folly, silliness, weakness.

simply *adv* **1** artlessly, plainly, sincerely, unaffectedly. **2** barely, merely, of itself, solely. **3** absolutely, alone.

simulate *vb* act, affect, ape, assume, counterfeit, dissemble, feign, mimic, pretend, sham.

simulation *n* counterfeiting, feigning, personation, pretence.

simultaneous *adj* coeval, coincident, concomitant, concurrent, contemporaneous, synchronous.

sin *vb* do wrong, err, transgress, trespass. • *n* delinquency, depravity, guilt, iniquity, misdeed, offence, transgression, unrighteousness, wickedness, wrong.

since *conj* as, because, considering, seeing that. • *adv* **1** ago, before this. **2** from that time. • *prep* after, from the time of, subsequently to.

sincere *adj* **1** pure, unmixed. **2** genuine, honest, real, true, unaffected, unfeigned, unvarnished. **3** artless, candid, direct, frank, guileless, hearty, honest, ingenuous, open, plain, single, straightforward, truthful, undissembling, upright, whole-hearted.
adj antonym insincere.

sincerity *n* artlessness, candour, earnestness, frankness, genuineness, guilelessness, honesty, ingenuousness, probity, truth, truthfulness, unaffectedness, veracity.
n antonym insincerity.

sinew *n* **1** ligament, tendon. **2** brawn, muscle, nerve, strength.

sinewy *adj* able-bodied, brawny, firm, Herculean, muscular, nervous, powerful, robust, stalwart, strapping, strong, sturdy, vigorous, wiry.

sinful *adj* bad, criminal, depraved, immoral, iniquitous, mischievous, peccant, transgressive, unholy, unrighteous, wicked, wrong.
adj antonyms righteous, sinless.

sinfulness *n* corruption, criminality, depravity, iniquity, irreligion, ungodliness, unholiness, unrighteousness, wickedness.

sing *vb* cantillate, carol, chant, hum, hymn, intone, lilt, troll, warble, yodel.

singe *vb* burn, scorch, sear.

singer *n* cantor, caroler, chanter, gleeman, prima donna, minstrel, psalmodist, songster, vocalist.

single *vb* (*with* out) choose, pick, select, single. • *adj* **1** alone, isolated, one only, sole, solitary. **2** individual, particular, separate. **3** celibate, unmarried, unwedded. **4** pure, simple, uncompounded, unmixed. **5** honest, ingenuous, sincere, unbiased, uncorrupt, upright.

single-handed *adj* alone, by one's self, unaided, unassisted.

single-minded *adj* artless, candid, guileless, ingenuous, sincere.

singleness *n* **1** individuality, unity. **2** purity, simplicity. **3** ingenuousness, integrity, sincerity, uprightness.

singular *adj* **1** eminent, exceptional, extraordinary, rare, remarkable, strange, uncommon, unusual, unwonted. **2** particular, unexampled, unparalleled, unprecedented. **3** unaccountable. **4** bizarre, curious, eccentric, fantastic, odd, peculiar, queer. **5** individual, single. **6** not complex, single, uncompounded, unique.
adj antonyms normal, usual.

singularity *n* **1** aberration, abnormality, irregularity, oddness, rareness, rarity, strangeness, uncommonness. **2** characteristic, idiosyncrasy, individuality, particularity, peculiarity. **3** eccentricity, oddity.

sinister *adj* **1** baleful, injurious, untoward. **2** boding ill, inauspicious, ominous, unlucky. **3** left, on the left hand.

sink *vb* **1** droop, drop, fall, founder, go down, submerge, subside. **2** enter, penetrate. **3** collapse, fail. **4** decay, decline, decrease, dwindle, give way, languish, lose strength. **5** engulf, immerse, merge, submerge, submerse. **6** dig, excavate, scoop out. **7** abase, bring down, crush, debase, degrade, depress, diminish, lessen, lower, overbear. **8** destroy, overthrow, overwhelm, reduce, ruin, swamp, waste. • *n* basin, cloaca, drain.

vb antonyms float, rise, uplift.

sinless *adj* faultless, guiltless, immaculate, impeccable, innocent, spotless, unblemished, undefiled, unspotted, unsullied, untarnished.

adj antonym sinful.

sinner *n* criminal, delinquent, evildoer, offender, reprobate, wrongdoer.

sinuosity *n* crook, curvature, flexure, sinus, tortuosity, winding.

sinuous *adj* bending, crooked, curved, curvilinear, flexuous, serpentine, sinuate, sinuated, tortuous, undulating, wavy, winding.

sip *vb* **1** drink, suck up, sup. **2** absorb, drink in. • *n* small draught, taste.

sire *vb* **1** father, reproduce. **2** author, breed, conceive, create, generate, originate, produce, propagate. • *n* **1** father, male parent, progenitor. **2** man, male person. **3** sir, sirrah. **4** author, begetter, creator, father, generator, originator.

siren *adj* alluring, bewitching, fascinating, seducing, tempting. • *n* **1** mermaid. **2** charmer, Circe, seducer, seductress, tempter, temptress.

sit *vb* **1** be, remain, repose, rest, stay. **2** bear on, lie, rest. **3** abide, dwell, settle. **4** perch. **5** brood, incubate. **6** become, be suited, fit.

site *vb* locate, place, position, situate, station. • *n* ground, locality, location, place, position, seat, situation, spot, station, whereabouts.

sitting *n* meeting, session.

situation *n* **1** ground, locality, location, place, position, seat, site, spot, whereabouts. **2** case, category, circumstances, condition, juncture, plight, predicament, state. **3** employment, office, place, post, station.

size *n* amplitude, bigness, bulk, dimensions, expanse, greatness, largeness, magnitude, mass, volume.

skeleton *n* **1** framework. **2** draft, outline, sketch.

sketch *vb* **1** design, draft, draw out. **2** delineate, depict, paint, portray, represent. • *n* delineation, design, draft, drawing, outline, plan, skeleton.

sketchy *adj* crude, incomplete, unfinished.

adj antonym full.

skilful *adj* able, accomplished, adept, adroit, apt, clever, competent, conversant, cunning, deft, dexterous, dextrous, expert, handy, ingenious, masterly, practised, proficient, qualified, quick, ready, skilled, trained, versed, well-versed.

skill *n* **1** ability, address, adroitness, aptitude, aptness, art, cleverness, deftness, dexterity, expertise, expertness, facility, ingenuity, knack, quickness, readiness, skilfulness. **2** discernment, discrimination, knowledge, understanding, wit.

skim *vb* **1** brush, glance, graze, kiss, scrape, scratch, sweep, touch lightly. **2** coast, flow, fly, glide, sail, scud, whisk. **3** dip into, glance at, scan, skip, thumb over, touch upon.

skin *vb* **1** pare, peel. **2** decorticate, excoriate, flay. • *n* **1** cuticle, cutis, derm, epidermis, hide, integument, pellicle, pelt. **2** hull, husk, peel, rind.

skinflint *n* churl, curmudgeon, lickpenny, miser, niggard, scrimp.

skinny *adj* emaciated, lank, lean, poor, shrivelled, shrunk, thin.

adj antonym fat.

skip *vb* **1** bound, caper, frisk, gambol, hop, jump, leap, spring. **2** disregard, intermit, miss, neglect, omit, pass over, skim. • *n* bound, caper, frisk, gambol, hop, jump, leap, spring.

skirmish *vb* battle, brush, collide, combat, contest, fight, scuffle, tussle. • *n* affair, affray, battle, brush, collision, combat, conflict, contest, encounter, fight, scuffle, tussle.

skirt *vb* **1** border, bound, edge, fringe, hem, march, rim. **2** circumnavigate, circumvent, flank, go along. • *n* **1** border, boundary, edge, margin, rim, verge. **2** flap, kilt, overskirt, petticoat.

skittish *adj* **1** changeable, fickle, inconstant. **2** hasty, volatile, wanton. **3** shy, timid, timorous.

skulk *vb* hide, lurk, slink, sneak.

skulker *n* **1** lurker, sneak. **2** shirk, slacker, malingerer.

skull *n* brain pan, cranium.

sky *n* empyrean, firmament, heaven, heavens, welkin.

sky-blue *adj* azure, cerulean, sapphire, sky-coloured.

skylarking *n* carousing, frolicking, sporting.

slab *adj* slimy, thick, viscous. • *n* **1** beam, board, layer, panel, plank, slat, table, tablet. **2** mire, mud, puddle, slime.

slabber *vb* **1** drivel, slaver, slobber. **2** drop, let fall, shed, spill.

slack *vb* **1** ease off, let up. **2** abate, ease up, relax, slacken. **3** malinger, shirk. **4** choke, damp, extinguish, smother, stifle. • *adj* **1** backward, careless, inattentive, lax, negligent, remiss. **2** abated, dilatory, diminished, lingering, slow, tardy. **3** loose, relaxed. **4** dull, idle, inactive, quiet, sluggish. • *n* **1** excess, leeway, looseness, play. **2** coal dust, culm, residue.

adj antonyms busy, diligent, quick, rigid, stiff, taut.

slacken *vb* **1** abate, diminish, lessen, lower, mitigate, moderate, neglect, remit, relieve, retard, slack. **2** loosen, relax. **3** flag, slow down. **4** bridle, check, control, curb, repress, restrain.

slackness *n* **1** looseness. **2** inattention, negligence, remissness. **3** slowness, tardiness.

slander *vb* **1** asperse, backbite, belie, brand, calumniate, decry, defame, libel, malign, reproach, scandalize, traduce, vilify. **2** detract from, disparage. • *n* aspersion, backbiting, calumny, defamation, detraction, libel, obloquy, scandal, vilification.

vb antonyms glorify, praise.

slanderous *adj* calumnious, defamatory, false, libellous, malicious, maligning.

slang *n* argo, cant, jargon, lingo.

slant *vb* incline, lean, lie obliquely, list, slope. • *n* inclination, slope, steep, tilt.

slap *vb* dab, clap, pat, smack, spank, strike. • *adv* instantly, quickly, plumply. • *n* blow, clap.

slapdash *adv* haphazardly, hurriedly, precipitately.

slash *vb* cut, gash, slit. • *n* cut, gash, slit.

slashed *adj* **1** cut, slit. **2** (*bot*) jagged, laciniate, multifid.

slattern *adj* slatternly, slovenly, sluttish. • *n* drab, slut, sloven, trollop.

slatternly *adj* dirty, slattern, slovenly, sluttish, unclean, untidy. • *adv* carelessly, negligently, sluttishly.

slaughter *vb* butcher, kill, massacre, murder, slay. • *n* bloodshed, butchery, carnage, havoc, killing, massacre, murder, slaying.

slaughterer *n* assassin, butcher, cutthroat, destroyer, killer, murderer, slayer.

slave *vb* drudge, moil, toil. • *n* **1** captive, dependant, henchman, helot, peon, serf, thrall, vassal, villein. **2** drudge, menial.

slavery *n* **1** bondage, bond-service, captivity, enslavement, enthralment, serfdom, servitude, thraldom, vassalage, villeinage. **2** drudgery, mean labour.

n antonym freedom.

slavish *adj* **1** abject, beggarly, base, cringing, fawning, grovelling, low, mean, obsequious, servile, sycophantic. **2** drudging, laborious, menial, servile.

slay *vb* **1** assassinate, butcher, dispatch, kill, massacre, murder, slaughter. **2** destroy, ruin.

slayer *n* assassin, destroyer, killer, murderer, slaughterer.

sledge *n* **1** drag, sled. **2** cutter, pung, sleigh.

sleek *adj* glossy, satin, silken, silky, smooth.

sleekly *adv* evenly, glossily, nicely, smoothly.

sleep *vb* catnap, doze, drowse, nap, slumber. • *n* dormancy, hypnosis, lethargy, repose, rest, slumber.

sleeping *adj* dormant, inactive, quiescent.

sleepwalker *n* night-walker, noctambulist, somnambulist.

sleepwalking *n* somnambulism.

sleepy *adj* **1** comatose, dozy, drowsy, heavy, lethargic, nodding, somnolent. **2** narcotic, opiate, slumberous, somniferous, somnific, soporiferous, soporific. **3** dull, heavy, inactive, lazy, slow, sluggish, torpid.

adj antonyms alert, awake, restless, wakeful.

sleight *n* adroitness, dexterity, manoeuvring.

sleight of hand *n* conjuring, hocus-pocus, jugglery, legerdemain, prestidigitation.

slender *adj* **1** lank, lithe, narrow, skinny, slim, spindly, thin. **2** feeble, fine, flimsy, fragile, slight, tenuous, weak. **3** inconsiderable, moderate, small, trivial. **4** exiguous, inadequate, insufficient, lean, meagre, pitiful, scanty. **5** abstemious, light, simple, spare, sparing.

adj antonyms considerable, fat, thick.

slice *vb* **1** cut, divide, part, section. **2** cut off, sever. • *n* chop, collop, piece.

slick *adj* **1** glassy, glossy, polished, sleek, smooth. **2** alert, clever, cunning, shrewd, slippery, unctuous. *vb* burnish, gloss, lacquer, polish, shine, sleek, varnish. **3** grease, lubricate, oil.

slide vb glide, move smoothly, slip. • n glide, glissade, skid, slip.

sliding adj gliding, slippery, uncertain. • n backsliding, falling, fault, lapse, transgression.

slight vb **1** cold-shoulder, disdain, disregard, neglect, snub. **2** overlook. **3** scamp, skimp, slur. • adj **1** inconsiderable, insignificant, little, paltry, petty, small, trifling, trivial, unimportant, unsubstantial. **2** delicate, feeble, frail, gentle, weak. **3** careless, cursory, desultory, hasty, hurried, negligent, scanty, superficial. **4** flimsy, perishable. **5** slender, slim. • n discourtesy, disregard, disrespect, inattention, indignity, neglect. vb antonyms compliment, flatter. adj antonyms considerable, large, major, significant.

slightingly adv contemptuously, disrespectfully, scornfully, slightly.

slightly adv **1** inconsiderably, little, somewhat. **2** feebly, slenderly, weakly. **3** cursorily, hastily, negligently, superficially.

slim vb bant, diet, lose weight, reduce, slenderize. • adj **1** gaunt, lank, lithe, narrow, skinny, slender, spare. **2** inconsiderable, paltry, poor, slight, trifling, trivial, unsubstantial, weak. **3** insufficient, meagre. adj antonyms chubby, fat, strong.

slime n mire, mud, ooze, sludge.

slimy adj **1** miry, muddy, oozy. **2** clammy, gelatinous, glutinous, gummy, lubricious, mucilaginous, mucous, ropy, slabby, viscid, viscous.

sling vb **1** cast, fling, hurl, throw. **2** hang up, suspend.

slink vb skulk, slip away, sneak, steal away.

slip vb **1** glide, slide. **2** err, mistake, trip. **3** lose, omit. **4** disengage, throw off. **5** escape, let go, loose, loosen, release. • n **1** glide, slide, slipping. **2** blunder, lapse, misstep, mistake, oversight, peccadillo, trip. **3** backsliding, error, fault, impropriety, indiscretion, transgression. **4** desertion, escape. **5** cord, leash, strap, string. **6** case, covering, wrapper.

slippery adj **1** glib, slithery, smooth. **2** changeable, insecure, mutable, perilous, shaky, uncertain, unsafe, unstable, unsteady. **3** cunning, dishonest, elusive, faithless, false, knavish, perfidious, shifty, treacherous.

slipshod adj careless, shuffling, slovenly, untidy. adj antonyms careful, fastidious, neat, tidy.

slit vb **1** cut. **2** divide, rend, slash, split, sunder. • n cut, gash.

slobber vb **1** drivel, drool, slabber, slaver. **2** daub, obscure, smear, stain.

slobbery adj dank, floody, moist, muddy, sloppy, wet.

slope vb incline, slant, tilt. • n acclivity, cant, declivity, glacis, grade, gradient, incline, inclination, obliquity, pitch, ramp.

sloping adj aslant, bevelled, declivitous, inclining, oblique, shelving, slanting.

sloppy adj muddy, slabby, splashy, slobbery, splashy, wet.

sloth n **1** dilatoriness, slowness, tardiness. **2** idleness, inaction, inactivity, indolence, inertness, laziness, lumpishness, slothfulness, sluggishness, supineness, torpor. n antonyms diligence, industriousness, sedulity.

slothful adj dronish, idle, inactive, indolent, inert, lazy, lumpish, slack, sluggish, supine, torpid. adj antonyms diligent, industrious, sedulous.

slouch vb **1** droop, loll, slump. **2** shamble, shuffle. • n **1** malingerer, shirker, slacker. **2** shamble, shuffle, stoop.

slouching adj awkward, clownish, loutish, lubberly, uncouth, ungainly.

slough[1] n **1** bog, fen, marsh, morass, quagmire. **2** dejection, depression, despondence, despondency.

slough[2] vb **1** cast, desquamate, excuviate, moult, shed, throw off. **2** cast off, discard, divest, jettison, reject. • n cast, desquamation.

sloven n slattern, slob, slouch, slut.

slovenly adj **1** unclean, untidy. **2** blowsy, disorderly, dowdy, frowsy, loose, slatternly, tacky, unkempt, untidy. **3** careless, heedless, lazy, negligent, perfunctory.

slow vb **1** abate, brake, check, decelerate, diminish, lessen, mitigate, moderate, modulate, reduce, weaken. **2** delay, detain, retard. **3** ease, ease up, relax, slack, slacken, slack off. • adj **1** deliberate, gradual. **2** dead, dull, heavy, inactive, inert, sluggish, stupid. **3** behindhand, late, tardy, unready. **4** delaying, dilatory, lingering, slack. adj antonyms active, fast, quick, rapid, swift.

sludge *n* **1** mire, mud. **2** slosh, slush.

sluggish *adj* **1** dronish, drowsy, idle, inactive, indolent, inert, languid, lazy, listless, lumpish, phlegmatic, slothful, torpid. **2** slow. **3** dull, stupid, supine, tame.

adj antonyms brisk, dynamic, eager, quick, vigorous.

sluice *vb* drain, drench, flood, flush, irrigate. • *n* floodgate, opening, vent.

slumber *vb* catnap, doze, nap, repose, rest, sleep. • *n* catnap, doze, nap, repose, rest, siesta, sleep.

slump *vb* **1** droop, drop, fall, flop, founder, sag, sink, sink down. **2** decline, depreciate, deteriorate, ebb, fail, fall away, lose ground, recede, slide, slip, subside, wane. • *n* **1** droop, drop, fall, flop, lowering, sag, sinkage. **2** decline, depreciation, deterioration, downturn, downtrend, subsidence, ebb, falling off, wane. **3** crash, recession, smash.

n antonym boom.

slur *vb* **1** asperse, calumniate, disparage, depreciate, reproach, traduce. **2** conceal, disregard, gloss over, obscure, pass over, slight. • *n* **1** mark, stain. **2** brand, disgrace, reproach, stain, stigma. **3** innuendo.

slush *n* slosh, sludge.

slushy *vb* plashy, sloppy, sloshy, sludgy.

slut *n* drab, slattern, sloven, trollop.

sluttish *adj* careless, dirty, disorderly, unclean, untidy.

sly *adj* **1** artful, crafty, cunning, insidious, subtle, wily. **2** astute, cautious, shrewd. **3** arch, knowing, clandestine, secret, stealthy, underhand.

adj antonyms frank, honest, open, straightforward.

smack[1] *vb* smell, taste. • *n* **1** flavour, savour, tang, taste, tincture. **2** dash, infusion, little, space, soupçon, sprinkling, tinge, touch. **3** smattering.

smack[2] *vb* **1** slap, strike. **2** crack, slash, snap. **3** buss, kiss. • *n* **1** crack, slap, slash, snap. **2** buss, kiss.

small *adj* **1** diminutive, Lilliputian, little, miniature, petite, pygmy, tiny, wee. **2** infinitesimal, microscopic, minute. **3** inappreciable, inconsiderable, insignificant, petty, trifling, trivial, unimportant. **4** moderate, paltry, scanty, slender. **5** faint, feeble, puny, slight, weak. **6** illiberal, mean, narrow, narrow-minded, paltry, selfish, ungenerous, unworthy.

adj antonyms big, huge, large.

small talk *n* chat, conversation, gossip.

smart[1] *vb* **1** hurt, pain, sting. **2** suffer. • *adj* keen, painful, poignant, pricking, pungent, severe, sharp, stinging.

smart[2] *adj* **1** active, agile, brisk, fresh, lively, nimble, quick, spirited, sprightly, spry. **2** effective, efficient, energetic, forcible, vigorous. **3** adroit, alert, clever, dexterous, dextrous, expert, intelligent, stirring. **4** acute, apt, pertinent, ready, witty. **5** chic, dapper, fine, natty, showy, spruce, trim.

adj antonyms dowdy, dumb, slow, stupid, unfashionable, untidy.

smartness *n* **1** acuteness, keenness, poignancy, pungency, severity, sharpness. **2** efficiency, energy, force, vigour. **3** activity, agility, briskness, liveliness, nimbleness, sprightliness, spryness, vivacity. **4** alertness, cleverness, dexterity, expertise, expertness, intelligence, quickness. **5** acuteness, aptness, pertinency, wit, wittiness. **6** chic, nattiness, spruceness, trimness.

smash *vb* break, crush, dash, mash, shatter. • *n* **1** crash, debacle, destruction, ruin. **2** bankruptcy, failure.

smattering *n* dabbling, smatter, sprinkling.

smear *vb* **1** bedaub, begrime, besmear, daub, plaster, smudge. **2** contaminate, pollute, smirch, smut, soil, stain, sully, tarnish. • *n* **1** blot, blotch, daub, patch, smirch, smudge, spot, stain. **2** calumny, defamation, libel, slander.

smell *vb* scent, sniff, stench, stink. • *n* **1** aroma, bouquet, fragrance, fume, odour, perfume, redolence, scent, stench, stink. **2** sniff, snuff.

smelt *vb* fuse, melt.

smile *vb* grin, laugh, simper, smirk. • *n* grin, simper, smirk.

smite *vb* **1** beat, box, collide, cuff, knock, strike, wallop, whack. **2** destroy, kill, slay. **3** afflict, chasten, punish. **4** blast, destroy.

smitten *adj* **1** attracted, captivated, charmed, enamoured, fascinated, taken. **2** destroyed, killed, slain. **3** smit, struck. **4** afflicted, chastened, punished.

smock *n* **1** chemise, shift, slip. **2** blouse, gaberdine.

smoke *vb* **1** emit, exhale, reek, steam. **2** fumigate, smudge. **3** discover, find out, smell out. • *n* **1** effluvium, exhalation, fume, mist, reek, smother, steam, vapour. **2** fumigation, smudge.

smoky *adj* **1** fuliginous, fumid, fumy, smudgy. **2** begrimed, blackened, dark, reeky, sooty, tanned.

smooth *vb* **1** flatten, level, plane. **2** ease, lubricate. **3** extenuate, palliate, soften. **4** allay, alleviate, assuage, calm, mitigate, mollify. • *adj* **1** even, flat, level, plane, polished, unruffled, unwrinkled. **2** glabrous, glossy, satiny, silky, sleek, soft, velvet. **3** euphonious, flowing, liquid, mellifluent. **4** fluent, glib, voluble. **5** bland, flattering, ingratiating, insinuating, mild, oily, smooth-tongued, soothing, suave, unctuous.
vb antonym roughen.
adj antonyms coarse, harsh, irregular, rough, unsteady.

smoothly *adv* **1** evenly. **2** easily, readily, unobstructedly. **3** blandly, flatteringly, gently, mildly, pleasantly, softly, soothingly.

smooth-tongued *adj* adulatory, cozening, flattering, plausible, smooth, smooth-spoken.

smother *vb* **1** choke, stifle, suffocate. **2** conceal, deaden, extinguish, hide, keep down, repress, suppress. **3** smoke, smoulder.

smudge *vb* besmear, blacken, blur, smear, smut, smutch, soil, spot, stain. • *n* blur, blot, smear, smut, spot, stain.

smug *adj* **1** complacent, self-satisfied. **2** neat, nice, spruce, trim.
adj antonym modest.

smuggler *n* contrabandist, runner.

smut *vb* blacken, smouch, smudge, soil, stain, sully, taint, tarnish. • *n* dirt, **1** smudge, smutch, soot. **2** nastiness, obscenity, ribaldry, smuttiness. **3** pornography.

smutty *adj* **1** coarse, gross, immodest, impure, indecent, indelicate, loose, nasty. **2** dirty, foul, nasty, soiled, stained.
adj antonyms clean, decent.

snack *n* bite, light meal, nibble.

snag *vb* catch, enmesh, entangle, hook, snare, sniggle, tangle. • *n* **1** knarl, knob, knot, projection, protuberance, snub. **2** catch, difficulty, drawback, hitch, rub, shortcoming, weakness. **3** obstacle.

snaky *adj* **1** serpentine, snaking, winding. **2** artful, cunning, deceitful, insinuating, sly, subtle.

snap *vb* **1** break, fracture. **2** bite, catch at, seize, snatch at, snip. **3** crack. **4** crackle, crepitate, decrepitate, pop. • *adj* casual, cursory, hasty, offhand, sudden, superficial. • *n* **1** bite, catch, nip, seizure. **2** catch,

clasp, fastening, lock. **3** crack, fillip, flick, flip, smack. **4** briskness, energy, verve, vim.

snappish *adj* acrimonious, captious, churlish, crabbed, cross, crusty, froward, irascible, ill-tempered, peevish, perverse, pettish, petulant, snarling, splenetic, surly, tart, testy, touchy, waspish.

snare *vb* catch, ensnare, entangle, entrap. • *n* catch, gin, net, noose, springe, toil, trap, wile.

snarl[1] *vb* girn, gnarl, growl, grumble, murmur. • *n* growl, grumble.

snarl[2] *vb* **1** complicate, disorder, entangle, knot. **3** confuse, embarrass, ensnare. • *n* **1** complication, disorder, entanglement, tangle. **2** difficulty, embarrassment, intricacy.

snatch *vb* catch, clutch, grasp, grip, pluck, pull, seize, snip, twich, wrest, wring, • *n* **1** bit, fragment, part, portion. **2** catch, effort.

sneak *vb* **1** lurk, skulk, slink, steal. **2** crouch, truckle. • *adj* clandestine, concealed, covert, hidden, secret, sly, underhand. • *n* **1** informer, telltale. **2** lurker, shirk.

sneaky *adj* **1** furtive, skulking, slinking. **2** abject, crouching, grovelling, mean. **3** clandestine, concealed, covert, hidden, secret, sly, underhand.

sneer *vb* **1** flout, gibe, jeer, mock, rail, scoff. **2** (*with* at) deride, despise, disdain, laugh at, mock, rail at, scoff, spurn. • *n* flouting, gibe, jeer, scoff.

snicker *vb* giggle, laugh, snigger, titter.

sniff *vb* **1** breathe, inhale, snuff. **2** scent, smell.

snip *vb* **1** clip, cut, nip. **2** snap, snatch. • *n* **1** bit, fragment, particle, piece, shred. **2** share, snack.

snivel *vb* blubber, cry, fret, sniffle, snuffle, weep, whimper, whine.

snob *n* climber, toady.

snooze *vb* catnap, doze, drowse, nap, sleep, slumber. • *n* catnap, nap, sleep, slumber.

snout *n* **1** muzzle, nose. **2** nozzle.

snowy *adj* immaculate, pure, spotless, unblemished, unstained, unsullied, white.

snub[1] *vb* abash, cold-shoulder, cut, discomfit, humble, humiliate, mortify, slight, take down. • *n* check, rebuke, slight.

snub[2] *vb* check, clip, cut short, dock, nip, prune, stunt. • *adj* pug, retroussé, snubbed, squashed, squat, stubby, turned-up.

snuff¹ *vb* **1** breathe, inhale, sniff. **2** scent, smell. **2** snort.

snuff² *vb* (*with* out) annihilate, destroy, efface, extinguish, obliterate.

snuffle *vb* **1** sniffle. **2** snort, snuff.

snug *adj* **1** close, concealed. **2** comfortable, compact, convenient, neat, trim.

snuggle *vb* cuddle, nestle, nuzzle.

so *adv* **1** thus, with equal reason. **2** in such a manner. **3** in this way, likewise. **4** as it is, as it was, such. **5** for this reason, therefore. **6** be it so, thus be it. • *conj* in case that, on condition that, provided that.

soak *vb* **1** drench, moisten, permeate, saturate, wet. **2** absorb, imbibe. **3** imbue, macerate, steep.

soar *vb* ascend, fly aloft, glide, mount, rise, tower.
vb antonym plummet.

sob *vb* cry, sigh convulsively, weep.

sober *vb* (*with* up) calm down, collect oneself, compose oneself, control oneself, cool off, master, moderate, simmer down. • *adj* **1** abstemious, abstinent, temperate, unintoxicated. **2** rational, reasonable, sane, sound. **3** calm, collected, composed, cool, dispassionate, moderate, rational, regular, restrained, steady, temperate, unimpassioned, unruffled, well-regulated. **4** demure, grave, quiet, sedate, serious, solemn, sombre, staid. **5** dark, drab, dull-looking, quiet, sad, subdued.
adj antonyms drunk, excited, frivolous, gay, intemperate, irrational.

sobriety *n* **1** abstemiousness, abstinence, soberness, temperance. **2** calmness, coolness, gravity, sedateness, sober-mindedness, staidness, thoughtfulness. **3** gravity, seriousness, solemnity.
n antonyms drunkenness, excitement, frivolity.

sobriquet *n* appellation, nickname, nom de plume, pseudonym.

sociability *n* companionableness, comradeship, good fellowship, sociality.

sociable *adj* accessible, affable, communicative, companionable, conversable, friendly, genial, neighbourly, social.

social *adj* **1** civic, civil. **2** accessible, affable, communicative, companionable, familiar, friendly, hospitable, neighbourly, sociable. **3** convivial, festive, gregarious. • *n* conversazione, gathering, get-together, party, reception, soiree.

society *n* **1** association, companionship, company, converse, fellowship. **2** the community, populace, the public, the world. **3** élite, monde. **4** body, brotherhood, copartnership, corporation, club, fraternity, partnership, sodality, union.

sodden *adj* **1** drenched, saturated, soaked, steeped, wet. **2** boiled, decocted, seethed, stewed.

sofa *n* couch, davenport, divan, ottoman, settee.

soft *adj* **1** impressible, malleable, plastic, pliable, yielding. **2** downy, fleecy, velvety, mushy, pulpy, squashy. **3** compliant, facile, irresolute, submissive, undecided, weak. **4** bland, mild, gentle, kind, lenient, softhearted, tender. **5** delicate. **6** easy, even, quiet, smooth-going, steady. **7** effeminate, luxurious, unmanly. **8** dulcet, fluty, mellifluous, melodious, smooth. • *interj* hold, stop.
adj antonyms hard, harsh, heavy, loud, rigid, rough, severe, strict.

soften *vb* **1** intenerate, mellow, melt, tenderize. **2** abate, allay, alleviate, appease, assuage, balm, blunt, calm, dull, ease, lessen, make easy, mitigate, moderate, mollify, qualify, quell, quiet, relent, relieve, soothe, still, temper. **3** extenuate, modify, palliate, qualify. **4** enervate, weaken.

soil¹ *n* **1** earth, ground loam, mould. **2** country, land.

soil² *vb* bedaub, begrime, bemire, besmear, bespatter, contaminate, daub, defile, dirty, foul, pollute, smirch, stain, sully, taint, tarnish. • *n* **1** blemish, defilement, dirt, filth, foulness. **2** blot, spot, stain, taint, tarnish.

sojourn *vb* abide, dwell, live, lodge, remain, reside, rest, stay, stop, tarry, visit. • *n* residence, stay.

solace *vb* **1** cheer, comfort, console, soothe. **2** allay, assuage, mitigate, relieve, soften. • *n* alleviation, cheer, comfort, consolation, relief.

soldier *n* **1** fighting man, man-at-arms, warrior. **2** GI, private.

soldierly *adj* **1** martial, military, warlike. **2** brave, courageous, gallant, heroic, honourable, intrepid, valiant.

sole *adj* alone, individual, one, only, single, solitary, unique.
adj antonyms multiple, shared.

solecism *n* barbarism, blunder, error, faux pas, impropriety, incongruity, mistake, slip.

solemn *adj* **1** ceremonial, formal, ritual. **2** devotional, devout, religious, reverential, sacred. **3** earnest, grave, serious, sober. **4** august, awe-inspiring, awful, grand, imposing, impressive, majestic, stately, venerable.
adj antonyms frivolous, gay, light-hearted.

solemnity *n* **1** celebration, ceremony, observance, office, rite. **2** awfulness, sacredness, sanctity. **3** gravity, impressiveness, seriousness.

solemnize *vb* celebrate, commemorate, honour, keep, observe.

solicit *vb* **1** appeal to, ask, beg, beseech, conjure, crave, entreat, implore, importune, petition, pray, press, request, supplicate, urge. **2** arouse, awaken, entice, excite, invite, summon. **3** canvass, seek.

solicitation *n* **1** address, appeal, asking, entreaty, importunity, insistence, petition, request, suit, supplication, urgency. **2** bidding, call, invitation, summons.

solicitor *n* **1** attorney, law agent, lawyer. **2** asker, canvasser, drummer, petitioner, solicitant.

solicitous *adj* anxious, apprehensive, careful, concerned, disturbed, eager, troubled, uneasy.

solicitude *n* anxiety, care, carefulness, concern, perplexity, trouble.

solid *adj* **1** congealed, firm, hard, impenetrable, rock-like. **2** compact, dense, impermeable, massed. **3** cubic. **4** sound, stable, stout, strong, substantial. **5** just, real, true, valid, weighty. **6** dependable, faithful, reliable, safe, staunch, steadfast, trustworthy, well established.
adj antonyms broken, insubstantial, liquid.

solidarity *n* communion of interests, community, consolidation, fellowship, joint interest, mutual responsibility.

solidify *vb* compact, congeal, consolidate, harden, petrify.

solidity *n* **1** compactness, consistency, density, firmness, hardness, solidness. **2** fullness. **3** massiveness, stability, strength. **4** dependability, gravity, justice, reliability, soundness, steadiness, validity, weight. **5** cubic content, volume.

soliloquy *n* monologue.

solitariness *n* **1** isolation, privacy, reclusion, retirement, seclusion. **2** loneliness, solitude.

solitary *adj* **1** alone, companionless, lone, lonely, only, separate, unaccompanied. **2** individual, single, sole. **3** desert, deserted, desolate, isolated, lonely, remote, retired, secluded, unfrequented.
adj antonyms accompanied, gregarious.

solitude *n* **1** isolation, loneliness, privacy, recluseness, retiredness, retirement, seclusion, solitariness. **2** desert, waste, wilderness.
n antonym companionship.

solution *n* **1** answer, clue, disentanglement, elucidation, explication, explanation, key, resolution, unravelling, unriddling. **2** disintegration, dissolution, liquefaction, melting, resolution, separation. **3** breach, disconnection, discontinuance, disjunction, disruption.

solve *vb* clear, clear up, disentangle, elucidate, explain, expound, interpret, make plain, resolve, unfold.

solvent *n* diluent, dissolvent, menstruum.

somatic *adj* bodily, corporeal.

sombre *adj* **1** cloudy, dark, dismal, dull, dusky, gloomy, murky, overcast, rayless, shady, sunless. **2** doleful, funereal, grave, lugubrious, melancholy, mournful, sad, sober.

some *adj* **1** a, an, any, one. **2** about, near. **3** certain, little, moderate, part, several.

somebody *n* **1** one, someone, something. **2** celebrity, VIP.

somehow *adv* in some way.

something *n* **1** part, portion, thing. **2** somebody. **3** affair, event, matter.

sometime *adj* former, late. • *adv* **1** formerly, once. **2** now and then, at one time or other, sometimes.

sometimes *adv* **1** at intervals, at times, now and then, occasionally. **2** at a past period, formerly, once.
adv antonyms always, never.

somewhat *adv* in some degree, more or less, rather, something. • *n* something, a little, more or less, part.

somewhere *adv* here and there, in one place or another, in some place.

somnambulism *n* sleepwalking, somnambulation.

somnambulist *n* night-walker, noctambulist, sleepwalker, somnambulator, somnambule.

somniferous *adj* narcotic, opiate, slumberous, somnific, soporific, soporiferous.

somnolence *n* doziness, drowsiness, sleepiness, somnolency.

somnolent *adj* dozy, drowsy, sleepy.

son *n* cadet, heir, junior, scion.

song *n* **1** aria, ballad, canticle, carol, ditty, glee, lay, lullaby, snatch. **2** descant, melody. **3** anthem, hymn, poem, psalm, strain. **4** poesy, poetry, verse.

sonorous *adj* **1** full-toned, resonant, resounding, ringing, sounding. **2** high-sounding, loud.

soon *adv* **1** anon, before long, by and by, in a short time, presently, shortly. **2** betimes, early, forthwith, promptly, quick. **3** gladly, lief, readily, willingly.

soot *n* carbon, crock, dust.

soothe *vb* **1** cajole, flatter, humour. **2** appease, assuage, balm, calm, compose, lull, mollify, pacify, quiet, soften, still, tranquillize. **3** allay, alleviate, blunt, check, deaden, dull, ease, lessen, mitigate, moderate, palliate, qualify, relieve, repress, soften, subdue, temper.

vb antonyms annoy, irritate, vex.

soothsayer *n* augur, diviner, foreteller, necromancer, predictor, prophet, seer, sorcerer, vaticinator.

sooty *adj* black, dark, dusky, fuliginous, murky, sable.

sophism *n* casuistry, fallacy, paralogism, paralogy, quibble, specious argument.

sophist *n* quibbler.

sophistical *adj* casuistical, fallacious, illogical, quibbling, subtle, unsound.

soporific *adj* dormitive, hypnotic, narcotic, opiate, sleepy, slumberous, somnific, somniferous, soporiferous, soporous.

soppy *adj* **1** drenched, saturated, soaked, sopped. **2** emotional, mawkish, sentimental.

soprano *n* (*mus*) descant, discant, treble.

sorcerer *n* charmer, conjurer, diviner, enchanter, juggler, magician, necromancers, seer, shaman, soothsayer, thaumaturgist, wizard.

sorcery *n* black art, charm, divination, enchantment, necromancy, occultism, shamanism, spell, thaumaturgy, voodoo, witchcraft.

sordid *adj* base, degraded, low, mean, vile.

sore *adj* **1** irritated, painful, raw, tender, ulcerated. **2** aggrieved, galled, grieved, hurt, irritable, vexed. **3** afflictive, distressing, severe, sharp, violent. • *n* **1** abscess, boil, fester, gathering, imposthume, pustule, ulcer. **2** affliction, grief, pain, sorrow, trouble.

sorely *adv* greatly, grievously, severely, violently.

sorrily *adv* despicably, meanly, pitiably, poorly, wretchedly.

sorrow *vb* bemoan, bewail, grieve, lament, mourn, weep. • *n* affliction, dolour, grief, heartache, mourning, sadness, trouble, woe.

vb antonym rejoice.

n antonyms happiness, joy.

sorrowful *adj* **1** afflicted, dejected, depressed, grieved, grieving, heartsore, sad. **2** baleful, distressing, grievous, lamentable, melancholy, mournful, painful. **3** disconsolate, dismal, doleful, dolorous, drear, dreary, lugubrious, melancholy, piteous, rueful, woebegone, woeful.

adj antonyms happy, joyful.

sorry *adj* **1** afflicted, dejected, grieved, pained, poor, sorrowful. **2** distressing, pitiful. **3** chagrined, mortified, pained, regretful, remorseful, sad, vexed. **4** abject, base, beggarly, contemptible, despicable, low, mean, paltry, insignificant, miserable, shabby, worthless, wretched.

adj antonym glad.

sort *vb* **1** arrange, assort, class, classify, distribute, order. **2** conjoin, join, put together. **3** choose, elect, pick out, select. **4** associate, consort, fraternize. **5** accord, agree with, fit, suit. • *n* **1** character, class, denomination, description, kind, nature, order, race, rank, species, type. **2** manner, way.

sortie *n* attack, foray, raid, sally.

so-so *adj* indifferent, mediocre, middling, ordinary, passable, tolerable.

sot *n* **1** blockhead, dolt, dullard, dunce, fool, simpleton. **2** drunkard, tippler, toper.

sottish *adj* **1** doltish, dull, foolish, senseless, simple, stupid. **2** befuddled, besotted, drunken, insensate, senseless, tipsy.

sotto voce *adv* in a low voice, in an undertone, softly.

sough *n* **1** murmur, sigh. **2** breath, breeze, waft.

soul *n* **1** mind, psyche, spirit. **2** being, person. **3** embodiment, essence, personification, spirit, vital principle. **4** ardour, energy, fervour, inspiration, vitality.

soulless *adj* dead, expressionless, lifeless, unfeeling.

sound¹ *adj* entire, intact, unbroken, unhurt, unimpaired, **1** uninjured, unmutilated, whole. **2** hale, hardy, healthy, hearty, vigorous. **3** good, perfect, undecayed. **4** sane, well-balanced. **5** correct, orthodox, right, solid, valid, well-founded. **6** legal. **7** deep, fast, profound, unbroken, undisturbed. **8** forcible, lusty, severe, stout.

sound² *n* channel, narrows, strait.
adj antonyms shaky, unfit, unreliable, unsound.

sound³ *vb* **1** resound. **2** appear, seem. **3** play on. **4** express, pronounce, utter. **5** announce, celebrate, proclaim, publish, spread. • *n* noise, note, tone, voice, whisper.

sound⁴ *vb* **1** fathom, gauge, measure, test. **2** examine, probe, search, test, try.

sounding *adj* **1** audible, resonant, resounding, ringing, sonorous. **2** imposing, significant.

soundless *adj* **1** dumb, noiseless, silent. **2** abysmal, bottomless, deep, profound, unfathomable, unsounded.

soundly *adv* **1** satisfactorily, thoroughly, well. **2** healthily, heartily. **3** forcibly, lustily, severely, smartly, stoutly. **4** correctly, rightly, truly. **5** firmly, strongly. **6** deeply, fast, profoundly.

soundness *n* **1** entireness, entirety, integrity, wholeness. **2** healthiness, vigour, saneness, sanity. **3** correctness, orthodoxy, rectitude, reliability, truth, validity. **4** firmness, solidity, strength, validity.

soup *n* broth, consommé, purée.

sour *vb* **1** acidulate. **2** embitter, envenom. • *adj* **1** acetose, acetous, acid, astringent, pricked, sharp, tart, vinegary. **2** acrimonious, crabbed, cross, crusty, fretful, glum, ill-humoured, ill-natured, ill-tempered, peevish, pettish, petulant, snarling, surly. **3** bitter, disagreeable, unpleasant. **4** austere, dismal, gloomy, morose, sad, sullen. **5** bad, coagulated, curdled, musty, rancid, turned.
adj antonyms good-natured, sweet.

source *n* **1** beginning, fountain, fountainhead, head, origin, rise, root, spring, well. **2** cause, original.

sourness *n* **1** acidity, sharpness, tartness. **2** acrimony, asperity, churlishness, crabbedness, crossness, discontent, harshness, moroseness, peevishness.

souse *vb* **1** pickle. **2** dip, douse, immerse, plunge, submerge.

souvenir *n* keepsake, memento, remembrance, reminder.

sovereign *adj* **1** imperial, monarchical, princely, regal, royal, supreme. **2** chief, commanding, excellent, highest, paramount, predominant, principal, supreme, utmost. **3** efficacious, effectual. • *n* **1** autocrat, monarch, suzerain. **2** emperor, empress, king, lord, potentate, prince, princess, queen, ruler.

sovereignty *n* authority, dominion, empire, power, rule, supremacy, sway.

sow *vb* **1** scatter, spread, strew. **2** disperse, disseminate, propagate, spread abroad. **3** plant. **4** besprinkle, scatter.

space *n* **1** expanse, expansion, extension, extent, proportions, spread. **2** accommodation, capacity, room, place. **3** distance, interspace, interval.

spacious *adj* **1** extended, extensive, vast, wide. **2** ample, broad, capacious, commodious, large, roomy, wide.
adj antonyms confined, cramped, narrow, small.

span *vb* compass, cross, encompass, measure, overlay. • *n* **1** brief period, spell. **2** pair, team, yoke.

spank *vb* slap, strike.

spar¹ *n* beam, boom, pole, (*naut*) sprit, yard.

spar² *vb* **1** box, fight. **2** argue, bicker, contend, dispute, quarrel, spat, squabble, wrangle.

spare *vb* **1** lay aside, lay by, reserve, save, set apart, set aside. **2** dispense with, do without, part with. **3** forbear, omit, refrain, withhold. **4** exempt, forgive, keep from. **5** afford, allow, give, grant. **6** save. **7** economize, pinch. • *adj* **1** frugal, scanty, sparing, stinted. **2** chary, parsimonious. **3** emaciated, gaunt, lank, lean, meagre, poor, thin, scraggy, skinny. **4** additional, extra, supernumerary.
adj antonyms corpulent, necessary, profuse.

sparing *adj* **1** little, scanty, scarce. **2** abstemious, meagre, spare. **3** chary, economical, frugal, parsimonious, saving. **4** compassionate, forgiving, lenient, merciful.
adj antonyms lavish, liberal, unsparing.

spark *vb* **1** scintillate, sparkle. **2** begin, fire, incite, instigate, kindle, light, set off, start, touch off, trigger. • *n* **1** scintilla, scintillation, sparkle. **2** beginning, element, germ, seed.

sparkle *vb* **1** coruscate, flash, gleam, glisten, glister, glitter, radiate, scintillate, shine, twinkle. **2** bubble, effervesce, foam, froth. • *n* **1** glint, scintillation, spark. **2** luminosity, lustre.

sparkling *adj* **1** brilliant, flashing, glistening, glittering, glittery, twinkling. **2** bubbling, effervescing, eloquent, foaming, frothing, mantling. **3** brilliant, glowing, lively, nervous, piquant, racy, spirited, sprightly, witty.

sparse *adj* dispersed, infrequent, scanty, scattered, sporadic, thin.

spartan *adj* **1** bold, brave, chivalric, courageous, daring, dauntless, doughty, fearless, hardy, heroic, intrepid, lion-hearted, undaunted, valiant, valorous. **2** austere, exacting, hard, severe, tough, unsparing. **3** enduring, long-suffering, self-controlled, stoic.

spasm *n* **1** contraction, cramp, crick, twitch. **2** fit, paroxysm, seizure, throe.

spasmodic *adj* **1** erratic, fitful, intermittent, irregular, sporadic. **2** convulsive, paroxysmal, spasmodical, violent.

spat *vb* argue, bicker, dispute, jangle, quarrel, spar, squabble, wrangle.

spatter *vb* **1** bespatter, besprinkle, plash, splash, sprinkle. **2** spit, sputter.

spawn *vb* bring forth, generate, produce. • *n* **1** eggs, roe. **2** fruit, offspring, product.

speak *vb* **1** articulate, deliver, enunciate, express, pronounce, utter. **2** announce, confer, declare, disclose, mention, say, tell. **3** celebrate, make known, proclaim, speak abroad. **4** accost, address, greet, hail. **5** exhibit. **6** argue, converse, dispute, talk. **7** declaim, discourse, hold forth, harangue, orate, plead, spout, treat.

speaker *n* **1** discourse, elocutionist, orator, prolocutor, spokesman. **2** chairman, presiding officer.

speaking *adj* **1** rhetorical, talking. **2** eloquent, expressive. **3** lifelike. • *n* **1** discourse, talk, utterance. **2** declamation, elocution, oratory.

spear *n* **1** dart, gaff, harpoon, javelin, lance, pike. **2** shoot, spire.

special *adj* **1** specific, specifical. **2** especial, individual, particular, peculiar, unique. **3** exceptional, extraordinary, marked, particular, uncommon. **4** appropriate, express. *adj antonyms* common, normal, ordinary, usual.

speciality, specialty *n* **1** particularity. **2** feature, forte, pet subject.

species *n* **1** assemblage, class, collection, group. **2** description, kind, sort, variety. **3** (*law*) fashion, figure, form, shape.

specific *adj* **1** characteristic, especial, particular, peculiar. **2** definite, limited, precise, specified. *adj antonyms* general, vague.

specification *n* **1** characterization, designation. **2** details, particularization.

specify *vb* define, designate, detail, indicate, individualize, name, show, particularize.

specimen *n* copy, example, model, pattern, sample.

specious *adj* **1** manifest, obvious, open, showy. **2** flimsy, illusory, ostensible, plausible, sophistical.

speck *n* **1** blemish, blot, flaw, speckle, spot, stain. **2** atom, bit, corpuscle, mite, mote, particle, scintilla.

spectacle *n* **1** display, exhibition, pageant, parade, representation, review, scene, show, sight. **2** curiosity, marvel, phenomenon, wonder.

spectacles *npl* glasses, goggles, shades.

spectator *n* beholder, bystander, observer, onlooker, witness. *n antonyms* contestant, participant, player.

spectral *adj* eerie, ghostlike, ghostly, phantomlike, shadowy, spooky, weird, wraithlike.

spectre, specter *n* apparition, banshee, ghost, goblin, hobgoblin, phantom, shade, shadow, spirit, sprite, wraith.

spectrum *n* appearance, image, representation.

speculate *vb* **1** cogitate, conjecture, contemplate, imagine, meditate, muse, ponder, reflect, ruminate, theorize, think. **2** bet, gamble, hazard, risk, trade, venture.

speculation *n* **1** contemplation, intellectualization. **2** conjecture, hypothesis, scheme, supposition, reasoning, reflection, theory, view.

speculative *adj* **1** contemplative, philosophical, speculatory, unpractical. **2** ideal, imaginary, theoretical. **3** hazardous, risky, unsecured.

speculator *n* **1** speculatist, theorist, theorizer. **2** adventurer, dealer, gambler, trader.

speech *n* **1** articulation, language, words. **2** dialect, idiom, locution, tongue. **3** conversation, oral communication, parlance, talk, verbal intercourse. **4** mention, observation, remark, saying. **5** address, declaration, discourse, harangue, oration, palaver.

speechless *adj* **1** dumb, gagged, inarticulate, mute, silent. **2** dazed, dumbfounded, flabbergasted, shocked.

speed *vb* **1** hasten, hurry, rush, scurry. **2** flourish, prosper, succeed, thrive. **3** accelerate, expedite, hasten, hurry, quicken, press forward, urge on. **4** carry through, dispatch, execute. **5** advance, aid, assist, help. **6** favour. • *n* **1** acceleration, celerity, dispatch, expedition, fleetness, haste, hurry, quickness, rapidity, swiftness, velocity. **2** good fortune, good luck, prosperity, success. **3** impetuosity.

vb antonyms delay, hamper, restrain, slow.

speedy *adj* **1** fast, fleet, flying, hasty, hurried, hurrying, nimble, quick, rapid, swift. **2** expeditious, prompt, quick. **3** approaching, early, near.

spell[1] *n* **1** charm, exorcism, hoodoo, incantation, jinx, witchery. **2** allure, bewitchment, captivation, enchantment, entrancement, fascination.

spell[2] *vb* decipher, interpret, read, unfold, unravel, unriddle.

spell[3] *n* fit, interval, period, round, season, stint, term, turn.

spellbound *adj* bewitched, charmed, enchanted, entranced, enthralled, fascinated.

spend *vb* **1** disburse, dispose of, expend, lay out, part with. **2** consume, dissipate, exhaust, lavish, squander, use up, wear, waste. **3** apply, bestow, devote, employ, pass.

vb antonyms hoard, save.

spendthrift *n* prodigal, spender, squanderer, waster.

n antonyms hoarder, miser, saver.

spent *adj* exhausted, fatigued, played out, used up, wearied, worn out.

spew *vb* **1** cast up, puke, throw up, vomit. **2** cast forth, eject.

spheral *adj* complete, perfect, symmetrical.

sphere *n* **1** ball, globe, orb, spheroid. **2** ambit, beat, bound, circle, circuit, compass, department, function, office, orbit, province, range, walk. **3** order, rank, standing. **4** country, domain, quarter, realm, region.

spherical *adj* **1** bulbous, globated, globous, globular, orbicular, rotund, round, spheroid. **2** planetary.

spice *n* **1** flavour, flavouring, relish, savour, taste. **2** admixture, dash, grain, infusion, particle, smack, soupçon, sprinkling, tincture.

spicily *adv* pungently, wittily.

spicy *adj* **1** aromatic, balmy, fragrant. **2** keen, piquant, pointed, pungent, sharp. **3** indelicate, off-colour, racy, risqué, sensational, suggestive.

adj antonym bland.

spill *vb* effuse, pour out, shed. • *n* accident, fall, tumble.

spin *vb* **1** twist. **2** draw out, extend. **3** lengthen, prolong, protract, spend. **4** pirouette, turn, twirl, whirl. • *n* **1** drive, joyride, ride. **2** auto-rotation, gyration, loop, revolution, rotation, turning, wheeling. **3** pirouette, reel, turn, wheel, whirl.

spindle *n* axis, shaft.

spine *n* **1** barb, prickle, thorn. **2** backbone. **3** ridge.

spinose *adj* briery, spinous, spiny, thorny.

spiny *adj* **1** briery, prickly, spinose, spinous, thorny. **2** difficult, perplexed, troublesome.

spiracle *n* aperture, blowhole, orifice, pore, vent.

spiral *adj* cochlear, cochleated, curled, helical, screw-shaped, spiry, winding. • *n* helix, winding, worm.

spire *n* **1** curl, spiral, twist, wreath. **2** steeple. **3** blade, shoot, spear, stalk. **4** apex, summit.

spirit *vb* **1** animate, encourage, excite, inspirit. **2** carry off, kidnap. • *n* **1** immaterial substance, life, vital essence. **2** person, soul. **3** angel, apparition, demon, elf, fairy, genius, ghost, phantom, shade, spectre, sprite. **4** disposition, frame of mind, humour, mood, temper. **5** spirits. **6** ardour, cheerfulness, courage, earnestness, energy, enterprise, enthusiasm, fire, force, mettle, resolution, vigour, vim, vivacity, zeal. **7** animation, cheerfulness, enterprise, esprit, glow, liveliness, piquancy, spice, spunk, vivacity, warmth. **8** drift, gist, intent, meaning, purport, sense, significance, tenor. **9** character, characteristic, complexion, essence, nature, quality, quintessence. **10** alcohol, liquor. **11** (*with* **the**) Comforter, Holy Ghost, Paraclete.

spirited *adj* active, alert, animated, ardent, bold, brisk, courageous, earnest, frisky, high-mettled, high-spirited, high-strung, lively, mettlesome, sprightly, vivacious.

adj antonyms lazy, spiritless, timid.

spiritless *adj* **1** breathless, dead, extinct, lifeless. **2** dejected, depressed, discouraged, dispirited, low-spirited. **3** apathetic, cold, dull, feeble, languid, phlegmatic, sluggish, soulless, torpid, unenterprising. **4** dull, frigid, heavy, insipid, prosaic, prosy, stupid, tame, uninteresting.

adj antonym spirited.

spiritual *adj* **1** ethereal, ghostly, immaterial incorporeal, psychical, supersensible. **2** ideal, moral, unwordly. **3** divine, holy, pure, sacred. **4** ecclesiastical.

adj antonyms material, physical.

spiritualize *vb* elevate, etherealize, purify, refine.

spit[1] *vb* impale, thrust through, transfix.

spit[2] *vb* **1** eject, throw out. **2** drivel, drool, expectorate, salivate, slobber, spawl, splutter. • *n* saliva, spawl, spittle, sputum.

spite *vb* **1** injure, mortify, thwart. **2** annoy, offend, vex. • *n* grudge, hate, hatred, ill-nature, ill-will, malevolence, malice, maliciousness, malignity, pique, rancour, spleen, venom, vindictiveness.

n antonyms affection, goodwill.

spiteful *adj* evil-minded, hateful, ill-disposed, ill-natured, malevolent, malicious, malign, malignant, rancorous.

adj antonyms affectionate, charitable.

splash *vb* dabble, dash, plash, spatter, splurge, swash, swish. • *n* blot, daub, spot.

splay *adj* broad, spreading out, turned out, wide.

spleen *n* anger, animosity, chagrin, gall, grudge, hatred, ill-humour, irascibility, malevolence, malice, malignity, peevishness, pique, rancour, spite.

splendid *adj* **1** beaming, bright, brilliant, effulgent, glowing, lustrous, radiant, refulgent, resplendent, shining. **2** dazzling, gorgeous, imposing, kingly, magnificent, pompous, showy, sumptuous, superb. **3** celebrated, conspicuous, distinguished, eminent, excellent, famous, glorious, illustrious, noble, pre-eminent, remarkable, signal. **4** grand, heroic, lofty, noble, sublime.

adj antonyms drab, ordinary, run-of-the-mill.

splendour *n* **1** brightness, brilliance, brilliancy, lustre, radiance, refulgence. **2** display, éclat, gorgeousness, grandeur, magnificence, parade, pomp, show, showiness, stateliness. **3** celebrity, eminence, fame, glory, grandeur, renown. **4** grandeur, loftiness, nobleness, sublimity.

splenetic *adj* **1** choleric, cross, fretful, irascible, irritable, peevish, pettish, petulant, snappish, testy, touchy, waspish. **2** churlish, crabbed, morose, sour, sulky, sullen. **3** gloomy, jaundiced.

splice *vb* braid, connect, join, knit, mortise.

splinter *vb* rend, shiver, sliver, split. • *n* fragment, piece.

split *vb* **1** cleave, rive. **2** break, burst, rend, splinter. **3** divide, part, separate, sunder. • *n* **1** crack, fissure, rent. **2** breach, division, separation.

splotch *n* blot, daub, smear, spot, stain.

splutter *vb* sputter, stammer, stutter.

spoil *vb* **1** despoil, fleece, loot, pilfer, plunder, ravage, rob, steal, strip, waste. **2** corrupt, damage, destroy, disfigure, harm, impair, injure, mar, ruin, vitiate. **3** decay, decompose.

spoils *npl* **1** booty, loot, pillage, plunder, prey. **2** rapine, robbery, spoliation, waste.

spoiler *n* **1** pillager, plunderer, robber. **2** corrupter, destroyer.

spokesman *n* mouthpiece, prolocutor, speaker.

spoliate *vb* despoil, destroy, loot, pillage, plunder, rob, spoil.

spoliation *n* **1** depradation, deprivation, despoliation, destruction, robbery. **2** destruction, devastation, pillage, plundering, rapine, ravagement.

sponge *vb* **1** cleanse, wipe. **2** efface, expunge, obliterate, rub out, wipe out.

sponger *n* hanger-on, parasite.

spongy *adj* **1** absorbent, porous, spongeous. **2** rainy, showery, wet. **3** drenched, marshy, saturated, soaked, wet.

sponsor *vb* back, capitalize, endorse, finance, guarantee, patronize, promote, support, stake, subsidize, take up, underwrite. • *n* **1** angel, backer, guarantor, patron, promoter, supporter, surety, underwriter. **2** godfather, godmother, godparent.

spontaneity *n* improvisation, impulsiveness, spontaneousness.

spontaneous *adj* free, gratuitous, impulsive, improvised, instinctive, self-acting, self-moving, unbidden, uncompelled, unconstrained, voluntary, willing.

adj antonyms forced, planned, studied.

sporadic *adj* dispersed, infrequent, isolated, rare, scattered, separate, spasmodic.

sport *vb* **1** caper, disport, frolic, gambol, have fun, make merry, play, romp, skip. **2** trifle. **3** display, exhibit. • *n* **1** amusement, diversion, entertainment, frolic, fun, gambol, game, jollity, joviality, merriment, merry-making, mirth, pastime, pleasantry, prank, recreation. **2** jest, joke. **3** derision, jeer, mockery, ridicule. **4** monstrosity.

sportive *adj* **1** frisky, frolicsome, gamesome, hilarious, lively, merry, playful, prankish, rollicking, sprightly, tricksy. **2** comic, facetious, funny, humorous, jocose, jocular, lively, ludicrous, mirthful, vivacious, waggish.

spot *vb* **1** besprinkle, dapple, dot, speck, stud, variegate. **2** blemish, disgrace, soil, splotch, stain, sully, tarnish. **3** detect, discern, espy, make out, observe, see, sight. • *n* **1** blot, dapple, fleck, freckle, maculation, mark, mottle, patch, pip, speck, speckle. **2** blemish, blotch, flaw, pock, splotch, stain, taint. **3** locality, place, site.

spotless *adj* **1** perfect, unspotted. **2** blameless, immaculate, innocent, irreproachable, pure, stainless, unblemished, unstained, untainted, untarnished.

spotted *adj* bespeckled, bespotted, dotted, flecked, freckled, speckled, spotty.

spousal *adj* bridal, conjugal, connubial, hymeneal, marital, matrimonial, nuptial, wedded.

spouse *n* companion, consort, husband, mate, partner, wife.

spout *vb* **1** gush, jet, pour out, spirit, spurt, squirt. **2** declaim, mouth, speak, utter. • *n* **1** conduit, tube. **2** beak, nose, nozzle, waterspout.

sprain *vb* overstrain, rick, strain, twist, wrench, wrick.

spray[1] *vb* atomize, besprinkle, douche, gush, jet, shower, splash, splatter, spout, sprinkle, squirt. • *n* aerosol, atomizer, douche, foam, froth, shower, sprinkler, spume.

spray[2] *n* bough, branch, shoot, sprig, twig.

spread *vb* **1** dilate, expand, extend, mantle, stretch. **2** diffuse, disperse, distribute, radiate, scatter, sprinkle, strew. **3** broadcast, circulate, disseminate, divulge, make known, make public, promulgate, propagate, publish. **4** open, unfold, unfurl. **5** cover, extend over, overspread. • *n* **1** compass, extent, range, reach, scope, stretch. **2** expansion, extension. **3** circulation, dissemination, propagation. **4** cloth, cover. **5** banquet, feast, meal.

vb antonyms close, compress, contain, fold.

spree *n* bacchanal, (*inf*) bender, binge, ca-

rousal, debauch, frolic, jamboree, jollification, orgy, revel, revelry, saturnalia.

sprig *n* **1** shoot, spray, twig. **2** lad, youth.

sprightliness *n* animation, activity, briskness, cheerfulness, gaiety, life, liveliness, nimbleness, vigour, vivacity.

sprightly *adj* airy, animated, blithe, blithesome, brisk, buoyant, cheerful, debonair, frolicsome, joyous, lively, mercurial, vigorous, vivacious.

adj antonym inactive.

spring *vb* **1** bound, hop, jump, leap, prance, vault. **2** arise, emerge, grow, issue, proceed, put forth, shoot forth, stem. **3** derive, descend, emanate, flow, originate, rise, start. **4** fly back, rebound, recoil. **5** bend, warp. **6** grow, thrive, wax. • *adj* hopping, jumping, resilient, springy. • *n* **1** bound, hop, jump, leap, vault. **2** elasticity, flexibility, resilience, resiliency, springiness. **3** fount, fountain, fountainhead, geyser, springhead, well. **4** cause, origin, original, principle, source. **5** seed time, springtime.

springe *n* gin, net, noose, snare, trap.

springiness *n* **1** elasticity, resilience, spring. **2** sponginess, wetness.

springy *adj* bouncing, bounding, elastic, rebounding, recoiling, resilient.

sprinkle *vb* **1** scatter, strew. **2** bedew, besprinkle, dust, powder, sand, spatter. **3** wash, cleanse, purify, shower.

sprinkling *n* **1** affusion, baptism, bedewing, spattering, splattering, spraying, wetting. **2** dash, scattering, seasoning, smack, soupçon, suggestion, tinge, touch, trace, vestige.

sprite *n* apparition, elf, fairy, ghost, goblin, hobgoblin, phantom, pixie, shade, spectre, spirit.

sprout *vb* burgeon, burst forth, germinate, grow, pullulate, push, put forth, ramify, shoot, shoot forth. • *n* shoot, sprig.

spruce *vb* **1** preen, prink. **2** adorn, deck, dress, smarten, trim. • *adj* dandyish, dapper, fine, foppish, jaunty, natty, neat, nice, smart, tidy, trig, trim.

adj antonyms dishevelled, untidy.

spry *adj* active, agile, alert, brisk, lively, nimble, prompt, quick, ready, smart, sprightly, stirring, supple.

adj antonyms doddering, inactive, lethargic.

spume *n* foam, froth, scum, spray.

spumy *adj* foamy, frothy, spumous.

spur *vb* **1** gallop, hasten, press on, prick.

2 animate, arouse, drive, goad, impel, incite, induce, instigate, rouse, stimulate, urge forward. • *n* **1** goad, point, prick, rowel. **2** fillip, impulse, incentive, incitement, inducement, instigation, motive, provocation, stimulus, whip. **3** gnarl, knob, knot, point, projection, snag.
vb antonym curb.
n antonym curb.

spurious *adj* bogus, counterfeit, deceitful, false, feigned, fictitious, make-believe, meretricious, mock, pretended, sham, supposititious, unauthentic.
adj antonyms authentic, genuine, real.

spurn *vb* **1** drive away, kick. **2** contemn, despise, disregard, flout, scorn, slight. **3** disdain, reject, repudiate.

spurt *vb* gush, jet, spirt, spout, spring out, stream out, well. • *n* **1** gush, jet, spout, squirt. **2** burst, dash, rush.

sputter *vb* spawl, spit, splutter, stammer.

spy *vb* **1** behold, discern, espy, see. **2** detect, discover, search out. **3** explore, inspect, scrutinize, search. **4** shadow, trail, watch. • *n* agent, detective, double agent, mole, scout, undercover agent.

squabble *vb* **1** brawl, fight, quarrel, scuffle, struggle, wrangle. **2** altercate, bicker, contend, dispute, jangle. • *n* brawl, dispute, fight, quarrel, rumpus, scrimmage.

squad *n* band, bevy, crew, gang, knot, lot, relay, set.

squalid *adj* dirty, filthy, foul, mucky, slovenly, unclean, unkempt.
adj antonyms clean, pleasant.

squalidness *n* filthiness, foulness, squalidity, squalor.

squall *vb* bawl, cry, cry out, scream, yell. • *n* **1** bawl, cry, outcry, scream, yell. **2** blast, flurry, gale, gust, hurricane, storm, tempest.

squally *adj* blustering, blustery, gusty, stormy, tempestuous, windy.

squander *vb* dissipate, expend, lavish, lose, misuse, scatter, spend, throw away, waste.

square *vb* **1** make square, quadrate. **2** accommodate, adapt, fit, mould, regulate, shape, suit. **3** adjust, balance, close, make even, settle. **4** accord, chime in, cohere, comport, fall in, fit, harmonize, quadrate, suit. • *adj* **1** four-square, quadrilateral, quadrate. **2** equal, equitable, exact, fair, honest, just, upright. **3** adjusted, balanced, even, settled. **4** true, suitable. • *n* **1** four-

sided figure, quadrate, rectangle, tetragon. **2** open area, parade, piazza, plaza.

squash *vb* crush, mash.

squashy *adj* pulpy, soft.

squat *vb* **1** cower, crouch. **2** occupy, plant, settle. • *adj* **1** cowering, crouching. **2** dumpy, pudgy, short, stocky, stubby, thickset.

squeal *vb* **1** creak, cry, howl, scream, screech, shriek, squawk, yell. **2** betray, inform on. • *n* creak, cry, howl, scream, screech, shriek, squawk, yell.

squeamish *adj* **1** nauseated, qualmish, queasy, sickish. **2** dainty, delicate, fastidious, finical, hypercritical, nice, over-nice, particular, priggish.

squeeze *vb* **1** clutch, compress, constrict, grip, nip, pinch, press. **2** drive, force. **3** crush, harass, oppress. **4** crowd, force through. **5** press. **6** (*with* out) extract. • *n* **1** congestion, crowd, crush, throng. **2** compression.

squelch *vb* crush, quash, quell, silence, squash, suppress.

squib *n* **1** firework, fuse. **2** lampoon, pasquinade, satire.

squint *vb* look askance, look obliquely, peer. • *adj* askew, aslant, crooked, oblique, skew, skewed, twisted.

squire *vb* accompany, attend, escort, wait on.

squirm *vb* twist, wriggle, writhe.

squirt *vb* eject, jet, splash, spurt.

stab *vb* **1** broach, gore, jab, pierce, pink, spear, stick, transfix, transpierce. **2** wound. • *n* **1** cut, jab, prick, thrust. **2** blow, dagger-stroke, injury, wound.

stability *n* **1** durability, firmness, fixedness, immovability, permanence, stableness, steadiness. **2** constancy, firmness, reliability.
n antonyms insecurity, instability, unsteadiness, weakness.

stable *adj* **1** established, fixed, immovable, immutable, invariable, permanent, unalterable, unchangeable. **2** constant, firm, staunch, steadfast, steady, unwavering. **3** abiding, durable, enduring, fast, lasting, permanent, perpetual, secure, sure.
adj antonyms shaky, unstable, weak, wobbly.

staff *n* **1** baton, cane, pole, rod, stick, wand. **2** bat, bludgeon, club, cudgel, mace. **3** prop, stay, support. **4** employees, personnel, team, workers, work force.

stage *vb* dramatize, perform, present, produce, put on. • *n* **1** dais, platform, rostrum, scaffold, staging, stand. **2** arena, field. **3** boards, playhouse, theatre. **4** degree, point, step. **5** diligence, omnibus, stagecoach.

stagey *adj* bombastic, declamatory, dramatic, melodramatic, ranting, theatrical.

stagger *vb* **1** reel, sway, totter. **2** alternate, fluctuate, overlap, vacillate, vary. **3** falter, hesitate, waver. **4** amaze, astonish, astound, confound, dumbfound, nonplus, pose, shock, surprise.

stagnant *adj* **1** close, motionless, quiet, standing. **2** dormant, dull, heavy, inactive, inert, sluggish, torpid.

stagnate *vb* decay, deteriorate, languish, rot, stand still, vegetate.

staid *adj* calm, composed, demure, grave, sedate, serious, settled, sober, solemn, steady, unadventurous.
adj antonyms debonair, frivolous, jaunty, sportive.

stain *vb* **1** blemish, blot, blotch, discolour, maculate, smirch, soil, splotch, spot, sully, tarnish. **2** colour, dye, tinge. **3** contaminate, corrupt, debase, defile, deprave, disgrace, dishonour, pollute, taint. • *n* **1** blemish, blot, defect, discolouration, flaw, imperfection, spot, tarnish. **2** contamination, disgrace, dishonour, infamy, pollution, reproach, shame, taint, tarnish.

stainless *adj* **1** spotless, unspotted, untarnished. **2** blameless, faultless, innocent, guiltless, pure, spotless, uncorrupted, unsullied.

stairs *npl* flight of steps, staircase, stairway.

stake[1] *vb* brace, mark, prop, secure, support. • *n* pale, palisade, peg, picket, post, stick.

stake[2] *vb* **1** finance, pledge, wager. **2** hazard, imperil, jeopardize, peril, risk, venture. • *n* **1** bet, pledge, wager. **2** adventure, hazard, risk, venture.

stale *adj* **1** flat, fusty, insipid, mawkish, mouldy, musty, sour, tasteless, vapid. **2** decayed, effete, faded, old, time-worn, worn-out. **3** common, commonplace, hackneyed, stereotyped, threadbare, trite.
adj antonym fresh.

stalk[1] *n* culm, pedicel, peduncle, petiole, shaft, spire, stem, stock.

stalk[2] *vb* **1** march, pace, stride, strut, swagger. **2** follow, hunt, shadow, track, walk stealthily.

stall[1] *n* **1** stable. **2** cell, compartment, recess. **3** booth, kiosk, shop, stand.

stall[2] *vb* **1** block, delay, equivocate, filibuster, hinder, postpone, procrastinate, temporize. **2** arrest, check, conk out, die, fail, halt, stick, stop.

stalwart *adj* **1** able-bodied, athletic, brawny, lusty, muscular, powerful, robust, sinewy, stout, strapping, strong, sturdy, vigorous. **2** bold, brave, daring, gallant, indomitable, intrepid, redoubtable, resolute, valiant, valorous. • *n* backer, member, partisan, supporter.

stamina *n* energy, force, lustiness, power, stoutness, strength, sturdiness, vigour.

stammer *vb* falter, hesitate, stutter. • *n* faltering, hesitation, stutter.

stamp *vb* brand, impress, imprint, mark, print. • *n* **1** brand, impress, impression, print. **2** cast, character, complexion, cut, description, fashion, form, kind, make, mould, sort, type.

stampede *vb* charge, flee, panic. • *n* charge, flight, rout, running away, rush.

stanch *see* **staunch**[1].

stanchion *n* prop, shore, stay, support.

stand *vb* **1** be erect, remain upright. **2** abide, be fixed, continue, endure, hold good, remain. **3** halt, pause, stop. **4** be firm, be resolute, stand ground, stay. **5** be valid, have force. **6** depend, have support, rest. **7** bear, brook, endure, suffer, sustain, weather. **8** abide, admit, await, submit, tolerate, yield. **9** fix, place, put, set upright. **10** (*with* **against**) oppose, resist, withstand. **11** (*with* **by**) be near, be present. **12** aid, assist, defend, help, side with, support. **13** defend, make good, justify, maintain, support, vindicate. **14** (*naut*) attend, be ready. **15** (*with* **fast**) be fixed, be immovable. **16** (*with* **for**) mean, represent, signify. **17** aid, defend, help, maintain, side with, support. **18** (*with* **off**) keep aloof, keep off. **19** not to comply. **20** (*with* **out**) be prominent, jut, project, protrude. **21** not comply, not yield, persist. **22** (*with* **up for**) defend, justify, support, sustain, uphold. **23** (*with* **with**) agree. • *n* **1** place, position, post, standing place, station. **2** halt, stay, stop. **3** dais, platform, rostrum. **4** booth, stall. **5** opposition, resistance.
vb antonym advance.
n antonym progress.

standard[1] *n* banner, colours, ensign, flag, gonfalon, pennon, streamer.

adj antonyms abnormal, irregular, unusual.

standard[2] *adj* 1 average, conventional, customary, normal, ordinary, regular, usual. 2 accepted, approved, authoritative, orthodox, received. 3 formulary, prescriptive, regulation. • *n* 1 canon, criterion, model, norm, rule, test, type. 2 gauge, measure, model, scale. 3 support, upright.

standing *adj* 1 established, fixed, immovable, settled. 2 durable, lasting, permanent. 3 motionless, stagnant. • *n* 1 position, stand, station. 2 continuance, duration, existence. 3 footing, ground, hold. 4 condition, estimation, rank, reputation, status.

adj antonyms horizontal, lying.

standpoint *n* point of view, viewpoint.

standstill *n* 1 cessation, interruption, stand, stop. 2 deadlock.

stanza *n* measure, staff, stave, strophe, verse.

staple *adj* basic, chief, essential, fundamental, main, primary, principal. • *n* 1 fibre, filament, pile, thread. 2 body, bulk, mass, substance.

adj antonym minor.

star *vb* 1 act, appear, feature, headline, lead, perform, play. 2 emphasize, highlight, stress, underline. • *adj* 1 leading, main, paramount, principal. 2 celebrated, illustrious, well-known. • *n* 1 heavenly body, luminary. 2 asterisk, pentacle, pentagram. 3 destiny, doom, fate, fortune, lot. 4 diva, headliner, hero, heroine, lead, leading lady, leading man, prima ballerina, prima donna, principal, protagonist.

starchy *adj* ceremonious, exact, formal, precise, prim, punctilious, rigid, starched, stiff.

stare *vb* gape, gaze, look intently, watch.

stark *adj* 1 rigid, stiff. 2 absolute, bare, downright, entire, gross, mere, pure, sheer, simple. • *adv* absolutely, completely, entirely, fully, wholly.

adj antonyms mild, slight.

adv antonyms mildly, slightly.

starry *adj* 1 astral, sidereal, star-spangled, stellar. 2 bright, brilliant, lustrous, shining, sparkling, twinkling.

start *vb* 1 begin, commence, inaugurate, initiate, institute. 2 discover, invent. 3 flinch, jump, shrink, startle, wince. 4 alarm, disturb, fright, rouse, scare. 5 depart, set off, take off. 6 arise, call forth, evoke, raise. 7 dislocate, move suddenly, spring. • *n* 1 beginning, commencement, inauguration, outset. 2 fit, jump, spasm, twitch. 3 impulse, sally.

vb antonyms finish, stop.

n antonyms finish, stop.

startle *vb* 1 flinch, shrink, start, wince. 2 affright, alarm, fright, frighten, scare, shock. 3 amaze, astonish, astound.

vb antonym calm.

startling *adj* abrupt, alarming, astonishing, shocking, sudden, surprising, unexpected, unforeseen, unheard of.

starvation *n* famine, famishment.

starve *vb* 1 famish, perish. 2 be in need, lack, want. 3 kill, subdue.

state *vb* affirm, assert, aver, declare, explain, expound, express, narrate, propound, recite, say, set forth, specify, voice. • *adj* civic, national, public. • *n* 1 case, circumstances, condition, pass, phase, plight, position, posture, predicament, situation, status. 2 condition, guise, mode, quality, rank. 3 dignity, glory, grandeur, magnificence, pageantry, parade, pomp, splendour. 4 body politic, civil community, commonwealth, nation, realm.

statecraft *n* diplomacy, political subtlety, state management, statesmanship.

stated *adj* 1 established, fixed, regular, settled. 2 detailed, set forth, specified.

stately *adj* 1 august, dignified, elevated, grand, imperial, imposing, lofty, magnificent, majestic, noble, princely, royal. 2 ceremonious, formal, magisterial, pompous, solemn.

adj antonyms informal, unimpressive.

statement *n* 1 account, allegation, announcement, communiqué, declaration, description, exposition, mention, narration, narrative, recital, relation, report, specification. 2 assertion, predication, proposition, pronouncement, thesis.

statesman *n* politician.

station *vb* establish, fix, locate, place, post, set. • *n* 1 location, place, position, lost, seat, situation. 2 business, employment, function, occupation, office. 3 character, condition, degree, dignity, footing, rank, standing, state, status. 4 depot, stop, terminal.

stationary *adj* fixed, motionless, permanent, quiescent, stable, standing, still.

statuary n carving, sculpture, statues.

statue n figurine, image, statuette.

stature n **1** height, physique, size, tallness. **2** altitude, consequence, elevation, eminence, prominence.

status n caste, condition, footing, position, rank, standing, station.

n antonym unimportance.

statute n act, decree, edict, enactment, law, ordinance, regulation.

staunch[1], **stanch** vb arrest, block, check, dam, plug, stem, stop.

adj antonyms unreliable, wavering, weak.

staunch[2] adj **1** firm, sound, stout, strong. **2** constant, faithful, firm, hearty, loyal, resolute, stable, steadfast, steady, strong, trustworthy, trusty, unwavering, zealous.

stave vb **1** break, burst. **2** (with off) adjourn, defer, delay, postpone, procrastinate, put off, waive.

stay vb **1** abide, dwell, lodge, rest, sojourn, tarry. **2** continue, halt, remain, stand still, stop. **3** attend, delay, linger, wait. **4** arrest, check, curb, hold, keep in, prevent, rein in, restrain, withhold. **5** delay, detain, hinder, obstruct. **6** hold up, prop, shore up, support, sustain, uphold. • n **1** delay, repose, rest, sojourn. **2** halt, stand, stop. **3** bar, check, curb, hindrance, impediment, interruption, obstacle, obstruction, restraint, stumbling block. **4** buttress, dependence, prop, staff, support, supporter.

stead n place, room.

steadfast adj **1** established, fast, firm, fixed, stable. **2** constant, faithful, implicit, persevering, pertinacious, resolute, resolved, staunch, steady, unhesitating, unreserved, unshaken, unwavering, wholehearted.

adj antonyms unreliable, wavering, weak.

steadiness n **1** constancy, firmness, perseverance, persistence, resolution, steadfastness. **2** fixedness, stability.

steady vb balance, counterbalance, secure, stabilize, support. • adj **1** firm, fixed, stable. **2** constant, equable, regular, undeviating, uniform, unremitting. **3** persevering, resolute, staunch, steadfast, unchangeable, unwavering.

adj antonyms unsteady, wavering.

steal vb **1** burglarize, burgle, crib, embezzle, filch, peculate, pilfer, plagiarize, poach, purloin, shoplift, thieve. **2** creep, sneak, pass stealthily.

vb antonym return.

stealing n burglary, larceny, peculation, shoplifting, robbery, theft, thievery.

stealth n secrecy, slyness, stealthiness.

stealthy adj clandestine, furtive, private, secret, skulking, sly, sneaking, surreptitious, underhand.

adj antonym open.

steam vb **1** emit vapour, fume. **2** evaporate, vaporize. **3** coddle, cook, poach. **4** navigate, sail. **5** be hot, sweat. • n **1** vapour. **2** effluvium, exhalation, fume, mist, reek, smoke.

steamboat n steamer, steamship.

steamy adj **1** misty, moist, vaporous. **2** erotic, voluptuous.

steed n charger, horse, mount.

steel vb **1** case-harden, edge. **2** brace, fortify, harden, make firm, nerve, strengthen.

steep[1] adj abrupt, precipitous, sheer, sloping, sudden. • n declivity, precipice.

adj antonyms gentle, moderate.

steep[2] vb digest, drench, imbrue, imbue, macerate, saturate, soak.

steeple n belfry, spire, tower, turret.

steer vb direct, conduct, govern, guide, pilot, point.

steersman n conductor, guide, helmsman, pilot.

stellar adj astral, starry, star-spangled, stellary.

stem[1] vb (with from) bud, descend, generate, originate, spring, sprout. • n **1** axis, stipe, trunk. **2** pedicel, peduncle, petiole, stalk. **3** branch, descendant, offspring, progeny, scion, shoot. **4** ancestry, descent, family, generation, line, lineage, pedigree, race, stock. **5** (naut) beak, bow, cutwater, forepart, prow. **6** helm, lookout. **7** etymon, radical, radix, origin, root.

stem[2] vb **1** breast, oppose, resist, withstand. **2** check, dam, oppose, staunch, stay, stop.

vb antonyms encourage, increase.

stench n bad smell, fetor, offensive odour, stink.

stenography n brachygraphy, shorthand, tachygraphy.

step vb pace, stride, tramp, tread, walk. • n **1** footstep, pace, stride. **2** stair, tread. **3** degree, gradation, grade, interval. **4** advance, advancement, progression. **5** act, action, deed, procedure, proceeding. **6** footprint, trace, track, vestige. **7** footfall, gait, pace, walk. **8** expedient, means, measure, method. **9** round, rundle, rung.

steppe n pampa, prairie, savannah.

sterile *adj* **1** barren, unfruitful, unproductive, unprolific. **2** bare, dry, empty, poor. **3** (*bot*) acarpous, male, staminate.
adj antonyms fruitful, septic.

sterility *n* barrenness, fruitlessness, unfruitfulness, unproductiveness.

sterling *adj* genuine, positive, pure, real, sound, standard, substantial, true.

stern[1] *adj* **1** austere, dour, forbidding, grim, severe. **2** bitter, cruel, hard, harsh, inflexible, relentless, rigid, rigorous, severe, strict, unrelenting. **3** immovable, incorruptible, steadfast, uncompromising.

stern[2] *n* **1** behind, breach, hind part, posterior, rear, tail. **2** (*naut*) counter, poop, rudderpost, tailpost. **3** butt, buttocks, fundament, rump.

sternness *n* **1** austerity, rigidity, severity. **2** asperity, cruelty, harshness, inflexibility, relentlessness, rigour.

sternum *n* (*anat*) breastbone.

stertorous *adj* hoarsely breathing, snoring.

stew *vb* boil, seethe, simmer, stive. • *n* **1** ragout. **2** confusion, difficulty, mess, scrape.

steward *n* **1** chamberlain, majordomo, seneschal. **2** manciple, purveyor.

stick[1] *vb* **1** gore, penetrate, pierce, puncture, spear, stab, transfix. **2** infix, insert, thrust. **3** attach, cement, glue, paste. **4** fix in, set. **5** adhere, cleave, cling, hold. **6** abide, persist, remain, stay, stop. **7** doubt, hesitate, scruple, stickle, waver. **8** (*with* by) adhere to, be faithful, support. • *n* prick, stab, thrust.
vb antonym unstick.

stick[2] *n* **1** birch, rod, switch. **2** bat, bludgeon, club, cudgel, shillelah. **3** cane, staff, walking stick. **4** cue, pole, spar, stake.

stickiness *n* adhesiveness, glutinousness, tenacity, viscosity, viscousness.

stickle *vb* **1** altercate, contend, contest, struggle. **2** doubt, hesitate, scruple, stick, waver.

sticky *adj* adhesive, clinging, gluey, glutinous, gummy, mucilaginous, tenacious, viscid, viscous.
adj antonyms cool, dry, easy.

stiff *adj* **1** inflexible, rigid, stark, unbending, unyielding. **2** firm, tenacious, thick. **3** obstinate, pertinacious, strong, stubborn. **4** absolute, austere, dogmatic, inexorable, peremptory, positive, rigorous, severe, straitlaced, strict, stringent, uncompromising. **5** ceremonious, chilling, con-

strained, formal, frigid, prim, punctilious, stately, starchy, stilted. **6** abrupt, cramped, crude, graceless, harsh, inelegant.
adj antonyms flexible, graceful, informal, mild.

stiff-necked *adj* contumacious, crossgrained, dogged, headstrong, intractable, mulish, obdurate, obstinate, stubborn, unruly.

stiffness *n* **1** hardness, inflexibility, rigidity, rigidness, rigour, starkness. **2** compactness, consistence, denseness, density, thickness. **3** inflexibility, obstinacy, pertinacity, stubbornness. **4** austerity, harshness, rigorousness, severity, sternness, strictness. **5** constraint, formality, frigidity, precision, primness, tenseness.

stifle *vb* **1** choke, smother, suffocate. **2** check, deaden, destroy, extinguish, quench, repress, stop, suppress. **3** conceal, gag, hush, muffle, muzzle, silence, smother, still.
vb antonym encourage.

stigma *n* blot, blur, brand, disgrace, dishonour, reproach, shame, spot, stain, taint, tarnish.
n antonym credit.

stigmatize *vb* brand, defame, discredit, disgrace, dishonour, post, reproach, slur, vilify.

stiletto *n* **1** dagger, dirk, poniard, stylet. **2** bodkin, piercer.

still[1] *vb* **1** hush, muffle, silence, stifle. **2** allay, appease, calm, compose, lull, pacify, quiet, smooth, tranquillize. **3** calm, check, immobilize, restrain, stop, subdue, suppress. • *adj* **1** hushed, mum, mute, noiseless, silent. **2** calm, placid, quiet, serene, stilly, tranquil, unruffled. **3** inert, motionless, quiescent, stagnant, stationary. • *n* **1** hush, lull, peace, quiet, quietness, quietude, silence, stillness, tranquillity. **2** picture, photograph, shot.

still[2] *n* **1** distillery, still-house. **2** distillatory, retort, stillatory.

still[3] *adv, conj* **1** till now, to this time, yet. **2** however, nevertheless, notwithstanding. **3** always, continually, ever, habitually, uniformly. **4** after that, again, in continuance.

stilted *adj* bombastic, fustian, grandiloquent, grandiose, high-flown, high-sounding, inflated, magniloquent, pompous, pretentious, swelling, tumid, turgid.

stimulant *adj* exciting, stimulating,

stimulative. • *n* **1** bracer, cordial, pick-me-up, tonic. **2** fillip, incentive, provocative, spur, stimulus.

stimulate *vb* animate, arouse, awaken, brace, encourage, energize, excite, fire, foment, goad, impel, incite, inflame, inspirit, instigate, kindle, prick, prompt, provoke, rally, rouse, set on, spur, stir up, urge, whet, work up.
vb antonym discourage.

stimulus *n* encouragement, fillip, goad, incentive, incitement, motivation, motive, provocation, spur, stimulant.
n antonym discouragement.

sting *vb* **1** hurt, nettle, prick, wound. **2** afflict, cut, pain.

stinging *adj* **1** acute, painful, piercing. **2** biting, nipping, pungent, tingling.

stingy *adj* avaricious, close, close-fisted, covetous, grudging, mean, miserly, narrow-hearted, niggardly, parsimonious, penurious.
adj antonym generous.

stink *vb* emit a stench, reek, smell bad. • *n* bad smell, fetor, offensive odour, stench.

stint *vb* **1** bound, confine, limit, restrain. **2** begrudge, pinch, scrimp, skimp, straiten. **3** cease, desist, stop. • *n* **1** bound, limit, restraint. **2** lot, period, project, quota, share, shift, stretch, task, time, turn.

stipend *n* allowance, compensation, emolument, fee, hire, honorarium, pay, remuneration, salary, wages.

stipulate *vb* agree, bargain, condition, contract, covenant, engage, provide, settle terms.
vb antonym imply.

stipulation *n* agreement, bargain, concordat, condition, contract, convention, covenant, engagement, indenture, obligation, pact.

stir *vb* **1** budge, change place, go, move. **2** agitate, bestir, disturb, prod. **3** argue, discuss, moot, raise, start. **4** animate, arouse, awaken, excite, goad, incite, instigate, prompt, provoke, quicken, rouse, spur, stimulate. **5** appear, happen, turn up. **6** get up, rise. **7** (*with* **up**) animate, awaken, incite, instigate, move, provoke, quicken, rouse, stimulate. • *n* **1** activity, ado, agitation, bustle, confusion, excitement, fidget, flurry, fuss, hurry, movement. **2** commotion, disorder, disturbance, tumult, uproar.
vb antonyms bore, calm, stay.
n antonym calm.

stirring *adj* **1** active, brisk, diligent, industrious, lively, smart. **2** animating, arousing, awakening, exciting, quickening, stimulating.

stitch *vb* backstitch, baste, bind, embroider, fell, hem, seam, sew, tack, whip.

stive *vb* **1** stow, stuff. **2** boil, seethe, stew. **3** make close, hot or sultry.

stock *vb* **1** fill, furnish, store, supply. **2** accumulate, garner, hoard, lay in, reposit, reserve, save, treasure up. • *adj* permanent, standard, standing. • *n* **1** assets, capital, commodities, fund, principal, shares. **2** accumulation, hoard, inventory, merchandise, provision, range, reserve, store, supply. **3** ancestry, breed, descent, family, house, line, lineage, parentage, pedigree, race. **4** cravat, neckcloth. **5** butt, haft, hand. **6** block, log, pillar, post, stake. **7** stalk, stem, trunk.
adj antonym original.

stockholder *n* shareholder.

stocking *n* hose, sock.

stock market *n* **1** stock exchange. **2** cattle market.

stocks *npl* **1** funds, public funds, public securities. **2** shares.

stockstill *adj* dead-still, immobile, motionless, stationary, still, unmoving.

stocky *adj* chubby, chunky, dumpy, plump, short, stout, stubby, thickset.

stoic, stoical *adj* apathetic, cold-blooded, impassive, imperturbable, passionless, patient, philosophic, philosophical, phlegmatic, unimpassioned.
adj antonyms anxious, depressed, furious, irascible.

stoicism *n* apathy, coldness, coolness, impassivity, indifference, insensibility, nonchalance, phlegm.

stolen *adj* **1** filched, pilfered, purloined. **2** clandestine, furtive, secret, sly, stealthy, surreptitious.

stolid *adj* blockish, doltish, dull, foolish, heavy, obtuse, slow, stockish, stupid.
adj antonyms interested, lively.

stolidity *n* doltishness, dullness, foolishness, obtuseness, stolidness, stupidity.

stomach *vb* abide, bear, brook, endure, put up with, stand, submit to, suffer, swallow, tolerate. • *n* **1** abdomen, belly, gut, paunch, pot, tummy. **2** appetite, desire, inclination, keenness, liking, relish, taste.

stone *vb* **1** cover, face, slate, tile. **2** lapidate, pelt. • *n* **1** boulder, cobble, gravel, pebble, rock. **2** gem, jewel, precious stone. **3** cenotaph, gravestone, monument, tombstone. **4** nut, pit. **5** adamant, agate, flint, gneiss, granite, marble, slate, etc.

stony *adj* **1** gritty, hard, lapidose, lithic, petrous, rocky. **2** adamantine, flinty, hard, inflexible, obdurate. **3** cruel, hard-hearted, inexorable, pitiless, stony-hearted, unfeeling, unrelenting.

adj antonyms forgiving, friendly, softhearted.

stoop *vb* **1** bend forward, bend down, bow, lean, sag, slouch, slump. **2** abase, cower, cringe, give in, submit, succumb, surrender. **3** condescend, deign, descend, vouchsafe. **4** fall, sink. • *n* **1** bend, inclination, sag, slouch, slump. **2** descent, swoop.

stop *vb* **1** block, blockade, close, close up, obstruct, occlude. **2** arrest, check, halt, hold, pause, stall, stay. **3** bar, delay, embargo, hinder, impede, intercept, interrupt, obstruct, preclude, prevent, repress, restrain, staunch, suppress, thwart. **4** break off, cease, desist, discontinue, forbear, give over, leave off, refrain from. **5** intermit, quiet, quieten, terminate. **6** lodge, tarry. • *n* **1** halt, intermission, pause, respite, rest, stoppage, suspension, truce. **2** block, cessation, check, hindrance, interruption, obstruction, repression. **3** bar, impediment, obstacle. **4** full stop, point.

vb antonyms advance, continue, start.

n antonyms continuation, start.

stopcock *n* cock, faucet, tap.

stoppage *n* arrest, block, check, closure, hindrance, interruption, obstruction, prevention.

stopper *n* cork, plug, stopple.

store *vb* **1** accumulate, amass, cache, deposit, garner, hoard, husband, lay by, lay in, lay up, put by, reserve, save, store up, stow away, treasure up. **2** furnish, provide, replenish, stock, supply. • *n* **1** accumulation, cache, deposit, fund, hoard, provision, reserve, stock, supply, treasure, treasury. **2** abundance, plenty. **3** storehouse. **4** emporium, market, shop.

vb antonym use.

n antonym scarcity.

storehouse *n* depository, depot, godown, magazine, repository, store, warehouse.

storm *vb* **1** assail, assault, attack. **2** blow violently. **3** fume, rage, rampage, rant,

rave, tear. • *n* **1** blizzard, gale, hurricane, squall, tempest, tornado, typhoon, whirlwind. **2** agitation, clamour, commotion, disturbance, insurrection, outbreak, sedition, tumult, turmoil. **3** adversity, affliction, calamity, distress. **4** assault, attack, brunt, onset, onslaught. **5** violence.

n antonym calm.

storminess *n* inclemency, roughness, tempestuousness.

stormy *adj* **1** blustering, boisterous, gusty, squally, tempestuous, windy. **2** passionate, riotous, rough, turbulent, violent, wild. **3** agitated, furious.

adj antonym calm.

story *n* **1** annals, chronicle, history, record. **2** account, narration, narrative, recital, record, rehearsal, relation, report, statement, tale. **3** fable, fiction, novel, romance. **4** anecdote, incident, legend, tale. **5** canard, fabrication, falsehood, fib, figure, invention, lie, untruth.

storyteller *n* bard, chronicler, narrator, raconteur.

stout *adj* **1** able-bodied, athletic, brawny, lusty, robust, sinewy, stalwart, strong, sturdy, vigorous. **2** courageous, hardy, indomitable, stouthearted. **3** contumacious, obstinate, proud, resolute, stubborn. **4** compact, firm, solid, staunch. **5** bouncing, bulky, burly, chubby, corpulent, fat, heavy, jolly, large, obese, plump, portly, stocky, strapping, thickset.

adj antonyms slim, timid, weak.

stouthearted *adj* **1** fearless, heroic, redoubtable. **2** bold, brave, courageous, dauntless, doughty, firm, gallant, hardy, indomitable, intrepid, resolute, valiant, valorous.

stow *vb* load, pack, put away, store, stuff.

straddle *vb* bestride.

straggle *vb* **1** rove, wander. **2** deviate, digress, ramble, range, roam, stray, stroll.

straggling *adj* **1** rambling, roving, straying, strolling, wandering. **2** scattered.

straight *adj* **1** direct, near, rectilinear, right, short, undeviating, unswerving. **2** erect, perpendicular, plumb, right, upright, vertical. **3** equitable, fair, honest, honourable, just, square, straightforward. • *adv* at once, directly, forthwith, immediately, straightaway, straightway, without delay.

adj antonyms circuitous, dilute, dishonest, evasive, indirect, roundabout.

straightaway *adv* at once, directly, forthwith, immediately, speedily, straight, suddenly, without delay.

straighten *vb* arrange, make straight, neaten, order, tidy.

straight-laced *see* **strait-laced**.

strain[1] *vb* 1 draw tightly, make tense, stretch, tighten. 2 injure, sprain, wrench. 3 exert, overexert, overtax, rack. 4 embrace, fold, hug, press, squeeze. 5 compel, constrain, force. 6 dilute, distil, drain, filter, filtrate, ooze, percolate, purify, separate. 7 fatigue, overtask, overwork, task, tax, tire. • *n* 1 stress, tenseness, tension, tensity. 2 effort, exertion, force, overexertion. 3 burden, task, tax. 4 sprain, wrench. 5 lay, melody, movement, snatch, song, stave, tune.

strain[2] *n* 1 manner, style, tone, vein. 2 disposition, tendency, trait, turn. 3 descent, extraction, family, lineage, pedigree, race, stock.

strait *adj* 1 close, confined, constrained, constricted, contracted, narrow. 2 rigid, rigorous, severe, strict. 3 difficult, distressful, grievous, straitened. • *n* channel, narrows, pass, sound.

straits *npl* crisis, difficulty, dilemma, distress, embarrassment, emergency, exigency, extremity, hardship, pass, perplexity, pinch, plight, predicament.

straiten *vb* 1 confine, constrain, constrict, contract, limit. 2 narrow. 3 intensify, stretch. 4 distress, embarrass, perplex, pinch, press.

straitened *adj* distressed, embarrassed limited, perplexed, pinched.
adj antonyms easy, well-off.

strait-laced, straight-laced *adj* austere, formal, prim, rigid, rigorous, stern, stiff, strict, uncompromising.
adj antonyms broad-minded, easy-going.

straitness *n* 1 narrowness, rigour, severity, strictness. 2 difficulty, distress, trouble. 3 insufficiency, narrowness, scarcity, want.

strand[1] *vb* abandon, beach, be wrecked, cast away, go aground, ground, maroon, run aground, wreck. • *n* beach, coast, shore.

strand[2] *n* braid, cord, fibre, filament, line, rope, string, tress.

stranded *adj* aground, ashore, cast away, lost, shipwrecked, wrecked.

strange *adj* 1 alien, exotic, far-fetched, foreign, outlandish, remote. 2 new, novel. 3 curious, exceptional, extraordinary, irregular, odd, particular, peculiar, rare,

singular, surprising, uncommon, unusual. 4 abnormal, anomalous, extraordinary, inconceivable, incredible, inexplicable, marvellous, mysterious, preternatural, unaccountable, unbelievable, unheard of, unique, unnatural, wonderful. 5 bizarre, droll, grotesque, quaint, queer. 6 inexperienced, unacquainted, unfamiliar, unknown. 7 bashful, distant, distrustful, reserved, shy, uncommunicative.
adj antonyms comfortable, common, familiar, ordinary.

strangeness *n* 1 foreignness. 2 bashfulness, coldness, distance, reserve, shyness, uncommunicativeness. 3 eccentricity, grotesqueness, oddness, singularity, uncommonness, uncouthness.

stranger *n* 1 alien, foreigner, newcomer, immigrant, outsider. 2 guest, visitor.
n antonyms local, native.

strangle *vb* 1 choke, contract, smother, squeeze, stifle, suffocate, throttle, tighten. 2 keep back, quiet, repress, still, suppress.

strap *vb* 1 beat, thrash, whip. 2 bind, fasten, sharpen, strop. • *n* 1 thong. 2 band, ligature, strip, tie. 3 razor-strap, strop.

strapping *adj* big, burly, large, lusty, stalwart, stout, strong, tall.

stratagem *n* artifice, cunning, device, dodge, finesse, intrigue, machination, manoeuvre, plan, plot, ruse, scheme, trick, wile.

strategic, strategical *adj* 1 calculated, deliberate, diplomatic, manoeuvring, planned, politic, tactical. 2 critical, decisive, key, vital.

strategy *n* generalship, manoeuvring, plan, policy, stratagem, tactics.

stratum *n* band, bed, layer.

straw *n* 1 culm, stalk, stem. 2 button, farthing, fig, penny, pin, rush, snap.

stray *vb* deviate, digress, err, meander, ramble, range, roam, rove, straggle, stroll, swerve, transgress, wander. • *adj* 1 abandoned, lost, strayed, wandering. 2 accidental, erratic, random, scattered.

streak *vb* 1 band, bar, striate, stripe, vein. 2 dart, dash, flash, hurtle, run, speed, sprint, stream, tear. • *n* 1 band, bar, belt, layer, line, strip, stripe, thread, trace, vein. 2 cast, grain, tone, touch, vein. 3 beam, bolt, dart, dash, flare, flash, ray, stream.

streaky *adj* streaked, striped, veined.

stream *vb* 1 course, flow, glide, pour, run, spout. 2 emit, pour out, shed. 3 emanate, go forth, issue, radiate. **4** extend, float, stretch out, wave. • *n* **1** brook, burn, race, rill, rivulet, run, runlet, runnel, trickle. **2** course, current, flow, flux, race, rush, tide, torrent, wake, wash. **3** beam, gleam, patch, radiation, ray, streak.

streamer *n* banner, colours, ensign, flag, pennon, standard.

street *n* avenue, highway, road, way.

strength *n* **1** force, might, main, nerve, potency, power, vigour. **2** hardness, solidity, toughness. **3** impregnability, proof. **4** brawn, grit, healthy, lustiness, muscle, robustness, sinew, stamina, thews, vigorousness. **5** animation, courage, determination, firmness, fortitude, resolution, spirit. **6** cogency, efficacy, soundness, validity. **7** emphasis, energy. **8** security, stay, support. **9** brightness, brilliance, clearness, intensity, vitality, vividness. **10** body, excellence, virtue. **11** impetuosity, vehemence, violence. **12** boldness.

n antonyms timidness, weakness.

strengthen *vb* **1** buttress, recruit, reinforce. **2** fortify. **3** brace, energize, harden, nerve, steel, stimulate. **4** freshen, invigorate, vitalize. **5** animate, encourage. **6** clench, clinch, confirm, corroborate, establish, fix, justify, sustain, support.

vb antonym weaken.

strenuous *adj* **1** active, ardent, eager, earnest, energetic, resolute, vigorous, zealous. **2** bold, determined, doughty, intrepid, resolute, spirited, strong, valiant.

adj antonyms easy, effortless.

stress *vb* **1** accent, accentuate, emphasize, highlight, point up, underline, underscore. **2** bear, bear upon, press, pressurize. **3** pull, rack, strain, stretch, tense, tug. • *n* **1** accent, accentuation, emphasis. **2** effort, force, pull, strain, tension, tug. **3** boisterousness, severity, violence. **4** pressure, urgency.

vb antonym relax.

n antonym relaxation.

stretch *vb* **1** brace, screw, strain, tense, tighten. **2** elongate, extend, lengthen, protract, pull. **3** display, distend, expand, spread, unfold, widen. **4** sprain, strain. **5** distort, exaggerate, misrepresent. • *n* **1** compass, extension, extent, range, reach, scope. **2** effort, exertion, strain, struggle. **3** course, direction.

vb antonyms relax, squeeze.

strict *adj* **1** close, strained, tense, tight. **2** accurate, careful, close, exact, literal, particular, precise, scrupulous. **3** austere, inflexible, harsh, orthodox, puritanical, rigid, rigorous, severe, stern, strait-laced, stringent, uncompromising, unyielding.

adj antonyms easy-going, flexible, mild.

stricture *n* animadversion, censure, denunciation, criticism, compression, constriction, contraction.

strife *n* battle, combat, conflict, contention, contest, discord, quarrel, struggle, warfare.

n antonym peace.

strike *vb* **1** bang, beat, belabour, box, buffet, cudgel, cuff, hit, knock, lash, pound, punch, rap, slap, slug, smite, thump, whip. **2** impress, imprint, stamp. **3** afflict, chastise, deal, give, inflict, punish. **4** affect, astonish, electrify, stun. **5** clash, collide, dash, touch. **6** surrender, yield. **7** mutiny, rebel, rise.

stringent *adj* binding, contracting, rigid, rigorous, severe, strict.

strip[1] *n* piece, ribbon, shred, slip.

vb antonyms cover, provide.

strip[2] *vb* **1** denude, hull, skin, uncover. **2** bereave, deprive, deforest, desolate, despoil, devastate, disarm, dismantle, disrobe, divest, expose, fleece, loot, shave. **3** plunder, pillage, ransack, rob, sack, spoil. **4** disrobe, uncover, undress.

strive *vb* **1** aim, attempt, endeavour, exert, labour, strain, struggle, toil. **2** contend, contest, fight, tussle, wrestle. **3** compete, cope.

stroke[1] *n* **1** blow, glance, hit, impact, knock, lash, pat, percussion, rap, shot, switch, thump. **2** attack, paralysis, stroke. **3** affliction, damage, hardship, hurt, injury, misfortune, reverse, visitation. **4** dash, feat, masterstroke, touch.

stroke[2] *vb* caress, feel, palpate, pet, knead, massage, nuzzle, rub, touch.

stroll *vb* loiter, lounge, ramble, range, rove, saunter, straggle, stray, wander. • *n* excursion, promenade, ramble, rambling, roving, tour, trip, walk, wandering.

strong *adj* **1** energetic, forcible, powerful, robust, sturdy. **2** able, enduring. **3** cogent, firm, valid.

adj antonyms mild, weak.

structure *vb* arrange, constitute, construct, make, organize. • *n* **1** arrangement, conformation, configuration, constitution, construction, form, formation, make, organization. **2** anatomy, composition, texture. **3** building, edifice, fabric, framework, pile.

struggle *vb* **1** aim, endeavour, exert, labour, strive, toil, try. **2** battle, contend, contest, fight, wrestle. **3** agonize, flounder, writhe. • *n* **1** effort, endeavour, exertion, labour, pains. **2** battle, conflict, contention, contest, fight, strife. **3** agony, contortions, distress.
vb antonyms give in, rest.
n antonyms ease, submission.

stubborn *adj* **1** contumacious, dogged, headstrong, heady, inflexible, intractable, mulish, obdurate, obstinate, perverse, positive, refractory, ungovernable, unmanageable, unruly, unyielding, willful. **2** constant, enduring, firm, hardy, persevering, persistent, steady, stoical, uncomplaining, unremitting. **3** firm, hard, inflexible, stiff, strong, tough, unpliant, studied.
adj antonym compliant.

studious *adj* **1** contemplative, meditative, reflective, thoughtful. **2** assiduous, attentive, desirous, diligent, eager, lettered, scholarly, zealous.

study *vb* **1** cogitate, meditate, muse, ponder, reflect, think. **2** analyse, contemplate, examine, investigate, ponder, probe, scrutinize, search, sift, weigh. • *n* **1** exercise, inquiry, investigation, reading, research, stumble. **2** cogitation, consideration, contemplation, examination, meditation, reflection, thought. **3** stun. **4** model, object, representation, sketch. **5** den, library, office, studio.

stunning *adj* **1** deafening, stentorian. **2** dumbfounding, stupefying.
adj antonyms poor, ugly.

stunted *adj* checked, diminutive, dwarfed, dwarfish, lilliputian, little, nipped, small, undersized.

stupendous *adj* **1** amazing, astonishing, astounding, marvellous, overwhelming, surprising, wonderful. **2** enormous, huge, immense, monstrous, prodigious, towering, tremendous, vast.

stupid *adj* brainless, crass, doltish, dull, foolish, idiotic, inane, inept, obtuse, pointless, prosaic, senseless, simple, slow, sluggish, stolid, tedious, tiresome, witless.
adj antonyms alert, clever.

stupor *n* coma, confusion, daze, lethargy, narcosis, numbness, stupefaction, torpor.
n antonym alertness.

sturdy *adj* **1** bold, determined, dogged, firm, hardy, obstinate, persevering, pertinacious, resolute, stiff, stubborn, sturdy. **2** athletic, brawny, forcible, lusty, muscular, powerful, robust, stalwart, stout, strong, thickset, vigorous, well-set.
adj antonyms decrepit, puny.

style *vb* address, call, characterize, denominate, designate, dub, entitle, name, term. • *n* **1** dedication, expression, phraseology, turn. **2** cast, character, fashion, form, genre, make, manner, method, mode, model, shape, vogue, way. **3** appellation, denomination, designation, name, title. **4** chic, elegance, smartness. **5** pen, pin, point, stylus.
n antonym inelegance.

stylish *adj* chic, courtly, elegant, fashionable, genteel, modish, polished, smart.

suave *adj* affable, agreeable, amiable, bland, courteous, debonair, delightful, glib, gracious, mild, pleasant, smooth, sweet, oily, unctuous, urbane.
adj antonym unsophisticated.

subdue *vb* **1** beat, bend, break, bow, conquer, control, crush, defeat, discomfit, foil, master, overbear, overcome, overpower, overwhelm, quell, rout, subject, subjugate, surmount, vanquish, worst. **2** allay, choke, curb, mellow, moderate, mollify, reduce, repress, restrain, soften, suppress, temper.
vb antonym arouse.

subject *vb* **1** control, master, overcome, reduce, subdue, subjugate, tame. **2** enslave, enthral. **3** abandon, refer, submit, surrender. • *adj* **1** beneath, subjacent, underneath. **2** dependent, enslaved, inferior, servile, subjected, subordinate, subservient. **3** conditional, obedient, submissive. **4** disposed, exposed to, liable, obnoxious, prone. • *n* **1** dependent, henchman, liegeman, slave, subordinate. **2** matter, point, subject matter, theme, thesis, topic. **3** nominative, premise. **4** case, object, patient, recipient. **5** ego, mind, self, thinking.
adj antonyms free, insusceptible, superior.
n antonym master.

subjoin *vb* add, affix, annex, append, join, suffix.

subjugate *vb* conquer, enslave, enthral, master, overcome, overpower, overthrow, subdue, subject, vanquish.

sublimate *vb* alter, change, repress.

sublime *adj* **1** aloft, elevated, high, sacred. **2** eminent, exalted, grand, great, lofty, mighty. **3** august, glorious, magnificent, majestic, noble, stately, solemn, sublunary. **4** elated, elevated, eloquent, exhilarated, raised.

adj antonym lowly.

submission *n* **1** capitulation, cession, relinquishment, surrender, yielding. **2** acquiescence, compliance, obedience, resignation. **3** deference, homage, humility, lowliness, obeisance, passiveness, prostration, self-abasement, submissiveness.

submissive *adj* **1** amenable, compliant, docile, pliant, tame, tractable, yielding. **2** acquiescent, long-suffering, obedient, passive, patient, resigned, unassertive, uncomplaining. **3** deferential, humble, lowly, meek, obsequious, prostrate, self-abasing.

adj antonym intractable.

submit *vb* **1** cede, defer, endure, resign, subject, surrender, yield. **2** commit, propose, refer. **3** offer. **4**

vb antonym struggle.

acquiesce, bend, capitulate, comply, stoop, succumb.

subordinate *adj* ancillary, dependent, inferior, junior, minor, secondary, subject, subservient, subsidiary. • *n* assistant, dependant, inferior, subject, underling.

adj antonym superior.

n antonym superior, superiority.

subscribe *vb* **1** accede, approve, agree, assent, consent, yield. **2** contribute, donate, give, offer, promise.

subscription *n* aid, assistance, contribution, donation, gift, offering.

subsequent *adj* after, attendant, ensuing, later, latter, following, posterior, sequent, succeeding.

adj antonym previous.

subservient *adj* **1** inferior, obsequious, servile, subject, subordinate. **2** accessory, aiding, auxiliary, conducive, contributory, helpful, instrumental, serviceable, useful.

subside *vb* **1** settle, sink. **2** abate, decline, decrease, diminish, drop, ebb, fall, intermit, lapse, lessen, lower, lull, wane.

vb antonym increase.

subsidence *n* **1** settling, sinking. **2** abatement, decline, decrease, descent, ebb, diminution, lessening.

subsidiary *adj* adjutant, aiding, assistant, auxiliary, cooperative, corroborative, helping, subordinate, subservient.

subsidize *vb* aid, finance, fund, sponsor, support, underwrite.

subsidy *n* aid, bounty, grant, subvention, support, underwriting.

subsist *vb* **1** be, breathe, consist, exist, inhere, live, prevail. **2** abide, continue, endure, persist, remain. **3** feed, maintain, ration, support.

subsistence *n* aliment, food, livelihood, living, maintenance, meat, nourishment, nutriment, provision, rations, support, sustenance, victuals.

substance *n* **1** actuality, element, groundwork, hypostasis, reality, substratum. **2** burden, content, core, drift, essence, gist, heart, import, meaning, pith, sense, significance, solidity, soul, sum, weight. **3** estate, income, means, property, resources, wealth.

substantial *adj* **1** actual, considerable, essential, existent, hypostatic, pithy, potential, real, subsistent, virtual. **2** concrete, durable, positive, solid, tangible, true. **3** corporeal, bodily, material. **4** bulky, firm, goodly, heavy, large, massive, notable, significant, sizable, solid, sound, stable, stout, strong, well-made. **5** cogent, just, efficient, influential, valid, weighty.

adj antonyms insignificant, small.

substantially *adv* adequately, essentially, firmly, materially, positively, really, truly.

substantiate *vb* actualize, confirm, corroborate, establish, prove, ratify, verify.

vb antonym disprove.

subterfuge *n* artifice, evasion, excuse, expedient, mask, pretence, pretext, quirk, shift, shuffle, sophistry, trick.

n antonyms honesty, openness.

subtle *adj* **1** arch, artful, astute, crafty, crooked, cunning, designing, diplomatic, intriguing, insinuating, sly, tricky, wily. **2** clever, ingenious. **3** acute, deep, discerning, discriminating, keen, profound, sagacious, shrewd. **4** airy, delicate, ethereal, light, nice, rare, refined, slender, subtle, thin, volatile.

adj antonyms open, unsubtle.

subtlety *n* **1** artfulness, artifice, astuteness, craft, craftiness, cunning, guile, subtleness. **2** acumen, acuteness, cleverness, discernment, intelligence, keenness, sagacity, sharpness, shrewdness. **3** attenuation, delicacy, fitness, nicety, rareness, refinement.

subtract *vb* deduct, detract, diminish, remove, take, withdraw.

vb antonyms add, add to.

suburbs *npl* environs, confines, neighbourhood, outskirts, precincts, purlieus, vicinage.

subversive *adj* destructive, overthrowing, pervasive, ruining, upsetting. • *n* collaborator, dissident, insurrectionist, saboteur, terrorist, traitor.

subvert *vb* **1** invert, overset, overthrow, overturn, reverse, upset. **2** demolish, destroy, extinguish, raze, ruin. **3** confound, corrupt, injure, pervert.

vb antonyms boost, uphold.

succeed *vb* **1** ensue, follow, inherit, replace. **2** flourish, gain, hit, prevail, prosper, thrive, win.

vb antonyms fail, precede.

success *n* **1** attainment, issue, result. **2** fortune, happiness, hit, luck, prosperity, triumph.

n antonym failure.

successful *adj* auspicious, booming, felicitous, fortunate, happy, lucky, prosperous, victorious, winning.

adj antonym unsuccessful.

succession *n* **1** chain, concatenation, cycle, consecution, following, procession, progression, rotation, round, sequence, series, suite. **2** descent, entail, inheritance, lineage, race, reversion.

succinct *adj* brief, compact, compendious, concise, condensed, curt, laconic, pithy, short, summary, terse.

adj antonym wordy.

succour *vb* **1** aid, assist, help, relieve. **2** cherish, comfort, encourage, foster, nurse. • *n* aid, assistance, help, relief, support.

succulent *adj* juicy, luscious, lush, nutritive, sappy.

succumb *vb* capitulate, die, submit, surrender, yield.

sudden *adj* **1** abrupt, hasty, hurried, immediate, instantaneous, rash, unanticipated, unexpected, unforeseen, unusual. **2** brief, momentary, quick, rapid.

adj antonym slow.

sue *vb* **1** charge, court, indict, prosecute, solicit, summon, woo. **2** appeal, beg, demand, entreat, implore, petition, plead, pray, supplicate.

suffer *vb* **1** feel, undergo. **2** bear, endure, sustain, tolerate. **3** admit, allow, indulge, let, permit.

sufferable *adj* allowable, bearable, endurable, permissible, tolerable.

sufferance *n* **1** endurance, inconvenience, misery, pain, suffering. **2** long-suffering, moderation, patience, submission. **3** allowance, permission, toleration.

suffice *vb* avail, content, satisfy, serve.

sufficient *adj* **1** adequate, ample, commensurate, competent, enough, full, plenteous, satisfactory. **2** able, equal, fit, qualified, responsible.

adj antonyms insufficient, poor.

suffocate *vb* asphyxiate, choke, smother, stifle, strangle.

suffrage *n* **1** ballot, franchise, voice, vote. **2** approval, attestation, consent, testimonial, witness.

suggest *vb* advise, allude, hint, indicate, insinuate, intimate, move, present, prompt, propose, propound, recommend.

vb antonyms demonstrate, order.

suggestion *n* allusion, hint, indication, insinuation, intimation, presentation, prompting, proposal, recommendation, reminder.

n antonyms demonstration, order.

suit *vb* **1** accommodate, adapt, adjust, fashion, fit, level, match. **2** accord, become, befit, gratify, harmonize, please, satisfy, tally. • *n* **1** appeal, entreaty, invocation, petition, prayer, request, solicitation, supplication. **2** courtship, wooing. **3** action, case, cause, process, prosecution, trial. **4** clothing, costume, habit.

vb antonyms clash, displease.

suitable *adj* adapted, accordant, agreeable, answerable, apposite, applicable, appropriate, apt, becoming, befitting, conformable, congruous, convenient, consonant, correspondent, decent, due, eligible, expedient, fit, fitting, just, meet, pertinent, proper, relevant, seemly, worthy.

adj antonym unsuitable.

suite *n* **1** attendants, bodyguard, convoy, cortege, court, escort, followers, staff, retainers, retinue, train. **2** collection, series, set, suit. **3** apartment, rooms.

sulky *adj* aloof, churlish, cross, crossgrained, dogged, grouchy, ill-humoured,

ill-tempered, moody, morose, perverse, sour, spleenish, spleeny, splenetic, sullen, surly, vexatious, wayward.
adj antonym cheerful.

sullen *adj* 1 cross, crusty, glum, grumpy, ill-tempered, moody, morose, sore, sour, sulky. 2 cheerless, cloudy, dark, depressing, dismal, foreboding, funereal, gloomy, lowering, melancholy, mournful, sombre. 3 dull, heavy, slow, sluggish. 4 intractable, obstinate, perverse, refractory, stubborn, vexatious. 5 baleful, evil, inauspicious, malign, malignant, sinister, unlucky, unpropitious.
adj antonym cheerful.

sully *vb* blemish, blot, contaminate, deface, defame, dirty, disgrace, dishonour, foul, smirch, soil, slur, spot, stain, tarnish.

sultry *adj* close, damp, hot, humid, muggy, oppressive, stifling, stuffy, sweltering.
adj antonyms cold, cool.

sum *vb* 1 add, calculate, compute, reckon. 2 collect, comprehend, condense, epitomize, summarize. • *n* 1 aggregate, amount, total, totality, whole. 2 compendium, substance, summary. 3 acme, completion, height, summit.

summary *adj* 1 brief, compendious, concise, curt, laconic, pithy, short, succinct, terse. 2 brief, quick, rapid. • *n* abridgement, abstract, brief, compendium, digest, epitome, precis, résumé, syllabus, synopsis.
adj antonym lengthy.

summit *n* acme, apex, cap, climax, crest, crown, pinnacle, top, vertex, zenith.
n antonyms bottom, nadir.

summon *vb* 1 arouse, bid, call, cite, invite, invoke, rouse. 2 convene, convoke. 3 charge, indict, prosecute, subpoena, sue.
vb antonym dismiss.

sumptuous *adj* costly, dear, expensive, gorgeous, grand, lavish, luxurious, magnificent, munificent, pompous, prodigal, rich, showy, splendid, stately, superb.

sunburnt *adj* bronzed, brown, ruddy, tanned.

sunder *vb* break, disconnect, disjoin, dissociate, dissever, disunited, divide, part, separate, sever.

sundry *adj* different, divers, several, some, various.

sunny *adj* 1 bright, brilliant, clear, fine, luminous, radiant, shining, unclouded, warm. 2 cheerful, genial, happy, joyful, mild, optimistic, pleasant, smiling.
adj antonym gloomy.

super *adj* excellent, incomparable, magnificent, marvellous, splendid, superb, terrific, wonderful.

superannuated *adj* aged, anile, antiquated, decrepit, disqualified, doting, effete, imbecile, passé, retired, rusty, time-worn, unfit.
adj antonym young.

superb *adj* august, beautiful, elegant, exquisite, grand, gorgeous, imposing, magnificent, majestic, noble, pompous, rich, showy, splendid, stately, sumptuous.
adj antonym poor.

supercilious *adj* arrogant, condescending, contemptuous, dictatorial, domineering, haughty, high, imperious, insolent, intolerant, lofty, lordly, magisterial, overbearing, overweening, proud, scornful, vainglorious.
adj antonym humble.

superficial *adj* external, flimsy, shallow, untrustworthy.
adj antonym detailed.

superfluity *n* excess, exuberance, redundancy, superabundance, surfeit.

superfluous *adj* excessive, redundant, unnecessary.

superintend *vb* administer, conduct, control, direct, inspect, manage, overlook, oversee, supervise.

superintendence *n* care, charge, control, direction, guidance, government, inspection, management, oversight, supervision, surveillance.

superior *adj* 1 better, greater, high, higher, finer, paramount, supreme, ultra, upper. 2 chief, foremost, principal. 3 distinguished, matchless, noble, pre-eminent, preferable, sovereign, surpassing, unrivalled, unsurpassed. 4 predominant, prevalent. • *n* boss, chief, director, head, higher-up, leader, manager, principal, senior, supervisor.
adj antonyms humble, inferior.
n antonyms inferior, junior.

superiority *n* 1 advantage, ascendency, lead, odds, predominance, pre-eminence, prevalence, transcendence. 2 excellence, nobility, worthiness.
n antonym inferiority.

superlative *adj* consummate, greatest, incomparable, peerless, pre-eminent, supreme, surpassing, transcendent.
adj antonym poor.

supernatural *adj* abnormal, marvellous,

metaphysical, miraculous, otherworldly, preternatural, unearthly.

adj antonym natural.

supernumerary *adj* excessive, odd, redundant, superfluous.

supersede *vb* 1 annul, neutralize, obviate, overrule, suspend. 2 displace, remove, replace, succeed, supplant.

supervise *vb* administer, conduct, control, direct, inspect, manage, overlook, oversee, superintend.

supine *adj* apathetic, careless, drowsy, dull, idle, indifferent, indolent, inert, languid, lethargic, listless, lumpish, lazy, negligent, otiose, prostrate, recumbent, sleepy, slothful, sluggish, spineless, torpid.

supplant *vb* 1 overpower, overthrow, undermine. 2 displace, remove, replace, supersede.

supple *adj* 1 elastic, flexible, limber, lithe, pliable, pliant. 2 compliant, humble, submissive, yielding. 3 adulatory, cringing, fawning, flattering, grovelling, obsequious, oily, parasitical, servile, slavish, sycophantic.

adj antonym rigid.

supplement *vb* add, augment, extend, reinforce, supply. • *n* addendum, addition, appendix, codicil, complement, continuation, postscript.

vb antonym deplete.

suppliant *adj* begging, beseeching, entreating, imploring, precatory, praying, suing, supplicating. • *n* applicant, petitioner, solicitor, suitor, supplicant.

supplicate *vb* beg, beseech, crave, entreat, implore, importune, petition, pray, solicit.

supplication *n* 1 invocation, orison, petition, prayer. 2 entreaty, petition, prayer, request, solicitation.

supply *vb* 1 endue, equip, furnish, minister, outfit, provide, replenish, stock, store. 2 afford, accommodate, contribute, furnish, give, grant, yield. • *n* hoard, provision, reserve, stock, store.

vb antonym take.

n antonym lack.

support *vb* 1 brace, cradle, pillow, prop, sustain, uphold. 2 bear, endure, undergo, suffer, tolerate. 3 cherish, keep, maintain, nourish, nurture. 4 act, assume, carry, perform, play, represent. 5 accredit, confirm, corroborate, substantiate, verify. 6 abet, advocate, aid, approve, assist, back, befriend, champion, countenance, encour-

age, favour, float, hold, patronize, relieve, reinforce, succour, vindicate. • *n* 1 bolster, brace, buttress, foothold, guy, hold, prop, purchase, shore, stay, substructure, supporter, underpinning. 2 groundwork, mainstay, staff. 3 base, basis, bed, foundation. 4 keeping, living, livelihood, maintenance, subsistence, sustenance. 5 confirmation, evidence. 6 aid, assistance, backing, behalf, championship, comfort, countenance, encouragement, favour, help, patronage, succour.

vb antonyms contradict, oppose.

n antonym opposition.

suppose *vb* 1 apprehend, believe, conceive, conclude, consider, conjecture, deem, imagine, judge, presume, presuppose, think. 2 assume, hypothesize. 3 imply, posit, predicate, think. 4 fancy, opine, speculate, surmise, suspect, theorize, wean.

vb antonym know.

supposition *n* 1 conjecture, guess, guesswork, presumption, surmise. 2 assumption, hypothesis, postulation, theory, thesis. 3 doubt, uncertainty.

n antonym knowledge.

suppress *vb* 1 choke, crush, destroy, overwhelm, overpower, overthrow, quash, quell, quench, smother, stifle, subdue, withhold. 2 arrest, inhibit, obstruct, repress, restrain, stop. 3 conceal, extinguish, keep, retain, secret, silence, stifle, strangle.

vb antonyms encourage, incite.

supremacy *n* ascendancy, domination, headship, lordship, mastery, predominance, pre-eminence, primacy, sovereignty.

supreme *adj* chief, dominant, first, greatest, highest, leading, paramount, predominant, pre-eminent, principal, sovereign.

adj antonyms lowly, poor, slight.

sure *adj* 1 assured, certain, confident, positive. 2 accurate, dependable, effective, honest, infallible, precise, reliable, trustworthy, undeniable, undoubted, unmistakable, well-proven. 3 guaranteed, inevitable, irrevocable. 4 fast, firm, safe, secure, stable, steady.

adj antonyms doubtful, unsure.

surely *adv* 1 assuredly, certainly, infallibly, sure, undoubtedly. 2 firmly, safely, securely, steadily.

surety *n* bail, bond, certainty, guarantee, pledge, safety, security.

surfeit *vb* **1** cram, gorge, overfeed, sate, satiate. **2** cloy, nauseate, pall. • *n* excess, fullness, glut, oppression, plethora, satiation, satiety, superabundance, superfluity.

surge *vb* billow, rise, rush, sweep, swell, swirl, tower. • *n* billow, breaker, roller, wave, white horse.

surly *adj* **1** churlish, crabbed, cross, crusty, discourteous, fretful, gruff, grumpy, harsh, ill-natured, ill-tempered, morose, peevish, perverse, pettish, petulant, rough, rude, snappish, snarling, sour, sullen, testy, touchy, uncivil, ungracious, waspish. **2** dark, tempestuous.
adj antonym pleasant.

surmise *vb* believe, conclude, conjecture, consider, divine, fancy, guess, imagine, presume, suppose, think, suspect. • *n* conclusion, conjecture, doubt, guess, notion, possibility, supposition, suspicion, thought.
vb antonym know.
n antonym certainty.

surmount *vb* **1** clear, climb, crown, overtop, scale, top, vault. **2** conquer, master, overcome, overpower, subdue, vanquish. **3** exceed, overpass, pass, surpass, transcend.

surpass *vb* beat, cap, eclipse, exceed, excel, outdo, outmatch, outnumber, outrun, outstrip, override, overshadow, overtop, outshine, surmount, transcend.

surplus *adj* additional, leftover, remaining, spare, superfluous, supernumerary, supplementary. • *n* balance, excess, overplus, remainder, residue, superabundance, surfeit.
adj antonym essential.
n antonym lack.

surprise *vb* amaze, astonish, astound, bewilder, confuse, disconcert, dumbfound, startle, stun. • *n* amazement, astonishment, blow, shock, wonder.
n antonym composure.

surprising *adj* amazing, astonishing, astounding, extraordinary, marvellous, unexpected, remarkable, startling, strange, unexpected, wonderful.

surrender *vb* **1** cede, sacrifice, yield. **2** abdicate, abandon, forgo, relinquish, renounce, resign, waive. **3** capitulate, comply, succumb. • *n* abandonment, capitulation, cession, delivery, relinquishment, renunciation, resignation, yielding.
vb antonyms fight on.

surreptitious *adj* clandestine, fraudulent, furtive, secret, sly, stealthy, unauthorized, underhand.
adj antonym open.

surround *vb* beset, circumscribe, compass, embrace, encircle, encompass, environ, girdle, hem, invest, loop.

surveillance *n* care, charge, control, direction, inspection, management, oversight, superintendence, supervision, surveyorship, vigilance, watch.

survey *vb* **1** contemplate, observe, overlook, reconnoitre, review, scan, scout, view. **2** examine, inspect, scrutinize. **3** oversee, supervise. **4** estimate, measure, plan, plot, prospect. • *n* **1** prospect, retrospect, sight, view. **2** examination, inspection, reconnaissance, review. **3** estimating, measuring, planning, plotting, prospecting, work-study.

survive *vb* endure, last, outlast, outlive.
vb antonym succumb.

susceptible *adj* capable, excitable, impressible, impressionable, inclined, predisposed, receptive, sensitive.
adj antonyms impregnable, resistant.

suspect *vb* **1** believe, conclude, conjecture, fancy, guess, imagine, judge, suppose, surmise, think. **2** distrust, doubt, mistrust. • *adj* doubtful, dubious, suspicious.
adj antonyms acceptable, innocent, straightforward.

suspend *vb* **1** append, hang, sling, swing. **2** adjourn, arrest, defer, delay, discontinue, hinder, intermit, interrupt, postpone, stay, withhold. **3** debar, dismiss, rusticate.
vb antonyms continue, expedite, reinstate, restore.

suspicion *n* **1** assumption, conjecture, dash, guess, hint, inkling, suggestion, supposition, surmise, trace. **2** apprehension, distrust, doubt, fear, jealousy, misgiving, mistrust.

suspicious *adj* **1** distrustful, jealous, mistrustful, suspect, suspecting. **2** doubtful, questionable.
adj antonyms innocent, trustful, unexceptionable.

sustain *vb* **1** bear, bolster, fortify, prop, strengthen, support, uphold. **2** maintain, nourish, perpetuate, preserve. **3** aid, assist, comfort, relieve. **4** brave, endure, suffer, undergo. **5** approve, confirm, ratify, sanction, validate. **6** confirm, establish, justify, prove.

sustenance *n* **1** maintenance, subsistence, support. **2** aliment, bread, food, nourishment, nutriment, nutrition, provisions, supplies, victuals.

swagger *vb* bluster, boast, brag, bully, flourish, hector, ruffle, strut, swell, vapour. • *n* airs, arrogance, bluster, boastfulness, braggadocio, ruffling, strut.

n antonyms diffidence, modesty, restraint.

swain *n* **1** clown, countryman, hind, peasant, rustic. **2** adorer, gallant, inamorata, lover, suitor, wooer.

swallow *vb* **1** bolt, devour, drink, eat, englut, engorge, gobble, gorge, gulp, imbibe, ingurgitate, swamp. **2** absorb, appropriate, arrogate, devour, engulf, submerge. **3** consume, employ, occupy. **4** brook, digest, endure, pocket, stomach. **5** recant, renounce, retract. • *n* **1** gullet, oesophagus, throat. **2** inclination, liking, palate, relish, taste. **3** deglutition, draught, gulp, mouthful, taste.

swamp *vb* **1** engulf, overwhelm, sink. **2** capsize, embarrass, overset, ruin, upset, wreck. • *n* bog, fen, marsh, morass, quagmire, slough.

sward *n* grass, lawn, sod, turf.

swarm *vb* abound, crowd, teem, throng. • *n* cloud, concourse, crowd, drove, flock, hive, horde, host, mass, multitude, press, shoal, throng.

swarthy *adj* black, brown, dark, darkskinned, dusky, tawny.

adj antonyms fair, pale.

sway *vb* **1** balance, brandish, move, poise, rock, roll, swing, wave, wield. **2** bend, bias, influence, persuade, turn, urge. **3** control, dominate, direct, govern, guide, manage, rule. **4** hoist, raise. **5** incline, lean, lurch, yaw. • *n* **1** ascendency, authority, command, control, domination, dominion, empire, government, mastership, mastery, omnipotence, predominance, power, rule, sovereignty. **2** bias, direction, influence, weight. **3** preponderance, preponderation. **4** oscillation, sweep, swing, wag, wave.

swear *vb* **1** affirm, attest, avow, declare, depose, promise, say, state, testify, vow. **2** blaspheme, curse.

sweep *vb* **1** clean, brush. **2** graze, touch. **3** rake, scour, traverse. • *n* **1** amplitude, compass, drive, movement, range, reach, scope. **2** destruction, devastation, havoc, ravage. **3** curvature, curve.

sweeping *adj* broad, comprehensive, exaggerated, extensive, extravagant, general, unqualified, wholesale.

sweet *adj* **1** candied, cloying, honeyed, luscious, sugary, saccharine. **2** balmy, fragrant, odorous, redolent, spicy. **3** harmonious, dulcet, mellifluous, mellow, melodious, musical, pleasant, soft, tuneful, silver-toned, silvery. **4** beautiful, fair, lovely. **5** agreeable, charming, delightful, grateful, gratifying. **6** affectionate, amiable, attractive, engaging, gentle, mild, lovable, winning. **7** benignant, serene. **8** clean, fresh, pure, sound. • *n* **1** fragrance, perfume, redolence. **2** blessing, delight, enjoyment, gratification, joy, pleasure. **3** candy, treat.

swell *vb* **1** belly, bloat, bulge, dilate, distend, expand, inflate, intumesce, puff, swell, tumefy. **2** augment, enlarge, increase. **3** heave, rise, surge. **4** strut, swagger. • *n* **1** swelling. **2** augmentation, excrescence, protuberance. **3** ascent, elevation, hill, rise. **4** force, intensity, power. **5** billows, surge, undulation, waves. **6** beau, blade, buck, coxcomb, dandy, exquisite, fop, popinjay.

vb antonyms contract, dwindle, shrink.

swerve *vb* **1** deflect, depart, deviate, stray, turn, wander. **2** bend, incline, yield. **3** climb, swarm, wind.

swift *adj* **1** expeditious, fast, fleet, flying, quick, rapid, speedy. **2** alert, eager, forward, prompt, ready, zealous. **3** instant, sudden.

adj antonyms slow, sluggish, tardy.

swiftness *n* celerity, expedition, fleetness, quickness, rapidity, speed, velocity.

swindle *vb* cheat, con, cozen, deceive, defraud, diddle, dupe, embezzle, forge, gull, hoax, overreach, steal, trick, victimize. • *n* cheat, con, deceit, deception, fraud, hoax, imposition, knavery, roguery, trickery.

swindler *n* blackleg, cheat, defaulter, embezzler, faker, fraud, impostor, jockey, knave, peculator, rogue, sharper, trickster.

swing *vb* **1** oscillate, sway, vibrate, wave. **2** dangle, depend, hang. **3** brandish, flourish, whirl. **4** administer, manage. • *n* **1** fluctuation, oscillation, sway, undulation, vibration. **2** elbow-room, freedom, margin, play, range, scope, sweep. **3** bias, tendency.

swoop *vb* descend, pounce, rush, seize, stoop, sweep. • *n* **1** clutch, pounce, seizure. **2** stoop, descent.

sword *n* brand, broadsword, claymore, cutlass, epee, falchion, foil, hanger, rapier, sabre, scimitar.

sybarite *n* epicure, voluptuary.

sycophancy *n* adulation, cringing, fawning, flattery, grovelling, obsequiousness, servility.

sycophant *n* cringer, fawner, flunky, hanger-on, lickspittle, parasite, spaniel, toady, wheedler.

syllabus *n* abridgement, abstract, breviary, brief, compendium, digest, epitome, outline, summary, synopsis.

symbol *n* badge, emblem, exponent, figure, mark, picture, representation, representative, sign, token, type.

symbolic, symbolical *adj* emblematic, figurative, hieroglyphic, representative, significant, typical.

symmetry *n* balance, congruity, evenness, harmony, order, parallelism, proportion, regularity, shapeliness.

n antonyms asymmetry, irregularity.

sympathetic *adj* affectionate, commiserating, compassionate, condoling, kind, pitiful, tender.

adj antonyms antipathetic, callous, indifferent, unsympathetic.

sympathy *n* **1** accord, affinity, agreement, communion, concert, concord, congeniality, correlation, correspondence, harmony, reciprocity, union. **2** commiseration, compassion, condolence, fellow-feeling, kindliness, pity, tenderness, thoughtfulness.

n antonyms callousness, disharmony, incompatibility, indifference.

symptom *n* diagnostic, indication, mark, note, prognostic, sign, token.

symptomatic *adj* characteristic, indicative, symbolic, suggestive.

synonymous *adj* equipollent, equivalent, identical, interchangeable, similar, tantamount.

adj antonyms antonymous, dissimilar, opposite.

synopsis *n* abridgement, abstract, compendium, digest, epitome, outline, precis, résumé, summary, syllabus.

system *n* method, order, plan.

systematic *adj* methodic, methodical, orderly, regular.

adj antonyms disorderly, inefficient, unsystematic.

T

tab *n* **1** flap, tag. **2** account, bill, invoice, statement.

tabby *adj* (*cat*) mottled, striped.

table *vb* enter, move, propose, submit, suggest. • *n* **1** plate, slab, tablet. **2** board, counter, desk, stand. **3** catalogue, chart, compendium, index, list, schedule, syllabus, synopsis, tabulation. **4** diet, fare, food, victuals.

tablet 1 slab, stone. **2** notepad. **3** cap, capsule, lozenge, pill, tablet.

tableau *n* picture, scene, representation.

taboo *vb* forbid, interdict, prohibit, proscribe. • *adj* banned, forbidden, inviolable, outlawed, prohibited, proscribed. • *n* ban, interdict, prohibition, proscription.
adj antonym acceptable.

tacit *adj* implicit, implied, inferred, silent, understood, unexpressed, unspoken.
adj antonyms explicit, express, spoken, stated.

taciturn *adj* close, dumb, laconic, mum, reserved, reticent, silent, tight-lipped, uncommunicative.
adj antonyms communicative, forthcoming, sociable, talkative.

tack *vb* **1** add, affix, append, attach, fasten, tag. **2** gybe, yaw, zigzag. • *n* **1** nail, pin, staple. **2** bearing, course, direction, heading, path, plan, procedure.

tackle *vb* **1** attach, grapple, seize. **2** attempt, try, undertake. • *n* apparatus, cordage, equipment, furniture, gear, harness, implements, rigging, tackling, tools, weapons.

tact *n* address, adroitness, cleverness, dexterity, diplomacy, discernment, finesse, insight, knack, perception, skill, understanding.
n antonyms clumsiness, indiscretion, tactlessness.

tail *vb* dog, follow, shadow, stalk, track. • *adj* abridged, curtailed, limited, reduced. • *n* **1** appendage, conclusion, end, extremity, stub. **2** flap, skirt. **3** queue, retinue, train.

taint *vb* **1** imbue, impregnate. **2** contaminate, corrupt, defile, inflect, mildew, pollute, poison, spoil, touch. **3** blot, stain, sully, tarnish. • *n* **1** stain, tincture, tinge, touch. **2** contamination, corruption, defilement, depravation, infection, pollution. **3** blemish, defect, fault, flaw, spot.

take *vb* **1** accept, obtain, procure, receive. **2** clasp, clutch, grasp, grip, gripe, seize, snatch. **3** filch, misappropriate, pilfer, purloin, steal. **4** abstract, apprehend, appropriate, arrest, bag, capture, ensnare, entrap. **5** attack, befall, smite. **6** capture, carry off, conquer, gain, win. **7** allure, attract, bewitch, captivate, charm, delight, enchant, engage, fascinate, interest, please. **8** consider, hold, interrupt, suppose, regard, understand. **9** choose, elect, espouse, select. **10** employ, expend, use. **11** claim, demand, necessitate, require. **12** bear, endure, experience, feel, perceive, tolerate. **13** deduce, derive, detect, discover, draw. **14** carry, conduct, convey, lead, transfer. **15** clear, surmount. **16** drink, eat, imbibe, inhale, swallow. • *n* proceeds, profits, return, revenue, takings, yield.

tale *n* **1** account, fable, legend, narration, novel, parable, recital, rehearsal, relation, romance, story, yarn. **2** catalogue, count, enumeration, numbering, reckoning, tally.

talent *n* ableness, ability, aptitude, capacity, cleverness, endowment, faculty, forte, genius, gift, knack, parts, power, turn.
n antonyms inability, ineptitude, weakness.

tall *adj* **1** big, elevated, giant, great, high, lanky, lofty, steep, towering. **2** absurd, dubious, exaggerated, implausible, improbable, incredible, preposterous, unbelievable. **3** difficult, hard

talk *vb* chatter, communicate, confer, confess, converse, declaim, discuss, gossip, pontificate, speak. • *n* chatter, communication, conversation, diction, gossip, jargon, language, rumour, speech, utterance.

talkative *adj* chatty, communicative, garrulous, loquacious, voluble.
adj antonyms reserved, taciturn.

tally *vb* accord, agree, conform, coincide, correspond, harmonize, match, square, suit. • *n* **1** match, mate. **2** check, counterpart, muster, roll call. **3** account, reckoning.
vb antonyms differ, disagree.

tame *vb* **1** domesticate, reclaim, train. **2** conquer, master, overcome, repress, subdue, subjugate. • *adj* **1** docile, domestic, domesticated, gentle, mild, reclaimed. **2** broken, crushed, meek, subdued, unresisting, submissive. **3** barren, commonplace, dull, feeble, flat, insipid, jejune, languid, lean, poor, prosaic, prosy, spiritless, tedious, uninteresting, vapid.
adj antonyms exciting, rebellious, unmanageable, wild.

tamper *vb* **1** alter, conquer, dabble, damage, interfere, meddle. **2** intrigue, seduce, suborn.

tang *n* **1** aftertaste, flavour, relish, savour, smack, taste. **2** keenness, nip, sting.

tangible *adj* **1** corporeal, material, palpable, tactile, touchable. **2** actual, certain, embodied, evident, obvious, open, perceptible, plain, positive, real, sensible, solid, stable, substantial.
adj antonym intangible.

tangle *vb* **1** complicate, entangle, intertwine, interweave, mat, perplex, snarl. **2** catch, ensnare, entrap, involve, catch. **3** embarrass, embroil, perplex. • *n* **1** complication, disorder, intricacy, jumble, perplexity, snarl. **2** dilemma, embarrassment, quandary, perplexity.
vb antonym disentangle.

tantalize *vb* balk, disappoint, frustrate, irritate, provoke, tease, torment, vex.
vb antonym satisfy.

tantamount *adj* equal, equivalent, synonymous.

tantrum *n* fit, ill-humour, outburst, paroxysm, temper, whim.

tap[1] *vb* knock, pat, rap, strike, tip, touch. • *n* pat, tip, rap, touch.

tap[2] *vb* **1** broach, draw off, extract, pierce. **2** draw on, exploit, mine, use, utilize. **3** bug, eavesdrop, listen in. • *n* **1** faucet, plug, spigot, spout, stopcock, valve. **2** bug, listening device, transmitter.

tardiness *n* delay, dilatoriness, lateness, procrastination, slackness, slowness.

tardy *adj* **1** slow, sluggish, snail-like. **2** backward, behindhand, dilatory, late, loitering, overdue, slack.
adj antonyms prompt, punctual.

tarn *n* bog, fen, marsh, morass, swamp.

tarnish *vb* blemish, deface, defame, dim, discolour, dull, slur, smear, soil, stain, sully. • *n* blemish, blot, soiling, spot, stain.

vb antonyms brighten, enhance, polish up.
n antonyms brightness, polish.

tarry *vb* **1** delay, dally, linger, loiter, remain, stay, stop, wait. **2** defer. **3** abide, lodge, rest, sojourn.

tart *adj* **1** acid, acidulous, acrid, astringent, piquant, pungent, sharp, sour. **2** acrimonious, caustic, crabbed, curt, harsh, ill-humoured, ill-tempered, keen, petulant, sarcastic, severe, snappish, testy.

task *vb* burden, overwork, strain, tax. • *n* **1** drudgery, labour, toil, work. **2** business, charge, chore, duty, employment, enterprise, job, mission, stint, undertaking. **3** assignment, exercise, lesson.

taste *vb* **1** experience, feel, perceive, undergo. **2** relish, savour, sip. • *n* **1** flavour, gusto, relish, savour, smack, piquancy. **2** admixture, bit, dash, fragment, hint, infusion, morsel, mouthful, sample, shade, sprinkling, suggestion, tincture. **3** appetite, desire, fondness, liking, partiality, predilection. **4** acumen, cultivation, culture, delicacy, discernment, discrimination, elegance, fine-feeling, grace, judgement, polish, refinement. **5** manner, style.

tasteful *adj* **1** appetizing, delicious, flavoursome, palatable, savoury, tasty, toothsome. **2** aesthetic, artistic, attractive, elegant.
adj antonym tasteless.

tasteless *adj* **1** flat, insipid, savourless, stale, watery. **2** dull, mawkish, uninteresting, vapid.
adj antonym tasteful.

tattle *vb* **1** babble, chat, chatter, jabber, prate, prattle. **2** blab, gossip, inform. • *n* gabble, gossip, prate, prattle, tittle-tattle, twaddle.

taunt *vb* censure, chaff, deride, flout, jeer, mock, scoff, sneer, revile, reproach, ridicule, twit, upbraid. • *n* censure, derision, gibe, insult, jeer, quip, quirk, reproach, ridicule, scoff.

taut *adj* strained, stretched, tense, tight.
adj antonyms loose, relaxed, slack.

tautology *n* iteration, pleonasm, redundancy, reiteration, repetition, verbosity, wordiness.
n antonyms economy, succinctness.

tavern *n* bar, chophouse, hostelry, inn, pub, public house.

tawdry *adj* flashy, gaudy, garish, glittering, loud, meretricious, ostentatious, showy.
adj antonyms excellent, fine, superior.

tax *vb* **1** burden, demand, exact, load, overtax, require, strain, task. **2** accuse, charge. • *n* **1** assessment, custom, duty, excise, impost, levy, rate, taxation, toll, tribute. **2** burden, charge, demand, requisition, strain. **3** accusation, censure.

teach *vb* **1** catechize, coach, discipline, drill, edify, educate, enlighten, inform, indoctrinate, initiate, instruct, ground, prime, school, train, tutor. **2** communicate, disseminate, explain, expound, impart, implant, inculcate, infuse, instil, interpret, preach, propagate. **3** admonish, advise, counsel, direct, guide, signify, show.

teacher *n* **1** coach, educator, inculcator, informant, instructor, master, pedagogue, preceptor, schoolteacher, trainer, tutor. **2** adviser, counsellor, guide, mentor. **3** pastor, preacher.

tear *vb* **1** burst, slit, rive, rend, rip. **2** claw, lacerate, mangle, shatter, rend, wound. **3** sever, sunder. **4** fume, rage, rant, rave. • *n* fissure, laceration, rent, rip, wrench.

tease *vb* annoy, badger, beg, bother, chafe, chagrin, disturb, harass, harry, hector, importune, irritate, molest, pester, plague, provoke, tantalize, torment, trouble, vex, worry.

tedious *adj* **1** dull, fatiguing, irksome, monotonous, tiresome, trying, uninteresting, wearisome. **2** dilatory, slow, sluggish, tardy. *adj antonyms* exciting, interesting.

teem *vb* **1** abound, bear, produce, swarm. **2** discharge, empty, overflow. *vb antonyms* lack, want.

teeming *adj* abounding, fraught, full, overflowing, pregnant, prolific, replete, swarming. *adj antonyms* lacking, rare, sparse.

tell *vb* **1** compute, count, enumerate, number, reckon. **2** describe, narrate, recount, rehearse, relate, report. **3** acknowledge, announce, betray, confess, declare, disclose, divulge, inform, own, reveal. **4** acquaint, communicate, instruct, teach. **5** discern, discover, distinguish. **6** express, mention, publish, speak, state, utter.

temper *vb* **1** modify, qualify. **2** appease, assuage, calm, mitigate, mollify, moderate, pacify, restrain, soften, soothe. **3** accommodate, adapt, adjust, fit, suit. • *n* **1** character, constitution, nature, organization, quality, structure, temperament, type. **2** disposition, frame, grain, humour, mood, spirits, tone, vein. **3** calmness, composure, equanimity, moderation, tranquillity. **4** anger, ill-temper, irritation, spleen, passion.

temperament *n* character, constitution, disposition, habit, idiosyncrasy, nature, organization, temper.

temperate *adj* **1** abstemious, ascetic, austere, chaste, continent, frugal, moderate, self-controlled, self-denying, sparing. **2** calm, cool, dispassionate, mild, sober, sedate. *adj antonyms* excessive, extreme, intemperate.

tempest *n* **1** cyclone, gale, hurricane, squall, storm, tornado. **2** commotion, disturbance, excitement, perturbation, tumult, turmoil.

temporal *adj* **1** civil, lay, mundane, political, profane, secular, terrestrial, worldly. **2** brief, ephemeral, evanescent, fleeting, momentary, short-lived, temporal, transient, transitory. *adj antonym* spiritual.

temporary *adj* brief, ephemeral, evanescent, fleeting, impermanent, momentary, short-lived, transient, transitory. *adj antonyms* everlasting, permanent.

tempt *vb* **1** prove, test, try. **2** allure, decoy, entice, induce, inveigle, persuade, seduce. **3** dispose, incite, incline, instigate, lead, prompt, provoke. *vb antonyms* discourage, dissuade.

tempting *adj* alluring, attractive, enticing, inviting, seductive.

tenable *adj* defensible, maintainable, rational, reasonable, sound.

tenacious *adj* **1** retentive, unforgetful. **2** adhesive, clinging, cohesive, firm, glutinous, gummy, resisting, retentive, sticky, strong, tough, unyielding, viscous. **3** dogged, fast, obstinate, opinionated, opinionative, pertinacious, persistent, resolute, stubborn, unwavering. *adj antonyms* loose, slack, weak.

tenacity *n* **1** retentiveness, tenaciousness. **2** adhesiveness, cohesiveness, gumminess, toughness, stickiness, strength, viscidity. **3** doggedness, firmness, obstinacy, perseverance, persistency, pertinacity, resolution, stubbornness. *n antonyms* looseness, slackness, weakness.

tend[1] *vb* accompany, attend, graze, guard, keep, protect, shepherd, watch.

tend² *vb* **1** aim, exert, gravitate, head, incline, influence, lead, lean, point, trend, verge. **2** conduce, contribute.

vb antonym neglect.

tendency *n* aim, aptitude, bearing, bent, bias, course, determination, disposition, direction, drift, gravitation, inclination, leaning, liability, predisposition, proclivity, proneness, propensity, scope, set, susceptibility, turn, twist, warp.

tender¹ *vb* bid, offer, present, proffer, propose, suggest, volunteer. • *n* **1** bid, offer, proffer, proposal. **2** currency, money.

tender² *adj* **1** callow, delicate, effeminate, feeble, feminine, fragile, immature, infantile, soft, weak, young. **2** affectionate, compassionate, gentle, humane, kind, lenient, loving, merciful, mild, pitiful, sensitive, sympathetic, tender-hearted. **3** affecting, disagreeable, painful, pathetic, touching, unpleasant.

adj antonyms callous, chewy, hard, harsh, rough, severe, tough.

tenebrous *adj* cloudy, dark, darksome, dusky, gloomy, murky, obscure, shadowy, shady, sombre, tenebrious.

tenement *n* abode, apartment, domicile, dwelling, flat, house.

tenet *n* belief, creed, position, dogma, doctrine, notion, opinion, position, principle, view.

tenor *n* **1** cast, character, cut, fashion, form, manner, mood, nature, stamp, tendency, trend, tone. **2** drift, gist, import, intent, meaning, purport, sense, significance, spirit.

tense *vb* flex, strain, tauten, tighten. • *adj* **1** rigid, stiff, strained, stretched, taut, tight. **2** excited, highly strung, intent, nervous, rapt.

vb antonyms loosen, relax.

adj antonyms calm, lax, loose, relaxed.

tentative *adj* essaying, experimental, provisional, testing, toying.

adj antonyms conclusive, decisive, definite, final.

tenure *n* holding, occupancy, occupation, possession, tenancy, tenement, use.

term *vb* call, christen, denominate, designate, dub, entitle, name, phrase, style. • *n* **1** bound, boundary, bourn, confine, limit, mete, terminus. **2** duration, period, season, semester, span, spell, termination, time. **3** denomination, expression, locution, name, phrase, word.

terminal *adj* **1** bounding, limiting. **2** final, terminating, ultimate. • *n* **1** end, extremity, termination. **2** bound, limit. **3** airport, depot, station, terminus.

adj antonym initial.

terminate *vb* **1** bound, limit. **2** end, finish, close, complete, conclude. **3** eventuate, issue, prove.

vb antonyms begin, initiate, start.

termination *n* **1** ending, suffix. **2** bound, extend, limit. **3** end, completion, conclusion, consequence, effect, issue, outcome, result.

terms *npl* conditions, provisions, stipulations.

terrestrial *adj* earthly, global, mundane, subastral, subcelestial, sublunar, sublunary, tellurian, worldly. • *n* earthling, human.

terrible *adj* **1** appalling, dire, dreadful, fearful, formidable, frightful, gruesome, hideous, horrible, horrid, shocking, terrific, tremendous. **2** alarming, awe-inspiring, awful, dread. **3** great, excessive, extreme, severe.

adj antonyms great, pleasant, superb, wonderful.

terrific *adj* **1** marvellous, sensational, superb. **2** immense, intense. **3** alarming, dreadful, formidable, frightful, terrible, tremendous.

terrify *vb* affright, alarm, appal, daunt, dismay, fright, frighten, horrify, scare, shock, startle, terrorize.

territory *n* country, district, domain, dominion, division, land, place, province, quarter, region, section, tract.

terror *n* affright, alarm, anxiety, awe, consternation, dismay, dread, fear, fright, horror, intimidation, panic, terrorism.

n antonyms long-winded, prolix, repetitious.

terse *adj* brief, compact, concise, laconic, neat, pithy, polished, sententious, short, smooth, succinct.

test *vb* **1** assay. **2** examine, prove, try. • *n* **1** attempt, essay, examination, experiment, ordeal, proof, trial. **2** criterion, standard, touchstone. **3** example, exhibition. **4** discrimination, distinction, judgment.

testify *vb* affirm, assert, asseverate, attest, avow, certify, corroborate, declare, depose, evidence, state, swear.

testimonial *n* **1** certificate, credential, recommendation, voucher. **2** monument, record.

testimony *n* **1** affirmation, attestation, confession, confirmation, corroboration, declaration, deposition, profession. **2** evidence, proof, witness.

testy *adj* captious, choleric, cross, fretful, hasty, irascible, irritable, quick, peevish, peppery, pettish, petulant, snappish, splenetic, touchy, waspish.
adj antonyms even-tempered, good-humored.

tetchy *adj* crabbed, cross, fretful, irritable, peevish, sullen, touchy.

tether *vb* chain, fasten, picket, stake, tie. • *n* chain, fastening, rope.

text *n* copy, subject, theme, thesis, topic, treatise.

texture *n* **1** fabric, web, weft. **2** character, coarseness, composition, constitution, fibre, fineness, grain, make-up, nap, organization, structure, tissue.

thankful *adj* appreciative, beholden, grateful, indebted, obliged.
adj antonyms thankless, unappreciative, ungrateful.

thankfulness *n* appreciation, gratefulness, gratitude.

thankless *adj* profitless, ungracious, ungrateful, unthankful.

thaw *vb* dissolve, liquefy, melt, soften, unbend.
vb antonym freeze.

theatre *n* **1** opera house, playhouse. **2** arena, scene, seat, stage.

theatrical *adj* **1** dramatic, dramaturgic, dramaturgical, histrionic, scenic, spectacular. **2** affected, ceremonious, meretricious, ostentatious, pompous, showy, stagy, stilted, unnatural.

theft *n* depredation, embezzlement, fraud, larceny, peculation, pilfering, purloining, robbery, spoliation, stealing, swindling, thieving.

theme *n* composition, essay, motif, subject, text, thesis, topic, treatise.

theoretical *adj* abstract, conjectural, doctrinaire, ideal, hypothetical, pure, speculative, unapplied.
adj antonyms applied, concrete, practical.

theory *n* **1** assumption, conjecture, hypothesis, idea, plan, postulation, principle, scheme, speculation, surmise, system. **2** doctrine, philosophy, science. **3** explanation, exposition, philosophy, rationale.
n antonyms certainty, practice.

therefore *adv* accordingly, afterward, consequently, hence, so, subsequently, then, thence, whence.

thesaurus *n* dictionary, encyclopedia, repository, storehouse, treasure.

thick *adj* **1** bulky, chunky, dumpy, plump, solid, squab, squat, stubby, thickset. **2** clotted, coagulated, crass, dense, dull, gross, heavy, viscous. **3** blurred, cloudy, dirty, foggy, hazy, indistinguishable, misty, obscure, vaporous. **4** muddy, roiled, turbid. **5** abundant, frequent, multitudinous, numerous. **6** close, compact, crowded, set, thickset. **7** confused, guttural, hoarse, inarticulate, indistinct. **8** dim, dull, weak. **9** familiar, friendly, intimate, neighbourly, well-acquainted. • *adv* **1** fast, frequently, quick. **2** closely, densely, thickly. • *n* centre, middle, midst.
adj antonyms brainy, clever, slender, slight, slim, thin, watery.

thicket *n* clump, coppice, copse, covert, forest, grove, jungle, shrubbery, underbrush, undergrowth, wood, woodland.

thief *n* **1** filcher, pilferer, lifter, marauder, purloiner, robber, shark, stealer. **2** burglar, corsair, defaulter, defrauder, embezzler, footpad, highwayman, housebreaker, kidnapper, pickpocket, pirate, poacher, privateer, sharper, swindler, peculator.

thieve *vb* cheat, embezzle, peculate, pilfer, plunder, purloin, rob, steal, swindle.

thin *vb* attenuate, dilute, diminish, prune, reduce, refine, weaken. • *adj* attenuated, bony, emaciated, fine, fleshless, flimsy, gaunt, haggard, lank, lanky, lean, meagre, peaked, pinched, poor, scanty, scraggy, scrawny, slender, slight, slim, small, sparse, spindly.
adj antonyms broad, dense, fat, solid, strong, thick.

thing *n* **1** being, body, contrivance, creature, entity, object, something, substance. **2** act, action, affair, arrangement, circumstance, concern, deed, event, matter, occurrence, transaction.

think *vb* **1** cogitate, contemplate, dream, meditate, muse, ponder, reflect, ruminate, speculate. **2** consider, deliberate, reason, undertake. **3** apprehend, believe, conceive, conclude, deem, determine, fancy, hold, imagine, judge, opine, presume, reckon, suppose, surmise. **4** design, intend, mean, purpose. **5** account, count, deem, esteem, hold, regard. **6** compass, design, plan, plot. • *n* assessment, contemplation, deliberation, meditation, opinion, reasoning, reflection.

thirst *n* **1** appetite, craving, desire, hunger, longing, yearning. **2** aridity, drought, dryness.

thirsty *adj* **1** arid, dry, parched. **2** eager, greedy, hungry, longing, yearning.

thorn *n* **1** prickle, spine. **2** annoyance, bane, care, evil, infliction, nettle, nuisance, plague, torment, trouble, scourge.

thorny *adj* **1** briary, briery, prickly, spinose, spinous, spiny. **2** barbed, pointed, prickling, sharp, spiky. **3** annoying, difficult, harassing, perplexing, rugged, troublesome, trying, vexatious.

thorough *adj* **1** absolute, arrant, complete, downright, entire, exhaustive, finished, perfect, radical, sweeping, total unmitigated, utter. **2** accurate, correct, reliable, trustworthy.
adj antonyms careless, haphazard, partial.

though *conj* admitting, allowing, although, granted, granting, if, notwithstanding, still. • *adv* however, nevertheless, still, yet.

thought *n* **1** absorption, cogitation, engrossment, meditation, musing, reflection, reverie, rumination. **2** contemplation, intellect, ratiocination, thinking, thoughtfulness. **3** application, conception, consideration, deliberation, idea, pondering, speculation, study. **4** consciousness, imagination, intellect, perception, understanding. **5** conceit, fancy, notion. **6** conclusion, judgment, motion, opinion, sentiment, supposition, view. **7** anxiety, attention, care, concern, provision, regard, solicitude, thoughtfulness. **8** design, expectation, intention, purpose.

thoughtful *adj* **1** absorbed, contemplative, deliberative, dreamy, engrossed, introspective, pensive, philosophic, reflecting, reflective, sedate, speculative. **2** attentive, careful, cautious, circumspect, considerate, discreet, heedful, friendly, kind-hearted, kindly, mindful, neighbourly, provident, prudent, regardful, watchful, wary. **3** quiet, serious, sober, studious.
adj antonym thoughtless.

thoughtless *adj* **1** careless, casual, flighty, heedless, improvident, inattentive, inconsiderate, neglectful, negligent, precipitate, rash, reckless, regardless, remiss, trifling,

unmindful, unthinking. **2** blank, blockish, dull, insensate, stupid, vacant, vacuous.
adj antonym thoughtful.

thrash *vb* beat, bruise, conquer, defeat, drub, flog, lash, maul, pommel, punish, thwack, trounce, wallop, whip.

thread *vb* **1** course, direction, drift, tenor. **2** reeve, trace. • *n* **1** cord, fibre, filament, hair, line, twist. **2** pile, staple.

threadbare *adj* **1** napless, old, seedy, worn. **2** common, commonplace, hackneyed, stale, trite, worn-out.
adj antonyms fresh, luxurious, new, plush.

threat *n* commination, defiance, denunciation, fulmination, intimidation, menace, thunder, thunderbolt.

threaten *vb* **1** denounce, endanger, fulminate, intimidate, menace, thunder. **2** augur, forebode, foreshadow, indicate, portend, presage, prognosticate, warn.

threshold *n* **1** doorsill, sill. **2** door, entrance, gate. **3** beginning, commencement, opening, outset, start.

thrift *n* **1** economy, frugality, parsimony, saving, thriftiness. **2** gain, luck, profit, prosperity, success.
n antonyms profligacy, waste.

thriftless *adj* extravagant, improvident, lavish, profuse, prodigal, shiftless, unthrifty, wasteful.

thrifty *adj* **1** careful, economical, frugal, provident, saving, sparing. **2** flourishing, prosperous, thriving, vigorous.
adj antonyms prodigal, profligate, thriftless, wasteful.

thrill *vb* affect, agitate, electrify, inspire, move, penetrate, pierce, rouse, stir, touch. • *n* excitement, sensation, shock, tingling, tremor.

thrilling *adj* affecting, exciting, gripping, moving, sensational, touching.

thrive *vb* advance, batten, bloom, boom, flourish, prosper, succeed.
vb antonyms die, fail, languish, stagnate.

throng *vb* congregate, crowd, fill, flock, pack, press, swarm. • *n* assemblage, concourse, congregation, crowd, horde, host, mob, multitude, swarm.

throttle *vb* choke, silence, strangle, suffocate.

throw *vb* cast, chuck, dart, fling, hurl, lance, launch, overturn, pitch, pitchfork, send, sling, toss, whirl. • *n* **1** cast, fling, hurl, launch, pitch, sling, toss, whirl. **2** chance, gamble, try, venture.

thrust *vb* clap, dig, drive, force, impel, jam, plunge, poke, prod, propel, push, ram, run, shove, stick. • *n* dig, jab, lunge, pass, plunge, poke, propulsion, push, shove, stab, tilt.

thump *vb* bang, batter, beat, belabour, knock, punch, strike, thrash, thwack, whack. • *n* blow, knock, punch, strike, stroke.

thwart *vb* 1 baffle, balk, contravene, counteract, cross, defeat, disconcert, frustrate, hinder, impede, oppose, obstruct, oppugn. 2 cross, intersect, traverse.
vb antonyms abet, aid, assist.

tickle *vb* amuse, delight, divert, enliven, gladden, gratify, please, rejoice, titillate.

ticklish *adj* 1 dangerous, precarious, risky, tottering, uncertain, unstable, unsteady. 2 critical, delicate, difficult, nice.
adj antonyms easy, straightforward.

tide *n* course, current, ebb, flow, stream.

tidings *npl* advice, greetings, information, intelligence, news, report, word.

tidy *vb* clean, neaten, order, straighten. • *adj* clean, neat, orderly, shipshape, spruce, trig, trim.
adj antonyms disorganized, untidy.

tie *vb* 1 bind, confine, fasten, knot, lock, manacle, secure, shackle, fetter, yoke. 2 complicate, entangle, interlace, knit. 3 connect, hold, join, link, unite. 4 constrain, oblige, restrain, restrict. • *n* 1 band, fastening, knot, ligament, ligature. 2 allegiance, bond, obligation. 3 bow, cravat, necktie.

tier *n* level, line, rank, row, series.

tiff *n* fit, fume, passion, pet, miff, rage.

tight *adj* 1 close, compact, fast, firm. 2 taut, tense, stretched. 3 impassable, narrow, strait.
adj antonyms lax, loose, slack; sober.

till *vb* cultivate, plough, harrow.

tillage *n* agriculture, cultivation, culture, farming, geoponics, husbandry.

tilt *vb* 1 cant, incline, slant, slope, tip. 2 forge, hammer. 3 point, thrust. 4 joust, rush. • *n* 1 awning, canopy, tent. 2 lunge, pass, thrust. 3 cant, inclination, slant, slope, tip.

time *vb* clock, control, count, measure, regulate, schedule. • *n* 1 duration, interim, interval, season, span, spell, tenure, term, while. 2 aeon, age, date, epoch, eon, era. 3 term. 4 cycle, dynasty, reign. 5 confine-ment, delivery, parturition. 6 measure, rhythm.

timely *adj* acceptable, appropriate, apropos, early, opportune, prompt, punctual, seasonable, well-timed.
adj antonym ill-timed, inappropriate, unfavorable.

timid *adj* 1 afraid, cowardly, faint-hearted, fearful, irresolute, meticulous, nervous, pusillanimous, skittish, timorous, unadventurous. 2 bashful, coy, diffident, modest, shame-faced, shrinking.
adj antonyms audacious, bold, brave.

tincture *vb* 1 colour, dye, shade, stain, tinge, tint. 2 flavour, season. 3 imbue, impregnate, impress, infuse. • *n* 1 grain, hue, shade, stain, tinge, tint, tone. 2 flavour, smack, spice, taste. 3 admixture, dash, infusion, seasoning, sprinkling, touch.

tinge *vb* 1 colour, dye, stain, tincture, tint. 2 imbue, impregnate, impress, infuse. • *n* 1 cast, colour, dye, hue, shade, stain, tincture, tint. 2 flavour, smack, spice, quality, taste.

tint *n* cast, colour, complexion, dye, hue, shade, tinge, tone.

tiny *adj* diminutive, dwarfish, Lilliputian, little, microscopic, miniature, minute, puny, pygmy, small, wee.
adj antonyms big, immense.

tip[1] *n* apex, cap, end, extremity, peak, pinnacle, point, top, vertex.

tip[2] *vb* 1 incline, overturn, tilt. 2 dispose of, dump. • *n* 1 donation, fee, gift, gratuity, perquisite, reward. 2 inclination, slant. 3 hint, pointer, suggestion. 4 strike, tap.

tirade *n* abuse, denunciation, diatribe, harangue, outburst.

tire *vb* 1 exhaust, fag, fatigue, harass, jade, weary. 2 bore, bother, irk.
vb antonyms energize, enliven, exhilarate, invigorate, refresh.

tiresome *adj* annoying, arduous, boring, dull, exhausting, fatiguing, fagging, humdrum, irksome, laborious, monotonous, tedious, wearisome, vexatious.
adj antonyms easy, interesting, stimulating.

tissue *n* 1 cloth, fabric. 2 membrane, network, structure, texture, web. 3 accumulation, chain, collection, combination, conglomeration, mass, series, set.

titanic *adj* colossal, Cyclopean, enormous, gigantic, herculean, huge, immense, mighty, monstrous, prodigious, stupendous, vast.

title vb call, designate, name, style, term. • n **1** caption, legend, head, heading. **2** appellation, application, cognomen, completion, denomination, designation, epithet, name. **3** claim, due, ownership, part, possession, prerogative, privilege, right.

tittle n atom, bit, grain, iota, jot, mite, particle, scrap, speck, whit.

tittle-tattle vb, n babble, cackle, chatter, discourse, gabble, gossip, prattle.

toast vb **1** brown, dry, heat. **2** honour, pledge, propose, salute. • n **1** compliment, drink, pledge, salutation, salute. **2** favourite, pet.

toil vb drudge, labour, strive, work. • n **1** drudgery, effort, exertion, exhaustion, grinding, labour, pains, travail, work. **2** gin, net, noose, snare, spring, trap.

token adj nominal, superficial, symbolic. • n **1** badge, evidence, index, indication, manifestation, mark, note, sign, symbol, trace, trait. **2** keepsake, memento, memorial, reminder, souvenir.

tolerable adj **1** bearable, endurable, sufferable, supportable. **2** fair, indifferent, middling, ordinary, passable, so-so.

tolerance n endurance, receptivity, sufferance, toleration.

tolerate vb **1** admit, allow, indulge, let, permit, receive. **2** abide, brook, endure, suffer.

toll¹ n **1** assessment, charge, customs, demand, dues, duty, fee, impost, levy, rate, tax, tribute. **2** cost, damage, loss.

toll² vb chime, knell, peal, ring, sound. • n chime, knell, peal, ring, ringing, tolling.

tomb n catacomb, charnel house, crypt, grave, mausoleum, sepulchre, vault.

tone vb blend, harmonize, match, suit. • n **1** note, sound. **2** accent, cadence, emphasis, inflection, intonation, modulation. **3** key, mood, strain, temper. **4** elasticity, energy, force, health, strength, tension, vigour. **5** cast, colour, manner, hue, shade, style, tint. **6** drift, tenor.

tongue n **1** accent, dialect, language, utterance, vernacular. **2** discourse, parlance, speech, talk. **3** nation, race.

too adv additionally, also, further, likewise, moreover, overmuch.

toothsome adj agreeable, dainty, delicious, luscious, nice, palatable, savoury.

top vb **1** cap, head, tip. **2** ride, surmount. **3** outgo, surpass. • adj apical, best, chief,

culminating, finest, first, foremost, highest, leading, prime, principal, topmost, uppermost. • n acme, apex, crest, crown, head, meridian, pinnacle, summit, surface, vertex, zenith.

n antonyms base, bottom, nadir.

topic n **1** business, question, subject, text, theme, thesis. **2** division, head, subdivision. **3** commonplace, dictum, maxim, precept, proposition, principle, rule. **4** arrangement, scheme.

topple vb fall, overturn, tumble, upset.

torment vb **1** annoy, agonize, distress, excruciate, pain, rack, torture. **2** badger, fret, harass, harry, irritate, nettle, plague, provoke, tantalize, tease, trouble, vex, worry. • n agony, anguish, pang, rack, torture.

tornado n blizzard, cyclone, gale, hurricane, storm, tempest, typhoon, whirlwind.

torpid adj **1** benumbed, lethargic, motionless, numb. **2** apathetic, dormant, dull, inactive, indolent, inert, listless, sleepy, slothful, sluggish, stupid.

adj antonyms active, lively, vigorous.

torpor n **1** coma, insensibility, lethargy, numbness, torpidity. **2** inaction, inactivity, inertness, sluggishness, stupidity.

n antonyms activity, animation, vigor.

torrid adj **1** arid, burnt, dried, parched. **2** burning, fiery, hot, parching, scorching, sultry, tropical, violent.

adj antonym arctic.

tortuous adj **1** crooked, curved, curvilineal, curvilinear, serpentine, sinuate, sinuated, sinuous, twisted, winding. **2** ambiguous, circuitous, crooked, deceitful, indirect, perverse, roundabout.

adj antonyms straight, straightforward.

torture vb agonize, distress, excruciate, pain, rack, torment. • n agony, anguish, distress, pain, pang, rack, torment.

toss vb **1** cast, fling, hurl, pitch, throw. **2** agitate, rock, shake. **3** disquiet, harass, try. **4** roll, writhe. • n cast, fling, pitch, throw.

total vb add, amount to, reach, reckon. • adj **1** complete, entire, full, whole. **2** integral, undivided. • n aggregate, all, gross, lump, mass, sum, totality, whole.

adj antonyms limited, partial, restricted.

totter vb **1** falter, reel, stagger, vacillate. **2** lean, oscillate, reel, rock, shake, sway, tremble, waver. **3** fail, fall, flag.

touch vb **1** feel, graze, handle, hit, pat, strike, tap. **2** concern, interest, regard. **3** affect, impress, move, stir. **4** grasp, reach, stretch. **5** melt, mollify, soften. **6** afflict, distress, hurt, injure, molest, sting, wound. • *n* **1** hint, smack, suggestion, suspicion, taste, trace. **2** blow, contract, hit, pat, tap.

touchiness *n* fretfulness, irritability, irascibility, peevishness, pettishness, petulance, snappishness, spleen, testiness.

touching *adj* **1** affecting, heart-rending, impressive, melting, moving, pathetic, pitiable, tender. **2** abutting, adjacent, bordering, tangent.

touchy *adj* choleric, cross, fretful, hot-tempered, irascible, irritable, peevish, petulant, quick-tempered, snappish, splenetic, tetchy, testy, waspish.

adj antonyms calm, imperturbable, serene, unflappable.

tough *adj* **1** adhesive, cohesive, flexible, tenacious. **2** coriaceous, leathery. **3** clammy, ropy, sticky, viscous. **4** inflexible, intractable, rigid, stiff. **5** callous, hard, obdurate, stubborn. **6** difficult, formidable, hard, troublesome. • *n* brute, bully, hooligan, ruffian, thug.

adj antonyms brittle, delicate, fragile, liberal, soft, tender, vulnerable, weak.

tour *vb* journey, perambulate, travel, visit. • *n* circuit, course, excursion, expedition, journey, perambulation, pilgrimage, round.

tow *vb* drag, draw, haul, pull, tug. • *n* drag, lift, pull.

tower *vb* mount, rise, soar, transcend. • *n* **1** belfry, bell tower, column, minaret, spire, steeple, turret. **2** castle, citadel, fortress, stronghold. **3** pillar, refuge, rock, support.

towering *adj* **1** elevated, lofty. **2** excessive, extreme, prodigious, violent.

adj antonyms minor, small, trivial.

toy *vb* dally, play, sport, trifle, wanton. • *n* **1** bauble, doll, gewgaw, gimmick, knick-knack, plaything, puppet, trinket. **2** bagatelle, bubble, trifle. **3** play, sport.

trace *vb* **1** follow, track, train. **2** copy, deduce, delineate, derive, describe, draw, sketch. • *n* **1** evidence, footmark, footprint, footstep, impression, mark, remains, sign, token, track, trail, vestige, wake. **2** memorial, record. **3** bit, dash, flavour, hint, suspicion, streak, tinge.

track *vb* chase, draw, follow, pursue, scent, track, trail. • *n* **1** footmark, footprint, footstep, spoor, trace, vestige. **2** course,

pathway, rails, road, runway, trace, trail, wake, way.

trackless *adj* pathless, solitary, unfrequented, unused.

tract[1] *n* **1** area, district, quarter, region, territory. **2** parcel, patch, part, piece, plot, portion.

tract[2] *n* disquisition, dissertation, essay, homily, pamphlet, sermon, thesis, tractate, treatise.

tractable *adj* **1** amenable, docile, governable, manageable, submissive, willing, yielding. **2** adaptable, ductile, malleable, plastic, tractile.

adj antonyms headstrong, intractable, obstinate, refractory, stubborn, unruly, wilful.

trade *vb* bargain, barter, chaffer, deal, exchange, interchange, sell, traffic. • *n* **1** bargaining, barter, business, commerce, dealing, traffic. **2** avocation, calling, craft, employment, occupation, office, profession, pursuit, vocation.

traditional *adj* accustomed, apocryphal, customary, established, historic, legendary, old, oral, transmitted, uncertain, unverified, unwritten.

traduce *vb* abuse, asperse, blemish, brand, calumniate, decry, defame, depreciate, disparage, revile, malign, slander, vilify.

traducer *n* calumniator, defamer, detractor, slanderer, vilifier.

traffic *vb* bargain, barter, chaffer, deal, exchange, trade. • *n* barter, business, chaffer, commerce, exchange, intercourse, trade, transportation, truck.

tragedy *n* **1** drama, play. **2** adversity, calamity, catastrophe, disaster, misfortune.

n antonyms prosperity, success, triumph.

tragic *adj* **1** dramatic. **2** calamitous, catastrophic, disastrous, dreadful, fatal, grievous, heart-breaking, mournful, sad, shocking, sorrowful.

adj antonyms comic, successful, triumphant.

trail *vb* **1** follow, hunt, trace, track. **2** drag, draw, float, flow, haul, pull. • *n* footmark, footprint, footstep, mark, trace, track.

train *vb* **1** drag, draw, haul, trail, tug. **2** allure, entice. **3** discipline, drill, educate, exercise, instruct, school, teach. **4** accustom, break in, familiarize, habituate, inure, prepare, rehearse, use. • *n* **1** trail, wake. **2** entourage, cortege, followers, retinue, staff, suite. **3** chain, consecution, sequel, series, set, succession. **4** course, method, order, process. **5** allure, artifice, device, enticement, lure, persuasion, stratagem, trap.

trait *n* **1** line, mark, stroke, touch. **2** characteristic, feature, lineage, particularity, peculiarity, quality.

traitor *n* **1** apostate, betrayer, deceiver, Judas, miscreant, quisling, renegade, turncoat. **2** conspirator, deserter, insurgent, mutineer, rebel, revolutionary.

traitorous *adj* **1** faithless, false, perfidious, recreant, treacherous. **2** insidious, treasonable.

adj antonyms faithful, loyal, patriotic.

tramp *vb* hike, march, plod, trudge, walk. • *n* **1** excursion, journey, march, walk. **2** homeless person, tramper, vagabond, vagrant.

trample *vb* **1** crush, tread. **2** scorn, spurn.

trance *n* **1** dream, ecstasy, hypnosis, rapture. **2** catalepsy, coma.

tranquil *adj* calm, hushed, peaceful, placid, quiet, serene, still, undisturbed, unmoved, unperturbed, unruffled, untroubled.

adj antonyms agitated, disturbed, noisy, troubled.

tranquillity *n* calmness, peace, peacefulness, placidity, placidness, quiet, quietness, serenity, stillness, tranquilness.

tranquillize *vb* allay, appease, assuage, calm, compose, hush, lay, lull, moderate, pacify, quell, quiet, silence, soothe, still.

transact *vb* conduct, dispatch, enact, execute, do, manage, negotiate, perform, treat.

transaction *n* **1** act, action, conduct, doing, management, negotiation, performance. **2** affair, business, deal, dealing, incident, event, job, matter, occurrence, procedure, proceeding.

transcend *vb* **1** exceed, overlap, overstep, pass, transgress. **2** excel, outstrip, outrival, outvie, overtop, surmount, surpass.

transcendent *adj* **1** consummate, inimitable, peerless, pre-eminent, supereminent, surpassing, unequalled, unparalleled, unrivalled, unsurpassed. **2** metempiric, metempirical, noumenal, super-sensible.

transcript *n* duplicate, engrossment, rescript.

transfer *vb* **1** convey, dispatch, move, remove, send, translate, transmit, transplant, transport. **2** alienate, assign, cede, confer, convey, consign, deed, devise, displace, forward, grant, pass, relegate. • *n* alienation, assignment, bequest, carriage, cession, change, conveyance, copy, demise, gift, grant, move, relegation, removal, shift, shipment, transference, transferring, transit, transmission, transportation.

transfigure *vb* change, convert, dignify, idealize, metamorphose, transform.

transform *vb* **1** alter, change, metamorphose, transfigure. **2** convert, resolve, translate, transmogrify, transmute.

vb antonym preserve.

transgress *vb* **1** exceed, transcend, overpass, overstep. **2** break, contravene, disobey, infringe, violate. **3** err, intrude, offend, sin, slip, trespass.

transgression *n* **1** breach, disobedience, encroachment, infraction, infringement, transgression, violation. **2** crime, delinquency, error, fault, iniquity, misdeed, misdemeanour, misdoing,

offence, sin, slip, trespass, wrongdoing.

transient *adj* **1** diurnal, ephemeral, evanescent, fleeting, fugitive, impertinent, meteoric, mortal, passing, perishable, short-lived, temporary, transitory, volatile. **2** hasty, imperfect, momentary, short.

adj antonym permanent.

transitory *adj* brief, ephemeral, evanescent, fleeting, flitting, momentary, passing, short, temporary, transient.

translate *vb* **1** remove, transfer, transport. **2** construe, decipher, decode, interpret, render, turn.

translucent *adj* diaphanous, hyaline, pellucid, semi-opaque, semi-transparent.

adj antonym opaque.

transmit *vb* **1** forward, remit, send. **2** communicate, conduct, radiate. **3** bear, carry, convey.

vb antonym receive.

transparent *adj* **1** bright, clear, diaphanous, limpid, lucid. **2** crystalline, hyaline, pellucid, serene, translucent, unclouded. **3** open, porous. **4** evident, obvious, manifest, patent.

adj antonyms ambiguous, opaque, unclear.

transpire *vb* **1** befall, chance, happen, occur. **2** evaporate, exhale.

transport *vb* **1** bear, carry, cart, conduct, convey, fetch, remove, ship, take, transfer, truck. **2** banish, expel. **3** beatify, delight, enrapture, entrance, ravish. • *n* **1** carriage, conveyance, movement, transportation, transporting. **2** beatification, beatitude, bliss, ecstasy, felicity, happiness, rapture, ravishment. **3** frenzy, passion, vehemence, warmth.

vb antonyms bore, leave.

n antonym boredom.

trap *vb* **1** catch, ensnare, entrap, noose, snare, springe. **2** ambush, deceive, dupe, trick. **3** enmesh, tangle, trepan. • *n* **1** gin, snare, springe, toil. **2** ambush, artifice, pitfall, stratagem, trepan.

trappings *npl* **1** adornments, decorations, dress, embellishments, frippery, gear, livery, ornaments, paraphernalia, rigging. **2** accoutrements, caparisons, equipment, gear.

trash *n* **1** dregs, dross, garbage, refuse, rubbish, trumpery, waste. **2** balderdash, nonsense, twaddle.

n antonym sense.

travel *vb* **1** journey, peregrinate, ramble, roam, rove, tour, voyage, walk, wander. **2** go, move, pass. • *n* excursion, expedition, journey, peregrination, ramble, tour, trip, voyage, walk.

vb antonym stay.

traveller *n* excursionist, explorer, globetrotter, itinerant, passenger, pilgrim, rover, sightseer, tourist, trekker, tripper, voyager, wanderer, wayfarer.

traverse *vb* **1** contravene, counteract, defeat, frustrate, obstruct, oppose, thwart. **2** ford, pass, play, range.

travesty *vb* imitate, parody, take off. • *n* burlesque, caricature, imitation, parody, take-off.

treacherous *adj* deceitful, disloyal, faithless, false, false-hearted, insidious, perfidious, recreant, sly, traitorous, treasonable, unfaithful, unreliable, unsafe, untrustworthy.

treachery *n* betrayal, deceitfulness, disloyalty, double-dealing, faithlessness, foul play, infidelity, insidiousness, perfidiousness, treason, perfidy.

n antonyms dependability, loyalty.

treason *n* betrayal, disloyalty, perfidy, sedition, traitorousness, treachery.

n antonym loyalty.

treasonable *adj* disloyal, traitorous, treacherous.

treasure *vb* **1** accumulate, collect, garner, hoard, husband, save, store. **2** cherish, idolize, prize, value, worship. • *n* **1** cash, funds, jewels, money, riches, savings, valuables, wealth. **2** abundance, reserve, stock, store.

vb antonym disparage.

treasurer *n* banker, bursar, purser, receiver, trustee.

treat *vb* **1** entertain, feast, gratify, refresh. **2** attend, doctor, dose, handle, manage, serve. **3** bargain, covenant, negotiate, parley. • *n* **1** banquet, entertainment, feast. **2** delight, enjoyment, entertainment, gratification, luxury, pleasure, refreshment.

n antonym drag.

treatise *n* commentary, discourse, dissertation, disquisition, monograph, tractate.

treatment *n* **1** usage, use. **2** dealing, handling, management, manipulation. **3** doctoring, therapy.

treaty *n* agreement, alliance, bargain, compact, concordat, convention, covenant, entente, league, pact.

tremble *vb* quake, quaver, quiver, shake, shiver, shudder, vibrate, wobble. • *n* quake, quiver, shake, shiver, shudder, tremor, vibration, wobble.

n antonym steadiness.

tremendous *adj* **1** colossal, enormous, huge, immense. **2** excellent, marvellous, wonderful. **3** alarming, appalling, awful, dreadful, fearful, frightful, horrid, horrible, terrible.

adj antonyms boring, dreadful, run-of-the-mill, tiny.

tremor *n* agitation, quaking, quivering, shaking, trembling, trepidation, tremulousness, vibration.

n antonym steadiness.

tremulous *adj* afraid, fearful, quavering, quivering, shaking, shaky, shivering, timid, trembling, vibrating.

adj antonyms calm, firm.

trench *vb* **1** carve, cut. **2** ditch, channel, entrench, furrow. • *n* **1** channel, ditch, drain, furrow, gutter, moat, pit, sewer, trough. **2** dugout, entrenchment, fortification.

trenchant *adj* **1** cutting, keen, sharp. **2** acute, biting, caustic, crisp, incisive, pointed, piquant, pungent, sarcastic, sententious, severe, unsparing, vigorous.

adj antonym woolly.

trend *vb* drift, gravitate, incline, lean, run, stretch, sweep, tend, turn. • *n* bent, course, direction, drift, inclination, set, leaning, tendency, trending.

trepidation *n* **1** agitation, quaking, quivering,

shaking, trembling, tremor. **2** dismay, excitement, fear, perturbation, tremulousness.

n antonym calm.

trespass *vb* **1** encroach, infringe, intrude, trench. **2** offend, sin, transgress. • *n* **1** encroachment, infringement, injury, intrusion, invasion. **2** crime, delinquency, error, fault, sin, misdeed, misdemeanour, offence, transgression. **3** trespasser.

vb antonyms keep to, obey.

trial *adj* experimental, exploratory, testing. • *n* **1** examination, experiment, test. **2** experience, knowledge. **3** aim, attempt, effort, endeavour, essay, exertion, struggle. **4** assay, criterion, ordeal, prohibition, proof, test, touchstone. **5** affliction, burden, chagrin, dolour, distress, grief, hardship, heartache, inclination, misery, mortification, pain, sorrow, suffering, tribulation, trouble, unhappiness, vexation, woe, wretchedness. **6** action, case, cause, hearing, suit.

tribe *n* **1** clan, family, lineage, race, sept, stock. **2** class, distinction, division, order.

tribulation *n* adversity, affliction, distress, grief, misery, pain, sorrow, suffering, trial, trouble, unhappiness, woe, wretchedness.

n antonyms happiness, rest.

tribunal *n* **1** bench, judgement seat. **2** assizes, bar, court, judicature, session.

tribute *n* **1** subsidy, tax. **2** custom, duty, excise, impost, tax, toll. **3** contribution, grant, offering.

n antonyms blame.

trice *n* flash, instant, jiffy, moment, second, twinkling.

trick *vb* cheat, circumvent, cozen, deceive, defraud, delude, diddle, dupe, fob, gull, hoax, overreach. • *n* **1** artifice, blind, deceit, deception, dodge, fake, feint, fraud, game, hoax, imposture, manoeuvre, shift, ruse, swindle, stratagem, wile. **2** antic, caper, craft, deftness, gambol, sleight. **3** habit, mannerism, peculiarity, practice.

trickle *vb* distil, dribble, drip, drop, ooze, percolate, seep. • *n* dribble, drip, percolation, seepage.

vb antonyms gush, stream.

n antonyms gush, stream.

tricky *adj* artful, cunning, deceitful, deceptive, subtle, trickish.

adj antonyms easy, honest.

trifle *vb* dally, dawdle, fool, fribble, palter, play, potter, toy. • *n* **1** bagatelle, bauble,

bean, fig, nothing, triviality. **2** iota, jot, modicum, particle, trace.

trifling *adj* empty, frippery, frivolous, inconsiderable, insignificant, nugatory, petty, piddling, shallow, slight, small, trivial, unimportant, worthless.

adj antonym important.

trill *vb* shake, quaver, warble. • *n* quaver, shake, tremolo, warbling.

trim *vb* **1** adjust, arrange, prepare. **2** balance, equalize, fill. **3** adorn, array, bedeck, decorate, dress, embellish, garnish, ornament. **4** clip, curtail, cut, lop, mow, poll, prune, shave, shear. **5** berate, chastise, chide, rebuke, reprimand, reprove, trounce. **6** fluctuate, hedge, shift, shuffle, vacillate. • *adj* **1** compact, neat, nice, shapely, snug, tidy, well-adjusted, well-ordered. **2** chic, elegant, finical, smart, spruce. • *n* **1** dress, embellishment, gear, ornaments, trappings, trimmings. **2** case, condition, order, plight, state.

adj antonym scruffy.

trinket *n* bagatelle, bauble, bijoux, gewgaw, gimcrack, knick-knack, toy, trifle.

trinkets *npl* bijouterie, jewellery, jewels, ornaments.

trip *vb* **1** caper, dance, frisk, hop, skip. **2** misstep, stumble. **3** bungle, blunder, err, fail, mistake. **4** overthrow, supplant, upset. **5** catch, convict, detect. • *n* **1** hop, skip. **2** lurch, misstep, stumble. **3** blunder, bungle, error, failure, fault, lapse, miss, mistake, oversight, slip. **4** circuit, excursion, expedition, jaunt, journey, ramble, route, stroll, tour.

trite *adj* banal, beaten, common, commonplace, hackneyed, old, ordinary, stale, stereotyped, threadbare, usual, worn.

adj antonym original.

triturate *vb* **1** beat, bray, bruise, grind, pound, rub, thrash. **2** comminute, levigate, pulverize.

triumph *vb* **1** exult, rejoice. **2** prevail, succeed, win. **3** flourish, prosper, thrive. **4** boast, brag, crow, gloat, swagger, vaunt. • *n* **1** celebration, exultation, joy, jubilation, jubilee, ovation. **2** accomplishment, achievement, conquest, success, victory.

vb antonym fail.

n antonym disaster.

triumphant *adj* boastful, conquering, elated, exultant, exulting, jubilant, rejoicing, successful, victorious.

adj antonyms defeated, humble.

trivial *adj* frivolous, gimcrack, immaterial, inconsiderable, insignificant, light, little, nugatory, paltry, petty, small, slight, slim, trifling, trumpery, unimportant.
adj antonym significant.

trollop *n* prostitute, slattern, slut, whore.

troop *vb* crowd, flock, muster, throng. • *n* 1 company, crowd, flock, herd, multitude, number, throng. 2 band, body, party, squad, troupe.

trophy *n* laurels, medal, palm, prize.

troth *n* 1 candour, sincerity, truth, veracity, verity. 2 allegiance, belief, faith, fidelity, word. 3 betrothal.

trouble *vb* 1 agitate, confuse, derange, disarrange, disorder, disturb. 2 afflict, ail, annoy, badger, concern, disquiet, distress, fret, grieve, harass, molest, perplex, perturb, pester, plague, torment, vex, worry. • *n* 1 adversity, affliction, calamity, distress, dolour, grief, hardship, misfortune, misery, pain, sorrow, suffering, tribulation, woe. 2 ado, annoyance, anxiety, bother, care, discomfort, embarrassment, fuss, inconvenience, irritation, pains, perplexity, plague, torment, vexation, worry. 3 commotion, disturbance, row. 4 bewilderment, disquietude, embarrassment, perplexity, uneasiness.
vb antonyms help, reassure.
n antonyms calm, peace.

troublesome *adj* 1 annoying, distressing, disturbing, galling, grievous, harassing, painful, perplexing, vexatious, worrisome. 2 burdensome, irksome, tiresome, wearisome. 3 importunate, intrusive, teasing. 4 arduous, difficult, hard, inconvenient, trying, unwieldy.
adj antonyms easy, helpful, polite.

troublous *adj* agitated, disquieted, disturbed, perturbed, tumultuous, turbulent.

trough *n* 1 hutch, manger. 2 channel, depression, hollow, furrow.

truant *vb* be absent, desert, dodge, malinger, shirk, skive. • *n* absentee, deserter, idler, laggard, loiterer, lounger, malingerer, quitter, runaway, shirker, vagabond.

truce *n* armistice, breathing space, cessation, delay, intermission, lull, pause, recess, reprieve, respite, rest.
n antonym hostilities.

truck *vb* barter, deal, exchange, trade, traffic. • *n* lorry, van, wagon.

truckle *vb* 1 roll, trundle. 2 cringe, crouch, fawn, knuckle, stoop, submit, yield.

truculent *adj* 1 barbarous, bloodthirsty, ferocious, fierce, savage. 2 cruel, malevolent, relentless. 3 destructive, deadly, fatal, ruthless.
adj antonyms co-operative, good-natured.

true *adj* 1 actual, unaffected, authentic, genuine, legitimate, pure, real, rightful, sincere, sound, truthful, veritable. 2 substantial, veracious. 3 constant, faithful, loyal, staunch, steady. 4 equitable, honest, honourable, just, upright, trusty, trustworthy, virtuous. 5 accurate, correct, even, exact, right, straight, undeviating. • *adv* good, well.
adj antonyms faithless, false, inaccurate.
adv antonyms falsely, inaccurately.

truism *n* axiom, commonplace, platitude.

trumpery *adj* pinchbeck, rubbishy, trashy, trifling, worthless. • *n* 1 deceit, deception, falsehood, humbug, imposture. 2 frippery, rubbish, stuff, trash, trifles.

truncheon *n* 1 club, cudgel, nightstick, partisan, staff. 2 baton, wand.

trunk *n* 1 body, bole, butt, shaft, stalk, stem, stock, torso. 2 box, chest, coffer.

trundle *vb* bowl, revolve, roll, spin, truckle, wheel.

truss *vb* bind, bundle, close, cram, hang, pack. • *n* 1 bundle, package, packet. 2 apparatus, bandage, support.
vb antonym untie.

trust *vb* 1 confide, depend, expect, hope, rely. 2 believe, credit. 3 commit, entrust. • *n* 1 belief, confidence, credence, faith. 2 credit, tick. 3 charge, deposit. 4 commission, duty, errand. 5 assurance, conviction, expectation, hope, reliance, security.
vb antonym mistrust.
n antonym mistrust.

trustful *adj* 1 confiding, trusting, unquestioning, unsuspecting. 2 faithful, trustworthy, trusty.

trustworthy *adj* confidential, constant, credible, dependable, faithful, firm, honest, incorrupt, upright, reliable, responsible, straightforward, staunch, true, trusty, uncorrupt, upright.
adj antonym unreliable.

truth *n* 1 fact, reality, veracity. 2 actuality, authenticity, realism. 3 canon, law, oracle, principle. 4 right, truthfulness, veracity. 5 candour, fidelity, frankness, honesty, honour, ingenuousness, integrity, probity, sincerity, virtue. 6 constancy, devotion, faith, fealty, loyalty, steadfastness. **7** accuracy, correctness, exactitude, exactness, nicety, precision, regularity, trueness. *n antonym* falsehood.

truthful *adj* **1** correct, reliable, true, trustworthy, veracious. **2** artless, candid, frank, guileless, honest, ingenuous, open, sincere, straightforward, trusty. *adj antonym* untruthful.

try *vb* **1** examine, prove, test. **2** attempt, essay. **3** adjudicate, adjudge, examine, hear. **4** purify, refine. **5** sample, sift, smell, taste. **6** aim, attempt, endeavour, seek, strain, strive. • *n* attempt, effort, endeavour, experiment, trial.

trying *adj* **1** difficult, fatiguing, hard, irksome, tiresome, wearisome. **2** afflicting, afflictive, calamitous, deplorable, dire, distressing, grievous, hard, painful, sad, severe. *adj antonym* calming.

tryst *n* appointment, assignation, rendezvous.

tube *n* bore, bronchus, cylinder, duct, hollow, hose, pipe, pipette, worm.

tuft *n* **1** brush, bunch, crest, feather, knot, plume, topknot, tussock. **2** clump, cluster, group.

tug *vb* **1** drag, draw, haul, pull, tow, wrench. **2** labour, strive, struggle. • *n* drag, haul, pull, tow, wrench.

tuition *n* education, instruction, schooling, teaching, training.

tumble *vb* **1** heave, pitch, roll, toss, wallow. **2** fall, sprawl, stumble, topple, trip. **3** derange, disarrange, dishevel, disorder, disturb, rumple, tousle. • *n* collapse, drop, fall, plunge, spill, stumble, trip.

tumbler *n* **1** acrobat, juggler. **2** glass.

tumid *adj* **1** bloated, distended, enlarged, puffed-up, swelled, swollen, turgid. **2** bombastic, declamatory, fustian, grandiloquent, grandiose, high-flown, inflated, pompous, puffy, rhetorical, stilted, swelling.

tumour *n* boil, carbuncle, swelling, tumefaction.

tumult *n* ado, affray, agitation, altercation, bluster, brawl, disturbance, ferment, flurry, feud, fracas, fray, fuss, hubbub, huddle, hurly-burly, melee, noise, perturbation, pother, quarrel, racket, riot, row, squabble, stir, turbulence, turmoil, uproar. *n antonym* calm.

tumultuous *adj* blustery, breezy, bustling, confused, disorderly, disturbed, riotous, turbulent, unruly.

tune *vb* **1** accord, attune, harmonize, modulate. **2** adapt, adjust, attune. • *n* **1** air, aria, melody, strain, tone. **2** agreement, concord, harmony. **3** accord, order.

tuneful *adj* dulcet, harmonious, melodious, musical.

turbid *adj* foul, impure, muddy, thick, unsettled. *adj antonym* clear.

turbulence *n* **1** agitation, commotion, confusion, disorder, disturbance, excitement, tumult, tumultuousness, turmoil, unruliness, uproar. **2** insubordination, insurrection, mutiny, rebellion, riot, sedition.

turbulent *adj* **1** agitated, disturbed, restless, tumultuous, wild. **2** blatant, blustering, boisterous, brawling, disorderly, obstreperous, tumultuous, uproarious, vociferous. **3** factious, insubordinate, insurgent, mutinous, raging, rebellious, refractory, revolutionary, riotous, seditious, stormy, violent. *adj antonym* calm.

turf *n* **1** grass, greensward, sod, sward. **2** horse racing, racecourse, race-ground.

turgid *adj* **1** bloated, distended, protuberant, puffed-up, swelled, swollen, tumid. **2** bombastic, declamatory, diffuse, digressive, fustian, high-flown, inflated, grandiloquent, grandiose, ostentatious, pompous, puffy, rhetorical, stilted.

turmoil *n* activity, agitation, bustle, commotion, confusion, disorder, disturbance, ferment, flurry, huddle, hubbub, hurly-burly, noise, trouble, tumult, turbulence, uproar. *n antonym* calm.

turn *vb* **1** revolve, rotate. **2** bend, cast, defect, inflict, round, spin, sway, swivel, twirl, twist, wheel. **3** crank, grind, wind. **4** deflect, divert, transfer, warp. **5** form, mould, shape. **6** adapt, fit, manoeuvre, suit. **7** alter, change, conform, metamorphose, transform, transmute, vary. **8** convert, persuade, prejudice. **9** construe, render, translate. **10** depend, hang, hinge, pivot. **11** eventuate, issue, result, terminate. **12** acidify, curdle, ferment. • *n* **1** cycle, gyration, revolution, rotation, round. **2** bending, deflection, deviation, diversion, doubling, flection, flexion, flexure, reel, retroversion, slew, spin, sweep, swing, swirl, swivel, turning, twist, twirl, whirl, winding. **3** alteration, change, variation, vicissitude. **4** bend, circuit, drive, ramble, run, round, stroll. **5** bout, hand, innings, opportunity, shift, spell. **6** act, action, deed, office. **7** convenience, occasion, purpose. **8** cast, fashion, form, guise, manner, mould, phase, shape. **9** aptitude, bent, bias, disposition, faculty, genius, gift, inclination, leaning, proclivity, proneness, propensity, talent, tendency.

turncoat *n* apostate, backslider, deserter, recreant, renegade, traitor, wretch.

turpitude *n* baseness, degradation, depravity, vileness, wickedness.

turret *n* cupola, minaret, pinnacle.

tussle *vb* conflict, contend, contest, scuffle, struggle, wrestle. • *n* conflict, contest, fight, scuffle, struggle.

tutelage *n* care, charge, dependence, guardianship, protection, teaching, tutorage, tutorship, wardship.

tutor *vb* **1** coach, educate, instruct, teach. **2** discipline, train. • *n* coach, governess, governor, instructor, master, preceptor, schoolteacher, teacher.

twaddle *vb* chatter, gabble, maunder, prate, prattle. • *n* balderdash, chatter, flummery, gabble, gibberish, gobbledegook, gossip, jargon, moonshine, nonsense, platitude, prate, prattle, rigmarole, stuff, tattle.

tweak *vb, n* jerk, pinch, pull, twinge, twitch.

twig[1] *n* bough, branch, offshoot, shoot, slip, spray, sprig, stick, switch.

twig[2] *vb* catch on, comprehend, discover, grasp, realize, recognize, see, understand.

twin *vb* couple, link, match, pair. • *adj* double, doubled, duplicate, geminate, identical, matched, matching, second, twain. • *n* corollary, double, duplicate, fellow, likeness, match.

twine *vb* **1** embrace, encircle, entwine, interlace, surround, wreathe. **2** bend, meander, wind. **3** coil, twist. • *n* **1** convolution, coil, twist. **2** embrace, twining, winding. **3** cord, string.

twinge *vb* pinch, tweak, twitch. • *n* **1** pinch, tweak, twitch. **2** gripe, pang, spasm.

twinkle *vb* **1** blink, twink, wink. **2** flash, glimmer, scintillate, sparkle. • *n* **1** blink, flash, gleam, glimmer, scintillation, sparkle. **2** flash, instant, jiffy, moment, second, tick, trice, twinkling.

twinkling *n* **1** flashing, sparkling, twinkle. **2** flash, instant, jiffy, moment, second, tick, trice.

twirl *vb* revolve, rotate, spin, turn, twist, twirl. • *n* convolution, revolution, turn, twist, whirling.

twist *vb* **1** purl, rotate, spin, twine. **2** complicate, contort, convolute, distort, pervert, screw, wring. **3** coil, writhe. **4** encircle, wind, wreathe. • *n* **1** coil, curl, spin, twine. **2** braid, roll. **3** change, complication, development, variation. **4** bend, convolution, turn. **5** defect, distortion, flaw, imperfection. **6** jerk, pull, sprain, wrench. **7** aberration, characteristic, eccentricity, oddity, peculiarity, quirk.

twit[1] *vb* banter, blame, censure, reproach, taunt, tease, upbraid.

twit[2] *n* blockhead, fool, idiot, nincompoop, nitwit.

twitch *vb* jerk, pluck, pull, snatch. • *n* **1** jerk, pull. **2** contraction, pull, quiver, spasm, twitching.

type *n* **1** emblem, mark, stamp. **2** adumbration, image, representation, representative, shadow, sign, symbol, token. **3** archetype, exemplar, model, original, pattern, prototype, protoplast, standard. **4** character, form, kind, nature, sort. **5** figure, letter, text, typography.

typical *adj* emblematic, exemplary, figurative, ideal, indicative, model, representative, symbolic, true.

adj antonyms atypical, untypical.

typify *vb* betoken, denote, embody, exemplify, figure, image, indicate, represent, signify.

tyrannical *adj* **1** absolute, arbitrary, autocratic, cruel, despotic, dictatorial, domineering, high, imperious, irresponsible, severe, tyrannical, unjust. **2** galling, grinding, inhuman, oppressive, overbearing, severe.

adj antonyms liberal, tolerant.

tyranny *n* absolutism, autocracy, despotism, dictatorship, harshness, oppression.

tyrant *n* autocrat, despot, dictator, oppressor.

tyro *n* **1** beginner, learner, neophyte, novice. **2** dabbler, smatterer.

U

ubiquitous *adj* omnipresent, present, universal.
adj antonym rare.

udder *n* nipple, pap, teat.

ugly *adj* **1** crooked, homely, ill-favoured, plain, ordinary, unlovely, unprepossessing, unshapely, unsightly. **2** forbidding, frightful, gruesome, hideous, horrible, horrid, loathsome, monstrous, shocking, terrible, repellent, repulsive. **3** bad-tempered, cantankerous, churlish, cross, quarrelsome, spiteful, surly, vicious.
adj antonyms beautiful, charming, good, pretty.

ulcer *n* boil, fester, gathering, pustule, sore.

ulterior *adj* **1** beyond, distant, farther. **2** hidden, personal, secret, selfish, undisclosed.

ultimate *adj* conclusive, decisive, eventual, extreme, farthest, final, last. • *n* acme, consummation, culmination, height, peak, pink, quintessence, summit.

ultra *adj* advanced, beyond, extreme, radical.

umbrage *n* **1** shadow, shade. **2** anger, displeasure, dissatisfaction, dudgeon, injury, offence, pique, resentment.

umpire *vb* adjudicate, arbitrate, judge, referee. • *n* adjudicator, arbiter, arbitrator, judge, referee.

unabashed *adj* bold, brazen, confident, unblushing, undaunted, undismayed.
adj antonyms abashed, sheepish.

unable *adj* impotent, incapable, incompetent, powerless, weak.

unacceptable *adj* disagreeable, distasteful, offensive, unpleasant, unsatisfactory, unwelcome.

unaccommodating *adj* disobliging, noncompliant, uncivil, ungracious.

unaccomplished *adj* **1** incomplete, unachieved, undone, unperformed, unexecuted, unfinished. **2** ill-educated, uncultivated, unpolished.

unaccountable *adj* **1** inexplicable, incomprehensible, inscrutable, mysterious, unintelligible. **2** irresponsible, unanswerable.
adj antonyms accountable, explicable.

unaccustomed *adj* **1** uninitiated, unskilled, unused. **2** foreign, new, strange, unfamiliar, unusual.

unaffected *adj* **1** artless, honest, naive, natural, plain, simple, sincere, real, unfeigned. **2** chaste, pure, unadorned. **3** insensible, unchanged, unimpressed, unmoved, unstirred, untouched.
adj antonyms affected, unnatural; impressed, moved.

unanimity *n* accord, agreement, concert, concord, harmony, union, unity.

unanimous *adj* agreeing, concordant, harmonious, like-minded, solid, united.
adj antonyms disunited, split.

unassuming *adj* humble, modest, reserved, unobtrusive, unpretending, unpretentious.
adj antonyms assuming, presumptuous, pretentious.

unattainable *adj* inaccessible, unobtainable.

unavailing *adj* abortive, fruitless, futile, ineffectual, ineffective, inept, nugatory, unsuccessful, useless, vain.
adj antonyms productive, successful.

unbalanced *adj* **1** unsound, unsteady. **2** unadjusted, unsettled.
adj antonym balanced.

unbearable *adj* insufferable, insupportable, unendurable.
adj antonyms acceptable, bearable.

unbecoming *adj* inappropriate, indecent, indecorous, improper, unbefitting, unbeseeming, unseemly, unsuitable.
adj antonyms becoming, seemly.

unbelief *n* **1** disbelief, dissent, distrust, incredulity, incredulousness, miscreance, miscreancy, nonconformity. **2** doubt, freethinking, infidelity, scepticism.

unbeliever *n* agnostic, deist, disbeliever, doubter, heathen, infidel, sceptic.

unbending *adj* **1** inflexible, rigid, stiff, unpliant, unyielding. **2** firm, obstinate, resolute, stubborn.
adj antonyms approachable, friendly, relaxed.

unbiased *adj* disinterested, impartial, indifferent, neutral, uninfluenced, unprejudiced, unwarped.
adj antonym biased.

unbind *vb* **1** loose, undo, unfasten, unloose, untie. **2** free, unchain, unfetter.

unblemished *adj* faultless, guiltless, immaculate, impeccable, innocent, intact, perfect, pure, sinless, spotless, stainless, undefiled, unspotted, unsullied, untarnished.
adj antonyms blemished, flawed, imperfect.

unblushing *adj* boldfaced, impudent, shameless.

unbounded *adj* 1 absolute, boundless, endless, immeasurable, immense, infinite, interminable, measureless, unlimited, vast. 2 immoderate, uncontrolled, unrestrained, unrestricted.

unbridled *adj* dissolute, intractable, lax, licensed, licentious, loose, uncontrolled, ungovernable, unrestrained, violent, wanton.

unbroken *adj* 1 complete, entire, even, full, intact, unimpaired. 2 constant, continuous, fast, profound, sound, successive, undisturbed. 3 inviolate, unbetrayed, unviolated.
adj antonyms cowed, fitful, intermittent.

unbuckle *vb* loose, unfasten, unloose.

uncanny *adj* 1 inopportune, unsafe. 2 eerie, eery, ghostly, unearthly, unnatural, weird.

unceremonious *adj* 1 abrupt, bluff, blunt, brusque, course, curt, gruff, plain, rough, rude, ungracious. 2 casual, familiar, informal, offhand, unconstrained.

uncertain *adj* 1 ambiguous, doubtful, dubious, equivocal, indefinite, indeterminate, indistinct, questionable, unsettled. 2 insecure, precarious, problematical. 3 capricious, changeable, desultory, fitful, fluctuating, irregular, mutable, shaky, slippery, unreliable, variable.
adj antonym certain.

unchaste *adj* dissolute, incontinent, indecent, immoral, lascivious, lecherous, libidinous, lewd, loose, obscene, wanton.

unchecked *adj* uncurbed, unhampered, unhindered, unobstructed, unrestrained, untrammelled.

uncivil *adj* bearish, blunt, boorish, brusque, discourteous, disobliging, disrespectful, gruff, ill-bred, ill-mannered, impolite, irreverent, rough, rude, uncomplaisant, uncourteous, uncouth, ungentle, ungracious, unmannered, unseemly.
adj antonym civil.

unclean *adj* 1 abominable, beastly, dirty, filthy, foul, grimy, grubby, miry, muddy, nasty, offensive, purulent, repulsive, soiled, sullied. 2 improper, indecent, indecorous, obscene, polluted, risqué, sinful, smutty, unholy, uncleanly.
adj antonym clean.

uncomfortable *adj* 1 disagreeable, displeasing, disquieted, distressing, disturbed, uneasy, unpleasant, restless. 2 cheerless, close, oppressive. 3 dismal, miserable, unhappy.
adj antonyms comfortable, easy.

uncommon *adj* choice, exceptional, extraordinary, infrequent, noteworthy, odd, original, queer, rare, remarkable, scarce, singular, strange, unexampled, unfamiliar, unusual, unwonted.
adj antonym common.

uncommunicative *adj* close, inconversable, reserved, reticent, taciturn, unsociable, unsocial.

uncomplaining *adj* long-suffering, meek, patient, resigned, tolerant.

uncompromising *adj* inflexible, narrow, obstinate, orthodox, rigid, stiff, strict, unyielding.
adj antonyms flexible, open-minded.

unconcerned *adj* apathetic, careless, indifferent.
adj antonym concerned.

unconditional *adj* absolute, categorical, complete, entire, free, full, positive, unlimited, unqualified, unreserved, unrestricted.
adj antonym conditional.

uncongenial *adj* antagonistic, discordant, displeasing, ill-assorted, incompatible, inharmonious, mismatched, unsuited, unsympathetic.
adj antonym congenial.

uncouth *adj* 1 awkward, boorish, clownish, clumsy, gawky, inelegant, loutish, lubberly, rough, rude, uncourtly, ungainly, unpolished, unrefined, unseemly. 2 odd, outlandish, strange, unfamiliar, unusual.
adj antonyms polished, polite, refined, urbane.

uncover *vb* 1 denude, divest, lay bare, strip. 2 disclose, discover, expose, reveal, unmask, unveil. 3 bare, doff. 4 open, unclose, unseal.
vb antonyms conceal, cover, suppress.

unctuous *adj* 1 adipose, greasy, oily, fat, fatty, oleaginous, pinguid, sebaceous. 2 bland, lubricious, smooth, slippery. 3 bland, fawning, glib, obsequious, plausible, servile, suave, sycophantic. **4** fervid, gushing.

uncultivated *adj* **1** fallow, uncultured, unreclaimed, untilled. **2** homely, ignorant, illiterate, rude, uncivilized, uncultured, uneducated, unfit, unlettered, unpolished, unread, unready, unrefined, untaught. **3** rough, savage, sylvan, uncouth, wild.

undaunted *adj* bold, brave, courageous, dauntless, fearless, intrepid, plucky, resolute, undismayed.
adj antonyms cowed, timorous.

undefiled *adj* **1** clean, immaculate, pure, spotless, stainless, unblemished, unspotted, unsullied, untarnished. **2** honest, innocent, inviolate, pure, uncorrupted, unpolluted, unstained.

undemonstrative *adj* calm, composed, demure, impassive, modest, placid, quiet, reserved, sedate, sober, staid, tranquil.

undeniable *adj* certain, conclusive, evident, incontestable, incontrovertible, indisputable, indubitable, obvious, unquestionable.

under *prep* below, beneath, inferior to, lower than, subordinate to, underneath. • *adv* below, beneath, down, lower.

underestimate *vb* belittle, underrate, undervalue.

undergo *vb* bear, endure, experience, suffer, sustain.

underhand *adj* clandestine, deceitful, disingenuous, fraudulent, hidden, secret, sly, stealthy, underhanded, unfair. • *adv* **1** clandestinely, privately, secretly, slyly, stealthily, surreptitiously. **2** fraudulently, unfairly.
adj antonym above board.

underling *n* agent, inferior, servant, subordinate.

undermine *vb* **1** excavate, mine, sap. **2** demoralize, foil, frustrate, thwart, weaken.
vb antonyms fortify, strengthen.

understand *vb* **1** apprehend, catch, comprehend, conceive, discern, grasp, know, penetrate, perceive, see, seize, twig. **2** assume, interpret, take. **3** imply, mean.
vb antonym misunderstand.

understanding *adj* compassionate, considerate, forgiving, kind, kindly, patient, sympathetic, tolerant. • *n* brains, comprehension, discernment, faculty, intellect, intelligence, judgement, knowledge, mind, reason, sense.

adj antonyms impatient, insensitive, intolerant, unsympathetic.

undertake *vb* **1** assume, attempt, begin, embark on, engage in, enter upon, take in hand. **2** agree, bargain, contract, covenant, engage, guarantee, promise, stipulate.

undertaking *n* adventure, affair, attempt, business, effort, endeavour, engagement, enterprise, essay, move, project, task, venture.

undesigned *adj* spontaneous, unintended, unintentional, unplanned, unpremeditated.

undigested *adj* **1** crude, ill-advised, ill-considered, ill-judged. **2** confused, disorderly, ill-arranged, unmethodical.

undivided *adj* **1** complete, entire, whole. **2** one, united.

undo *vb* **1** annul, cancel, frustrate, invalidate, neutralize, nullify, offset, reverse. **2** disengage, loose, unfasten, unmake, unravel, untie. **3** crush, destroy, overturn, ruin.

undoubted *adj* incontrovertible, indisputable, indubitable, undisputed, unquestionable, unquestioned.

undress *vb* denude, dismantle, disrobe, unclothe, unrobe, peel, strip. • *n* **1** disarray, nakedness, nudity. **2** mufti, negligee.

undue *adj* **1** illegal, illegitimate, improper, unlawful, excessive, disproportionate, immoderate, unsuitable. **2** unfit.

undulation *n* billowing, fluctuation, pulsation, ripple, wave.

undying *adj* deathless, endless, immortal, imperishable.
adj antonyms impermanent, inconstant.

unearthly *adj* preternatural, supernatural, uncanny, weird.

uneasy *adj* **1** disquieted, disturbed, fidgety, impatient, perturbed, restless, restive, unquiet, worried. **2** awkward, stiff, ungainly, ungraceful. **3** constraining, cramping, disagreeable, uncomfortable.
adj antonyms calm, composed.

unending *adj* endless, eternal, everlasting, interminable, never-ending, perpetual, unceasing.

unequal *adj* disproportionate, disproportioned, ill-matched, inferior, irregular, insufficient, not alike, uneven.
adj antonym equal.

unequalled *adj* exceeding, incomparable, inimitable, matchless, new, nonpareil, novel, paramount, peerless, pre-eminent, superlative, surpassing, transcendent, unheard of, unique, unparalleled, unrivalled.

unequivocal *adj* **1** absolute, certain, clear, evident, incontestable, indubitable, positive. **2** explicit, unambiguous, unmistakable.
adj antonyms ambiguous, vague.

uneven *adj* **1** hilly, jagged, lumpy, ragged, rough, rugged, stony. **2** motley, unequal, variable, variegated.
adj antonym even.

uneventful *adj* commonplace, dull, eventless, humdrum, quiet, monotonous, smooth, uninteresting.

unexceptionable *adj* excellent, faultless, good, irreproachable.

unexpected *adj* abrupt, sudden, unforeseen.
adj antonyms expected, normal, predictable.

unfair *adj* dishonest, dishonourable, faithless, false, hypocritical, inequitable, insincere, oblique, one-sided, partial, unequal, unjust, wrongful.
adj antonym fair.

unfaithful *adj* **1** adulterous, derelict, deceitful, dishonest, disloyal, false, faithless, fickle, perfidious, treacherous, unreliable. **2** negligent. **3** changeable, inconstant, untrue.
adj antonyms faithful, loyal.

unfamiliar *adj* bizarre, foreign, new, novel, outlandish, queer, singular, strange, uncommon, unusual.
adj antonyms customary, familiar.

unfashionable *adj* antiquated, destitute, disused, obsolete, old-fashioned, unconventional.

unfavourable *adj* **1** adverse, contrary, disadvantageous, discouraging, ill, inauspicious, inimical, inopportune, indisposed, malign, sinister, unfriendly, unlucky, unpropitious, untimely. **2** foul, inclement.

unfeeling *adj* **1** apathetic, callous, heartless, insensible, numb, obdurate, torpid, unconscious, unimpressionable. **2** adamantine, cold-blooded, cruel, hard, merciless, pitiless, stony, unkind, unsympathetic.
adj antonym concerned.

unfit *vb* disable, disqualify, incapacitate. • *adj* **1** improper, inappropriate, incompetent, inconsistent, unsuitable. **2** ill-equipped, inadequate, incapable, unqualified, useless. **3** debilitated, feeble, flabby, unhealthy, unsound.

adj antonyms competent, fit, suitable.

unflagging *adj* constant, indefatigable, never-ending, persevering, steady, unfaltering, unremitting, untiring, unwearied.

unflinching *adj* firm, resolute, steady, unshrinking.

unfold *vb* **1** display, expand, open, separate, unfurl, unroll. **2** declare, disclose, reveal, tell. **3** decipher, develop, disentangle, evolve, explain, illustrate, interpret, resolve, unravel.
vb antonyms fold, suppress, withhold, wrap.

unfortunate *adj* **1** hapless, ill-fated, ill-starred, infelicitous, luckless, unhappy, unlucky, unprosperous, unsuccessful, wretched. **2** calamitous, deplorable, disastrous. **3** inappropriate, inexpedient.
adj antonym fortunate.

unfrequented *adj* abandoned, deserted, forsaken, lone, solitary, uninhabited, unoccupied.

unfruitful *adj* **1** barren, fruitless, sterile. **2** infecund, unprolific. **3** unprofitable, unproductive.

ungainly *adj* awkward, boorish, clownish, clumsy, gawky, inelegant, loutish, lubberly, lumbering, slouching, stiff, uncourtly, uncouth, ungraceful.
adj antonyms elegant, graceful.

ungentlemanly *adj* ill-bred, impolite, rude, uncivil, ungentle, ungracious, unmannerly.

unhappy *adj* afflicted, disastrous, dismal, distressed, drear, evil, inauspicious, miserable, painful, unfortunate, wretched.
adj antonyms fortunate, happy.

unhealthy *adj* ailing, diseased, feeble, indisposed, infirm, poorly, sickly, toxic, unsanitary, unsound, toxic, venomous.
adj antonyms healthy, hygienic, robust, salubrious.

uniform *adj* alike, constant, even, equable, equal, smooth, steady, regular, unbroken, unchanged, undeviating, unvaried, unvarying. • *n* costume, dress, livery, outfit, regalia, suit.
adj antonyms changing, colorful, varied.

uniformity *n* **1** constancy, continuity, permanence, regularity, sameness, stability. **2** accordance, agreement, conformity, consistency, unanimity.

unimportant *adj* immaterial, inappreciable, inconsequent, inconsequential, inconsiderable, indifferent, insignificant, mediocre, minor, paltry, petty, small, slight, trifling, trivial.

adj antonym important.

unintentional *adj* accidental, casual, fortuitous, inadvertent, involuntary, spontaneous, undesigned, unmeant, unplanned, unpremeditated, unthinking.

adj antonyms deliberate, intentional.

uninterrupted *adj* continuous, endless, incessant, perpetual, unceasing.

union *n* **1** coalescence, coalition, combination, conjunction, coupling, fusion, incorporation, joining, junction, unification, uniting. **2** agreement, concert, concord, concurrence, harmony, unanimity, unity. **3** alliance, association, club, confederacy, federation, guild, league.

n antonyms alienation, disunity, estrangement, separation.

unique *adj* choice, exceptional, matchless, only, peculiar, rare, single, sole, singular, uncommon, unexampled, unmatched.

adj antonym commonplace.

unison *n* accord, accordance, agreement, concord, harmony.

n antonyms disharmony, polyphony.

unite *vb* **1** amalgamate, attach, blend, centralize, coalesce, confederate, consolidate, embody, fuse, incorporate, merge, weld. **2** associate, conjoin, connect, couple, link, marry. **3** combine, join. **4** harmonize, reconcile. **5** agree, concert, concur, cooperate, fraternize.

vb antonyms separate, sever.

universal *adj* **1** all-reaching, catholic, cosmic, encyclopedic, general, ubiquitous, unlimited. **2** all, complete, entire, total, whole.

unjust *adj* **1** inequitable, injurious, partial, unequal, unfair, unwarranted, wrong, wrongful. **2** flagitious, heinous, influenced, iniquitous, nefarious, unrighteous, wicked. **3** biased, prejudiced.

unjustifiable *adj* **1** indefensible, unjust, unreasonable, unwarrantable. **2** inexcusable, unpardonable.

adj antonym justifiable.

unknown *adj* **1** unappreciated, unascertained. **2** undiscovered, unexplored, uninvestigated. **3** concealed, dark, enigmatic, hidden, mysterious, mystic. **4** anonymous, incognito, inglorious, nameless, obscure, undistinguished, unheralded, unnoted.

adj antonyms familiar, known.

unladylike *adj* ill-bred, impolite, rude, uncivil, ungentle, ungracious, unmannerly.

unlamented *adj* unmourned, unregretted.

unlimited *adj* **1** boundless, infinite, interminable, limitless, measureless, unbounded. **2** absolute, full, unconfined, unconstrained, unrestricted. **3** indefinite, undefined.

adj antonyms circumscribed, limited.

unlucky *adj* **1** baleful, disastrous, ill-fated, ill-starred, luckless, unfortunate, unprosperous, unsuccessful. **2** ill-omened, inauspicious. **3** miserable, unhappy.

adj antonym lucky.

unmanageable *adj* **1** awkward, cumbersome, inconvenient, unwieldy. **2** intractable, unruly, unworkable, vicious. **3** difficult, impractical.

adj antonyms docile, manageable.

unmatched *adj* matchless, unequalled, unparalleled, unrivalled.

unmitigated *adj* absolute, complete, consummate, perfect, sheer, stark, thorough, unqualified, utter.

unnatural *adj* **1** aberrant, abnormal, anomalous, foreign, irregular, prodigious, uncommon. **2** brutal, cold, heartless, inhuman, unfeeling, unusual. **3** affected, artificial, constrained, forced, insincere, self-conscious, stilted, strained. **4** factitious.

adj antonyms acceptable, natural, normal.

unpleasant *adj* disagreeable, displeasing, distasteful, obnoxious, offensive, repulsive, unlovely, ungrateful, unacceptable, unpalatable, unwelcome.

adj antonym pleasant.

unpremeditated *adj* extempore, impromptu, offhand, spontaneous, undesigned, unintentional, unstudied.

adj antonym premeditated.

unprincipled *adj* bad, crooked, dishonest, fraudulent, immoral, iniquitous, knavish, lawless, profligate, rascally, roguish, thievish, trickish, tricky, unscrupulous, vicious, villainous, wicked.

adj antonym ethical.

unqualified *adj* **1** disqualified, incompetent, ineligible, unadapted, unfit. **2** absolute, certain, consummate, decided, direct, downright, full, outright, unconditional, unmeasured, unrestricted, unmitigated. **3** exaggerated, sweeping.

adj antonyms conditional, tentative.

unreal *adj* chimerical, dreamlike, fanciful,

flimsy, ghostly, illusory, insubstantial, nebulous, shadowy, spectral, visionary, unsubstantial.

adj antonyms genuine, real.

unreasonable *adj* absurd, excessive, exorbitant, foolish, ill-judged, illogical, immoderate, impractical, injudicious, irrational, nonsensical, preposterous, senseless, silly, stupid, unfair, unreasoning, unwarrantable, unwise.

adj antonyms moderate, rational, reasonable.

unreliable *adj* fallible, fickle, irresponsible, treacherous, uncertain, undependable, unstable, unsure, untrustworthy.

adj antonym reliable.

unremitting *adj* assiduous, constant, continual, diligent, incessant, indefatigable, persevering, sedulous, unabating, unceasing.

unrepentant *adj* abandoned, callous, graceless, hardened, impenitent, incorrigible, irreclaimable, lost, obdurate, profligate, recreant, seared, shameless.

adj antonyms penitent, repentant.

unrequited *adj* unanswered, unreturned, unrewarded.

unreserved *adj* 1 absolute, entire, full, unlimited. 2 above-board, artless, candid, communicative, fair, frank, guileless, honest, ingenuous, open, sincere, single-minded, undesigning. 3 demonstrative, emotional, open-hearted.

unresisting *adj* compliant, long-suffering, non-resistant, obedient, passive, patient, submissive, yielding.

unresponsive *adj* irresponsive, unsympathetic.

adj antonyms responsive, sympathetic.

unrestrained *adj* 1 unbridled, unchecked, uncurbed, unfettered, unhindered, unobstructed, unreserved. 2 broad, dissolute, incontinent, inordinate, lax, lewd, licentious, loose, wanton. 3 lawless, wild.

adj antonym inhibited.

unrestricted *adj* 1 free, unbridled, unconditional, unconfined, uncurbed, unfettered, unlimited, unqualified, unrestrained. 2 clear, open, public, unobstructed.

unrevealed *adj* hidden, occult, secret, undiscovered, unknown.

unrewarded *adj* unpaid, unrecompensed.

unriddle *vb* explain, expound, solve, unfold, unravel.

unrighteous *adj* 1 evil, sinful, ungodly, unholy, vicious, wicked, wrong. 2 heinous, inequitable, iniquitous, nefarious, unfair, unjust.

unripe *adj* 1 crude, green, hard, immature, premature, sour. 2 incomplete, unfinished.

unrivalled *adj* incomparable, inimitable, matchless, peerless, unequalled, unexampled, unique, unparalleled.

unrobe *vb* disrobe, undress.

unroll *vb* 1 develop, discover, evolve, open, unfold. 2 display, lay open.

unromantic *adj* literal, matter-of-fact, prosaic.

unroot *vb* eradicate, extirpate, root out, uproot.

unruffled *adj* 1 calm, peaceful, placid, quiet, serene, smooth, still, tranquil. 2 collected, composed, cool, imperturbable, peaceful, philosophical, placid, tranquil, undisturbed, unexcited, unmoved.

adj antonyms anxious, troubled.

unruly *adj* 1 disobedient, disorderly, fractious, headstrong, insubordinate, intractable, mutinous, obstreperous, rebellious, refractory, riotous, seditious, turbulent, ungovernable, unmanageable, wanton, wild. 2 lawless, obstinate, rebellious, stubborn, vicious.

adj antonym manageable.

unsafe *adj* dangerous, hazardous, insecure, perilous, precarious, risky, treacherous, uncertain, unprotected.

adj antonyms safe, secure.

unsaid *adj* tacit, unmentioned, unspoken, unuttered.

unsanctified *adj* profane, unhallowed, unholy.

unsatisfactory *adj* 1 insufficient. 2 disappointing. 3 faulty, feeble, imperfect, poor, weak.

adj antonym satisfactory.

unsatisfied *adj* 1 insatiate, unsated, unsatiated, unstaunched. 2 discontented, displeased, dissatisfied, malcontent. 3 undischarged, unpaid, unperformed, unrendered.

unsavoury *adj* 1 flat, insipid, mawkish, savourless, tasteless, unflavoured, unpalatable, vapid. 2 disagreeable, disgusting, distasteful, nasty, nauseating, nauseous, offensive, rank, revolting, sickening, uninviting, unpleasing.

unscathed *adj* unharmed, uninjured.

unschooled *adj* 1 ignorant, uneducated, uninstructed. 2 undisciplined, untrained.

unscrupulous *adj* dishonest, reckless, ruthless, unconscientious, unprincipled, unrestrained.
adj antonym scrupulous.

unsealed *adj* open, unclosed.

unsearchable *adj* hidden, incomprehensible, inscrutable, mysterious.

unseasonable *adj* 1 ill-timed, inappropriate, infelicitous, inopportune, untimely. 2 late, too late. 3 inexpedient, undesirable, unfit, ungrateful, unsuitable, unwelcome. 4 premature, too early.

unseasonably *adv* malapropos, unsuitably, untimely.

unseasoned *adj* 1 inexperienced, unaccustomed, unqualified, untrained. 2 immoderate, inordinate, irregular. 3 green. 4 fresh, unsalted.

unseeing *adj* blind, sightless.

unseemly *adj* improper, indecent, inappropriate, indecorous, unbecoming, uncomely, unfit, unmeet, unsuitable.
adj antonyms decorous, seemly.

unseen *adj* 1 undiscerned, undiscovered, unobserved, unperceived. 2 imperceptible, indiscoverable, invisible, latent.

unselfish *adj* altruistic, devoted, disinterested, generous, high-minded, impersonal, liberal, magnanimous, self-denying, self-forgetful, selfless, self-sacrificing.
adj antonym selfish.

unserviceable *adj* 1 ill-conditioned, unsound, useless. 2 profitless, unprofitable.

unsettle *vb* confuse, derange, disarrange, disconcert, disorder, disturb, trouble, unbalance, unfix, unhinge, upset.

unsettled *adj* 1 changeable, fickle, inconstant, restless, transient, unstable, unsteady, vacillating, wavering. 2 inequable, unequal. 3 feculent, muddy, roiled, roily, turbid. 4 adrift, afloat, homeless, unestablished, uninhabited. 5 open, tentative, unadjusted, undecided, undetermined. 6 due, outstanding, owing, unpaid. 7 perturbed, troubled, unnerved.
adj antonyms certain, composed, settled.

unshackle *vb* emancipate, liberate, loose, release, set free, unbind, unchain, unfetter.

unshaken *adj* constant, firm, resolute, steadfast, steady, unmoved.

unshapen *adj* deformed, grotesque, ill-formed, ill-made, ill-shaped, misshapen, shapeless, ugly, uncouth.

unsheltered *adj* exposed, unprotected.

unshrinking *adj* firm, determined, persisting, resolute, unblenching, unflinching.

unshroud *vb* discover, expose, reveal, uncover.

unsightly *adj* deformed, disagreeable, hideous, repellent, repulsive, ugly.
adj antonym pleasing.

unskilful, unskillful *adj* awkward, bungling, clumsy, inapt, inexpert, maladroit, rough, rude, unhandy, unskilled, unversed.

unskilled *adj* 1 inexperienced, raw, undisciplined, undrilled, uneducated, unexercised, unpractised, unprepared, unschooled. 2 unskilful.

unslaked *adj* unquenched, unslacked.

unsleeping *adj* unslumbering, vigilant, wakeful, watchful.

unsmirched *adj* undefiled, unpolluted, unspotted.

unsociable *adj* 1 distant, reserved, retiring, segregative, shy, solitary, standoffish, taciturn, uncommunicative, uncompanionable, ungenial, unsocial. 2 inhospitable, misanthropic, morose.

unsoiled *adj* clean, spotless, unspotted, unstained, unsullied, untarnished.

unsophisticated *adj* 1 genuine, pure, unadulterated. 2 good, guileless, innocent, unpolluted. 3 artless, honest, ingenuous, naive, natural, simple, sincere, straightforward, unaffected, unstudied.
adj antonyms complex, pretentious, sophisticated.

unsound *adj* 1 decayed, defective, impaired, imperfect, rotten, thin, wasted, weak. 2 broken, disturbed, light, restless. 3 diseased, feeble, infirm, morbid, poorly, sickly, unhealthy, weak. 4 deceitful, erroneous, fallacious, false, faulty, hollow, illogical, incorrect, invalid, ill-advised, irrational, questionable, sophistical, unreasonable, unsubstantial, untenable, wrong. 5 dishonest, false, insincere, unfaithful, untrustworthy, untrue. 6 insubstantial, unreal. 7 heretical, heterodox, unorthodox.
adj antonyms safe, sound.

unsparing *adj* 1 bountiful, generous, lavish, liberal, profuse, ungrudging. 2 harsh, inexorable, relentless, rigorous, ruthless, severe, uncompromising, unforgiving.

unspeakable *adj* indescribable, ineffable, inexpressible, unutterable.

unspiritual *adj* bodily, carnal, fleshly, sensual.

unspotted *adj* 1 clean, spotless, unsoiled, unstained, unsullied, untarnished. 2 faultless, immaculate, innocent, pure, stainless, unblemished, uncorrupted, undefiled, untainted.

unstable *adj* 1 infirm, insecure, precarious, top-heavy, tottering, unbalanced, unballasted, unreliable, unsafe, unsettled, unsteady. 2 changeable, erratic, fickle, inconstant, irresolute, mercurial, mutable, vacillating, variable, wavering, weak, volatile.—*also* **instable**.

adj antonyms stable, steady.

unstained *adj* 1 colourless, uncoloured, undyed, untinged. 2 clean, spotless, unspotted.

unsteady *adj* 1 fluctuating, oscillating, unsettled. 2 insecure, precarious, unstable. 3 changeable, desultory, ever-changing, fickle, inconstant, irresolute, mutable, unreliable, variable, wavering. 4 drunken, jumpy, tottering, vacillating, wobbly, tipsy.

adj antonyms firm, steady.

unstinted *adj* abundant, ample, bountiful, full, large, lavish, plentiful, prodigal, profuse.

unstrung *adj* overcome, shaken, unnerved, weak.

unstudied *adj* 1 extempore, extemporaneous, impromptu, offhand, spontaneous, unpremeditated. 2 inexpert, unskilled, unversed.

unsubdued *adj* unbowed, unbroken, unconquered, untamed.

unsubmissive *adj* disobedient, contumacious, indocile, insubordinate, obstinate, perverse, refractory, uncomplying, ungovernable, unmanageable, unruly, unyielding.

unsubstantial *adj* 1 airy, flimsy, gaseous, gossamery, light, slight, tenuous, thin, vaporous. 2 apparitional, bodiless, chimerical, cloudbuilt, dreamlike, empty, fantastical, ideal, illusory, imaginary, imponderable, spectral, unreal, vague, visionary. 3 erroneous, fallacious, flimsy, groundless, illogical, unfounded, ungrounded, unsound, untenable, weak.

unsuccessful *adj* 1 abortive, bootless, fruitless, futile, ineffectual, profitless, unavailing, vain. 2 ill-fated, ill-starred, luckless, unfortunate, unhappy, unlucky, unprosperous.

adj antonyms effective, successful.

unsuitable *adj* 1 ill-adapted, inappropriate, malapropos, unfit, unsatisfactory, unsuited. 2 improper, inapplicable, inapt, incongruous, inexpedient, infelicitous, unbecoming, unfitting.

adj antonyms seemly, suitable.

unsuited *adj* unadapted, unfitted, unqualified.

unsullied *adj* 1 chaste, clean, spotless, unsoiled, unspotted, unstained, untarnished. 2 immaculate, pure, stainless, unblemished, uncorrupted, undefiled, untainted, untouched, virginal.

unsupplied *adj* destitute, unfurnished, unprovided.

unsupported *adj* 1 unaided, unassisted. 2 unbacked, unseconded, unsustained, unupheld.

unsurpassed *adj* matchless, peerless, unequalled, unexampled, unexcelled, unmatched, unparalleled, unrivalled.

unsusceptible *adj* apathetic, cold, impassive, insusceptible, phlegmatic, stoical, unimpressible, unimpressionable.

unsuspecting *adj* confiding, credulous, trusting, unsuspicious.

adj antonyms conscious, knowing.

unsuspicious *adj* confiding, credulous, gullible, simple, trustful, unsuspecting.

unsustainable *adj* 1 insupportable, intolerable. 2 controvertible, erroneous, unmaintainable, untenable.

unswerving *adj* 1 direct, straight, undeviating. 2 constant, determined, firm, resolute, staunch, steadfast, steady, stable, unwavering.

adj antonyms irresolute, tentative.

unsymmetrical *adj* amorphous, asymmetric, disproportionate, formless, irregular, unbalanced.

unsystematic, unsystematical *adj* casual, disorderly, haphazard, irregular, planless, unmethodical.

untainted *adj* 1 chaste, clean, faultless, fresh, healthy, pure, sweet, wholesome. 2 spotless, unsoiled, unstained, unsullied, untarnished. 3 immaculate, stainless, unblemished, uncorrupted, undefiled, unspotted.

untamable *adj* unconquerable.

untamed *adj* fierce, unbroken, wild.

adj antonyms domesticated, tame.

untangle *vb* disentangle, explain, explicate.

untarnished *adj* 1 chaste, clean, spotless,

unsoiled, unspotted, unstained, unsullied.
2 immaculate, pure, spotless, stainless, unblemished, uncorrupted, undefiled, unspotted, unsullied, untainted, virginal, virtuous.

untaught *adj* **1** illiterate, unenlightened, uninformed, unlettered. **2** ignorant, inexperienced, undisciplined, undrilled, uneducated, uninitiated, uninstructed, untutored.

untenable *adj* **1** indefensible, unmaintainable, unsound. **2** fallacious, hollow, illogical, indefensible, insupportable, unjustifiable, weak.
adj antonyms sound, tenable.

untenanted *adj* deserted, empty, tenantless, uninhabited, unoccupied.

unthinking *adj* **1** careless, heedless, inconsiderate, thoughtless, unreasoning, unreflecting. **2** automatic, mechanical.

unthoughtful *adj* careless, heedless, inconsiderable, thoughtless.

unthrifty *adj* extravagant, improvident, lavish, prodigal, profuse, thriftless, wasteful.

untidy *adj* careless, disorderly, dowdy, frumpy, mussy, slatternly, slovenly, unkempt, unneat.
adj antonyms systematic, tidy.

untie *vb* **1** free, loose, loosen, unbind, unfasten, unknot, unloose. **2** clear, resolve, solve, unfold.

until *adv, conj* **1** till, to the time when. **2** to the place, point, state or degree that.
• *prep* till, to.

untimely *adj* **1** ill-timed, immature, inconvenient, inopportune, mistimed, premature, unseasonable, unsuitable. **2** ill-considered, inauspicious, uncalled for, unfortunate. • *adv* unseasonably, unsuitably.
adj antonyms opportune, timely.

untinged *adj* achromatic, colourless, hueless, uncoloured, undyed, unstained.

untiring *adj* persevering, incessant, indefatigable, patient, tireless, unceasing, unfatiguable, unflagging, unremitting, unwearied, unwearying.

untold *adj* **1** countless, incalculable, innumerable, uncounted, unnumbered. **2** unrelated, unrevealed.

untouched *adj* **1** intact, scatheless, unharmed, unhurt, uninjured, unscathed. **2** insensible, unaffected, unmoved, unstirred.

untoward *adj* **1** adverse, intractable, perverse, refractory, stubborn, unfortunate. **2** annoying, ill-timed, inconvenient, unmanageable, vexatious. **3** awkward, uncouth, ungainly, ungraceful.
adj antonyms auspicious, suitable.

untrained *adj* green, ignorant, inexperienced, raw, unbroken, undisciplined, undrilled, uneducated, uninstructed, unpractised, unskilled, untaught, untutored.

untrammelled *adj* free, unhampered.

untried *adj* **1** fresh, inexperienced, maiden, new, unassayed, unattempted, unattested, virgin. **2** undecided.

untrodden *adj* pathless, trackless, unbeaten.

untroubled *adj* calm, careless, composed, peaceful, serene, smooth, tranquil, undisturbed, unvexed.

untrue *adj* **1** contrary, false, inaccurate, wrong. **2** disloyal, faithless, perfidious, recreant, treacherous, unfaithful.

untrustworthy *adj* **1** deceitful, dishonest, inaccurate, rotten, slippery, treacherous, undependable, unreliable. **2** disloyal, false. **3** deceptive, fallible, illusive, questionable.
adj antonyms reliable, trustworthy.

untruth *n* **1** error, faithlessness, falsehood, falsity, incorrectness, inveracity, treachery. **2** deceit, deception, fabrication, fib, fiction, forgery, imposture, invention, lie, misrepresentation, misstatement, story.

untutored *adj* **1** ignorant, inexperienced, undisciplined, undrilled, uneducated, uninitiated, uninstructed, untaught. **2** artless, natural, simple, unsophisticated.
adj antonyms educated, trained.

untwist *vb* disentangle, disentwine, ravel, unravel, unwreathe.

unused *adj* **1** idle, unemployed, untried. **2** new, unaccustomed, unfamiliar.

unusual *adj* abnormal, curious, exceptional, extraordinary, odd, peculiar, queer, rare, recherché, remarkable, singular, strange, unaccustomed, uncommon, unwonted.
adj antonyms normal, usual.

unutterable *adj* incommunicable, indescribable, ineffable, inexpressible, unspeakable.

unvarnished *adj* **1** unpolished. **2** candid, plain, simple, true, unadorned, unembellished.

unvarying *adj* constant, invariable, unchanging.

unveil *vb* disclose, expose, reveal, show, uncover, unmask.

unveracious *adj* false, lying, mendacious, untruthful.

unversed *adj* **1** inexperienced, raw, undisciplined, undrilled, uneducated, unexercised, unpractised, unprepared, unschooled. **2** unskilful.

unviolated *adj* inviolate, unbetrayed, unbroken.

unwarlike *adj* pacific, peaceful.

unwarped *adj* impartial, unbiased, undistorted, unprejudiced.

unwarrantable *adj* improper, indefensible, unjustifiable.

unwary *adj* careless, hasty, heedless, imprudent, incautious, indiscreet, precipitate, rash, reckless, remiss, uncircumspect, unguarded.

adj antonyms cautious, wary.

unwavering *adj* **1** constant, determined, firm, fixed, resolute, settled, staunch, steadfast, steady, unhesitating.

unwearied *adj* unfatigued. **2** constant, continual, incessant, indefatigable, persevering, persistent, unceasing, unremitting, untiring.

unwelcome *adj* disagreeable, unacceptable, ungrateful, unpleasant, unpleasing.

unwell *adj* ailing, delicate, diseased, ill, indisposed, sick.

unwept *adj* unlamented, unmourned, unregretted.

unwholesome *adj* **1** baneful, deleterious, injurious, insalubrious, noisome, noxious, poisonous, unhealthful, unhealthy. **2** injudicious, pernicious, unsound. **3** corrupt, tainted.

unwieldy *adj* bulky, clumsy, cumbersome, cumbrous, elephantine, heavy, hulking, large, massy, ponderous, unmanageable, weighty.

adj antonyms dainty, neat, petite.

unwilling *adj* **1** averse, backward, disinclined, indisposed, laggard, loath, opposed, recalcitrant, reluctant. **2** forced, grudging.

adj antonyms enthusiastic, willing.

unwind *vb* **1** unravel, unreel, untwine, wind off. **2** disentangle.

unwise *adj* brainless, foolish, ill-advised, ill-judged, impolitic, imprudent, indiscreet, injudicious, inexpedient, senseless, silly, stupid, unwary, weak.

adj antonyms prudent, wise.

unwitnessed *adj* unknown, unseen, unspied.

unwittingly *adv* ignorantly, inadvertently, unconsciously, undesignedly, unintentionally, unknowingly.

adj antonyms conscious, deliberate, knowing, witting.

unwonted *adj* **1** infrequent, rare, uncommon, unusual. **2** unaccustomed, unused.

adj antonyms usual, wonted.

unworthy *adj* **1** undeserving. **2** bad, base, blameworthy, worthless. **3** shameful, unbecoming, vile. **4** contemptible, derogatory, despicable, discreditable, mean, paltry, reprehensible, shabby.

unwrap *vb* open, unfold.

unwrinkled *adj* smooth, unforrowed.

unwritten *adj* **1** oral, traditional, unrecorded. **2** conventional, customary.

unwrought *adj* crude, rough, rude, unfashioned, unformed.

unyielding *adj* **1** constant, determined, indomitable, inflexible, pertinacious, resolute, staunch, steadfast, steady, tenacious, uncompromising, unwavering. **2** headstrong, intractable, obstinate, perverse, self-willed, stiff, stubborn, wayward, wilful. **3** adamantine, firm, grim, hard, immovable, implastic, inexorable, relentless, rigid, unbending.

adj antonyms flexible, yielding.

unyoke *vb* disconnect, disjoin, part, separate.

unyoked *adj* **1** disconnected, separated. **2** licentious, loose, unrestrained.

up *v* increase. • *adj* **1** high, ascending. **2** awake. **3** improving. • *adv* upward, upwards, upward, upwardly, upwards

upbraid *vb* accuse, blame, chide, condemn, criticize, denounce, fault, reproach, reprove, revile, scold, taunt, twit.

vb antonyms commend, praise.

upheaval *n* **1** elevation, upthrow. **2** cataclysm, convulsion, disorder, eruption, explosion, outburst, overthrow.

uphill *adj* **1** ascending, upward. **2** arduous, difficult, hard, laborious, strenuous, toilsome, wearisome.

uphold *vb* **1** elevate, raise. **2** bear up, hold up, support, sustain. **3** advocate, aid, champion, countenance, defend, justify, maintain, vindicate.

upland *n* down, fell, ridge, plateau.

uplift *vb* **1** raise, upraise. **2** animate, elevate, inspire, lift, refine. • *n* **1** ascent, climb, elevation, lift, rise, upthrust. **2** exaltation, inspiration, uplifting. **3** improvement, refinement.

upon *prep* **1** on, on top of, over. **2** about, concerning, on the subject of, relating to. **3** immediately after, with.

upper hand *n* advantage, ascendancy, control, dominion, mastership, mastery, preeminence, rule, superiority, supremacy, whip hand.

uppermost *adj* foremost, highest, loftiest, supreme, topmost, upmost.

uppish *adj* arrogant, assuming, haughty, perky, proud, smart.

adj antonyms diffident, unassertive.

upright *adj* **1** erect, perpendicular, vertical. **2** conscientious, equitable, fair, faithful, good, honest, honourable, incorruptible, just, pure, righteous, straightforward, true, trustworthy, upstanding, virtuous.

adj antonyms dishonest, flat, horizontal, prone, supine.

uprightness *n* **1** erectness, perpendicularity, verticality. **2** equity, fairness, goodness, honesty, honour, incorruptibility, integrity, justice, probity, rectitude, righteousness, straightforwardness, trustiness, trustworthiness, virtue, worth.

uproar *n* clamour, commotion, confusion, din, disturbance, fracas, hubbub, hurly-burly, noise, pandemonium, racket, riot, tumult, turmoil, vociferation.

uproarious *adj* boisterous, clamorous, loud, noisy, obstreperous, riotous, tumultuous.

adj antonym sedate.

uproot *vb* eradicate, extirpate, root out.

upset *vb* **1** capsize, invert, overthrow, overtumble, overturn, spill, tip over, topple, turn turtle. **2** agitate, confound, confuse, discompose, disconcert, distress, disturb, embarrass, excite, fluster, muddle, overwhelm, perturb, shock, startle, trouble, unnerve, unsettle. **3** checkmate, defeat, overthrow, revolutionize, subvert. **4** foil, frustrate, nonplus, thwart. • *adj* **1** disproved, exposed, overthrown. **2** bothered, confused, disconcerted, flustered, mixed-up, perturbed. **3** shocked, startled, unsettled. **4** beaten, defeated, overcome, overpowered, overthrown. **5** discomfited, distressed, discomposed, overexcited, overwrought, shaken, troubled, unnerved. • *n* **1** confutation, refutation. **2** foiling, frustration, overthrow, revolution, revulsion, ruin, subversion, thwarting.

upshot *n* conclusion, consummation, effect, end, event, issue, outcome, result, termination.

upside down *adj* bottom side up, bottom up, confused, head over heels, inverted, topsy-turvy.

upstart *n* adventurer, arriviste, parvenu, snob, social cimber, yuppie.

upturned *adj* **1** raised, uplifted. **2** retroussé.

upward *adj* ascending, climbing, mounting, rising, uphill. • *adv* **1** above, aloft, overhead, up. **2** heavenwards, skywards.

urbane *adj* civil, complaisant, courteous, courtly, elegant, mannerly, polished, polite, refined, smooth, suave, well-mannered.

adj antonyms gauche, uncouth.

urbanity *n* amenity, civility, complaisance, courtesy, politeness, smoothness, suavity.

urchin *n* brat, child, kid, ragamuffin, rascal, scrap, squirt, tad.

urge *vb* **1** crowd, drive, force on, impel, press, press on, push, push on. **2** beg, beseech, conjure, entreat, exhort, implore, importune, ply, solicit, tease. **3** animate, egg on, encourage, goad, hurry, incite, instigate, quicken, spur, stimulate. • *n* compulsion, desire, drive, impulse, longing, pressure, wish, yearning.

vb antonyms deter, dissuade.

n antonym disinclination.

urgency *n* **1** drive, emergency, exigency, haste, necessity, press, pressure, push, stress. **2** clamorousness, entreaty, insistence, importunity, instance, solicitation. **3** goad, incitement, spur, stimulus.

urgent *adj* cogent, critical, crucial, crying, exigent, immediate, imperative, important, importunate, insistent, instant, pertinacious, pressing, serious.

urinal *n* chamber, chamber pot, lavatory, pot, potty, toilet.

urinate *vb* make water, pee, pee-pee, piddle, piss, stale, wee.

usage *n* **1** treatment. **2** consuetude, custom, fashion, habit, method, mode, practice, prescription, tradition, use.

use *vb* **1** administer, apply, avail oneself of, drive, employ, handle, improve, make use of, manipulate, occupy, operate, ply, put into action, take advantage of, turn to account, wield, work. **2** exercise, exert, exploit, practice, profit by, utilize. **3** absorb, consume, exhaust, expend, swallow up, waste, wear out. **4** accustom, familiarize, habituate, harden, inure, train. **5** act toward, behave toward, deal with, manage, treat. **6** be accustomed, be wont. • *n* **1** appliance, application, consumption, conversion, disposal, exercise, employ, employment, practice, utilization. **2** adaptability, advantage, avail, benefit, convenience, profit, service, usefulness, utility, wear. **3** exigency, necessity, indispensability, need, occasion, requisiteness. **4** custom, habit, handling, method, treatment, usage, way.

useful *adj* **1** active, advantageous, available, availing, beneficial, commodious, conducive, contributory, convenient, effective, good, helpful, instrumental, operative, practical, profitable, remunerative, salutary, suitable, serviceable, utilitarian. **2** available, helpful, serviceable, valuable.
adj antonym useless.

usefulness *n* advantage, profit, serviceableness, utility, value.

useless *adj* **1** abortive, bootless, fruitless, futile, helpless, idle, incapable, incompetent, ineffective, ineffectual, inutile, nugatory, null, profitless, unavailing, unprofitable, unproductive, unserviceable, valueless, worthless. **2** good for nothing, waste.
adj antonym useful.

usher *vb* **1** announce, forerun, herald, induct, introduce, precede. **2** conduct, direct, escort, shepherd, show. • *n* attendant, conductor, escort, shepherd, squire.

usual *adj* accustomed, common, customary, everyday, familiar, frequent, general, habitual, normal, ordinary, prevailing, prevalent, regular, wonted.
adj antonyms unheard-of, unusual.

usurp *vb* appropriate, arrogate, assume, seize.

usurpation *n* assumption, dispossession, infringement, seizure.

usury *n* **1** interest. **2** exploitation, extortion, profiteering.

utensil *n* device, implement, instrument, tool.

utility *n* **1** advantageousness, avail, benefit, profit, service, use, usefulness. **2** happiness, welfare.
n antonym inutility.

utilize *vb* employ, exploit, make use of, put to use, turn to account, use.

utmost *adj* **1** extreme, farthest, highest, last, main, most distant, remotest. **2** greatest, uttermost. • *n* best, extreme, maximum, most.

Utopian *adj* air-built, air-drawn, chimerical, fanciful, ideal, imaginary, visionary, unreal.

utricle *n* bladder, cyst, sac, vesicle.

utter[1] *adj* complete, entire, perfect, total. **2** absolute, blank, diametric, downright, final, peremptory, sheer, stark, thorough, thoroughgoing, unconditional, unqualified, total.

utter[2] *vb* **1** articulate, breathe, deliver, disclose, divulge, emit, enunciate, express, give forth, pronounce, reveal, speak, talk, tell, voice. **2** announce, circulate, declare, issue, publish.

utterance *n* articulation, delivery, disclosure, emission, expression, pronouncement, pronunciation, publication, speech.

utterly *adv* absolutely, altogether, completely, downright, entirely, quite, totally, unconditionally, wholly.

uttermost *adj* **1** extreme, farthest. **2** greatest, utmost.

V

vacant *adj* **1** blank, empty, unfilled, void. **2** disengaged, free, unemployed, unoccupied, unencumbered. **3** thoughtless, unmeaning, unthinking, unreflective. **4** uninhabited, untenanted.
adj antonyms engaged, occupied.

vacate *vb* **1** abandon, evacuate, relinquish, surrender. **2** abolish, abrogate, annul, cancel, disannul, invalidate, nullify, overrule, quash, rescind.

vacillate *vb* dither, fluctuate, hesitate, oscillate, rock, sway, waver.

vacillation *n* faltering, fluctuation, hesitation, inconstancy, indecision, irresolution, reeling, rocking, staggering, swaying, unsteadiness, wavering.

vacuity *n* **1** emptiness, inanition, vacancy. **2** emptiness, vacancy, vacuum, void. **3** expressionlessness, inanity, nihility.

vacuous *adj* **1** empty, empty-headed, unfilled, vacant, void. **2** inane, unintelligent.

vacuum *n* emptiness, vacuity, void.

vagabond *adj* footloose, idle, meandering, rambling, roving, roaming, strolling, vagrant, wandering. • *n* beggar, castaway, landloper, loafer, lounger, nomad, outcast, tramp, vagrant, wanderer.

vagary *n* caprice, crotchet, fancy, freak, humour, whim.

vagrant *adj* erratic, itinerant, roaming, roving, nomadic, strolling, unsettled, wandering. • *n* beggar, castaway, landloper, loafer, lounger, nomad, outcast, tramp, vagabond, wanderer.

vague *adj* ambiguous, confused, dim, doubtful, indefinite, ill-defined, indistinct, lax, loose, obscure, uncertain, undetermined, unfixed, unsettled.
adj antonyms certain, clear, definite.

vain *adj* **1** baseless, delusive, dreamy, empty, false, imaginary, shadowy, suppositional, unsubstantial, unreal, void. **2** abortive, bootless, fruitless, futile, ineffectual, nugatory, profitless, unavailing, unprofitable. **3** trivial, unessential, unimportant, unsatisfactory, unsatisfying, useless, vapid, worthless. **4** arrogant, conceited, egotistical, flushed, high, inflated, opinionated, ostentatious, overweening, proud, self-confident, self-opinionated, vainglorious. **5** gaudy, glittering, gorgeous, showy.
adj antonyms modest, self-effacing.

valediction *n* adieu, farewell, goodbye, leave-taking.

valet *n* attendant, flunky, groom, lackey, servant.

valetudinarian *adj* delicate, feeble, frail, infirm, sickly.

valiant *adj* bold, brave, chivalrous, courageous, daring, dauntless, doughty, fearless, gallant, heroic, intrepid, lion-hearted, redoubtable, Spartan, valorous, undaunted.
adj antonym cowardly.

valid *adj* binding, cogent, conclusive, efficacious, efficient, good, grave, important, just, logical, powerful, solid, sound, strong, substantial, sufficient, weighty.
adj antonym invalid.

valley *n* basin, bottom, canyon, dale, dell, dingle, glen, hollow, ravine, strath, vale.

valorous *adj* bold, brave, courageous, dauntless, doughty, intrepid, stout.

valour *n* boldness, bravery, courage, daring, gallantry, heroism, prowess, spirit.

valuable *adj* **1** advantageous, precious, profitable, useful. **2** costly, expensive, rich. **3** admirable, estimable, worthy. • *n* heirloom, treasure.
adj antonyms useless, valueless.

value *vb* **1** account, appraise, assess, estimate, price, rate, reckon. **2** appreciate, esteem, prize, regard, treasure. • *n* **1** avail, importance, usefulness, utility, worth. **2** cost, equivalent, price, rate. **3** estimation, excellence, importance, merit, valuation.
vb antonyms disregard, neglect, undervalue.

valueless *adj* miserable, useless, worthless.

vandal *n* barbarian, destroyer, savage.

vandalism *n* barbarism, barbarity, savagery.

vanish *vb* disappear, dissolve, fade, melt.
vb antonyms appear, materialize.

vanity *n* **1** emptiness, falsity, foolishness, futility, hollowness, insanity, triviality, unreality, worthlessness. **2** arrogance, conceit, egotism, ostentation, self-conceit.
n antonyms modesty, worth.

vanquish *vb* **1** conquer, defeat, outwit,

overcome, overpower, overthrow, subdue, subjugate. **2** crush, discomfit, foil, master, quell, rout, worst.

vapid *adj* **1** dead, flat, insipid, lifeless, savourless, spiritless, stale, tasteless. **2** dull, feeble, jejune, languid, meagre, prosaic, prosy, tame.

adj antonyms interesting, vigorous.

vapour *n* **1** cloud, exhalation, fog, fume, mist, rack, reek, smoke, steam. **2** daydream, dream, fantasy, phantom, vagary, vision, whim, whimsy.

variable *adj* **1** changeable, mutable, shifting. **2** aberrant, alterable, capricious, fickle, fitful, floating, fluctuating, inconstant, mobile, mutable, protean, restless, shifting, unsteady, vacillating, wavering.

adj antonym invariable.

variance *n* disagreement, difference, discord, dissension, incompatibility, jarring, strife.

variation *n* **1** alteration, change, modification. **2** departure, deviation, difference, discrepancy, innovation. **3** contrariety, discordance.

n antonyms monotony, similitude, uniformity.

variegated *adj* chequered, dappled, diversified, flecked, kaleidoscopic, mottled, multicoloured, pied, spotted, striped.

variety *n* **1** difference, dissimilarity, diversity, diversification, medley, miscellany, mixture, multiplicity, variation. **2** kind, sort.

n antonyms monotony, similitude, uniformity.

various *adj* different, diverse, manifold, many, numerous, several, sundry.

varnish *vb* **1** enamel, glaze, japan, lacquer. **2** adorn, decorate, embellish, garnish, gild, polish. **3** disguise, excuse, extenuate, gloss over, palliate. • *n* **1** enamel, lacquer, stain. **2** cover, extenuation, gloss.

vary *vb* **1** alter, metamorphose, transform. **2** alternate, exchange, rotate. **3** diversify, modify, variegate. **4** depart, deviate, swerve.

vassal *n* bondman, liegeman, retainer, serf, slave, subject, thrall.

vast *adj* **1** boundless, infinite, measureless, spacious, wide. **2** colossal, enormous, gigantic, huge, immense, mighty, monstrous, prodigious, tremendous. **3** extraordinary, remarkable.

vaticination *n* augury, divination, prediction, prognostication, prophecy.

vault[1] *vb* arch, bend, curve, span. • *n* **1** cupola, curve, dome. **2** catacomb, cell, cellar, crypt, dungeon, tomb. **3** depository, strongroom.

vault[2] *vb* **1** bound, jump, leap, spring. **2** tumble, turn. • *n* bound, leap, jump, spring.

vaunt *vb* advertise, boast, brag, display, exult, flaunt, flourish, parade.

vb antonyms belittle, minimize.

veer *vb* change, shift, turn.

vegetate *vb* **1** blossom, develop, flourish, flower, germinate, grow, shoot, sprout, swell. **2** bask, hibernate, idle, stagnate.

vehemence *n* **1** impetuosity, violence. **2** ardour, eagerness, earnestness, enthusiasm, fervency, fervour, heat, keenness, passion, warmth, zeal. **3** force, intensity.

vehement *adj* **1** furious, high, hot, impetuous, passionate, rampant, violent. **2** ardent, burning, eager, earnest, enthusiastic, fervid, fiery, keen, passionate, sanguine, zealous. **3** forcible, mighty, powerful, strong.

adj antonyms apathetic, indifferent.

veil *vb* cloak, conceal, cover, curtain, envelop, hide, invest, mask, screen, shroud. • *n* **1** cover, curtain, film, shade, screen. **2** blind, cloak, disguise, mask, muffler, visor.

vb antonyms expose, uncover.

vein *n* **1** course, current, lode, seam, streak, stripe, thread, wave. **2** bent, character, faculty, humour, mood, talent, turn.

velocity *n* acceleration, celerity, expedition, fleetness, haste, quickness, rapidity, speed, swiftness.

velvety *adj* delicate, downy, smooth, soft.

venal *adj* corrupt, mean, purchasable, sordid.

adj antonym incorruptible.

vend *vb* dispose, flog, hawk, retail, sell.

venerable *adj* **1** grave, respected, revered, sage, wise. **2** awful, dread, dreadful. **3** aged, old, patriarchal.

venerate *vb* adore, esteem, honour, respect, revere.

vb antonyms anathematize, disregard, execrate.

veneration *n* adoration, devotion, esteem, respect, reverence, worship.

vengeance *n* retaliation, retribution, revenge.

n antonym forgiveness.

venial *adj* allowed, excusable, pardonable, permitted, trivial.

venom *n* **1** poison, virus. **2** acerbity, acrimony, bitterness, gall, hate, ill-will, malevolence, malice, maliciousness, malignity, rancour, spite, virulence.

venomous *adj* **1** deadly, poisonous, septic, toxic, virulent. **2** caustic, malicious, malignant, mischievous, noxious, spiteful.

vent *vb* emit, express, release, utter. • *n* **1** air hole, hole, mouth, opening, orifice. **2** air pipe, air tube, aperture, blowhole, bunghole, hydrant, plug, spiracle, spout, tap, orifice. **3** effusion, emission, escape, outlet, passage. **4** discharge, expression, utterance.

ventilate *vb* **1** aerate, air, freshen, oxygenate, purify. **2** fan, winnow. **3** canvass, comment, discuss, examine, publish, review, scrutinize.

venture *vb* adventure, dare, hazard, imperil, jeopardize, presume, risk, speculate, test, try, undertake. • *n* adventure, chance, hazard, jeopardy, peril, risk, speculation, stake.

veracious *adj* **1** reliable, straightforward, true, trustworthy, truthful. **2** credible, genuine, honest, unfeigned.

veracity *n* accuracy, candour, correctness, credibility, exactness, fidelity, frankness, honesty, ingenuousness, probity, sincerity, trueness, truth, truthfulness.

verbal *adj* nuncupative, oral, spoken, unwritten.

verbose *adj* diffusive, long-winded, loquacious, talkative, wordy.
adj antonyms economical, laconic, succinct.

verdant *adj* **1** fresh, green, verdure, verdurous. **2** green, inexperienced, raw, unsophisticated.

verdict *n* answer, decision, finding, judgement, opinion, sentence.

verge *vb* **1** bear, incline, lean, slope, tend. **2** approach, border, skirt. • *n* **1** mace, rod, staff. **2** border, boundary, brink, confine, edge, extreme, limit, margin. **3** edge, eve, point.

verification *n* authentication, attestation, confirmation, corroboration.

verify *vb* attest, authenticate, confirm, corroborate, prove, substantiate.
vb antonyms discredit, invalidate.

verily *adv* absolutely, actually, confidently, indeed, positively, really, truly.

verity *n* certainty, reality, truth, truthfulness.

vernacular *adj* common, indigenous, local, mother, native, vulgar. • *n* cant, dialect, jargon, patois, speech.

versatile *adj* adaptable, protean, plastic, varied.
adj antonym inflexible.

versed *adj* able, accomplished, acquainted, clever, conversant, practised, proficient, qualified, skilful, skilled, trained.

version *n* interpretation, reading, rendering, translation.

vertex *n* apex, crown, height, summit, top, zenith.

vertical *adj* erect, perpendicular, plumb, steep, upright.
adj antonym horizontal.

vertigo *n* dizziness, giddiness.

verve *n* animation, ardour, energy, enthusiasm, force, rapture, spirit.
n antonym apathy.

very *adv* absolutely, enormously, excessively, hugely, remarkably, surpassingly. • *adj* **1** actual, exact, identical, precise, same. **2** bare, mere, plain, pure, simple.
adv antonyms hardly, scarcely, slightly.

vesicle *n* bladder, blister, cell, cyst, follicle.

vest *vb* **1** clothe, cover, dress, envelop. **2** endow, furnish, invest. • *n* dress, garment, robe, vestment, vesture, waistcoat.

vestibule *n* anteroom, entrance hall, lobby, porch.

vestige *n* evidence, footprint, footstep, mark, record, relic, sign, token.

veteran *adj* adept, aged, experienced, disciplined, seasoned, old. • *n* **1** campaigner, old soldier. **2** master, past master, old-timer, old-stager.

veto *vb* ban, embargo, forbid, interdict, negate, prohibit. • *n* ban, embargo, interdict, prohibition, refusal.
vb antonyms approve, sanction.
n antonyms approval, assent.

vex *vb* **1** annoy, badger, bother, chafe, cross, distress, gall, harass, harry, hector, molest, perplex, pester, plague, tease, torment, trouble, roil, spite, worry. **2** affront, displease, fret, irk, irritate, nettle, offend, provoke. **3** agitate, disquiet, disturb.
vb antonym soothe.

vexation *n* **1** affliction, agitation, chagrin, discomfort, displeasure, disquiet, distress, grief, irritation, pique, sorrow, trouble. **2** annoyance, curse, nuisance, plague, torment. **3** damage, troubling, vexing.

vexed *adj* afflicted, agitated, annoyed, bothered, disquieted, harassed, irritated, perplexed, plagued, provoked, troubled, worried.

vibrate *vb* **1** oscillate, sway, swing, undulate, wave. **2** impinge, quiver, sound, thrill. **3** fluctuate, hesitate, vacillate, waver.

vibration *n* nutation, oscillation, vibration.

vicarious *adj* commissioned, delegated, indirect, second-hand, substituted.

vice *n* **1** blemish, defect, failing, fault, imperfection, infirmity. **2** badness, corruption, depravation, depravity, error, evil, immorality, iniquity, laxity, obliquity, sin, viciousness, vileness, wickedness.

n antonym virtue.

vicinity *n* **1** nearness, proximity. **2** locality, neighbourhood, vicinage.

vicious *adj* **1** abandoned, atrocious, bad, corrupt, degenerate, demoralized, depraved, devilish, diabolical, evil, flagrant, hellish, immoral, iniquitous, mischievous, profligate, shameless, sinful, unprincipled, wicked. **2** malicious, spiteful, venomous. **3** foul, impure. **4** debased, faulty. **5** contrary, refractory.

adj antonyms gentle, good, virtuous.

viciousness *n* badness, corruption, depravity, immorality, profligacy.

vicissitude *n* **1** alteration, interchange. **2** change, fluctuation, mutation, revolution, variation.

victim *n* **1** martyr, sacrifice, sufferer. **2** prey. **3** cat's-paw, cull, cully, dupe, gull, gudgeon, puppet.

victimize *vb* bamboozle, befool, beguile, cheat, circumvent, cozen, deceive, defraud, diddle, dupe, fool, gull, hoax, hoodwink, overreach, swindle, trick.

victor *n* champion, conqueror, vanquisher, winner.

n antonyms loser, vanquished.

victorious *adj* conquering, successful, triumphant, winning.

victory *n* achievement, conquest, mastery, triumph.

n antonyms defeat, loss.

vie *vb* compete, contend, emulate, rival, strive.

view *vb* **1** behold, contemplate, eye, inspect, scan, survey. **2** consider, inspect, regard, study. • *n* **1** inspection, observation, regard, sight. **2** outlook, panorama, perspective, prospect, range, scene, survey, vista. **3** aim, intent, intention, design, drift, object, purpose, scope. **4** belief, conception, impression, idea, judgement, notion, opinion, sentiment, theory. **5** appearance, aspect, show.

vigilance *n* alertness, attentiveness, carefulness, caution, circumspection, observance, watchfulness.

vigilant *adj* alert, attentive, careless, cautious, circumspect, unsleeping, wakeful, watchful.

adj antonyms careless, forgetful, lax, negligent.

vigorous *adj* **1** lusty, powerful, strong. **2** active, alert, cordial, energetic, forcible, strenuous, vehement, vivid, virile. **3** brisk, hale, hardy, robust, sound, sturdy, healthy. **4** fresh, flourishing. **5** bold, emphatic, impassioned, lively, nervous, piquant, pointed, severe, sparkling, spirited, trenchant.

adj antonyms feeble, lethargic, weak.

vigour *n* **1** activity, efficacy, energy, force, might, potency, power, spirit, strength. **2** bloom, elasticity, haleness, health, heartiness, pep, punch, robustness, soundness, thriftiness, tone, vim, vitality. **3** enthusiasm, freshness, fire, intensity, liveliness, piquancy, strenuousness, vehemence, verve, raciness.

vile *adj* **1** abject, base, beastly, beggarly, brutish, contemptible, despicable, disgusting, grovelling, ignoble, low, odious, paltry, pitiful, repulsive, scurvy, shabby, slavish, sorry, ugly. **2** bad, evil, foul, gross, impure, iniquitous, lewd, obscene, sinful, vicious, wicked. **3** cheap, mean, miserable, valueless, worthless.

vilify *vb* abuse, asperse, backbite, berate, blacken, blemish, brand, calumniate, decry, defame, disparage, lampoon, libel, malign, revile, scandalize, slander, slur, traduce, vituperate.

vb antonyms adore, compliment, eulogize, glorify.

villain *n* blackguard, knave, miscreant, rascal, reprobate, rogue, ruffian, scamp, scapegrace, scoundrel.

n antonyms angel, goody, hero, heroine.

villainous *adj* **1** base, mean, vile. **2** corrupt, depraved, knavish, unprincipled, wicked. **3** atrocious, heinous, outrageous, sinful. **4** mischievous, sorry.

adj antonyms angelic, good, heroic.

vindicate *vb* **1** defend, justify, uphold.

2 advocate, avenge, assert, maintain, right, support.

vindication *n* apology, excuse, defence, justification.

n antonyms accusation, conviction.

vindictive *adj* avenging, grudgeful, implacable, malevolent, malicious, malignant, retaliative, revengeful, spiteful, unforgiving, unrelenting, vengeful.

violate *vb* **1** hurt, injure. **2** break, disobey, infringe, invade. **3** desecrate, pollute, profane. **4** abuse, debauch, defile, deflower, outrage, ravish, transgress.

vb antonyms obey, observe, uphold.

violent *adj* **1** boisterous, demented, forceful, forcible, frenzied, furious, high, hot, impetuous, insane, intense, stormy, tumultuous, turbulent, vehement, wild. **2** fierce, fiery, fuming, heady, heavy, infuriate, passionate, obstreperous, strong, raging, rampant, rank, rapid, raving, refractory, roaring, rough, tearing, towering, ungovernable. **3** accidental, unnatural. **4** desperate, extreme, outrageous, unjust. **5** acute, exquisite, poignant, sharp.

adj antonyms calm, gentle, moderate, passive, peaceful.

virago *n* amazon, brawler, fury, shrew, tartar, vixen.

virgin *adj* **1** chaste, maidenly, modest, pure, undefiled, stainless, unpolluted, vestal, virginal. **2** fresh, maiden, untouched, unused. • *n* celibate, damsel, girl, lass, maid, maiden.

virile *adj* forceful, manly, masculine, robust, vigorous.

adj antonyms effeminate, impotent, weak.

virtual *adj* constructive, equivalent, essential, implicit, implied, indirect, practical, substantial.

virtue *n* **1** chastity, goodness, grace, morality, purity. **2** efficacy, excellence, honesty, integrity, justice, probity, quality, rectitude, worth.

n antonym vice.

virtuous *adj* **1** blameless, equitable, exemplary, excellent, good, honest, moral, noble, righteous, upright, worthy. **2** chaste, continent, immaculate, innocent, modest, pure, undefiled. **3** efficacious, powerful.

adj antonyms bad, dishonest, immoral, vicious, wicked.

virulent *adj* **1** deadly, malignant, poisonous, toxic, venomous. **2** acrid, acrimonious, bitter, caustic.

visage *n* aspect, countenance, face, guise, physiognomy, semblance.

viscera *n* bowels, entrails, guts, intestines.

viscous *adj* adhesive, clammy, glutinous, ropy, slimy, sticky, tenacious.

visible *adj* **1** observable, perceivable, perceptible, seeable, visual. **2** apparent, clear, conspicuous, discoverable, distinct, evident, manifest, noticeable, obvious, open, palpable, patent, plain, revealed, unhidden, unmistakable.

vision *n* **1** eyesight, seeing, sight. **2** eyeshot, ken. **3** apparition, chimera, dream, ghost, hallucination, illusion, phantom, spectre.

visionary *adj* **1** imaginative, impractical, quixotic, romantic. **2** chimerical, dreamy, fancied, fanciful, fantastic, ideal, illusory, imaginary, romantic, shadowy, unsubstantial, utopian, wild. • *n* dreamer, enthusiast, fanatic, idealist, optimist, theorist, zealot.

n antonym pragmatist.

vital *adj* **1** basic, cardinal, essential, indispensable, necessary, needful. **2** animate, alive, existing, life giving, living. **3** paramount.

adj antonyms inessential, peripheral, unimportant.

vitality *n* animation, life, strength, vigour, virility.

vitiate *vb* adulterate, contaminate, corrupt, debase, defile, degrade, deprave, deteriorate, impair, infect, injure, invalidate, poison, pollute, spoil.

vb antonym purify.

vitiation *n* adulteration, corruption, degeneracy, degeneration, degradation, depravation, deterioration, impairment, injury, invalidation, perversion, pollution, prostitution.

vituperate *vb* abuse, berate, blame, censure, denounce, overwhelm, rate, revile, scold, upbraid, vilify.

vituperation *n* abuse, blame, censure, invective, reproach, railing, reviling, scolding, upbraiding.

n antonyms acclaim, eulogy, praise.

vivacious *adj* active, animated, breezy, brisk, buxom, cheerful, frolicsome, gay, jocund, light-hearted, lively, merry, mirthful, spirited, sportive, sprightly.

adj antonym languid.

vivacity *n* animation, cheer, cheerfulness, gaiety, liveliness, sprightliness.

vivid *adj* **1** active, animated, bright, brilliant,

clear, intense, fresh, lively, living, lucid, quick, sprightly, strong. **2** expressive, graphic, striking, telling.
adj antonyms dull, lifeless.

vivify *vb* animate, arouse, awake, quicken, vitalize.

vixen *n* brawler, scold, shrew, spitfire, tartar, virago.

vocabulary *n* **1** dictionary, glossary, lexicon, wordbook. **2** language, terms, words.

vocation *n* **1** call, citation, injunction, summons. **2** business, calling, employment, occupation, profession, pursuit, trade.

vociferate *vb* bawl, bellow, clamour, cry, exclaim, rant, shout, yell.

vociferous *adj* blatant, clamorous, loud, noisy, obstreperous, ranting, stunning, uproarious.

vogue *adj* fashionable, modish, stylish, trendy. • *n* custom, fashion, favour, mode, practice, repute, style, usage, way.

voice *vb* declare, express, say, utter. • *n* **1** speech, tongue, utterance. **2** noise, notes, sound. **3** opinion, option, preference, suffrage, vote. **4** accent, articulation, enunciation, inflection, intonation, modulation, pronunciation, tone. **5** expression, language, words.

void *vb* **1** clear, eject, emit, empty, evacuate. • *adj* blank, empty, hollow, vacant. **2** clear, destitute, devoid, free, lacking, wanting, without. **3** inept, ineffectual, invalid, nugatory, null. **4** imaginary, unreal, vain. • *n* abyss, blank, chasm, emptiness, hole, vacuum.
vb antonyms fill, validate.
adj antonyms full, valid.

volatile *adj* **1** gaseous, incoercible. **2** airy, buoyant, frivolous, gay, jolly, lively, sprightly, vivacious. **3** capricious, changeable, fickle, flighty, flyaway, giddy, harebrained, inconstant, light-headed, mercurial, reckless, unsteady, whimsical, wild.
adj antonyms constant, steady.

volition *n* choice, determination, discretion, option, preference, will.

volley *n* **1** fusillade, round, salvo. **2** blast, burst, discharge, emission, explosion, outbreak, report, shower, storm.

voluble *adj* fluent, garrulous, glib, loquacious, talkative.

volume *n* **1** book, tome. **2** amplitude, body, bulk, compass, dimension, size, substance, vastness. **3** fullness, power, quantity.

voluminous *adj* **1** ample, big, bulky, full, great, large. **2** copious, diffuse, discursive, flowing.
adj antonyms scanty, slight.

voluntary *adj* **1** free, spontaneous, unasked, unbidden, unforced. **2** deliberate, designed, intended, purposed. **3** discretionary, optional, willing.
adj antonyms compulsory, forced, involuntary, unwilling.

volunteer *vb* offer, present, proffer, propose, tender.

voluptuary *n* epicure, hedonist, sensualist.

voluptuous *adj* carnal, effeminate, epicurean, fleshy, licentious, luxurious, sensual, sybaritic.
adj antonym ascetic.

vomit *vb* discharge, eject, emit, puke, regurgitate, spew, throw up.

voracious *adj* devouring, edacious, greedy, hungry, rapacious, ravenous.

vortex *n* eddy, maelstrom, whirl, whirlpool.

votary *adj* devoted, promised. • *n* adherent, devotee, enthusiast, follower, supporter, votarist, zealot.

vote *vb* **1** ballot, elect, opt, return. **2** judge, pronounce, propose, suggest. • *n* ballot, franchise, poll, referendum, suffrage, voice.

vouch *vb* affirm, asseverate, attest, aver, declare, guarantee, support, uphold, verify, warrant.

vouchsafe *vb* accord, cede, deign, grant, stoop, yield.

vow *vb* **1** consecrate, dedicate, devote. **2** asseverate. • *n* oath, pledge, promise.

voyage *vb* cruise, journey, navigate, ply, sail. • *n* crossing, cruise, excursion, journey, passage, sail, trip.

vulgar *adj* **1** base-born, common, ignoble, lowly, plebeian. **2** boorish, cheap, coarse, discourteous, flashy, homespun, garish, gaudy, ill-bred, inelegant, loud, rustic, showy, tawdry, uncultivated, unrefined. **3** general, ordinary, popular, public. **4** base, broad, loose, low, gross, mean, ribald, vile. **5** inelegant, unauthorized.
adj antonyms correct, decent, elegant, noble, polite, refined.

vulgarity *n* baseness, coarseness, grossness, meanness, rudeness.

vulnerable *adj* accessible, assailable, defenceless, exposed, weak.
adj antonyms protected, strong.

W

waddle *vb* toddle, toggle, waggle, wiggle, wobble.

waft *vb* bear, carry, convey, float, transmit, transport. • *n* breath, breeze, draught, puff.

wag[1] *vb* **1** shake, sway, waggle. **2** oscillate, vibrate, waver. **3** advance, move, progress, stir. • *n* flutter, nod, oscillation, vibration.

wag[2] *n* humorist, jester, joker, wit.

wage *vb* **1** bet, hazard, lay, stake, wager. **2** conduct, undertake.

wager *vb* back, bet, gamble, lay, pledge, risk, stake. • *n* bet, gamble, pledge, risk, stake.

wages *npl* allowance, compensation, earnings, emolument, hire, pay, payment, remuneration, salary, stipend.

waggish *adj* **1** frolicsome, gamesome, mischievous, roguish, tricksy. **2** comical, droll, facetious, funny, humorous, jocular, jocose, merry, sportive.
adj antonyms grave, serious, staid.

wagon *n* cart, lorry, truck, van, waggon, wain.

wail *vb* **1** bemoan, deplore, lament, mourn. **2** cry, howl, weep. • *n* complaint, cry, lamentation, moan, wailing.

waist *n* bodice, corsage, waistline.

wait *vb* **1** delay, linger, pause, remain, rest, stay, tarry. **2** attend, minister, serve. **3** abide, await, expect, look for. • *n* delay, halt, holdup, pause, respite, rest, stay, stop.
vb antonyms depart, go, leave.

waiter, waitress *n* attendant, lackey, servant, servitor, steward, valet.

waive *vb* **1** defer, forgo, surrender, relinquish, remit, renounce. **2** desert, reject.
vb antonyms claim, maintain.

wake[1] *vb* **1** arise, awake, awaken. **2** activate, animate, arouse, awaken, excite, kindle, provoke, stimulate. • *n* vigil, watch, watching.
vb antonyms relax, sleep.

wake[2] *n* course, path, rear, track, trail, wash.

wakeful *adj* **1** awake, sleepless, restless. **2** alert, observant, vigilant, wary, watchful.

wale *n* ridge, streak, stripe, welt, whelk.

walk *vb* advance, depart, go, march, move, pace, saunter, step, stride, stroll, tramp.

• *n* **1** amble, carriage, gait, step. **2** beat, career, course, department, field, province. **3** conduct, procedure. **4** alley, avenue, cloister, esplanade, footpath, path, pathway, pavement, promenade, range, sidewalk, way. **5** constitutional, excursion, hike, ramble, saunter, stroll, tramp, turn.

wall *n* escarp, parapet, plane, upright.

wallet *n* bag, knapsack, pocketbook, purse, sack.

wan *adj* ashen, bloodless, cadaverous, colourless, haggard, pale, pallid.

wand *n* baton, mace, truncheon, sceptre.

wander *vb* **1** forage, prowl, ramble, range, roam, rove, stroll. **2** deviate, digress, straggle, stray. **3** moon, rave. • *n* amble, cruise, excursion, ramble, stroll.

wane *vb* **1** abate, decrease, ebb, subside. **2** decline, fail, sink. • *n* **1** decrease, diminution, lessening. **2** decay, declension, decline, failure.
vb antonyms increase, wax.
n antonym increase.

want *vb* **1** crave, desire, need, require, wish. **2** fail, lack, neglect, omit. • *n* **1** absence, defect, default, deficiency, lack. **2** defectiveness, failure, inadequacy, insufficiency, meagreness, paucity, poverty, scantiness, scarcity, shortness. **3** requirement. **4** craving, desire, longing, wish. **5** destitution, distress, indigence, necessity, need, penury, poverty, privation, straits.
vb antonyms abundance, plenty, riches.

wanton *vb* **1** caper, disport, frisk, frolic, play, revel, romp, sport. **2** dally, flirt, toy, trifle. • *adj* **1** free, loose, unchecked, unrestrained, wandering. **2** abounding, exuberant, luxuriant, overgrown, rampant. **3** airy, capricious, coltish, frisky, playful, skittish, sportive. **4** dissolute, irregular, licentious, loose. **5** carnal, immoral, incontinent, lascivious, lecherous, lewd, libidinous, light, lustful, prurient, salacious, unchaste. **6** careless, gratuitous, groundless, heedless, inconsiderate, needless, perverse, reckless, wayward, wilful.

war *vb* battle, campaign, combat, contend, crusade, engage, fight, strive. • *n* contention, enmity, hostility, strife, warfare.

n antonym peace.

warble *vb* sing, trill, yodel. • *n* carol, chant, hymn, hum.

ward *vb* **1** guard, watch. **2** defend, fend, parry, protect, repel. • *n* **1** care, charge, guard, guardianship, watch. **2** defender, guardian, keeper, protector, warden. **3** custody. **4** defence, garrison, protection. **5** minor, pupil. **6** district, division, precinct, quarter. **7** apartment, cubicle.

warehouse *n* depot, magazine, repository, store, storehouse.

wares *npl* commodities, goods, merchandise, movables.

warfare *n* battle, conflict, contest, discord, engagement, fray, hostilities, strife, struggle, war.

warily *adv* carefully, cautiously, charily, circumspectly, heedfully, watchfully, vigilantly.

wariness *n* care, caution, circumspection, foresight, thought, vigilance.

n antonyms heedlessness, recklessness, thoughtlessness.

warlike *adj* bellicose, belligerent, combative, hostile, inimical, martial, military, soldierly, watchful.

adj antonym peaceable.

warm *vb* **1** heat, roast, toast. **2** animate, chafe, excite, rouse. • *adj* **1** lukewarm, tepid. **2** genial, mild, pleasant, sunny. **3** close, muggy, oppressive. **4** affectionate, ardent, cordial, eager, earnest, enthusiastic, fervent, fervid, glowing, hearty, hot, zealous. **5** excited, fiery, flushed, furious, hasty, keen, lively, passionate, quick, vehement, violent.

vb antonym cool.

adj antonyms cool, indifferent, unfriendly.

warmth *n* **1** glow, tepidity. **2** ardour, fervency, fervour, zeal. **3** animation, cordiality, eagerness, earnestness, enthusiasm, excitement, fervency, fever, fire, flush, heat, intensity, passion, spirit, vehemence.

n antonyms coldness, coolness, unfriendliness.

warn *vb* **1** caution, forewarn. **2** admonish, advise. **3** apprise, inform, notify. **4** bid, call, summon.

warning *adj* admonitory, cautionary, cautioning, monitory. • *n* **1** admonition, advice, caveat, caution, monition.

2 information, notice. **3** augury, indication, intimation, omen, portent, presage, prognostic, sign, symptom. **4** call, summons. **5** example, lesson, sample.

warp *vb* bend, bias, contort, deviate, distort, pervert, swerve, turn, twist. • *n* bent, bias, cast, crook, distortion, inclination, leaning, quirk, sheer, skew, slant, slew, swerve, twist, turn.

vb antonym straighten.

warrant *vb* **1** answer for, certify, guarantee, secure. **2** affirm, assure, attest, avouch, declare, justify, state. **3** authorize, justify, license, maintain, sanction, support, sustain, uphold. • *n* **1** guarantee, pledge, security, surety, warranty. **2** authentication, authority, commission, verification. **3** order, pass, permit, summons, subpoena, voucher, writ.

warrantable *adj* admissible, allowable, defensible, justifiable, lawful, permissible, proper, right, vindicable.

warrior *n* champion, captain, fighter, hero, soldier.

wary *adj* careful, cautious, chary, circumspect, discreet, guarded, heedful, prudent, scrupulous, vigilant, watchful.

adj antonyms careless, foolhardy, heedless, reckless, unwary.

wash *vb* **1** purify, purge. **2** moisten, wet. **3** bathe, clean, flush, irrigate, lap, lave, rinse, sluice. **4** colour, stain, tint. • *n* **1** ablution, bathing, cleansing, lavation, washing. **2** bog, fen, marsh, swamp, quagmire. **3** bath, embrocation, lotion. **4** laundry, washing.

washy *adj* **1** damp, diluted, moist, oozy, sloppy, thin, watery, weak. **2** feeble, jejune, pointless, poor, spiritless, trashy, trumpery, unmeaning, vapid, worthless.

waspish *adj* **1** choleric, fretful, irascible, irritable, peevish, petulant, snappish, testy, touchy. **2** slender, slim, small-waisted.

waste *vb* **1** consume, corrode, decrease, diminish, emaciate, wear. **2** absorb, deplete, devour, dissipate, drain, empty, exhaust, expend, lavish, lose, misspend, misuse, scatter, spend, squander. **3** demolish, desolate, destroy, devastate, devour, dilapidate, harry, pillage, plunder, ravage, ruin, scour, strip. **4** damage, impair, injure. **5** decay, dwindle, perish, wither. • *adj* **1** bare, desolated, destroyed, devastated, empty, ravaged, ruined, spoiled, stripped, void. **2** dismal, dreary, forlorn. **3** abandoned, bare, barren, uncultivated, unimproved, uninhabited, untilled, wild. **4** useless, valueless, worthless. **5** exuberant, superfluous. • *n* **1** consumption, decrement, diminution, dissipation, exhaustion, expenditure, loss, wasting. **2** destruction, dispersion, extravagance, loss, squandering, wanton. **3** decay, desolation, destruction, devastation, havoc, pillage, ravage, ruin. **4** chaff, debris, detritus, dross, excrement, husks, junk, matter, offal, refuse, rubbish, trash, wastrel, worthlessness. **5** barrenness, desert, expanse, solitude, wild, wilderness.

wasteful *adj* **1** destructive, ruinous. **2** extravagant, improvident, lavish, prodigal, profuse, squandering, thriftless, unthrifty.

adj antonyms economical, frugal, thrifty.

watch *vb* **1** attend, guard, keep, oversee, protect, superintend, tend. **2** eye, mark, observe. • *n* **1** espial, guard, outlook, wakefulness, watchfulness, watching, vigil, ward. **2** alertness, attention, inspection, observation, surveillance. **3** guard, picket, sentinel, sentry, watchman. **4** pocket watch, ticker, timepiece, wristwatch.

watchful *adj* alert, attentive, awake, careful, circumspect, guarded, heedful, observant, vigilant, wakeful, wary.

adj antonym inattentive.

watchword *n* catchword, cry, motto, password, shibboleth, word.

waterfall *n* cascade, cataract, fall, linn.

watery *adj* **1** diluted, thin, waterish, weak. **2** insipid, spiritless, tasteful, vapid. **3** moist, wet.

adj antonyms solid, strong.

wave *vb* **1** float, flutter, heave, shake, sway, undulate, wallow. **2** brandish, flaunt, flourish, swing. **3** beckon, signal. • *n* **1** billow, bore, breaker, flood, flush, ripple, roll, surge, swell, tide, undulation. **2** flourish, gesture, sway. **3** convolution, curl, roll, unevenness.

waver *vb* **1** flicker, float, undulate, wave. **2** reel, totter. **3** falter, fluctuate, flutter, hesitate, oscillate, quiver, vacillate.

vb antonyms decide, stand.

wax *vb* become, grow, increase, mount, rise.

vb antonym wane.

way *n* **1** advance, journey, march, progression, transit, trend. **2** access, alley, artery, avenue, beat, channel, course, highroad, highway, passage, path, road, route, street, track, trail. **3** fashion, manner, means, method, mode, system. **4** distance, interval, space, stretch. **5** behaviour, custom, form, guise, habit, habitude, practice, process, style, usage. **6** device, plan, scheme.

wayfarer *n* itinerant, nomad, passenger, pilgrim, rambler, traveller, walker, wanderer.

wayward *adj* capricious, captious, contrary, forward, headstrong, intractable, obstinate, perverse, refractory, stubborn, unruly, wilful.

adj antonyms complaisant, good-natured.

weak *adj* **1** debilitated, delicate, enfeebled, enervated, exhausted, faint, feeble, fragile, frail, infirm, invalid, languid, languishing, shaky, sickly, spent, strengthless, tender, unhealthy, unsound, wasted, weakly. **2** accessible, defenceless, unprotected, vulnerable. **3** light, soft, unstressed. **4** boneless, cowardly, infirm. **5** compliant, irresolute, pliable, pliant, undecided, undetermined, unsettled, unstable, unsteady, vacillating, wavering, yielding. **6** childish, foolish, imbecile, senseless, shallow, silly, simple, stupid, weak-minded, witless. **7** erring, foolish, indiscreet, injudicious, unwise. **8** gentle, indistinct, low, small. **9** adulterated, attenuated, diluted, insipid, tasteless, thin, watery. **10** flimsy, frivolous, poor, sleazy, slight, trifling. **11** futile, illogical, inconclusive, ineffective, ineffectual, inefficient, lame, unconvincing, unsatisfactory, unsupported, unsustained, vague, vain. **12** unsafe, unsound, unsubstantial, untrustworthy. **13** helpless, impotent, powerless. **14** breakable, brittle, delicate, frangible. **15** inconsiderable, puny, slender, slight, small.

adj antonym strong.

weaken *vb* **1** cramp, cripple, debilitate, devitalize, enervate, enfeeble, invalidate, relax, sap, shake, stagger, undermine, unman, unnerve, unstring. **2** adulterate, attenuate, debase, depress, dilute, exhaust, impair, impoverish, lessen, lower, reduce.

vb antonym strengthen.

weakness *n* **1** debility, feebleness, fragility, frailty, infirmity, languor, softness. **2** defect, failing, fault, flaw. **3** fondness, inclination, liking.

n antonyms dislike, strength.

weal *n* **1** advantage, good, happiness, interest, profit, utility, prosperity, welfare. **2** ridge, streak, stripe.

wealth *n* **1** assets, capital, cash, fortune, funds, goods, money, possessions, property, riches, treasure. **2** abundance, affluence, opulence, plenty, profusion.

n antonym poverty.

wean *vb* alienate, detach, disengage, withdraw.

wear *vb* **1** bear, carry, don. **2** endure, last. **3** consume, impair, rub, use, waste. • *n* **1** corrosion, deterioration, disintegration, erosion, wear and tear. **2** consumption, use. **3** apparel, array, attire, clothes, clothing, dress, garb, gear.

wearied *adj* apathetic, bored, exhausted, fagged, fatigued, jaded, tired, weary, worn.

weariness *n* apathy, boredom, ennui, exhaustion, fatigue, languor, lassitude, monotony, prostration, sameness, tedium.

n antonym freshness.

wearisome *adj* annoying, boring, dull, exhausting, fatiguing, humdrum, irksome, monotonous, prolix, prosaic, slow, tedious, tiresome, troublesome, trying, uninteresting, vexatious.

adj antonym refreshing.

weary *vb* debilitate, exhaust, fag, fatigue, harass, jade, tire. • *adj* **1** apathetic, bored, drowsy, exhausted, jaded, spent, tired, worn. **2** irksome, tiresome, wearisome.

adj antonyms excited, fresh, lively.

weave *vb* **1** braid, entwine, interlace, lace, mat, plait, pleat, twine. **2** compose, construct, fabricate, make.

wed *vb* contract, couple, espouse, marry, unite.

vb antonym divorce.

wedding *n* bridal, espousal, marriage, nuptials.

wedlock *n* marriage, matrimony.

ween *vb* fancy, imagine, suppose, think.

weep *vb* bemoan, bewail, complain, cry, lament, sob.

vb antonym rejoice.

weigh *vb* **1** balance, counterbalance, lift, raise. **2** consider, deliberate, esteem, examine, study.

vb antonyms cut no ice, hearten.

weight *vb* **1** ballast, burden, fill, freight, load. **2** weigh. • *n* **1** gravity, heaviness, heft, tonnage. **2** burden, load, pressure. **3** consequence, efficacy, emphasis, importance, impressiveness, influence, moment, pith, power, significance, value.

vb antonym lighten.

n antonym lightness.

weighty *adj* **1** heavy, massive, onerous, ponderous, unwieldy. **2** considerable, efficacious, forcible, grave, important, influential, serious, significant.

weird *adj* eerie, ghostly, strange, supernatural, uncanny, unearthly, witching.

adj antonym normal.

welcome *vb* embrace, greet, hail, receive. • *adj* acceptable, agreeable, grateful, gratifying, pleasant, pleasing, satisfying. • *n* greeting, reception, salutation.

vb antonyms reject, snub.

adj antonym unwelcome.

welfare *n* advantage, affluence, benefit, happiness, profit, prosperity, success, thrift, weal, wellbeing.

n antonym harm.

well[1] *vb* flow, gush, issue, jet, pour, spring. • *n* **1** fount, fountain, reservoir, spring, wellhead, wellspring. **2** origin, source. **3** hole, pit, shaft.

well[2] *adj* **1** hale, healthy, hearty, sound. **2** fortunate, good, happy, profitable, satisfactory, useful. • *adv* **1** accurately, adequately, correctly, efficiently, properly, suitably. **2** abundantly, considerably, fully, thoroughly. **3** agreeably, commendably, favourably, worthily.

adj antonyms bad, ill.

adv antonym badly.

wellbeing *n* comfort, good, happiness, health, prosperity, welfare.

welter *vb* flounder, roll, toss, wallow. • *n* confusion, jumble, mess.

wet *vb* dabble, damp, dampen, dip, drench, moisten, saturate, soak, sprinkle, water. • *adj* **1** clammy, damp, dank, dewy, dripping, humid, moist. **2** rainy, showery, sprinkly. • *n* dampness, humidity, moisture, wetness.

vb antonym dry.

adj antonyms dry, resolute, strong.

n antonyms dryness.

whack *vb, n* bang, beat, rap, strike, thrash, thump, thwack.

wharf *n* dock, pier, quay.

wheedle *vb* cajole, coax, flatter, inveigle, lure.

vb antonym force.

wheel *vb* gyrate, revolve, roll, rotate, spin,

swing, turn, twist, whirl, wind. • *n* circle, revolution, roll, rotation, spin, turn, twirl.

whet *vb* 1 grind, sharpen. 2 arouse, awaken, excite, provoke, rouse, stimulate. 3 animate, inspire, kindle, quicken, warm.

whiff *vb, n* blast, gust, puff.

whim *n* caprice, crotchet, fancy, freak, frolic, humour, notion, quirk, sport, vagary, whimsy, wish.

whimsical *adj* capricious, crotchety, eccentric, erratic, fanciful, frolicsome, odd, peculiar, quaint, singular.

adj antonym sensible.

whine *vb* cry, grumble, mewl, moan, snivel, wail, whimper. • *n* complaint, cry, grumble, moan, sob, wail, whimper.

whip *vb* 1 beat, lash, strike. 2 flagellate, flog, goad, horsewhip, scourge, slash. 3 hurt, sting. 4 jerk, snap, snatch, whisk. • *n* bullwhip, cane, crop, horsewhip, knout, lash, scourge, switch, thong.

whipping *n* beating, castigation, dusting, flagellation, flogging, thrashing.

whirl *vb* gyrate, pirouette, roll, revolve, rotate, turn, twirl, twist, wheel. • *n* eddy, flurry, flutter, gyration, rotation, spin, swirl, twirl, vortex.

n antonym calm.

whit *n* atom, bit, grain, iota, jot, mite, particle, scrap, speck, tittle.

white *adj* 1 argent, canescent, chalky, frosty, hoary, ivory, milky, silver, snowy. 2 grey, pale, pallid, wan. 3 candid, clean, chaste, immaculate, innocent, pure, spotless, unblemished.

whole *adj* 1 all, complete, entire, intact, integral, total, undivided. 2 faultless, firm, good, perfect, strong, unbroken, undivided, uninjured. 3 healthy, sound, well. • *adv* entire, in one. • *n* aggregate, all, amount, ensemble, entirety, gross, sum, total, totality.

adj antonyms damaged, ill, partial.

n antonym part.

wholesome *adj* 1 healthy, healthful, invigorating, nourishing, nutritious, salubrious, salutary. 2 beneficial, good, helpful, improving, salutary. 3 fresh, sound, sweet.

adj antonym unwholesome.

wholly *adv* altogether, completely, entirely, fully, totally, utterly.

adv antonym partly.

whoop *vb* halloo, hoot, roar, shout, yell. • *n* bellow, hoot, roar, shout, yell.

wicked *adj* 1 abandoned, abominable, depraved, devilish, godless, graceless, immoral, impious, infamous, irreligious, irreverent, profane, sinful, ungodly, unholy, unprincipled, unrighteous, vicious, vile, worthless. 2 atrocious, bad, black, criminal, dark, evil, heinous, ill, iniquitous, monstrous, nefarious, unjust, villainous.

adj antonyms good, harmless, modest, upright.

wide *adj* 1 ample, broad, capacious, comprehensive, distended, expanded, large, spacious, vast. 2 distant, remote. 3 prevalent, rife, widespread. • *adv* completely, farthest, fully.

adj antonyms limited, narrow.

adv antonym on target.

wield *vb* 1 brandish, flourish, handle, manipulate, ply, work. 2 control, manage, sway, use.

wild *adj* 1 feral, undomesticated, untamed. 2 desert, desolate, native, rough, rude, uncultivated. 3 barbarous, ferocious, fierce, savage, uncivilized. 4 dense, luxuriant, rank. 5 disorderly, distracted, frantic, frenzied, furious, impetuous, irregular, mad, outrageous, raving, turbulent, ungoverned, uncontrolled, violent. 6 dissipated, fast, flighty, foolish, giddy, harebrained, heedless, ill-advised, inconsiderate, reckless, thoughtless, unwise. 7 boisterous, rough, stormy. 8 crazy, extravagant, fanciful, grotesque, imaginary, strange. • *n* desert, waste, wilderness.

adj antonyms civilized, peaceful, sane, sensible, tame, unenthusiastic.

wilderness *n* desert, waste, wild.

wilful *adj* 1 cantankerous, contumacious, dogged, headstrong, heady, inflexible, intractable, mulish, obdurate, obstinate, perverse, pig-headed, refractory, self-willed, stubborn, unruly, unyielding. 2 arbitrary, capricious. 3 deliberate, intended, intentional, planned, premeditated.

adj antonyms complaisant, good-natured.

will *vb* 1 bid, command, decree, direct, enjoin, ordain. 2 choose, desire, elect, wish. 3 bequeath, convey, demise, devise, leave. • *n* 1 decision, determination, resoluteness, resolution, self-reliance. 2 desire, disposition, inclination, intent, pleasure, purpose, volition, wish. 3 behest, command, decree, demand, direction, order, request, requirement.

willing *adj* **1** adaptable, amenable, compliant, desirous, disposed, inclined, minded. **2** deliberate, free, intentional, spontaneous, unasked, unbidden, voluntary. **3** cordial, eager, forward, prompt, ready.
adj antonym unwilling.

willingly *adv* cheerfully, gladly, readily, spontaneously, voluntarily.

wily *adj* arch, artful, crafty, crooked, cunning, deceitful, designing, diplomatic, foxy, insidious, intriguing, politic, sly, subtle, treacherous, tricky.
adj antonym guileless.

win *vb* **1** accomplish, achieve, acquire, catch, earn, effect, gain, gather, get, make, obtain, procure, reach, realize, reclaim, recover. **2** gain, succeed, surpass, triumph. **3** arrive. **4** allure, attract, convince, influence, persuade. • *n* conquest, success, triumph, victory.
vb antonym lose.
n antonym defeat.

wind[1] *n* **1** air, blast, breeze, draught, gust, hurricane, whiff, zephyr. **2** breath, breathing, expiration, inspiration, respiration. **2** flatulence, gas, windiness.

wind[2] *vb* **1** coil, crank, encircle, involve, reel, roll, turn, twine, twist. **2** bend, curve, meander, zigzag. • *n* bend, curve, meander, twist, zigzag.

winding *adj* circuitous, devious, flexuose, flexuous, meandering, serpentine, tortuous, turning, twisting. • *n* bend, curve, meander, turn, twist.

windy *adj* **1** breezy, blowy, blustering, boisterous, draughty, gusty, squally, stormy, tempestuous. **2** airy, empty, hollow, inflated.
adj antonyms calm, fearless, modest.

winning *adj* **1** alluring, attractive, bewitching, brilliant, captivating, charming, dazzling, delightful, enchanting, engaging, fascinating, lovely, persuasive, pleasing, prepossessing. **2** conquering, triumphant, victorious.

winnow *vb* cull, glean, divide, fan, part, select, separate, sift.

winsome *adj* blithe, blithesome, bonny, buoyant, charming, cheerful, debonair, jocund, light-hearted, lively, lovable, merry, pleasant, sportive, winning.
adj antonym unattractive.

wintry *adj* arctic, boreal, brumal, cold, frosty, icy, snowy.

wipe *vb* clean, dry, mop, rub. • *n* **1** mop, rub, blow, hit, strike. **2** gibe, jeer, sarcasm, sneer, taunt.

wisdom *n* **1** depth, discernment, far-sightedness, foresight, insight, judgement, judiciousness, prescience, profundity, prudence, sagacity, sapience, sense, solidity, understanding, wiseness. **2** attainment, edification, enlightenment, erudition, information, knowledge, learning, lore, scholarship. **3** reason.
n antonym folly.

wise *adj* **1** deep, discerning, enlightened, intelligent, judicious, penetrating, philosophical, profound, rational, seasonable, sensible, sage, sapient, solid, sound. **2** erudite, informed, knowing, learned, scholarly. **3** crafty, cunning, designing, foxy, politic, sly, subtle, wary, wily.
adj antonym foolish.

wish *vb* **1** covet, desire, hanker, list, long. **2** bid, command, desire, direct, intend, mean, order, want. • *n* **1** behest, desire, intention, mind, pleasure, want, will. **2** craving, desire, hankering, inclination, liking, longing, want, yearning.
vb antonyms dislike, fear.
n antonyms dislike, fear.

wistful *adj* **1** contemplative, engrossed, meditative, musing, pensive, reflective, thoughtful. **2** desirous, eager, earnest, longing.

wit *n* **1** genius, intellect, intelligence, reason, sense, understanding. **2** brightness, banter, cleverness, drollery, facetiousness, fun, humour, jocularity, piquancy, point, raillery, satire, sparkle, whim. **3** conceit, epigram, jest, joke, pleasantry, quip, quirk, repartee, sally, witticism. **4** humorist, joker, wag.
n antonyms seriousness, stupidity.

witch *n* **1** charmer, enchantress, fascinator, sorceress. **2** crone, hag, sibyl.

witchcraft *n* conjuration, enchantment, magic, necromancy, sorcery, spell.

withdraw *vb* **1** abstract, deduct, remove, retire, separate, sequester, sequestrate, subduct, subtract. **2** disengage, wean. **3** abjure, recall, recant, relinquish, resign, retract, revoke. **4** abdicate, decamp, depart, dissociate, retire, shrink, vacate.
vb antonyms advance, deposit, persist.

wither *vb* **1** contract, droop, dry, sear, shrivel, wilt, wizen. **2** decay, decline, languish, pine, waste.
vb antonyms boost, thrive.

withhold *vb* check, detain, hinder, repress, restrain, retain, suppress.

vb antonyms accord, give.

withstand *vb* confront, defy, face, oppose, resist.

vb antonyms collapse, yield.

witless *adj* daft, dull, foolish, halfwitted, obtuse, senseless, shallow, silly, stupid, unintelligent.

witness *vb* corroborate, mark, note, notice, observe, see. • *n* **1** attestation, conformation, corroboration, evidence, proof, testimony. **2** beholder, bystander, corroborator, deponent, eyewitness, onlooker, spectator, testifier.

witty *adj* **1** bright, clever, droll, facetious, funny, humorous, jocose, jocular, pleasant, waggish. **2** alert, penetrating, quick, sparkling, sprightly.

adj antonyms dull, unamusing.

wizard *n* charmer, diviner, conjurer, enchanter, magician, necromancer, seer, soothsayer, sorcerer.

woe *n* affliction, agony, anguish, bitterness, depression, distress, dole, grief, heartache, melancholy, misery, sorrow, torture, tribulation, trouble, unhappiness, wretchedness.

n antonym joy.

woeful *adj* **1** afflicted, agonized, anguished, burdened, disconsolate, distressed, melancholy, miserable, mournful, piteous, sad, sorrowful, troubled, unhappy, wretched. **2** afflicting, afflictive, calamitous, deplorable, depressing, disastrous, distressing, dreadful, tragic, tragical, grievous, lamentable, pitiable, saddening.

wonder *vb* **1** admire, gape, marvel. **2** conjecture, ponder, query, question, speculate. • *n* amazement, astonishment, awe, bewilderment, curiosity, marvel, miracle, prodigy, surprise, stupefaction, wonderment.

n antonyms disinterest, ordinariness.

wonderful *adj* amazing, astonishing, astounding, awe-inspiring, awesome, awful, extraordinary, marvellous, miraculous, portentous, prodigious, startling, stupendous, surprising.

adj antonyms ordinary, rotten.

wont *adj* accustomed, customary, familiar, habitual, ordinary, usual. • *n* custom, habit, practice, rule, usage.

wonted *adj* accustomed, common, conventional, customary, everyday, familiar, frequent, habitual, ordinary, regular, usual.

wood *n* coppice, copse, covert, forest, greenwood, grove, spinney, thicket, woodland.

word *vb* express, phrase, put, say, state, term, utter. • *n* **1** expression, name, phrase, term, utterance. **2** account, advice, information, intelligence, message, news, report, tidings. **3** affirmation, assertion, averment, avowal, declaration, statement. **4** conversation, speech. **5** agreement, assurance, engagement, parole, pledge, plight, promise. **6** behest, bidding, command, direction, order, precept. **7** countersign, password, signal, watchword.

wordy *adj* circumlocutory, diffuse, garrulous, inflated, lengthened, long-winded, loquacious, periphrastic, rambling, talkative, tedious, verbose, windy.

adj antonyms concise, laconic.

work *vb* **1** act, operate. **2** drudge, fag, grind, grub, labour, slave, sweat, toil. **3** move, perform, succeed. **4** aim, attempt, strive, try. **5** effervesce, ferment, leaven, rise. **6** accomplish, beget, cause, effect, engender, manage, originate, produce. **7** exert, strain. **8** embroider, stitch. • *n* **1** exertion, drudgery, grind, labour, pain, toil. **2** business, employment, function, occupation, task. **3** action, accomplishment, achievement, composition, deed, feat, fruit, handiwork, opus, performance, product, production. **4** fabric, manufacture. **5** ferment, leaven. **6** management, treatment.

vb antonyms fail, play, rest.

n antonyms hobby, play, rest.

workman *n* **1** journeyman, employee, labourer, operative, worker, wright. **2** artisan, craftsman, mechanic.

world *n* cosmos, creation, earth, globe, nature, planet, sphere, universe.

worldly *adj* **1** common, earthly, human, mundane, sublunary, terrestrial. **2** carnal, fleshly, profane, secular, temporal. **3** ambitious, grovelling, irreligious, selfish, proud, sordid, unsanctified, unspiritual. **4** sophisticated, worldly-wise.

adj antonym unworldly.

worry *vb* annoy, badger, bait, beset, bore, bother, chafe, disquiet, disturb, fret, gall, harass, harry, hector, infest, irritate, molest, persecute, pester, plague, tease, torment, trouble, vex. • *n* annoyance, anxiety, apprehensiveness, care, concern, disquiet, fear, misgiving, perplexity, solicitude, trouble, uneasiness, vexation.

vb antonyms comfort, reassure.

n antonyms comfort, reassurance.

worship *vb* **1** adore, esteem, honour, revere, venerate. **2** deify, idolize. **3** aspire, pray. • *n* **1** adoration, devotion, esteem, homage, idolatry, idolizing, respect, reverence. **2** aspiration, exultation, invocation, laud, praise, prayer, supplication.

vb antonym despise.

n antonym vilification.

worst *vb* beat, choke, conquer, crush, defeat, discomfit, foil, master, overpower, overthrow, quell, rout, subdue, subjugate, vanquish.

worth *n* **1** account, character, credit, desert, excellence, importance, integrity, merit, nobleness, worthiness, virtue. **2** cost, estimation, price, value.

n antonym worthlessness.

worthless *adj* **1** futile, meritless, miserable, nugatory, paltry, poor, trifling, unproductive, unsalable, unserviceable, useless, valueless, wretched. **2** abject, base, corrupt, degraded, ignoble, low, mean, vile.

adj antonym valuable.

worthy *adj* **1** deserving, fit, suitable. **2** estimable, excellent, exemplary, good, honest, honourable, reputable, righteous, upright, virtuous. • *n* celebrity, dignitary, luminary, notability, personage, somebody, VIP.

adj antonyms disreputable, unworthy.

wound *vb* **1** damage, harm, hurt, injure. **2** cut, gall, harrow, irritate, lacerate, pain, prick, stab. **3** annoy, mortify, offend. • *n* **1** blow, hurt, injury. **2** damage, detriment. **2** anguish, grief, pain, pang, torture.

wraith *n* apparition, ghost, phantom, spectre, vision.

wrangle *vb* argue, bicker, brawl, cavil, dispute, jangle, jar, quarrel, squabble, spar, spat. • *n* altercation, argument, bickering, brawl, contest, controversy, jar, quarrel, squabble.

vb antonym agree.

n antonym agreement.

wrap *vb* cloak, cover, encase, envelop, muffle, swathe, wind. • *n* blanket, cape, cloak, cover, overcoat, shawl.

vb antonym unwrap.

wrath *n* anger, choler, exasperation, fury, heat, resentment, indignation, ire, irritation, offence, passion, rage.

n antonyms calm, pleasure.

wrathful *adj* angry, enraged, exasperated, furious, hot, indignant, infuriated, irate, mad, passionate, provoked, rageful.

wreak *vb* execute, exercise, indulge, inflict, work.

wreath *n* chaplet, curl, festoon, garland, ring, twine.

wreathe *vb* encircle, festoon, garland, intertwine, surround, twine, twist.

wreck *vb* **1** founder, shipwreck, strand. **2** blast, blight, break, devastate, ruin, spoil. • *n* crash, desolation, destruction, perdition, prostration, ruin, shipwreck, smash, undoing.

vb antonyms repair, save.

wrench *vb* **1** distort, pervert, twist, wrest, wring. **2** sprain, strain. **3** extort, extract. • *n* **1** twist, wring. **2** sprain, strain. **2** monkey wrench, spanner.

wrest *vb* force, pull, strain, twist, wrench, wring.

wrestle *vb* contend, contest, grapple, strive, struggle.

wretch *n* **1** outcast, pariah, pilgarlic, troglodyte, vagabond, victim, sufferer. **2** beggar, criminal, hound, knave, miscreant, rascal, ruffian, rogue, scoundrel, villain.

wretched *adj* **1** afflicted, comfortless, distressed, forlorn, sad, unfortunate, unhappy, woebegone. **2** afflicting, calamitous, deplorable, depressing, pitiable, sad, saddening, shocking, sorrowful. **3** bad, beggarly, contemptible, mean, paltry, pitiful, poor, shabby, sorry, vile, worthless.

adj antonyms excellent, happy.

wring *vb* **1** contort, twist, wrench. **2** extort, force, wrest. **3** anguish, distress, harass, pain, rack, torture.

wrinkle[1] *vb* cockle, corrugate, crease, gather, pucker, rumple. • *n* cockle, corrugation, crease, crimp, crinkle, crumple, fold, furrow, gather, plait, ridge, rumple.

wrinkle[2] *n* **1** caprice, fancy, notion, quirk, whim. **2** device, tip, trick.

writ *n* decree, order, subpoena, summons.

write *vb* compose, copy, indite, inscribe, pen, scrawl, scribble, transcribe.

writer *n* amanuensis, author, clerk, penman, scribe, secretary.

writhe *vb* contort, distort, squirm, twist, wriggle.

written *adj* composed, indited, inscribed, penned, transcribed.

wrong *vb* abuse, encroach, injure, maltreat, oppress. • *adj* **1** inequitable, unfair, unjust, wrongful. **2** bad, criminal, evil, guilty, immoral, improper, iniquitous, reprehensible, sinful, vicious, wicked. **3** amiss, improper, inappropriate, unfit, unsuitable. **4** erroneous, false, faulty, inaccurate, incorrect, mistaken, untrue. • *adv* amiss, erroneously, falsely, faultily, improperly, inaccurately, incorrectly, wrongly. • *n* **1** foul, grievance, inequity, injury, injustice, trespass, unfairness. **2** blame, crime, dishonesty, evil, guilt, immorality, iniquity, misdeed, misdoing, sin, transgression, unrighteousness, vice, wickedness, wrongdoing. **3** error, falsity.

adj antonym right.

adv antonym right.

n antonym right.

wroth *adj* angry, enraged, exasperated, furious, incensed, indignant, irate, passionate, provoked, resentful.

wrought *adj* done, effected, performed, worked.

wry *adj* askew, awry, contorted, crooked, distorted, twisted.

adj antonym straight.

XYZ

xanthous *adj* blonde, fair, light-complexioned, xanthic, yellow.

xiphoid *adj* ensiform, gladiate, sword-like, sword-shaped.

Xmas *n* Christmas, Christmastide, Noel, Yule, Yuletide.

X-ray *n* roentgen ray, röntgen ray.

xylograph *n* cut, woodcut, wood engraving.

xylographer *n* wood engraver.

xylophagous *adj* wood-eating, wood-nourished.

yap *vb* bark, cry, yelp. • *n* bark, cry, yelp.

yard *n* close, compound, court, courtyard, enclosure, garden.

yarn *n* anecdote, boasting, fabrication, narrative, story, tale, untruth.

yawn *vb* dehisce, gape, open wide. • *n* gap, gape, gulf.

yearn *vb* crave, desire, hanker after, long for.

yell *vb* bawl, bellow, cry out, howl, roar, scream, screech, shriek, squeal.• *n* cry, howl, roar, scream, screech, shriek.
vb antonym whisper.
n antonym whisper.

yellow *adj* aureate, gilded, gilt, gold, golden, lemon, primrose, saffron, xanthic, xanthous.

yelp *vb* 1 bark, howl, yap. 2 complain, bitch, grouse. • *n* bark, sharp cry, howl.

yet *adv* at last, besides, further, however, over and above, so far, still, thus far, ultimately. • *conj* moreover, nevertheless, notwithstanding, now.

yield *vb* 1 afford, bear, bestow, communicate, confer, fetch, furnish, impart, produce, render, supply. 2 accede, accord, acknowledge, acquiesce, allow, assent, comply, concede, give, grant, permit. 3 abandon, abdicate, cede, forgo, give up, let go, quit, relax, relinquish, resign, submit, succumb, surrender, waive. • *n* earnings, income, output, produce, profit, return, revenue.

yielding *adj* 1 accommodating, acquiescent, affable, compliant, complaisant, easy, manageable, obedient, passive, submissive, unresisting. 2 bending, flexible, flexile, plastic, pliant, soft, supple, tractable.

3 fertile, productive.
adj antonyms obstinate, solid.

yoke *vb* associate, bracket, connect, couple, harness, interlink, join, link, unite. • *n* 1 bond, chain, ligature, link, tie, union. 2 bondage, dependence, enslavement, service, servitude, subjection, vassalage. 3 couple, pair.
vb antonym unhitch.

yokel *n* boor, bumpkin, countryman, peasant, rustic.
n antonyms sophisticate, towny.

yore *adj* ancient, antique, old, olden. • *n* long ago, long since, olden times.

young *adj* green, ignorant, inexperienced, juvenile, new, recent, youthful. • *n* 1 young people, youth. 2 babies, issue, brood, offspring, progeny, spawn.
adj antonym old.
n antonym parents.

youngster *n* adolescent, boy, girl, lad, lass, stripling, youth.
n antonym oldie.

youth *n* 1 adolescence, childhood, immaturity, juvenile, juvenility, minority, nonage, pupillage, wardship. 2 boy, girl, lad, lass, schoolboy, schoolgirl, slip, sprig, stripling, youngster.

youthful *adj* boyish, childish, girlish, immature, juvenile, puerile, young.
adj antonyms aged, languorous.

zany *adj* 1 comic, comical, crazy, droll, eccentric, funny, imaginative, scatterbrained. 2 clownish, foolish, ludicrous, silly. • *n* buffoon, clown, droll, fool, harlequin, jester, punch.
adj antonym serious.

zeal *n* alacrity, ardour, cordiality, devotedness, devotion, earnestness, eagerness, energy, enthusiasm, fervour, glow, heartiness, intensity, jealousness, passion, soul, spirit, warmth.
n antonym apathy.

zealot *n* bigot, devotee, fanatic, freak, partisan.

zealous *adj* ardent, burning, devoted, eager, earnest, enthusiastic, fervent, fiery, forward, glowing, jealous, keen, passionate,

prompt, ready, swift, warm.
adj antonym apathetic.

zenith *n* acme, apex, climax, culmination, heyday, pinnacle, prime, summit, top, utmost, height.
n antonym nadir.

zero *n* cipher, naught, nadir, nil, nothing, nought.

zest *n* **1** appetite, enjoyment, exhilaration, gusto, liking, piquancy, relish, thrill. **2** edge, flavour, salt, savour, tang, taste. **3** appetizer, sauce.
n antonym apathy.

zone *n* **1** band, belt, cincture, girdle, girth. **2** circuit, clime, region.

zymotic *adj* bacterial, fermentative, germinating.